The Neoliberal Age?

The Neoliberal Age?

Britain since the 1970s

Edited by

Aled Davies, Ben Jackson
and Florence Sutcliffe-Braithwaite

UCLPRESS

First published in 2021 by
UCL Press
University College London
Gower Street
London WC1E 6BT

Available to download free: www.uclpress.co.uk

A CIP catalogue record for this book is available from The British Library.

ISBN: 978-1-78735-687-0 (Hbk.)
ISBN: 978-1-78735-686-3 (Pbk.)
ISBN: 978-1-78735-685-6 (PDF)
ISBN: 978-1-78735-688-7 (epub)
ISBN: 978-1-78735-689-4 (mobi)
DOI: https://doi.org/10.14324/111.9781787356856

Contents

List of figures

List of tables

List of abbreviations

ASI	Adam Smith Institute
BBC	British Broadcasting Corporation
BSA	Building Societies Association
BSC	British Steel Corporation
CAT	City Action Team
CBI	Confederation of British Industry
CCC	Caribbean Chamber of Commerce
CPO	Compulsory Purchase Order
CPRS	Central Policy Review Staff
CPS	Centre for Policy Studies
CRE	Commission for Racial Equality
EHRC	Equality and Human Rights Commission
EU	European Union
FIS	Family Income Supplement
GDP	Gross Domestic Product
GLC	Greater London Council
ICI	Imperial Chemical Industries
IEA	Institute of Economic Affairs
IFS	Institute for Fiscal Studies
IMF	International Monetary Fund
IoD	Institute of Directors
IPG	Industrial Policy Group
JAC	Judicial Appointments Commission
MKDC	Milton Keynes Development Corporation
MPS	Mont Pèlerin Society
NAIRU	Non-Accelerating Inflation Rate of Unemployment
NCB	National Coal Board
NEB	National Enterprise Board
NEC	National Executive Committee (Labour Party)
NHS	National Health Service
NIT	Negative Income Tax

NLWIA	North London West Indian Association
NMW	National Minimum Wage
NUM	National Union of Mineworkers
OBR	Office for Budgetary Responsibility
OECD	Organisation for Economic Co-operation and Development
OPEC	Organization of Petroleum Exporting Countries
OWAAD	Organisation of Women of African and Asian Descent
PFI	Private Finance Initiative
RPM	Resale Price Maintenance
SBS	Southall Black Sisters
SERPS	State Earnings Related Pension Scheme
SPD	Sozialdemokratische Partei Deutschlands
STUC	Scottish Trades Union Congress
TGWU	Transport and General Workers' Union
TUC	Trades Union Congress
VAT	Value Added Tax
WFTC	Working Families Tax Credit
WI	Women's Institute
WISC	West Indian Standing Conference

List of contributors

Aled Davies is a Career Development Fellow in Modern History at Jesus College, University of Oxford. He is the author of *The City of London and Social Democracy: The political economy of finance in Britain, 1959–1979* (Oxford University Press, 2017).

David Edgerton is Hans Rausing Professor of the History of Science and Technology and Professor of Modern British History at King's College London. His most recent book is *The Rise and Fall of the British Nation: A twentieth-century history* (Penguin, 2018).

James Freeman is Lecturer in the Digital Humanities (History) at the University of Bristol. As a historian of contemporary British politics, his research brings together histories of political rhetoric, Conservatism and 'neoliberalism'.

Ben Jackson is Associate Professor of Modern History at Oxford University. He is co-editor of *Making Thatcher's Britain* (Cambridge University Press, 2012) and author of *The Case for Scottish Independence: A history of nationalist political thought in modern Scotland* (Cambridge University Press, 2020).

Helen McCarthy is Reader in Modern and Contemporary British History at the University of Cambridge and a Fellow of St John's College. She is the author of *Double Lives: A history of working motherhood* (Bloomsbury, 2020).

Sarah Mass is Assistant Professor in the Department of History at Sam Houston State University. She is currently working on her first monograph, a study of retailing and citizenship in twentieth-century Britain.

Guy Ortolano is Professor of History at New York University. He is the author of *Thatcher's Progress: From social democracy to market liberalism through an English New Town* (Cambridge University Press, 2019).

Jim Phillips is Professor of Economic and Social History at the University of Glasgow. He is the author of *Scottish Coal Miners in the Twentieth Century* (Edinburgh University Press, 2019) and co-author, with Valerie Wright and Jim Tomlinson, of *Deindustrialisation and the Moral Economy in Scotland* (Edinburgh University Press, 2021).

Bernhard Rieger is Professor of European History at Leiden University and Honorary Professor of Modern and Contemporary History at UCL. He is currently working on a comparative and transnational history of workfare since the 1960s entitled 'Making Society Work Again'.

Neil Rollings is Professor of Economic and Business History at the University of Glasgow. He has written widely on business–government relations in the United Kingdom in the twentieth century.

Tehila Sasson is Assistant Professor of History at Emory University. Previously she was a Past & Present Postdoctoral Fellow at the Institute for Historical Research, London, and a research associate with the Centre for History and Economics at the University of Cambridge.

Camilla Schofield is Associate Professor in Modern History at the University of East Anglia. She is the author of *Enoch Powell and the Making of Postcolonial Britain* (Cambridge University Press, 2013) and co-editor, with Dan Geary and Jennifer Sutton, of *Global White Nationalism: From apartheid to Trump* (Manchester University Press, 2020). She is currently writing a history of equality law in twentieth-century Britain.

Peter Sloman is Senior Lecturer in British Politics at the University of Cambridge and the author of *Transfer State: The idea of a guaranteed income and the politics of redistribution in modern Britain* (Oxford University Press, 2019).

Florence Sutcliffe-Braithwaite is Associate Professor of Twentieth-Century British History at UCL and the author of *Class, Politics and the Decline of Deference in England, 1968–2000* (Oxford University Press, 2018).

Jim Tomlinson is Professor of Economic and Social History at the University of Glasgow. He has published widely on the historical political economy of modern Britain, most recently *Managing the Economy, Managing the People: Narratives of British economic life from Beveridge to Brexit* (Oxford University Press, 2017) and *Dundee and the Empire: Juteopolis 1850–1939* (Edinburgh University Press, 2014).

Rob Waters is Lecturer in Modern British History at Queen Mary University of London. He is the author of *Thinking Black: Britain, 1964–1985* (University of California Press, 2018).

Mark Wickham-Jones is Professor of Political Science at the University of Bristol. He is the author of *Whatever Happened to Party Government?* (University of Michigan Press, 2018).

Acknowledgements

The editors would like to thank the Economic History Society, the Royal Historical Society and UCL History Department for generously funding the conference out of which this collection grew, and University College, Oxford for providing further funding for the book. We would also like to thank all the participants at the conference, and the anonymous reviewer for UCL Press, for their intellectual input, and all the authors in the book for their hard work in bringing the volume together. We are hugely grateful to Alfie Steer for his research assistance as we finalised the manuscript and to Oliver Gough for indexing the book. Particular thanks to Chris Penfold, our editor at UCL Press, for his support and patience during the preparation of the book.

1

Introduction: a neoliberal age?

Florence Sutcliffe-Braithwaite,
Aled Davies and Ben Jackson

Britain's recent past is frequently characterised – in both public and academic debates – as an era of 'neoliberalism'. This descriptor is often associated with a wider global transformation in politics, economics and everyday life that is said to have taken hold from the 1970s onwards. In the British case (but also in the wider global story) it is most commonly argued that neoliberalism originated as a right-wing ideology in favour of free markets and against the welfare state, an ideology that was peddled by political economists, think tanks and politicians from the 1930s onwards, and that finally transformed Britain (and the world) in the 1970s and 1980s. Neoliberalism has supposedly remained dominant until the present, although the financial crisis in 2008, and the rise of nationalist 'populism' in the 2010s, are now sometimes identified as possible endpoints of the neoliberal age (the jury remains out on this periodisation).[1] This book subjects this commonplace understanding of recent British history to a more sustained and in-depth analysis, suggesting that the standard account oversimplifies in several regards, and identifying other metanarratives we must attend to in order to understand Britain in this period.

The introduction to this book falls into five parts. The first of these examines the different conceptual approaches to the category of 'neoliberalism' that are prevalent within the social sciences and history. The second part focuses on how neoliberalism has come to form the central descriptive and explanatory category for understanding the late twentieth century in many survey histories of modern Britain and highlights some of the key critiques of this framing. In the final three sections, we then explore how neoliberalism fits within three major strands of the historiography of contemporary Britain: political and intellectual history, social and cultural history, and economic history. These different fields, of course, overlap, but separating them out does, nonetheless, form a useful heuristic device. While there are some important subjects that we have (inevitably) neglected – such as a four nations perspective (though Jim Phillips considers the different political and cultural trajectory of Scotland in the period), national identity, European integration, democracy and law and order – the chapters gathered here offer a broad perspective on some of the areas and debates currently animating most historical work, and together they add up to more than the sum of their parts. The final three sections of this introduction draw together recent historiography and the arguments made in this volume, offering some initial answers to the central questions of the book: how useful is the category 'neoliberalism' to understanding Britain since *c.* 1970? And what alternative causes and categories must we look at if we want to understand the period since the 1970s more fully?

Approaches to neoliberalism

The adoption of 'neoliberalism' by historians in recent years reflects its development, since the late twentieth century, as a key critical concept within the social sciences. As in contemporary political discourse, the term has generated a great deal of debate and discussion over its meaning and validity. Fortunately, this has been a highly productive and sophisticated interdisciplinary examination of the concept that is in stark contrast with the simplistic disagreement that often characterises public and political debate over the term.[2] As Angus Burgin has argued, one important benefit of the concept of neoliberalism is that it has facilitated a constructive dialogue between historians and social scientists after a period in which the methodological gap between the two had been widening.[3] Analysts of neoliberalism in different disciplines have shared three fundamental questions: what is neoliberalism (a body of ideas; a political project; a governmentality; a form of capitalism); how coherent is/was neoliberalism; and what are/were its causes? In attempting to answer these questions anthropologists, geographers, historians, political economists, sociologists and others have come to recognise the value of neoliberalism as an analytical concept, while also revealing its complexities, inconsistencies and contradictions. It is evident that diverse disciplinary epistemologies and approaches have produced distinctly different answers to the questions of coherence and causation. At the risk of oversimplification, it is possible to distil this literature into three strands focused on the ideological and political, economic, and social and cultural aspects of neoliberalism.[4]

Neoliberalism as political ideology

Intellectual historians and political theorists have focused on the development of neoliberalism as an ideological movement – identifying its origins and then tracing the transfer of its ideas into politics and public policy throughout the second half of the twentieth century. The most significant contribution of this now extensive literature has been to identify both diversity *and* coherence within neoliberal thought. Neoliberalism is recognised as a response to the global crisis of liberalism in the 1930s. This led to the formation of a 'neoliberal thought collective', which was formalised at the first meeting of the Mont Pèlerin Society (MPS) in 1947. Neoliberals believed that economic planning threatened to destroy the only means by which individual liberty could be secured: free and competitive markets. The novelty of the neoliberal response was that rather than arguing for a return to the limited 'night-watchman' state of laissez-faire liberalism, neoliberals believed that the state should be repurposed and redeployed to *create and uphold* markets and competition. The neoliberal movement was anchored in this fundamental insight, but its participants developed a diverse range of approaches and priorities in pursuit of the restoration of individual freedom and the market order. Scholars now usually divide 'neoliberal' thought into at least three schools: the German ordo-liberals, the Austrian School associated with Friedrich Hayek and the Chicago School associated with Milton Friedman.[5]

Beyond a pure history of ideas, scholars of neoliberalism have focused on how neoliberal thought came to impact upon politics and policymaking around the world. A crude summary of this literature (examined in greater depth by Ben Jackson in this volume) is that these ideas were promoted by the effectively organised and well-funded transnational neoliberal movement and were then adopted by sympathetic politicians and translated into national policymaking environments as the economic turbulence of the 1970s delegitimised the more social democratic policy norms adopted in the 1930s and 1940s.[6] The United Kingdom and the United States were at the forefront of this ideological triumph. It is also argued that neoliberal ideas colonised key sites of social scientific authority and expertise, notably the discipline of economics, and the international economic and financial institutions of the World Bank and the International Monetary Fund (IMF).[7] As Will Davies has argued, the cumulative effect of this change in economic expertise was to generate a powerful legitimising language for states, one which presented neoliberal policy objectives as attractive instantiations of a competitive political and economic order. Inequality was a necessary corollary of this competition.[8]

The strand of scholarship on neoliberalism that focuses on ideology and activism therefore draws attention to the role of political agency in the economic and social transformations of the last 50 years or so. This is a literature that identifies specific historical actors with a consequential role in public debate and state decision-making, an emphasis that is congruent with historians' traditional interest in the contingent character of the juncture points that shape historical outcomes. However, it is also an approach that tends to focus on elites at the expense of both grassroots mobilisations and seemingly less 'political' social changes that can, in fact, have quite significant political implications. In emphasising transformations in political ideology, this approach can also draw attention away from long- and short-term economic changes.

Neoliberalism as a form of capitalism

As might be expected, the importance of ideas is relegated to secondary status in Marxist analyses of neoliberalism. Instead, the emphasis is placed on the collapse of class compromise in the 1960s, which generated a 'crisis of capitalist accumulation' and compelled the capitalist class to construct a new, flexible 'regime of accumulation'. According to David Harvey, and Gérard Duménil and Dominique Lévy, the chief proponents of this interpretation, neoliberal ideas were simply the 'vehicle for the restoration of class power' in the 1970s and beyond.[9] These ideas promoted reforms to the management of capitalism that enabled its globalisation and 'financialisation' in pursuit of the restoration of profitability.[10] Other scholars whose work is informed by Marxism, such as Andrew Glyn, follow a similar line of argument without using the term 'neoliberalism'. Like Harvey et al., Glyn suggests that a crisis of profitability in the late 1960s and 1970s was the key cause of the shifts in political economy seen in the late twentieth century.[11] This crisis of profitability interacted with existing dynamics in economic development – particularly globalisation, deindustrialisation and the growth of the financial sector – to create the political economy of the late twentieth century.

Aside from Marxist-inspired accounts, there are alternative explanations of neoliberalism that emphasise the importance of economic factors. One such interpretation holds that neoliberal policies were the product of the globalisation of capitalism that took off in the 1960s in the form of multinational business and the liberation of financial markets from national control. This transferred power to globalised capital, which offered the rewards of inward investment to countries that pursued 'responsible' policies of low taxation, balanced budgets, inflation control and limited regulation of private markets.[12] While this analysis de-emphasises ideology, other scholars, by contrast, have integrated economic with ideological explanations. Mark Blyth, for example, has argued that the 'stagflation' crisis of the 1970s generated a political-economic problem that neoliberal ideas were able to *define* and subsequently provide a coherent solution to (for example, replacing Keynesianism with monetarism as the dominant macroeconomic policymaking framework).[13] This interpretation thus synthesises an economic perspective with the ideological one discussed in the previous section.[14]

In each of these accounts, neoliberalism is interpreted as a response to, or even a function of, the changing material conditions of capitalism in the late twentieth century. Such economic accounts in effect provide a structural history of this period, placing causal weight on large-scale material changes in the nature of production, an approach familiar to those economic and social historians who have long advocated the benefits of a Marxist or structural economic perspective. Of course, the disadvantages of such a perspective are also familiar to historians: the grand scale of this analysis can downplay the importance of social and cultural change and the role of politics in mediating between broad economic trends and the everyday lived experience of citizens in different states.

Neoliberal governmentality

The third main approach to the study of neoliberalism is inspired by Michel Foucault's lectures on the topic in the late 1970s, first published in English in 2008, and by his concept of 'governmentality'.[15] According to this view, neoliberalism should be understood as a 'rationality' in which 'generalised competition' has become a societal norm, and in which individual subjectivity has been reformed according to the ideal of entrepreneurialism.[16] As the anthropologist Carla Freeman puts it:

> . . . neoliberal flexibility is not reducible to the restructuring of labour processes or the free-floating circulation of capital to rationalize and expand the parameters of the global assembly line, but has reached into the recesses of kinship, citizenship, mind and body such that feeling and subjectivity itself is being constituted, managed, and experienced in new ways.[17]

This remaking of society has not been achieved simply as a top-down, state-led project but has been produced by power dispersed across multiple sites of knowledge, and in a variety of agencies.[18] This has served to guide and mould 'the ways in which people conduct themselves'.[19]

This analysis has tended to reject the notion of a coherent 'Neoliberalism with a big "N"', but instead to see it as an 'abstract, mobile, and dynamic' logic that is assembled in varied forms according to different contexts.[20] Neoliberalism can be perceived in the cultural logics governing not only politics and policy, but also identities, subjectivities and everyday life.[21] Unlike the ideological and economic accounts, this view of neoliberalism as a logic or effect that saturates modern society offers more of a map or a description of deep-rooted cultural change than an explicit account of causation, but it follows methods similar to those employed by social and cultural historians who have also been influenced by Foucault. Unlike the ideological and economic approaches discussed earlier, the governmentality literature provides a lens through which to interrogate neoliberalism as a phenomenon that reshapes everyday life, and not just large-scale economic change or elite decision-making. Hence scholars taking this approach have examined how processes of financialisation have transformed individuals' relationship to money, debt and saving;[22] how individuals have been encouraged to be 'entrepreneurs of the self';[23] and how neoliberalism has transformed democracy and models of citizenship in an individualistic direction.[24]

*

The aim of this book is not only to contribute to the historiography of modern Britain, but also to respond to this broader interdisciplinary, international literature on neoliberalism.[25] The following pages focus on the application of these different approaches to one detailed national case study. It is an exercise that helps to reveal both the analytical strengths of this vast body of work on neoliberalism, and the tensions within it. Furthermore, the chapters presented in this book encourage us to place the question of neoliberalism in a wider perspective, and in doing so they raise the question of whether to depart altogether from a framework that prioritises neoliberalism as the central historical development of this period.[26] The remainder of this introduction sets the scene for the subsequent chapters by investigating how the approaches to the study of neoliberalism outlined above speak (or at times do not speak) to the existing historiography of contemporary Britain and the chapters collected in this volume.

The dominance of the political in narratives of twentieth-century Britain

Synthetic, narrative works about Britain in the twentieth century generally reflect the standard story of neoliberalism set out at the start of this introduction. Most survey histories divide the post-war period into three phases: first, the triumph of 'social democracy' in the post-war settlement; second, a period of political and economic crisis during the 1970s; and, finally, the triumph of 'neoliberalism'. This is the case even in revisionist histories; for example, Selina Todd's analysis of working-class life and politics in the period 1910–2010 challenges many of the common assumptions of political and social history, but nevertheless conforms to an historical arc which has 1976 (the IMF loan to Britain) and 1979 (the election of Margaret Thatcher) as its key turning points, ushering in 'neoliberal times'.[27] James Vernon's 2017 textbook, *Modern Britain: 1750 to the present*, also identifies 1976 as a turning point, and the final section of the book is entitled 'The neoliberal revolution and the making of *Homo Economicus*'. Vernon argues that the neoliberal revolution 'largely dismantled' the institutions of social democracy, replaced its governing logic with a new one ('to allow markets to transform government as well as economic and social life') and ultimately 'created a new type of person – *homo economicus* – who understood themselves and the world in purely economistic terms'. The examples he draws on to demonstrate this are phenomena such as jogging and self-improvement culture.[28]

Popular histories of post-war Britain, including those of Dominic Sandbrook, Andy Beckett and Andy McSmith, follow this pattern even more strongly; there is little sense that these authors have any overarching interpretative framework outside the political.[29] In Andy Beckett's *Promised You a Miracle*, it is presented as obvious that the main question one might ask of the oeuvre of the pop band ABC is the extent to which it was 'Thatcherite'.[30] More than perhaps any other period, post-war British history is dominated by a periodisation and narrative structure taken from *political* history. This is a structure that derives directly from political accounts that were generated contemporaneously – in particular, by the Conservative Party. In the period after Clement Attlee's shock victory in the 1945 general election, the Conservative Party made a concerted effort to construct a public image of itself as a party that had changed: a party which had taken defeat as a wake-up call and accepted the core goals and institutions set up by the Labour government. This was something of a fiction – in fact, before the election of 1945 many in the Conservative Party were already sympathetic to much of this policy platform. But it was the narrative that was important.[31] Then, in the 1970s, in order to justify their own political project, Keith Joseph and Margaret Thatcher constructed a narrative of a 'progressive consensus' in British politics, allegedly encompassing the mainstream of both the Labour and Tory parties. Thatcher claimed in 1975 that the consensus consisted in 'the doctrine that the state should be active on many fronts: in promoting equality, in the provision of social welfare, and in the redistribution of wealth and incomes', and that 'these views have been held in varying degrees by all political parties, in schools and universities, and among social commentators generally', but that they were 'now being questioned right across the same broad spectrum'.[32] Thatcher and her allies argued that they were smashing that consensus and introducing a real alternative into British politics, one which could reverse the 'decline' Britain had supposedly been experiencing for the previous 30 years. It was the Conservatives who constructed the broad outline of a narrative of 'social-democratic consensus', 'decline' and 'neoliberal revolution' (although the 'social-democratic' and 'neoliberal' descriptors have been more recent additions). That fact should inevitably lead historians to question its utility as an interpretative framework. The concept of 'consensus' has been widely critiqued since at least Harriet Jones and Michael Kandiah's 1996 book *The Myth of Consensus*.[33] The idea of 'decline' has been problematised by Jim Tomlinson, who argues we should think of 'declinism' not 'decline'.[34] The category of 'neoliberalism' is now also coming under scrutiny.

Beyond this, the narrative of a transition from social democracy to neoliberalism, or from consensus to Thatcherism, has a number of additional weaknesses. Firstly, as David Edgerton argues in this volume, and in his recent book *The Rise and Fall of the British Nation*, the characterisation of Britain from *c*. 1945–75 as 'social democratic' implies that the most salient features of the political economy of this period were Keynesianism and the welfare state; as Edgerton argues, this characterisation misses out key features of the British economic model, in particular the uniquely 'national' character of the economy in this period, and its resurgent globalisation in the period after *c*. 1970.[35] Secondly, the use of the term 'neoliberal' to describe contemporary Britain produces a confusion between description and causal analysis. To describe the period as 'neoliberal' produces a tendency to view the transformations seen in the period as the result of 'neoliberal' ideology and ideologues: the description presupposes causation. And thirdly, using 'neoliberalism' as the dominant grand narrative to describe the period means we tend to read all social and cultural change as the result of the discursive, political and economic changes associated with 'neoliberalism'. In fact, we must attend to other social, cultural, economic and technological dynamics at work to properly understand the period. Doing so will enable us to appreciate longer-term processes and lessen our reliance on the 1970s as a turning point or moment of disjuncture. As recent work has begun to talk of the 'mid-twentieth century' as a coherent period for some purposes, questioning the view of the Second World War as transformative, so we should do the same for the 1970s.[36]

Though the political has dominated synthetic narratives of twentieth-century British history, historians have offered important new readings of the nature and periodisation of Britain after 1945: as noted, Edgerton suggests the alternative categories of national and global to characterise the economy, and Tomlinson posits deindustrialisation as a metanarrative for Britain after *c.* 1955.[37] Meanwhile Jon Lawrence and Emily Robinson et al. have suggested that the rise of 'popular individualism' from the 1950s onwards was a motor of change in Britain's politics as well as its social norms.[38] Building on such work, this volume offers a more complex and nuanced account of the causes and character of the period since *c.* 1970. Detailed, empirical case studies explore the utility of the category of 'neoliberalism' in intellectual, political, economic, social and cultural histories of Britain, and in doing so they open up the possibility of integrating these often disconnected areas. The volume thus offers a more grounded account of the human agents and the structural forces at work in bringing about the transformation of Britain. It presents alternative accounts of causation, as well as a more variegated characterisation of Britain in this period.

Intellectual and political history

Intellectual historians have been quickest to take up the task of analysing neoliberalism, and there is a well-developed literature in this field, which is surveyed by Ben Jackson in this volume. As we have seen, intellectual historians have examined the political economists and other thinkers grouped under the label 'neoliberal', unpicking intellectual lineages but also emphasising the diversity, and at times the contradictions, in neoliberal discourse.[39] Where some have suggested that 'neoliberal' is too fuzzy a term to be useful, Philip Mirowski has argued that it makes sense to use the term 'neoliberal thought collective' to describe the transnational network of thinkers gathered by the Mont Pèlerin Society and associated think tanks. As with Mirowski's work, many intellectual histories take a transnational approach, reflecting the fact that neoliberal thinking crossed national boundaries from its earliest days. This transnationalism has been especially valuable in helping historians to avoid taking too parochial a view of Britain's post-war history.

Building on the work of intellectual historians, many scholars have, in recent years, complicated our accounts of the impact of neoliberal thought on British politics, starting with the Thatcher years. Some of the foundational and most influential scholarly treatments of Thatcherism distinguished the Thatcher government from earlier periods of British political history precisely because of its unusually ideological character. This is most notable in the classic work of Stuart Hall and Andrew Gamble. While they did not, in fact, use the specific term 'neoliberalism' in their writings of the 1980s and 1990s, they deployed cognate ideas such as 'the New Right' or 'monetarist philosophy' to characterise the ideological objectives of the Thatcherite elements of the Conservative Party.[40] Recent histories of specific policy areas have bolstered and deepened, but also in certain respects problematised, this analysis by offering more nuanced treatments of the precise nature of the neoliberalism which influenced Thatcherism in practice. Hugh Pemberton, Aled Davies and James Freeman's examination of pensions policy suggests that it was, in fact, ordo-liberal logic which was most evident in the Thatcherite pensions reforms.[41] Florence Sutcliffe-Braithwaite and Matthew Grimley have focused on the personal beliefs inculcated by Thatcher's Methodist, small-town, lower-middle-class upbringing, stressing the interplay of these ideas with neoliberal ones in the shaping of 'Thatcherism'.[42] Adrian Williamson has examined a range of economic policy areas to show that, in many spheres, there was little new about Thatcherism and much continuity with the thinking of the Conservative Party over the previous 15 years.[43] David Rooney has shown that the Thatcher governments took an interest in the neoliberal idea of using urban road pricing as a way to tackle congestion but ultimately discarded the idea because of their ideological commitment to low taxation and individual freedom, and the car-owning nature of their voter base.[44]

A bracing strand of scepticism about the ideological character of Thatcherism has also been introduced to this debate in the work of Richard Vinen, who has argued that the interpretation pioneered by Gamble and Hall places too much emphasis on the self-promoting writings of journalists and think-tank personnel rather than focusing on the decision-making of leading Cabinet ministers and the civil service.[45] Vinen's point is well taken and it is certainly fair to conclude that Thatcherism was about more than just neoliberalism, and that it was not always in tune with every brand of 'neoliberal' ideas. Nonetheless, as Ben Jackson points out in his chapter, these debates would benefit from a greater level of precision about how ideology and public policy interact with each other. Jackson demonstrates that it is important to distinguish between a variety of ways in which neoliberal ideas influenced politics in this period, ranging from the provision of new technical concepts for policymakers, to the promotion of particular partisan public interpretations of events, and to the development of specific policy ideas that were taken up by government. Jackson argues that along each of these dimensions a clear, though delimited case for the ideological influence of neoliberalism can be made, but that it should be combined with an acknowledgement of the importance of other intellectual influences, and of the role of economic and social change in setting broad constraints on the path of public policy. In his chapter in this volume, James Freeman traces how neoliberal ideas were picked up by Conservatives in the 1970s and 1980s as a toolkit for finding new ways to achieve old goals, and to revive a flagging party.[46] However, he argues, historians might do well to move away from a preoccupation with the 'influence' of neoliberal ideas on policy under Thatcher and turn instead to an exploration of the historically specific points at which Conservatism and neoliberalism interfaced with one another, considering, for example, how separate developments within the Conservative and neoliberal traditions increased the potential compatibility of the two, and how Conservatives selectively read and appropriated neoliberal ideas to solve particular political problems that the party was confronting.

In analyses of the success and failure of 'Thatcherism', many have emphasised the fact that, for all that her governments transformed Britain, Thatcher's 'revolution' was far from complete. As early as 1989, Ivor Crewe wrote of Thatcher's attempts to change British values as 'the crusade that failed'.[47] Though she did succeed in changing the balance of spending on different elements of the welfare state, Thatcher did not permanently shrink overall government spending as a proportion of GDP.[48] As Stephen Brooke has suggested, we can see 'the stubborn persistence of social democracy in the attempt, for example, to construct a different world of social democracy at the local level' in the 1980s, as well as in support for the National Health Service (NHS) and the revolt against the Poll Tax.[49] This work cumulatively contributes to a view of Thatcherism not as the inevitable solution to a pervasive crisis of the 1970s, or the outcome of decades of development of 'neoliberal' political economy promoted by a core of right-wing ideologues,[50] but as a complex, messy amalgam of older right-wing tenets with newer neoliberal ideas, which had some successes, but which was far from completely 'triumphant' in the 1980s.[51]

At a dinner in 2002, Thatcher was asked what she saw as her greatest achievement; she replied, 'Tony Blair and New Labour. We forced our opponents to change their minds.'[52] Debate has raged over the extent to which New Labour can be seen as 'neoliberal' or Thatcherite, as a renewed form of social democracy or as a genuine 'Third Way'.[53] Indeed, it seems likely that the very prominence of the concept of 'neoliberalism' from the late 1990s onwards in part reflected a need to explain why 'free market' principles and policies continued to exercise considerable political influence even as the parties that were their initial sponsors, such as the British Conservatives and the Republicans in the US, were ejected from office by a new generation of centre-left governments. The persistence of an underlying neoliberal ideology and/or policy regime irrespective of which party was in government offered one influential interpretation of the politics of the 1990s and 2000s.[54] In this volume, Mark Wickham-Jones re-evaluates the debates over this question at the time and uses party documents and first-person accounts of the period when Labour was preparing for power in 1996–7 in order to assess to what extent the term 'neoliberal' is useful here. He points out that the Labour Party has traditionally had a fairly accommodationist attitude towards the market economy; this attitude long pre-dated the rise of neoliberalism. Furthermore, Wickham-Jones argues that although New Labour's rhetoric shifted towards a more market-based approach, its policy record was more nuanced and harder to stereotype as ideologically on the right.

Several other chapters also examine the continuities and discontinuities between neoliberal thought, Thatcherism and New Labour in particular policy areas. Peter Sloman examines the expansion of transfer payments (such as housing benefit and tax credits) in the 1970s and 1980s, suggesting that these represent not a failure of neoliberalism, but rather the triumph of an ideology of 'redistributive market liberalism'. He argues that some neoliberals always suggested that cash transfers to the poor were the best way to enable everyone to participate in markets to meet all their needs, and that Thatcher recognised that transfers were politically necessary to defuse potential tensions as she rolled back collective welfare provision and restructured labour markets. New Labour was subsequently reconciled to the practicality of using fiscal transfers to tackle poverty in the context of a growing economy and rising inequality. Sloman thus suggests that a particular strand of neoliberal thinking did come to dominate in this policy area. By contrast, in his examination of unemployment policy, Bernhard Rieger argues that both Thatcherite and

New Labour policies on unemployment were influenced by a neoliberal desire to impose economic incentives on the unemployed, but that both were also profoundly influenced by much longer-standing moralising traditions on both sides of the political divide.

In their respective chapters on work and housing in this period, Jim Phillips and Guy Ortolano suggest that neoliberalism was far from a dominant force. Ortolano examines housing in post-war Britain through the lens of Milton Keynes's development corporation. He argues that while the development corporation held to a vision of a 'property-owning social democracy', encompassing both public and private housing, in practice its ability to deliver this was challenged by economic and political pressures from 1976 onwards, and increasingly stymied by the cuts and policy changes of the Thatcher government. Phillips examines the complex forces shaping experiences of work in Britain. He argues that while deindustrialisation was already transforming the British labour force before the 1980s, it was accelerated by deliberate actions taken by the Thatcher governments, which also intervened to obscure the 'real' level of unemployment. Under New Labour, government policy continued to structure experiences of work in significant ways, not all of which have roots in neoliberal ways of thinking about the economy. In particular, the advent of the minimum wage was an important moment of pushback against the neoliberal focus on the free market. Finally, Camilla Schofield, Rob Waters and Florence Sutcliffe-Braithwaite, in their examination of New Labour policy on race and racism, trace some continuities with Thatcherism, and some congruities with neoliberal logic, but also point to significant continuities between New Labour and the radical New Urban Left of the 1980s. While the period of 'modernisation' from *c.* 1983–97 does appear as an important moment of inflection, then, there were still continuities on the left across this period. At most, New Labour can be characterised as *in part* shaped by neoliberalism.

Further complicating the picture, historians have begun to trace the pre-history of 'neoliberal' ideas (or at least ideas which came to be seen as 'neoliberal') such as individual freedom, choice and the market on the left of British politics before 1979, disrupting the idea that the neoliberal revolution was engineered solely from the right. Ben Jackson has traced 'neoliberal' ideas within the Liberal Party and even the Labour Party before Thatcher's election as Prime Minister. As he points out, in 1976, Jim Callaghan famously told the Labour Party conference that Britain could no longer 'spend [its] way out of a recession'.[55] But the left had been generating some rather 'neoliberal' ideas even before this conversion to a monetarist analysis of government spending. As Jackson shows, Peter Jay, thought to have written the key passage of Callaghan's 1976 speech, developed a form of 'market socialism' in the 1970s which was monetarist, anti-corporatist and anti-trade union monopoly, but still committed to democratic and egalitarian outcomes.[56]

Other scholars have traced a line of influence from the broader new left politics of the 1960s and 1970s into the neoliberal revolution of the 1980s. The politics of the new social movements and 'expressive revolution' of the 1960s and 1970s helped to undermine the structures and institutions of the welfare state by elaborating critiques of the paternalism, patriarchy, racism, sexism and ableism which were found in those institutions. Feminist, anti-racist and disabled activists critiqued social security rules, racism and sexism in schools, the disempowering of disabled people and a host of other forms of oppression and discrimination.[57] Community activists critiqued the centralised, bureaucratic social democratic state and argued for devolved services shaped by, and run by and for, local people.[58] Some of the architects and planners most associated with modernist attempts to engineer new urban environments in the 1950s and 1960s came to critique those grand plans by the early 1970s and helped unpick this modernist planning project alongside right-wing neoliberals;[59] the conceptualisation of 'multiple deprivation' and the focus on deprived 'inner-city' areas that flowed from it in the 1970s fractured the universal principle of the welfare state, making inner-city areas compete with each other to evidence the highest levels of deprivation;[60] and it was new left thinkers who first developed the idea of doing away with urban planning, an idea which subsequently migrated onto the right and found form in the shape of the Enterprise Zones that transformed some British cities in the 1980s.[61] Champions of worker participation and control in industry, who came from both left and right, critiqued the corporatist settlement of the post-war years. As Alistair Reid has written, the 'social-democratic state . . . was being torn apart from within by its own beneficiaries, something which the old left . . . could not really understand'.[62]

These accounts suggest a more complex and contingent view of the transformations of the 1970s and 1980s: Thatcher was just one outcome, and there were other 'roads not taken'; New Labour operated in a post-Thatcherite landscape, but it was not simply a vehicle for neoliberal ideas. But these accounts also push us towards another (apparently somewhat contradictory) conclusion: Thatcherism might have been the outcome of some very contingent and unstable developments, but some moves in the direction of 'neoliberal' ideas were probably on the cards even if Callaghan had gone to the country and won in late 1978, before the Winter of Discontent, or if Thatcher had been toppled in the early 1980s at a moment when she was weak and precarious. Certain ideas we now see as part of 'neoliberal' Britain were being incubated on the left as well as on the right of politics before 1979. That view is bolstered further when we make international comparisons; shifts that can be characterised broadly as 'neoliberal' were seen in much of the West during this period, under Reagan in the US but also under governments of the left in Australia, New Zealand and Spain, and even under François Mitterrand in France with the 'austerity turn' in 1983.[63]

Economic history

Historians of Britain's political economy have tended to push back against ideas-centric accounts of the transition to neoliberalism and to argue that material forces and structural transformations have been central to the remaking of Britain in the final third of the twentieth century. They have not, however, produced narrowly determinist accounts, but have instead sought to emphasise how politics has interacted with specific domestic and international economic conditions.

The most well-developed 'economic' aspect of the historiography concerns the crisis of economic management in Britain during the 1970s. In particular, the concurrent rise in unemployment and inflation in the mid-1970s challenged the established methods of 'managing the economy' as they had been developed since the war: fine-tuning a balance between full employment and minimal inflation.[64] The politics of incomes policies – working through trade unions and employers in an attempt to limit wage growth to control inflation – overwhelmed the Heath government in 1973–4 and undermined the Callaghan government in 1978–9.[65] Furthermore, the inflation problem combined with a deficit in the nation's current account and a substantial growth in public borrowing to trigger a collapse in the value of sterling in 1976. All three of these macroeconomic indicators had been severely affected by the global spike in the price of oil engineered by the Organization of Petroleum Exporting Countries (OPEC) in 1973–4. The resulting cuts to public expenditure by the Labour government were the price to pay for accessing IMF credit.[66] This crisis is commonly thought to signal the end of the post-war Keynesian-corporatist settlement. Jim Tomlinson has argued that this proclaimed death of Keynesianism, and its replacement with 'monetarism', is inaccurate and simplistic;[67] and, in his contribution to this book, Neil Rollings shows how, despite the common view that Thatcher rejected the accommodationist, consensual tendencies of the Confederation of British

Industry (CBI), her government maintained a close relationship with the organisation throughout the 1980s as a means of keeping pay levels under control without having to resort to formal incomes policies. Nevertheless, this story of corporatist Keynesianism's crisis and abandonment in the 1970s remains fairly well entrenched.

There is much work left to be done on the exact nature of the economic policymaking revolution in the 1970s and 1980s.[68] However, recent historical work has also sought to understand the rise of neoliberalism as the product of deeper and wider structural conditions. As Aled Davies argues, at least part of the neoliberal turn in economic government (e.g. reducing taxes on wealth and high incomes; de/re-regulating markets; reducing the power of trade unions; and prioritising the control of inflation over employment) can be understood as a capitalist revolt against state intervention in the economy that was triggered by a steep decline in profits in the middle of the decade.[69] This analysis draws on earlier work by Andrew Glyn, as well as Adam Przeworski's assessment of the power relations upon which post-war social democracy was based.[70] This rather blunt materialist explanation should not be taken too far, but it is an important reminder that even if we reject the simple idea that the dynamics of capitalism autonomously *determine* politics, society and culture, those dynamics cannot be ignored. The work of Jackson and Rollings on the relationship between British business groups and neoliberal ideas, Davies on the influence of monetarist economics in the City's financial markets, and Jacob Ward on the pressure financial institutions in the City of London exerted in order to bring about the privatisation of BT offers a significant avenue for future exploration of the relationship between the material and the ideological components of this period.[71] Emma Barrett's study of elite stockbrokers Cazenove and Co. demonstrates further complexities in the relation between politics, ideology and financial institutions, arguing that while Cazenove adapted to the Thatcherite reforms to Britain's financial sector, the firm made good use of elite social networks to entrench many of its privileges and traditions.[72]

Beyond the domestic British economy, changes to the international economic order have also been identified as a cause of the transformation of Britain in the late twentieth century. It can be argued that the linked dynamics of expanded global trade, the multi-nationalisation of business and the resurgence of global finance weakened the material conditions of post-war interventionist, nationalist economic policy. This was a gradual process that pre-dated the 1970s: for example, technological change, particularly the communications and information technology revolution, was a significant factor enabling the incipient re-globalisation of the world economy from the 1960s onwards. Yet a focus on technology should not obscure the *political* drivers of this process: for example, the integration of Britain within the European Economic Community required a liberalisation of capital movements, and under the partial leadership of the Thatcher governments the European project became a means by which international trade and investment barriers were dismantled in the 1980s.[73]

Britain's earlier role in reconstituting globalised finance (which had been constrained by nation states through controls on the free movement of capital) is especially notable. As discussed in Davies's chapter, which draws on the work of Catherine Schenk, Gary Burn, Jeremy Green and others, the City of London's banking establishment (overseen by the Bank of England) constructed an 'offshore' financial system that served the interests of the City in its effort to revive itself as a global financial centre. This coincided with a demand for global credit and investment facilities from multinational enterprises and national governments; it also assisted the US in managing its financial role as the Western hegemonic power. The development of these 'Euromarkets' generated flows of 'hot money' that destabilised and ultimately contributed to the collapse of the Bretton Woods system of fixed exchange rates between 1971 and 1973. This liberated states from the discipline of maintaining their currency parities (a constraint that frustrated growth-oriented post-war British governments). But after a vast expansion of sovereign lending to finance the massive current account deficits created by the oil price rise of 1973, nation states were then subjected to the discipline of global financial markets whose willingness to finance governments was determined by the perceived commitment of those governments to control inflation. Britain's recourse to the IMF in 1976 must be placed in this context.

Rather than looking to 'neoliberalism', an alternative way to think about the political economy of Britain in the late twentieth century is to see it as a product of rapid deindustrialisation and the transition to a service-based economy after 1970. Tomlinson has argued that many of the key features of neoliberal Britain, such as wage inequality and work insecurity, are the product of the decline of industrial employment.[74] For Avner Offer, the disappearance of a 'proletarian mode of production' underpinned the rhetorical remaking of workers into consumers.[75] The loss of industrial jobs made the Thatcher governments' task of weakening trade unions easier, and the stagnation in average incomes caused by the disappearance of stable employment in industry forced households to rely on credit and asset ownership (particularly mortgage-financed home ownership) to maintain their position relative to accelerating pay growth at the top of the income scale.[76] This latter outcome suggests that the 'financialisation' of British society was a rational coping mechanism in the face of fundamental economic change, although as the work of Amy Edwards and of Kieran Heinemann has demonstrated, pressure to adopt individualist saving and investment strategies came from a host of sources and could be traced back throughout the twentieth century.[77] Stuart Aveyard, Paul Corthorn and Sean O'Connell have also provided an essential history of the politics of credit in twentieth-century Britain that demonstrates the diverse, complex and long-term origins of credit liberalisation since the 1970s.[78]

Deindustrialisation may have also served as a constraint on the neoliberal political project. As Tomlinson argues in his chapter in this book, another fundamental effect of deindustrialisation was to compromise the ability of politicians to implement the neoliberal 'rollback' of the welfare state. As deindustrialisation increased inequality and created larger numbers of unskilled or semi-skilled workers on low wages in the service sector, it created a situation where governments, unless they were willing to preside over a vast expansion of relative – and even absolute – poverty, were forced to subsidise wages. This began with Edward Heath's Family Income Supplement in the early 1970s and culminated in New Labour's tax credit programmes and the huge expansion of housing benefit.

Centring deindustrialisation as a driver of change in post-war Britain prompts us, of course, to ask what caused the disappearance of industrial work after 1970. An orthodox economist would point to technological change, relative factor costs (enabled by globalisation) and the increased demand for services in an affluent economy. Evidence of the decline of industrial jobs throughout the developed world could be used to prove this point, suggesting that 'neoliberalism' is a distraction from the more fundamental, autonomous transformation of global capitalism. There are, however, distinctions to be made between the pace of deindustrialisation in Britain relative to other countries. Comparative political economists have argued that different models of capitalism have produced these divergent economic outcomes. In the most commonly known typology, Britain is identified (alongside the US) as the archetypal 'liberal market economy', in contrast to other 'co-ordinated market economies' (most notably Germany).[79] Yet the functionalist 'varieties of capitalism' model of Hall and Soskice, while useful as a descriptive characterisation of the international economy at the start of this millennium, is unsatisfactorily ahistorical.

One might argue that the more enthusiastic embrace of liberal economic policies in Britain from the 1980s was a legacy of its imperial position in the second half of the nineteenth century, in which the City of

London became the central financial hub of the world economy.[80] While its power within Britain was subdued following the 1931 financial crash and the 1944 Bretton Woods agreement, the Euromarket revival allowed the globally oriented City to reassert its power vis-à-vis the state but also provided the platform for a post-industrial national economic strategy. In this context the City of London effectively organised itself as a coherent lobby group in the 1960s and 1970s, drawing on the legacy and ideals of the City's pre-1931 global financial freedom (kept aflame in the Bank of England), which were repurposed to meet the demands of post-war economic politics. Davies has described the activities of the *invisible exports* campaign that began in the late 1950s and which asserted that the City offered a solution to British economic decline: its capacity to provide *services* to the world offered an alternative to the nation's internationally uncompetitive industrial sector.[81] From this perspective, we might say that the neoliberal reformation was driven by an embrace of a post-industrial *vision* of future national prosperity. Yet in his chapter in this volume, Davies suggests that this was not necessarily a conscious 'choice' by the Thatcher government: the acceleration of deindustrialisation during the Thatcherite monetarist experiment left the British state with little option but to cling to the service sector as a national lifesaver.

Empire and decolonisation are also emphasised in Tehila Sasson's chapter; as Sasson suggests, important recent work by several scholars demonstrates the connections between the processes of decolonisation and financialisation, deindustrialisation and the changing labour market in Britain. James Vernon has argued that deregulation, outsourcing and 'flexibilisation' can be seen as the result of 'a particular conjuncture of decolonization, a new state-sanctioned biopolitics of racialized immigration controls and changing forms of racialized neoliberal capitalism'.[82] Vanessa Ogle has shown that the end of empires led to the flight of white capital into expanding tax havens, driving financialisation and also setting the scene for the development of discourses and practices of development aid and modernisation in the global South.[83] In her chapter, Sasson develops these arguments further, suggesting that 'microfinance' initiatives pioneered in the global South, and imbued with a neoliberal rationality, were subsequently imported into Britain and shaped New Labour's thinking about 'financial inclusion'. Empire and decolonisation thus formed important – and intertwined – influences on the development of key facets of the 'neoliberal' economy in Britain before and after the 1970s.

An examination of British economic history tends to push against the ideas- and politics-centric accounts of the neoliberal transformation of Britain, by encouraging historians to recognise the changing structural conditions of British and global capitalism, and the role of material interests. However, historians working in this area have not resorted to monocausal material explanations of the rise of neoliberalism in Britain and have been alive to how economic dynamics interacted with neoliberal ideas, the imperatives of national statecraft, long-term social changes, and the legacy of Britain's imperial past and the process of decolonisation.

Social and cultural history

As we saw above, one way of narrating the social and cultural history of late twentieth- and early twenty-first-century Britain is as a 'neoliberal' period, one where, as James Vernon traces, new individualistic forms of self-fashioning, and cultures of greed and selfishness, came to dominate.[84] Work, family and community are said to have been relentlessly colonised and distorted by the demands of neoliberal economies and ideologies. The image of the call centre is perhaps paradigmatic of this view of contemporary culture: rows of isolated workers, alienated from their work and from one another, servicing the demands of consumers and of globalised and financialised capitalism, un-unionised and disempowered, competing to complete the most calls and meet their sales targets.[85] Historical studies of neoliberal cultures and subjectivities are not as far advanced, yet, as historical studies of neoliberal ideas, political movements and economic structures; however, this is a field into which historians are beginning to move. Historians working in this field have often taken as their starting point the tradition of social and cultural theory inspired by Foucault. Nikolas Rose, for example, has depicted neoliberalism as a mode of liberal governmentality that compels the individual to be free: to embrace autonomy, choice and personal responsibility, and to treat herself as an enterprise (to become 'an entrepreneur of oneself').[86] Others have examined the development of neoliberal culture and neoliberal subjectivities through the lens of 'neoliberal sensibilities'. Ellen Boucher, for example, has suggested that studying public reactions to the threat of nuclear war in the 1980s uncovers an emerging 'neoliberal sensibility', focused on assessing risk and taking personal responsibility; this sensibility, Boucher suggests, was not completely dominant or totalising, but it was one important pattern of thought and feeling.[87]

At the same time, as we saw above, many scholars have suggested that the new left politics of the 1960s and 1970s, the emphasis on individual self-expression and gratification of the 1960s counter-culture and the 'spirit of 68' fed into the advent of Thatcherism or neoliberalism in the 1980s.[88] This suggests that neoliberalism alone may not be enough to explain the shifts in society, culture and subjectivities of late twentieth-century Britain. Instead, we should think about modern British history in terms of several cross-cutting metanarratives which interacted, but none of which ever had overall primacy.[89] One such trend, which cuts across the rise of neoliberal ideas and policies, is the rise of individualism and the decline of deference, which Sutcliffe-Braithwaite has argued had long roots and diverse drivers in post-war Britain – from the right as well as the left – and which played into Thatcher's hands in some ways.[90] James Hinton's work, based on Mass Observation sources from the Second World War and from the 1980s, also points to rising individualism, as well as growing self-reflexivity and ideas about self-fulfilment as long-term developments spanning the entire period.[91] What this suggests is that we should not ask whether all the social and cultural phenomena of the late twentieth century were 'neoliberal'; rather, we should examine them on their own terms, looking not simply to 'neoliberalism' as an explanation, but to longer and more varied roots. This book contributes to this work and thus complicates depictions of British culture and society in this period as 'neoliberal'.

Studies of the family and neoliberalism have stressed the tensions between the impulse towards individualism in neoliberal thinking and the requirement, in practice, for the family to deliver the housework and childcare needed to keep the neoliberal economy working. Melinda Cooper has examined how, in the US, neoliberal thinkers adopted the discourse of 'family values' because, far from wanting to create a world of atomised individuals, their economic model required the family to shoulder the burden of responsibility for caring for its members as the state retreated from that responsibility.[92] Helen McCarthy's chapter in this book examines the pressures on women as wives and mothers in late twentieth-century Britain. She finds that 'responsibilisation' (sometimes identified as a defining feature of 'neoliberalism') was, in fact, a continuous theme in conceptualisations of women as mothers and workers: even in the 1950s and 1960s, there were many endorsements of married women's work – but only where the women involved also used private resources to take responsibility for the home and children first. When it comes to state provision of childcare, Thatcher's policies (or lack thereof) were nothing new; here, New Labour marked a distinctive break, introducing a National Childcare Strategy in 1998. But this was an ideologically messy document, justifying itself more often by reference to the need to tackle childhood inequalities than the need to create an equal playing field for women workers. Women were still to a large extent 'responsibilised', and, as globalisation and deindustrialisation changed labour markets, they were more and more required to work in order to meet the needs of the family budget. Despite this long-running top-down effort at 'responsibilisation', however, turning to look at women's subjectivities in this period, McCarthy suggests that there was no capitulation to the stringent demands of responsibilisation at home and in work: women subverted the demand that they should be 'superwomen' with humour, scepticism and ambivalence.

One of the key arguments made in literature on 'neoliberal' subjectivities concerns the development of entrepreneurial practices. Historical studies, though, challenge – or at least complicate – this story. In this volume, Bernhard Rieger points to the ways in which Thatcher's governments attempted to promote entrepreneurialism among the unemployed, but he also emphasises that this was not the Thatcherites' only approach to the out-of-work, who were more often treated punitively. Tehila Sasson also examines how new government-endorsed financial institutions encouraged new forms of financial subjectivity and risk-taking in the late twentieth century. By contrast, Sarah Mass shifts her focus away from government and towards society, tracing the development of 'outsider' commercial actors buying and selling in informal spaces such as Sunday markets between 1945 and 1975. She argues that we should not see these 'entrepreneurial subjectivities' as 'neoliberal' or 'proto-neoliberal'. These entrepreneurs in the informal economy presented themselves as flexible alternatives to the inflexible provision made by vested interests in the public and private sector, and called for the deregulation of retail, but they based their case not on neoliberal ideology, but rather on claims about the nature of the modern 'ordinary working family' and the right of individuals to flexibility in shopping and to cheap goods.

Camilla Schofield, Rob Waters and Florence Sutcliffe-Braithwaite also examine the theme of entrepreneurship, examining the transition of individuals from Black and anti-racist activism in the 1970s and 1980s into the emerging sector of race relations consultancy. They demonstrate how Black activism was rearticulated in the 1980s, partly under the influence of neoliberal ideas, but also because of the money the Thatcher governments funnelled into Black, anti-racist and ethnic groups for pragmatic reasons in the aftermath of the urban uprisings of 1981. Black enterprise was emphasised, but this did not represent an imposition from outside Black culture: Schofield et al. examine Black businessmen and activists in the 1970s who articulated a distinctive anti-racism linked inextricably to entrepreneurship, and who had roots in and connections to the radical Black activism of the 1960s and 1970s. Furthermore, as Schofield has argued in earlier work, individualism – often seen as the natural correlate of Thatcherism and neoliberalism – was in fact incubated and encouraged by the left-wing apparatus of race relations legislation in 1960s and 1970s Britain.[93] Work on the social and cultural history of post-war Britain thus complicates narratives of the rise of 'neoliberal subjectivities', suggesting that developments such as entrepreneurship and individualism had more diverse and complicated causes; it also shows how partial the reach of neoliberalism into British society and institutions was.

Chapter structure and conclusion

Many of the chapters in this book move between intellectual, political, social and cultural history. The book is designed so that each chapter stands alone; however, the chapters also work consecutively to develop and interrogate a series of arguments. In the introductory section, David Edgerton problematises the description of Britain from 1945 to 1979 as 'social democratic' and from 1979 as 'neoliberal', while Ben Jackson provides a counterpoint, arguing for a more precise calibration of the influence of neoliberal ideas on British politics after the 1970s. The second section examines the welfare state, with Peter Sloman and Jim Tomlinson offering contrasting analyses of how 'neoliberal' the welfare state became after the 1970s, and Bernhard Rieger tracing discontinuities in the approaches of Thatcherites and New Labour. In the section on work and family, Helen McCarthy (examining women's work and feminism) and Jim Phillips (examining work and trade unionism) also trace continuity and change in policy on work and welfare and stress the significant instances of resistance to 'neoliberal' forms of subjectification. Sarah Mass examines the supposedly 'neoliberal' emphasis on flexible shopping in the late twentieth century, arguing it can be traced back to small-scale entrepreneurs in the decades before the 1980s, and suggesting important alternative sources for shifts in subjectivities and in the economy in this period.

In the section on politics, Camilla Schofield, Florence Sutcliffe-Braithwaite and Rob Waters continue the focus on entrepreneurialism, tracing antecedents for Black enterprise culture in Britain in the 1960s and 1970s, and suggesting neoliberalism was only one influence on New Labour's anti-racist politics. Mark Wickham-Jones and James Freeman also trace long-term continuities in Labour and Conservative politics, while also mapping the influence of neoliberalism on both. Writing on political economy, Neil Rollings and Aled Davies examine the impact of organised business and the City of London on the direction of the British economy in the post-war period; Davies and Guy Ortolano both focus on the housing market, demonstrating how secular economic change as well as Thatcherite policy transformed housing after the 1970s. Finally, Tehila Sasson in her afterword argues for the utility of the term 'neoliberal' but suggests that we should see neoliberalism as having 'many lives', not one single story.

The chapters in this book do not all take the same view of 'neoliberalism', or of its utility as a category to understand Britain after *c.* 1970. But taken together, and read alongside other recent historical scholarship on neoliberalism, they suggest that the story of the 'rise and triumph of neoliberalism', which is often repeated in contemporary political discourse, and which often structures survey histories of Britain after 1945, is partial and problematic. As Philip Mirowski has argued, it makes sense to talk about a 'neoliberal thought collective' which had significant success in influencing political discourse and public policy. What this book suggests, however, is that it is not particularly helpful to describe the late twentieth century as straightforwardly a 'neoliberal' period. This can tend to imply that neoliberal ideology was the main driver of the changes seen in this period when, as many of our contributors show, material interests, economic processes, technological changes and cross-cutting trends such as the rise of individualism were also important in shaping the politics, economics, society and culture of Britain after the 1970s.[94] This decade is rightly seen as a crucial turning point in modern British history but the reasons for this are complex, reflecting both short- and long-term factors that are variously political, economic, social and cultural in character. For this reason, 'neoliberalism' should be one, but not the only, category used to understand Britain since the 1970s.

Notes

1 For recent statements to this effect in public debate, see, for example, Jeremy Corbyn, Speech, Labour Party Conference (27 September 2017), https://www.newstatesman.com/politics/staggers/2017/09/jeremy-corbyns-2017-conference-speech-full (accessed 21 June 2021); and Stephen Metcalf, 'Neoliberalism: The idea that swallowed the world', *The Guardian* (18 August 2017), https://www.theguardian.com/news/2017/aug/18/neoliberalism-the-idea-that-changed-the-world (accessed 21 June 2021). For a similar account of the US context, see Gary Gerstle, 'The rise and fall(?) of America's neoliberal order', *Transactions of the Royal Historical Society*, 28 (2018), 241–64.

2 For a sophisticated critique of the use of neoliberalism as a concept in the social sciences, see Rajesh Venugopal, 'Neoliberalism as concept', *Economy and Society*, 44 (2015), 165–87; and for a powerful defence of the term, see Philip Mirowski, 'The political movement that dared not

speak its own name: The neoliberal thought collective under erasure', Institute for New Economic Thinking Working Paper (23 September 2014), https://www.ineteconomics.org/uploads/papers/WP23-Mirowski.pdf (accessed 21 June 2021).

3 Angus Burgin, 'The neoliberal turn', Oxford Political Thought Seminar Paper (November 2019).

4 For a more comprehensive overview of the extensive literature on neoliberalism and the opportunities for future research, see Kean Birch, *A Research Agenda for Neoliberalism* (Cheltenham, Edward Elgar, 2017); Simon Springer, Kean Birch and Julie MacLeavy (eds), *The Handbook of Neoliberalism* (London, Routledge, 2016); and Damien Cahill, Melinda Cooper, Martijn Konings and David Primrose (eds), *The SAGE Handbook of Neoliberalism* (Los Angeles, SAGE, 2018).

5 Philip Mirowski and Dieter Plehwe (eds), *The Road from Mont Pèlerin: The making of the neoliberal thought collective* (Cambridge, MA, Harvard University Press, 2009); Ben Jackson, 'At the origins of neo-liberalism: The free economy and the strong state, 1930–47', *Historical Journal*, 53 (2010), 129–51; Angus Burgin, *The Great Persuasion* (Cambridge, MA, Harvard University Press, 2012); Quinn Slobodian, *Globalists: The end of empire and the birth of neoliberalism* (Cambridge, MA, Harvard University Press, 2018); and Thomas Biebricher, *The Political Theory of Neoliberalism* (Stanford, CA, Stanford University Press, 2019).

6 Dieter Plehwe, Bernhard Walpen and Gisela Neunhöffer (eds), *Neo-Liberal Hegemony: A global critique* (London, Routledge, 2005); Mirowski and Plehwe, *Road from Mont Pèlerin*; Kim Phillips-Fein, *Invisible Hands* (New York, W. W. Norton, 2010); and Ben Jackson, 'The think tank archipelago: Thatcherism and neo-liberalism', in Ben Jackson and Robert Saunders (eds), *Making Thatcher's Britain* (Cambridge, Cambridge University Press, 2012), 43–61.

7 Yahya M. Madra and Fikret Adaman, 'Neoliberal turn in the discipline of economics: Depoliticization through economization', in Damien Cahill, Melinda Cooper, Martijn Konings and David Primrose (eds), *The SAGE Handbook of Neoliberalism* (Los Angeles, SAGE, 2018), 113–28; Avner Offer and Gabriel Söderberg, *The Nobel Factor: The prize in economics, social democracy, and the market turn* (Princeton, NJ, Princeton University Press, 2016); and Jeffrey M. Chwieroth, 'Testing and measuring the role of ideas: The case of neoliberalism in the International Monetary Fund', *International Studies Quarterly*, 51 (2007), 5–30.

8 William Davies, *The Limits of Neoliberalism* (London, SAGE, 2014).

9 David Harvey, *A Brief History of Neoliberalism* (Oxford, Oxford University Press, 2005).

10 Gérard Duménil and Dominique Lévy, *The Crisis of Neoliberalism* (Cambridge, MA, Harvard University Press, 2011); and Gérard Duménil and Dominique Lévy, *Capital Resurgent* (Cambridge, MA, Harvard University Press, 2004).

11 Andrew Glyn, *Capitalism Unleashed: Finance, Globalisation and Welfare* (Oxford, Oxford University Press, 2008).

12 See, for example, Susan Strange, *The Retreat of the State: The diffusion of power in the world economy* (Cambridge, Cambridge University Press, 1996); and Philip G. Cerny, 'The dynamics of financial globalization: Technology, market structure, and policy response', *Policy Sciences*, 27 (1994), 319–42.

13 Mark Blyth, *Great Transformations: Economic ideas and institutional change in the twentieth century* (Cambridge, Cambridge University Press, 2002), 126–248.

14 As discussed in greater detail with respect to the case of Britain by Peter A. Hall, 'The movement from Keynesianism to monetarism: Institutional analysis and British economic policy in the 1970s', in Sven Steinmo, Kathleen Thelen and Frank Longstreth (eds), *Structuring Politics: Historical institutionalism in comparative analysis* (Cambridge, Cambridge University Press, 1992), 90–113; and Peter A. Hall, 'Policy paradigms, social learning and the state: The case of economic policy making in Britain', *Comparative Politics*, 25 (1993), 284–92.

15 Michel Foucault, *The Birth of Biopolitics: Lectures at the Collège de France, 1978–1979*, trans. Graham Burchell (London, Routledge, 2008); Thomas Lemke, '"The Birth of Bio-Politics": Michel Foucault's lecture at the Collège de France on neo-liberal governmentality', *Economy and Society*, 30 (2001), 190–207; and Nikolas Rose, Pat O'Malley and Mariana Valverde, 'Governmentality', *Annual Review of Law and Social Science*, 2 (2006), 83–104.

16 Pierre Dardot and Christian Laval, *The New Way of the World: On neo-liberal society*, trans. Gregory Elliott (London, Verso, 2013), 4–6.

17 Carla Freeman, 'Embodying and affecting neoliberalism', in Francis E. Mascia-Lees (ed.), *A Companion to the Anthropology of the Body and Embodiment* (Oxford, Wiley-Blackwell, 2011), 356.

18 Nikolas Rose, *Governing the Soul: The shaping of the private self* (London, Free Association Books, 1999).

19 Ilpo Helén, 'Review essay: Welfare and its vicissitudes: Nikolas Rose, *Powers of Freedom*, Mitchell Dean, *Governmentality*', *Acta Sociologica*, 43 (2000), 157–64, at 158.

20 Aihwa Ong, *Neoliberalism as Exception: Mutations in citizenship and sovereignty* (Durham, NC, Duke University Press, 2006).

21 Julie A. Wilson, *Neoliberalism* (New York, Routledge, 2018).

22 Paul Langley, *The Everyday Life of Global Finance: Saving and borrowing in Anglo-America* (Oxford, Oxford University Press, 2009); and Randy Martin, *Financialization of Daily Life* (Philadelphia, Temple University Press, 2002).

23 Tim Christiaens, 'The entrepreneur of the self beyond Foucault's neoliberal homo oeconomicus', *European Journal of Social Theory*, 23 (2020), 493–511.

24 Wendy Brown, *Undoing the Demos: Neoliberalism's stealth revolution* (Durham, NC, Duke University Press, 2015); and Ong, *Neoliberalism as Exception*.

25 For recent transnational discussions of neoliberalism by historians grappling with this literature, see 'Forum I: Neoliberalism as a concept of contemporary history', *Journal of Modern European History*, 17 (2019), 381–411; Iain Stewart, 'On recent developments in the new historiography of (neo) liberalism', *Contemporary European History*, 29 (2020), 116–24; 'Special section: Social histories of neoliberalism', *Journal of Social History*, 53 (2019); and Ben Jackson, 'Putting neoliberalism in its place', *Modern Intellectual History*, published online 17 February 2021, at https://doi.org/10.1017/S1479244321000032 (accessed 21 June 2021).

26 Guy Ortolano, *Thatcher's Progress* (Cambridge, Cambridge University Press, 2019), 30, stresses the benefits of triangulating between a global or transnational scale and a local or national one for similar reasons.

27 Selina Todd, *The People: The rise and fall of the working class, 1910–2010* (London, John Murray, 2015), new afterword in 2015 paperback edition, 404.

28 James Vernon, *Modern Britain: 1750 to the present* (Cambridge, Cambridge University Press, 2017), 476–97.

29 Dominic Sandbrook, *Seasons in the Sun: The battle for Britain, 1974–1979* (London, Allen Lane, 2012); Dominic Sandbrook, *Who Dares Wins: Britain, 1979–1982* (London, Allen Lane, 2019); Andy Beckett, *When the Lights Went Out: Britain in the seventies* (London, Faber and Faber, 2009); Andy Beckett, *Promised You a Miracle: Why 1980–82 made modern Britain* (London, Allen Lane, 2015); and Andy McSmith, *No Such Thing as Society: Britain in the turmoil of the 1980s* (London, Constable, 2011).

30 Beckett, *Promised You a Miracle*, 185–91.

31 John Ramsden, 'A party for owners or a party for earners? How far did the British Conservative Party really change after 1945?', *Transactions of the Royal Historical Society*, 37 (1987), 49–63.

32 Margaret Thatcher, Speech to the Institute for Socio-Economic Studies, 'Let our children grow tall', 15 September 1975, MTF, 102769, http://www.margaretthatcher.org/document/102769 (accessed 21 June 2021).

33 Harriet Jones and Michael Kandiah (eds), *The Myth of Consensus: New views on British history, 1945–64* (Basingstoke, Macmillan, 1996).

34 Jim Tomlinson, *The Politics of Decline: Understanding postwar Britain* (London, Routledge, 2014); and Jim Tomlinson, 'De-industrialization not decline: A new meta-narrative for post-war Britain', *Twentieth Century British History*, 27 (2016), 76–99.

35 David Edgerton, *The Rise and Fall of the British Nation: A twentieth-century history* (London, Allen Lane, 2018).

36 For examples, see Ben Jones, *The Working Class in Mid Twentieth-Century England: Community, identity and social memory* (Manchester, Manchester University Press, 2012); Emily Robinson, Camilla Schofield, Florence Sutcliffe-Braithwaite and Natalie Thomlinson, 'Telling stories about post-war Britain: Popular individualism and the "crisis" of the 1970s', *Twentieth Century British History*, 28 (2017), 268–304; and Vernon, *Modern Britain*, 351–472.

37 Tomlinson, 'De-industrialization not decline'.

38 Jon Lawrence, 'Paternalism, class, and the British path to modernity', in Simon Gunn and James Vernon (eds), *The Peculiarities of Liberal Modernity in Imperial Britain* (Berkeley, University of California Press, 2011), 147–64, at 163; see also Robinson et al., 'Telling stories'; and Florence Sutcliffe-Braithwaite, *Class, Politics and the Decline of Deference in England, 1968–2000* (Oxford, Oxford University Press, 2018).

39 Ben Jackson, 'Freedom, the common good, and the rule of law: Lippmann and Hayek on economic planning', *Journal of the History of Ideas*, 73 (2012), 47–68; Ben Jackson, 'At the origins of neo-liberalism'; Mirowski and Plehwe, *Road from Mont Pèlerin*; Rachel S. Turner, *Neo-Liberal Ideology: History, concepts and politics* (Edinburgh, Edinburgh University Press, 2008); Daniel Stedman Jones, *Masters of the Universe: Hayek, Friedman, and the birth of neoliberal politics* (Princeton, NJ, Princeton University Press, 2012); Burgin, *Great Persuasion*; and Slobodian, *Globalists*.

40 Stuart Hall, 'The great moving right show', *Marxism Today* (January 1979), 14–20; and Andrew Gamble, *The Free Economy and the Strong State*, 2nd ed. (Basingstoke, Palgrave, 1994). Both Hall and Gamble later shifted to using 'neoliberalism': Stuart Hall, 'The neoliberal revolution', *Soundings*, 48 (2011), 9–27; and Andrew Gamble, 'Neoliberalism', *Capital and Class*, 25 (2001), 127–34.

41 Aled Davies, James Freeman and Hugh Pemberton, '"Everyman a capitalist" or "free to choose"? Exploring the tensions within Thatcherite neoliberalism', *Historical Journal*, 61 (2018), 477–501; and Aled Davies, 'Pension funds and the politics of ownership in Britain, c.1970–86', *Twentieth Century British History*, 30 (2019), 93–105.

42 Florence Sutcliffe-Braithwaite, 'Neo-liberalism and morality in the making of Thatcherite social policy', *Historical Journal*, 55 (2012), 497–520; and Matthew Grimley, 'Thatcherism, morality and religion', in Ben Jackson and Robert Saunders (eds), *Making Thatcher's Britain* (Cambridge, Cambridge University Press, 2012), 78–94.

43 Adrian Williamson, *Conservative Economic Policymaking and the Birth of Thatcherism, 1964–1979* (Basingstoke, Palgrave, 2015); see also Jim Tomlinson, 'Tale of a death exaggerated: How Keynesian policies survived the 1970s', *Contemporary British History*, 21 (2007), 429–48.

44 David Rooney, 'The political economy of congestion: Road pricing and the neoliberal project, 1952–2003', *Twentieth Century British History*, 25 (2014), 628–50.

45 Richard Vinen, *Thatcher's Britain* (London, Simon & Schuster, 2009).

46 See also Matthew Francis, '"A crusade to enfranchise the many?" Thatcherism and the "property-owning democracy"', *Twentieth Century British History*, 23 (2012), 275–97.

47 Ivor Crewe, 'Values: The crusade that failed', in Dennis Kavanagh and Anthony Seldon (eds), *The Thatcher Effect: A decade of change* (Oxford, Oxford University Press, 1989), 239–50.

48 Rowena Crawford, Carl Emmerson and Gemma Tetlow, *A Survey of Public Spending in the UK* (London, Institute for Fiscal Studies, 2009).

49 Stephen Brooke, 'Living in "new times": Historicizing 1980s Britain', *History Compass*, 12 (2014), 20–32, at 27.

50 See Richard Cockett, *Thinking the Unthinkable: Think-tanks and the economic counter-revolution, 1931–83* (London, HarperCollins, 1994), for the view that Thatcherism was the fulfilment of neoliberal thinkers' plans.

51 This is the view that emerges from E. H. H. Green's important work; see E. H. H. Green, *Thatcher* (London, Hodder and Stoughton, 2006).

52 Conor Burns, 'Margaret Thatcher's greatest achievement: New Labour', *ConservativeHome* (11 April 2008), https://conservativehome.blogs.com/centreright/2008/04/making-history.html (accessed 21 June 2021).

53 Colin Hay, *The Political Economy of New Labour: Labouring under false pretences?* (Manchester, Manchester University Press, 1999); Ben Clift and Jim Tomlinson, 'Credible Keynesianism? New Labour macroeconomic policy and the political economy of coarse tuning', *British Journal of Political Science*, 37 (2007), 47–69; Hall, 'Neoliberal revolution'; and Stephanie Mudge, *Leftism Reinvented: Western parties from socialism to neoliberalism* (Cambridge, MA, Harvard University Press, 2018).

54 For studies of public policy which trace continuities from the 1980s into the New Labour years, see, for example, Brett Christophers, *The New Enclosure: The appropriation of public land in neoliberal Britain* (New York, Verso, 2018); and Timothy P. R. Weaver, *Blazing the Neoliberal Trail: Urban political development in the United States and the United Kingdom* (Philadelphia, University of Pennsylvania Press, 2016).

55 James Callaghan, Speech, Labour Party Conference (1976), http://www.britishpoliticalspeech.org/speech-archive.htm?speech=174 (accessed 21 June 2021).

56 Ben Jackson, 'Currents of neoliberalism: British political ideologies and the New Right, c. 1955–79', *English Historical Review*, 131 (2016), 823–50.

57 Adam Lent, *British Social Movements since 1945: Sex, colour, peace and power* (Basingstoke, Palgrave, 2001).

58 David Ellis, 'On taking (back) control: Lessons from community action in 1970s Britain', *Renewal*, 25 (2017), 53–61; and Daisy Payling, '"Socialist republic of South Yorkshire": Grassroots activism and left-wing solidarity in 1980s Sheffield', *Twentieth Century British History*, 25 (2014), 602–27.

59 Otto Saumarez Smith, 'The inner city crisis and the end of urban modernism in 1970s Britain', *Twentieth Century British History*, 27 (2016), 578–98.

60 Aaron Andrews, 'Multiple deprivation, the inner city, and the fracturing of the welfare state: Glasgow, c.1968–78', *Twentieth Century British History*, 29 (2018), 605–24.

61 Sam Wetherell, 'Freedom planned: Enterprise zones and non-planning in post-war Britain', *Twentieth Century British History*, 27 (2016), 266–89.

62 Alastair J. Reid, 'The dialectics of liberation: The Old Left, the New Left and the counter-culture', in David Feldman and Jon Lawrence (eds), *Structures and Transformations in Modern British History* (Cambridge, Cambridge University Press, 2011), 261–80.

63 Daniel Rodgers, *Age of Fracture* (Cambridge, MA, Harvard University Press, 2011); Gerstle, 'Rise and fall(?)'; Andrew Glyn (ed.), *Social Democracy in Neo-Liberal Times: The left and economic policy since 1980* (Oxford, Oxford University Press, 2001); and Mudge, *Leftism Reinvented?*.

64 The extent to which British post-war macroeconomic policy was 'Keynesian' has been discussed at length. See Alan Booth, 'New revisionists and the Keynesian era in British economic policy', *Economic History Review*, 454 (2001), 346–66. On the breakdown of Keynesianism in the 1970s, see Michael J. Oliver and Hugh Pemberton, 'Learning and change in 20th-century British economic policy', *Governance*, 17 (2004), 428–32.

65 For recent work on this, see Williamson, *Conservative Economic Policymaking*, 89–125; and John Shepherd, *Crisis? What Crisis? The Callaghan government and the British 'Winter of Discontent'* (Manchester, Manchester University Press, 2016).

66 Mark D. Harmon, *The British Labour Government and the 1976 IMF Crisis* (Basingstoke, Palgrave Macmillan, 1998); Kevin Hickson, *The IMF Crisis of 1976 and British Politics* (London, I.B. Tauris, 2005); and Douglas Wass, *Decline to Fall: The making of British macro-economic policy and the 1976 IMF crisis* (Oxford, Oxford University Press, 2008).

67 Tomlinson, 'Tale of a death exaggerated'.

68 See, for example, Duncan Needham, *UK Monetary Policy from Devaluation to Thatcher, 1967–1982* (Basingstoke, Palgrave Macmillan, 2014).

69 Aled Davies, *The City of London and Social Democracy: The political economy of finance in Britain, 1959–1979* (Oxford, Oxford University Press, 2017), 127–39.

70 Adam Przeworski, *Capitalism and Social Democracy* (Cambridge, Cambridge University Press, 1985).

71 Jackson, 'The think-tank archipelago'; Neil Rollings, 'Cracks in the post-war Keynesian settlement? The role of organised business in the rise of neoliberalism before Margaret Thatcher', *Twentieth Century British History*, 24 (2013), 637–59; Davies, *City of London*, 181–214; and Jacob Ward, 'Financing the information age: London TeleCity, the legacy of IT-82, and the selling of British Telecom', *Twentieth Century British History*, 30 (2019), 424–46.

72 Emma Barrett, 'King Caz: Cazenove, Thatcherism, and the 1980s financial revolution', *Twentieth Century British History*, 30 (2018), 108–31.

73 Stephen Wall, 'Making the single market', *Journal of European Integration History*, 16 (2010), 57–64.

74 Tomlinson, 'De-industrialization not decline', 76–99.

75 Avner Offer, 'British manual workers: From producers to consumers, c.1950–2000', *Contemporary British History*, 22 (2008), 537–71.

76 Colin Crouch, 'Privatised Keynesianism: An unacknowledged policy regime', *British Journal of Politics and International Relations*, 11 (2009), 382–99.

77 Amy Edwards, '"Manufacturing capitalists": The wider share ownership council and the problem of "popular capitalism", 1958–92', *Twentieth Century British History*, 27 (2016), 100–23; Amy Edwards, '"Financial consumerism": Citizenship, consumerism and capital ownership in the 1980s', *Contemporary British History*, 31 (2017), 210–29 ; Kieran Heinemann, 'Investment, speculation and popular stock market engagement in 20th-century Britain', *Archiv für Sozialgeschichte*, 56 (2016), 249–72; and Kieran Heinemann, *Playing the Market: Retail investment and speculation in twentieth-century Britain* (Oxford, Oxford University Press, 2021).

78 Stuart Aveyard, Paul Corthorn and Sean O'Connell, *The Politics of Consumer Credit in the UK, 1938–1992* (Oxford, Oxford University Press, 2018).

79 Peter A. Hall and David Soskice (eds), *Varieties of Capitalism: The institutional foundations of comparative advantage* (Oxford, Oxford University Press, 2001).

80 David Coates, 'The UK: Less a liberal market economy, more a post-imperial one', *Capital & Class*, 30 (2014), 171–82.

81 Davies, *City of London*, 181–214.

82 James Vernon, 'Heathrow and the making of neoliberal Britain', *Past & Present*, 252 (2021), 213–47.

83 Vanessa Ogle, '"Funk money": The end of empires, the expansion of tax havens, and decolonization as an economic and financial event', *Past & Present*, 249 (2020), 213–49.

84 Vernon, *Modern Britain*.

85 See, for example, Jamie Woodcock, *Working the Phones: Control and resistance in call centres* (London, Pluto Press, 2016); and Anthony Lloyd, 'Efficiency, productivity and targets: The gap between ideology and reality in the call centre', *Critical Sociology*, 46 (2020), 83–96.

86 See Rose, *Governing the Soul*; and Rose et al., 'Governmentality', 83–104.

87 Ellen Boucher, 'Anticipating Armageddon: Nuclear risk and the neoliberal sensibility in Thatcher's Britain', *American Historical Review*, 124 (2019), 1221–45.

88 Thomas Frank, *One Market under God: Extreme capitalism, market populism and the end of economic democracy* (London, Vintage, 2002); Joseph Heath and Andrew Potter, *The Rebel Sell: How the counterculture became consumer culture* (Chichester, Capstone, 2006); Kristin Ross, *May '68 and Its Afterlives* (Chicago, University of Chicago Press, 2002); Richard Cockett, 'The New Right and the 1960s: "The dialectics of liberation"', in Geoff Andrews (ed.), *New Left, New Right and Beyond: Taking the sixties seriously* (Basingstoke, Palgrave, 1999), 85–105; and Eve Chiapello and Luc Boltanski, *The New Spirit of Capitalism*, trans. Gregory Elliot (London, Verso, 2007).

89 Robinson et al., 'Telling stories'. See also Chris Hilliard in Florence Sutcliffe-Braithwaite, Chris Hilliard, Christienna Fryar, Mo Moulton and Mark Hampton, '*Modern Britain, 1750 to the Present* by James Vernon', *Twentieth Century British History*, 30 (2019), 264–84.

90 Sutcliffe-Braithwaite, *Class, Politics, and the Decline of Deference*. See also Robinson et al., 'Telling stories'; and Jon Lawrence, *Me, Me, Me? The search for community in post-war England* (Oxford, Oxford University Press, 2019). On the long roots of changes in selfhood and subjectivity, see Charles Taylor, *Sources of the Self: The making of modern identity* (Cambridge, Cambridge University Press, 1989).

91 James Hinton, *Seven Lives from Mass Observation: Britain in the late twentieth century* (Oxford, Oxford University Press, 2016); and James Hinton, *Nine Wartime Lives: Mass Observation and the making of the modern self* (Oxford, Oxford University Press, 2010).

92 Melinda Cooper, *Family Values: Between neoliberalism and the new social conservatism* (New York, Zone Books, 2017). Ben Jackson has made similar points with respect to the UK: 'Free markets and feminism: The neo-liberal defence of the male breadwinner model in Britain, c. 1980–97', *Women's History Review*, 28 (2019), 297–316.

93 Robinson et al., 'Telling stories'.

94 There are therefore parallels between the arguments of this book and the similar points made about the history of neoliberalism in the Americas and Germany respectively in Amy Offner, *Sorting Out the Mixed Economy* (Princeton, NJ, Princeton University Press, 2019); and Julian Germann, *Unwitting Architect* (Stanford, CA, Stanford University Press, 2021).

2

What came between new liberalism and neoliberalism? Rethinking Keynesianism, the welfare state and social democracy

David Edgerton*

The *new neoliberalism* is an ugly neologism, but it captures a crucial problem with the term 'neoliberalism' and how it is understood in relation to British history. *Neoliberalism* is supposed, in most of the extensive literature on it, to appear very much later than, and to be different from, both liberalism and the British 'new liberalism' of the early twentieth century.[1] Furthermore, neoliberalism is thought to have followed something that succeeded new liberalism. Various terms are used to describe this post-new liberal and pre-neoliberal phase, usually said to date from 1945 to the late 1970s or early 1980s: they are usually Keynesianism, the welfare state and, in recent years, social democracy, often used in combination and defined circularly.[2] The usages of Keynesianism and welfare state clearly pre-date the advent of the common usage of neoliberalism. However, social democracy as a descriptor of a form of polity-economy-society seems only to have come into significant use among historians with the rising use of the term neoliberalism. Curiously, Keynesianism and the (Beveridgean) welfare state are, in a standard historiographical cliché, identified as direct descendants of new liberalism, while British social democracy is typically characterised as Keynesianism and the welfare state.[3] In short, we are in a conceptual mess. In this chapter I hope to bring some clarity to these issues by enquiring into the meaning, scope and logical consistency of the concepts, their relationship with each other, and how well they map onto what we know of the history of the UK since 1945. I want to show that the terms are not innocent, but that their influence and significance arise from the grip that very particular historiographical traditions have had on our understanding of twentieth-century British history.[4]

I suggest that the concepts Keynesianism, the welfare state and social democracy, along with related ones, are in practice unhelpful analytical terms which should be abandoned as general descriptors (though certainly not as narrower, well-specified technical terms). By implication, neoliberalism, which too often relies on a contrast with them, for this and other reasons, is also best dispensed with. I echo Daniel Wincott's critique of 'epochalism' in thinking about these issues.[5] I also argue, with Jim Tomlinson, that the claims made for the usual chronologies of the welfare state and Keynesianism are misleading, especially but not only in that neither disappeared when neoliberalism, according to standard accounts of neoliberalism, replaced them: the concept of neoliberalism suspect for this reason alone.[6] I also suggest that neoliberalism should not be used because, in all its common variants, it misses key elements of radical changes that have been visited on the UK since the 1980s.

These concepts appear to be well grounded and capable of being applied in serious theoretical and analytical work. Yet they have very particular or very general meanings, and changeable ones. Most are not actors' terms, but analysts', and many have shifted from being negative to positive descriptions, from aspirations to descriptions of reality. They are typically poorly defined, and while they refer to mere parts, they are often misleadingly made to stand for the whole. Keynesianism and welfare state, and now social democracy, are closely related to other concepts, which in itself lends them authority. Thus affluence, it is often suggested, was the result of Keynesianism and the welfare state. The post-war consensus and the post-war settlement are in both cases, historians suggest, mainly agreements about Keynesianism and the welfare state.[7] But these concepts, far from being neutral descriptive and/or analytical terms, are in fact embodiments of very particular and strongly interdependent historiographical and ideological assumptions.

These terms are also thought to be powerful because they are (or in some cases are becoming) terms of art in the historiography of the post-war UK. But their claims to usefulness as general descriptions of economy, society and polity are not as historiographically secure as they seem.[8] Their usage needs to be understood as the result of the dominance of a particular kind of social democratic historiography of post-war Britain, which tells that history in very particular ways, stressing Keynesianism and the welfare state, and seeing these as the products of what is seen as *the* creative force of the time – social democracy. But British historiography could have been very different. In a blistering 1993 article, the sociologist W. G. Runciman asked the question: when, in the twentieth century, did the British capitalist mode of production change? He had no truck with terms such as Keynesianism or social democracy and their implied chronologies.[9] He is clear that there was one huge change with permanent effects, which took place between 1915 and 1922 and involved the creation of the welfare state, a new corporate economy and large trade unions and the establishment of mass suffrage. By contrast, changes in 1945 and 1979 were trivial: he suggests that neither nationalisation nor privatisation made much difference and that the new mode of production established early in the century continued in existence. It is both a very necessary corrective and a reminder of how much of history is driven by arguments about chronology.[10] His argument is not as wrong as it must appear to the student of British history. But in this chapter I also argue for breaks in 1945 and 1979, though not for the reasons most of their advocates suggest, or that Runciman considers.

Social democracy

Social democracy has long been a term of art on the left. As every socialist knows, before 1914 many Marxist parties styled themselves as Social Democratic parties (in Germany, Russia and the UK, for example), and since the First World War social democracy was the term for non-communist socialist parties, the most important of which, in terms of size, was the German Social Democratic Party (the SPD), and, after 1945, the British Labour Party. It was a term commonly used *critically* in reference to such parties by those further to the left, as in David Howell's *British Social Democracy*.[11] In the pages of *Marxism Today* in the 1980s the term was still used in this way by, for example, Stuart Hall.[12] If for the left it was a term of critique, it was also used positively by the right of the Labour Party, to distinguish itself from the left (which in response sometimes styled itself democratic socialist). The revisionists of the 1950s used it of themselves, and in 1981 a right-wing splinter group from Labour was called the Social Democratic Party.

While there is obvious authority for, and value in, labelling parties or fractions of parties as social democratic, it is not obvious that they ever created societies which ought to be so labelled. Eric Hobsbawm made, in passing, a crucial point. As he noted, '[t]he Soviet systems are the only ones which actually claimed to have established fully socialist economies and societies. To the best of my knowledge no social-democratic government or party, however radical or long-lived, has ever made such a claim.'[13] I have no reason to challenge that conclusion. Certainly, it is implausible that the social democrats of Germany or France or Italy would ever make such a claim for their nation, given how rarely and/or how late Social Democrats achieved office compared with Christian Democrats or Gaullists. A Labour Party claim to have created a social democracy, given that Labour was in office for only roughly half the period between 1945 and 1979, would be only a little less unlikely.

However, a number of students of modern capitalism have used the term as a descriptor for a phase of capitalism. In 1981 Andrew Gamble used 'social democracy' to describe a common trend in 'most capitalist states' to have universal suffrage and increased public spending, while clearly remaining essentially capitalist, and consequently having a particular kind of politics.[14] In his pioneering 1988 book on the politics of Thatcherism, Gamble used the term to cover most advanced Western economies, as the political and social superstructure which best accommodated Fordism. It was a richer definition than Keynesianism and welfare, to be sure.[15] Jeffry Frieden's 2007 history of capitalism sees social democracy as a means of saving capitalism from itself, starting in the 1930s with Scandinavian Social Democratic governments and the US New Deal, calling it a moderate anti-capitalism, which after 1945 was to be found even among European Christian Democrats, who extended the welfare state and intervened in industry.[16] More recently, Branko Milanović has developed a three-period model of capitalism – classical, social democratic and liberal meritocratic – defined in terms of returns to capital and labour.[17] Much less well defined, social democracy appears in work by Tony Judt. His collection of essays *Ill Fares the Land* uses the term repeatedly in the sense of a general Western European practice since 1945.[18] It has to be said that his discussion is shot through with conflicting and changing, vague definitions.[19] By contrast, his earlier *Postwar* uses the term, and sparingly, in the classical sense.[20] More recently Thomas Piketty has used the term for the period 1950–80 (its 'golden age'), covering countries ranging from Sweden to the US to Argentina, defining it as a period of low inequality and a large fiscal and social state (which, I note below, is not a workable definition).[21]

Among historians of the UK, the term social democracy was very rarely used to describe the nation as a whole but has been coming into limited use in the last decade. In 1991, Paul Addison wrote in a review in *Twentieth Century British History* that '[t]he rise and fall of Keynesian social democracy is one of the central problems of twentieth century British history'.[22] Roger Middleton labelled the last and fourth part of a

1996 book 'The rise and fall of Keynesian Social Democracy'.[23] But after around 2010 it became a little more common, including in *Twentieth Century British History*. There James Vernon wrote that '[t]he social democracy that my parents and I grew up with in Britain – where the state managed a mixed economy and sought to deliver full employment and universal forms of welfare – was shared in various forms across much of the world'.[24] In the same journal, others have since 'complicated the "rise and decline" narrative of social democracy' or written of the 'transition from post-war welfarism and social democracy' or 'the social democracy of the post-1945 welfare state'.[25]

Social democracy is defined in this recent literature in varying ways. James Vernon's definition is intimately connected to the welfare state: the Beveridge report, he writes, 'became the foundation of a new post-war social democratic settlement', while recognising that social democracy was 'compromised' by anti-democratic tendencies, and differences in gender, class and race.[26] Others see it somewhat differently. Aled Davies argues for a post-war 'social democratic economic policy' of industrial modernisation, and a 'social democratic political economy'.[27] He takes the Labour Party to have created, from 1945, a 'social democratic state' which lasted to the 1970s.[28] The aim was to 'achieve the fundamental goal of a modern industrial economy in which export-led growth could resist national decline by overcoming the endemic deficit in the nation's balance of payments; as well as providing stable, productive and well-paid employment for all'.[29] But here social democratic political economy is defined as the standard historians' account of post-war economic policy – and nothing in the argument claims it is specifically social democratic. Guy Ortolano contrasts social democracy with market liberalism, as *co-existing tendencies* within the post-war UK, encouraging or opposing the extension of the state, specifically the welfare state, while recognising that there are those who see only a very weak social democracy in the post-war UK.[30] More concretely, in the case of housing he identifies social democracy with mixed private and public housing, addressing, therefore, the crucial importance of ownership in social democratic politics and aspirations. He notes and rejects the historiographical focus on the origins of market liberalism and the degeneration of social democracy, supporting the claims of Davies and Edgerton that social democracy (as a party and intellectual programme) remained, or even became, dynamic in the 1970s.[31]

Chronology is part of definition. British social democracy is usually dated from 1945 (or 1940) to 1979. For Andrew Gamble, 'the war established social democracy in Britain', specifically in 1940.[32] However,

Vernon's textbook gives it a heterodox beginning in 1931 (when it was, oddly, a matter of protection, support for distressed areas, colonial trade and a state-managed economy), though established as common sense from 1945 (with a radically new welfare state, and a new imperialism), and argues it lasted into the 1970s.[33] By contrast, Scott Newton depicts a social democracy (though the definition is not clear) created by the Tories in the early 1960s, and which lasted until the Thatcher years.[34]

It seems to me that using the term social democracy in this new, broad sense has not in fact generally brought much new to the table of British history (and I will suggest below what else it might bring). It has done little more than re-label the welfare state and Keynesianism, and some other aspects of economic policy, to contrast it with what came before and later. This is nevertheless problematic, for two key reasons.

The first is that it ignores traditions of historiography which would deny, for important reasons, the applicability not only of the term, but of the underlying meanings it now conveys. Some historians have long maintained that precisely because of the centrality of Keynesianism and Beveridgean welfare, the UK was not, and could not be, social democratic. Thus Patrick Joyce, writing recently, referred to the 'myth of social democracy'.[35] Historians of the left have, as Joyce does, long insisted on what might be called a new liberal continuity thesis. This argument emphasises the importance of Edwardian new liberal innovations to the post-war welfare state and notes the ways in which Keynesianism restrained modernising state intervention. Both Keynes and Beveridge are characterised as new liberals. The implicit claim, surely correct, is that social democracy must mean something other than Keynesianism and Beveridgean welfare.

The second point is more complex. It is that this usage of 'social democratic' does not recognise that the historiography which labels the post-war UK as Keynesian and a welfare state is a very particular one, dating from the 1960s, and which can itself be called social democratic, in the sense of Labour revisionist. These histories celebrated Keynesianism and the welfare state, linked them and told the story of twentieth-century British history as the triumph of these two elements after 1945. It was a history focused on the civil state which systematically excluded the Cold War, and the warfare state, and indeed the private sector, except under the distorting lens of decline. It sometimes feels as if by definition all change of any value was the work of social democrats or resulted in social democracy.[36] This work still defines for many historians what British history is, and the context in which sub-elements should be studied.[37] The evaluation may now be generally less positive than in the past, but the key themes of broad historical understanding are (apart from empire) much the same.

A social democratic governmentality?

If social democratic historiography has its limitations, could the concept of social democracy help further illuminate British history? I believe so. We can ask, for example, what it would take to show that the UK could usefully be described as social democratic after 1945? We could ask, did it follow a social democratic foreign policy or defence policy? Interestingly, it is highly unlikely anyone has ever made this claim. Restricting the argument to the domestic sphere, we would need to show, I think, that the Labour Party, the Labour movement, developed and implemented a distinctively social democratic (rather than Keynesian or Beveridgean) method of economic and social calculation. Was there a social democratic governmentality?

Such a governmentality, or aspiration to it, is hard to find. One looks in vain (until the 1970s) for an elaborated set of arguments from the left for alternative ways of running the economy, except for making general arguments about planning and putting the interests of the nation first.[38] For example, the Labour Party made only minimal proposals for taking private industries into public ownership after the 1945 general election, and did not do so again until the early 1970s. It is interesting too how little attention is given in subsequent accounts to Labour policy for nationalised industries or to the significance for the power of property of the privatisations after 1979.[39]

That said, there were huge transfers to the public sector in the late 1940s, giving the state enormous leverage in investment, in everything from public housing to electricity generation. Yet there was little discussion of these programmes, excepting perhaps housing, by the Labour Party and the left at least until the 1970s. There were no distinctive Labour criteria for nationalised industries, though they were nationalised on the basis that they should indeed be run on principles recognising their systemic national and perhaps class significance. Post-war governments produced criteria which merely aped the profit criteria for private firms, which often made nationalised industries unprofitable when they did what they were supposed to do – behave differently from a private enterprise.[40] This is not to say that nationalised industries and other state enterprises did not, in fact, operate to distinctly national and other criteria – they did, most notably in buying British and ignoring the costs of doing so; the point here is that these crucial issues were not the subject of sustained analysis on the left. To put it another way, the Labour Party generally relied on state experts rather than on its own, including in economics. Indeed, it is crucial to understanding the nature of post-war expertise, including that associated with the public sector, not to assume that it was somehow social democratic in spirit, although it often is.

The exception that proves the rule is the post-Beveridge economics and sociology of the welfare state. There was a left tradition of investigation and policy prescription operating on assumptions about what was best for the nation, and which were aimed at correcting systematic inequalities created by capitalism. For example, in criticising the notion of the National Health Service (NHS) as a cost to the individual through taxation, and private medicine as a saving to the taxpayer, it was argued that both private and public medicine cost the nation money, and the issue was which system was more equitable and more efficient. Thus, the NHS, it was argued, was a cheap as well as equitable way of providing the nation with the health care it might otherwise provide itself by less equitable and more expensive private means. Similarly, a universal national state pension scheme of a generous kind might well be the most efficient from a national point of view. This was, indeed, the argument made by Labour welfare specialists in the late 1950s in arguing for a new National Superannuation scheme, one which rejected the key Beveridgean principle of the fixed contribution and benefit.[41] The policy never came into practice, and it was only in the 1970s, with the State Earnings Related Pension Scheme (SERPS), that a limited version came (temporarily) into play in a world in which the private occupational pension now dominated. This and other measures radically (and, as it turned out, temporarily) increased the generosity of the welfare state in the 1970s.[42] That transformation of the welfare state is barely known, but it is important to note its significance, and to understand that the reforms of the 1980s were in part restorations of the welfare state of the 1950s and early 1960s.[43] This argument is consonant with Richard Vinen's important claim that Thatcherism was in many ways a return to the consensus of the 1950s and 1960s, one broken by the left in the 1970s.[44] We need to ask, given Avner Offer's definition of social democracy as provision for life-cycle dependency by transfers through progressive taxation (rather than private savings through the market), whether even by this criterion the UK was ever social democratic.[45]

After all, the National Superannuation scheme was decisively rejected by the Conservatives, who favoured the expansion of private pensions which grew dramatically. There was, in any case, always a non-social democratic economics and sociology of welfare in play, for example doctors and others who continued to oppose the NHS, including health economists, through the 1950s into the 1960s and 1970s.[46] Furthermore, much of the application of efficiency thinking to the NHS was the sort of work study and operational research already in use in government and industry to reduce costs.[47]

Another way of defining social democracy would be in terms of a systematic recognition of the existence of labour and capital, with mechanisms to ensure that the voices and interests of labour are represented, constraining the power of capital and increasing that of labour. To be sure, there was a good deal of tripartism after 1945, but of a limited kind, which was obviously, as was corporatism more generally, not necessarily social democratic in this sense at all. It was not until the 1970s that Labour intellectuals, trade unions and others proposed new practices, exemplified in plans for 'industrial democracy', the social contract and planning agreements, which might count as such.[48] In the British case it is rather striking that there was a change in the tone and nature of capital–labour relations, but that this seems mostly due to economic conditions rather than new governing practices. Differentials of income were very substantially reduced from the 1940s into the 1970s, though of course never anything like as much as social democrats wanted.[49]

Another way of approaching the issue would be to look for measures designed to restrict the prerogatives of property. Keynes himself held that his theory had major implications for capital. If the rich were not needed to drive investment, then interest rates could and should be held low, which would lead to the euthanasia of the rentier, the functionless investor.[50] And indeed, the 1930s, the war and, importantly, the post-war years were periods of low real interest rates, and the distribution of wealth became more equal, until the 1980s. But it is equally notable that wealth taxes (as opposed to taxes on income from wealth) remained minimal, and that the state subsidised private ownership of some capital, notably in housing. The rentier was constrained but was not dead, and the social democratic politics of property were very much more moderate than Keynes' own.

What was Keynesian welfarism?

The British case is often taken as an exemplary one for Keynesianism and welfare and social democracy. But comparative assessment across

Western Europe suggests a variegated picture from which it is very difficult to conclude that the British case is indeed exemplary, or that such forms are in fact truly transnational, except at the most trivial level. Was Keynesianism, whatever it is taken to be, the norm across Western Europe (or 'the Western world') after 1945? Was the UK more, or less, Keynesian than the norm? What did that imply for state intervention? It is very hard to say. For welfare the story is much clearer. Comparatively speaking, within Western Europe, the UK was a low spender on welfare, in the 1950s and later too.[51] Furthermore, most continental welfare states organised welfare on a different model from the UK. With regard to social democracy generally, it is tellingly completely unclear where the UK stands comparatively, though for some aspects, British social democracy is seen as comparatively weak (the institutionalisation of corporatism, the existence of a social democratic 'pillar', the authority of the trade unions), especially in comparison with Scandinavia.

Just as the comparative question had no easy answer, nor has the straightforward definitional question as to whether the post-war UK is usefully described as Keynesian or a welfare state. These seemingly self-explanatory terms, rich with meaning, are in fact very problematic, in terms of what they are understood to mean. It is unclear, once one looks carefully, when Keynesianism and welfarism can be deemed to have started or ended.[52]

Implicit and explicit definitions of Keynesianism vary. Sometimes a very wide definition is used as a label for all economic policy, including nationalisation and sometimes even the welfare state. It has been suggested that Keynesianism even created the concept of a national economy. At other times Keynesianism is defined narrowly, as demand management, to argue that because policy was Keynesian in this sense it ignored 'the supply side' or did not lead to a 'developmental state'. There are good grounds for defining it narrowly, not least because Keynes, and most Keynesians, wanted macroeconomic intervention to make the liberal market economy work better, not to replace it. They had no brief for nationalisation or radical industrial policy. Even defined narrowly, Keynesianism is used misleadingly to suggest that managing the total level of demand in the economy was the way in which government managed to generate the historically unprecedented rates of economic growth (well over 2% GDP growth per annum on average) with historically low rates of unemployment, even though demand management was used mainly, as in the Second World War, to restrain inflation rather than to promote growth. It was more stop than go. The idea that Keynesians were inflationists, and those opposed to inflation were anti-Keynesian, is false.[53]

The question of when Keynesianism started is not straightforward. Although many have been tempted by the idea that the British Second World War economy was run on Keynesian lines, that is to misunderstand it. Indeed, it has been plausibly argued that Keynesianism represents a discontinuity with wartime and immediate post-war practice and only becomes significant with the removal of controls from the very late 1940s.[54] Keynesianism, in this sense, was the policy of 1950s Tories, not 1940s Labour. But as will be noted below, even in the Conservative years, economic policy involved many different elements, many of which had nothing to do with Keynesianism.

The welfare state is similarly defined in varying ways.[55] In its application is taken to have been, for example, the principal cause for lifting the British people out of poverty, when the most likely cause was higher wages. It is also strongly associated with state spending as a whole, and a new phase in the history of such spending, even though what was most novel in British public spending in the 1940s and 1950s was high levels of warfare spending.

When did the welfare state begin? is a tellingly problematic question. It cannot be in the Second World War itself, since the war was fought with a pre-war welfare system. That system was very elaborate. It was a Beveridgean working-class welfare state created in the 1920s. It cannot thus be said to have started from 1945. What Beveridge did in the Second World War was to plan to extend the system to the whole population. Indeed, it remained based on the regressive national insurance system, a poll tax, and aiming for a subsistence level benefit (though the NHS was not). Social democratic experts on the social services like Richard Titmuss did not see the UK as a welfare state.[56] It could be argued that a new kind of welfare state was introduced not in the 1940s, but in the 1960s and especially the 1970s with the rejection of the Beveridgean flat-rate principle.

It is even doubtful if, as is often implied, Keynesianism or welfarism were at the centre of post-war politics, even of the Labour Party, or of the consensus. The economy was discussed in terms of exports and imports, and above all the difference between them – the balance of trade and of payments – as well as investment, planning and production, at least as much as in terms of budget deficits or surpluses. Welfare policy was not the main focus of politics or policy, even rhetorically, even for the Labour Party. The first time Labour had used the term 'welfare state' in a manifesto was in 1955. But this is what it said:

> In order to strengthen our Welfare State still further and at the same time to play our part in assisting the under-developed areas of the

> world, our own production must rise every year. Only a government prepared to plan the nation's resources can do this. Labour will ensure that the claims of investment and modernisation come first.[57]

The Conservative manifesto of that year paired the welfare state with military expenditure:

> In an armed Welfare State the demands on taxable resources cannot be light. This makes it all the more necessary that government, central and local, should be run economically. There are today over 50,000 fewer civil servants and four fewer Ministries than when we took over. Conservatives will persist in the drive for simpler and less expensive administration.[58]

There were exceptions, notably the 1959 Labour manifesto, the work of the Gaitskellite social democratic revisionists, which was *uniquely* welfarist.

If the beginnings of the Keynesian welfare state are not as clear as the labelling implies, nor are the endings. Macroeconomic control of the economy hardly disappeared after 1979 – the rationale might have changed, but Keynesians are entitled to argue that the economy continued to behave in Keynesian ways. Keynesian policy instruments continued to be used into the 1990s and beyond, as Jim Tomlinson has eloquently argued.[59] In any case, the fiscal size of the state did not shrink to where it had been in, say, the 1930s. Indeed, it did not even shrink back to 1960s levels for very many years, and then only temporarily. In the case of welfare spending specifically, the picture is more dramatic – the proportion of GDP devoted to welfare increased from the 1970s to today. What did change, in the 1980s, was the generosity of the system to individuals, and radically so, returning the system to the post-war norm. The most obviously social democratic element of welfare, the NHS (state-owned, run by para-state employees [excepting general practitioners], providing universal services, funded by mildly progressive tax) very obviously expanded in the supposedly post-welfarist era, even if key elements would be undermined through trusts, private finance initiatives (PFI) and contracting out.

The point can be illustrated by looking again at Piketty's definitions of social democracy. He defines it as a period of reduced inequality, the golden age being 1950–80, *and* by high taxation and social spending, a large 'fiscal and social state'. For Piketty and for many others it seems obvious that the two definitions coincide chronologically. But as Piketty's own figures show all too clearly, while inequality started to increase quite radically from around 1980, the fiscal and social state was usually stable in size in relation to GDP, and in many cases growing. In fact, for all his illustrative cases, including the UK, the fiscal state was larger in 2010 than in 1970.[60] His argument might be better put like this: in the period 1950–80, in many places, inequality fell as the fiscal and social state *expanded* rapidly. However, from 1980 inequality increased, with a stable or growing fiscal and social state. They are not coincident indicators. It is a serious mistake to believe that welfare systems were designed to reduce, or succeeded in reducing, inequality.

Neoliberalism

Neoliberalism is a term which should, I think, not be used. As well as being a catch-all critical term, and not usually an advocate's category, neoliberalism, by focusing attention on limited and often misconstrued aspects of the great transition of the 1980s, misunderstands those changes, and their extent, in important ways. Firstly, neoliberalism is commonly defined as post-Keynesianism and post-welfarism and post-social democracy, without appreciating the multiple weaknesses of such a definition. Secondly, it is also used in a host of other contradictory or at least very different ways. It is often taken to be a set of *ideas* – dating to the 1930s – arguing for relying on market mechanism, which were then applied from the 1980s onwards.[61] Or, it is suggested, that neoliberalism involved the creation of a new, entrepreneurial *homo economicus*. In another version, neoliberalism is associated with the bureaucratism of the New Public Management. It is usually taken to be one thing, overlooking the differences between 'Austrian' thinking, and for example anti-Keynesian neoclassical liberal economics.[62] This conceptual apparatus hardly does justice to changes which have taken place since the 1980s, globally or in the UK. Notably, these framings do not address the changing relative power of capital, property and labour since the 1970s.[63] Modern hypercapitalism (to use Piketty's term) is centrally a matter of rebalancing the world in favour of capital, rather than the product of a new entrepreneurship or the power of markets qua markets.

But there is a deeper conceptual and periodisation problem. In Michel Foucault's brilliant analysis, neoliberalism was both a post-Nazi phenomenon which arose in nations which had never been liberal, and a US-centred critique of the non-liberal New Deal, post-war welfarism and the Great Society programmes. For him neoliberalism was both German 'ordo-liberalism', which was influential in what was called the 'social market economy' of Germany from the 1950s, and in the US a new economics of work focused on the worker as entrepreneur.[64] All this in itself throws a huge spanner into the standard argument that the UK and Western Europe/the Western world were social democratic between say 1945 and the 1980s, and neoliberal after that.[65] There is, however, a another problem which Foucault's argument makes clear. For Foucault, neoliberalism was not centrally post-social democratic but rather post-non-liberal and post-nationalist. Indeed, a vital part of the Hayekian critique of socialism was that it was in fact nationalist. (It is worth noting that *Road to Serfdom* did not recognise any new liberalism – as Keith Tribe notes, Britain had, in Friedrich Hayek's view, been corrupted by German (nationalist) thought, not by anything that came from liberalism.)[66] A vital part of Austrian neoliberalism, as Quinn Slobodian's recent examination rightly stresses, is its sustained critique of economic nationalism.[67] Pushing for a cosmopolitan capitalism as opposed to a national (and a potentially democratic) capitalism was a central concern. There is an obvious case to be made that national protection increased in many places in the world after 1945, and that the first great moves to liberalisation (post-war West Germany excepted) came in the formerly very national protectionist (and not obviously social democratic) Southern Cone nations in the early 1970s.

A national economy

We need to ask, recalling Foucault and Slobodian, whether we might also cast post-war British history as a case of nationalism (perhaps with a social democratic twist) replacing liberalism and new liberalism, and this economic nationalism being replaced by a revitalised liberalism. It's a question which most histories of twentieth-century Britain would answer with a bemused, perhaps outraged: NO! For British nationalism, economic or any other kind, barely exists in the history books. But as I have argued elsewhere, we need to take it seriously, especially between 1945 and the 1970s.[68]

I go further than the now-common argument that Keynesianism, and national accounting, constructed the national economy. The national economy was constituted primarily by economic barriers, sustained by nationalist and imperialist ideologies. Unfortunately, in the British case, this process, so familiar around the world, has been nearly invisible to British historians.[69] This is in part because it was not the result of a political movement, nor was it associated with an intellectual, as Keynesianism obviously was. But it is also because a central argument of much left social democratic (and here the term is most definitely admissible) and Marxist political economy has been that British capitalism has been unusually liberal and cosmopolitan/imperial and therefore, crucially, not national enough.[70] The consequence was, in this account, that the British national productive economy was undermined. The state's interventions, it is argued in this view, were limited to macro-economic Keynesianism and welfarism. The problem was, in effect, that there was no real post-new-liberal moment at all.[71] Some influential responses to Thatcherism certainly suggested it was a radical manifestation of a very long-standing aversion to national economic development in favour of cosmopolitan finance.[72]

Contrary to this thesis, I have argued there was a British national economy with a developmental state. There is a case for seeing it start with the introduction of general tariffs and general imperial preference in 1931/2, but that is, I think, better seen as a shift to an imperial rather than a national economy. It might be thought, from the histories, that the Second World War economy was a national economy, but in many ways the UK became more dependent than ever on overseas supply, not least now from the US.[73] The year 1945 saw a real break, I argue, with the end of Lend-Lease and the sudden need for the national economy to export in order to import. Although the years from the 1940s were the peak of imperial trade, the rhetoric was now national, and efforts were made to reduce imperial trade as well. From the 1940s into the late 1960s the proportion of trade to GDP was pushed down, as imports were reduced.[74] It was also a period, contrary to what is usually implied, of net emigration, not immigration. National policies to promote exports, and restrict imports, had the consequence that the post-war UK was more industrialised than it had ever been in its history, with the highest ever proportions of output and employment accounted for by manufacturing. Conceptually, the economy was highly national in that the balance of payments was seen as a national profit and loss account.[75] This economic nationalism in the context of imperial preference was not the preferred outcome of either liberals or imperialists. Indeed, as Alan Milward showed, the elite wanted to get away from both imperial and national economics, but only succeeded in doing so in the 1970s.[76]

The national economy also had a developmental state transforming the nationalised infrastructure of the nation. It took until the 1970s for modern trains, mines, electricity generation, post offices and telephone systems to be put in place, nearly all powered by nationally made equipment. On top of that, a dynamic national private capitalism was created in part by state action – resulting in an economy growing at unprecedented and still unmatched rates. Apart from state provision of infrastructure and energy, and generic support for education, there was direct state investment, investment grants and the use of the tax system to direct economic activity, particularly in favour of manufacturing.

All this highlights that Keynesian new liberalism was hardly the only economic ideology in play after 1945 and makes the point that the technocrats of the post-war UK were not mainly, or even mostly, liberals or social democrats. Many were pursuing a conservative vision of British modernity. One needs to think only of the aeronautical engineers and the aircraft industry to establish the point, though it applies very much more broadly.[77] For example, what was social democratic about the experts promoting motorways and motorisation?[78]

Thatcher's economy – another view

In this light it is significant and odd that British nationalism barely exists in the lexicon of British politics, except in relation to two important cases, Enoch Powell and Margaret Thatcher. But, as well as being nationalists, they were economic liberals who generally disdained economic nationalism. Powell certainly recognised British economic nationalism and its characteristic forms (for example the obsession with the balance of payments, and declinism). The Thatcher governments dismantled the remaining apparatus of economic nationalism, from the abolition of exchange controls to the promotion of the single market and myriad other initiatives, for example the welcoming of Japanese carmakers into the UK. The balance of payments, which went into historically massive deficits, not least in manufactures, was no longer a cause for concern. It ceased to be contentious to import coal. All this was hardly accidental.

Of course, the economic opening to the world was not the only aspect of Thatcherism, but it was decisive and sustained. However, Thatcherism also represented a rulers' revolt, a radical strengthening of the power of wealth, and the wealth of the powerful, and a new economic form where, for example, privatised infrastructure was a means of extracting profit on an unprecedented scale. As Brett Christophers shows, a new form of rentier capitalism of huge scope has emerged.[79] Not for nothing did Denis Healey call Thatcher 'la Pasionaria of privilege'.[80] Understanding the importance of the opening up to the world, and the new politics of property, helps make clear what Thatcherism was not.

Thatcherism did not transform the rate of growth of the British economy, nor did it unleash a radical new British entrepreneurialism, or indeed consumer sovereignty in a national market.[81]

Paradoxically the move to economic internationalism was made possible by previous state investment, by the success of the state, not by its failure. Thatcher inherited, uniquely in modern British history, a nation self-sufficient in food, an exporter of wheat and meat (a point not noted in social democratic or left histories). She also inherited a nation which was about to become, for the first time since 1939, a net exporter of energy. This epochal post-war transformation has barely registered in political discourse or the history books.[82] The implications were extraordinary: the UK no longer needed to be a net exporter of manufactures. The post-war national reconstruction programme was crucial to Thatcher for a second reason. There was a mass of modern public capital that had not been there in 1950, or 1960, or even 1970. As well as the cases mentioned above, council houses, in their millions, now existed, ready to be sold in unprecedented quantities. Furthermore, the devastations to the productive economy caused by government policy were only sustainable because the government inherited a newly comprehensive and, by historical British standards, generous welfare state created in the 1970s. There was an extensive safety net onto which many millions could and did fall. The official number of unemployed rose to more than three million and stayed at that level for years. The number of people on invalidity and sickness benefit doubled between 1980 and 1993, to two million people.[83]

Conclusion

That the Second World War or the late 1940s inaugurated Keynesianism and the welfare state and was therefore social democratic, and that this was superseded by a neoliberal era which was non- or even anti-Keynesian and which rolled back the welfare state, is a commonplace in British historiography. It rests on shaky foundations and is the result of, and has resulted in, an underpowered analysis of post-war history. Keynesianism, the welfare state and social democracy did exist, but not in ways or at times which justify any or all of them standing for the whole political-economic-social system. The conventional understanding of neoliberalism as the successor to this badly articulated social democracy is similarly limited and limiting, and the term probably should not be used at all.

Keynesianism, welfare state social democracy and neoliberalism are hardly the only keywords of modern British historiography which should be challenged. 'New liberalism', 'the people's budget', 'the war to end war', 'appeasement', 'Britain alone', 'people's war', 'consensus', 'post-war settlement', 'affluence', 'stop-go', 'decline', 'Thatcherism', 'monetarism' and, indeed, 'empire' are similarly open to challenge. They embody very particular analytical frames, but these are difficult to see because they are seen as British history itself. That is why there is a notable lack of debate between interpretations – where such debates have occurred they have largely been skirmishes over particular cases. One reason is that historiography overemphasises what has been visible in the public sphere and to the centre left.[84] While there are serious interpretative works on twentieth-century Britain which take distinct views, they are not the subject of extended debate as to their conclusions or their merits and are barely known to curricula.[85] They deserve to be. For the idea that the post-war UK was Keynesian and a welfare state is very much the product of historians' imaginations; so too is the notion that it should be described as social democratic, and indeed that it should not.

Notes

* I would like to record my deep appreciation for Patrick Joyce and Colin Gordon, organisers of the Foucault Life and Politics workshops, for providing the immensely stimulating context without which this paper would not have been written, as well as the organisers of the conference which has led to this book. I am also grateful to Aled Davies, Alex Hutton, Tom Kelsey, Kit Kowol, Gabriel Mesevage, Avner Offer, Richard Vinen and Jon Wilson for their comments and suggestions on drafts.

1 Pierre Dardot and Christian Laval, *The New Way of the World: On neoliberal society* (London, Verso, 2013), 46–7, makes the point that new liberalism and the later but overlapping *neoliberalism,* as ideas, were both committed to saving liberalism, but by different means – the first exemplified for them by Keynes, by increasing state intervention, the second by using the state to maximise the operation of markets. But while they insist on the difference between liberalism and neoliberalism, they have no account of what came between them historically – other than odd references to Fordism and welfare states and so on.

2 Sometimes, however, *neoliberal* means simply a wide variety of liberalisms in play from 1945, as in Ben Jackson, 'Currents of neo-liberalism: British political ideologies and the New Right, c.1955–1979', *English Historical Review*, 131 (2016), 823–50.

3 For a rich, not only British-focused, argument to this effect, see Ben Jackson, 'Social democracy' in Michael Freeden and Marc Stears (eds), *The Oxford Handbook of Political Ideologies* (Oxford, Oxford University Press, 2013), 348–63.

4 On which see Emily Robinson, *The Language of Progressive Politics in Modern Britain* (London, Palgrave Macmillan, 2017).

5 Daniel Wincott, 'The (golden) age of the welfare state: Interrogating a conventional wisdom', *Public Administration*, 91 (2013), 806–22.

6 Jim Tomlinson, *Managing the Economy, Managing the People: Narratives of economic life in Britain from Beveridge to Brexit* (Oxford, Oxford University Press, 2017), 229–30.

7 On affluence, see Stuart Middleton, '"Affluence" and the left in Britain, *c.*1958–1974', *English Historical Review*, 129 (2014), 107–38; on consensus, see Richard Toye, 'From "consensus" to

"common ground": The rhetoric of the postwar settlement and its collapse', *Journal of Contemporary History*, 48 (2013), 3–23.

8 For the neglect of the important British warfare state after 1945 in the literature, and how it was possible for historiography and the social sciences to so systematically neglect such a crucial and obviously significant part of the state, see David Edgerton, *Warfare State: Britain, 1920–1970* (Cambridge, Cambridge University Press, 2005), especially chapter 7.

9 Walter G. Runciman, 'Has British capitalism changed since the First World War?', *British Journal of Sociology*, 44 (1993), 53–67.

10 Thanks to Daniel Wincott.

11 David Howell, *British Social Democracy: A study in development and decay* (London, Croom Helm, 1976).

12 Stuart Hall, 'The great moving right show', *Marxism Today* (January 1979), 14–20.

13 Eric Hobsbawm, 'Out of the ashes', *Marxism Today* (April 1991), 19.

14 Andrew Gamble, *Britain in Decline: Economic policy, political strategy and the British state* (London, Macmillan, 1981), 186–7. See p. 185 for its party political senses.

15 Andrew Gamble, *The Free Economy and the Strong State: The politics of Thatcherism* (London, Macmillan, 1988). Thanks to Jon Wilson.

16 Jeffry A. Frieden, *Global Capitalism: Its rise and fall in the twentieth century* (New York, Norton, 2007), 229–50, 297–300. It is particularly interesting in noting that small countries, very exposed to world trade, could be among the most social democratic – he has in mind the Nordics.

17 Branko Milanović, *Capitalism Alone* (Cambridge, MA, Belknap Press, 2019).

18 Tony Judt, *Ill Fares the Land* (London, Penguin, 2010). An expansion of a lecture: Tony Judt, 'What is living and what is dead in social democracy?', *New York Review of Books* (17 December 2009).

19 Dylan Riley, 'Tony Judt: A cooler look', *New Left Review* (September–October 2011).

20 Tony Judt, *Postwar* (London, Penguin, 2005).

21 Thomas Piketty, *Capital and Ideology* (Cambridge, MA, Belknap Press, 2020), 487–91. In the following pages Piketty does discuss in effect many other rich dimensions of social democracy but they are not included in the definition.

22 Paul Addison, 'The intellectual origins of the Keynesian revolution', *Twentieth Century British History*, 2 (1991), 89–94.

23 Roger Middleton, *Government versus the Market: The growth of the public sector, economic management and British economic performance c.1890–1979* (Cheltenham, Edward Elgar, 1996).

24 For example James Vernon, 'The local, the imperial and the global: Repositioning twentieth-century Britain and the brief life of its social democracy', *Twentieth Century British History*, 21 (2010), 375–418, at 418: 'I have suggested that the central historical problem in twentieth-century Britain was not the strange death of liberal England but the brief life of social democracy.'

25 Gillian Murray, 'Community business in Scotland: An alternative vision of "enterprise culture", 1979–97', *Twentieth Century British History*, 30 (2019), 585–606, at 586; Alistair Kefford, 'Housing the citizen-consumer in post-war Britain: The Parker Morris Report, affluence and the even briefer life of social democracy', *Twentieth Century British History*, 29 (2018), 225–58, at 226; and Tom Hulme, 'Putting the city back into citizenship: Civics education and local government in Britain, 1918–45', *Twentieth Century British History*, 26 (2015), 26–51 at 26.

26 James Vernon, *Modern Britain: 1750 to the present* (Cambridge, Cambridge University Press, 2017), 372, 378–9.

27 Aled Davies, *The City of London and Social Democracy: The political economy of finance in Britain 1959–1979* (Oxford, Oxford University Press, 2017), 1.

28 Davies, *The City of London*, 5.

29 Davies, *The City of London*, 18.

30 Guy Ortolano, *Thatcher's Progress: From social democracy to market liberalism through an English New Town* (Cambridge, Cambridge University Press, 2019), 17–19. He identifies a 'broadly social democratic political culture' (28); he refers to a deep 'social democratic project' identified with the welfare state (29). See also 33–4 where social democracy contains within it both consumerism and individualism.

31 Ortolano, *Thatcher's Progress*, 21, citing Davies, *City of London* and David Edgerton, *The Rise and Fall of the British Nation: A twentieth-century history* (London, Allen Lane, 2018).

32 Gamble, *Britain in Decline*, 103.
33 Vernon, *Modern Britain*, chapters 10 and 11.
34 Scott Newton, *The Reinvention of Britain 1960–2016: A political and economic history* (London, Routledge, 2017).
35 Patrick Joyce, *The State of Freedom: A social history of the British state since 1800* (Cambridge, Cambridge University Press, 2013), 322 ff, passim.
36 For a critique of the surprisingly common assumption that most change in twentieth-century Britain came from progressive liberals or social democrats, see Edgerton, *Rise and Fall of the British Nation*.
37 See, for example, Peter Clarke, *Hope and Glory: Britain 1900–2000* (London, Penguin, 1996, 2004); Vernon, *Modern Britain*; and Pat Thane, *Divided Kingdom: A history of Britain, 1900 to the present* (Cambridge, Cambridge University Press, 2018).
38 See Edgerton, *Rise and Fall of the British Nation*.
39 Ortolano, *Thatcher's Progress*, is an exception as noted above.
40 Alec Nove, *Efficiency Criteria for Nationalised Industries* (London, George Allen & Unwin, 1973).
41 See, for example, Sally Sheard, *The Passionate Economist: How Brian Abel-Smith shaped global health and social welfare* (Bristol, Policy Press, 2013).
42 Daniel Wincott, 'Images of welfare in law and society: The British welfare state in comparative perspective', *Journal of Law and Society*, 38 (2011), 343–75; and Wincott, '(Golden) age of the welfare state', 806–22.
43 For an attempt to sketch out these arguments, see Edgerton, *Rise and Fall of the British Nation*, 302–6, 460–2.
44 Richard Vinen, *Thatcher's Britain: The politics and social upheaval of the Thatcher era* (London, Simon & Schuster, 2013).
45 Avner Offer, 'The market turn: From social democracy to market liberalism', *Economic History Review*, 70 (2017), 1051–71.
46 Andrew Seaton, 'Against the "sacred cow": NHS opposition and the fellowship for freedom in medicine, 1948–72', *Twentieth Century British History*, 26 (2015), 424–49.
47 Stephen M. Davies, 'Promoting productivity in the National Health Service, 1950 to 1966', *Contemporary British History*, 31 (2017), 47–68.
48 Tomlinson, *Managing the Economy*, 69, also makes the point that the 1970s were the high point of social democracy. See also Edgerton, *Rise and Fall of the British Nation*, chapter 16.
49 But only if a qualifier to a term descriptive of the system – as in Milanović's 'social-democratic capitalism'.
50 See John Maynard Keynes, *The General Theory of Employment, Interest and Money* (London, Macmillan, 1936), chapter 24, 'Concluding notes'. Thanks to Tom Kelsey. Ironically, through nationalisation Labour created purer rentiers than the old owners of nationalised industries. They exchanged shares for more secure government bonds.
51 José Harris, 'Enterprise and welfare states: A comparative perspective', *Transactions of the Royal Historical Society*, 40 (1990), 180
52 Wincott, '(Golden) age of the welfare state', 806–22.
53 E. H. H. Green, 'The Treasury resignations of 1958: A reconsideration', *Twentieth Century British History*, 11 (2000), 409–30.
54 Neil Rollings, '"The Reichstag method of governing"? The Attlee governments and permanent economic controls', in Helen Mercer and Neil Rollings (eds), *Labour Governments and Private Industry* (Edinburgh, Edinburgh University Press, 1992).
55 On the term 'welfare state', see Edgerton, *Warfare State*, 59–60; Klaus Jørn Petersen and Henrik Petersen, 'Confusion and divergence: Origins and meanings of the term "welfare state" in Germany and Britain, 1840–1940', *Journal of European Social Policy*, 23 (2013), 37–51; and Daniel Wincott, 'Original and imitated or elusive and limited? Towards a genealogy of the welfare state idea in Britain', in Daniel Béland and Klaus Petersen (eds), *Analysing Social Policy Concepts and Language: Comparative and transnational perspectives* (Bristol, Policy Press, 2014), 127–42.
56 See Richard Titmuss, *Essays on the 'Welfare State'* (London, Allen & Unwin, 1958).
57 Labour Party, *Forward with Labour: Labour's policy for the consideration of the nation* (1955).
58 Conservative Party, *United for Peace and Progress: The Conservative and Unionist Party's policy: A personal statement by the Prime Minister* (1955).
59 Jim Tomlinson, 'Tale of a death exaggerated: How Keynesian policies survived the 1970s', *Contemporary British History*, 21 (2007), 429–48.

60 Piketty, *Capital and Ideology*, 457.

61 One might add that many accounts of neoliberalism are inversions of the very limited and intellectualised stories the neoliberals told of themselves. Amy C. Offner, *Sorting Out the Mixed Economy: The rise and fall of welfare and developmental states in the Americas* (Princeton, NJ, Princeton University Press, 2019), 283–5, 289.

62 David Edgerton and Kirsty Hughes, 'The poverty of science: A critical analysis of scientific and industrial policy under Mrs Thatcher', *Public Administration*, 67 (1989), 419–33.

63 Though some, such as David Harvey, define neoliberalism as a renewal of the power of capital, a global phenomenon emerging out of the crisis of capitalist accumulation of the 1970s, rather than merely the result of a change in ideas. David Harvey, *A Brief History of Neoliberalism* (Oxford, Oxford University Press, 2005). See also Milanović, *Capitalism Alone*.

64 Michel Foucault, *The Birth of Biopolitics: Lectures at the Collège de France, 1978–1979*, trans. Graham Burchell (London, Routledge, 2008).

65 Of course, in reality, many, including Foucault, understood the distinctiveness of West Germany's 'social market economy' and its ordo-liberalism, and indeed did not subscribe to this model at all.

66 See Keith Tribe, 'Liberalism and neoliberalism in Britain, 1930–1980', in Philip Mirowski and Dieter Plehwe (eds), *The Road from Mont Pèlerin: The making of the neoliberal thought collective* (Cambridge, MA, Harvard University Press, 2009). More generally Tribe notes that the British neoliberals of the 1940s and 1950s and subsequently had no grasp of economic realities.

67 Quinn Slobodian, *Globalists: The end of empire and the birth of neoliberalism* (Cambridge, MA, Harvard University Press, 2018).

68 Edgerton, *Rise and Fall of the British Nation*.

69 This is an argument made in Edgerton, *Rise and Fall of the British Nation*. The broader context of the spread of import substitution industrialisation (ISI) and the shrinkage of trade in post-colonial and Latin American states after 1945 is well described in Frieden, *Global Capitalism*, chapter 13.

70 Tom Nairn, 'The left against Europe?', *New Left Review* (September 1972); and Bob Rowthorn, 'Imperialism in the seventies: Unity or rivalry?', *New Left Review* (September 1971). For the general argument for the centrality of the nationalist critique to the left, see Edgerton, *Rise and Fall of the British Nation*, 385–94.

71 John Eatwell, *Whatever Happened to Britain? The economics of decline* (London, Duckworth, 1982), especially chapter 4 on the 'Keynesian ideology'.

72 Eatwell, *Whatever Happened*, 142 and passim, is a good example of this argument. See also Perry Anderson, 'The figures of descent', *New Left Review* (January–February 1987), 20–77.

73 For the standard national view, see Angus Calder, *The People's War: Britain 1939–1945* (London, Deutsch, 1969). For a critique, and the alternative non-national view, registering the internationalist and imperialist aspects, see David Edgerton, *Britain's War Machine: Weapons, resources and experts in the Second World War* (London, Allen Lane, 2011).

74 The key work is George Brennan and Alan Milward, *Britain's Place in the World: Import controls 1945–60* (London, Routledge, 2003).

75 On this, see Tomlinson, *Managing the Economy*, chapter 9.

76 Alan S. Milward, *The Rise and Fall of a National Strategy 1945–1963: The UK and the European Community, Volume 1* (London, Routledge, 2002).

77 See David Edgerton, *England and the Aeroplane: Militarism, modernity and machines* (London, Penguin, 1991, 2013); Edgerton, *Warfare State*; and Waqar S. H. Zaidi, 'The Janus-face of techno-nationalism: Barnes Wallis and the "strength of England"', *Technology and Culture*, 49 (2008), 62–88.

78 On which point see Otto Saumarez Smith, *Boom Cities: Architect-planners and the politics of radical urban renewal in 1960s Britain* (Oxford, Oxford University Press, 2019). Ortolano, *Thatcher's Progress*, notes that while there is much to be said for the social democratic origins of Milton Keynes – not least the social democratic politics of the chair of the New Town, and its architect – the model was, as he shows, something like Los Angeles, accommodating and using the motor car, which suggests another set of ideologies, since the US and the motor car are not usually thought of as social democratic.

79 Brett Christophers, *Rentier Capitalism: Who owns the economy, and who pays for it?* (London, Verso, 2020).

80 House of Commons Debates, *Hansard* (22 January 1975), vol. 884, col. 1553. La Pasionaria was the nickname given to Dolores Ibárruri, a famous Spanish communist politician.

81 See Edgerton, *Rise and Fall of the British Nation*, for this perspective, and also more recent work focusing on wealth, rather than markets, notably Grace Blakeley, *Stolen: How to save the world from financialisation* (London, Repeater, 2019). See also the vital work on the 'foundational economy' and what has happened to it: Foundational Economy Collective, *Foundational Economy: The infrastructure of everyday life* (Manchester, Manchester University Press, 2018).

82 Bob Rowthorn and John Wells, *De-Industrialisation and Foreign Trade* (Cambridge, Cambridge University Press, 1987), 100–1.

83 See, for example, Institute for Fiscal Studies, online resources at https://www.ifs.org.uk/tools_and_resources/fiscal_facts (accessed 21 June 2021), specifically Employment and Support Allowance, Incapacity Benefit, Invalidity Benefit and Sickness Benefit at https://www.ifs.org.uk/uploads/publications/ff/ib_2020.xlsx (accessed 24 January 2021).

84 On the question of what is visible and what is not, see Edgerton, *Rise and Fall of the British Nation*, xxxvi–xxxvii.

85 For a discussion of a number of such works, see Edgerton, *Rise and Fall of the British Nation*, 592–600. See also Robinson, *Language of Progressive Politics* and David Edgerton, 'The nationalisation of British history: Historians, nationalism and the myths of 1940', *English Historical Review*, 136 (2021), n.p.

3
Intellectual histories of neoliberalism and their limits

Ben Jackson*

Writing in 1989, Maurice Cowling penned a memorable account of the 'sources of the New Right' in British politics since the Second World War. A participant in some of the circles that he delineated, Cowling sketched a vivid portrait of the small group of intellectuals, politicians and activists who, he said, had been instrumental in rallying Conservative opinion to mount a concerted counter-offensive against the 'liberal collectivism' established in 1940. This 'New Right' constituted 'about 50 people' in total '(mainly graduates, and mostly men)', and had 'five faces': the revivalist market liberal economists centred around the Institute of Economic Affairs (IEA); the opponents of progressive education, comprehensive schools and university radicalism who coalesced around the publication of the Black Papers; the intellectuals and MPs who supported Enoch Powell and then Margaret Thatcher (including by founding the think tank the Centre for Policy Studies [CPS]); the small group of Conservative academics (including Cowling himself) who were associated particularly with the London School of Economics, Peterhouse, Cambridge and the journal *The Salisbury Review*; and, finally, the intellectually inclined journalists who promulgated New Right opinion across the national British press in the 1970s and 1980s, particularly in *The Telegraph* but also in *The Times* and most other influential British newspapers of the period.[1] Cowling recognised that there were severe limits to the impact of such intellectual endeavours on political and social life, but he nonetheless insisted that even the seemingly pragmatic Conservative Party required 'reserves of belief which can be called up without having to be created on each particular occasion'. Fostering such 'reserves of belief', argued Cowling, had been the important accomplishment of the New Right.[2]

The term 'neoliberalism' had not yet come into widespread use at the time Cowling wrote, but there is considerable overlap between Cowling's enthusiastic reconstruction of the intellectual roots of his New Right and the many accounts of late modern British history that ascribe significant causal weight to neoliberal ideology. Like Cowling, some of the most influential works on Britain after the 1970s have stressed the importance of a variety of academics, journalists, think tanks and freelance activists in generating the distinctive policy agenda that has dominated British politics since then. The most un-Cowling-like figures Andrew Gamble and Stuart Hall pioneered in the pages of *Marxism Today* and later academic publications a fecund analysis of Thatcherism as a distinctively ideological project that sought to refashion public policy and political discourse in a style that would be more favourable to the interests of the Conservative Party. Whereas Cowling himself said little about the wider international context of this turn towards a more muscular form of Conservatism, Gamble and Hall conceptualised Thatcherism as the local embodiment of a global ideological counter-offensive by market liberals.[3] This line of argument dovetails with the work undertaken more recently by intellectual historians, which has documented in detail the creation of an influential body of economic and political theory by the 'neoliberal thought collective' organised around the Mont Pèlerin Society (MPS), the international discussion group founded by Friedrich Hayek in 1947 to revive market liberalism.[4]

Scepticism about intellectual history

In spite of this widespread interest in the ideology of neoliberalism, other historians have nonetheless expressed reservations about how influential such ideas really were.[5] This is particularly the case in the field of modern British history, where two different strands of the burgeoning scholarship on the late twentieth century have created a pincer movement against this preoccupation with the intellectual roots of Thatcherism.[6] One strand originates in the field of political history and offers a high political account of the 1980s that is doubtful about the extent to which senior politicians and civil servants meaningfully engaged with the New Right intelligentsia identified by Cowling. Perhaps the most important variant of this argument has been elaborated by Richard Vinen. Among other things, Vinen has argued that historians and political scientists have paid disproportionate attention to think tanks and intellectuals compared with the more consequential role played by government ministers and civil servants. These latter figures, Vinen argues, were more obviously central to government decision-making than the obscure scribblers emphasised by commentators fascinated by ideas.[7] Yet in a curious twist, this interpretation of Thatcherism is itself somewhat Cowlingite in flavour, as it asserts the autonomy of the 'high political' domain at the expense of a wider analysis of economic, social and intellectual forces, a point that Cowling himself had famously used as a guiding principle when writing his histories of modern British politics.[8] Indeed, Cowling had raised precisely this point in his article on the New Right:

> Until enough of the archives are open, including the private archives of politicians, it will be difficult to know how Mrs Thatcher succeeded after 1979 in effecting changes which Mr Heath had promised in 1966 but had failed to deliver in office. It may well turn out that the existence of an independent intelligentsia was unimportant, and that what mattered was the opinions of civil servants and of the political heavyweights – Mr Nigel Lawson, Sir Geoffrey Howe, Lord Joseph and, pre-eminently, Mrs Thatcher herself – after the acquiescence of the last three under Mr Heath.[9]

While this strand of political history has sought to minimise the importance of ideological argument to the politics of Thatcherism, a second strand of scholarship has striven to downplay the significance of party politics and state decision-making altogether. Social and economic historians have aimed to 'decentre' the 1980s and 1990s by focusing on larger economic, social and discursive changes that they argue are of more fundamental causal significance than the neoliberal ideology given star billing in many of the standard histories of the late twentieth century.[10] One important economic claim that has been pressed in the literature on the global rise of neoliberalism is that material changes in capitalist production and class interests should bear the bulk of the explanatory weight in accounting for the neoliberal trend in public policy after the 1970s.[11] With respect to Britain, a powerful version of this wider interpretation has been made by Aled Davies, who has shown that the changing structure of the financial sector in the 1960s and 1970s – with the growth of institutional investors, a liberalisation of the banking sector and the rise of unregulated global capital markets in London – undermined key elements of the post-war economic model and facilitated a shift in economic policy in a neoliberal direction.[12]

A more radical strand of economic analysis denies not just that ideology was important in the rise of neoliberalism but that 'neoliberalism' itself is an overrated category for conceptualising economic change in the late twentieth century. Jim Tomlinson, for example, has drawn attention to the importance of the economics of deindustrialisation in this period – a process that he sees as largely independent of the actions of particular governments and which (he argues) produced much of the social and economic tumult usually attributed to the Thatcher government and 'neoliberalism'.[13] Similarly, David Edgerton has argued that economic change in modern British history is best described as a transition from a mid-twentieth-century nationalist and industrial model of the economy to an internationalist, service-sector economy that emerged under the Thatcher government after the state became self-sufficient in food and energy and was therefore much less dependent on earnings from manufacturing exports.[14]

This economic analysis can be placed alongside the work of social historians who have detailed the decline of social deference in the post-war period. Historians such as Florence Sutcliffe-Braithwaite and Jon Lawrence have argued that the 1960s and 1970s saw the emergence of a new egalitarian spirit centred around the idea of 'ordinariness', which rejected established class hierarchies and prioritised individual autonomy and authenticity. This new social morality formed the context for Thatcherism, in that the individualism promoted by those governments was one way of formulating a political project that could appeal to these deeply rooted popular sentiments, but from this perspective Thatcherism and neoliberalism look much more like a product of this underlying social change rather than the cause of it.[15] Like the economic histories, the new social histories of this period detect more deep-rooted, long-range trends that lie beneath the dramatic political events of the 1980s and suggest that a preoccupation with the personalities, policies and ideology of the Thatcher government obscures these more fundamental changes in Britain and around the world in the late twentieth century.

These are all salutary and important points, which deserve serious consideration in any historical account of this period. However, in this chapter I want to respond to this scholarship by reformulating the importance of intellectual history to our understanding of Britain after the 1970s. But I want to do so in a way that steers the debate away from the more exuberantly idealist accounts of the 1980s towards a more constrained account of how the history of ideas can complement the important insights that we can glean from the study of high politics, the economy and social change.[16] Scepticism about the social significance of ideas is of course a perennial theme in historical study that has generated in turn many compelling and ingenious answers from historians of a more idealist bent.[17] But one of the difficulties with resolving our specific question of whether neoliberal ideology should be seen as causally significant is that critics of the importance of ideas sometimes misunderstand what intellectual historians see as the distinctive contribution of their approach. In fact, there are a variety of ways in which ideas matter to the political life of modern societies and it is only by enumerating them, and distinguishing between them, that we can make progress in identifying the contribution of the history of ideas to the study of late twentieth-century Britain. In order to gauge the limits of intellectual history for our period, it is first necessary to make a reckoning with what precisely the study of neoliberal ideas *can* tell us.

The historiography of neoliberalism

One preliminary point to stress is that the most recent wave of scholarship on the intellectual history of neoliberalism is precisely trying to avoid a charge of gross idealism by integrating the study of ideas with a more sociological account of the networks that mobilised behind neoliberal ideas and of the social functions performed by intellectuals and think tanks across a variety of national contexts in the post-war period. The pioneering research on the MPS, and on the rise of neoliberalism in the US and Europe, has been distinguished from earlier work on this topic precisely because it has identified neoliberalism as a movement of ideas that publicised its ideology through a specific set of institutions that mobilised both intellectual and material resources in order to reshape elite opinion. This analysis of what Philip Mirowski and Dieter Plehwe have dubbed 'the neoliberal thought collective' uses the tools of social research to track the network of intellectuals who founded the MPS. It is significant that Mirowski and Plehwe adopted the term 'thought collective' from the sociology of science. Following Ludwig Fleck, a 'thought collective' refers to a community of thinkers who develop a shared set of ideas as a result of repeated intellectual interaction – highlighting that intellectual production is a collective enterprise that unfolds through social networks rather than in the solitary minds of great thinkers.[18] The 'thought collective' that coalesced around the MPS drew on the material resources of like-minded figures in the business world to construct a global alliance of think tanks and advocacy organisations whose role was to promote the neoliberal policy prospectus to elites around the world.[19]

This was a strategy that drew on Hayek's diagnosis of political change in his 1949 essay 'The intellectuals and socialism'. Hayek argued that changes in intellectual fashion were politically consequential because the boundaries of what is considered to be feasible in public policy were defined by a group of public intellectuals – journalists, novelists, certain academics, technical experts of various kinds – who broadcast to a wider audience their own perception of what were the most valid political and economic theories (without necessarily themselves having the expertise to adjudicate on this question). In Hayek's view, the success of socialism was explained by the widespread adoption of socialist ideas and attitudes by these 'second-hand dealers in ideas' over the course of the first half of the twentieth century. The neoliberal strategy, as it developed over the 1950s and 1960s, was therefore to counteract the intellectual growth of socialism by broadcasting market liberal ideas to elites (and to a lesser extent the public) through new public policy organisations – think tanks – that sat at the interface between academic knowledge and political debate and in effect contested the status of the left-leaning social sciences that had made such headway in the public sphere in the decades after the Second World War.[20] Such a project required considerable financial investment and assiduous political networking, both of which the 'thought collective' was able to build up over the course of the 1960s and 1970s.

The argument for the importance of neoliberal ideas is therefore a much more nuanced one than is sometimes supposed, insofar as it rests on this wider analysis of the social context of the generation of political ideas. In effect, the claim of intellectual historians is not that ideas were in and of themselves causally significant, but rather that ideas served as a key element in the neoliberal right's political strategy and succeeded in gaining a wide social purchase because they were effectively marketed by well-funded and highly strategic policy entrepreneurs. This was a transnational process and, in the case of Britain, there is a sense in which this represents an Americanisation of British political debate, since the most prestigious neoliberal figures and ideas tended to be transferred to Britain after being germinated in the US.[21]

A second preliminary point is that this new intellectual history has also stressed the internal diversity of neoliberalism. Neoliberal thought was the product of intellectual collaboration across national boundaries, but it also comprised several distinct strands of argument that reflected these diverse national origins and were at times in tension with one another. Austrian economists such as Hayek, for example, elaborated a strong form of economic individualism and a priori reasoning that was highly sceptical of the use of economic statistics or even the pursuit of macroeconomic policy by the state, both of which were key features of the work of the 'Chicago School' of economics associated with figures such as

Milton Friedman. Meanwhile, the 'ordo-liberal' tradition developed in Germany by economists such as Walter Eucken and Wilhelm Röpke incorporated a powerful role for the state in maintaining market freedom, for example by enforcing strong anti-monopoly policies, precisely the point that economists from Chicago such as George Stigler sought to contest in post-war policy debates in the US.[22] Other important strands of neoliberalism have also been identified. Quinn Slobodian, for example, has drawn attention to what he has called the 'Geneva School', which overlaps in membership with some of the groups mentioned earlier, but which focused on problems of global rather than domestic economic order. Slobodian has demonstrated that an important strand of neoliberalism has sought to 'encase' markets in institutions of global economic governance that would prevent sovereign states from disrupting private property rights and market transactions.[23] Likewise, the 'Virginia School' associated with James Buchanan, which focused on public choice theory and the economic analysis of political institutions, has recently become the subject of considerable debate.[24] At one level, this internal ideological diversity makes the story of neoliberalism's influence much more complex, since it is necessary to dig more deeply into the precise ideological connotations of particular arguments and policies and to be aware of the extent to which there was no straightforwardly homogeneous 'neoliberalism'. Neoliberalism was in any case a distinctive kind of ideology, which (as we have seen) was created not as part of a social movement, but initially as an elite-led effort to fight back against the ideological success of the left. Neoliberals were therefore at first detached from existing political factions – and to enter public debate in an influential way, they had to synthesise their ideas with pre-existing ideological traditions. This process meant that different currents of neoliberalism became available in public debate in Britain and elsewhere as liberals, conservatives and even socialists absorbed aspects of neoliberal theory into their political thought.[25]

Amid this dizzying array of differing forms of neoliberalism, however, it is also important to remember that neoliberal theorists and their political allies shared a lot in common as well, not least in the opponents that they saw themselves as arrayed against: the social democratic state bureaucracy, trade unions, the Soviet bloc, post-colonial movements and left-wing intellectuals and experts. One way of reconciling this mix of commonality and diversity within neoliberal ideology is to think of it as an alliance between different intellectual tendencies that were concerned about the various ways in which, over the course of the twentieth century, popular politics had eroded the liberating and efficient powers of the market. Neoliberals were therefore, as William Davies has put it, ultimately pursuing 'the disenchantment of politics by economics' in order to 'replace political judgement with economic evaluation', a project that was ultimately capable of a variety of theorisations and practical instantiations.[26]

Varieties of intellectual influence

The nature of neoliberalism and its influence is therefore far from a straightforward issue. In the rest of the chapter I will seek to navigate this complexity by developing a working typology that distinguishes between four different ways in which historians of this period can usefully engage with the history of neoliberal thought when telling the story of Britain in the late twentieth century. Firstly, and minimally, the study of ideology is itself one important way of documenting wider social and economic changes. The intellectual output of writers, thinkers, politicians and activists forms a substantial body of source material for understanding how contending elites in a society understood the times in which they lived and the fundamental political ideals that they sought to pursue to reform and improve that society. Such texts can also offer the clearest and most systematic exposition of debates that otherwise remain implicit or inchoate in popular discourse. From this perspective, the palpable growth of advocacy for neoliberalism during the 1970s and 1980s is itself a signifier of the way in which market economics emerged as a challenger to the model of the British state that evolved in the mid-twentieth century. Without making any claim about wider political influence, such source material simply offers the historian a means of accessing the most detailed statements of the ways in which unvarnished capitalism began to shift from an old-fashioned worldview to an appealing option for the future. For example, leading advocates of neoliberalism in Britain, such as Arthur Seldon, the Editorial Director of the IEA, believed that the lived experience of post-war capitalism was fundamentally at odds with the top-down logic of the social democratic state because it gave individuals the capacity to make choices for themselves, as consumers, rather than simply accepting what they were given by state-run services. The British people, Seldon argued in 1966, now enjoyed much greater 'freedom of choice for their food and drinks, their clothes, their furniture and household equipment'. Since the average man and woman were now 'treated like lords and ladies at the grocer's, the hairdresser's and on the plane to their fortnight in Spain', it was unlikely that they will 'tolerate much longer being treated as servile, cap-in-hand supplicants in the local state school, the doctor's surgery, the hospital'. Hostility to the paternalism of state-provided welfare, Seldon concluded, would therefore increase as incomes rose.[27] The attractions of market-based forms of freedom – and their presumed appeal to certain electoral groups – can therefore in part be documented through an investigation of the way they were expressed in public debate.

Secondly, some of the scepticism about the importance of ideas noted earlier neglects the extent to which the capacity to engage in argument about public policy depends on fundamental conceptual innovations among technical specialists that in turn provide the very categories that structure that debate. When new political agendas are formulated, as they were in the 1970s and 1980s, whether they are pushed to the forefront of policymaking by material pressures or by high political manoeuvres, they nonetheless require intellectual content with sufficient technocratic authority to make the proposed policies appear credible to financial markets, civil servants, the media and (to a lesser extent) the public. They therefore must draw on the specialised language developed by professional intellectuals of various sorts, whether located in think tanks, academia or the higher echelons of the media. This is a particularly acute need in the case of economic policy, where a workable governing economic strategy requires a level of technical detail that can only be provided by specialists in the field. Professional economists are therefore the principal group of intellectuals who, from the mid-twentieth century onwards, have been able to act as the authoritative interpreters of a body of knowledge that has a direct relationship with policymaking. The precise influence of academic economics on economic policymaking is of course a complex one, but my specific focus here is on the way in which changes at a broad level in economic theory reshape public policy.[28] My argument is not at this stage the more fine-grained one that specific ideas shape specific policy proposals, rather it is that deep conceptual shifts open up new spaces in political argument.

A useful illustration of this point is the well-ventilated debate about monetarism. The history of neoliberalism is inextricably bound up with the history of new ideas about macroeconomic management, especially the rise of monetarism as an alternative to what is sometimes rather crudely referred to as 'Keynesianism'. As Jim Bulpitt pointed out many years ago, monetarism proved politically useful for the Conservative Party because it prescribed a new form of counter-inflationary statecraft that departed from a reliance on negotiating wage increases with trade unions (a practice that was widely believed to disadvantage the

Conservative Party electorally in the 1970s).[29] In essence, Bulpitt identified the high political rationale for economic policy change that has been widely discussed by historians and political scientists ever since.[30] But while it is correct to note that monetarism became politically useful to the Conservative Party for this reason, this does not mean that a more idealist account of monetarism is irrelevant to a historical explanation of its rise. As we have seen, the technocratic character of economic policy is such that it is not possible simply to adopt *any* economic idea as state policy unless it carries with it a degree of scientific authority, as perceived by government and central bank officials, financial markets and economic commentators. Any story about why monetarism emerged as a policy option in Britain in the 1970s – whether relating to the condition of the British economy, party interest, the role of financial markets and so on – therefore must start by acknowledging that the concept of something called 'monetarism' existed because it had been constructed in the first place by a number of technically qualified economists, notably Milton Friedman, who popularised the term and set out a range of arguments for it.

In particular, it seems clear that Friedman's famous 1967 presidential address to the American Economic Association, 'The role of monetary policy', had an important international agenda-setting impact in highlighting the case he (and others) had made in hitherto specialised publications that there was no long-run trade-off between inflation and unemployment since workers come to expect price rises and to demand that their wages keep pace with inflation. While there is a considerable debate about the theoretical originality of this lecture (or its lack of it), and its subsequent reception among economists, Friedman's address was nonetheless widely perceived by policymakers and in elite public debate in the 1970s as signifying an important shift in economic opinion.[31] The continued application of inflationary stimulus, Friedman was understood to have argued, cannot push unemployment below its 'natural' rate. Instead, Friedman popularised the adoption of monetary rules to control inflation and to focus government policy on ensuring monetary stability rather than lowering unemployment.[32] The complexities of implementing this theoretical design were formidable and caused enormous problems for the Thatcher government in practice,[33] but the point nonetheless stands that intellectual history is a necessary ingredient of this larger historical story because it enables us to identify the precise concepts and theories that were then taken up in policy debate, and to track how these concepts and theories provided political actors with new languages with which to legitimise their actions. Intellectual history is therefore in part about a stage a few steps removed from the exigencies of political decision-making insofar as it reconstructs the formation of the broad conceptual space in which that decision-making takes place.

A third way in which ideas are salient to historical explanation is that it is only through language that social change can itself be interpreted. That is to say, the study of ideas is not only, as I suggested earlier, a means by which underlying social change can be registered, it is also a way to understand how historical actors imprinted a particular meaning on this social change and constructed compelling narratives about the political action necessary to rectify the problems they diagnosed. In one sense, this is to agree with much of the neo-Cowlingite picture painted by historians such as Richard Vinen, which focuses on the capacity of leading politicians, not least Margaret Thatcher herself, to use rhetoric as an effective weapon in the struggle for power. A 'high politics' analysis of Thatcherism is an ally of the intellectual history of this period insofar as both approaches agree that focusing purely on shifting economic interests or exogenous social change cannot offer a full account. This is because both political and intellectual historians follow the linguistic turn insofar as they see interests as only legible to historical actors through a process of conceptualisation and interpretation that necessarily relies on ideas (an insight that has of course also been recognised by social historians ever since the early debates about the linguistic turn in the 1980s).[34] In the case of political history, more emphasis is placed on the way in which leading political figures construct coalitions of support and frame policy debates through careful use of public speech.[35] For intellectual historians, the focus falls more on the fine-grained analysis of the writings of professional ideologists, whether formally employed as academics, journalists, policy experts or even politicians. But there is no reason to see these two approaches as contradictory, as some political historians seem to suggest in the case of Thatcherism. We might instead see them as complementary, in part because politicians inevitably draw on and render in more demotic form the language first set out at a more abstract level in specialised books and periodicals, and in part because the intellectuals also take their lead from the politicians and develop new arguments that extend and reinforce the positioning first laid out in a more popular form in political speeches.

To give one example of the former process, in the late 1960s Enoch Powell made a robust public case for market liberalism (and nationalism) that drew on a close acquaintance with neoliberal political and economic theory (Powell was a long-standing MPS member). Powell was an important forerunner of elements of Thatcherism, though he was markedly less successful than Keith Joseph or Thatcher in framing public debate in Britain in neoliberal terms – in part because he spoke as an outsider, lacking the authority of a leading figure in a party aspiring to form a government, and in part because the economic context – only a few years into a new Labour administration – could not yet be as persuasively portrayed as a systematic crisis as it could be in the later 1970s.[36]

Keith Joseph played a more significant role as an outrider for what became Thatcherism in the 1970s, initially making a series of important speeches in 1974 that set out an early version of what became the Thatcherite analysis of Britain's decline during the post-war period. These speeches were written in collaboration with his adviser, Alfred Sherman, as well as with the input of sympathetic economists and journalists such as Alan Walters and Samuel Brittan.[37] All of these figures had close connections to the alternative intellectual infrastructure developed by neoliberals over the 1960s and 1970s – Walters, for example, was a member of the MPS (and later an adviser to Margaret Thatcher in government), and Brittan had been deploying the ideas of figures such as Hayek and Friedman in his journalism in the *Financial Times* throughout the 1970s.[38] Joseph's speeches were punctuated by references to IEA pamphlets and works by economists associated with the MPS, forming an overall analysis that clearly owed a great deal to the political and economic theory of neoliberalism. As Joseph himself wrote to Ralph Harris at the IEA during his summer holiday in the middle of writing and delivering these speeches: 'I'm steeping myself in Hayek – and am ashamed not to have read the great *Constitution of Liberty* long ago.' He also reported that he was reading Friedman's IEA pamphlet, *Monetary Correction*, and various other IEA pamphlets he had taken with him.[39] The central argument of Joseph's speeches was that Britain's economic turbulence in the 1970s – or Britain's 'decline', as Joseph would have seen it – was the product of systemic flaws in the economic and social policy of the British state, flaws which he diagnosed as related to a failure to exercise appropriate control over inflation via monetary policy and the expansion of government activity into the economy in a way that had distorted market price signals and incentives.[40] Similar points about the artful use of political language to construct a particular interpretation of the economic crisis of the 1970s have also been made by Robert Saunders in relation to the speeches of Margaret Thatcher and by Colin Hay with respect to the popular press.[41] James Freeman's chapter in this book gives several other important examples of the way in which Conservative politicians such as Thatcher and Joseph 'interfaced' with neoliberal (as well as neoconservative) ideas in their speechwriting through contact with figures such as Sherman, and William and Shirley Letwin (who were both former students of Hayek), and through their own reading. Given the numerous interconnections that can be documented between the realm of more abstract intellectual argument and political speech, it therefore seems more fruitful to treat these approaches to the analysis of political language as complementary rather than antagonistic.

A fourth way in which ideas influence political outcomes is a much narrower one: when it can be demonstrated that specific policy innovations or decisions drew on ideas that were initially elaborated by think tanks or political writers. This is often the hardest category to document and is perhaps the form of influence that sceptics of intellectual history have in mind when they suggest that ideological accounts of Thatcherism are overblown. It is certainly important to be cautious when making claims about the specific influence of intellectuals on decision-making which occurs amid the extraordinary pressures that face governments, when politicians and their advisers and officials daily face new headwinds that buffet them off course. Yet even here there are examples of neoliberal ideas being deployed directly by politicians and their advisers in state policymaking, examples which usually demonstrate the important mediating role played by think tanks in connecting the ideological domain with practical policymaking. The reason that ideology enters the decision-making equation at this high political level is precisely because of the pressures and complexity of state policy formation: amid this tumult it is necessary to have a 'heuristic' that can guide political action in an agreed strategic direction without having to litigate that overall strategy on each occasion.[42] In the case of the Thatcher governments, such a rough rule of thumb was often related to the desire to increase consumer choice, widen asset ownership and increase market competition. In practice, this ideological orientation was not always successful, but it does provide an important insight into how decisions were taken by the Conservatives in power. Several examples of this have been documented in the literature on Thatcherism.

Matthew Francis, for example, has shown that the precise form taken by the Thatcher government's privatisation policies reflected an ideological preference for widening private property ownership that went beyond traditional Conservative statecraft or economic necessity to reveal a Conservatism that had been deeply influenced by neoliberalism. Each of the privatisations was designed to offer preferential access to ownership to 'ordinary' individuals, whether through employee share ownership, priority for small investors or significant discounts on the purchase of council houses (often in the face of objections from the Treasury, on the grounds that this approach would not maximise government revenue). These choices in policy design reflected an extended discussion within the Conservative Party from the 1970s about the relationship between democracy and ownership and a marked shift in the thinking of key Conservatives towards the neoliberal argument that the wider personal choice facilitated by private property ownership represented a deeper form of democratic control than voting or political participation.[43]

Charles Lockwood has identified a second example: the introduction of compulsory competitive tendering for local government services. This idea was pushed up the political agenda by the Adam Smith Institute (ASI) in 1980, in a pamphlet authored by the future Conservative MP Michael Forsyth (who at that time was a councillor on Westminster City Council). Drawing on the public choice theory of MPS member Gordon Tullock, Forsyth argued that introducing competitive tendering for core functions of local government would serve as a way to introduce market competition into council services while avoiding the full-scale political row that would ensue if services were straightforwardly privatised. Thatcher's Policy Unit ordered 20,000 copies of the pamphlet to circulate to Conservative local authorities. The scope of compulsory competitive tendering was increased over time by the Conservatives in government from 1980 onwards, with certain Conservative councils acting as pioneers who would go much further than the legislative requirements laid down by central government.[44]

A third example, which I have discussed elsewhere, was the Major government's introduction of vouchers for nursery education in 1995. The decision to create a voucher system for nurseries was a straightforward reflection of the wider debate among Conservative intellectuals and think tanks about the importance of introducing a market for childcare services in Britain rather than a universal taxpayer-funded system. Pamphlets by the CPS and the ASI had made this point in the run-up to the government's pivot towards offering greater financial support for working parents. The author of the ASI pamphlet, David Soskin, ran a chain of private nurseries, and shortly after writing the report for the ASI he went to work in the Number 10 Policy Unit for John Major, thus providing a particularly clear example of the way in which neoliberal think tanks mobilised social networks and ideas in a politically effective way.[45]

A fourth, more ambiguous, example, uncovered by Aled Davies, James Freeman and Hugh Pemberton, concerns the important role played by the CPS in the Thatcher government's pension policy. Figures associated with the CPS and the wider neoliberal policy community, such as Nigel Vinson and Philip Chappell, made considerable headway in internal government debates by arguing for a radical extension of personal responsibility into pensions. Rather than accepting the collective and institutional character of pension funds that had developed by the 1980s, they argued that the Thatcher government should seek to introduce individualised pension funds that were owned and managed by individual workers themselves. This proposal was not in fact implemented in full, in part because of internal opposition within government but also because of the severe practical difficulties that emerged in putting such a radical vision into practice. However, as Davies, Freeman and Pemberton have shown, the pension reforms enacted by the Thatcher government did take up ideas of individual choice derived from neoliberal theory. Rather than the initial idea of creating a nation of individual investors, a new vision emerged of a pension system that furnished consumers with the freedom to choose between different pension providers. As Davies, Freeman and Pemberton put it, Thatcherism emerges from this case study as a '*pathway* through the diverse array of neoliberal ideas', a political project that evolved in the making as it drew on certain strands of neoliberalism and traditional British Conservatism to overcome both internal ideological tensions and practical obstacles.[46]

The limits of neoliberalism

The case for the importance of neoliberal ideas in shaping the political trajectory of Britain since the 1970s is therefore a strong one, but (as the example of pensions policy shows) it is crucial to qualify this statement by recognising that the influence of neoliberalism was also a limited one, which should not be used straightforwardly to capture the entirety of British historical experience between the 1970s and today. Firstly, intellectual history by its nature tends to focus on the elaboration of ideas among elites, so this approach has tended to pay less attention to the way in which neoliberal ideas circulated among the wider public.[47] Public opinion research certainly gives good reason to think that some key neoliberal tenets were not in fact widely accepted by the electorate.[48] The work of social historians who have drawn on social surveys has likewise suggested that 'popular individualism' in Britain was not the same as Thatcherite individualism but rather provided a social context that Thatcherites were able to tap into rhetorically without always accurately representing it.[49] Secondly, neoliberalism was not the only influential ideology in public life in the late twentieth century. A full account of the period would have to consider how other politically powerful ideas made a social impact (and interacted with neoliberalism). Foremost among these other ideas would undoubtedly be feminism, multiculturalism, nationalism (British, Scottish, Welsh, Irish, English) and the more general rise of human rights in political and legal discourse.[50] With respect to economic policy, the rise of New Keynesianism, which sought to retrieve insights from Keynes in the wake of the monetarist counter-offensive, also furnished political debate on the centre left during the 1990s with an influential and distinctive set of economic ideas.[51] All of these bodies of thought were in some respects in tension with neoliberalism and pushed public life in directions that neoliberals were highly critical of but found themselves unable to stop. Thirdly, while ideas help historical actors to conceptualise and direct social change, there are always structural limits to political action set by the economic, demographic and institutional context. The extent, and political implications, of 'deindustrialisation' were malleable to some extent, for example, but as a broad economic wave it undoubtedly swept over Britain just as it did all other advanced industrialised states in the late twentieth century. However, it *did* matter that in the British case key state decisions were taken by a government that had become convinced that it was less important to worry about the distribution of economic prosperity and security between social classes than to foster individual economic responsibility and improve the incentives for wealth creation, which is where neoliberalism enters the story once again, as the key ideological influence on this distinctive orientation of the Thatcher government.[52]

All of this suggests that the preoccupation in some of the historiography on Britain after the 1970s with an apparent contrast between neoliberal ideas and political or economic interests is too abstract. As Andrew Gamble has observed, it is a mistake to think about ideas 'as some prime mover opposed to interests' since 'no context can be understood apart from the ideas that are constitutive of it'.[53] The most promising avenue of enquiry for historians is therefore to focus more closely on the way in which ideas (including, but not only, neoliberal ones) interact with particular social and economic contexts rather than seeking to prioritise one over the other.

Notes

* I am grateful to Aled Davies for his comments on an earlier draft of this chapter.

1 Maurice Cowling, 'Sources of the New Right: Irony, geniality and malice', *Encounter* (November 1989), 3, 11.

2 Cowling, 'Sources of the New Right', 12.

3 Stuart Hall, 'The great moving right show', *Marxism Today* (January 1979), 14–20; Stuart Hall and Martin Jacques (eds), *The Politics of Thatcherism* (London, Lawrence and Wishart, 1983); and Andrew Gamble, *The Free Economy and the Strong State*, 2nd ed. (Basingstoke, Palgrave, 1994). Another influential early work in this vein is Richard Cockett, *Thinking the Unthinkable: Think tanks and the economic counter-revolution, 1931–83* (London, HarperCollins, 1995).

4 Philip Mirowski and Dieter Plehwe (eds), *The Road from Mont Pèlerin: The making of the neoliberal thought collective* (Cambridge, MA, Harvard University Press, 2009); Ben Jackson, 'At the origins of neo-liberalism: The free economy and the strong state, 1930–47', *Historical Journal*, 53 (2010), 129–51; Angus Burgin, *The Great Persuasion* (Cambridge, MA, Harvard University Press, 2012); Daniel Stedman Jones, *Masters of the Universe: Hayek, Friedman and the birth of neo-liberal politics* (Princeton, NJ, Princeton University Press, 2012); Philip Mirowski, *Never Let a Serious Crisis Go to Waste* (London, Verso, 2013); Quinn Slobodian, *Globalists: The end of empire and the birth of neoliberalism* (Cambridge, MA, Harvard University Press, 2018); and Jessica Whyte, *The Morals of the Market: Human rights and the rise of neoliberalism* (London, Verso, 2019). I have summarised some of this literature in 'Putting neoliberalism in its place', *Modern Intellectual History*, published online 17 February 2021, http://dx.doi.org/10.1017/S1479244321000032.

5 The very employment of the term 'neoliberalism' is itself controversial, as some excellent scholars are doubtful of the word's utility. I remain unrepentant in thinking that the term is a useful one to describe a historically specific movement in economic and political ideas in the late twentieth century, for the reasons persuasively set out by Philip Mirowski, 'The political movement that dared not speak its own name: The neoliberal thought collective under erasure', Institute for New Economic Thinking Working Paper (23 September 2014), https://www.ineteconomics.org/uploads/papers/WP23-Mirowski.pdf (accessed 21 June 2021). But people of goodwill will continue to disagree on this point, and readers averse to the term might simply substitute 'market liberal' for 'neoliberal' if they prefer, as modelled for example by Avner Offer, 'The market turn: From social democracy to market liberalism', *Economic History Review*, 70 (2017), 1051–71; and Guy Ortolano, *Thatcher's Progress: From social democracy to market liberalism through an English new town* (Cambridge, Cambridge University Press, 2019).

6 For a sceptical view about the influence of neoliberal ideas in the context of the Americas that parallels some of the debates in modern British history, see Amy Offner, *Sorting Out the Mixed Economy: The rise and fall of welfare and developmental states in the Americas* (Princeton, NJ, Princeton University Press, 2019).

7 Richard Vinen, *Thatcher's Britain: The politics and social upheaval of the Thatcher era* (London, Simon & Schuster, 2009), 34–8. See also Adrian Williamson, *Conservative Economic Policy-Making and the Birth of Thatcherism, 1964–79* (Basingstoke, Palgrave, 2015), 13–15, 44–7; and Richard Vinen, 'War of position? The Thatcher government's preparation for the 1984 miners' strike', *English Historical Review*, 134 (2019), 147–8.

8 Maurice Cowling, *1867: Disraeli, Gladstone and revolution* (Cambridge, Cambridge University Press, 1967); Maurice Cowling, *The Impact of Labour, 1920–24* (Cambridge, Cambridge University Press, 1971); and Maurice Cowling, *The Impact of Hitler* (Cambridge, Cambridge University Press, 1975). This brief description oversimplifies Cowling's own position, however, as detailed by David Craig, '"High politics" and the "new political history"', *Historical Journal*, 53 (2010), 453–75.

9 Cowling, 'Sources of the New Right', 7–8.

10 Matthew Hilton, Chris Moores and Florence Sutcliffe-Braithwaite, '*New Times* revisited: Britain in the 1980s', *Contemporary British History*, 31 (2017), 145–65.

11 Gérard Duménil and Dominique Lévy, *Capital Resurgent* (Cambridge, MA, Harvard University Press, 2004); Gérard Duménil and Dominique Lévy, *The Crisis of Neoliberalism* (Cambridge, MA, Harvard University Press, 2011); and David Harvey, *A Brief History of Neoliberalism* (Oxford, Oxford University Press, 2005).

12 Aled Davies, *The City of London and Social Democracy: The political economy of finance, 1959–79* (Oxford, Oxford University Press, 2017); see also Davies's chapter in this book. For an interpretation that similarly stresses the importance of credit liberalisation for the global neoliberal wave, see Offer, 'The market turn', 1051–71.

13 Jim Tomlinson, 'Deindustrialisation not decline: A new meta-narrative for post-war British history', *Twentieth Century British History*, 27 (2016), 76–99. See also Tomlinson's chapter in this book.

14 David Edgerton, *The Rise and Fall of the British Nation* (London, Allen Lane, 2018). See also Edgerton's chapter in this book.

15 Jon Lawrence, 'Paternalism, class, and the British path to modernity', in Simon Gunn and James Vernon (eds), *The Peculiarities of Liberal Modernity in Imperial Britain* (Berkeley, University of California Press, 2011), 147–64; Florence Sutcliffe-Braithwaite and Jon Lawrence, 'Margaret Thatcher and the decline of class politics', in Ben Jackson and Robert Saunders (eds), *Making Thatcher's Britain* (Cambridge, Cambridge University Press, 2012), 132–47; Emily Robinson, Camilla Schofield, Florence Sutcliffe-Braithwaite and Natalie Thomlinson, 'Telling stories about post-war Britain: Popular individualism and the "crisis" of the 1970s', *Twentieth Century British History*, 28 (2017), 268–304; Florence Sutcliffe-Braithwaite, *Class, Politics and the Decline of Deference in England, 1968–2000* (Oxford, Oxford University Press, 2018); and Jon Lawrence, *Me, Me, Me: The search for community in post-war England* (Oxford, Oxford University Press, 2019).

16 For a cognate approach to this topic, which I follow in the footsteps of, see Ortolano, *Thatcher's Progress*, and Ortolano's chapter in this book.

17 Seminal answers which have influenced my approach here include Quentin Skinner, 'Moral principles and social change', in his *Visions of Politics, Volume 1* (Cambridge, Cambridge University Press, 2002), 145–57; Gareth Stedman Jones, 'Rethinking Chartism', in his *Languages of Class* (Cambridge, Cambridge University Press, 1983), 90–178; Michael Freeden, 'The stranger at the feast: Ideology and public policy in twentieth century Britain', *Twentieth Century British History*, 1 (1990), 9–34; Philip Williamson, *Stanley Baldwin* (Cambridge, Cambridge University Press, 1999), 12–18; and Samuel Moyn, 'Imaginary intellectual history', in Darrin McMahon and Samuel Moyn (eds), *Rethinking Modern European Intellectual History* (Oxford, Oxford University Press, 2014), 112–30.

18 Dieter Plehwe, 'Introduction', and Philip Mirowski, 'Postface: Defining neoliberalism', in Philip Mirowski and Dieter Plehwe (eds), *The Road from Mont Pèlerin* (Cambridge, MA, Harvard University Press, 2009), 1–42, at 35 fn 5 and 417–56, at 428–9.

19 Dieter Plehwe, Bernhard Walpen and Gisela Neunhöffer (eds), *Neo-Liberal Hegemony: A global critique* (London, Routledge, 2005); Mirowski and Plehwe (eds), *Road from Mont Pèlerin*; and Kim Phillips-Fein, *Invisible Hands* (New York, W. W. Norton, 2010).

20 F. A. Hayek, 'The intellectuals and socialism', *University of Chicago Law Review* (Spring 1949), 417–33; and Thomas Medvetz, *Think Tanks in America* (Chicago, University of Chicago Press, 2012).

21 For accounts of the British case in this methodological vein, see Keith Tribe, 'Liberalism and neo-liberalism in Britain', in Philip Mirowski and Dieter Plehwe (eds), *The Road from Mont Pèlerin* (Cambridge, MA, Harvard University Press, 2009), 68–97; Ben Jackson, 'The think tank archipelago: Thatcherism and neo-liberalism', in Ben Jackson and Robert Saunders (eds), *Making Thatcher's Britain* (Cambridge, Cambridge University Press, 2012), 43–61; and Neil Rollings, 'Cracks in the post-war Keynesian settlement? The role of organised business in Britain in the rise of neoliberalism before Margaret Thatcher', *Twentieth Century British History*, 24 (2013), 637–59. See also Rollings's chapter in this book.

22 Overviews of these different variants of neoliberal thought can be found in Plehwe and Mirowski (eds), *Road from Mont Pèlerin*; Robert Van Horn, Philip Mirowski and Thomas Stapleford (eds), *Building Chicago Economics* (Cambridge, Cambridge University Press, 2011); Burgin, *Great Persuasion*; Joseph Hien and Christian Joerges (eds), *Ordoliberalism, Law and the Rule of Economics* (London, Bloomsbury, 2017); Thomas Biebricher, *The Political Theory of Neo-Liberalism* (Stanford, CA, Stanford University Press, 2019); and Janek Wasserman, *The Austrian School* (New Haven, CT, Yale University Press, 2019). For discussion of how these different intellectual strands fed into British neoliberalism, see Robert Ledger, *Neo-Liberal Thought and Thatcherism: 'A transition from here to there'?* (London, Routledge, 2017).

23 Slobodian, *Globalists*, 7–13.

24 Nancy MacLean, *Democracy in Chains* (London, Penguin, 2017); Henry Farrell and Steven Teles, 'When politics drives scholarship', *Boston Review* (30 August 2017), http://bostonreview.net/class-inequality/henry-farrell-steven-m-teles-when-politics-drives-scholarship (accessed 21 June 2021); Jean-Baptiste Fleury and Alain Marciano, 'The sound of silence: A review essay of Nancy MacLean's *Democracy in Chains*', *Journal of Economic Literature*, 56 (2018), 1492–1537; and Philip Mirowski, 'The Eighteenth Brumaire of James Buchanan', *boundary 2*, 46 (2019), 197–219.

25 Florence Sutcliffe-Braithwaite, 'Neo-liberalism and morality in the making of Thatcherite social policy', *Historical Journal*, 55 (2012), 497–520; Ben Jackson, 'Currents of neo-liberalism:

British political ideologies and the New Right, c. 1955–79', *English Historical Review*, 131 (2016), 823–50; and Stephanie Mudge, *Leftism Reinvented: Western parties from socialism to neoliberalism* (Cambridge, MA, Harvard University Press, 2018).

26 William Davies, *The Limits of Neo-Liberalism* (London, SAGE, 2014), 2–3.

27 Arthur Seldon, 'What kind of welfare?', *Spectator* (18 March 1966), 320–1.

28 Roger Middleton, *Charlatans or Saviours? Economists and the British economy from Marshall to Meade* (Cheltenham, Edward Elgar, 1998); and Marion Fourcade, *Economists and Societies: Discipline and profession in the United States, Britain and France, 1890s to 1990s* (Princeton, NJ, Princeton University Press, 2009).

29 Jim Bulpitt, 'The discipline of the new democracy: Mrs Thatcher's domestic statecraft', *Political Studies*, 34 (1986), 19–39.

30 Gamble, *Free Economy and the Strong State*; and Jim Tomlinson, 'Thatcher, monetarism and the politics of inflation', in Ben Jackson and Robert Saunders (eds), *Making Thatcher's Britain* (Cambridge, Cambridge University Press, 2012), 62–77.

31 James Forder, *Macroeconomics and the Phillips Curve* (Oxford, Oxford University Press, 2014); James Forder and Kardin Sømme, 'Explaining the fame of Friedman's Presidential Address', *Cambridge Journal of Economics*, 43 (2019), 1683–1700; and Beatrice Cherrier and Aurélien Goutsmedt, 'The making and dissemination of Milton Friedman's 1967 AEA Presidential Address', *The Undercover Economist* (27 November 2017), https://beatricecherrier.wordpress.com/2017/11/27/the-friedman-legacy-on-the-making-and-dissemination-of-milton-friedman-1967-aea-presidential-address/ (accessed 7 August 2020).

32 Milton Friedman, 'The role of monetary policy', *American Economic Review*, 58 (1968), 1–17.

33 These complexities have been described by Jim Tomlinson, 'Mrs Thatcher's macroeconomic adventurism 1979–81', *British Politics*, 2 (2007), 3–19; and Duncan Needham and Anthony Hotson (eds), *Expansionary Fiscal Contraction: The Thatcher government's 1981 budget in perspective* (Cambridge, Cambridge University Press, 2014).

34 This point has been well summarised in the context of neoliberalism by Biebricher, *Political Theory of Neo-Liberalism*, 195–7. For the linguistic turn in British social and political history, see, for example, Patrick Joyce, *Visions of the People: Industrial England and the question of class c.1848–1914* (Cambridge, Cambridge University Press, 1991); James Vernon, *Politics and the People: A study in English political culture, 1815–1867* (Cambridge, Cambridge University Press, 1993); and Jon Lawrence, *Speaking for the People: Party, language and popular politics in England, 1867–1914* (Cambridge, Cambridge University Press, 1998).

35 Williamson, *Stanley Baldwin*, 12–18.

36 Camilla Schofield, *Enoch Powell and the Making of Postcolonial Britain* (Cambridge, Cambridge University Press, 2009); and Paul Corthorn, *Enoch Powell: Politics and ideas in modern Britain* (Oxford, Oxford University Press, 2019).

37 Andrew Denham and Mark Garnett, *Keith Joseph* (Chesham, Acumen, 2001), 255–7.

38 Roger Middleton, 'Brittan on Britain: "The economic contradictions of democracy" redux', *Historical Journal*, 54 (2011), 1141–68; and Jackson, 'Think tank archipelago', 50, 54.

39 Keith Joseph to Ralph Harris, 8 August 1974, IEA Papers, Hoover Institution Archive, Stanford University, 295/12; and Milton Friedman, *Monetary Correction* (London, IEA, 1974).

40 Keith Joseph, *Reversing the Trend: Seven speeches by Sir Keith Joseph* (London, Barry Allen, 1975).

41 Robert Saunders, '"Crisis, what crisis?" Thatcherism and the seventies', in Ben Jackson and Robert Saunders (eds), *Making Thatcher's Britain* (Cambridge, Cambridge University Press, 2012), 25–42; Colin Hay, 'Narrating crisis: The discursive construction of the Winter of Discontent', *Sociology*, 30 (1996), 253–77; and Colin Hay, 'Chronicles of a death foretold: The Winter of Discontent and construction of the crisis of British Keynesianism', *Parliamentary Affairs*, 63 (2010), 446–70.

42 Biebricher, *Political Theory of Neo-Liberalism*, 198–200.

43 Matthew Francis, '"A crusade to enfranchise the many?" Thatcherism and the "property-owning democracy"', *Twentieth Century British History*, 23 (2012), 275–97.

44 Charles Lockwood, 'The British New Right and the problem of public opinion, c. 1965–87' (PhD thesis, Cambridge University, 2020), 232–3; Michael Forsyth, *Re-Servicing Britain* (London, Adam Smith Institute, 1980); and Kate Ascher, *The Politics of Privatisation* (Basingstoke, Macmillan, 1987).

45 Ben Jackson, 'Free markets and feminism: The neo-liberal defence of the male bread-winner model in British politics, 1980–97', *Women's History Review*, 28 (2019), 297–316.

46 Aled Davies, James Freeman and Hugh Pemberton, '"Everyman a capitalist" or "free to choose"? Exploring the tensions within Thatcherite individualism', *Historical Journal*, 61 (2018), 477–501, at 500, emphasis in original; see also Aled Davies, 'Pension funds and the politics of ownership in Britain, c. 1970–86', *Twentieth Century British History*, 30 (2019), 93–105.

47 One important study of Thatcherite values at a more grassroots level is Chris Moores, 'Thatcher's troops? Neighbourhood watch schemes and the search for "ordinary" Thatcherism in 1980s Britain', *Contemporary British History*, 31 (2017), 230–55.

48 Ivor Crewe, 'Values: The crusade that failed', in Dennis Kavanagh and Anthony Seldon (eds), *The Thatcher Effect* (Oxford, Oxford University Press, 1989), 239–50.

49 Sutcliffe-Braithwaite, *Class, Politics and the Decline of Deference*, 145–72.

50 See, for example, Eve Setch, 'The face of metropolitan feminism: The London Women's Liberation Workshop, 1969–79', *Twentieth Century British History*, 13 (2002), 171–90; Richard Bourke, *Peace in Ireland: The war of ideas* (London, Pimlico, 2003); Michael Kenny, *The Politics of English Nationhood* (Oxford, Oxford University Press, 2014); Lucy Delap, 'Feminist bookshops, reading cultures and the women's liberation movement in Great Britain, c.1974–2000', *History Workshop Journal*, 81 (2016), 171–96; Natalie Thomlinson, *Race, Ethnicity and the Women's Movement in England, 1968–1993* (Basingstoke, Palgrave, 2016); Chris Moores, *Civil Liberties and Human Rights in Twentieth-Century Britain* (Cambridge, Cambridge University Press, 2017); Sarah Stoller, 'Forging a politics of care: Theorising household work in the British women's liberation movement', *History Workshop Journal*, 85 (2018), 95–119; Rob Waters, *Thinking Black: Britain 1964–85* (Oakland, University of California Press, 2018); Ben Jackson, *The Case for Scottish Independence: A history of nationalist political thought in modern Scotland* (Cambridge, Cambridge University Press, 2020); and Max Shock, 'Renewing left-wing ideas in late twentieth-century Britain: *Marxism Today*, c. 1977–1994' (DPhil thesis, Oxford University, 2020).

51 Will Hutton, 'New Keynesianism and New Labour', in Andrew Gamble and Tony Wright (eds), *The New Social Democracy* (Oxford, Wiley/Political Quarterly, 1999), 97–102; Philip Arestis and Malcolm Sawyer, 'The economic analysis underlying the "Third Way"', *New Political Economy*, 6 (2001), 258–78; Ben Clift and Jim Tomlinson, 'Credible Keynesianism: New Labour macroeconomic policy and the political economy of coarse tuning', *British Journal of Political Science*, 37 (2007), 47–69; and Dan Corry, 'Where is the British centre-left now on macro policy?', *Renewal*, 21 (2013), 34–45.

52 As documented for example by Jim Phillips, 'Deindustrialisation and the moral economy of the Scottish coalfields, 1947 to 1991', *International Labor and Working-Class History*, 84 (2013), 99–115; Bernhard Rieger, 'Making Britain work again: Unemployment and the remaking of British social policy in the eighties', *English Historical Review*, 133 (2018), 634–66; and Felix Römer, 'Poverty, inequality statistics, and knowledge politics under Thatcher', *English Historical Review* (forthcoming).

53 Andrew Gamble, 'Europe and America', in Ben Jackson and Robert Saunders (eds), *Making Thatcher's Britain* (Cambridge, Cambridge University Press, 2012), 218–33, at 229.

Part I
Welfare State and Social Policy

4

Welfare in a neoliberal age: the politics of redistributive market liberalism

Peter Sloman

In spring 1947, Milton Friedman made his first trip outside the US to speak at a gathering of free-market intellectuals in the Swiss resort of Mont Pèlerin.[1] Friedman took with him a paper on 'Taxation, poverty and income distribution', which he presented to the conference on Tuesday 8 April and which proposed that Western governments should attempt to tackle poverty through a Negative Income Tax (NIT) programme. Friedman pointed out that the growth of state intervention and trade unionism over the previous half-century had largely been driven by the 'desire to eliminate poverty' and economic insecurity. If the liberals gathered at Mont Pèlerin wanted to 'break up unions' and restore a market-based economic order, they would have to 'combat the evils which unions were designed to counteract' in another way, since 'no democratic society' would 'tolerate people starving to death, if there is food with which to feed them'. Anticipating an argument he would develop in *Capitalism and Freedom* (1962), Friedman presented NIT as a 'substitute' for other forms of social provision but denied that it was merely a political 'expedient'. Cash transfers offered an attractive way of establishing a minimum income floor which would allow all citizens to exercise consumer choice in the market.[2]

Friedman's NIT proposal was endorsed by his Chicago colleague (and brother-in-law) Aaron Director and welcomed by Karl Popper, who thought it 'an attractive alternative to socialism'.[3] Other delegates at the Mont Pèlerin meeting, however, were much more sceptical. The Swiss economist William Rappard, for instance, thought Friedman's plan to 'subsidise the poor' would have 'the worst possible psychological effects': discouraging work and adding to the burden on 'the good citizen, who pays his taxes'.[4] Friedrich Hayek also pointed out that conceptions of poverty varied sharply between countries and argued that a minimum income should only be provided in return for work 'under semi-military conditions'.[5] Friedman's Midwestern optimism about the possibility of poverty relief thus ran up against the age-old republican fear of 'decadence' and demoralisation. The Mont Pèlerin Society's (MPS) statement of aims, agreed after long debate at the end of the conference, concluded that 'further study' was needed of whether it was possible to establish 'minimum standards by means not inimical to initiative and the functioning of the market'.[6]

The controversy over Friedman's NIT scheme highlights an enduring tension in neoliberal thought over the proper extent and purpose of redistribution. Friedman's 1947 paper is a classic exposition of what John Kay has called 'redistributive market liberalism': the belief that the distribution of income and wealth is a legitimate object of political action, but that the state 'should discharge this responsibility with as little interference as possible in the workings of the free market'.[7] As the neoliberal movement founded at Mont Pèlerin has become aligned with New Right politics since the 1960s and 1970s, Friedman's vision has largely been supplanted by a moralistic conservatism which asserts the legitimacy of market outcomes and blames poverty on individual failure or cultural pathology.[8] At the same time, however, cash transfers to low-income households have become more extensive than they ever were in the middle decades of the twentieth century. Exploring this paradox reminds us of the complex relationship between 'neoliberalism as doctrine' and the messy realities of post-industrial public policy.[9]

The conjunction of anti-welfarist discourse with welfarist practice is not unique to the UK, but it is perhaps particularly striking in Britain. At the level of ideology and discourse, the ascendancy of free-market ideas in British politics has been closely tied up with a conservative critique of redistribution, powerfully articulated by Margaret Thatcher, as Florence Sutcliffe-Braithwaite has shown.[10] Despite this rhetoric, however, Conservative and New Labour governments have presided over a significant expansion in the redistributive role of the British state. As market incomes from wages, salaries and investments have become increasingly unequal since the late 1970s, the rise in the Gini coefficient has been cushioned by the impact of taxes and transfers (figure 4.1). In particular, cash benefits to working-age adults and children have more than trebled in real terms since 1979, mainly through the expansion of means-tested benefits and tax credits for low- and middle-income households (figure 4.2).[11] The period since 2010 has been characterised

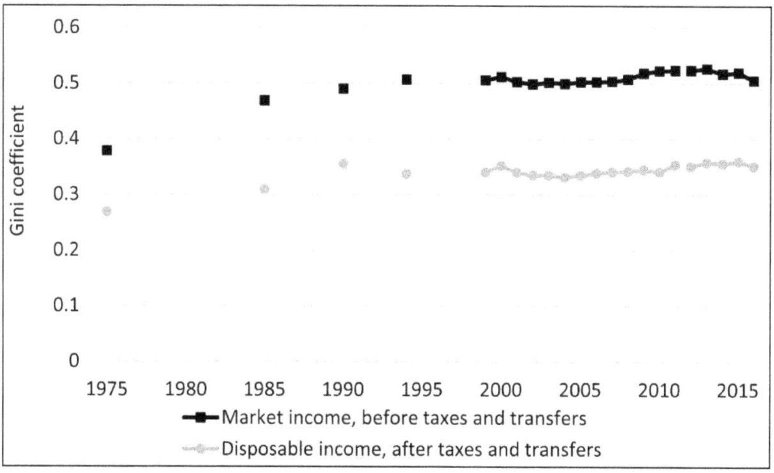

Figure 4.1 Income inequality in Britain, 1975–2016: Gini coefficients for market and disposable income

Source: OECD Statistics database

http://www.oecd.org/social/income-distribution-database.htm (accessed 25 June 2021).

Note: The OECD dataset on UK income inequality comprises intermittent figures from 1975 to 1999 and an annual series from 1999 onwards. The OECD adopted a new definition of income in 2012, so the data series before and after this date are not strictly comparable.

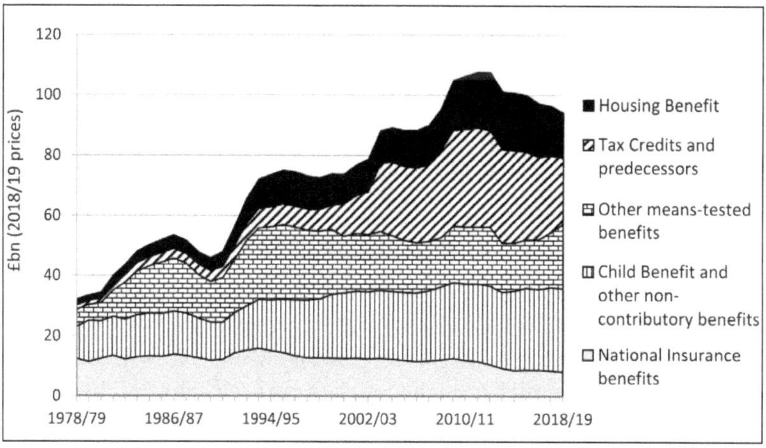

Figure 4.2 Transfer payments to working-age adults and children in Great Britain, 1978/9–2018/19 (real terms, £bn, 2018/19 prices)

Source: Author's calculations based on Department for Work and Pensions, 'Benefit Expenditure and Caseload Tables', Autumn Budget 2018

http://www.gov.uk/government/publications/benefit-expenditure-and-caseload-tables-2018 (accessed 25 June 2021).

both by efforts to rein in this spending through welfare cuts, and by the rationalisation of means-tested benefits into a single monthly payment through the introduction of Universal Credit.

This chapter examines how Friedman's strand of neoliberal thought has contributed to British welfare policy since the Second World War, with a particular focus on the system of cash transfers to working-age households.[12] Changes to the benefit system have, of course, reflected a number of factors, including the impact of deindustrialisation and demographic change, which accounted for much of the growth of social security spending during the 1980s and 1990s – as Jim Tomlinson and Jim Phillips show elsewhere in this volume.[13] Likewise, the development of in-work benefits has been combined with increasingly demanding employment and job search conditions, designed to 'activate' the unemployed for low-paid work (an approach which Friedman, incidentally, repudiated).[14] Despite this complexity, however, the impact of redistributive market liberalism can be clearly discerned. The post-industrial British state has come to make extensive use of cash transfers to alleviate the inequality generated by a financialised and service-based liberal market economy. The wave of interest in 'pre-distribution' since the 2008 financial crisis suggests a growing awareness of the limitations of this strategy.[15]

Redistributive market liberalism in British social thought, *c.* 1945–79

As the editors note in their introduction, neoliberalism has become an increasingly contested category in the humanities and social sciences, as sociologists and cultural theorists have taken it out of the realm of political ideas and deployed it as a master key for understanding a range of contemporary phenomena. Neoliberalism is perhaps best understood, for our purposes, as the doctrine (or set of ideas) associated with the Mont Pèlerin 'thought collective', even though the term itself has rarely been used within the movement since the late 1950s.[16] Although neoliberal doctrine has varied over time and between thinkers, the movement has long been centred on the promotion of market pricing as an allocation device – reflecting the core analytical insight of neoclassical economics. The socialist calculation debate of the 1930s reinforced market liberals' conviction that a decentralised market economy was generally more efficient (and responsive to consumer demands) than collective provision of goods and services. As Ben Jackson has shown, many founding MPS members also emphasised their distance from what they saw as the laissez-faire liberalism of the nineteenth century. Hayek and Friedman were *neo*liberals because they recognised that some forms of economic management, regulation and social provision were necessary both to create competitive markets and to secure political support for the capitalist system.[17]

It is difficult to identify an organised neoliberal movement in Britain before the Institute of Economic Affairs (IEA) was formed in the mid-1950s, as Keith Tribe and George Peden have noted, but British economists featured prominently in the MPS from the beginning.[18] Twenty-four of the 121 individuals listed in the MPS's 1948 membership list, for instance, were based in the UK, including no fewer than eight at the London School of Economics: Hayek, Popper, Lionel Robbins, Ronald Coase, Ronald Edwards, Frank Paish, Sir Arnold Plant and the economic historian T. S. Ashton.[19] In the context of the late 1940s, these and other market-oriented economists reacted strongly against the expansion of public ownership and the Attlee government's attempts to use wartime controls as a basis for peacetime economic planning. Far from being frozen out by a collectivist consensus, as heroic narratives such as Richard Cockett's *Thinking the Unthinkable* (1994) have implied, these free-market economists influenced policy debates in a variety of ways through public lectures, newspaper articles, and links with the Conservative and Liberal parties.[20]

The idea of establishing a minimum income through cash transfers played an important political role for the first generation of neoliberals. In Britain, as in much of the Western world, the growth of state intervention and trade union power in the first half of the twentieth century had been accompanied by a significant narrowing of income and wealth differentials, and the 1945–51 Labour government used a discourse of 'fair shares for all' to justify the maintenance of collective provision and rationing.[21] Many working-class voters seemed to view the debate over planning in class terms, as the economist Honor Croome observed in a 1949 article; the political challenge for market liberals was to break this linkage and show that the removal of rationing and price subsidies need not reverse the trend towards social equality.[22] Just as Keynesian demand management promised to reconcile capitalism with full employment, so fiscal redistribution could reconcile market mechanisms with a continued assault on poverty.[23] Indeed, the French writer and MPS member Bertrand de Jouvenel argued that the redistributive effects of the Attlee government's policies were 'oblique' rather than 'vertical'. A 'pure' form of redistribution 'would merely transfer income from the richer to the poorer', and 'could conceivably be achieved by a simple reverse-tax or subsidy handed to the recipients of lower incomes'.[24]

Proposals for a guaranteed income dovetailed with the tradition of 'poverty line' research associated with Seebohm Rowntree and A. L.

Bowley, which focused on quantifying the minimum income required to cover households' subsistence needs.[25] As José Harris has pointed out, the 'materialism' of the nineteenth-century English poor law continued to pervade post-war social security policy through the flat-rate structure of National Insurance benefits (which William Beveridge based, in a roundabout way, on Rowntree's scales) and the survival of means-tested National Assistance.[26] At the same time, redistributive market liberalism conflicted sharply with other strands in British social thought, such as the trade unions' strong commitment to the male-breadwinner 'family wage' as the foundation of household income. The bitter debates over Family Allowances during the 1920s and 1930s showed that many trade unionists saw in-work benefits as an affront to the dignity and independence of working men, which would undermine the pursuit of higher wages through collective bargaining.[27] Public provision of services such as health care, education and housing, by contrast, disguised the state's role in subsidising working-class living standards. Many socialist thinkers also emphasised the scope for achieving economies of scale through state provision. R. H. Tawney, for instance, argued that 'collective expenditure makes possible results which would be unattainable, were an identical sum distributed . . . in fractional additions to individual incomes'.[28]

Despite these political obstacles, early neoliberals were able to argue with some force that the distributional effects of market-based reforms – such as the price increases which would follow the removal of rationing – could be offset through the tax and benefit systems. This approach enabled them to make common cause with left-leaning economists such as James Meade, who urged the Attlee government to move away from physical planning and focus on tackling inequality in other ways – for instance, through death duties, educational reform and perhaps even a universal basic income.[29] It also reassured Conservative politicians that they could present liberalisation as a way of expanding consumer choice for all social groups, not just the better-off. The Tory Chancellor R. A. Butler, for instance, cut the £400 million food subsidy programme which he had inherited from Labour in his 1952 budget and used some of the savings to increase pensions and Family Allowances.[30] As the post-war housing shortage eased, the 1951–64 Conservative government also reined in general council house subsidies and pressed local authorities to target support on the poorest tenants through rent rebate schemes.[31]

Some of the most radical British neoliberals shared Friedman's hope that a guaranteed minimum income would pave the way for the wholesale marketisation of public services, particularly in a context of rising consumer 'affluence'. Peter Goldman of the Conservative Research Department, for instance, argued than the government should remove state provision from the middle class and focus on providing a 'safety net' for 'the shiftless or luckless 5 per cent', while Arthur Seldon of the IEA believed that an NIT scheme would make it easier to introduce charges for public services and then move towards a private market.[32] Even the Liberal Party leader Jo Grimond looked forward to a time 'when the only Social Service is a straight payment to bring everyone's income (including that of children) up to a national minimum'.[33] In practice, however, movement in this direction was cautious and incremental. Although the removal of rationing and food subsidies was a political success, the Macmillan government's attempt to liberalise the rented housing market under the 1957 Rent Act turned into a fiasco, and many Tories grudgingly accepted that the National Health Service (NHS) and state education were relatively cost-effective as well as being popular with voters.[34] The principle that full-time workers should not receive means-tested benefits also remained a significant obstacle to wage supplementation, as Jim Tomlinson notes in his chapter. When Edward Heath crossed this Rubicon by creating the Family Income Supplement (FIS) in 1971 – a very limited measure designed to help about 190,000 families at a cost of £6 million a year – the scheme attracted intense criticism from across the political spectrum.[35] On the right, Enoch Powell accused the government of reviving the 'evil' of the early nineteenth-century Speenhamland system; on the left, the Trades Union Congress condemned FIS as 'a direct and explicit subsidy to low wages'.[36] Jack Jones of the Transport and General Workers' Union also warned Labour colleagues that the unions could not be expected to moderate their pay demands to take account of universal benefits such as Family Allowances: 'To rely unduly on changes in social benefits' to eliminate poverty would 'make virtual State pensioners of hundreds of thousands of ordinary, healthy men and women'.[37]

The 'golden age' of the post-war welfare state thus presents us with a paradox. At an intellectual level, Conservative and Liberal thought was strongly influenced by redistributive market liberalism, and commentators such as Samuel Brittan and Michael Young frequently echoed Friedman's argument that poverty could be tackled most effectively by a guaranteed minimum income.[38] At the level of policy, however, social security spending rose only from 4 per cent of GDP in the late 1940s to about 7 per cent in the mid-1970s, half of it devoted to state pensions and two-thirds of it channelled through Beveridge's contributory National Insurance system. Insofar as the British state engaged in fiscal redistribution in

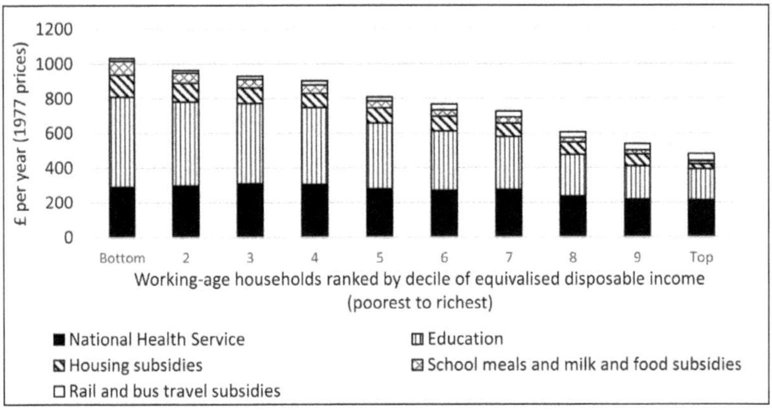

Figure 4.3 Cash value of benefits in kind (£) to working-age households by equivalised disposable income decile, 1977

Source: Author's calculations based on Office for National Statistics, 'Effects of taxes and benefits on household income: Historical datasets' (20 June 2018), https://www.ons.gov.uk/peoplepopulationandcommunity/personalandhouseholdfinances/incomeandwealth/datasets/theeffectsoftaxesandbenefitsonhouseholdincomehistoricaldatasets (accessed 25 June 2021).

this period, it did so primarily on the tax side, using highly progressive marginal rates of income tax to pay for education, health care and other forms of collective provision. Spending on these benefits in kind was somewhat progressive, as figure 4.3 shows, though this partly reflected life-cycle effects: for instance, poorer households benefited more from education and school meals because they were more likely to contain children. In any case, so far as disposable incomes were concerned, cash transfers from the rich were more important than cash transfers to the poor. The relatively low Gini coefficients of the 1960s and 1970s should thus be understood largely as the product of earnings compression in the context of full employment, national pay bargaining, progressive taxation and strong trade union organisation in manufacturing industry.

Thatcherism and social security: reluctant redistributors

Attitudes to redistribution hardened within the Conservative Party during the course of the 1970s, especially after Margaret Thatcher succeeded Edward Heath as Tory leader in January 1975. As Sutcliffe-Braithwaite has argued, Thatcher's 'vision of moral rejuvenation' through self-reliance and property ownership squeezed out the redistributive strand of neoliberal thought associated with Friedman.[39] Where Heathite

Conservatives had embraced selective benefits as a source of distributional 'balance', Thatcher worried about the growth of social security spending and thought a guaranteed minimum income would become 'a shirker's charter'.[40] This moralistic individualism manifested itself in a number of ways during Thatcher's 11 years in power, as Bernhard Rieger shows in his chapter: in the whittling-back of out-of-work benefits, the development of new forms of welfare conditionality and dramatic cuts to the top rate of income tax in the 1979 and 1988 budgets.[41] Despite this ideological shift, however, redistributive market liberalism did not go away. Indeed, cash transfers have become much more central to British public policy since 1979 than they ever were during the post-war 'golden age'.

It is clear from the aggregate statistics in figure 4.2 that economic change has been an important driver of this expansion. Much of the growth of benefit spending on working-age households has been concentrated in the periods during and after the 1980–1, 1990–1 and 2008–9 recessions, when unemployment rose sharply. During the 1980s and early 1990s, in particular, the unemployment benefit system 'buckled under the weight of unprecedented inflows' and many older manual workers became long-term social security claimants, especially in those regions which were hit most heavily by the decline of coal and manufacturing employment.[42] Yet the structural changes associated with deindustrialisation – and exacerbated by the Thatcher government's monetarist policies – do not tell the whole story. As unemployment (and hence unemployment benefit spending) has declined, Conservative and New Labour governments have rolled forward in-work benefits as an instrument of economic and social policy. As a result, reductions in real-terms welfare spending during periods of economic recovery have only partly reversed the previous expansions.

Under the Conservative governments of 1979–97, the use of cash transfers as a policy tool was cautious and reluctant, reflecting Thatcher's deep hostility to redistribution and the government's declared intention of reducing welfare dependency. Even so, means-tested benefits remained an important tool of Conservative statecraft; indeed, in some respects the Thatcher government's radicalism made them more important than they had been in 1951–64 or 1970–4. Not only did monetarism and changes to trade union law reduce workers' bargaining power and so widen pre-tax inequalities, but a host of other Thatcherite policies – such as increases in VAT and National Insurance contributions, cuts to fuel and transport subsidies, and the introduction of the Poll Tax – imposed direct and tangible costs on poorer households. Shrewder

Conservative ministers and Whitehall officials recognised that it was easier to implement these regressive reforms if the losers would be protected by a means-tested safety net.[43] As Norman Fowler pointed out to Thatcher in 1985, increased demand for benefits partly reflected the fact that the system was 'having to pick up other people's bills' as a result of cuts in other public services.[44] By the late 1980s, even Thatcher found it politically useful to rebut accusations that she was indifferent to poverty and inequality by pointing to 'record levels' of social security spending.[45]

The use of means-tested benefits to 'flank' and legitimate free-market reforms was particularly clear in housing and employment policy. The creation of housing benefit in 1982 unified the systems of rent rebates (for council tenants) and rent allowances (for private tenants) which the Heath government had introduced a decade earlier and brought them under the control of the Department of Health and Social Security: as Fowler explained, it seemed best for this 'form of income support' to be 'considered in the context of the social security benefit structure . . . as a whole'.[46] When the Conservatives went on to deregulate private lettings under the 1988 Housing Act, housing minister Sir George Young used the existence of housing benefit to justify the move to market rents: 'If people cannot afford to pay that market rent, housing benefit will take the strain.'[47] As average rental costs rose – roughly trebling in real terms between 1979 and 1997 – cuts in spending on council house subsidies were more than offset by the rising cost of housing benefit.[48] By 1996/7 the housing benefit bill came to £11.4 billion a year, two-thirds of which went to working-age households.

In-work benefits also formed an integral part of the Thatcher government's labour market strategy, as Chris Grover has shown.[49] As the manufacturing sector contracted during the 1980s, Thatcherite ministers such as Nigel Lawson insisted that 'the rediscovery of the enterprise culture' and the removal of 'rigidities and distortions' through supply-side reforms was the only sustainable way of creating new jobs.[50] Lawson was particularly keen to emulate the US's success in expanding service-sector employment, including part-time and casual jobs in fields such as retail and hospitality. As the Central Policy Review Staff pointed out, however, the 'aim of increasing real wage flexibility' was 'likely to run into conflict with trade unions and often with the public's sense of fairness'. The replacement of FIS with the more generous Family Credit in 1988 was partly designed to defuse these concerns, improving incentives for men and women with children to take low-paid jobs and 'breaking the linkage in the public mind between low pay and family poverty'.[51] Once in place,

Family Credit grew rapidly, redistributing £2.1 billion a year to 714,000 households by 1996/7. Indeed, the Conservatives even promised to 'protect' its value as part of a 'Family Benefits Guarantee' in their 1997 manifesto.[52]

New Labour, social democracy and the child poverty agenda

In quantitative terms, cash transfers peaked as a share of disposable household income for all working-age households under the Thatcher government (at 15 per cent in 1984) and for the poorest decile of working-age households under John Major's government (at 70 per cent in 1993), but these figures were partly the result of high unemployment levels. Fiscal redistribution fitted much more comfortably with Tony Blair's 'Third Way' politics than with the harsher impulses of Thatcherism.[53] If New Labour should be seen as 'a social democratic response to issues made prominent by the New Right', as Mark Bevir has suggested, then the prospect of reducing poverty through the tax and benefit systems played an important role in reconciling Labour politicians (and voters) to market liberalism.[54] To be sure, the Labour Party's strategy for achieving social justice remained as eclectic as it had been under Clement Attlee or Harold Wilson, combining efforts to raise skills (through education policy) and tackle low pay (through the National Minimum Wage) with spending on benefits and public services (especially the NHS). Nevertheless, the emphasis tilted perceptibly away from the wage politics which had dominated the party's outlook for much of the twentieth century. There would be no revival of Britain's old industrial base, no 'beer and sandwiches' with trade union leaders in Number 10 and no attempt to reverse the decline of collective bargaining.[55]

Characterisations of New Labour as a neoliberal project risk veering into simplistic caricature, as Mark Wickham-Jones points out in his chapter. In practice, the Blair government's 'neoliberalism' consisted largely in its acceptance of the political economy which had emerged during the 1980s and early 1990s, in which the City of London, consumer credit and housing wealth became major drivers of an 'Anglo-liberal growth model' and service-sector employers took up the slack in the labour market.[56] This policy choice was shaped by a heavy dose of political pragmatism, including the belief that good relations with business would help restore Labour's reputation for economic competence. It was also underpinned by the growing acceptance of mainstream (neoclassical) microeconomics – together with its characteristic 'policy devices' and 'styles of reasoning' – as the government's primary toolkit for policy analysis.[57] Gordon Brown's Treasury saw markets as 'a powerful means of advancing the public interest' and focused on establishing stable macroeconomic conditions while dealing with market failures – 'ensuring dynamic properly functioning markets . . . with low barriers to entry and free mobility of capital and labour'.[58]

The influence of neoclassical economics was particularly evident in New Labour's approach to the labour market. Despite the Labour Party's long-standing links with the trade unions, the 'stagflation' of the 1970s and the mass unemployment of the early 1980s had prompted many social democratic economists to see wage rigidity as a serious problem. The work of Richard Layard, Steve Nickell and Richard Jackman at the LSE Centre for Labour Economics was particularly influential in applying the concept of the Non-Accelerating Inflation Rate of Unemployment (NAIRU) to Britain and persuading Labour to refine rather than reverse the Thatcher government's efforts to promote labour market flexibility.[59] Blair and Brown thus embraced the 'work first' approach to active labour market policy canvassed by the Organisation for Economic Co-operation and Development's 1994 Jobs Study, and though they maintained the commitment to a minimum wage which they had inherited from Neil Kinnock and John Smith, they kept its initial rate down (to £3.60 an hour in 1999) in order to limit the impact on job creation.[60] Accepting the growth of low-skilled service jobs allowed Brown to reduce unemployment without stoking the inflationary pressures which had accompanied full employment in the 1960s and 1970s, and so to deliver on his promise of 'no return to boom and bust' – at least until the 2008 financial crisis.

Taken by itself, however, New Labour's embrace of the 'Anglo-liberal growth model' offered little hope of arresting or reversing the rise in income inequality which the UK had experienced under Thatcher and Major, and to which economists such as Tony Atkinson and think tanks such as the Institute for Fiscal Studies (IFS) had increasingly drawn attention.[61] Blair and Brown's public discourse focused on 'tackling the root causes of poverty and inequality' through welfare-to-work and investment in human capital, but Brown, at least, recognised that cash transfers had an important part to play in supporting low-paid workers while these long-term measures bore fruit.[62] Brown was particularly impressed by the way the Earned Income Tax Credit provided 'a top-up for low wages' in the US, and he sought to emulate this by replacing Family Credit with tax credits delivered through the pay packet.[63] When

Blair set out the goal of ending child poverty in a generation in his March 1999 Beveridge Lecture, tax credits became the centrepiece of a wide-ranging child poverty strategy.[64] Picking up on a proposal by Tony Atkinson, the Treasury and Department of Social Security turned Blair's goal into a precise income-based target: reducing the proportion of children in households with less than 60 per cent of median equivalised income by a quarter by 2004, halving it by 2010, and pushing it as close to zero as possible – so that it was at least among the lowest levels in Europe – by 2020.[65] Brown expanded tax credits in successive budgets, taking advantage of the falling cost of out-of-work benefits and revenue from tax reforms (such as the abolition of Married Couples' Allowance) and fiscal drag, until the system was distributing almost £30 billion a year by 2010 – an average of more than £4,000 a year to 6.25 million households.[66]

Despite New Labour's avowed commitment to tackling poverty at its root, decomposition analysis by Richard Dickens suggests that increased spending on tax credits and other benefits was by far the most important factor in driving progress towards the child poverty target. If benefits had remained unchanged, the child poverty rate (before housing costs) would have risen from 26.2 per cent in 1997/8 to 29.0 per cent in 2008/9 as a result of changes in population structure, wages and work patterns; instead, it fell to 21.1 per cent.[67] Indeed, the Family Resources Survey – on which these figures are based – only captures about 85 per cent of benefit income, so the true impact may have been even greater.[68] Of course, such an analysis cannot account for the wider economic effects of tax credits and other welfare-to-work measures, and some critics suggest that they may have contributed to wage stagnation by encouraging firms to adopt 'low-road' production strategies.[69] Nevertheless, there are good reasons for thinking that the use of tax receipts from the City of London to pay for transfers to low-paid workers with children played a significant role in stabilising 'Anglo-liberal capitalism' in the run-up to the financial crisis.[70] Tax credits also provided a useful fiscal stabiliser after 2008, as the Brown government used above-inflation increases in Child Tax Credit to cushion the impact of the recession on low- and middle-income households.[71]

Conclusion

In a 2017 article for *American Affairs*, the cultural theorist Nancy Fraser launched a forceful attack on what she called 'progressive neoliberalism'.[72] Building on her earlier analysis of 'the redistribution-recognition dilemma', Fraser argued that Third Way politicians such as Bill Clinton and Tony Blair had used a 'liberal-meritocratic politics of recognition' – the 'superficially egalitarian and emancipatory' championing of 'feminism, antiracism, multiculturalism, environmentalism' and gay rights – to 'seduce major currents of progressive social movements into the new hegemonic bloc' and give 'an expropriative, plutocratic economic program . . . the patina of legitimacy'.[73] Whatever the merits of Fraser's broader analysis, the implication that 'progressive neoliberals' have ignored distributional issues is wholly misleading. In Britain, at least, redistribution through cash transfers and public services has played an essential role in mitigating the social effects of industrial decline and global competition. Under the influence of economists such as Atkinson and Nicholas Barr, governments now routinely apply the tools of economic analysis to the welfare state and use microsimulation models to quantify the impact of policy changes on household incomes.[74]

The 'actually existing neoliberalism' which has emerged in Britain since the 1980s thus bears a closer resemblance to Friedman's vision at Mont Pèlerin than either its supporters or its critics have usually recognised. This does not, however, mean that the use of transfer payments to flank and legitimate neoliberal policies has been wholly successful. Indeed, the experience of the last 20 years suggests that, as a political strategy, redistributive market liberalism runs up against three serious limitations. Firstly, the continuing cultural resonance of the Protestant work ethic means that cash transfers themselves face questions of legitimacy, including among potential beneficiaries of redistribution, as Brian Steensland has noted in the US.[75] Blair and Brown sought to sidestep the problem by focusing tax credits on working families with children, but this cultural framing became increasingly tenuous as the system expanded: after 2003, Child Tax Credit was paid directly to the main carer and made no distinction between families in and out of work. At the same time, New Labour's rhetorical assault on 'welfare' seems to have contributed to a hardening of public attitudes towards the unemployed, thereby laying the groundwork for an increasingly punitive system of benefit sanctions.[76] The introduction of Universal Credit may well exacerbate this problem, eroding distinctions between the so-called 'deserving' and 'undeserving' poor without providing the kind of genuinely comprehensive safety net which Friedman envisaged back in 1947.

The second problem with a strategy based on fiscal transfers is that it requires a continuing stream of tax revenues to offset market inequalities and so accentuates the 'structural dependence of the state on capital' which Marxist political economists have long warned about.[77] Although the expansion of working-age benefits in Britain has not provoked an overt tax revolt, it has clearly been constrained by politicians' sensitivity to the signals which tax rates send to investors and middle-class voters, and cuts to in-work benefits formed a major part of George Osborne's deficit-reduction programme. These fiscal pressures may become even more intense in the coming decades, as other parts of the welfare state (such as health care, pensions and social care) demand a growing share of national income.[78]

Beneath these two practical limitations lies the conceptual or even ethical weakness recently highlighted by Samuel Moyn: that the pursuit of a social minimum focuses on 'sufficiency' at the expense of broader questions about equity, economic power and the impact of rising inequality further up the income spectrum.[79] New Labour's approach to redistribution was particularly lopsided, as Blair and Brown largely abandoned the ethical critique of inequality which was so important to previous generations of British socialists.[80] Conceptions of distributive justice are, of course, a matter of political choice, but the downsides of a narrow focus on poverty alleviation have become increasingly apparent in recent years. Means-tested transfers such as Friedman's NIT may be 'efficient' in the sense that they represent the cheapest way of lifting households up to the poverty line, but they also expose claimants to high marginal tax rates, social stigma and uncertainty about benefit entitlement. Nor have technological advances – the great hope of generations of tax benefit reformers – entirely solved these problems, as the experience of Universal Credit shows.[81] A universal basic income would provide a more stable and predictable income floor, but most mainstream policymakers continue to be deterred by the cost.[82]

In the light of these challenges, it is not difficult to understand the appeal of 'pre-distribution' strategies which would engage more directly with the causes of inequality. Policies to lift the wage floor, increase housing supply and regulate prices (for instance in the utilities sector) all promise to reshape the distribution of market power and so reduce the need to alleviate poverty through cash transfers.[83] However desirable such an interventionist agenda might be, though, the immediate impact on the income distribution is likely to be relatively modest. For instance, projections by the Office for Budget Responsibility and the IFS suggested that the introduction of the National Living Wage would reduce working-age welfare spending by less than 1 per cent and would have very little impact on headline poverty and inequality measures.[84] Recurrent controversies over benefit cuts and the troubled rollout of Universal Credit have underlined how important cash transfers have become for millions of working-age households. The UK's current welfare system may be almost universally unloved, but unless there is a radical shift in the underlying economic model, some system of transfers to the working poor is likely to remain socially necessary and politically inevitable.

Notes

1 Milton Friedman and Rose D. Friedman, *Two Lucky People: Memoirs* (Chicago, University of Chicago Press, 1998), 158.
2 Friedman also revealed a youthful sympathy for Keynesian economics by pointing out that NIT would have a useful 'anti-cyclical effect' in a recession: 'Taxation, poverty and income distribution. Tuesday April 8th, 8.30 p.m.', notes of discussion, Mont Pèlerin Society records, 5.12, Hoover Institution Archives, Stanford University. See also Milton Friedman, *Capitalism and Freedom* (Chicago, University of Chicago Press, 1962), 190–5.
3 Director had set out his views on Tuesday 1 April, in response to Hayek's paper; see '"Free" enterprise or competitive order. Tuesday, April 1st, 4.30', notes of discussion, Mont Pèlerin Society records, 5.12.
4 'Taxation, poverty and income distribution', notes of discussion, Mont Pèlerin Society records, 5.12.
5 'Taxation, poverty and income distribution', notes of discussion, Mont Pèlerin Society records, 5.12.
6 Mont Pèlerin Society statement of aims (8 April 1947), https://www.montpelerin.org/statement-of-aims/ (accessed 25 March 2019).
7 John Kay, 'Staking a moral claim', *New Statesman* (11 October 1996), 18–20, at 18. See also Samuel Brittan, 'Redistributive market liberalism', in Samuel Brittan, *Essays, Moral, Political, and Economic* (Edinburgh, Edinburgh University Press, 1998), 22–32.
8 Alan Deacon, *Perspectives on Welfare: Ideas, ideologies and policy debates* (Buckingham, Open University Press, 2002); Peter Dorey, *British Conservatism: The politics and philosophy of inequality* (London, I.B. Tauris, 2011).
9 Rajesh Venugopal, 'Neoliberalism as concept', *Economy and Society*, 44 (2015), 165–87.
10 Florence Sutcliffe-Braithwaite, 'Neo-liberalism and morality in the making of Thatcherite social policy', *Historical Journal*, 55 (2012), 497–520.
11 Unless otherwise stated, all social security statistics are based on Department for Work and Pensions, 'Benefit expenditure and caseload tables', Autumn Budget 2018, http://www.gov.uk/government/publications/benefit-expenditure-and-caseload-tables-2018 (accessed 25 March 2019).
12 On this restructuring process, see Paul Gray and Nicholas Timmins, *Reforming Working-Age Social Security: Lessons for policy makers* (London, Social Security Advisory Committee/Institute for Government, 2018).
13 Christina Beatty and Steve Fothergill, 'The impact on welfare and public finances of job loss in industrial Britain', *Regional Studies, Regional Science*, 4 (2017), 161–80
14 Milton Friedman to Rep. David Dennis, 17 February 1970, Milton Friedman papers, 201.6, Hoover Institution Archives.
15 Jacob Hacker, 'The institutional foundations of middle-class democracy', in Policy Network, *Priorities for a New Political Economy: Memo to the left* (London, Policy Network, 2011), 33–7; Ed Miliband, 'The inequality problem', *London Review of Books* (4 February 2016), 19–20.
16 Philip Mirowski and Dieter Plehwe (eds), *The Road from Mont Pèlerin: The making of the neoliberal thought collective* (Cambridge, MA, Harvard University Press, 2009); Philip Mirowski, 'Neoliberalism: The movement that dare not speak its name', *American Affairs*, 2/1 (2018), 118–41.
17 Ben Jackson, 'At the origins of neo-liberalism: The free economy and the strong state, 1930–1947', *Historical Journal*, 53 (2010), 129–51.
18 Keith Tribe, 'Liberalism and neoliberalism in Britain, 1930–1980', in Philip Mirowski and Dieter Plehwe (eds), *The Road from Mont Pèlerin: The making of the neoliberal thought collective* (Cambridge, MA, Harvard University Press, 2009), 68–97; George Peden, 'Neoliberal economists and the British welfare state, 1942–1975', *Journal of the History of Economic Thought*, 39 (2017), 413–27.

19 *The Mont Pèlerin Society* booklet, October 1948, Mont Pèlerin Society records, 56.9.
20 Richard Cockett, *Thinking the Unthinkable: Think-tanks and the economic counter-revolution, 1931–1983* (London, HarperCollins, 1994); Peter Sloman, *The Liberal Party and the Economy, 1929–1964* (Oxford, Oxford University Press, 2015), 166–203, 220–3; Marion Fourcade, *Economists and Societies: Discipline and profession in the United States, Britain, & France, 1890s to 1990s* (Princeton, NJ, Princeton University Press, 2009), 129–84.
21 Jim Tomlinson, 'Distributional politics: The search for equality in Britain since the First World War', in Pat Hudson and Keith Tribe (eds), *The Contradictions of Capital in the Twenty-First Century: The Piketty opportunity* (Newcastle upon Tyne, Agenda Publishing, 2016), 167–91.
22 Honor Croome, 'Liberty, equality and full employment', *Lloyds Bank Review* (July 1949), 14–32.
23 On Keynesianism and the market, see E. H. H. Green, 'The Conservative Party and Keynes', in E. H. H. Green and Duncan Tanner (eds), *The Strange Survival of Liberal England: Political leaders, moral values and the reception of economic debate* (Cambridge, Cambridge University Press, 2007), 186–211.
24 Bertrand de Jouvenel, *The Ethics of Redistribution* (Cambridge, Cambridge University Press, 1951), 90, 72.
25 Ian Gazeley, *Poverty in Britain, 1900–1965* (Basingstoke, Palgrave Macmillan, 2003).
26 José Harris, 'From poor law to welfare state: A European perspective', in Donald Winch and Patrick K. O'Brien (eds), *The Political Economy of British Historical Experience, 1688–1914* (Oxford, Oxford University Press, 2002), 409–37, at 437; John H. Veit-Wilson, 'Muddle or mendacity? The Beveridge Committee and the poverty line', *Journal of Social Policy*, 21 (1992), 269–301.
27 Susan Pedersen, *Family, Dependence, and the Origins of the Welfare State: Britain and France, 1914–1945* (Cambridge, Cambridge University Press, 1993); Marjorie Levine-Clark, *Unemployment, Welfare, and Masculine Citizenship: 'So much honest poverty' in Britain, 1870–1930* (Basingstoke, Palgrave Macmillan, 2015).
28 R. H. Tawney, *Equality* (London, George Allen and Unwin, 1931), 170.
29 James Meade, *Planning and the Price Mechanism: The liberal-socialist solution* (London, George Allen and Unwin, 1948). Meade took a close interest in Juliet Rhys-Williams's basic income proposals: see Peter Sloman, 'Beveridge's rival: Juliet Rhys-Williams and the campaign for basic income, 1942–55', *Contemporary British History*, 30 (2016), 203–23.
30 R. C. Whiting, 'Income tax, the working class and party politics, 1948–1952', *Twentieth Century British History*, 8 (1997), 194–221.
31 Peter Malpass, *Reshaping Housing Policy: Subsidies, rents and residualisation* (London, Routledge, 1990), 89–113.
32 Peter Goldman, 'Preface', in Conservative Political Centre, *The Future of the Welfare State: Seven Oxford lectures* (London, Conservative Political Centre, 1958), 7–10, at 9; 'Liberalism at/through the Mont Pèlerin Society: The British experience', paper by Arthur Seldon, March 1985, Institute of Economic Affairs papers, 368.10, Hoover Institution Archives.
33 Joseph Grimond, *The Liberal Future* (London, Faber and Faber, 1959), 106.
34 Peter Weiler, 'The rise and fall of the Conservatives' "grand design for housing", 1951–64', *Contemporary British History*, 14 (2000), 122–50; Rodney Lowe, 'The replanning of the welfare state, 1957–1964', in Martin Francis and Ina Zweiniger-Bargielowska (eds), *The Conservatives and British Society, 1880–1980* (Cardiff, University of Wales Press, 1996), 255–73.
35 806 Parl. Deb. H. C. (5th ser.) (1970) cols. 217–30.
36 806 Parl. Deb. H. C. (5th ser.) (1970) cols. 260–5, at col. 265; Trades Union Congress, *Economic Review 1971* (London, Trades Union Congress, 1971), 30.
37 Jack Jones, 'Wages and social security', *New Statesman* (7 January 1972), 7.
38 Samuel Brittan, 'How to reform the welfare state', *The Observer* (10 November 1963), 3; New Society Open Group, *Social Reform in a Centrifugal Society* (London, New Society, 1969).
39 Sutcliffe-Braithwaite, 'Neo-liberalism and morality', 520.
40 Martin Daunton, *Just Taxes: The politics of taxation in Britain, 1914–1979* (Cambridge, Cambridge University Press, 2002), 325–8; Lord Young of Graffham to Nigel Lawson, 'Study of tax and social security systems', 6 June 1985, with annotations by Thatcher, TNA: PRO, PREM19/1640.
41 Bernhard Rieger, 'Making Britain work again: Unemployment and the remaking of British social policy in the eighties', *English Historical Review*, 133 (2018), 634–66.
42 Jonathan Portes, 'Welfare and work: Continuity and change', *National Institute Economic Review*, 221 (2012), F4–F9, at F6.

43 This point has been made in a comparative context by John Myles and Paul Pierson, 'Friedman's revenge: The reform of "liberal" welfare states in Canada and the United States', *Politics & Society*, 25 (1997), 443–72.

44 Norman Fowler to Prime Minister, 'Social security review', 1 February 1985, TNA: PRO, BN13/302.

45 Margaret Thatcher, Speech to Conservative Party Women's Conference (London, 25 May 1988), https://www.margaretthatcher.org/document/107248 (accessed 26 February 2019).

46 Norman Fowler in 13 Parl. Deb. H. C. (6th ser.) (1981) cols. 642–52, at col. 651.

47 184 Parl. Deb. H.C. (6th ser.) (1991) col. 940.

48 Chris Belfield, Daniel Chandler and Robert Joyce, *Housing: Trends in prices, costs and tenure* (London, Institute for Fiscal Studies, 2015), 12; John Hills, *Ends and Means: The future roles of social housing in England* (London, Centre for Analysis of Social Exclusion, 2007), 56.

49 Chris Grover, *Social Security and Wage Poverty: Historical and policy aspects of supplementing wages in Britain and beyond* (Basingstoke, Palgrave Macmillan, 2016), 108–26.

50 Nigel Lawson, 'The British experiment', Mais Lecture at City University Business School (18 June 1984), https://www.margaretthatcher.org/document/109504 (accessed 26 February 2019).

51 'Central Policy Review Staff: Report on unemployment', September 1982, TNA: PRO, CAB184/610.

52 Conservative Party, *You Can only Be Sure with the Conservatives* (London, Conservative Party, 1997).

53 John Kay, 'The left is still searching for a practical philosophy', *Financial Times* (5 May 2010), 13.

54 Mark Bevir, *New Labour: A critique* (Abingdon, Routledge, 2005), 84.

55 Martin Rhodes, 'Desperately seeking a solution: Social democracy, Thatcherism and the "Third Way" in British welfare', in Maurizio Ferrera and Martin Rhodes (eds), *Recasting European Welfare States* (London, Frank Cass, 2000), 161–86.

56 For the concept of an 'Anglo-liberal growth model', see Colin Hay, *The Failure of Anglo-Liberal Capitalism* (Basingstoke, Palgrave Macmillan, 2013).

57 Daniel Hirschman and Elizabeth Popp Berman, 'Do economists make policies? On the political effects of economics', *Socio-Economic Review*, 12/4 (2014), 779–811, at 781.

58 Ed Balls, Joe Grice and Gus O'Donnell, *Microeconomic Reform in Britain: Delivering opportunities for all* (Basingstoke, Palgrave Macmillan, 2004), 6, 8.

59 Richard Layard, Stephen Nickell and Richard Jackman, *Unemployment: Macroeconomic performance and the labour market* (Oxford, Oxford University Press, 1991).

60 Andrew Glyn and Stewart Wood, 'New Labour's economic policy', in Andrew Glyn (ed.), *Social Democracy in Neoliberal Times: The left and economic policy since 1980* (Oxford, Oxford University Press, 2001), 200–22.

61 Anthony B. Atkinson, 'What is happening to the distribution of income in the UK?', *Proceedings of the British Academy*, 82 (1992), 317–51; Alissa Goodman and Steve Webb, *For Richer, For Poorer: The changing distribution of income in the United Kingdom, 1961–91* (London, Institute for Fiscal Studies, 1994).

62 The quote is from Gordon Brown, 1996; see Martin Powell, 'Introduction', in Martin Powell (ed.), *New Labour, New Welfare State? The 'Third Way' in British social policy* (Bristol, Policy Press, 1999), 1–27, at 17. Brown's adviser Ed Balls particularly emphasised the need for wage supplements to draw unskilled men back into the labour market; see Ed Balls, 'Danger: Men not at work: Unemployment and non-employment in the UK and beyond', in Ed Balls and Paul Gregg, *Work and Welfare: Tackling the jobs deficit* (London, Institute for Public Policy Research, 1993), 1–30.

63 Paddy Ashdown, *The Ashdown Diaries., Volume I: 1988–1997* (London, Allen Lane, 2000), 486; Desmond King and Mark Wickham-Jones, 'Bridging the Atlantic: The Democratic (Party) origins of welfare to work', in Martin Powell (ed.), *New Labour, New Welfare State? The 'Third Way' in British social policy* (Bristol, Policy Press, 1999), 257–80.

64 The pledge to end child poverty had not been cleared with the Treasury beforehand, and Brownites believed that it was added to Blair's speech by a spin doctor to win a headline in the *Daily Mirror*: Steve Richards, *Whatever It Takes: The real story of Gordon Brown and New Labour* (London, Fourth Estate, 2010), 136–7.

65 Department for Work and Pensions, *Measuring Child Poverty* (London, Department for Work and Pensions, 2003); HM Treasury, *Child Poverty Review* (London, HM Treasury, 2004). For Atkinson's proposal, see Anthony B. Atkinson, 'Targeting poverty', *New Economy*, 5/1 (1998), 3–7.

66 HM Revenue and Customs, 'Child and working tax credits statistics: Finalised annual awards, 2009 to 2010' (May 2011), http://webarchive.nationalarchives.gov.uk/20121112124508/http://www.hmrc.gov.uk/stats/personal-tax-credits/cwtc-final-awards-may11.pdf. (accessed 19 July 2018).

67 Richard Dickens, 'Child poverty in Britain: Past lessons and future prospects', *National Institute Economic Review*, 218 (2011), R7–R19, at R15, table 4.

68 Adam Corlett, Stephen Clarke, Conor D'Arcy and John Wood, *The Living Standards Audit 2018* (London, Resolution Foundation, 2018), 48–74.

69 Bob Jessop, 'From Thatcherism to New Labour: Neo-liberalism, workfarism, and labour market regulation', in Henk Overbeek (ed.), *The Political Economy of European Employment: European integration and the transnationalization of the (un)employment question* (London, Routledge, 2003), 137–53; Ghazala Azmat, 'The incidence of an earned income tax credit: Evaluating the impact on wages in the UK', Centre for Economic Performance Discussion Paper No. 724 (May 2006); Carolyn Lloyd, Geoff Mason and Ken Mayhew (eds), *Low-Wage Work in the United Kingdom* (New York, Russell Sage Foundation, 2007).

70 Scott Lavery, *British Capitalism after the Crisis* (Basingstoke, Palgrave Macmillan, 2019), 101–4.

71 Paul Gregg, Alex Hurrell and Matthew Whittaker, *Creditworthy: Assessing the impact of tax credits in the last decade and considering what this means for Universal Credit* (London, Resolution Foundation, 2012), 16–20.

72 Nancy Fraser, 'From progressive neoliberalism to Trump – and beyond', *American Affairs*, 1/4 (2017), 46–64.

73 Nancy Fraser, 'From redistribution to recognition? Dilemmas of justice in a "post-socialist" age', *New Left Review* I/212 (1995), 68–93; Fraser, 'Neoliberalism to Trump'.

74 Nicholas Barr, *The Economics of the Welfare State* (London, Weidenfeld & Nicolson, 1987); Stuart Astill, 'Nicholas Adrian Barr (1943–)', in Robert A. Cord (ed.), *The Palgrave Companion to LSE Economics* (Basingstoke, Palgrave Macmillan, 2018), 805–30; Damian McBride, *Power Trip: A decade of policy, plots and spin* (London, Biteback Publishing, 2013), 62–9.

75 Brian Steensland, *The Failed Welfare Revolution: America's struggle over guaranteed income policy* (Princeton, NJ, Princeton University Press, 2008).

76 John Curtice, 'Thermostat or weathervane? Public reactions to spending and redistribution under New Labour', in Alison Park, John Curtice, Katarina Thomson, Miranda Phillips, Elizabeth Clery and Sarah Butt (eds), *British Social Attitudes: The 26th Report* (London, SAGE, 2010), 19–38.

77 James O'Connor, *The Fiscal Crisis of the State* (New York, St Martin's Press, 1973); Adam Przeworski and Michael Wallerstein, 'Structural dependence of the state on capital', *American Political Science Review*, 82/1 (1988), 11–29.

78 The Office for Budget Responsibility, for instance, projects that the cost of delivering existing government policy (excluding debt interest) will rise from 36.7 per cent of GDP in 2017/18 to 44.6 per cent in 2067/8, largely as a result of an ageing population and rising treatment costs: Office for Budget Responsibility, *Fiscal Sustainability Report, July 2018* (London, HMSO, 2018), 75.

79 Samuel Moyn, *Not Enough: Human rights in an unequal world* (Cambridge, MA, Harvard University Press, 2018).

80 Ben Jackson, *Equality and the British Left: A study in progressive political thought, 1900–64* (Manchester, Manchester University Press, 2007).

81 Jane Millar and Fran Bennett, 'Universal Credit: Assumptions, contradictions and virtual reality', *Social Policy and Society*, 16 (2017), 169–82.

82 Peter Sloman, 'Universal basic income in British politics: From a "vagabond's wage" to a global debate', *Journal of Social Policy*, 47 (2018), 625–42.

83 Claudia Chwalisz and Patrick Diamond (eds), *The Predistribution Agenda: Tackling inequality and supporting sustainable growth* (London, I.B. Tauris, 2015).

84 Office for Budget Responsibility, *Welfare Trends Report* (London, HMSO, 2016), Cm. 9341, 63; James Browne and Andrew Hood, *Living Standards, Poverty and Inequality in the UK: 2015–16 to 2020–21* (London, Institute for Fiscal Studies, 2016), 34–5.

5

The failures of neoliberalism in Britain since the 1970s: the limits on 'market forces' in a deindustrialising economy and a 'New Speenhamland'

Jim Tomlinson

Neoliberalism has become a widely used term to describe the trajectory of British economic policy since the end of the 1970s.[1] While there is no clear agreement on what exactly this portmanteau concept means, all uses rely on the broad notion of an ideology that believes in expanding the role of markets as allocation devices, and this may involve the use of the state to *create* markets, in areas where they might otherwise be weak or non-existent.[2] This chapter shows that since the 1970s, key elements of the promises of neoliberalism to strengthen the market have *not* been fulfilled, most obviously in the cases of labour and housing. As Peter Taylor-Gooby has written, one view of the legacy of Thatcherism is that, while 'the ideology grows ever stronger', the policies, by contrast, can be seen to have 'failed'.[3] This chapter thus shares the view that, in Jamie Peck's words, neoliberalisation has been 'an open-ended and *contradictory* process of politically assisted market rule'.[4]

In both labour and housing markets, outcomes have been deemed politically unacceptable by all governments, and as a result in the labour market we have seen an explosion of wage subsidies (for example family tax credits) coupled with much greater wage regulation by a National Minimum and then a 'New Living Wage'. In the housing market we have seen a parallel ballooning in spending on housing subsidies, as free-market rents are deemed 'unaffordable' and politically untenable. While the years of austerity since 2010 have seen significant cuts in both wage subsidies and housing benefit, they remain very substantial parts of total public spending, testimony to their entrenchment in the 'neoliberal era'.[5] In the same period, reversing previous positioning, direct undermining of the operation of the labour market by legal enforcement of wage minima has become a taken-for-granted feature of the policy agenda of all mainstream political parties.

Why has neoliberalism failed to deliver on its promises in such a striking fashion? The key argument made here is that this failure results from the constraints imposed on policymaking by economic change, most importantly the deindustrialisation of the British economy (see also Jim Phillips in this volume). The underlying point here is that the richest accounts of neoliberalism in Britain have focused insightful attention on the development of neoliberal *ideas*.[6] But rather less attention has been paid to the *conditions of implementation* for turning these ideas into policy.[7] This is a common problem in historical accounts of the development of economic policy, and an instructive parallel can be made with discussions of a previous shift in economic doctrine and policy, 'the rise of Keynesianism'.

At the end of the 1960s, triumphalist accounts of this rise traced a straightforward passage from the development of Keynes's doctrine in the 1930s to its perceived successful embodiment in the policies of the fully employed post-war 'consensus'.[8] In the wake of the crisis of that consensus in the 1970s, economic historians and others challenged that triumphalist narrative, arguing that the success of Keynesianism in post-war Britain required not just a revolution in economic theory, but a whole range of institutional and administrative changes. These included the construction of a highly centralised fiscal system, and the dominance of a Treasury able to deploy the statistics and instruments of national economic management.[9] But the success of this new policy regime in the 1950s and 1960s also relied more broadly on the buoyancy of the international economic system and the sharp rise in both private and public investment at home.[10]

The key message from this 'revisionism' was the need to always ask: under what historical conditions can programmes of economic reform be realised? What is the relationship between ideologies of economic reform and the economies that they seek to act upon?

If we start with these questions and look at neoliberalism, it is clear that, just as the initial success of Keynesianism relied on the economic conditions created by the Second World War, so the initial successes of neoliberalism were reliant as much on the political opportunities provided by the combined inflationary/fiscal/industrial relations crisis of the 1970s as they were on any theoretical innovations. These conditions allowed the Conservatives under Margaret Thatcher to combine elements of neoliberalism with their declinist analysis to argue for a fundamental shift in economic policy towards 'rolling back the state' in terms of public spending, seen as central to extending the role of market forces.[11]

But 'rolling back the state' proved much easier to proclaim as a goal than to deliver. Public spending proved hard to reduce (especially in the 1980s), and when it was cut (as in the 1990s) it quickly led to pressures forcing a sharp reversal of trend in the early 2000s; a similar reversal of many aspects of previous austerity was evident in the run-up to the 2019 general election.[12] Simultaneously, in the late twentieth and early twenty-first centuries, the economy was being transformed by sectoral changes and especially the decline of industrial employment. Thus, the economy proved much less malleable, much less reformable on neoliberal lines, than the triumphalism of the ideologues of the 1980s suggested – or, indeed, than is suggested by the laments of many of neoliberalism's opponents.

This chapter begins with the growth of wage subsidies from the 1970s, alongside the more recent expansion in housing subsidies, before outlining the move towards the current consensus on the desirability of the state setting legal minima for wages. The next section puts these changes in the context of a deindustrialising labour market and other aspects of Britain's recent economic development. The final part offers some general conclusions on neoliberalism in Britain.

The growth of wage and housing subsidies

In 1970 the Conservative government proposed to introduce a Family Income Supplement (FIS), which would give a (very small) subsidy to some low-wage families.[13] This policy initiative was in part a consequence of the 're-discovery of poverty' in the 1960s, a rediscovery that suggested the erosion of the basic Beveridge assumption that poverty was overwhelmingly due to 'interruption of earnings' (plus large families). In their landmark study, *The Poor and the Poorest,* Abel-Smith and Townsend showed that in 1960 about 40 per cent of households in poverty (those below 140 per cent of the then National Assistance level) had a working member. Most of these households also had a large number of children (four or more), but FIS was aimed at those who were deemed to be disincentivised from seeking work by the small gap between income in and out of employment.[14]

It was in this context that Enoch Powell, a pioneer of British neoliberalism, made a striking parliamentary speech that summarises the case against FIS, seeing the policy as fundamentally at odds with the commitment to free markets.[15]

> I do not think it can be denied that we are taking a decisive new step now by the overt and direct payment – if I may use old-fashioned but significant and appropriate language – of 'relief in supplementation of wages'. We are reminded that there is 'no new thing under the sun'. It was on 6th May, 1795, that the Berkshire Magistrates met at the Pelican Inn in Speenhamland . . . It is the principle that it is an act of fateful consequence to pay relief – cash supplementation of income – to persons in full-time employment; that it is something which is bound profoundly to distort the wage system and to frustrate the ambition – which seems to me to be almost indissociable from the idea of a free society – that a man should receive as near as may be the full value of his work in cash.[16]

As Peter Sloman points out, such wage subsidies were also criticised from the left, Barbara Castle proclaiming them 'repugnant in a modern society'.[17] The reasons for this hostility were grounded in the belief that subsidies failed to address the underlying causes of low wages and undermined the idea that collective bargaining could and should be the route to improved pay.

For the proponents of this policy there was a 'neoliberal' logic that led to the opposite conclusion to that of Powell. Given the view of the labour market as driven by market incentives, FIS was aimed at increasing the gap between the incomes of the unemployed and the employed, in order to encourage the former to seek work. Thus, the policy was at one with a long tradition of Conservative thinking, which saw unemployment as partly, at least, caused by a lack of incentives to seek work, and resulted, eventually, in the squeeze in the incomes of the unemployed under Conservatives after 1979.[18]

FIS was introduced in 1971, and on a very small scale. But in the 1980s, under the provisions of the Supplement and its successor, Family Credit, payments to low-wage households expanded rapidly. By the early 1990s, the scale of spending of this kind was a source of boasting by leading Conservatives: 'In just the past three years, the Government have tripled spending in cash terms on family credit. Since 1979, spending on benefits for families dependent on low-paid work has increased by 10 times in real terms. Today the average family credit payment is more than £30 a week.'[19]

In-work benefits saw spectacular further growth under New Labour.[20] This can be seen as the product of a characteristic New Labour amalgam of pro-market views about incentives with a social democratic desire to reduce poverty. (On tensions in New Labour's social welfare policies, see Bernhard Rieger in this volume). It allowed a substantial expansion of cash transfers targeted on household income, without arousing traditional Labour hostility to means testing.[21] Under this impetus expenditure per claimant on such benefits increased from approximately £500 in 1970 to £4,300 in 2000.[22]

The Conservatives in opposition were highly critical of New Labour's policies on poverty reduction but asserted that 'tax credits are an essential part of a modern welfare policy – it is obviously better to increase someone's income in work than to see them either in poverty or out of work'.[23] The leader of the Opposition spoke in similar terms of the failure of Labour's policies but coupled this with a proclaimed need to 'increase the working Tax Credit that couples receive'.[24] There was no hint in these arguments of a Powellite rejection of 'New Speenhamland'.

Total spending on tax credits and their predecessors rose from £1 billion to £30 billion in cash terms over the 30 years from the mid-1980s, an increase of around tenfold in real terms. Absolute spending peaked in 2014/15 and by 2019/20 had fallen to around £25 billion. The fall relative to GDP is greater, down to around 1.3 per cent from the peak of 1.8 per cent in 2011/12.[25]

After 2010, governmental attempts to reduce wage subsidies battled against trends creating increased eligibility, with wages stagnating or falling, while the costs of childcare rose. Serious cuts were imposed, but spending remained substantial.[26]

It is not only that these in-work benefits have come to greatly exceed payments made to the unemployed, but that the whole principle of post-war welfare has shifted. As noted above, the classic mid-twentieth-century Beveridge analysis of the sources of poverty suggested the problem fundamentally lay in 'interruption to earnings' (by unemployment, sickness or old age) along with large numbers of children, the latter to be addressed by 'Family Allowances' (later, Child Benefit).[27] This analysis always misrepresented the actualities of the labour market, not least in its barely qualified notion of the 'male-breadwinner household', a notion increasingly at odds with growing married women's labour market participation from the 1950s. But its fundamental idea that, normally, paid work would provide a route out of poverty has underpinned most modern liberal understandings of how society works down to the present day. The 'New Speenhamland' provision challenges this idea and in doing so gives a role for the state which is difficult to see as 'neoliberal' in character.

A year before the attack on 'relief in supplementation of wages' quoted above, Powell had similarly attacked housing subsidies as 'Speenhamland in Modern Dress'.[28] In this case, of course, he was not attacking a new departure in current policy, because subsidies for housing of some kind had been a feature of Britain since the First World War and the start of local authority provision of housing. This had been accompanied by subsidies to home ownership, ultimately underpinned by the desire, originating in the Conservative response to the emergence of a mass proletarian electorate, to create a 'property-owning democracy'.

In the first post-war decades, subsidies were focused upon public sector housebuilding on the one side, and a variety of tax concessions to house purchasers on the other. This double pressure greatly reduced the role of the private rented sector, which was reduced to a residual role in housing provision. But from the 1970s (beginning at the time of the public expenditure cuts under the Labour government that preceded the International Monetary Fund borrowing of 1976), public sector housebuilding was cut back hard. This trajectory was continued under the Thatcher government, accompanied by some degree of 'balancing' between the public and private sectors by reducing mortgage interest tax relief (MIRA), which was finally abolished in 2002, though other substantial tax advantages for home ownership were retained.[29]

Famously, the Thatcher government, through a 'Right to Buy' policy imposed on local authorities, sold off large parts of the public housing stock. Governments almost stopped being builders of houses, and the rhetoric of the time was that public money would subsidise families, not bricks and mortar. This led to the consolidation of existing rent subsidies into Housing Benefit in 1983, accompanied by incremental deregulation of rents over the 1980s and 1990s.[30] This combination meant a growing expenditure on this benefit as rents increased, in part reflecting rising house prices (on trend: the market was subject to a sharp cycle in the early 1990s). But a limit was put on this growth by the fact that the 'property-owning democracy' was being realised, with owner-occupation growing from 56.4 to its peak at 69.4 per cent of all tenures in the two decades after 1981.[31]

However, the most rapid acceleration of this spending came after the turn of the century.

The subsidising of home ownership had long created a race between house price inflation, driven by strong demand in combination with relatively inelastic supply, and affordability, underpinned by rising real incomes among large swathes of the population. But after the crash of 2007 the 'race' was increasingly 'won' by continuing house price inflation, making entry into the housing market impossible for many, and the home ownership ratio fell back sharply.

The corollary of this falling back, coupled to the radical reduction in the public housing stock, was that the strain was taken by private sector renting, which underwent a striking expansion. Owner-occupation had peaked at the turn of the century, but the sharp fall came in the wake of the financial crash, with social renting also continuing its long-run decline.[32]

Housing benefit spending increased from 0.8 per cent of GDP in 1983–4 to 1.5 per cent in 2013–14, fluctuating with the economic cycle, but on a generally upward trend over time.[33] Absolute levels of spending then peaked in 2015/16 at just under £22 billion. Without a change in policy, they are likely to fluctuate around this level down to 2022 on current policies, staying higher than previously forecast for reasons which make clear why the benefit has proved so hard to cut more seriously: '[T]he share of the population renting had continued to rise faster than forecast . . . employment growth has been much faster than expected but earnings growth had been much weaker . . . rent inflation . . . had been higher than expected.'[34]

The politics of wage regulation

Significant state intervention in wages began with the Trade Boards introduced by the 1906 Liberal government. The scope of the Boards was significantly extended at the end of the First World War and again after 1945. They were renamed Wages Councils but continued to be sector-specific and focused on a small number of industries where the labour market was deemed 'abnormal' and trade union presence limited. For much of the second half of the twentieth century, opposition to the idea of more ambitious wage regulation by a national statutory minimum wage came from both the Labour and Conservative parties.

On their side, Labour and the trade unions combined a historical scepticism about the desirability of state intervention in the labour market with a belief that wages should be determined by collective bargaining between trade unions and employers.[35] There were dissenting voices, and the issue was a perennial one for debate in labour circles, revived in the 1960s partly in response to the rediscovery of poverty.[36] But it was not until the 1980s, when an alliance between Rodney Bickerstaffe of the

National Union of Public Employees and the Low Pay Unit was formed, that Labour opposition was defeated, and a straightforward commitment to introduce legislation was included in the 1987 general election manifesto.[37]

As part of the post-war 'consensus' the Conservatives accepted Wages Councils down to the 1970s. But the radicalisation of Conservative economic thinking under Thatcher led to growing hostility, and the eventual abolition of most Wages Councils in the 1980s, with the Major government finishing the job in 1993. The press release accompanying this final abolition announced: 'Wages Councils were established in the early 1900s when there were no employment rights, no general health and safety legislation and little social security protection. They have no role to play in the 1990s.'[38]

Thus, despite presiding over a significant expansion of wage subsidies, into the 1990s the Conservatives emphasised a continuing ideological commitment to the idea of the market determination of wages, evident in the early 1990s when they made ferocious attacks on Labour's proposals for a statutory minimum wage. The title of a 1991 Conservative Research Department document summarised their argument: *The Minimum Wage: Labour's axe on jobs*.[39] In a House of Commons debate in 1992 the Conservatives amended a critical Opposition motion to deplore 'the commitment of Her Majesty's Opposition to a National Minimum Wage which would destroy jobs, thereby reducing opportunities and living standards for up to two million people'.[40]

Beyond the alleged impact on employment levels, opposition to minimum wages was part of a broader pro-market perspective, clearly articulated by ex-Prime Minister Thatcher:

> We have different ways of doing things. We do not have a minimum wage. Because if you do you get all the differentials throughout the place and up go your costs. We say something different. We say if you haven't enough after working on which to keep your family, we add to it from the tax-payer Family Credit so you can keep them in decency and keep them in a way in which you'd expect. That doesn't add to industrial costs.[41]

The New Labour government, following the change of heart on this matter in the previous decade, introduced legislation for a National Minimum Wage in 1998. The Conservatives fought bitterly, though unsuccessfully, to prevent this new law coming into force. Again, the ex-Prime Minister sought to bolster the case, attacking the new government:

> It's easy enough to take credit for the low unemployment your Conservative predecessors bequeathed you. But proving your left wing credentials with a National Minimum Wage, with a Working Time Directive, and with compulsory trade union recognition is to take a three-fold swipe at job creation.[42]

But around the time of this speech the Conservative opposition started to row back on its hostility to the new law. In 2000, the Shadow Chancellor, Michael Portillo, announced that the party was officially ending its opposition to the policy, while saying that the party remained 'concerned at the costs for business'.[43] In 2005, the new party leader, David Cameron, proclaimed: 'I think the minimum wage has been a success, yes. It turned out much better than people expected.'[44] There were still equivocations in Conservative ranks until 2015, when Chancellor Osborne announced a statutory 'New Living Wage', despite the continuing criticism from free-market think tanks.[45] In the view of writers for such think tanks, the consensus between the parties had opened up the possibility of 'a political bidding war' on the level to be set for the minimum wage.[46]

There was a logic at work in Osborne's position, if not an unambiguously neoliberal one, in seeking to reduce public spending on wage subsidies by shifting more of the costs of raising wages on to employers. In his budget speech he announced big cuts to working-age benefits, especially tax credits, noting that the latter had risen from 8 per cent of public spending in 1980 to 13 per cent in 2015. But the ambition was by no means to abolish these credits, rather the aim was to 'return tax credits to 2007/8 levels in real terms' (that is, the level before the financial crash). The announcement of the National Living Wage was coupled to a claim that its impact in raising unemployment (calculated at 60,000 by the Office for Budgetary Responsibility) would be offset by the creation of a million new jobs. Conscious of arguments about the cost to employers, the announcement included promises of continuing cuts in corporation tax for large business, and National Insurance cuts for small firms. The Chancellor also noted the steep rise in Housing Benefit and announced a cut in rents in the *social housing* sector – but there were to be no general rent controls in the private sector to cut claims for that benefit, to match the policy combination of a Living Wage being combined with cuts to tax credits.[47]

The shift just outlined means that in the 'neoliberal era' the leaderships of both main British political parties moved from believing that wages should be settled as far as possible without legal intervention to a position of strongly supporting a legal minimum wage. For Labour this was an important shift but emerged from a long-running debate; for the Conservatives it involved a striking volte-face.

Deindustrialisation and wage polarisation

The link between deindustrialisation and polarisation in the labour market has been outlined elsewhere.[48] This draws on well-known evidence from both economists and think tanks about the much greater dispersion of incomes in the service sector compared with industrial employment.[49]

Polarisation suggests, of course, growth at both ends of the wage distribution. Goos and Manning's data shows this very clearly for the years 1979–99, when the two most rapidly growing sectors of employment in Britain were care assistants and attendants (a 419 per cent increase) and software engineers (a 405 per cent increase).[50] Care assistants also registered the largest absolute increase in numbers at over 400,000. The biggest proportionate falls over the same period were among 'boring and drilling machine setters and setter operators' and coal miners. The wage polarising aspects of such changes are suggested by the fact that care assistants in 1979 typically earned around 25 per cent below the median national wage, and software engineers two-thirds above that median, while the manual occupations which shrank most offered wages closest to (about 20 per cent above) the middle of the distribution.[51]

The significance of this polarisation is profound. Of course, it has meant a rapid growth in well-paid and relatively stable employment for the academically qualified, while making it increasingly difficult for those without such qualifications to secure such conditions. For many of the latter, while the rhetoric of 'work is the route out of poverty' is still widely heard, it is plainly no longer true. As a result of the changes in the labour market brought about by deindustrialisation, growing in-work poverty has been a central feature of the post-industrial period. While the period of much larger-scale employment in industry did not guarantee an above-poverty income, most poverty was among non-workers (the sick and disabled, pensioners, single mothers), or those with unusually large families. Recent work suggests that a majority of the poor in the early twenty-first century were members of households with at least one member in work:

> [In 2014/15] there are 400,000 fewer pensioners in poverty, despite there being around 1.7 million more people aged 65 or over. There are 2 million more people in working families in poverty, now up to 7.4 million, than a decade earlier. In contrast the number in workless or retired families in poverty fell by half a million. As pensioner poverty is now at low levels, the rate of in-work poverty is the most distinctive characteristic of poverty today.[52]

In-work benefits are clearly far from rescuing all recipient households from poverty, but they were certainly used effectively to reduce those numbers under New Labour, and they contributed significantly to the overall fall in poverty, especially among families with children, in that period. (Part of the complex legacy of New Labour was a big fall in poverty combined with no reduction in overall income inequality, as very top incomes continued to accelerate away.)[53]

Thus, deindustrialisation has cut across neoliberal plans for state retreat from intervention in labour and housing markets. The slogan of 'making work pay' has been 'successfully' pursued by worsening the financial position of the unemployed, but the policy of seeking to keep those in employment out of poverty, or at least at lower levels of poverty, has required an expansion of state activity of a striking scale and scope.[54]

Actually existing neoliberalism

There is no one single measure of the implementation of neoliberalism. But it is useful to start with public expenditure as one key area where the impact of the desire to 'roll back the state' can be assessed.

As a context, it is worth noting that at the global level the clear trend has been for public spending to rise over the long run, driven primarily by rises in social welfare spending, with the highest levels both in absolute terms and relative to GDP in the richest countries, but with the same trend evident in most countries as GDP has risen.[55] Within the Organisation for Economic Co-operation and Development, it is clear that overall public spending has been broadly stable since 1980, but with a larger proportion of that spending going on social welfare as military spending and economic subsidies were squeezed.[56] Levels of social expenditure among this grouping tended to grow significantly following the financial crash of 2007/8, and then fall back in the following period of austerity, but to levels still above those prevalent before the crash.[57]

What has happened in Britain has broadly mirrored the experience of other rich countries. Total public spending, adjusted for inflation, has risen almost continuously in the years since the mid-1970s, and even in the recent, post-2010, era of cuts the absolute level has barely declined (see table 5.1 and table 5.2). Over the last 40 years total spending (adjusted for inflation) has grown around 250 per cent.

Measured as a share of GDP, public spending has fluctuated with the economic cycle, but with a downward trend from just under 50 per cent

Table 5.1 Key components of public spending as a share of GDP, 1978/9–2017/18

	1978/9	**2017/18**
Health	4%	7%
Military	4%	1.9%
Social security (pensioners)	5%	6%
Social security (non-pensioners)	3%	4.6%

Source: C. Emmerson, T. Pope and B. Zaranko, *Outlook for 2019 Spending Review*, briefing note 243 (London, IFS, 2019), 5.

Table 5.2 Public spending in crisis, recovery and austerity, 2007–19

	Total managed expenditure in 2017/18 prices (£ billions)
2006/7	697
2007/8	721
2008/9	766
2009/10	794
2010/11	804
2011/12	793
2012/13	794
2013/14	781
2014/15	789
2015/16	789
2016/17	787
2017/18	795
2018/19 (estimated)	798
2019/20 (estimated)	810

Source: OBR databank: Public sector finances.

in 1975/6 (the post-war peak) to around 40 per cent in 2016/17, though the fall in public investment (not least in housing) means *current* spending has fallen by perhaps 5 per cent of GDP. Post-2010 austerity plans would have taken the figure to around 38 per cent by 2020 (still higher than the levels of the 1980s and 1990s), but that project has now ended. Within these totals, spending on health care and education has risen significantly as a share of GDP. In social security the aim of squeezing the incomes of the unemployed has been carried through, but overall social security spending has risen more than in line with GDP.[58] Much of this has come from growing expenditure on pensions, but the most striking change, reversed but by no means eliminated after 2010, has, as noted above, been the rise in in-work benefits and Housing Benefit.

Thus, overall in the 'neoliberal era', state spending in absolute terms has risen by a substantial amount, especially on social welfare. That spending has risen partly at the expense of other programmes, especially the military. The 'shrinking of the state' under the austerity policies since 2010 has hit some areas of spending enormously hard. Most striking has been the relentless squeeze on local authority spending, which has clear political advantage for central government in shifting the political focus but has had major regressive effects.[59] There have also been very big cuts in working-age benefits. But we should not allow these recent changes to obscure the fact that the trend in the 'neoliberal era' has been, by any measure, for spending on welfare to rise; we have moved from what David Edgerton called a 'warfare state' in mid-twentieth-century Britain to one which, at least in quantitative terms, more than ever deserves the term 'welfare state'.[60]

Of course, the numbers are only part of the story. For the ideologues of the Institute of Economic Affairs (IEA) in the late 1950s and 1960s the key aim was an assault on the welfare state, by introducing markets to create 'choice in welfare' by breaking up the National Health Service (NHS) and introducing vouchers for schooling.[61] Neither of these has happened as envisaged, and it is important to register that failure against the original priorities of British neoliberalism. But plainly these services (and many other parts of the public sector) have been much affected by reorganisations which have aimed to mimic private sector patterns of 'purchasers' and 'providers'. It is striking that in many areas the impact of neoliberalism has not been to 'roll back' the state in quantitative terms, but to change how that state works.[62]

The reorganisation of the state has included widespread contracting out in order to lower wage costs, and this, paradoxically, has increased the numbers of those paid wages which have to be supplemented by in-work benefits, so that the state budget has 'taken with one hand and given with the other'. This outsourcing has also meant that the scale of employment reliant directly on the public purse has trended clearly *upwards* over most of the 'neoliberal era' despite the cuts in those officially defined as working in the public sector.[63]

The aim of this chapter has not been to deny that neoliberalism has had profound effects on British policy since the 1970s. Trade unions have been marginalised, and many markets deregulated, including many aspects of the labour market (see Jim Phillips in this volume). This contributed in a major way to the extraordinary rise in income inequality in Britain in the 1980s, a shift which has since been stabilised but not reversed.[64] The parallel deregulation of finance has not only underpinned a huge growth in personal debt (with both macroeconomic and social implications) but has also created a process of financialisation with a wide range of social and political effects.[65]

But alongside these effects, this chapter has argued that there is a fundamental clash between the marketisation ambitions of neoliberalism and the effects of the shifts in the labour market as a consequence of deindustrialisation. The latter has generated a polarised labour market, with wages at the bottom below those deemed 'politically acceptable'. From the 1980s onwards, governments spent substantial sums in wage subsidies, and the scale of these became a major problem for the ambition to reduce public spending in the post-crash 'austerity' era, given their scale. The tensions over this issue pushed the post-2010 Conservative-led governments into a policy completely at odds with neoliberalism, a statutory national 'living' wage.

Thus, in an ostensibly 'neoliberal' policy regime we have seen the development of two major interventions in the labour market, entirely absent in the preceding period of allegedly 'Keynesian/social democratic' predominance, plus a multiplication of subsidies in the housing market, much of that multiplication reflecting the inability of those in work to afford market-determined rents.

'Actually existing neoliberalism' looks very different from the outcomes aimed for by most neoliberal ideologues. Some dimensions of this failure are well known. The failure to cut back the NHS in ways which would have followed the beliefs of early advocates of neoliberalism is clear.[66] It is not hard to see why this particular failure has occurred. In Britain, neoliberalism may have found its political home in the Conservative Party and achieved considerable purchase as a result. But this linkage has also meant that the influence of this doctrine has been constrained in the policymaking process by Conservative statecraft.[67]

That statecraft includes some quite straightforward political calculation about the attractions of a free-at-the-point-of-use health care system to the great mass of voters, especially as those voters have on average become older, and hence had greater demands for such care. The demographic shift is also, of course, hugely important in explaining how pensions have become such a large and growing part of the social security budget, and why largely publicly funded 'social care' became the fastest-growing employment sector in the final decades of the twentieth century.

This chapter has sought to add to our understanding of the constraints on neoliberal policymaking by emphasising the role of an economic change that neoliberals did not foresee: deindustrialisation.[68] This change, evident across the whole industrial world, was the consequence of technological changes, changes in consumption patterns and, to a lesser extent, globalisation.[69] It began in the 1950s and has been at work in Britain right through the 'neoliberal era'. It is doubtful that within broad parameters the pace or scale of the change has been or could be much affected by policy measures.[70] In response to the change, what has emerged since the 1980s is a political consensus on dealing with its consequences for incomes through increased public spending and wage regulation.[71]

Notes

1 Thus, Stedman-Jones seeks to explain 'how the neoliberal faith in markets came to dominate politics in Britain and the US in the last quarter of the twentieth century up to the financial crisis of 2008': Daniel Stedman-Jones, *Masters of the Universe: Hayek, Friedman and the birth of neoliberal politics* (Princeton, NJ, Princeton University Press, 2012), 1.

2 Ben Jackson, 'At the origins of neo-liberalism: The free economy and the strong state, 1930–1947', *Historical Journal*, 53 (2010), 129–51.

3 Peter Taylor-Gooby, 'Commentary', in Stephen Farrall and Colin Hay (eds), *The Legacy of Thatcherism: Assessing and exploring Thatcherite social and economic policies* (Oxford, Oxford University Press, 2014), 100–7, at 104.

4 Jamie Peck, *Constructions of Neoliberal Reason* (Oxford, Oxford University Press, 2010), xii (emphasis added).

5 There have been claims that post-2010 welfare reforms heralded the demise of tax credits, but these changes do not mark the end of in-work benefits. Rather, 'Universal Credit . . . pursues some broadly similar aims to tax credits but with a rather different emphasis': Daniel Clegg, 'The demise of tax credits', *Political Quarterly*, 86 (2015), at 497.

6 Pioneered by Richard Cockett, *Thinking the Unthinkable: Think tanks and the economic counter-revolution, 1931–1983* (London, HarperCollins, 1995); and Keith Tribe, 'Liberalism and neoliberalism in Britain, 1830–1980', in Philip Mirowski and Dieter Plehwe (eds), *The Road from Mont Pèlerin: The making of the neoliberal thought collective* (Cambridge, MA, Harvard University Press, 2009), 68–97.

7 An important exception is Damien Cahill, *The End of Laissez-Faire? On the durability of embedded neoliberalism* (Cheltenham, Edward Elgar, 2016). The very terminology of 'neoliberalism' predisposes the debate towards emphasising the *doctrinal* aspects of policy determinants. The term 'market fundamentalism' is in many ways more helpful, as it emphasises the visceral, ideological anti-statism which animated much of this shift, rather than the 'rational' and doctrinal underpinnings.

8 Robert Lekachman, *The Age of Keynes: A biographical study* (New York, Random House, 1966); and Michael Stewart, *Keynes and After* (Harmondsworth, Penguin, 1972).

9 Roger Middleton, *Towards the Managed Economy* (London, Methuen, 1985); Jim Tomlinson, *Problems of British Economic Policy* (London, Methuen, 1981); and Neil Rollings, 'The "Keynesian revolution" and economic policy-making: A comment', *Economic History Review*, 38 (1985), 95–100.

10 R. C. O. Matthews, 'Why has Britain had full employment since the war?', *Economic Journal*, 78 (1968), 555–69. In a different register were discussions about 'Fordism', linking production systems to employment: Karel Williams, Colin Haslam and John Williams, 'Ford versus "Fordism": The beginning of mass production?' *Work, Employment & Society*, 6 (1992), 517–55.

11 Jim Tomlinson, *Managing the Economy, Managing the People: Narratives of economic life in Britain from Beveridge to Brexit* (Oxford, Oxford University Press, 2017), chapter 3.

12 Rowena Crawford, Paul Johnson and Ben Zaranko, *The Planning and Control of UK Public Expenditure, 1993–2015* (London, Institute for Fiscal Studies, 2018); and Jim Tomlinson, 'Britain since the 1970s: A transition to neo-liberalism?', in Julian Hoppitt, Adrian Leonard and Duncan Needham (eds), *Money and Markets: Essays in honour of Martin Daunton* (Woodbridge, Boydell and Brewer, 2019).

13 For the context, see Peter Sloman, '"The pragmatist's solution to poverty": The Heath government's tax credit scheme and the politics of social policy in the 1970s', *Twentieth Century British History*, 27 (2016), 220–41.

14 Brian Abel-Smith and Peter Townsend, *The Poor and the Poorest: A new analysis of the Ministry of Labour's Family Expenditure surveys of 1953–54 and 1960* (London, Bell, 1965), 49; and Ian Gazeley, Andrew Newell, Kevin Reynolds and Rebecca Searle, 'The poor and the poorest, 50 years on: Evidence from British Household Expenditure surveys of the 1950s and 1960s', *Journal of the Royal Statistical Society*, Series A, 180 (2016), 455–74.

15 On Powell's neoliberalism, see Paul Corthorn, *Enoch Powell: Politics and ideas in modern Britain* (Oxford, Oxford University Press, 2018). Reviewing this book, one of Thatcher's closest advisers stressed that '[i]n the 1960s, he (Powell) became the darling of the neoliberals. Ralph Harris and Arthur Seldon, the genial masterminds of the Institute of Economic Affairs, regarded him as their most potent advocate.' Ferdinand Mount, '*Enoch Powell: Politics and Ideas in Modern Britain* by Paul Corthorn', *London Review of Books* (September 2019), 7.

16 J. Enoch Powell, *Hansard* (10 November 1970), vol. 806, cols 262, 264–5.

17 Sloman, '"Pragmatist's solution"', 234. In the debate in which Powell made the above statement, the Labour Opposition (represented by Shirley Williams) responded to the introduction of FIS, saying 'this House, while welcoming measures to help families in poverty, believes the Government's Family Income Supplements Scheme will assist only a tiny minority, further extend the complex system of a means-tested society which is an essential element in the policy of Her Majesty's Government, and will do nothing to encourage employers to improve very low wages in certain occupations'. *Hansard*, vol. 806, col. 230.

18 Anthony B. Atkinson and John Micklewright. 'Turning the screw: Benefits for the unemployed, 1979–1988', in Anthony B. Atkinson (ed.), *Poverty and Social Security* (Brighton, Harvester Wheatsheaf, 1989), 125–57.

19 *Hansard* (9 July 1991), vol. 194, col. 794. Note that in this debate Labour speakers voiced scepticism about tax credits as opposed to a national minimum wage as a way of raising work incomes.

20 Richard Blundell and Hilary Hoynes, 'Has "in-work" benefit reform helped the labour market?', in David Card, Richard Blundell and Richard Freeman (eds), *Seeking a Premier Economy: The economic effects of British reforms 1980–2000* (Chicago, University of Chicago Press, 2004), 411–45.

21 Clegg, 'Demise', 495.

22 Blundell and Hoynes 'Has "in-work" benefit reform helped the labour market?', 426; and Matthew Whittaker, *The Shape of Things to Come: Charting the changing size and shape of the UK state* (London, Resolution Foundation, November 2019).

23 Conservative Party, *Making British Poverty History* (London, Conservative Party, 2008), 7.

24 David Cameron, 'Making British poverty history' (16 October 2007), https://conservative-speeches.sayit.mysociety.org/speech/599767 (accessed 13 March 2019).

25 Office for Budget Responsibility, 'Tax by tax, spend by spend: Welfare spending: tax credits' (15 May 2018), https://obr.uk/forecasts-in-depth/tax-by-tax-spend-by-spend/welfare-spending-tax-credits/ (accessed 8 March 2019).

26 Office for Budget Responsibility, *Welfare Trends Report* (2014), 12, 42, 51.
27 Anthony Cutler, Karel Williams and John Williams, *Keynes, Beveridge and Beyond* (London, Routledge and Kegan Paul, 1986).
28 J. Enoch Powell, 'A housing policy for Great Britain: Speech to Federation of Registered House-Builders conference' (28 November 1968), http://enochpowell.info/wp-content/uploads/Speeches/Oct-Dec%201968.pdf (accessed 8 March 2019).
29 MIRA cost the Exchequer £7.7 billion in 1990, more than was spent on *gross* social housing investment (i.e. ignoring receipts from council house sales): David Mullins and Alan Murie, *Housing Policy in the UK* (Basingstoke, Palgrave Macmillan, 2006), 51.
30 Mullins and Murie, *Housing Policy in the UK*, 39, 115–16.
31 Mullins and Murie, *Housing Policy in the UK*, 49. On the politics of house ownership, see Matthew Francis, '"A crusade to enfranchise the many". Thatcherism and the "property-owning democracy"', *Twentieth Century British History*, 23 (2012), 275–97.
32 Kate Barker, *Housing: Where's the plan?* (London, London Publishing Partnership, 2014), 3. The growth of private renting was also encouraged by post-crash low interest rates which left many small (and some not so small) savers and pensioners desperate to find assets with reasonable yields, leading to the 'buy to rent' phenomenon.
33 Office for Budget Responsibility, 'Tax by tax, spend by spend'.
34 Office for Budget Responsibility, 'Tax by tax, spend by spend', 5.
35 Roger Bowlby, 'Union policy towards minimum wage legislation in post-war Britain', *Industrial and Labour Relations Review*, 11 (1957), 72–84.
36 Discussion in government circles was restarted *before* Labour came to power in 1964, in the context of debates about alternative ways to reduce family poverty: 'Inter-departmental committee on National Minimum Wage', established May 1964, TNA: PRO T227/2092; for a flavour of the political debate within Labour, see 'National Minimum Wage', *Hansard* (5 June 1967), vol. 747, cols 613–15.
37 Jerold Waltman, *Minimum Wage Policy in Great Britain and the USA* (New York, Algora, 2008), 75–83.
38 Waltman, *Minimum Wage Policy*, 74.
39 Note that this stance was not limited to the Conservative Party; the IFS was also opposed on the grounds that few poor families would get a significant income increase from higher wages: Paul Johnson and Graham Stark, 'The effects of a minimum wage on family incomes', *Fiscal Studies*, 12 (1991), 88–93; however, by 1996 opinion was starting to shift: Amanda Gosling, 'The effects of a minimum wage on family incomes', *Fiscal Studies*, 12 (1991), 88–93.
40 *Hansard* (Commons) (9 July 1992), vol. 194, col. 791. This view was strongly supported by the Institute of Economic Affairs: David Forrest and Stanley Dennison, *Low Pay or No Pay?* (London, IEA, 1984).
41 Speech in Chelmsford, 22 March 1992, MTFW: Thatcher papers.
42 Speech at the International Free Enterprise meeting, 20 April 1999, MTFW: Thatcher papers.
43 Michael White, 'Portillo adjusts to political reality', *The Guardian* (4 February 2000).
44 Waltman, *Minimum Wage Policy*, 207.
45 Ryan Bourne and Len Shackleton, *And How Much Do You Earn? Public pressure for government regulation of pay* (London, IEA, 2016).
46 Len Shackleton, *Restructuring Minimum Wages: Complexity, compliance and a case for reform* (London, IEA, 2018), 5.
47 George Osborne, Summer Budget Speech (2015), https://www.gov.uk/government/speeches/chancellor-george-osbornes-summer-budget-2015-speech (accessed 13 March 2015).
48 Jim Tomlinson, 'De-industrialization not decline: A new meta-narrative for post-war British history', *Twentieth Century British History*, 27 (2016), 76–99.
49 Maarten Goos and Alan Manning, 'Lousy and lovely jobs: The rising polarization of work in Britain', *Review of Economics and Statistics*, 89 (2007), 118–33; Craig Holmes and Ken Mayhew, *The Changing Shape of the UK Job Market and its Implications for the Bottom Half of Earners* (London, Resolution Foundation, 2012); and Patrick Emmenegger, *The Age of Dualization* (Oxford, Oxford University Press, 2012).
50 Goos and Manning, 'Lousy and lovely jobs'.
51 Goos and Manning, 'Lousy and lovely jobs', 124–5.
52 Joseph Rowntree Foundation, *Monitoring Poverty and Social Exclusion* (London, Joseph Rowntree Foundation, 2016), 1–2.

53 John Hills, Tom Sefton and Kitty Stewart (eds), *Towards a More Equal Society: Poverty, inequality and policy since 1997* (Bristol, Policy Press, 2009), 21–45.

54 As with other policy areas, neoliberal attitudes towards poverty have been diverse and subject to change, both in how far it is perceived as a major problem, and how whatever support for the poor is deemed appropriate should be organised. But none of its ideologues envisaged minimum wages and wage and housing subsidies as the way forward: Jackson, 'At the origins'; and Ben Jackson, 'Currents of neo-liberalism: British political ideologies and the New Right, c.1955–1979', *English Historical Review*, 131 (2016), 823–50. More broadly on neoliberal economics and the welfare state, see Roger Backhouse, Bradley Bateman, Tamotsu Nishizawa and Dieter Plehwe (eds), *Liberalism and the Welfare State: Economists and arguments for the welfare state* (Oxford, Oxford University Press, 2017).

55 Steven Pinker, *Enlightenment Now: The case for reason, science, humanism and progress* (London, Penguin, 2019), 107–10.

56 Joseph Cohen and Miguel Centeno, 'Neoliberalism and patterns of economic performance, 1980–2000', *Annals of the American Academy of Political and Social Science*, 606 (2006), 37–41.

57 OECD, Social Expenditure 2017, http://www.oecd.org/social/expenditure.htm (accessed 13 March 2019).

58 Andrew Jowett and Michael Hardie, 'Longer term trends: Public sector finance' (London, Office for National Statistics, November 2014); and Office for Budget Responsibility, *Welfare Trends*, 5.

59 Anette Hastings, Nick Bailey, Glen Bramley and Maria Gannon, 'Austerity urbanism in England: The "regressive redistribution" of local government services and the impact on the poor and marginalised', *Environment and Planning*, 49 (2017), 2007–24.

60 David Edgerton, *Warfare State: Britain, 1920–1970* (Cambridge, Cambridge University Press, 2006).

61 Ralph Harris and Arthur Seldon, *Choice in Welfare* (London, IEA, 1963); and Ralph Harris and Arthur Seldon, *Welfare without the State: A quarter-century of suppressed public choice* (London, IEA, 1987). See also Nicholas Bosanquet, *After the New Right* (London, Heinemann, 1983), 75–83.

62 This is a parallel argument to that which emphasises how far the privatisation of industry has been accompanied by a massive extension of regulatory activity: Cahill, *End of Laissez-Faire?*, 14–30.

63 John Buchanan, Julie Froud, Sukhdev Johal, Adam Leaver and Karel Williams, 'Undisclosed and unsustainable: Problems of the UK National Business Model' (Manchester, Centre for Research in Economic and Social Change, 2009).

64 Chris Belfield, Jonathan Cribb, Andrew Hood and Robert Joyce, *Living Standards, Poverty and Inequality in the UK: 2016* (London, Institute for Fiscal Studies, 2016), 23–5.

65 Julie Froud, Sukhdev Johal, Johnna Montgomerie and Karel Williams, 'Escaping the tyranny of earned income? The failure of finance as social innovation', *New Political Economy*, 15 (2010), 147–64.

66 Stedman-Jones, *Masters of the Universe*, xi. How central such a cutback was to pioneer British neoliberals is emphasised in D. Collard, *The New Right: A critique* (London, Fabian Society, 1968).

67 Jim Bulpitt, 'The discipline of the new democracy: Mrs Thatcher's domestic statecraft', *Political Studies*, 34 (1989), 19–39.

68 There was a tendency for some neoliberals to welcome the onset of deindustrialisation when it became widely recognised in the 1980s, seeing it as part of a market-driven adjustment to Britain's comparative advantage in services: Samuel Brittan, 'Deindustrialization is good for the UK', *Financial Times* (3 July 1980); and Samuel Brittan, 'How British is the British sickness?', *Journal of Law and Economics*, 21 (1978), 249–50.

69 Jim Tomlinson, 'De-industrialization: Strengths and weaknesses as a key concept for understanding post-war British history', *Urban History*, 47 (2020), 199–219.

70 The policies of the Thatcher period undoubtedly seriously exacerbated industrial contraction, but they did not originate it. Jim Tomlinson, 'Deindustrialisation and "Thatcherism": Moral economy and unintended consequences', *Contemporary British History*, published online 30 August 2021, https://doi.org/10.1080/13619462.2021.1972416.

71 Criticism of the 'New Speenhamland' has been limited and seems to have come mainly from the left, for example: David Byrne, 'The "Speenhamland" poor laws were not about supporting the unemployed', *The Guardian* (20 June 2011).

6

British varieties of neoliberalism: unemployment policy from Thatcher to Blair

Bernhard Rieger

'A welfare system that puts limits on an individual's ability to find a job must be reformed. Modern Social Democrats want to transform the safety net of entitlements into a springboard to personal responsibility', Tony Blair declared jointly with German Chancellor Gerhard Schröder in June 1999 as they presented a programme for the 'modernization' of Europe.[1] In Germany, this memorandum triggered a stormy debate, in which the Schröder government faced accusations of opening Germany to 'neoliberalism'.[2] In Britain, meanwhile, the outline attracted far less attention – and not just because the British media took little interest in a political statement that was deliberately European in outlook. Rather, Britons had been exposed to government rhetoric about excessive 'entitlement' in the social security system and a supposed lack of 'responsibility' among welfare recipients since the late 1970s, when Margaret Thatcher moved into Downing Street. Unlike in Germany, where unification's social fallout necessitated a significant expansion of existing welfare arrangements, this language was already well established and hence hardly newsworthy in the UK. Indeed, nothing highlights the contrast between Britain's and Germany's welfare landscapes more clearly than the defence put forward by British intellectual advocates of the welfare policies outlined in the so-called Blair–Schröder paper. Where the German chancellor stood accused of promoting neoliberalism, doyen of third-way thinking Anthony Giddens characterised Blair's welfare reforms as 'not a continuation of neoliberalism, but an alternative political philosophy to it'.[3]

Such diverging assessments of the Third Way's relationship with neoliberalism point towards what has frequently been regarded as one of New Labour's defining features. Rather than opt for a pronounced, readily visible break, Blair's and Brown's governments often adopted policies that overlapped with the solutions of their Conservative predecessors. In particular, New Labour's rhetoric about the virtues of market mechanisms has underpinned impressions of considerable political continuities across the electoral watershed of 1997.[4] None other than Giddens counts among those who highlighted positive qualities of market mechanisms, asserting that 'markets do not always increase inequality, but can sometimes be the means of overcoming it'. Indeed, 'Social Democrats', he emphasised, 'need to overcome some of their worries and fears about markets'.[5] Irrespective of its insistence that it offered a fundamental alternative, New Labour's relationship with the market-friendly policies promoted by its predecessors is by no means clear.

Studying social policy allows us to take a closer look at conceptual continuities and differences between Conservative and Labour governments from Thatcher to Blair. Since welfare provisions regulate myriad relationships between individuals and markets, they cast light on the social significance Conservative and New Labour politicians assigned to the forces of supply and demand. An examination of changes in unemployment policy – a prominent public issue in the 1980s and 1990s – provides an apt case study to this end. Provision for those who had lost their jobs and struggled to regain employment not only brings into view their fraught relationship with the labour market; policies to reduce joblessness also sought to turn those excluded from the job market into market participants. In other words, unemployment policy is shot through with assumptions about market mechanisms, and welfare regulations – that is, state institutions – played crucial roles in shaping the frameworks within which those out of work were expected to conduct their lives, thereby positioning themselves vis-à-vis the labour market. A key question is thus not whether British politicians sought to 'roll back the state' to make space for markets since the 1980s, but whether and how policies mobilised state institutions to promote market mechanisms in new social contexts.[6]

The new approaches to combating unemployment developed by Conservatives and New Labour unfolded as the British labour market itself underwent significant transformations, a topic Jim Tomlinson treats in more detail in this volume. It was not simply that the size of the workforce increased from 24.7 million to 28.2 million between 1970 and 2004. Rather, the structure of the workforce changed in a manner that is frequently captured by the term 'deindustrialisation', a process that pre-dated the time period under consideration here. Between 1980 and 2001, the national share of manufacturing jobs fell from 15.1 to 13.7 per cent while service sector jobs expanded from 62.9 to 77.6 per cent. Beyond a growing share of female labour, Britain's post-industrial labour market was characterised by an ongoing polarisation towards what the economists Maarten Goos and Alan Manning have termed 'lousy and lovely jobs'. While highly skilled work in the private sector could command rising pay, the number of medium-skilled, safe jobs offering steady incomes diminished due to a new international division of labour as well as organisational and technological changes. At the same time, the proportion of low-skill occupations that followed no set routines and could not easily be rationalised away in areas such as hospitality, cleaning and other parts of the service sector increased substantially. The latter trend underpinned a growing low-wage sector in which employees found frequently precarious forms of employment that offered meagre incomes. In short, Britain saw the rise of pronounced inequalities in terms of incomes, skills and job security between the late 1970s and the new millennium.[7]

Whether the new political recipes designed to combat unemployment in a changing labour market were predicated on promoting what Wendy Brown has called 'a peculiar form of reason that configures . . . existence in economic terms' offers the leitmotif for assessing their neoliberal character.[8] The shifting neoliberal elements in British social policy in the 1980s and 1990s gain clearer contours through an analysis of how welfare provision for the unemployed construed relationships between individuals and the labour market. As we shall see, Conservatives and New Labour adopted different approaches to protecting those out of work from, as well as exposing them to, the forces of supply and demand. In this process, they confronted the unemployed with different expectations to configure themselves as *homines oeconomici* who were anchored in market relations. As early as the late 1970s, Michel Foucault considered a version of *homo economicus* with an 'entrepreneurial self' as one of neoliberalism's distinguishing features. Neoliberal forms of governance, according to Foucault, prompted individuals to conduct themselves as 'entrepreneurs of [themselves]', taking advantage of, and responding to, market mechanisms.[9] Whether and how British governments set about recasting institutional arrangements that had firmly shielded those out of work from market forces before the 1980s along neoliberal lines requires an analysis of both specific political initiatives as well as their ideological underpinnings.

'Personal responsibility is key': Conservative labour market policies from Thatcher to Major

Between the end of the Second World War and the 1980s, social policy towards the unemployed was based on the premise that those out of work were victims of economic circumstances beyond their control and therefore deserved compensation for their material hardship through 'Unemployment Benefit'. This welfare provision represented a firm individual entitlement because it was funded through a worker's contributions to National Insurance and thus acted as a form of protection against what was widely perceived as the vicissitudes of the job market. Initially, Unemployment Benefit was a flat-rate benefit paid for six months, but in 1967 the Labour government extended its duration to one year and added an 'earnings-related element', a component that recognised a person's previous income and thereby acknowledged their earlier employment status.[10] With memories of the deprivation suffered by workers during the interwar slump very much alive, post-war governments of both political stripes considered keeping unemployment at low levels to be one of their foremost political priorities. One scholar has observed that, until the 1970s, unemployment rates over 2 per cent had 'alarm bells ringing in . . . party headquarters'.[11] In the late 1960s and first half of the 1970s, British governments repeatedly combated unemployment through countercyclical spending and fiscal measures. These policies, however, not only missed their aim of reducing unemployment in a lasting fashion, but stoked inflation and exacerbated industrial strife. Similar to other Western European countries, Britain witnessed the erosion of the socio-economic post-war settlement by the late 1970s.

While British administrations had focused on preventing unemployment up to the mid-1970s, Thatcher's government pursued an altogether different economic policy from 1979. To reverse what was widely regarded as Britain's dramatic post-war economic 'decline', she and her allies hoped to re-invigorate market forces through policies ranging from reining in the trade union movement, to reducing public spending and direct taxes, to raising productivity and competitiveness. Above all, Thatcher saw a low rate of inflation as the foundation on which a prospering economy rested. To combat inflation, the government raised interest rates, cut public spending and increased indirect taxes in 1981, thereby deepening a recession triggered by the second oil crisis, which led to numerous business failures and a surge of unemployment. At 1.3 million when Thatcher took office in May 1979, the count rose to more than three million at the beginning of 1982, remaining above this mark until spring 1987.[12]

Thatcher paid considerable attention to unemployment, not least since it ranked as the nation's most pressing issue in opinion polls.[13] Unsurprisingly, the Conservatives around Thatcher rejected the Opposition's claim that the government was responsible for the UK's persistent joblessness. On the contrary, Thatcherites saw high unemployment as an indicator of long-standing distortions of the laws of supply and demand in the labour market. People were out of jobs, the argument ran, because the price of labour was too high. As a result, demand for labour from employers remained too weak to restore more people to work. Viewed from this angle, the solution appeared simple. Wages had to fall, or, as Keith Joseph stated in 1978, '[t]he initial [wage] flexibility has to be downward'.[14] This raised the question of what was responsible for Britain's supposedly excessive pay levels. Next to the unions with their bargaining power, the welfare state inflated wage levels, according to the government. As economist Patrick Minford argued in a study sponsored by Thatcher's administration in 1982, 'the operation of the unemployment benefit system' established a 'floor' below which wages could not fall. After all, 'a man', he explained, 'will very naturally expect to be re-employed at a wage after tax and work expenses which is at least as high as this benefit'.[15] Alan Walters, Thatcher's most trusted economic adviser, outlined the link between welfare payments and unemployment in a brief memo to the Prime Minister in 1981 by posing a rhetorical question: '[D]oes not everyone believe that were real wages to fall 10 to 15%, there would be the most dramatic reduction in unemployment?'[16]

In keeping with this line of reasoning, the Conservatives started reducing the real value of provisions available for the unemployed from 1980 onwards by levying income tax on Unemployment Benefit, by abolishing the 'earnings-related element' and by ending the uprating of benefits in line with inflation. In part, these cuts were motivated by a desire for household discipline during a recession that raised government expenditure from 45.3 per cent of GDP in 1978/9 to 48.1 per cent in 1981/2.[17] This increase resulted not least from public protests about exploding unemployment, to which the government reluctantly responded by expanding schemes such as the Community Programme – a publicly funded job-creation measure for the long-term unemployed – and the Youth Opportunities programme, which raised the number of subsidised vocational training places for jobless school leavers from 216,000 trainees to 553,000 between 1978/9 and 1981/2.[18] Yet as the Thatcher government saw itself compelled to alleviate unemployment through higher welfare expenditure, it simultaneously hoped to lay the foundations for a reduction of benefit rolls once the recession ended by decreasing the real-terms value of individual benefits. Lowering the value of individual benefits would, Thatcher and her allies hoped, remove distortions in the play of supply and demand on the labour market and prompt larger numbers of those out of work to seek employment at lower pay than in the 1970s. With its belief in the efficacy of market mechanisms in the medium term, this aspect of Conservative unemployment policy bore a decidedly neoliberal imprint.

At the same time, Thatcher's government complemented the promotion of low-income work with policies that combated unemployment by helping those out of work set up their own small businesses. Put differently, Conservative welfare policy encouraged those excluded from the labour market to create their own jobs by joining the marketplace as entrepreneurs. At the beginning of the recession, recipients of Unemployment Benefit were deterred from pursuing this avenue to employment because starting up an enterprise automatically resulted in the loss of welfare payments. To remove this obstacle, the administration launched a programme that not only allowed unemployed Britons who began a small enterprise to keep their welfare payment for a year but also subsidised their private venture with a weekly payment of £40 during this period. Launched as a trial in late 1981 and rolled out across the country in summer 1983, the 'Enterprise Allowance Scheme' hoped to turn those out of work into small-scale entrepreneurs.[19] The test phase of the programme in five areas across mainland Britain with high rates of joblessness revealed strong interest among the unemployed. In April 1982, local managers of the Employment Service in the test areas explained that the unemployed who wished to set up as plumbers, furniture makers, joiners and travel agents no longer operated in the 'black economy'. One of the early participants stressed the importance of the weekly £40 subsidy: 'Having the enterprise allowance makes a considerable difference . . . providing a guaranteed source of income on which to live while you get the business off the ground.' These positive assessments led *The Guardian*, which was otherwise harshly critical of the government's social policies, to commend this programme as an 'imaginative attempt' to combat unemployment. In March 1983, *The Times* also called for the scheme's national extension, condemning the prospect of another trial period of limited geographical reach as 'disgraceful'.[20]

Given Thatcher's background as a grocer's daughter who repeatedly extolled the virtues of economic 'independence', it is hardly surprising that ministers followed the trials with interest. The administration also paid close attention to the initiative because it linked with its measures to support small businesses through loan guarantees, tax breaks and training initiatives that aimed to invigorate Britain's supposedly underdeveloped 'entrepreneurial spirit'.[21] Nonetheless, the Enterprise Allowance had to overcome considerable resistance when Thatcher's inner circle considered its national expansion in late 1982. Ferdinand Mount, head of the Policy Unit at 10 Downing Street, wrote in December that 'this does seem like a waste of money [and] should be scrapped', because the combined payments of Unemployment Benefit and the start-up subsidy resulted in annual costs of £2,900 per person, thereby rendering the Enterprise Allowance Scheme significantly more expensive than, for example, the Community Programme.[22] Other advisers, including the former merchant banker John Sparrow, disagreed and pointed out that, unlike most publicly sponsored job-creation programmes, this initiative generated 'real jobs in the small firm sector' that would provide livelihoods beyond the period during which the government subsidised them. A recalculation revealed that annual costs fell to a mere £700 on the cautious assumption that a quarter of the businesses launched under the scheme would survive for three years. When seen in this light, the Enterprise Allowance emerged as the cheapest measure against unemployment at the time and was rolled out nationally in 1983.[23] After its national launch, the initiative enjoyed a veritable boom and was repeatedly expanded. In 1986, the government announced that it would fund no fewer than 100,000 places from June, an enthusiastic vote of confidence that reflected the finding that the scheme ran at 'zero cost', as the Chairman of the Manpower Services Commission stated, because three quarters of the start-ups remained in business after 18 months. Aided by the booming economy of the second half of the 1980s, 315,000 Britons had taken advantage of the subsidy by February 1988.[24]

One response to rising unemployment by the Thatcher government, then, consisted in promoting entrepreneurial selves in a literal manner by encouraging Britons without a job to create their own in the form of a small business. That the government offered an initial subsidy to would-be small businesspersons did not clash with its market-friendly credentials because the scheme, like other initiatives strengthening small companies at the time, was designed to enhance the country's entrepreneurial culture. Since an auspicious economic climate ensured the survival of a high proportion of businesses founded under the scheme, the government also recouped its start-up costs and had thus happened upon a cost-neutral policy that reduced unemployment by relying on market forces.

Meeting with a positive echo among the unemployed, as well as the progressive and conservative press, the Enterprise Allowance emerged as a highly popular neoliberal social policy of the Thatcher years.

Irrespective of this scheme's boost to the small-business sector, the Thatcher government became increasingly convinced that Britain's welfare regime required fundamental reform as unemployment still stood at 3.6 million in 1986, despite solid economic growth over the previous three years. Promoting small businesses and cutting the value of benefits alone could not solve Britain's sizeable unemployment problem. The Prime Minister was unlikely to be surprised by the persistence of pervasive joblessness because she ascribed detrimental effects to existing social security regulations. Indeed, she regarded them as nothing less than a moral provocation, because institutional arrangements linked various forms of benefits, allowing those out of work to be in a materially better position than many who were in employment. As a result, she charged as early as 1980, 'to be proudly but poorly independent is to be *worse* off, and full of resentment'.[25] Reversing the consequences of a welfare regime that supposedly discouraged self-reliance and individual effort emerged as a central concern of a Prime Minister with a Methodist background who considered these very qualities as the True North of a conservative moral compass.[26] In 1982, she impressed on Ferdinand Mount that 'we really have to address . . . the values of society . . . Personal responsibility is key.'[27]

Held in high esteem by Thatcher for his record as a businessman and appointed Secretary of State for Employment in 1985, David Young presented the Prime Minister with a plan that would 'tackle the will to work'. What Young euphemistically called in a secret note 'increasing incentives to work' required 'a combination of carrots and sticks, but', he impressed on Thatcher, 'we must exercise great care that the sticks are never seen'.[28] The punitive regime the government imposed on the unemployed in the mid-1980s centred on the stipulation that benefit recipients had to demonstrate that they were 'available' for work to be eligible for welfare payments. To test this legal criterion, Young instructed Jobcentres to call unemployed individuals for a formal interview at the end of which they were presented with a choice of undergoing training, signing up for a subsidised low-wage job, accepting temporary employment in the Community Programme or joining a 'Job Club', which offered help with targeted job searches. Crucially, those who failed to attend the interview or refused all four options could have their benefits withdrawn because they were not deemed 'available' for work and hence fell foul of the law.[29]

When unemployment eventually began to fall during the 'Lawson boom' of the second half of the 1980s, the administration was quick to credit its welfare reforms for this development. It was thus consistent that, in the late 1980s, the government continued along these disciplinarian lines by further tightening the eligibility criteria for Unemployment Benefit. From 1989 on, recipients of Unemployment Benefit had to demonstrate that they were 'actively seeking' work rather than being 'available' for work, as the law had previously stated. Moreover, Unemployment Benefit could now be stopped after 13 weeks if a person declined a 'suitable' job on the grounds that it paid significantly less than her or his previous occupation. These reforms culminated under John Major in 1996. His Cabinet reduced the duration of payments to half a year and renamed the benefit for the unemployed as a 'Jobseeker's Allowance', thereby recategorising an insurance-based form of social security with a term that suggests a drastically weakened entitlement to support.[30]

The Conservatives lowered the value of welfare payments, encouraged self-employment among a minority of the unemployed and adopted disciplinarian measures including the withdrawal of benefits to push the majority of those without jobs into wage work at lower income rates. Conservative welfare reforms thus pursued multiple approaches to combat unemployment. The promotion of small businesses aimed to nurture entrepreneurial selves by directly creating entrepreneurs. To this end, the government strengthened the market power of a minority of jobless Britons by subsidising their start-ups. The majority of those out of work, however, were turned into disempowered market participants. In addition to advancing a disciplinarian agenda, Thatcher's and Major's policies relied on lower wages to reduce unemployment by forcing those out of work to expose themselves to the laws of supply and demand in a crowded labour market. No matter whether intended to create empowered or disempowered market participants, these policies bore a profoundly neoliberal imprint because they aimed to remove barriers between the individual and the market rationalities that the government regarded as efficient tools for solving the social problem of unemployment. Overall, Thatcher and Major subscribed to a version of neoliberalism with profoundly conservative traits because not only was it predicated on a belief in the efficiency of markets, but it also affirmed fiscal discipline, individualism, self-dependence and hard work as key political and cultural virtues. In keeping with these core convictions, the Conservative reforms confronted those out of work with a far stronger obligation to find employment themselves, a trend that culminated in the Jobseeker's

Allowance's requirement to 'actively' engage in job searches. It was the unemployed themselves who had to take responsibility for their employment status on the labour market. In short, Thatcher's and Major's approach to unemployment policy was premised on a culturally conservative form of market fundamentalism.

Towards a 'risk-taking' work force: New Labour's New Deal

At first sight, there appear to be considerable similarities between the Conservatives' and New Labour's welfare regimes for the unemployed. Most significantly, the Labour government that assumed office in 1997 neither revoked the law that had recently created the new Jobseeker's Allowance nor changed significantly the conditions under which this benefit could be claimed. Policies to counter unemployment thus retained a pronouncedly disciplinarian quality after 1997. This continuity reflects a wider reorientation of the Labour Party since the late 1980s to heighten its electoral appeal to voters in the political centre ground, a process Mark Wickham-Jones treats in greater deal elsewhere in this volume. In addition to abolishing the highly symbolic Clause Four that committed Labour to nationalisation policies, Blair emphasised in opposition that a government led by him would abide by Conservative reforms of trade union legislation and pursue a firm law-and-order course by being 'tough on crime and the causes of crime'. The party leadership also repeatedly stressed its dedication to a 'competitive [economic] framework that would help [private companies] flourish in the global economy', as Robert Taylor has observed.[31] To prevent the Tories from portraying Labour as committed to costly social programmes that would require tax increases, the 1997 election manifesto pledged to observe the spending targets of Major's government while remaining largely silent on social security issues.[32] Before electoral victory in 1997, New Labour emphasised that it broke with key tenets of the 'old' Labour Party and moved closer to positions that overlapped with Conservative policies.

This reorientation, however, does not imply that New Labour entered office without a distinctive social agenda – and not just because the new administration raised the value of many benefits to alleviate poverty, which had become much more pronounced under the Conservatives. Unemployment policy exemplifies how the Labour government substantially diverged from its Conservative predecessors. Blair's administration turned the requirement to 'actively' seek work into the platform from which it launched its own schemes to combat unemployment. New Labour could pursue its initiatives under favourable economic conditions. After the recession of the early 1990s, which had seen unemployment rise back to over three million in early 1993, the count had fallen back to just over two million in spring 1997.[33] Rather than fight rising unemployment, New Labour's task consisted in amplifying a falling trend.

Under the heading the 'New Deal', which confidently invoked Franklin Delano Roosevelt's Depression-era social programmes, the government initiated a raft of measures targeting jobless Britons by demanding that, while receiving social security payments, they enhance their employability. The 'New Deal for Young People' was the first and most prominent of these programmes. Highlighted in the 1997 election manifesto as a measure against youth unemployment, it launched as a trial in January 1998 before national implementation in June that year. For recipients of Jobseeker's Allowance aged between 18 and 24, participation was obligatory, thereby extending the disciplinarian strategy that had characterised Conservative employment policy. At the same time, the Employment Agency emphasised the programme's supportive rather than punitive intentions. Describing the initiative as a 'key part of the Government's welfare to work strategy', a widely distributed official brochure stated that 'it aims to help young people gain the qualities and skills they need to increase their employability and get and keep jobs'.[34] Those enrolling in this New Deal could count on personal advice from a dedicated caseworker, who would assess a jobseeker's 'needs, ambitions and options' during an initial four-month period. Young people whom advisers considered not yet ready to work could expect individually tailored assistance, including 'intensive counselling' as well as courses to boost literacy and numeracy skills. Subsequently, participants entered a six-month period of work experience and training by following an occupational skills course, by taking up a job in the voluntary or environmental sector or by working for a private business. To render the programme financially attractive, young people who remained enrolled received payments that at least equalled, but in many cases exceeded, Jobseeker's Allowance and also covered job-related expenses such as travel costs.[35] Crucially, those who failed to secure permanent employment after the phase of occupational training and work experience received further assistance from a personal caseworker to 'build on the progress they made during the New Deal' with the ultimate aim of finding a 'suitable job', the Employment Agency pledged.[36]

With its upbeat tone and its emphasis on individualised assistance, the New Deal for Young People approached unemployed Britons as open to receiving help with obstacles in the labour market, rather than suspiciously focusing on the motivation to work, as Conservative social policy had done. In other words, the New Deal for Young People started from the premise that many benefit recipients were willing to work. The belief that jobless Britons drawing social security payments welcomed help with finding employment through training and work experience also characterised the programmes that targeted additional groups who suffered from disadvantages in the labour market. By 1999, the government had extended its welfare-to-work approach through mandatory training and personal counselling to long-term unemployed citizens aged over 25 as well as those looking for work who were older than 50. Moreover, disabled Britons as well as lone parents had the option of signing up to New Deals.[37] When the second Blair government entered office in 2001, almost 1.2 million Britons had participated in a New Deal initiative.[38]

Yet it was not just in its basic assumption about the motivation of the unemployed that New Labour's approach differed from Conservative strategies. Blair's administration also backed these initiatives with new resources. By investing £4 billion in the New Deal, £2.6 billion of which was raised by a 'windfall tax' on the privatised utilities, the Labour government devoted considerable additional financial means to welfare-to-work programmes during a time of economic expansion, where its predecessors had overseen an erosion of the value of benefits during a recession.[39] That New Labour made fiscal and institutional investments in the New Deals corresponded with further measures that directly addressed the material dimensions of joblessness. Britons with limited skills, who could expect only low incomes and who made up the majority of those looking for work, stood at the centre of New Labour's efforts. To ensure that low-income employment offered a guaranteed level of material rewards, the government passed legislation for a minimum wage at a rate of £3.60 per hour in 1999.[40] In November 1997, Gordon Brown had already announced an additional £300 million to create affordable childcare places for 'almost 1 million children', in support of the various New Deals. This measure aimed to promote work among those lone parents and married couples whose low incomes had previously been absorbed by childcare costs, thereby creating a 'poverty trap' that had left many working parents worse off than their peers on benefits.[41]

Moreover, from April 1999, low-income families with children could supplement their wages with 'Working Tax Credits' that guaranteed married couples with offspring and 'at least one full-time earner' a minimum annual income of £10,400 through a wage subsidy by the tax office.[42] That tax credits were first available for families with children reflected the government's dedication to fighting widespread child poverty, with the overall aim of reversing multigenerational patterns of social disadvantages. Indeed, one month before the introduction of Working Tax Credits, Blair had committed the government to the eradication of child poverty, which formed a central concern for the Social Exclusion Unit that the Prime Minister installed in 10 Downing Street.[43] In 2003, the government made tax credits available to low earners without children, too.[44] These measures resulted in significant costs. Between 1997 and 2007, annual expenditure for tax credits rose from £7 billion to almost £25 billion, thereby reaching almost half the size of the defence budget.[45] New Labour thus created new baselines for earnings at the lower end of the income scale both through direct interventions into pricing mechanisms in the labour market and through fiscal transfer payments.

That Blair's government pre-empted, and compensated for, what the administration regarded as shortcomings of market mechanisms, however, by no means signalled a turn against markets per se, nor towards redistribution policies that would have characterised 'old' Labour. In the Anglo-German outline of the Third Way, Blair explicitly dismissed 'the belief that the state should address damaging market failures' comprehensively because, in the past, this had 'all too often led to a disproportionate expansion of the government's reach'. As he declared 'a robust and competitive market framework' a central policy aim, he expressly addressed the issue of those out of work. Reducing unemployment rates, he explained, 'will be easier' if 'labour markets are working properly'. A 'low-wage sector' was necessary to this end, he continued, because it 'make[s] low-skill jobs' available for a group that had long been disproportionately at risk of unemployment: those lacking training and professional qualifications. This low-wage sector, Blair hoped, would allow previously unemployed individuals to work their way towards more lucrative employment in the medium term: '[L]ow-paid work [is] better than no work because [it] ease[s] the transition from unemployment to jobs.'[46] In keeping with the left's ideological reorientation since the late 1980s, Blair explicitly affirmed market rationales as positive social forces, not just in general terms but specifically with regard to unemployment, because he hoped they would promote upward social mobility.

At the same time, Blair insisted that market mechanisms had to operate within boundaries. Since a 'market economy' should not give rise to a 'market society', he explained, 'replenish[ing] low incomes' among those on low-income jobs became the responsibility of the tax and benefits system. Before those holding badly paid positions could embark on their upward social trajectory, they deserved help that compensated for their willingness to expose themselves to the forces of supply and demand on the labour market.[47] Blair credited market mechanisms with an economic efficiency that extended only partially to the social realm, because they could leave substantial groups in material deprivation. Blair advocated a political economy of 'redistributive market liberalism', in which, according to economist John Kay, the state has 'a dominant role in income distribution, but should discharge its responsibility with as little interference as possible in the workings of the free market' for goods and services.[48] As Peter Sloman highlights in his chapter in this volume, New Labour's variant of redistributive market liberalism focused on anti-poverty measures among the working population in the low-wage labour market. In the case of New Labour, the laws of supply and demand reached the limits of their social expediency when low-wage labour failed to offer rewards that sustained individuals' motivation to work or look for it. In effect, Blair's government promoted the laws of supply and demand in the labour market by moderating their social effects at the lower end of the social spectrum. Rather than pay people to be out of work, New Labour compensated those who exposed themselves to unfavourable market constellations, with the ultimate aim that these employees would subsequently leave the low-wage sector behind.

New Labour advanced two justifications for its approach to unemployment policy. Firstly, it emphasised the individual obligation to work, which was reflected by the compulsory nature of the New Deal for many jobless Britons. As Tony Blair explained in 1998, New Labour's employment policies were part and parcel of a protracted recalibration of the relationship between individual rights and responsibilities. 'In recent decades, responsibility and duty were the preserves of the Right', he wrote, with an eye to the Thatcher and Major administrations and their eulogies of individual independence. Blair regarded this Conservative insistence on individual responsibility as a reaction against the 'Old Left', which had allegedly 'for too long' separated 'the demand for rights from the state . . . from the duties of citizenship'. In his eyes, no other social provision symbolised this discrepancy more strongly than the circumstance that, before Thatcher's premiership, 'unemployment benefits were often paid without strong reciprocal obligations'.[49]

In a 1996 speech, Blair, by contrast, started from the premise that 'duty is the cornerstone of a decent society'. Conceiving of individual responsibilities and entitlements as mutually constitutive, he declared that 'the rights we receive should reflect the duties we owe'. As he outlined the relationship between duties and rights that formed the core of New Labour's approach to welfare, he linked individualism to the notion of the 'public good' by invoking Christian motifs: '[I]t is from a sense of individual duty that we connect to the greater good – a principle the Church celebrates in the sacrament of communion.'[50] Blair's explicit appeal to Catholicism may have been unusual for a Labour politician speaking on social policy, but other New Labour figures also drew attention to welfare's moral dimension within a market economy. Anthony Giddens, for instance, argued that markets required strong political and moral moorings: '[M]arkets can't even function without a social and ethical framework – which they themselves cannot provide.'[51] New Labour thus embedded the political economy of 'redistributive market liberalism' in a moral economy that hinged on a reciprocal relationship between individual rights and responsibilities.

While Blair's concept of duty at first glance resembles Thatcher's outlook, due to both leaders' Christian faiths, there existed significant differences between them. To begin with, New Labour's public rhetoric placed less emphasis on the culturally conservative virtues, such as thrift and self-denial, that had underpinned Thatcher's praise of the 'proudly but poorly independent'. Nor did it embrace the Conservatives' habitual moral condemnation of single mothers, as the special employment initiatives aimed to support lone parents indicate.[52] More importantly, New Labour saw the duty to work as an integral element of a long-term strategy to promote social cohesion by expanding opportunities among disadvantaged groups – a theme that had been conspicuously absent from Conservative welfare rhetoric. Junior Minister for Employment and Equal Opportunities Margaret Hodge stressed in 2000 that social cohesion required redistribution through the tax and benefits system, albeit not through 'a politics of envy' that had allegedly guided 'Old Labour' when it '"punish[ed]" the rich by curtailing ambition'. Rather than pursue equality of outcome, the government characterised its approach as a 'politics of need' that targeted structural causes of poverty.[53] 'Based on the mantra that "work is the best route out of poverty"', Hodge explained, the 'Welfare to Work agenda' formed 'a central feature of our redistribution agenda'. While the government acknowledged that for those 'whose levels of poverty are too great or too ingrained, the hand out is their only lifeline', it strove primarily for 'equality based on the hand up, not the hand out'. To underline her egalitarian credentials, Hodge stressed that her party was committed to combating the unfair treatment frequently encountered by the disabled, women and, most notably, racial minorities: '[T]he disadvantage and discrimination people face must be central to an equality agenda.'[54] In other words, New Labour hoped to put in place a welfare system that allowed all those at the bottom of the social hierarchy to pull themselves up.

As a New Labour signature policy, facilitating the entry of the socially disadvantaged into the labour market was designed to strengthen social cohesion and enhance the government's wider anti-poverty strategy. 'Opportunity for all' emerged as a key social policy phrase in the late 1990s. Beyond initiatives against child poverty to break multigenerational deprivation, the government relied on training programmes to improve the prospects of adults lacking a job.[55] For New Labour, the development of skills provided far more than an entrance key to the labour market that, if cultivated, could lead to the social advancement that began with subsidised low-wage work. Qualifications also functioned as a personal insurance policy against the vagaries of the contemporary economy that commentators characterised as demanding multiple job changes over the course of a working life. According to Giddens, both the shift towards a post-industrial labour market and 'the high rate of business formation and dissolution . . . characteristic of a dynamic society' made employment less stable than in the 1950s and 1960s, thereby creating new personal risks. Blair argued along similar lines that 'in a more insecure and demanding labour market . . . people will change jobs more often', because workers were in greater danger of losing their paid positions.[56] In this socio-economic environment, the welfare state, Giddens pledged, faced the challenge of helping individuals cope not just by offering 'protection when things go wrong' but by providing them with the 'material and moral capabilities to move through major periods of transition in their lives'.[57] The New Deal, with its emphasis on training and individual advice, was designed to allow employees to respond more effectively to the existential challenges of an unpredictable post-industrial labour market.

Giddens, for one, went one step further and urged that 'effective risk management (individual or collective)' ought to go beyond protecting individuals against the negative consequences of change such as job losses. While 'risk taking' had long been praised as an integral dimension of 'entrepreneurial activity', Giddens pointed out that 'the same applies to the labour force'. After all, ordinary workers faced numerous risks, too. He urged welfare reformers to 'harness . . . the positive or energetic side of risk and provid[e] resources for risk taking' on a larger scale. Since moving from welfare to work involved abandoning familiar forms of material security, entering the job market amounted for many to a 'risk-infused activity' that policymakers, Giddens suggested, should encourage in a similar fashion as entrepreneurialism. It was thus only consistent to regard welfare arrangements as part of a 'social investment state' that would strengthen workers' competitive position.[58] Blair resorted to the same business-inspired rhetoric when stressing the importance of 'investment in human and social capital' through training and other initiatives.[59] While Conservative social policy conceived entrepreneurial values as the preserve of the minority of Britons who responded to unemployment by starting a business, New Labour expected far more citizens – not least those in and out of work at the lower end of the social scale – to cultivate entrepreneurial selves. To this end, Blair's and Brown's governments assigned multiple roles to the welfare state: they cast it as an investor in entrepreneurial virtues to strengthen the market power of working Britons and as a compensating institution that offset the material consequences of market operations among low-income groups. In contrast to Conservative policies predicated on a market fundamentalism that strongly affirmed the social efficiency of the forces of supply and demand, New Labour's progressive version of neoliberalism embraced a more sceptical attitude to market operations in the social arena, emphasising the need to empower a broad range of market participants as well as the need to redress social inequities.

Conclusion

Both differences and similarities marked the varieties of neoliberalism promoted by Conservative and New Labour social policies between the late 1970s and the turn of the millennium. In its employment policies, Blair's government retained Thatcher's disciplinarian stipulation that the unemployed 'actively' seek work or risk losing their benefits. New Labour, however, diverged from its predecessors by offering those searching for work significantly more support in the form of training and personal advice. This contrast between New Labour and the Conservatives reflects their respective understandings of markets. While they shared optimistic assumptions about the efficiency of market rationales in economic contexts, New Labour insisted on modifying the laws of supply and demand in the social realm, where, as persistent poverty demonstrated to Blair and his adherents, this economic mechanism worked only imperfectly. Since Conservatives more readily accepted the social outcomes of market operations, they showed little concern for inequality as a social issue and expected benefit recipients to enter the labour market irrespective of the implications for individuals' income and status. New Labour, meanwhile, emphasised the need for transfer payments for Britons in low-wage employment as a compensation for exposing themselves to market rationales on unfavourable terms. Compared with the Conservatives, New Labour displayed more scepticism about markets as socially efficient and expedient institutions.

In keeping with its strategy of expanding individual opportunity and advancing social cohesion, New Labour's unemployment policy provided additional resources for training and personal advice. Developing individual skills, policymakers expected, would grant those outside, or at the margins of, the labour market improved chances to assert themselves. By aiming to create empowered market participants with entrepreneurial traits on a broad scale, New Labour's unemployment policy also responded to a perceived need to prepare employees for a job market that offered significantly less stable employment than in the past. Conservative policy, by contrast, had restricted the promotion of entrepreneurial selves to the minority among the unemployed who were willing to start a small business. The majority of those out of work, by contrast, were faced with conservative policies that turned benefit recipients into disempowered market participants who had to expose themselves to the forces of supply and demand at the price of low incomes.

While the Conservatives and New Labour employed state institutions to promote market mechanisms in their social policies, they pursued differing approaches. These reflected their respective assessments of the expediency of markets in the social realm as well as contrasting moral economies that balanced individual duties and entitlements in different ways. Regarding the majority of those out of work as unwilling to return to the labour market, Thatcherite policy mobilised the state to enforce an individual obligation to independence through work and self-dependence. New Labour's policy initiatives revolved around notions that saw individual duties and entitlements in more reciprocal terms. Assuming that those out of work welcomed the opportunity to return to the labour market, it assigned a stronger redistributive task to the state to ensure that citizens became market participants. New Labour complemented the Conservatives' disciplinarian approach through initiatives that cast the state in the role of an investor.

In 1997, a culturally conservative neoliberalism founded on market fundamentalism gave way to a progressive version founded on a more ambivalent assessment of the efficiency of markets in the social realm. The unemployment policies of successive governments have thus implemented a neoliberal turn based on differing moral economies, as well as understandings of the market, to expose millions of Britons to market rationales. This sustained shift yielded considerable social effects. Benefit cuts and eroding legal protection through welfare reform under Thatcher contributed to Britain's significantly rising income inequality during the 1980s, when the Gini indicator rose by 34 per cent from 0.267 to 0.35.[60] New Labour's minimum wage regulations and tax credits may have stopped this trend but could not reverse it. Reducing income inequality would have required tax policies targeting higher incomes, which New Labour explicitly ruled out. Moreover, high income inequality also derived from the polarising post-industrial labour market that, among other things, witnessed an expansion of low-skilled, precarious and low-wage jobs in the service sector. Indeed, New Labour's decision to subsidise low-income work through tax credits did little to counteract the proliferation of 'lousy' jobs. Rather, it may actually have inadvertently stoked this trend by ensuring a steady supply of workers who were required by New Labour's welfare regime to seek work in this very sector of the labour market.[61] Viewed from this angle, Giddens's characterisation of the 'Third Way' as an attack on 'neoliberalism' is simultaneously right and wrong: right, because New Labour modified Thatcherite social policy significantly; and wrong, because Blair's (and subsequently Brown's) governments still placed considerable trust in market rationales to reduce unemployment. And by placing this trust in market rationales at a time when many of those out of work confronted an increasingly inauspicious labour market, New Labour contributed to the proliferation of forms of employment that have frequently been identified as a source of widespread political and social discontent in the UK for offering not just low incomes but little job security.

Notes

1 Tony Blair and Gerhard Schröder, *Europe: The Third Way/Die neue Mitte* (Johannesburg, Friedrich Ebert Foundation, 1999), 10.
2 See the report in *Frankfurter Allgemeine Zeitung* (10 June 1999), 10.
3 Anthony Giddens, *The Third Way and Its Critics* (Cambridge, Polity Press, 2000), 32.
4 For explorations of the relationship between New Labour and its predecessors, see Vernon Bogdanor, 'Social democracy', in Anthony Seldon (ed.), *Blair's Britain, 1997–2007* (Cambridge, Cambridge University Press, 2008), 164–82, esp. 168–9; and Robert Taylor, 'New Labour, new capitalism', in Anthony Seldon (ed.), *Blair's Britain, 1997–2007* (Cambridge, Cambridge University Press, 2008), 214–40, esp. 222–4.
5 Giddens, *Third Way and Its Critics*, 32–3.
6 Taylor, 'New Labour, new capitalism', 214–15. The active promotion of market mechanisms through state institutions is considered one of the key features of neoliberalism in general. For a particularly scholarly argument along these lines, see Quinn Slobodian, *Globalists: The end of empire and the birth of neoliberalism* (Cambridge, MA, Harvard University Press, 2018), 5–7.

'Rolling back the state' was, of course, central to Thatcherite rhetoric. See still E. H. H. Green, *Ideologies of Conservatism: Conservative political ideas in the twentieth century* (Oxford, Oxford University Press, 2002), 214–39, esp. 223–9.

7 See Office for National Statistics, LFS: In Employment: UK: All: Aged 16–64: Thousands: SA, https://www.ons.gov.uk/employmentandlabourmarket/peopleinwork/employmentandemployeetypes/timeseries/lf2g/lms (accessed 9 September 2019); Maarten Goos and Alan Manning, 'Lousy and lovely jobs: The rising polarization of jobs in Britain', *Review of Economics and Statistics*, 89 (2007), 118–33; Geoff Mason, Ken Mayhew, Matthew Osborne and Philip Stevens, 'Low pay, labour market institutions, and job quality in the United Kingdom', in Carolyn Lloyd, Geoff Mason and Ken Mayhew (eds), *Low-Wage Work in the United Kingdom* (New York, Russell Sage Foundation, 2008), 41–95, esp. 50; and Nicholas Crafts, Ian Gazeley and Andrew Newell, *Work and Pay in 20th Century Britain* (Oxford, Oxford University Press, 2007), 39.

8 Wendy Brown, *Undoing the Demos: Neoliberalism's stealth revolution* (Brooklyn, NY, Zone Books, 2015), 17.

9 Michel Foucault, *The Birth of Biopolitics: Lectures at the Collège de France, 1978–9* (Basingstoke, Palgrave Macmillan, 2015), 226–7, 267–86. For a sociological exploration, see Ulrich Bröckling, *The Entrepreneurial Self: Fabricating a new type of subject* (London, SAGE, 2016).

10 For more detail, see Bernhard Rieger, 'Making Britain work again: Unemployment and the remaking of British social policy in the eighties', *English Historical Review*, 133 (2018), 634–66, esp. 648–9.

11 Noel Thompson, 'Economic ideas and the development of economic opinion', in Richard Coopey and Nicholas Woodward (eds), *Britain in the 1970s: The troubled decade* (New York, St Martin's Press, 1996), 55–80, at 56.

12 James Denman and Paul MacDonald, 'Unemployment statistics from 1881 to the present day', *Labour Market Trends*, 104 (January 1996), 5–18, at 10–11.

13 Richard Vinen, *Thatcher's Britain: The politics and social upheaval of the Thatcher era* (London, Simon & Schuster, 2010), 132.

14 Keith Joseph, *Conditions for Fuller Employment* (London, Centre for Policy Studies, 1978), 6–7.

15 Patrick Minford, *Unemployment: Cause and cure* (Oxford, Wiley-Blackwell, 1983), 26.

16 Alan Walters, 'Unemployment measures proposed in E(81)74', 8 July 1981, paragraph 4, TNA: PREM 19/525.

17 Joan Brown, *Victims or Villains? Social security benefits in unemployment* (York, Joseph Rowntree Memorial Trust, 1990), 51–2.

18 David Stuart Edwards, 'The history and politics of the Youth Opportunities programme, 1978–1983' (PhD thesis, Institute of Education, London, 1985), 160.

19 For the initial announcement of this scheme, see *The Times* (14 November 1981), 1.

20 *The Guardian* (30 April 1982), 19; and *The Times* (4 March 1983), 17.

21 For an overview of these schemes, see *The Times* (3 June 1982), 18.

22 Policy Unit to Prime Minister, note, 22 December 1982, 2, TNA: PREM 19/1157.

23 John Sparrow to Prime Minister, note, 20 December 1982, 1, TNA: PREM 19/1157; CPRS, Unemployment Measures, note, 23 February 1983, 12, TNA: PREM 19/1161; and Ferdinand Mount to Prime Minister, note, 25 February 1983, 1, TNA: PREM 19/1161.

24 *The Times* (19 March 1986), 22; *The Guardian* (23 October 1986), 24; and *The Times* (16 February 1988), 4.

25 Handwritten comment by Margaret Thatcher on 'Minute to the Prime Minister', 5 December 1980 (emphasis in the original), TNA: PREM 19/523.

26 Matthew Grimley, 'Thatcherism, morality and religion', in Ben Jackson and Robert Saunders (eds), *Making Thatcher's Britain* (Cambridge, Cambridge University Press, 2012), 74–94.

27 Ferdinand Mount, *Cold Cream: My early life and other mistakes* (London, Bloomsbury, 2009), 288–9.

28 David Young, 'Enterprise and employment', secret note, 1 November 1985, 4, TNA: PREM 19/1839; and David Young to Margaret Thatcher, note, 6 June 1985, 2, TNA, PREM 19/1569.

29 See David Price, *Office of Hope: A history of the Employment Service* (London, Policy Studies Institute, 2000), 243–8.

30 A straightforward account of the manifold changes is Brown, *Victims or Villains?* For a report on Jobseeker's Allowance, see *The Guardian* (11 January 1996), 6.

31 Taylor, 'New Labour, new capitalism', 214–40, at 217. On the wider reorientation, see Bogdanor, 'Social democracy'.

32 For the manifesto, see http://www.politicsresources.net/area/uk/man/lab97.htm (accessed 28 January 2019).
33 For the figures, see https://www.ons.gov.uk/employmentandlabourmarket/peoplenotinwork/unemployment/timeseries/mgsc/unem (accessed 4 March 2019).
34 Employment Agency, *What Is New Deal for Young People?* (London, 1998), 1.
35 Employment Agency, *What Is New Deal for Young People?*, 4–6.
36 Employment Agency, *What Is New Deal for Young People?*, 8.
37 Kitty Stewart, 'Equality and social justice', in Anthony Seldon (ed.), *Blair's Britain, 1997–2007* (Cambridge, Cambridge University Press, 2008), 408–35, esp. 409, 422.
38 Paul Bivand, 'New Deal jobs approach half million mark', *Working Brief*, 125 (2001), 8–9.
39 See Gordon Brown's announcement of funding for the New Deals on 25 November 1997 in House of Commons debate, *Hansard* (25 November 1997), series 6, vol. 301, cols 776–7.
40 For the legal text, see https://www.legislation.gov.uk/uksi/1999/584/contents/made (accessed 21 June 2021).
41 House of Commons, *Hansard* (25 November 1997), col. 777.
42 Department of Social Services, *Opportunity for All: Tackling poverty and social exclusion*, Cm 4445 (London, HMSO, 1999), 58.
43 Tony Blair, The Beveridge Lecture (London, Toynbee Hall, 1999), https://www.bristol.ac.uk/poverty/background.html (accessed 12 September 2019).
44 Tom Sefton, John Hills and Holly Sutherland, 'Poverty, inequality and redistribution', in John Hills and Kitty Stewart (eds), *Towards a More Equal Society? Poverty, inequality and policy since 1997* (Bristol, Policy Press, 2005), 21–45, at 22.
45 Office for Budget Responsibility, *Welfare Trends Report* (London, HMSO, 2016), 126.
46 Blair and Schröder, *Europe: The Third Way*, 11–12.
47 Blair and Schröder, *Europe: The Third Way*, 2.
48 John Kay, 'Staking a moral claim', *New Statesman* (11 October 1996), 18–20, at 20. For an extended exploration of the concept with respect to welfare benefits for working Britons, see Peter Sloman, 'Redistribution in an age of neoliberalism: Market economics, "poverty knowledge", and the growth of working-age benefits in Britain, c. 1979–2010', *Political Studies*, 67 (2018), 732–51.
49 Tony Blair, *The Third Way* (London, The Fabian Society, 1998), 4–5.
50 Tony Blair, 'The rights we enjoy, the duties we owe', in Tony Blair, *New Britain: My vision of a young country* (Cambridge, MA, Westview Press, 2004), 236; and Tony Blair, 'Why I am a Christian', in Tony Blair, *New Britain: My vision of a young country* (Cambridge, MA, Westview Press, 2004), 59.
51 Giddens, *Third Way and Its Critics*, 33.
52 Kirk Mann and Sasha Roseneil, '"Some mothers do 'ave 'em": Backlash and the gender politics of the underclass debate', *Journal of Gender Studies*, 3 (1994), 317–31.
53 Margaret Hodge, 'Equality and New Labour', *Renewal*, 8 (2000), 34–41, at 36.
54 Hodge, 'Equality and New Labour', 36–8.
55 Department of Social Services, *Opportunity for All*, 1.
56 Blair, *Third Way*, 9.
57 Anthony Giddens, *The Third Way: The renewal of social democracy* (Cambridge, Polity, 1998), 100.
58 Giddens, *The Third Way*, 116.
59 Blair and Schröder, *Europe: The Third Way*, 8–9.
60 Anthony B. Atkinson, *Inequality: What can be done?* (Cambridge, MA, Harvard University Press, 2015), 9.
61 Stewart, 'Equality and social justice', 430–2; and Goos and Manning, 'Lousy and lovely jobs'.

Part II
Work and Family

7

'I don't know how she does it!' Feminism, family and work in 'neoliberal' Britain

Helen McCarthy

In the autumn of 1970, shortly after becoming Secretary of State for Education, Margaret Thatcher gave an interview to *Business and Professional Woman* magazine about her 'double image'. Pictured cheerfully stirring a saucepan in her kitchen, Thatcher described her demanding schedule as a Cabinet minister and explained to readers how she juggled family and career:

> I don't switch off. I switch over. Last night for instance, I left the House early (I was home at about 8.45pm) then I had to get a meal and because we had visitors at the weekend, I had to catch up with the washing. I was ironing until about 11.30pm. Although things like sheets, towels and shirts go to the laundry, there is still a lot to be washed at home.

A nanny had looked after her twins when they were young, Thatcher further elaborated, and her services had proved indispensable: 'Any working mother *must* have competent and reliable domestic help', she advised, 'and be prepared for emergencies.' As a result, the magazine concluded, Margaret Thatcher had never been forced to choose between politics and housewifery because 'she has always organised her life so that things run smoothly at home when she is not there'.[1]

Viewed retrospectively, the 'intriguing blend of career woman and homebody' which Margaret Thatcher presented to readers of *Business and Professional Woman* seems to presage the politics of gender, family and work embraced by Conservative governments in the 1980s. As Prime Minister, Thatcher encouraged aspiration, individualism and enterprise but envisaged no positive role for the state in helping parents reconcile the pursuit of those values with their caring responsibilities in the home. There was no substantial public investment in childcare provision on Thatcher's watch and no strengthening of maternity rights or introduction of paternity leave.[2] Mothers who wanted to work were forced to find their own solutions, either by hiring domestic help, drawing on informal sources of childcare in the extended family or taking lower-paid part-time jobs which fitted around children's school hours. Cuts in social welfare budgets reinforced this picture of families thrown onto their own resources, translating into more demands on women's time as unpaid carers for children, elderly parents and perhaps even needy neighbours too. As a number of scholars have recently observed, the ideological project of Thatcherism rested on accommodating a radical commitment to market values with socially conservative visions of the family.[3] Women were free economic agents, but they could not disavow their traditional social obligations to kin and community. To paraphrase Thatcher, they had to switch over, not switch off.

This chapter asks how effectively 'neoliberalism' as an analytical category captures this contradictory situation for British women in the late twentieth century. It makes three arguments. First, the chapter interrogates the concept of 'responsibilisation', developed by theorists of governmentality to denote the ways in which collectively shared burdens became reframed as the responsibility of private individuals under conditions of neoliberalism. The concept has been deployed recently by feminist scholars to analyse state and employer attitudes towards the problem of reconciling family life and work. But where those scholars regard responsibilisation as a distinctive element of 'neoliberal' times, I argue that it has a much longer history stretching back to late nineteenth-century discourses of women's paid work.

Second, the chapter shows how an ideology of personal responsibility also shaped government policy on childcare long before the 1980s, further complicating accounts of 'neoliberalism' centred on the late twentieth century. With the partial exception of the two world wars, publicly provided childcare was conceptualised as meeting a residual welfare need rather than being seen as a universal service for working mothers. When provision expanded substantially in the late 1990s under New Labour, the mixed economy of market, family and state solutions was preserved, while the needs of working mothers hovered only partially in view, obscured by Labour's desire to tackle childhood inequalities and its communitarian rhetoric of 'strong' families. In other words, the childcare needs of working mothers were marginalised by governments throughout the post-war period, and not just by 'neoliberal' ones.

Finally, the chapter argues that, amid these continuities, the late twentieth century did produce a new neoliberal subject in the figure of the stressed-out working mother, as exemplified in Kate Reddy, the heroine of Allison's Pearson's best-selling 2002 novel, *I Don't Know How She Does It!* Locating the novel in the discourses of 'post-feminism' which became culturally resonant from the early 1990s, I argue that Reddy represents the marriage of market and maternalist values associated with neoliberalism but also points to the tensions within it. I suggest that the conflicts captured in Pearson's novel were the object of wider critique around the turn of the millennium, but that this critique mostly took the form of individual strategies pursued by women to defend the arena of personal life from the values of the market. These strategies continue to give women a means of coping with the contradictions of responsibilised working motherhood in the twenty-first century.

The 'responsibilisation' of the working mother

In her recent study of women managers, the sociologist Zoe Young emphasises the high levels of stress experienced by mothers negotiating 'flexible' working patterns with their employers. Non-regular arrangements are now a common feature of the workplace, but the pressure to make a success of these arrangements, Young argues, is felt primarily by women. Firms can take credit for being 'enlightened' or 'caring' employers, but when experiments in flexible working fail, the failure rests with the employee, who is understood to have demonstrated insufficient self-discipline, ingenuity or determination. Young shows how women, grateful for the opportunity to hold on to highly valued careers, shoulder the practical and emotional burdens of organising their lives around their jobs and blame themselves when things unravel. This, Young argues, represents a 'personalisation of responsibility' and also a 'personalisation of failure'.[4]

Other feminist scholars have made similar arguments about how neoliberalism forces women, as Rosalind Gill puts it, 'to bear full responsibility for their life biography no matter how severe the constraints upon their action'.[5] Neoliberal rationality rules that women must self-organise all aspects of their personal and professional lives around the pursuit of highly individualised goals. Catherine Rottenberg shows how these values structure popular self-help guides such as Sheryl Sandberg's

Lean In: Women, work and the will to lead (2013) and Ivanka Trump's *Women Who Work* (2017). Rottenberg describes these texts as 'neoliberal feminist manifestos' which offer no critique, actual or immanent, of the social, economic and political inequalities which women are encouraged to surmount through their own efforts.[6] For Angela McRobbie, the once-radical language of 'empowerment' and 'choice' has been reconfigured in popular and official rhetoric as a type of *faux*-feminism. 'How successful the individual heterosexual woman might be in achieving equality in relation to domestic labour and childcare', McRobbie observes, 'becomes a private affair, or rather evidence that she has chosen well or fortuitously from the range of possible partners.'[7]

A historical perspective helps to specify what, if anything, is peculiar about this early twenty-first-century moment for women. The notion that domestic labour constitutes women's 'natural' or primary sphere of activity is long-established, acquiring the particular form of the male breadwinner family under the development of capitalist industry in the early nineteenth century.[8] A significant proportion of married women did, in fact, continue to work for wages in the era of industrialisation: around 15–25 per cent according to later nineteenth-century census returns, although these almost certainly undercounted casual labour and home-work.[9] Victorians tended to condemn married women's employment, claiming that it depressed male wages, contributed to infant mortality and destroyed the home as a sanctuary from the market.[10] Much of the agitation to limit women's working hours or restrict them from 'dangerous' trades had the defence of the male breadwinner family as its objective.[11] Meanwhile, the panic over 'sweated' home-working in the 1890s and 1900s was overwhelmingly centred on the wage-earning wife.[12] How to support married women in their 'proper' work in the home, whether through securing a family wage for men or a system of state endowment for mothers, became a pressing question in progressive liberal, socialist and trade unionist circles in the early twentieth century.[13]

Yet Victorian working mothers also found their champions in liberal feminists who, rather like later 'neoliberal' ones, spoke the language of personal responsibility and choice. Middle-class suffragists including Lydia Becker, Millicent Garrett Fawcett, Jessie Boucherett and Ada Heather-Bigg campaigned against protective legislation from the 1870s, organising through such bodies as the Society for the Promotion of Employment of Women, the Vigilance Association for the Defence of Personal Rights and the Women's Industrial Defence League. They opposed any interference with the individual's economic liberty, arguing that factory legislation infantilised women and entrenched their inferior status and vulnerability in the labour market.[14] In their various pamphlets, tracts and letters to the press, these feminists painted a powerful counter-image of women's work which privileged capacity, resilience and self-help. This is well captured in Heather-Bigg's account of the Black Country nail-makers whom she met in 1886. These women were 'cheerful and robust', Heather-Bigg observed, 'liking their calling and ridiculing the notion of their alleged serfdom'. Located in workshops attached to the home, the nail trade was well suited to the wage-earning mother: 'Her place of toil stands in her own small garden plot, in which her children can play round her after school hours. Her home being adjacent, she can at any moment run in and out and attend to her maternal and household duties.'[15] Jessie Boucherett and Helen Blackburn promoted a similar vision of robust working motherhood in their impassioned plea against the Factory Acts in 1896. The factory inspector did not appreciate what wage-earning meant to these women, they argued:

> He did not see the women after their hard day's work sitting down to a good nourishing supper; he did not see them with their family enjoying their piece of Sunday beef; he knew nothing of the happiness and comfort produced by the wages of these poor women.[16]

In the 1920s and 1930s, liberal feminists continued to rail against protective legislation but by then had a further target to attack: the widespread enforcement of marriage bars across government and private industry. The Open Door Council and Lady Rhondda's Six Point Group spoke out against this discriminatory practice, arguing that marriage bars removed a woman's freedom to decide for herself whether matrimony (and likely maternity) was compatible with continued employment. As Nancy Astor, the first woman to take her seat in Parliament, put it during a Commons debate on marriage bars in 1927: 'We do not want the Government to tell us what we should do. It is a question between the woman and her husband, and has nothing to do with a third person outside.'[17] Feminist societies appearing before the Royal Commission on the Civil Service (1929–31) insisted that married women were far more capable than policymakers allowed. The Council of Women Civil Servants described the marriage bar as an anachronism based on 'outworn' assumptions about the difficulties of managing a double role as housewife and worker. 'Women of wide interests', the Council observed, 'and particularly those whose social and financial position gives them the possibility of freedom, are able to combine marriage with a career, apparently with ease, as is abundantly clear at the present day in the case of many women in public life.'[18]

This statement did not hide the fact that the Council had mostly well-educated, professionally trained women in mind. Although women in the Labour Party and trade union movement also opposed the marriage bar, they were suspicious of the implication that all that was necessary to create a level playing field in the workplace was the removal of artificial barriers. Middle-class feminists dwelt little on domestic practicalities, presupposing that the working mother could organise childcare and housework by paying someone else to do it. Such assumptions were self-evident to women with sizeable salaries or private incomes, but they were far less so for those living on low earnings in working-class homes. Proponents of the 'dual role' in the 1950s and 1960s (by which time the *middle-class* home was typically servantless, too) gave greater recognition to these realities but tended nonetheless to talk up women's capacity to care for families and hold jobs harmoniously. Alva Myrdal and Viola Klein, who popularised this idea in their 1956 book *Women's Two Roles*, suggested a phased model in which women devoted themselves to full-time home-making while their children were young and sought re-entry to the workforce later, usually in their forties. Myrdal and Klein argued for social services to support these dual-role mothers, including nursery schools and communal laundries, but they placed the strongest emphasis on the woman's own orientation to work and her ability to organise her life efficiently. No longer need women choose between family and job, Myrdal and Klein confidently predicted: 'The best of both worlds has come within their grasp, if only they reach out for it.'[19]

Much of the literature on professional women's careers published in the post-war decades adopted this dual-role paradigm with its onus on personal responsibility. In her popular 1957 book *Wives Who Went to College*, Judith Hubback instructed her reader 'to face the difficulties involved in combining marriage, motherhood and individualism and to work out her own solution in terms of her own circumstances, character and endowment'.[20] In a 1960 newspaper article, Viola Klein elaborated on the qualities which allowed women to succeed in the 'combined operation' of career and family:

> It would appear that what makes these women 'tick' is, first of all, their determination to make a success of their dual role. Where they are prompted by a sense of vocation, by a feeling of duty to fill a vacancy in one of the shortage occupations, or by a psychological need to get out of their homes for part of the day – whatever their motives, they are equally attached to their job and resolved to make it work.[21]

This foregrounding of notions of personal drive, resolution and determination seems to prefigure the later 'neoliberal' emphasis on self-reliance and self-regulation. Indeed, we might trace the genealogy of twenty-first-century exhortations to women to 'lean in' in this post-war literature, with its similar tendency to frame the problem of combining family and work as an issue of individual commitment rather than external constraints.[22] What sets the 'neoliberal' feminist position apart from these earlier 'liberal' formulations, however, is its attempt to collapse *all* distinctions between the public and private self, a theme to which the chapter returns. Before that, it is necessary to address another major historical continuity in the 'responsibilisation' of the working mother: state failure in the provision of high-quality and affordable childcare.

Family and market solutions to the childcare problem

During both world wars, the British state took the unusual step of heavily subsidising local authority nurseries for use by mothers working in essential industries. In mid-1918, there were more than 160 publicly funded crèches with room for 7,000 children. Provision during the later conflict was significantly higher: 72,000 full-time places by mid-1944, with an additional 138,000 part-time nursery school places.[23] These were temporary measures to meet the emergency: nearly all war nurseries closed in 1918 and again in 1945. Local authorities thereafter retreated to their peacetime remit of offering day care only to families in difficult circumstances, typically unmarried mothers, children with special needs or families requiring short-term care where a mother was incapacitated.[24] The 'normal' mother – that is to say, the married mother whose husband was in steady employment – had no claim on these services, however much she might want to work. One Medical Officer of Health told a conference in 1951 that the mother hoping 'to park out her child for a substantial proportion of the day in order to devote herself to her career' could not 'expect the State or the municipality to subsidize her'.[25] In the mid-1970s, this paradigm of welfarism still characterised public day care provision. As a nursery matron in Hackney commented, 'you've got to have a real problem to get your child a place – unmarried, divorced, a battered or handicapped child, a handicapped parent or particularly bad housing conditions. If you can't produce that sort of evidence you haven't a hope.'[26] For most families, childcare remained a private matter, as reiterated by the Department of Health in 1989: '[I]n the first instance it is the responsibility of the parents to make arrangements, including financial arrangements, for the day-care of pre-school children.'[27]

How do we explain the resilience of privacy and parental responsibility as the values underpinning childcare policy throughout the twentieth century? One answer is that such values formed an intrinsic feature of Britain's 'liberal' tradition in social policy, setting it apart from continental welfare states such as Sweden, Denmark and France, where spending on preschool care has been dramatically higher.[28] Yet as Vicky Randall has argued, the 'liberalness' of British social policy has varied between policy areas and over time. British governments *have* intervened in the sphere of family through extending maternal and infant welfare services during and after the First World War, introducing maternity benefits for the wives of insured men in 1911 and universal family allowances in 1945, and by gradually expanding nursery school education, albeit at a low level by European standards. The salient point about these policies is that they aimed to stabilise family life by supporting women in their primary role of bringing up healthy and well-adjusted children. They were not conceived as measures to help parents reconcile caring responsibilities with paid employment. When Lady Plowden published her influential 1967 report on primary education, she explicitly disavowed any day care function for nursery schools. 'It is no business of the educational service', she wrote, to 'encourage' mothers to work.[29] As Education Secretary, Margaret Thatcher endorsed this position, stressing the educational benefits of nursery schools but prioritising spending on part-time rather than full-time places, which were of limited use to mothers who wished to work.[30]

Maternalist ideology helped to entrench this way of conceptualising preschool provision in the British social welfare tradition. From the early twentieth century, feminists across the political spectrum argued for state action to aid motherhood, whether in the interests of empire, the welfare of the working-class family or raising the status of housewives dependent on male breadwinners.[31] Many of the local or central government measures targeting the family from 1900 were the result of campaigning by women in the Labour Party, the Women's Cooperative Guild or the 'housewives' associations' which proliferated between the wars.[32] Helping women to reconcile family and paid work was never a high priority for these organisations, who argued instead for greater recognition of women's unwaged domestic labour in the home. Maude Royden, an advocate of state endowment of motherhood, captured this logic well in 1917 when she insisted that housewives were already 'earning their living, and earning it hard' by caring for their families. The problem was 'that they sometimes do not get it, and never have a right to it that can be enforced'.[33]

These activists wished to increase state support for mothers, and their demands were often in tension with the liberal-feminist position which privileged non-discrimination in the labour market as the key to women's equality. Yet as Denise Riley has brilliantly shown, feminist-maternalist arguments were folded into the larger pronatalist politics of the 1940s which re-inscribed the male breadwinner norm in the post-war welfare settlement. By institutionalising married women's economic dependence on men, William Beveridge's system of social insurance and welfare services rendered invisible the 'real needs' of mothers doing both domestic labour in the home *and* paid work outside it.[34] Psychoanalytic theories of 'maternal attachment' popularised by experts such as John Bowlby and Donald Winnicott added further authority in the 1950s to old prescriptions about women's primary duty to their families.[35] These were deferred to by proponents of the dual role, who mostly forgot about Myrdal and Klein's proposals for communal laundries and neighbourhood nurseries, promoting instead part-time work for mothers with older children. Under this model, preschool care did not present itself as a major policy issue, as it was assumed that mothers would be at home full time when their children were young and would typically seek a job fitting around school hours thereafter.[36]

The dramatic expansion of part-time work from the 1950s thus played an important role in sustaining low levels of investment by governments of both left and right in preschool day care and in after-school clubs and holiday play-schemes for older children. By the end of the 1970s, over two-fifths of the female workforce and nearly 70 per cent of working mothers were employed part time.[37] Policymakers reasoned that mothers working short, flexible shifts could more easily arrange their own childcare in the family or community, which is what the majority of women had no choice but to do. One 1963 study found that two-thirds of working mothers with children under five entrusted them to the care of female relatives (mostly grandmothers), neighbours or local minders.[38] The apparently smooth functioning of these informal care networks, as evidenced in social surveys, helped to convince policymakers that state action was unnecessary; indeed, mothers seemed actively to *prefer* family or community-based care to local authority nurseries.[39] This preference was sometimes stated by officials as if self-evident, even though the wartime experience had revealed the complexity of measuring demand for nursery places and the multiple factors behind women's childcare decisions.[40]

From the 1970s it became much harder for policymakers to claim that working mothers neither wanted nor needed day care. Women were increasingly discarding the dual-role model and returning to work before their children went to school. In 1976, about a quarter of mothers with preschool-aged children were working – more than double the figure 15 years earlier. By the end of the decade, one in four mothers re-entered the labour market within a year of giving birth, in some cases taking advantage of new maternity rights enshrined in the 1975 Employment Protection Act.[41] A series of official reports and academic surveys identified a growing demand for day care, while calls were made for a comprehensive system of preschool provision by an emerging 'under-fives' lobby of progressively-minded local authorities, trade unions, childcare experts and academics.[42] As previously noted, this did not result in any major investment by Conservative governments in the 1980s, although Labour-controlled councils developed social democratic experiments in funding nursery care. The Greater London Council, for example, was funding 12 per cent of all full-time childcare places in the capital by 1986.[43] More significant from the perspective of national policy were the ideas emerging from neoliberal think tanks such as the Institute of Economic Affairs (IEA) and the Centre for Policy Studies (CPS), who began to explore how the market might be made to work better in Britain's under-resourced childcare sector. As Ben Jackson has shown, helping parents to become better consumers of childcare as an alternative to major public expenditure moved to the centre of Conservative policy by the mid-1990s. In a 1994 CPS pamphlet, Sheila Lawlor suggested that families should have wider opportunities to buy childcare through a universal system of vouchers, a mechanism for empowering public service users already much discussed by neoliberal policy thinkers in both the US and the UK. Similar proposals were put forward by the Adam Smith Institute and subsequently adopted by John Major's Cabinet, although limited to families with four-year-olds.[44]

Tony Blair's New Labour government purported to break from Major's piecemeal approach by launching a National Childcare Strategy in 1998. A Green Paper, *Meeting the Childcare Challenge*, explained that such a strategy was necessary due to the historic failure of private and voluntary providers to meet parental demand for high-quality and affordable childcare. Yet the Green Paper was careful to delimit the scope for state action. It noted how social change had disrupted traditional forms of family-based care and suggested that government's role was 'to fill gaps' in the formal sector:

> Parents will always have the primary responsibility for the care and well-being of their children. It is up to parents to decide what sort of childcare they want for their children. This is not a matter for the Government. But it is the Government's responsibility to ensure that parents have access to services to enable them to make genuine choices.[45]

Emphasis was placed on bringing new providers into the market through substantial grant-making and, on the demand side, via a childcare tax credit for working parents. In keeping with all post-war governments, Labour thus remained committed to a mixed economy of care in which families 'packaged' care from a variety of sources.[46]

Unlike its predecessors, however, New Labour was willing to allocate considerable levels of funding into directly provided services through its flagship Sure Start programme. This started as a £452 million initiative targeting disadvantaged areas but was subsequently rolled out more widely. Sure Start was frequently cited by politicians as proof of Labour's broader commitment to gender equality in the workplace, as exemplified by moves to extend maternity leave, introduce paid paternity leave and give carers a right to request flexible working hours. Yet the provision of day care was a relatively minor element of Sure Start in its early phase, which focused instead on home visiting, parenting skills, play opportunities, health services and support for parents and children with special needs. From around 2003, the emphasis shifted towards getting parents (particularly lone mothers) into work, with more centres offering childcare. Yet as Kitty Stewart notes in her survey of Labour's early years policies, some of Sure Start's earliest champions criticised this move away from the original focus 'on play, nurture and parenting support'.[47]

This captures a key tension in Labour's childcare agenda after 1997: was it intended to meet the working mother's need for affordable day care or to advance a wider social democratic commitment to tackling childhood inequalities? The language of *Meeting the Childcare Challenge* slipped constantly between these objectives in its opening pages. The 'crucial role' of the National Childcare Strategy was 'meeting the needs and enhancing the opportunities of children and their families' by giving children 'the best start in life' and parents 'genuine choices: to look after their children full-time, or to combine work, education or training with parenting in a balanced way'. The Green Paper first described the developmental benefits to children of good quality care, then the benefits to the economy of getting more parents into work, and only towards the end of the Executive Summary did it explicitly acknowledge that 'offering equal opportunities for parents, especially women' formed part of the Strategy's objectives.[48] As many feminist critics pointed out, New Labour was more comfortable invoking the communitarian language of 'children and families' than justifying its policies in terms of eradicating structural inequalities between women and men.[49] Yet judged from a historical perspective, this stance was in keeping with a long-established tendency in British social policy to view the interests of women and families as one and the same thing. This view was shared by Conservative and Labour governments during the period of post-war social democracy, as well as in the 'neoliberal' era of the 1980s and beyond.

Post-feminism and the neoliberal feminist subject

This ideological inheritance offers a useful starting point for thinking about 'post-feminism' as it emerged at the end of the twentieth century and 'neoliberal feminism' at the beginning of the twenty-first. Post-feminism has generally been characterised as a new sensibility, culturally resonant in Britain from the 1990s, which denies or downplays the persistence of structural gender inequalities and interprets women's actions as expressive at all times of free choice. This sensibility imagines a world in which feminism has delivered sexual equality, thus releasing women to embrace behaviours and lifestyles, from pole dancing to home baking, which might previously have been understood within a framework of patriarchal power.[50] This logic underpinned the 'preference theory' developed by sociologist Catherine Hakim in an influential body of academic work and popular writings purporting to explain enduring differences between men and women in relation to family and work. In an era of equal opportunities and the pill, Hakim argued, women's greater tendency to take time out from the labour market for child rearing, to work shorter hours and to cluster in lower-paid 'feminised' sectors of the economy reflected genuine preferences. A minority of women were true careerists, but the rest either adapted their work to fit with family needs or plumped wholeheartedly for full-time domesticity. 'No matter what carrots are offered', Hakim wrote in a large feature in the *Daily Mail* in 1996, 'some women will always want to stay at home.'[51]

Hakim's contributions belonged to a wider debate unfolding in the media and popular culture which dwelt upon the mixed legacy of second-wave feminism for women living in 1990s Britain. A slew of memoirs and manifestos pondered this subject, while the press attacked it more brashly, inviting readers to question whether women really could 'have it all'.[52] Journalists asked whether stay-at-home mothers were happier than working mothers or vice versa; whether women were squandering their freedoms by dropping out of the labour force for motherhood; and whether the 'new man', a figure much trumpeted in the 1980s, truly existed.[53] High-profile cases such as the 1997 firing of 'superwoman' Nicola Horlick, asset manager and mother of five, fed a media appetite for stories about sexism in the corporate workplace.[54] Allison Pearson introduced her fictional creation, Kate Reddy, into this highly charged discursive field in December 2000 when she started a regular column in the *Daily Telegraph* entitled 'I don't know how she does it!' The column charted Reddy's stressful life as a city fund manager and mother of two high-spirited children, wittily narrating her attempts to placate a surly nanny and resentful husband while managing her own guilty conscience and physical fatigue.[55] In 2002, Pearson made Reddy the heroine of a full-length novel of the same title, which sold millions of copies in the UK and overseas, was serialised on the radio and later turned into a Hollywood film.

The considerable popular impact of Pearson's novel makes it a useful waypoint on the ideological map of gender, family and work in late-millennium Britain. Viewed from one angle, Kate Reddy is the archetypal 'responsibilised' neoliberal subject. She takes it for granted that neither state nor employer will step in to help her juggle the multiple demands on her time and attention. She spends a large portion of her salary on childcare, always in the privatised form of nannies. Wider structural inequalities are effaced, not because Reddy is a classless figure but, counter-intuitively, because Pearson gives her a working-class backstory similar to her own rise from northern comprehensive to Cambridge University and eventually to Fleet Street. Kate's social mobility is a device which deflects the obvious critique – that the novel deals with privileged women and is written from inside that privilege – and allows Pearson to present her heroine as an 'ordinary' mother trying, like mothers always have, to provide for and look after her family.[56] Like the later imagined subjects of *Lean In* or *Women Who Work*, Kate Reddy, a high-achieving, white, heterosexual mother, is somehow made to stand for all working women.[57]

Reddy's problems are exacerbated by her ambivalence about the choices she has made regarding family and career. An essentialist maternalism underpins Reddy's reflections on why she cannot delegate more domestic labour to her husband: 'They could give you good jobs and maternity leave', she tells herself, 'but until they programmed a man to notice you were out of toilet paper the project was doomed. Women carry the puzzle of family life in their heads, *they just do*.'[58] This 'puzzle in their heads' line was a favoured phrase of Pearson's, much repeated in interviews and columns: 'Working women have become honorary men but remained mothers in their hearts', Pearson wrote in one piece: 'If we are lucky, we love our jobs, but we still want to make the right kind of birthday cake. We want to be needed and not to be needed . . . We don't want to do everything ourselves, but we want to do it properly, so we must do it ourselves.'[59] In the novel, Pearson frames this as an immovable problem to which feminism offers no answer. 'Do I believe in equality of the sexes?' Kate asks herself:

> I'm not so sure. I did once, with all the passionate certainty of someone very young who knew absolutely everything and therefore nothing at all. It was a nice idea, equality: noble, indisputably fair. But how the hell was it supposed to work?[60]

Kate eventually decides that it can't, and she finds a solution to her dilemma in defeat. At the end of the novel, she quits her city job, moves out of London and starts a small, part-time business which allows her to spend more time with her children.

On this reading, the politics of *I Don't Know How She Does It!* seem perfectly located at the neoliberal intersection of market values and social conservatism in late twentieth-century Britain. Kate Reddy creates wealth in the city and strives to be the perfect mother and wife at home. Like Thatcher, she doesn't switch off, she switches over. Yet an alternative reading might frame Pearson's novel as a portrait of the working mother *in crisis*, the unwilling *victim* of a cruel neoliberal order. The novel's revealing subtitle, little noted by reviewers, was 'A comedy about failure, a tragedy about success'. Kate's life is defined not by capacity or agency but by their absence as her life spins out of control. Her unhappiness seems to expose what happens to women when the wall between the public and the private self collapses and when the values of the market, symbolised by Kate's rapacious city employer, override the ethic of care, represented in the novel by her children. Their need for mothering, Kate reflects, 'is like the need for water or light. It has a devastating simplicity . . . Children change your heart: they never wrote that in the books.'[61] Feminists had, in fact, written extensively since the 1970s on this subject, defining mothering as a distinctive type of labour which was calibrated differently from waged work and generative of its own system of values.[62] Pearson's novel lacks the radical vision of these earlier feminist analyses, but it nonetheless shares something of their conviction that the relationships which make us most human are not reducible to the rationality of the market.

Situating *I Don't Know How She Does It!* in the wider popular literature on working motherhood between the 1980s and early 2000s reveals a rupture with the post-war 'dual-role' texts, most notably in its celebration of imperfection and the valorisation of women's *in*capacity. This is indicated in the very titles of books such as Libby Purves's *How Not to Be a Perfect Mother* (1984), Jill Black's *Working Mother's Survival Guide* (1989) and Shirley Conran's *Down with Superwoman* (1990), in which Conran explains how her iconic 1975 household manual which introduced 'Superwoman' to the reading public had been fatally misinterpreted. The original *Superwoman* title, Conran remarked, 'was used ironically to demolish a myth' – that of the 'demanding, exhausting, super-achiever that threatened to depress our lives'. It was now necessary 'to forget SUPERWOMAN' and remember that the real achiever was the woman 'who avoids doing too much'.[63] Instructing women to disavow perfection and develop their own strategies for 'coping' or 'surviving' the rigours of family and professional life did not in itself constitute a viable feminist politics. But it is possible to see how these texts might have given women permission to refuse, perhaps even laugh at, a damagingly unattainable ideal of femininity.[64]

Rottenberg and McRobbie might be right that something changed again around the turn of the millennium, with the emergence of a new type of 'neoliberal feminism' which concealed the extent of its capitulation to the status quo by appropriating the language of empowerment and agency.[65] And yet, while careful empirical studies such as Zoe Young's reveal the realities of stress in women's lives, we should not be too ready to assume the hegemonic power of neoliberal subjectivity in women's conceptions of themselves. Reflecting on the counsels of perfection found in texts such as *Lean In*, Jacqueline Rose perceptively notes how

> . . . the sheer amount of effort that goes into the stereotype . . . also bears witness to its vacuity, to the fact that it is hanging by a thread . . . I have never met a single mother (myself included) who is not far more complex, critical, at odds with the set of clichés she is meant effortlessly to embody, than she is being encouraged – or rather instructed – to think.[66]

We find evidence of this sceptical posture as early as 1970, when one reader of *Business and Professional Woman* expressed her infuriation with the magazine's portrait of Margaret Thatcher as an exemplary working mother. In a letter to the editor, Mary Kalugerovich of Bathgate poured scorn on 'those paragons who put the rest of us to shame', pointing out how they all relied upon expensive help in the home to maintain their image of domestic order:

> Here is the TV personality who goes off to the studio at 8am and returns at 7pm, but makes a point of spending half-an-hour with her baby daughter at bedtime . . . A 'wonderful au pair' copes with the other 23 and a half hours. Here is the theatrical mother who goes off between plays for a month's holiday in the Mediterranean with her husband. The family is left behind of course, in the care of a 'marvellous housekeeper.' And even . . . Mrs Margaret Thatcher declares that one needs a nanny. Ain't it the truth![67]

As a mother with a part-time job, Kalugerovich was doing her best to manage without the aid of au pairs or nannies or housekeepers and was exhausted as a result. 'Dilettantes' such as Margaret Thatcher, she thought, should keep a respectful silence. 'Instead, will the real working mothers please stand up. Or better still, sit down. They need the rest.'[68]

Conclusion

The ideological formation which we might call 'neoliberalism' does not straightforwardly capture the situation of British women at the end of the twentieth century or the beginning of the twenty-first. As this chapter has shown, working mothers had been 'responsibilised' since at least the late nineteenth century by a liberal feminism which privileged the capacity of the wage-earning woman, and by a maternalist feminism which framed women's true 'work' as the rearing of children. When the state intervened more actively to support family life in the 1940s, it institutionalised women's primary status as that of home-maker and caregiver, leaving wage-earning mothers marginalised and unsupported. This gendered welfare settlement began to unravel in the 1970s as maternal employment rates rose, 'equal opportunities' became enshrined in law, and the ideas and vocabulary of Women's Liberation diffused unevenly into the wider culture. Yet those earlier traditions of conceptualising women as in turn waged workers, state-endowed mothers and the eternal dependants of men left a complex and contested legacy for policymaking and for women's own subjectivities in the 1980s and beyond.

This legacy is evident in the 'post-feminist' discourses of the 1990s, and in the 'neoliberal feminist' manifestos of Sandberg or Trump. Yet, as the final section of this chapter argued, it was present, too, in a wider discursive field in which women were encouraged – often playfully, wittily, irreverently – to debunk the 'myth' of perfection and refuse the feelings of guilt and inadequacy which were its inevitable product. Individual as opposed to collective or institutional strategies for managing family and work always had (have still) limited political potential, especially when regarded as necessary for mothers but not fathers. Yet the contradictions of caring and providing for a family in a system which does not recognise the needs of working parents might still prove transformative. In her recent history of mothering, Sarah Knott advocates 'a defence of caring under capitalism, uttered by caregivers of every persuasion – adoptive, biological and employed; female, male, lesbian, gay, trans and the rest' as a way forward which avoids reifying an essentialist conception of women's maternal role.[69] Without such a coalition behind them, it seems likely that women will be forced to follow Margaret Thatcher's advice – to switch over, rather than to switch off – for many decades to come.

Notes

1 'Mrs Thatcher's double image', *Business and Professional Woman* (Autumn 1970), 4–5.

2 For social policy affecting the family in the 1980s, see Gillian Pascall, 'Women and the family in the British welfare state: The Thatcher/Major legacy', *Social Policy & Administration*, 31 (1997), 290–305; and Joni Lovenduski and Vicky Randall, *Contemporary Feminist Politics: Women and power in Britain* (Oxford, Oxford University Press, 1993).

3 Ben Jackson, 'Free markets and feminism: The neo-liberal defence of the male bread-winner model in British politics, 1980–97', *Women's History Review*, 28 (2019), 297–316; Melinda Cooper, *Family Values: Between neoliberalism and the new social conservatism* (New York, Zone Books, 2017); and Florence Sutcliffe-Braithwaite, 'Neo-liberalism and morality in the making of Thatcherite social policy', *Historical Journal*, 55 (2012), 497–520.

4 Zoe Young, *Women's Work: How mothers manage flexible working in careers and family life* (Bristol, Bristol University Press, 2018), 164.

5 Rosalind Gill, 'Culture and subjectivity in neoliberal and postfeminist times', *Subjectivity*, 25 (2008), 432–45, at 436. See also Jessica Ringrose and Valerie Walkerdine, 'Regulating the abject', *Feminist Media Studies*, 8 (2008), 227–46.

6 See Catherine Rottenberg, 'The rise of neoliberal feminism', *Cultural Studies*, 28 (2014), 418–37; and Catherine Rottenberg, '*Women Who Work:* The limits of the neoliberal feminist paradigm', *Gender, Work and Organisation*, 26 (2018), 1–10.

7 Angela McRobbie, *The Aftermath of Feminism: Gender, culture and social change* (London, SAGE, 2009), 81.

8 Colin Creighton, 'The rise and decline of the "male breadwinner family" in Britain', *Cambridge Journal of Economics*, 23 (1999), 519–41.

9 John McKay, 'Married women and work in nineteenth-century Lancashire: The evidence of the 1851 and 1861 census reports', in Nigel Goose (ed.), *Women's Work in Industrial England: Regional and local perspectives* (Hatfield, Local Population Studies, 2007), 164–81. The extent to which census data undercounted married women's employment should not, however, be overstated, as recently argued in Edward Higgs and Amanda Wilkinson, 'Women, occupations and work in the Victorian censuses revisited', *History Workshop Journal*, 87 (2016), 17–38.

10 Margaret Hewitt, *Wives and Mothers in Victorian Industry* (London, Rockcliff, 1958).

11 Sonya Rose, *Limited Livelihoods: Gender and class in nineteenth-century England* (London, Rockliff, 1992); Barbara Harrison, *Not Only the 'Dangerous Trades': Women's work and health in Britain, 1880–1914* (London, Taylor and Francis, 1996); and Carolyn Malone, 'Gendered discourse and the making of protective labor legislation in England, 1830–1914', *Journal of British Studies*, 73 (1998), 166–91.

12 Jenny Morris, *Women Workers and the Sweated Trades: The origins of minimum wage legislation* (Aldershot, Gower, 1986); and Sheila Blackburn, *A Fair Day's Wage for a Fair Day's Work? Sweated labour and the origins of minimum wage legislation in Britain* (Aldershot, Ashgate, 2007), especially chapter 3.

13 Susan Pedersen, *Family, Dependence, and the Origins of the Welfare State: Britain and France 1914–1945* (Cambridge, Cambridge University Press, 1993).

14 Rosemary Feurer, 'The meaning of "sisterhood": the British women's movement and protective labour legislation', *Victorian Studies*, 31 (1988), 233–60; Ellen Mappen, 'Strategies for change: Social feminist approaches to problems of women's work', in Angela V. John (ed.), *Unequal Opportunities: Women's employment in England, 1800–1918* (Oxford, Basil Blackwell, 1986); and Angela V. John, *By the Sweat of Their Brow: Women workers at Victorian coal mines* (London, Routledge and Kegan Paul, 1984), especially chapter 5.

15 Ada Heather-Bigg, 'Female labour in the nail trade', *Fortnightly Review* (June 1886), 831, 833.

16 Jessie Boucherett and Helen Blackburn, *The Condition of Working Women and the Factory Acts* (London, Elliot Stock, 1896), 25.

17 House of Commons debate on the Married Women (Employment) Bill, *Hansard* (29 April 1927).

18 Statement submitted by the Council of Women Civil Servants (Higher Grades) to the Royal Commission on the Civil Service, October 1930, 31 TNA: T169/20. For an excellent account of struggles over the marriage bar in local government and the civil service, see Helen Glew, *Gender, Rhetoric and Regulation: Women's work in the civil service and the London County Council, 1900–55* (Manchester, Manchester University Press, 2016).

19 Alva Myrdal and Viola Klein, *Women's Two Roles: Home and work* (London, Routledge and Kegan Paul, 1956), xvi.

20 Judith Hubback, *Wives Who Went to College* (London, Heinemann, 1957), 87.

21 Viola Klein, 'A double life', *Manchester Guardian* (30 October 1964), 10.

22 Rottenberg's claim that 'the ability to happily balance public and private aspects of the self' has only recently been established as a new gender norm ignores this earlier history of professional women's efforts to find an equilibrium between home and work. Catherine Rottenberg, 'Happiness and the liberal imagination: How Superwoman became balanced', *Feminist Studies*, 40 (2014), 144–68.

23 Penny Summerfield, *Women Workers in the Second World War: Production and patriarchy in conflict* (London, Croom Helm, 1984).

24 Vicky Randall, *The Politics of Child Daycare in Britain* (Oxford, Oxford University Press, 2000); and Angela Davis, *Pre-school Childcare in England, 1939–2010: Theory, practice and experience* (Manchester, Manchester University Press, 2015).

25 Hugh Paul, 'Day nurseries', *Journal of the Royal Sanitary Institute*, 71 (1951), 235.

26 Lindsay Mackie and Polly Pattullo, *Women at Work* (London, Tavistock, 1977), 121.

27 Cited in Pascall, 'Women and the family', 296.

28 See discussion in Randall, *Politics of Daycare*, 6–8.

29 Randall, *Politics of Daycare*, 130.

30 Anna Danzier Halperin, '"Cinderella of the education system": Margaret Thatcher's plan for nursery expansion in 1970s Britain', *Twentieth Century British History*, 29 (2018), 284–308.

31 Anna Davin, 'Imperialism and motherhood', *History Workshop Journal*, 5 (1978), 9–65; Jane Lewis, *The Politics of Motherhood: Child and maternal welfare in England, 1900–1939* (London, Croom Helm, 1980); Anna Davin, 'Models of equality for women: The case of state support for children in twentieth-century Britain', in Gisela Bock and Pat Thane (eds), *Maternity and Gender Policies: Women and the rise of the European welfare states 1880s–1950s* (London, Routledge, 1991), 73–92; Pat Thane, 'Visions of gender in the making of the British welfare state: The case of women in the British Labour Party and social policy, 1906–1945', in Gisela Bock and Pat Thane (eds), *Maternity and Gender Policies: Women and the rise of the European welfare states 1880s–1950s* (London, Routledge, 1991), 93–118; and Carol Dyhouse, *Feminism and the Family in England, 1880–1939* (Oxford, Basil Blackwell, 1989), chapter 2.

32 For housewives' associations, see Caitriona Beaumont, *Housewives and Citizens: Domesticity and the women's movement in England, 1928–1964* (Manchester, Manchester University Press, 2013).
33 Maude Royden, 'The woman's movement of the future', in Victor Gollancz (ed.), *The Making of Women: Oxford essays in feminism* (London, George Allen and Unwin, 1917), 142.
34 Denise Riley, '"The free mothers": Pronatalism and working women in industry at the end of the last war in Britain', *History Workshop Journal*, 11 (1981), 59–118.
35 For the cultural reach of Bowlby, see Michal Shapira, *The War Inside: Psychoanalysis, total war, and the making of the democratic self in postwar Britain* (Cambridge, Cambridge University Press, 2013); and Mathew Thomson, *Lost Freedom: The landscape of the child and the British post-war settlement* (Oxford, Oxford University Press, 2013).
36 See Helen McCarthy, 'Social science and married women's employment in post-war Britain', *Past & Present*, 233 (2016), 269–305.
37 Peter Moss, 'Parents at work', in Peter Moss and Nickie Fonda (eds), *Work and the Family* (London, Temple Smith, 1980), 22–67.
38 Simon Yudkin and Anthea Holme, *Working Mothers and Their Children: A study for the Council for Children's Welfare* (London, Sphere Books, 1963), chapter 3.
39 See McCarthy, 'Social science'.
40 For a helpful discussion of this problem in the context of wartime, see Summerfield, *Women Workers in the Second World War*, chapter 4.
41 *Services for Young Children with Working Mothers: Report by the Central Policy Review Staff* (July 1978), 38, CAB 184/396; and Davis, *Pre-school Childcare*, 3. See also Paul Gregg, Maria Gutiérrez-Domènech and Jane Waldfogel, 'The employment of married mothers in Great Britain, 1974–2000, *Economica*, 74 (2007), 842–64. Under the Employment Protection Act, female employees with two years of full-time service (or five years part-time) became eligible for 14 weeks of statutory maternity pay, plus the right to reinstatement for up to 29 weeks after the birth of their baby.
42 See Randall, *Politics of Daycare*, chapter 3.
43 Stephen Brooke, 'Space, emotions and the everyday: The affective ecology of 1980s London', *Twentieth Century British History*, 28 (2017), 110–42, at 111.
44 Jackson, 'Free markets and feminism'.
45 Department for Education and Employment, *Meeting the Childcare Challenge* (1998), Executive Summary, paragraph 7.
46 Jane Lewis, 'Developing early years childcare in England, 1997–2002: The choices for (working) mothers', *Social Policy and Administration*, 37 (2003), 219–38.
47 Kitty Stewart, *Labour's Record on the Under-Fives: Policy, spending and outcomes, 1997–2010* (LSE Working Paper, 2013), 25, http://sticerd.lse.ac.uk/dps/case/spcc/wp04.pdf (accessed 21 June 2021).
48 *Meeting the Childcare Challenge*, Executive Summary.
49 See, for example, Jane Franklin, 'After modernisation: Gender, the Third Way and the new politics', in Anna Coote (ed.), *The New Gender Agenda* (London, IPPR, 2000), 15–22.
50 See McRobbie, *Aftermath of Feminism*, introduction.
51 Catherine Hakim, 'Why so many long to look after a home and a family', *Daily Mail* (29 March 1996), 14–15. See also Catherine Hakim, 'Grateful slaves and self-made women: Fact and fantasy in women's work orientations', *European Sociological Review*, 7 (1991) 101–21; Catherine Hakim, 'Five feminist myths about women's employment', *British Journal of Sociology*, 46 (1995), 429–55; and Catherine Hakim, *Work–Lifestyle Choices in the 21st Century: Preference theory* (Oxford, Oxford University Press, 2000).
52 For feminist texts, see Ros Coward, *Our Treacherous Hearts: Why women let men get their own way* (London, Faber and Faber, 1992); Yvonne Roberts, *Mad about Women* (London, Virago, 1992); Kate Figes, *Because of Her Sex: The myth of equality for women in Britain* (London, Macmillan, 1994); Helen Wilkinson, *No Turning Back: Generations and the genderquake* (London, Demos, 1994); Maureen Freely, *What about Us? An open letter to the mothers feminism forgot* (London, Bloomsbury, 1995); Suzanne Moore, *Head over Heels* (London, Viking, 1996); Natasha Walter, *The New Feminism* (London, Little Brown, 1998); and Germaine Greer, *The Whole Woman* (London, Anchor, 2000).
53 See, for example, Lynda Lee Potter, 'Mums on a tightrope', *Daily Mail* (21 February 1990), 7; Jessica Davies, 'The myth of Superwoman', *Daily Mail* (14 November 1990), 12; Edward Verity, 'Mothers who work are just selfish, says Paula Yates', *Daily Mail* (15 January 1992), 3; and Janice Walmsley, 'The mothering wars', *Daily Mail* (5 May 1992), 14.

54 'Superwoman flies into job battle with might of the city', *Daily Express* (18 January 1997), 3.
55 'Look, can we cut to the chase?', *Daily Telegraph* (4 December 2000), 14.
56 See Pearson's comments to Julie Wheelwright, 'From here to maternity', *Scotland on Sunday* (7 July 2002).
57 For the centrality of 'middle-classness' to neoliberal feminism, see Angela McRobbie, 'Feminism, the family, and the new "mediated" maternalism', *New Formations*, 80/81 (2013), 119–37.
58 Allison Pearson, *I Don't Know How She Does It!* (London, Chatto and Windus, 2002), 190 (emphasis added).
59 Allison Pearson, 'The living hell of today's working mother', *Evening Standard* (5 April 2000).
60 Pearson, *I Don't Know How She Does It!*, 190. See also, at 273: 'Back in the Seventies, when they were fighting for women's rights, what did they think equal opportunities meant: that women would be entitled to spend as little time with their kids as men do?'.
61 Pearson, *I Don't Know How She Does It!*, 165–6. Pearson repeated this passage, word for word, in her own voice in a long *Guardian* feature about the book: Allison Pearson, 'Parents: Resistance is useless', *The Guardian* (3 July 2002).
62 Sarah Stoller, 'Forging a politics of care: Theorizing household work in the British women's liberation movement', *History Workshop Journal*, 85 (2018), 95–119.
63 Shirley Conran, *Down with Superwoman: The guide for everyone who hates housework* (London, Penguin, 1990), 4.
64 Fiona Gibson, 'Confessions of a slob mother', *The Observer*, 16 March 2003, https://www.theguardian.com/theobserver/2003/mar/16/featuresreview.review (accessed 12 July 2021).
65 Although the 'anti-perfection' genre of parenting books continued; see, for example, Daisy Waugh, *I Don't Know Why She Bothers: Guilt-free motherhood for thoroughly modern mothers* (London, Phoenix, 2013).
66 Jacqueline Rose, *Mothers: An essay on love and cruelty* (London, Faber and Faber, 2018), 18.
67 'I protest!', *Business and Professional Woman* (Winter 1970), 25.
68 'I protest!'.
69 Sarah Knott, *Mother: An unconventional history* (London, Viking, 2019), 258.

8

Workers' voice and the moral economy in Britain's 'neoliberal' age

Jim Phillips

Work has changed significantly in the UK since the 1970s. Industrial employment had already peaked – in coal, cotton, metals and shipbuilding in the late 1950s, and in manufacturing in the 1960s – but the trend to deindustrialisation accelerated rapidly in the early 1980s, more quickly than in other mature economies. Manufacturing employment fell on average by 3 per cent per annum in the UK from 1979–89, whereas in France it fell by 1.9 per cent per annum, in Italy by 1 per cent per annum and in the Federal Republic of Germany by only 0.1 per cent per annum.[1] Divergence between 'good' jobs and 'bad' jobs was furthered in the UK as in the US by the rising preponderance of less regulated private sector employment and the shrinkage of better regulated public sector employment.[2] Pessimistic accounts relate the emergence of precariousness in service sector employment to neoliberalism's iron grip on work, workers and workplaces in various mature economies, including the UK.[3]

This chapter examines changes to work in the UK since the 1970s with a critical eye. The influence of neoliberalism is queried and qualified. There was tension between neoliberalism's two core aims: freeing markets, while shrinking the state. Policy measures adopted by Margaret Thatcher's Conservative governments to liberalise markets for goods and services involved major economic disruption and a sustained growth of unemployment. This resulted in increased public expenditure on the maintenance of redundant workers. Countervailing tendencies were also evident in the tightened regulation of work and workers. Thatcher's reforms of employment and industrial relations law were guided by long-running dialogue involving free marketeer academics and anti-trade union business figures.[4] Friedrich Hayek's influence was highly significant.

Trade unions were depicted as monopolistic barriers to free markets, and their rights – or 'privileges', in Hayekian terms – were incrementally dismantled in the 1980s.[5] Thatcher's carefully constructed regulatory environment shifted the distribution of power in workplaces emphatically to employers, but is nevertheless interpreted as a state-activist variant of neoliberalism, to enforce market competition.[6] The extent and character of this activism raises an important question, however, about the real priorities of Thatcher's governments. In this chapter it is argued that the most important goal of employment policy was not market liberalisation but the narrowing of industrial democracy. Within workplaces, this meant suppressing trade union organisation and voice. Andrew Gamble's early formula for understanding the broad contours of Thatcherism, '*the free economy and the strong state*', therefore remains highly apt when applied to the world of work. The sovereignty of employers and the right of management to manage were bolstered and cemented by concerted state action. The changes affecting employment from the 1980s onwards were therefore not entirely or even largely a reflection of neoliberalism in practice. Debates about the neoliberal credentials of Thatcher's governments are therefore misdirected. Class conflict was the real issue.[7]

Neoliberalism's ascendancy was qualified also by the extent and longevity of the resistance which it encountered. Thatcher and her neoliberal supporters depicted citizens as self-responsible individuals with limited obligations to others. This characterisation acquired cultural as well as political capital.[8] Val Walkerdine wrote in the early twenty-first century that female 'low-paid manual and service workers' were being 'constantly enjoined to improve and remake themselves as the freed consumer, the "entrepreneur of themselves"'.[9] Yet the popular appeal and practical reach of this ideological turn in the UK can be overstated. Thatcher's parliamentary majorities were built on minority electoral support: less than 44 per cent of the vote in 1983 and just over 42 per cent in 1987. Opposition was strong in industrial areas of England, including London, a manufacturing city in the 1970s, along with Wales and Scotland. In these areas, Thatcherism's market liberalisation and attacks on workers' voice transgressed a popular sense of justice that had developed and gained significant traction since the 1940s. This popular moral economy can be traced in various mobilisations of workers in the 1970s. From London, two important episodes stand out. At Trico in west London, 400 women secured equal pay after a lengthy strike in 1976. The practices of their employer, a US multinational producing windscreen wipers and other accessories, were challenged as immoral and possibly illegal under the 1970 Equal Pay Act and the 1975 Sex Discrimination Act.[10] The Trico strike overlapped with longer and unsuccessful industrial action at the Grunwick photo-processing plant in north-west London, where a large majority of the 450 workers were women of South Asian origin. They accepted as legitimate the exchange of time and effort for money wages, but only where their rights to consultation were respected through trade union recognition, which the employer resisted.[11] The practical levers of the popular moral economy – effective trade union voice and state intervention to safeguard workers' rights, along with high levels of manual employment – were deactivated by Thatcherism. The collective agency of workers was further affected in negative terms by the rapid acceleration of deindustrialisation. This was the most important long-term change affecting employment after 1979 and is examined in this book by Jim Tomlinson. Worker-activists became highly animated by a sense of the established order being unfairly disturbed and dismantled by employers and policymakers. Their defence of this order was an important popular rejection of neoliberalism.[12]

The shrinking number of relatively well-paid jobs for workers with limited educational qualifications contributed to the development of significant social problems which remain troubling in ex-industrial communities in the 2010s and early 2020s, especially those outside the major cities.[13] The management of these difficulties limited the extension of neoliberalism, as did the survival of the public sector as a major employer. Examining policymaking in the 1990s and 2000s further highlights the moderate longer-run influence of neoliberalism. The Labour government's 1998 National Minimum Wage covered workers in all sectors of the economy. Neoliberalism admittedly attained greater material expression under the UK Conservative–Liberal Democrat coalition from 2010, with 'austerity' a convenient cloak for shrinking the public realm and upwardly distributing income and wealth.[14] Even in the late 2010s, however, neoliberalism's effects in the world of work were constrained. In policy terms it was a far from hegemonic force across the UK. The Scottish government in 2017 announced its support for four pilot basic income schemes, all in ex-industrial communities. A cross-party group in the Scottish Parliament was established to monitor the initiative,[15] which flowed from a strengthening critique of neoliberal employment regimes across the world in the 2010s.[16] In summer 2020, a working group composed of Public Health Scotland and local authority officials recommended a broader three-year pilot, with emphasis on universality, unconditionality and periodic cash payment to individuals rather than households.[17]

The remainder of this chapter is organised into three parts. The first and second parts analyse the linked acceleration of deindustrialisation and erosion of worker voice under Thatcherism. This involved a heightening of 'market-ness', breaching moral economy expectations that the state would maintain economic and employment security.[18] The contested process highlighted the government's real priority: narrowing industrial democracy. Selected groups of manual workers, notably coal miners and dockers, were isolated by the state, and their workplace rights and industry voice eroded. The final part of the chapter examines the limits of neoliberalism's practical reach in employment since the 1990s. The Labour governments from 1997 to 2010 acknowledged the failings of the free market as experienced by many wage-earners through tax credits for low earners as well as the National Minimum Wage. Political divergence between Scotland and England was also important. Scotland's devolved government adopted a distinct approach to employment. This was especially marked in the 2010s, when there were also important variations in trade union membership in the various regions and nations of the UK. These demonstrated the continuing influence of collective organisation in former areas of intensive industrial employment and countermanded further the practical extent of neoliberalism.

Deindustrialisation in the 1980s and 1990s

Employment structures in Scotland demonstrate the long pedigree of deindustrialisation in the UK, which pre-dated Thatcher's election by two decades. Table 8.1 shows the drawn-out nature of this process, summarising employment in selected sectors in Scotland from 1959 to 1996.

In coal, 'early onset' deindustrialisation was especially deep. Across Scotland, as in Northumberland, Durham and South Wales, there were major job losses in the 1960s, as the National Coal Board (NCB) concentrated operations in a smaller number of larger pits, with Nottinghamshire and Yorkshire, which enjoyed significant geological advantages, gaining a higher share of production and employment.[19] In Scotland, these changes were managed carefully by policymakers, with new industrial development encouraged through regional incentives to manufacturers willing to establish factories in the coalfields.[20] The shrinkage of coal jobs was broadly offset by the growth of employment in other industrial sectors, providing new opportunities for women as well as redundant miners.[21] Deindustrialisation accelerated rapidly from

Table 8.1 Employment in industrial sectors (1,000s) (percentage of total) in Scotland, 1959–96

	1959	1968	1978	1988	1996
Coal	85	36	21	6	1
Manufacturing	741.4 (34.0)	728.3 (33.1)	609 (29.5)	408 (21.4)	314 (15.6)
Construction	162.3	185.5	163	126	111
All industry[1]	988.7 (45.2)	949.8 (43.1)	793 (38.3)	540 (28.3)	426 (21.5)
Total employment	2,183	2,200	2,067	1,911	1,981

Sources: *Digest of Scottish Statistics*, 16 (October 1960), tables 29 and 30; *Scottish Abstract of Statistics*, 1 (1971), tables 43a, 45 and 47; *Scottish Abstract of Statistics*, 10 (1981), table 9.3; *Scottish Abstract of Statistics*, 18 (1989), tables 9.2 (a) and (b); *Scottish Abstract of Statistics*, 26 (1998), table 6B3; and Miles Oglethorpe, *Scottish Collieries* (Edinburgh, RCAHMS, 2006), 20.

[1] Coal, construction and manufacturing combined.

1979, and, in contrast to preceding governments, Thatcher's administrations were unwilling to take action that would preserve manual employment and working-class economic security. Industry share of jobs fell by 10 per cent in the decade from 1978, to just 28.3 per cent in Scotland in 1988, with serious losses in manufacturing. There was much lower government expenditure on trade and industry, with less support for the regional stimuli that had sustained employment diversification in the 1960s and 1970s. Reduced commitment in this area was neoliberal-inspired.[22] Keith Joseph, the Secretary of State for Industry from 1979 to 1981, sternly opposed subsidising industrial production and employment.[23] In December 1979 he surprised Scottish Trades Union Congress (STUC) officials when they met for the first time. Seeking remedies for escalating industrial job losses, they were rebuffed. Joseph argued that such state intervention had been 'tried and found wanting over the last 15 years'. It was not the government's responsibility, he added, to partially fund production of goods which consumers were not purchasing.[24]

Unemployment rose as deindustrialisation gathered pace. Across the UK, the official claimant count doubled to three million from 1979 to 1982. Lost industrial production and jobs were unintended consequences of limiting the money supply and reducing inflation, as Tomlinson's account in this volume details. Thatcher's 'economic adventurism' was brutal,[25] and the radical reduction of regional aid was not its only neoliberal element. Thatcherism's regressive and anti-collectivist tendencies were exemplified by income tax cuts and VAT rises, along with privatisation of publicly owned industries and utilities.[26] Britain became more unequal, with the Gini coefficient for income distribution increasing by about 50 per cent in just ten years, from 0.23 in 1977 to 0.34 in 1987, where it more or less remained for the next three decades.[27]

The state, to reiterate, nevertheless retained a powerful role under Thatcher, not least in public 'order' and military defence.[28] Moreover, government expenditure as a proportion of GDP increased after 1979, partly because of the rise in social security payments in the wake of accelerating deindustrialisation. The public sector also remained an important employer. In Scotland the share of women workers who were employed in the public sector barely shifted from 31.8 per cent in 1977 to 32.4 per cent in 1987.[29] If there was an ambition to shrink the state, this was unrealised in part because of the new demands made of welfare services by deindustrialisation. Many of those in local authority and social security employment were managing the social wounds of industrial job loss: unemployment and poverty. Table 8.2 shows that in Scotland women acquired a growing share of manufacturing employment during a period of expansion in the 1960s. Women retained this share, roughly one job in three, as manufacturing contracted, slowly in the 1970s and then more rapidly in the 1980s. The situation changed in the 1990s.

Women were increasingly concentrated by the 2000s in lower-paid jobs in private sector services, including work in the 'contracted-out' former public sector, where trade union recognition was less prevalent, and conditions of employment less attractive. Deindustrialisation

Table 8.2 Women's share of manufacturing employment in Scotland, 1959–2005

Year	Share (per cent)
1958–9	28.9
1968	32.3
1977–8	31.9
1987–8	32.5
1996	30.1
2005	26.4

Sources: As table 8.1, plus *Scottish Abstract of Statistics*, 26 (1998), table 6B; and Jim Campbell and Emily Thomson, 'Changing role of women in the Scottish economy', in Kenneth Gibb, Duncan Maclennan, Des McNulty and Michael Comerford (eds), *The Scottish Economy* (London, Routledge, 2018), 135–51.

contributed to the continued gender gap in rewards, as men regained a larger share of manufacturing jobs, and 42 per cent of women and just 13 per cent of men were working part-time.[30] This latter phenomenon was 'sticky'. The STUC Women's Advisory Committee observed in 1988 that 43 per cent of female employees were part-time. This structural disadvantage compounded gender inequalities in pay, occupational opportunity and workplace rights. The absence of non-statutory nursery provision, discussed by Helen McCarthy in the previous chapter of this book, was a 'scandal' and impeded female workers from moving into full-time employment. The limited presence of the state in this area was partly a reflection of union influence being diminished in the 1980s. The outcome, illustrating a salient feature of a liberalised labour market, was pronounced gender inequality in employment opportunities and rewards.[31]

Industrial job losses were accompanied by a substantial growth of hidden unemployment as people withdrew from economic activity altogether. They were neither claiming unemployment benefits nor actively seeking work. Most were officially registered as 'permanently sick'. In Fife the portion of adult males classified in this manner increased from 2.7 per cent in 1981 to 5.7 per cent in 1991 and 7.1 per cent in 2001.[32] In Glasgow the rate of permanent sickness among all adults increased even more quickly, from 3 per cent in 1981 to 9 per cent in 1991, with 11.2 per cent among men.[33] The permanently sick were incentivised to assume this identity by the benefits system. Incapacity entitlements were higher than unemployment benefits, the value of which was radically reduced in the 1980s. Those in receipt of incapacity benefits could also draw occupational pensions, if these came 'early' in connection with redundancy payments. Incapacity benefits were not means tested, and the earnings of other household members were unaffected. Most of the permanently sick were further motivated by the absence of job opportunities: they were unemployed in all but official categorisation and would have worked had suitable employment been available. Combining the permanently sick with unemployment benefit claimants and others who were seeking work produces a 'real' level of unemployment appreciably higher than the official tally. In Glasgow, among adults in the 1980s, this was consistently in the region of 22–25 per cent, about 6–8 per cent above the UK average. In the Scottish coalfields it was likewise high, ranging from 21.2 per cent in Fife to 30 per cent in Ayrshire, via 28.7 per cent in Lanarkshire. In the Lothians the problem was smaller, at 16 per cent, although still above the UK average.[34]

Thatcher's governments did not initiate deindustrialisation. But economic policy from 1979 certainly accelerated the contraction of industrial employment, and there were no significant efforts to maintain economic security in the regions adversely affected. Thatcherite efforts to stigmatise the unemployed as authors of their own problems appear to have had limited general impact on political attitudes in northern England, Scotland and Wales, where support for the Conservative Party was consistently lower than in southern England, London aside. As in the 1930s, unemployed workers in the 1980s tended to see their position in collective terms, albeit fatalistically.[35] Thatcher's governments arguably acknowledged that unemployment was not entirely a matter for the 'individuals' affected. Policy interventions to ameliorate the social effects of deindustrialisation, notably the increased expenditure on welfare benefits, pulled Thatcherism away from its idealised goal of a smaller state.

Management's 'right' to manage

A key element of Thatcherism, and arguably its core feature in relation to work, was 'restoring' the 'right of management to manage', liberated from state regulation and the trade union 'veto'.[36] This involved an assault on the popular moral economy by reversing the post-1945 trend in industrial relations to greater pluralism and shared authority in workplaces. Thatcher was a principal actor in resisting the Labour government's industrial democracy agenda in the mid-1970s, which included proposals for union-channel directors in large private sector manufacturing firms.[37] Union advocates saw enhanced worker involvement in corporate governance, particularly where investment and disinvestment decisions were being reached, as a means of arresting capital flight and deindustrialisation.[38] Business leaders were often unhappy about Thatcher's economic approach, especially those in manufacturing who were squeezed in the early 1980s by inflation and a buoyant pound. But generally they welcomed the 'creation of a climate where being the boss counted for something', as Martin Adeney and John Lloyd put it in 1986.[39] The government strongly privileged the interests of employers over those of employees. Starting with the Employment Act of 1980, a sequence of legal measures on strikes, picketing, closed shops and trade union regulations greatly reduced the scale and agency of organised labour. The closed shop was a particular target for neoliberals. Union membership as a condition of employment offended neoliberalism's individualised view of freedom. Hayek saw it as a coercive attempt by unions to impose costs on workers, employers and the public more broadly.[40] Unions defended the closed shop as protection against free-riders who accepted the benefits of membership opportunistically without sharing the costs. 'If you want a seat on the bus then you have to buy a ticket', was a common collectivist defence,[41] which neoliberals rejected. The Employment Acts of 1982 and 1988 made action to enforce the closed shop illegal. There was a significant fall in union membership, although this was more the consequence of deindustrialisation than the legislative reforms. Union density – the proportion of the workforce represented by trade unions – fell from 54.5 per cent in 1980 to 38.1 per cent in 1990.[42] Power shifted to employers, who were encouraged to control and reorganise work unilaterally.[43]

The government's incremental recasting of power relations in workplaces was coupled with two major attacks, against coal miners in 1984–5 and dockers in 1989. The wide range of questions involved in the miners' strike against job losses and colliery closures is reflected in its highly diverse literature. This encompasses the contested finances of the coal industry,[44] the vital involvement of women and the extent of changes in coalfield gender politics,[45] the role of the Labour Party, plus the contested strategy and tactics of the strikers.[46] The breadth of these issues arguably obscures the central point of contestation in the strike, which was union voice in the management of the nationalised industry. The National Union of Mineworkers (NUM) accepted pit closures in the 1960s and 1970s only after careful dialogue with the NCB and government. This was the popular post-Second World War moral economy in action. It resembled the thinking ascribed by E. P. Thompson to the plebeian 'crowd' which resisted the elevation of market-ness in food provision and wage-setting in eighteenth-century England.[47] Expectations of communal and individual security were cultivated by the nationalisation of coal in 1947. Changes to the economic order in the coalfields were only accepted by workers through agreement, negotiated with union representatives, and where collective security was maintained.[48] In Scotland, the NUM blocked further contraction of the industry from the late 1960s onwards because the alternative pathway to economic security for manual workers in the coalfields, inward investment from multinational manufacturers, was growing too slowly.[49] Job losses in coal could no longer be offset by new employment in other industry.[50] The strike of 1984–5 was an unsuccessful defence of the popular moral economy and union voice against the invasive force of determined government action. While dissembling about the scale of planned pit closures, and publicly claiming that the government was not involved in the dispute, Thatcher and her Cabinet privately vetoed any outcome that did not give the NCB freedom to close pits unilaterally on economic grounds. The 'most important requirement' of an agreement, Thatcher said in September 1984, was 'that it would not in any way fetter the NCB in arranging the closure, as and when necessary, of uneconomic pits'.[51]

In pursuit of this goal, the government mobilised the overwhelming resources of the state. Thatcher intervened directly in policing, preventing strikers from blockading power stations, steelworks and other pressure points, including collieries where miners were working.[52] The government pushed the NCB into a 'back to work' movement, spending heavily on financial incentives to strike-breakers and 'safe' transport to and from their workplace.[53] Complicated legal manoeuvres in England and Wales were also cultivated by the government. David Hart, a businessman and adviser to the Prime Minister, encouraged working miners to sue the NUM over the legality of the strike. In September 1984 the High Court in London restrained the NUM from characterising the strike as official. NUM leaders defied this restraint, leading in October to the sequestration of their union's assets in England and Wales, although not in Scotland, where separate legal jurisdiction ruled the strike lawful. Thatcher's papers show she followed closely the anti-strike litigation, which exacerbated the NUM's difficulties.[54] Little was left to chance in pursuit of victory, with a huge public expenditure commitment. Estimates broadly coalesce around £6 billion – about £16.5 billion in 2021 values – in disappearing production and tax revenues, replacement coal stocks and additional oil burn charges, along with reduced economic activity more generally, plus the huge expense of policing. This outweighed the NCB's projected financial losses for producing coal in the financial year of 1984–5, some £100 million, by a factor of *sixty to one*.[55] This 'worthwhile investment', in the words of Nigel Lawson, Chancellor of the Exchequer, was central to the government's larger ambition of redistributing resources and authority from employees to employers. Business was liberated, and market forces strengthened, but only because of the state's intensive attack on the integrity of trade unionism.[56]

The same ideological reasoning framed the government's approach to port transport. Dock work was transformed in the late 1960s and early 1970s by the containerisation revolution, which reduced radically the demand for labour. The number of dockers in all UK ports fell from 47,728 in 1965 to 18,186 in 1989.[57] Most ports in 1989 still operated under the National Dock Labour Scheme introduced in 1947 to provide security of income for workers and a reliable supply of labour for employers. A closed shop applied. The principal union, the Transport and General Workers'

Union (TGWU), had a joint role with employers in determining the scale of the registered workforce and was able to influence the management of work in Scheme ports. Employers resented this. During a big industrial dispute in 1967, the chairman of the London Ocean Trades Employers' Association lamented 'the absence of master and servant legal rights as enjoyed in all other industries'.[58] Thatcher's government likewise loathed the Scheme, with its union voice and guaranteed weekly income when shortfalls in port traffic meant that dockers were not fully deployed.

A dock strike in July 1984 briefly jeopardised the government's strategy for defeating the miners. Lengthy interruption of imports and exports would be far more disruptive than the miners' strike in isolation. Dockers were aggrieved that British Steel Corporation (BSC) employees had been directed to unload coal imports. This was contrary to the rules of the Scheme, which the TGWU officials correctly feared was being threatened. Thatcher advised her Cabinet colleagues to show the public that the 'pretext' for the dockers' strike was false. She claimed that they enjoyed 'extraordinary privileges' in job security and pay, with almost one-third of the 13,000 Scheme-registered workers surplus to 'the genuine requirements of their industry'. Keen to isolate the miners, however, Thatcher detailed the Secretary of State for Transport, Nicholas Ridley, to issue a parliamentary assurance that the government had 'no plans to abolish or change the National Dock Labour Scheme'.[59] Ridley did so,[60] but in 1989 the Scheme was abolished, ending joint regulation and guaranteed income for dockers.[61] Redundancies and unemployment followed. Managerial sovereignty subsequently exerted downward pressure on wages in the 1990s, and the intensification of work contributed to an increase in injuries and fatalities.[62] The new regime was typified on the Liverpool waterfront. In 1995, around 500 dockers employed by Mersey Docks and Harbours Board were sacked after refusing to cross a picket line established by 60 dockers in dispute with another employer, Torside Ltd. Energetic local activism for the dockers' reinstatement broadened into an impressive international campaign. This was unsuccessful, in that the dockers eventually accepted severance terms in 1998, but demonstrated the contested nature of the liberalisation of work, just as the miners' strike had done in 1984–5.[63]

There was a significant drop in measurable industrial action after 1979. Thatcher and her supporters claimed this demonstrated that their reforms had 'worked',[64] ignoring the implications of cross-national comparisons. Data collated at the International Institute of Social History shows that falling industrial action was common in most mature economies from the 1980s to the 2010s,[65] influenced by the twin forces of deindustrialisation and globalisation examined in Tomlinson's chapter. Any conclusion that workers had accepted Thatcherite reforms, becoming self-motivated 'economic' men and women, would therefore be contentious.[66] In 2006–7, almost three decades after Thatcher's election, Burberry workers at Treorchy, South Wales, campaigned at length – although unsuccessfully – to block plant closure and redundancy. The mobilisation was mounted in moral economy terms familiar from the 1980s. The workers argued that the factory 'belonged' to the community and the multinational company was behaving illegitimately as it moved production from South Wales to a lower-wage and lower-regulation environment in China. The popular moral economy had been attacked in the 1980s, but citizens in the twenty-first century were still asserting claims to workplace justice and employment security.[67]

The limits of neoliberalism since the 1990s

The Thatcher governments did not achieve a permanent revolution in economic policy in the UK, neoliberal or otherwise. John Major's Conservative governments and then the Tony Blair–Gordon Brown Labour governments engaged in various interventionist and expansionist measures.[68] These feature elsewhere in the volume, in the chapters by Bernhard Rieger, Peter Sloman and Tomlinson. Labour's crucial innovations were the National Minimum Wage (NMW) and tax credits for the low paid. Brown, contributing to the campaign against Scottish independence in 2014, cited the NMW as evidence of Britain's valuable 'sharing union'. The NMW narrowed differentials between regions and reduced the dangers of a 'race to the bottom' of the labour market. It was made possible, moreover, by the redistribution of wealth across nations within the UK as well as boundaries of income.[69] The NMW came into force in April 1999, when 1.9 million workers were being paid less than the initial £3.60 hourly rate for workers aged 21 and over. The measure was designed in part to counteract the liberalising damage of the Thatcher years, which included abolition of various sector-wide Wages Councils, which had been in place since the 1940s. These had been especially valuable in raising the wages floor in sectors where unions had found organisation of workers and recognition from employers difficult to achieve, notably in hospitality and retail.[70]

The NMW was one of Labour's main successes in government. Applicable to all workers, it was more comprehensive than the Wages Councils, which covered only selected sectors. The NMW settled at around 50 per cent of the median wage and directly benefited 7 per cent of the workforce. Labour also introduced limited employment and trade union protections. The Employment Relations Act of 1999 established a statutory right to union recognition where 40 per cent of eligible employees in a workplace voted in favour, so long as a majority of those participating in the ballot also did so. European Union-inspired legislation was brought forward providing for parental leave and improved rights to information and consultation.[71] Many Labour supporters were nevertheless disappointed by the modesty of this policy effort. The Thatcher laws constricting union action were not repealed. Paul Smith argues that Labour's agenda 'domesticated' unions, tightening controls on militancy and continuing Thatcherism's neoliberal direction of travel. European Commission regulations on working time and the protection of agency workers were introduced, but in diluted form. In similar fashion, unfair dismissal legislation in 1999 lowered the qualifying period to one year but was thereafter modified to ease the procedural burden on employers. Union membership continued to shrink, particularly in the private sector, although more slowly than in the 1980s and early 1990s.[72]

Labour's policy shortcomings were slight when measured against what followed under Conservative–Liberal and then Conservative governments at UK level after 2010. Prolonged austerity in public finances, along with further oppressive anti-trade union legislation and private sector employment practices, framed the growth of a highly insecure labour regime. This included zero-hours contracts, an unmistakably neoliberal feature which brutally transgressed residual popular moral economy expectations of security and shared workplace authority. The number of people on employment contracts with no weekly minimum hours increased from fewer than 200,000 in 2010 to 901,000 in 2017, according to the government's Labour Force Survey. This amounted to 2.8 per cent of workers. The Office for National Statistics reported in 2018 that this phenomenon was possibly peaking,[73] but the high visibility of the gig economy demonstrated the renewed practical influence of neoliberalism in the labour market. This involved a highly exploitative blend of bogus self-employment, lost wages coupled with fines for workers reporting sick, and digital-era mechanisms for policing employees.[74]

In policy terms, however, neoliberalism was not a hegemonic force across the UK. The Scottish government's support for research in 2017 on universal basic income, with pilot schemes in Edinburgh, Fife, Glasgow and North Ayrshire, was noted in the introduction. The Scottish government articulated a broad-based revulsion in Scotland arising from the UK government's benefit cuts and contentious reform of welfare, Universal Credit. The Scottish government used its limited powers under devolution to mitigate the negative impact on claimants of this benefit, enabling fortnightly rather than monthly payments, and for housing elements of the entitlement to go directly to landlords.[75] Political divergence between Scotland and England was also clear in the tone used by the Scottish government in matters relating to employment and trade unionism. Partnership with the STUC and its affiliates was emphasised in the 2014 White Paper on an Independent Scotland,[76] and in 2015 the government established the Fair Work Convention, an advisory and research body that endorsed the value of workplace union voice.[77]

The question of historical justice for the casualties of deindustrialisation was likewise pursued in a distinct manner in Scotland. In October 2016, the UK Home Secretary, Amber Rudd, refused to establish an inquiry into policing at the 'Battle of Orgreave', where South Yorkshire Constabulary initiated a violent confrontation with striking miners in June 1984 at the BSC coking plant near Rotherham.[78] In June 2018, by contrast, Michael Matheson, the Scottish government's Cabinet Secretary for Justice, announced an independent review of the impact of policing on affected communities in the strike in Scotland. The review, chaired by John Scott QC, began collecting evidence in August 2018. Public consultation meetings were held across the ex-coalfields in mining welfare institutes. Former strikers provided vivid testimony of police harassment, intimidation and physical violence. The unusually vindictive punishments in sheriff courts were also emphasised, along with the suspected collusion between police and the NCB to secure the dismissals from employment of strike activists.[79] Scott's report, published in October 2020, recommended a pardon for the 500-plus former miners convicted in Scotland for public order offences associated with their strike activism. The Scottish government accepted this recommendation in principle, with Matheson's successor as Cabinet Secretary for Justice, Humza Yousaf, advising Parliament that the necessary legislation would follow in 2021.[80]

These policy divergences on employment and trade unionism within the UK have deep roots. Devolution in Scotland drew much impetus in the 1960s from trade union concerns about the political management of deindustrialisation. These were a direct articulation of popular moral economy expectations. The STUC was an advocate of Home Rule for Scotland within the UK from the late 1960s onwards. Devolution was regarded as holding the potential for distinct policy approaches that could enhance economic security for manual workers and industrial communities. This objective became more urgent in the early 1970s, as Edward Heath's Conservative government allowed unemployment to escalate, with major industrial job losses on Clydeside.[81] One of this book's editors has elsewhere argued, with co-authors, that in Britain there was a notable trend to greater 'popular individualism' in the 1970s. This was not incompatible with all forms of collective action, but among industrial workers in England it appears to have contributed to an undermining of the peak-level authority of unions.[82] In Scotland, by contrast, public support for collective action in defence of working-class economic security remained less ambiguous. The Labour government elected in 1974 became more popular over time in Scotland just as its support drained in England. Scottish voters appreciated the government's prioritisation of income from industrial employment, protected by union organisation and policy action. This included major new investment in coal mining, the subsidised 'rescue' of car manufacturing at Linwood in Renfrewshire and the nationalisation of shipbuilding. At the 1979 general election, Labour's share of the vote in Scotland increased from 36.3 per cent in October 1974 to 41.5 per cent, whereas its share in England fell from 40.1 per cent to 36.7 per cent.[83] Further political divergence followed when Thatcher's governments oversaw the ending of deep coal mining in Scotland, the privatisation of shipbuilding with big job losses on the Clyde and the closure of various large-scale industrial enterprises, notably the Linwood car plant in 1981. Local Labour MPs and management representatives from Linwood met Joseph prior to closure, seeking financial help to keep 4,800 workers in a job. Neoliberal thought was translated into neoliberal inaction. 'Sir Keith was extremely reluctant to agree to do anything at all', the official minute of this meeting recorded.[84]

Historical traditions of collectivism were not extinguished in the neoliberal age. In the 2010s, Walkerdine examined the damage to working-class self-confidence in a South Wales steel-making community arising from deindustrialisation. Young men unable to follow in their fathers' footsteps became disengaged from economic activity, dismissing 'women's employment' in service sectors. Walkerdine concluded that deindustrialisation disrupted the intergenerational transmission of working-class traditions of solidarity.[85] This overlooked the findings of an important study by Huw Beynon, Rhys Davies and Steve Davies. In oral testimony citizens whose working lives had commenced in the 1990s, and with limited or even no industrial employment experience, reported the strong formative influence of older relatives, neighbours and colleagues.

A strong culture of trade union organisation and activism *had* passed from one generation to the next, so that collective bargaining in service occupations was more robust in South Wales than in many regions of England.[86] Labour Force Survey and Office for National Statistics data on union membership and collective bargaining, assembled and analysed by Gregor Gall, indicates that historical tradition had similar lasting effects on Clydeside too. In Strathclyde in 2017, collective bargaining coverage was higher than in regions of England with similar employment structures.[87] In a similar register, Tim Strangleman argues that collective identities formed in industrial society operate as a 'residual structure of feeling' in the incomplete transition to post-industrial society. These identities remained valuable resources for manual workers, encouraging them to act in ways that mitigated the negative effects of deindustrialisation, such as low pay and authoritarian employers, and minimised the practical influence on their lives of neoliberal ideology.[88]

Conclusion

Neoliberal thinking inspired policy-driven changes affecting employment and trade unionism from 1979 onwards. The Thatcher governments first elected in that year introduced a sequence of reforms to employment and industrial relations law that cumulatively diminished the agency of trade unions. These laws were consistent with Hayek's theorisation of unions as monopolistic and coercive restraints on the efficient functioning of the market. Legislative measures against the closed shop highlight the practical impact of neoliberal ideology. It was not acceptable in neoliberal terms to insist on union membership as a condition of employment. Neoliberalism was far from being the only influence on government policy, however. Diminishing the agency of trade unions and rebalancing authority in workplaces in favour of employers were more fundamental to Thatcherism than extending the practical reach of the free market. Concerted state action, backed by sometimes very hefty public expenditure, was undertaken in pursuit of this anti-trade union agenda. This took priority over neoliberal budget- and state-shrinking aspirations. The huge 'investment' required to defeat striking miners, to remove their union's voice from the management of the coal industry, demonstrated this element of Thatcherism in vivid form.

Thatcherism's active-state neoliberalism duly represented an assault on the popular moral economy that had developed in many industrial communities and localities in Britain after the Second World War.

The popular moral economy comprised two core expectations: individual and communal security, encouraged by state intervention; and meaningful voice in the taking of decisions affecting employment, through political and trade union representatives. Market liberalisation and the 'restoration' of employer sovereignty in workplaces in the 1980s marked significant incursions on this moral economy. The acceleration of deindustrialisation represented a further contravention of this moral economy, creating high levels of unemployment, especially in the coalfields and manufacturing towns. There was a neoliberal disinclination to stimulate or subsidise alternative employment. The key moral economy levers – robust trade unionism and interventionist state policy – were diminished in their effectiveness. Moral economy expectations nevertheless continued to inform political thinking and voting patterns among manual workers, at least in industrial localities. The Thatcher governments were compelled to expend substantial resources to mitigate the damage arising from lost jobs in coal and manufacturing. The notable increase in the volume of citizens classified as 'permanently sick', withdrawn from economic activity and in receipt of higher levels of benefit than those registered as out of work, was not a neoliberal phenomenon. The record of the Labour governments elected in 1997 further restricted the practical application of neoliberal ideas. Measures affecting employment and trade unionism were adopted to constrain free-market forces. The NMW was the most significant of these, providing coverage for all workers, and survived even the fresh neoliberal turn in UK-level policymaking after 2010. The Scottish government's distinct approach in the 2010s and 2020s was shaped by the continuing influence of collectivist traditions formed under industrialisation and the more vigorous health of popular moral economy expectations, evident at times also in South Wales. This political and social divergence highlighted the far from universal traction of neoliberalism in Britain, ideologically as well as practically.

Notes

1 Michael Kitson and Jonathan Michie, 'The de-industrial revolution: The rise and fall of UK manufacturing, 1870–2010', in Roderick Floud, Jane Humphries and Paul Johnson (eds), *The Cambridge Economic History of Modern Britain: Volume 2, 1870 to the present* (Cambridge, Cambridge University Press, 2014), 302–29, at 314.

2 Arne L. Kelleberg, *Good Jobs, Bad Jobs: The rise of polarized and precarious employment systems in the United States, 1970s–2000s* (New York, Russell Sage Foundation, 2011).

3 Guy Standing, *The Precariat: The new dangerous class* (London, Bloomsbury Academic, 2011).

4 Neil Rollings, 'Cracks in the post-war Keynesian settlement? The role of organised business in the rise of neoliberalism before Margaret Thatcher', *Twentieth Century British History*, 24 (2013), 637–59.

5 Jim Tomlinson, *Hayek and the Market* (London, Pluto Press, 1990), 87–96.

6 Jamie Peck, *Constructions of Neoliberal Reason* (Oxford, Oxford University Press, 2010); and Paul Smith, 'Order in British industrial relations: From Donovan to neoliberalism', *Historical Studies in Industrial Relations*, 31/32 (2011), 115–54.

7 Andrew Gamble, *The Free Economy and the Strong State: The politics of Thatcherism*, 2nd ed. (Basingstoke, Palgrave, 1994).

8 Andy Beckett, *Promised You a Miracle: Why 1980–82 made modern Britain* (London, Allen Lane, 2015), especially Part Four, 'Revolution in the head', 183–288.

9 Valerie Walkerdine, 'Reclassifying upward mobility: Femininity and the neo-liberal subject', *Gender and Education*, 15 (2003), 237–48, at 243.

10 George Stevenson, 'The forgotten strike: Equality, gender, and class in the Trico equal pay strike', *Labour History Review*, 81 (2016), 141–68.

11 Linda McDowell, Sundari Anitha and Ruth Pearson, 'Striking narratives: Class, gender and ethnicity in the "Great Grunwick Strike", London, UK, 1976–1978', *Women's History Review*, 23 (2014), 595–619.

12 Ewan Gibbs and Jim Phillips, 'Who owns a factory? Caterpillar tractors in Uddingston, 1956–1987', *Historical Studies in Industrial Relations*, 39 (2018), 111–37.

13 Mike Foden, Steve Fothergill and Tony Gore, *The State of the Coalfields: Economic and social conditions in the former mining communities of England, Scotland and Wales* (Sheffield, Coalfields Regeneration Trust and Sheffield Hallam University, 2014); and Social Value Lab, *The Scottish Coalfields in 2020. Report for the Coalfields Regeneration Trust* (Glasgow, Social Value Lab and Coalfields Regeneration Trust, 2020).

14 Polly Toynbee and David Walker, *Cameron's Coup: How the Tories took Britain to the brink* (London, Faber and Faber, 2015).

15 Scottish Parliament, Cross-Party Group, Basic Income, https://www.parliament.scot/msps/basic-income.aspx (accessed 16 April 2019).

16 Guy Standing, *Basic Income: And how we can make it happen* (London, Penguin, 2017).

17 *Assessing the Feasibility of Citizens' Basic Income Pilots in Scotland: Final report*, Prepared by the Citizens' Basic Income Feasibility Study Steering Group, June 2020, https://basicincome.scot/2020/06/10/draft-final-report-cbi-feasibility-study, 7–19 (accessed 12 August 2020).

18 David Marquand, *Mammon's Kingdom: An essay on Britain, now* (London, Allen Lane, 2014).

19 W. Ashworth, *The History of the British Coal Industry, Volume 5, 1946–1982: The nationalised industry* (Oxford, Oxford University Press, 1986), 253, 261, 264, table 6.2, Regional distribution of output and manpower, 1957 and 1972–3.

20 Peter Scott, 'Regional development and policy', in Roderick Floud and Paul Johnson (eds), *The Cambridge Economic History of Modern Britain, Volume 3: Structural change and growth, 1939–2000* (Cambridge, Cambridge University Press, 2004), 332–67, with detail at 338.

21 General Registry Office, *Census 1961 Scotland, Occupation and industry. County tables: Dundee, Clackmannan and Fife* (Edinburgh, HMSO, 1966), table 3; and General Registry Office, *Census 1971 Scotland. Economic Activity: County Tables, Part II* (Edinburgh, HMSO, 1975), table 3.

22 Jim Tomlinson, *Managing the Economy, Managing the People: Narratives of economic life in Britain from Beveridge to Brexit* (Oxford, Oxford University Press, 2017), 74–80.

23 John Biffen, 'Keith Joseph (1918–1994), Obituary', *The Guardian* (12 December 1994).

24 STUC General Council, Report of Meeting with Sir Keith Joseph, 10 December 1979, Glasgow Caledonian University Archives (GCUA).

25 Jim Tomlinson, 'Mrs Thatcher's macroeconomic adventurism, 1979–1981, and its political consequences', *British Politics*, 2 (2007), 3–19.

26 James Meek, *Private Island: Why Britain now belongs to someone else* (London, Verso, 2014), 8–24.

27 Anthony B. Atkinson, 'The distribution of income in the UK and OECD countries in the twentieth century', *Oxford Review of Economic Policy*, 15 (1999), 56–75.

28 Tomlinson, *Managing the Economy*, 74–80.

29 *Scottish Abstract of Statistics*, 10 (1981), table 9.3; and *Scottish Abstract of Statistics*, 18 (1989), tables 9.2 (a) and (b).

30 Jim Campbell and Emily Thomson, 'Changing role of women in the Scottish economy', in Kenneth Gibb, Duncan Maclennan, Des McNulty and Michael Comerford (eds), *The Scottish Economy* (London, Routledge, 2018), 135–51.

31 STUC Joint General Council/Women's Committee Seminar (October 1988), GCUA.

32 *Census 1981 Scotland: Report for Fife Region, Volume 1* (Edinburgh, HMSO, 1982), table 2; *1991 Census: Report for Fife Region, Part 2* (Edinburgh, HMSO, 1993), table 72; and *Scotland's Census 2001. Key Statistics for Council Areas and Health Boards Across Scotland* (Edinburgh, HMSO, 2003).

33 *Census 1981 Scotland. Report for Strathclyde Region, Volume 4* (Edinburgh, HMSO, 1983); and *1991 Census. Report for the Strathclyde Region, Part 2* (Edinburgh, HMSO, 1993), table 72.

34 Christine Beatty and Stephen Fothergill, 'Labour market adjustment in areas of chronic industrial decline: The case of the UK coalfields', *Regional Studies*, 30 (1996), 627–40.

35 Noel Whiteside, *Bad Times: Unemployment in British social and political history* (London, Faber Press, 1991).

36 Chris Howell, *Trade Unions and the State: The construction of industrial relations institutions in Britain, 1890–2000* (Princeton, NJ, Princeton University Press, 2005), 131–73.

37 Jim Phillips, 'UK business power and opposition to the Bullock Committee's 1977 proposals for worker directors', *Historical Studies in Industrial Relations*, 31/32 (2011), 1–30.

38 Department of Trade, *Committee of Inquiry on Industrial Democracy*, Cmnd. 6706 (London, HMSO, 1977), 20–2.

39 Martin Adeney and John Lloyd, *The Miners' Strike, 1984–5: Loss without limit* (London, Routledge and Kegan Paul, 1986), 3–4.

40 Tomlinson, *Hayek and the Market*, 87–96.

41 Tom Smith and Dave Howie, former engineering shop stewards at Timex, Dundee, Interview with Valerie Wright and Jim Phillips (Dundee, 3 July 2018).

42 Chris Wrigley, *British Trade Unions since 1933* (Cambridge, Cambridge University Press, 2002), 19–20, 74–8.

43 Paul Davies and Mark Freedland, *Labour Legislation and Public Policy: A contemporary history* (Oxford, Clarendon Press, 1993), 425–525.

44 Andrew Glyn, 'The economic case against pit closures', in D. Cooper and T. Hopper (eds), *Debating Coal Closures: Economic calculation in the coal dispute, 1984–5* (Cambridge, Cambridge University Press, 1988), 57–94.

45 Jean Spence and Carol Stephenson, '"Side by side with our men?" Women's activism, community and gender in the 1984–85 British miners' strike', *International Labor and Working Class History*, 75 (2009), 68–84; and Florence Sutcliffe-Braithwaite and Natalie Thomlinson, 'Women's activism during the miners' strike: Memories and legacies', *Contemporary British History*, 32 (2018), 78–100.

46 David Howell, 'Defiant dominoes: Working miners and the 1984–5 strike', in Ben Jackson and Robert Saunders (eds), *Making Thatcher's Britain* (Cambridge, Cambridge University Press, 2012), 148–64.

47 E. P. Thompson, 'The moral economy of the English crowd in the eighteenth century', *Past & Present*, 50 (1971), 76–136.

48 Ewan Gibbs, 'The moral economy of the Scottish coalfields: Managing deindustrialization under nationalization, c. 1947–1983', *Enterprise and Society*, 19 (2018), 124–52.

49 Jim Phillips, *Scottish Coal Miners in the Twentieth Century* (Edinburgh, Edinburgh University Press, 2019), 199–209.

50 STUC General Council, Economic Committee, 25 November 1969, GCUA.

51 Cabinet Ministerial Group on Coal (CMGC), 30 May, 11 July and 12 September 1984, CAB 130/1268, The National Archives, Kew (TNA).

52 CMGC, 8 May 1984, CAB 130/1268, TNA.

53 National Union of Mineworkers Scottish Area, Strike Committee, 29 October and 19 November 1984, National Mining Museum of Scotland.

54 (Andrew) Turnbull (Private Secretary to the Prime Minister) minute to MT, 'Meeting with David Hart', 7 September 1984, enclosing correspondence from D. Negus of Ellis-Fermour Solicitors, Derby, to David Hart, 30 August 1984, Margaret Thatcher Foundation, http://www.margaretthatcher.org/document/133524 (accessed 21 June 2021).

55 Coal Industry National Consultative Council, 6 March 1984, COAL 74/4783, TNA.

56 Peter Dorey, '"It was just like arming to face the threat of Hitler in the late 1930s": The Ridley Report and the Conservative Party's preparations for the 1984–85 miners' strike', *Historical Studies in Industrial Relations*, 34 (2013), 173–214.

57 National Ports Council, *Digest of Port Statistics* (London, National Ports Council, 1966), tables 10 and 11; and Department of the Environment, Transport and the Regions, *Focus on Ports* (London, HMSO, 2000), November 2000, 68.

58 London Ocean Trades Employers' Association, Executive Committee, 17 October 1967, LAB 10/3233, TNA.
59 CMGC, 11 and 16 July 1984, CAB 130/1268, TNA.
60 *Parliamentary Debates, Sixth Series, Commons*, 64, 33 (16 July 1984).
61 Department of Employment, *Employment in the Ports: The Dock Labour Scheme*, Cm. 664 (London, HMSO, 1989); and Peter Turnbull, Charles Woolfson and John Kelly, *Dock Strike: Conflict and restructuring in Britain's ports* (Aldershot, Avebury, 1992).
62 Peter Turnbull and Victoria Wass, 'The greatest game no more: Redundant dockers and the demise of "dock work"', *Work, Employment and Society*, 8 (1994), 487–506.
63 Brian Marren, 'The Liverpool dock strike, 1995–98: A resurgence of solidarity in the age of globalisation', *Labor History*, 57 (2016), 463–81.
64 Martina Sterber, 'Fundamentals at stake: The Conservatives, industrial relations and the rhetorical framing of the miners' strike in 1984–85', *Contemporary British History*, 32 (2018), 60–77.
65 Sjaak van der Velden, *Global Conflicts Dataverse* (International Institute of Social History), 2016, https://datasets.socialhistory.org/dataverse/labourconflicts (accessed 4 January 2019).
66 Peter Fleming, *The Death of Homo Economicus* (London, Pluto Press, 2017), 10–39.
67 Jean Jenkins, 'Hands not wanted: Closure, and the moral economy of protest, Treorchy, South Wales', *Historical Studies in Industrial Relations*, 38 (2017), 1–36.
68 Jim Tomlinson, 'Tale of a death exaggerated: How Keynesian policies survived the 1970s', *Contemporary British History*, 21 (2007), 429–48.
69 Gordon Brown, *My Scotland, Our Britain: A future worth sharing* (London, Simon & Schuster, 2014), 224–5.
70 *The National Minimum Wage. First Report of the Low Pay Commission*, Cm. 3976 (London, HMSO, June 1998), 22, 31–50, 205–8, 254–5.
71 William Brown, 'Industrial relations in Britain under New Labour, 1997–2010: A post mortem', *Journal of Industrial Relations*, 53 (2011), 402–13.
72 Smith, 'Order in British industrial relations', 149–51.
73 Office for National Statistics, 'Contracts that do not guarantee a minimum of hours' (April 2018), https://www.ons.gov.uk/employmentandlabourmarket/peopleinwork/earningsandworkinghours/articles/contractsthatdonotguaranteeaminimumnumberofhours/april2018#future-of-the-experimental-business-survey (accessed 24 April 2019).
74 UCATT, False Self Employment, https://www.ucatt.org.uk/false-self-employment (accessed 15 March 2017).
75 Scottish Government, 'Offering flexibility to Universal Credit recipients' (31 October 2018), https://www.gov.scot/news/offering-flexibility-to-universal-credit-recipients/ (accessed 24 April 2019).
76 Scottish Government, *Scotland's Future: Your guide to an independent Scotland* (Edinburgh, Scottish Government, 2013), 103–9.
77 Fair Work Convention, 'Effective voice', https://www.fairworkconvention.scot/the-fair-work-framework/effective-voice/ (accessed 24 April 2019).
78 Michael Conn, 'Absent Amber Rudd accused of "bitter betrayal" over Orgreave', *The Guardian* (1 November 2016).
79 Author notes of Public Consultation Meeting, Fallin Miners Welfare Society and Social Club (5 December 2018).
80 Scottish Government, *Independent Review – Impact on Communities of the Policing of the Miners' Strike, 1984–85* (Edinburgh, Scottish Government, 2020); and Scottish Government, Miners' strike review: Justice Secretary update to Parliament 28 October 2020, https://www.gov.scot/publications/miners-strike-review-justice-secretary-update-parliament-28-october-2020 (accessed 28 October 2020).
81 STUC General Council, Scottish Assembly on Unemployment, 14 February 1972, List of Speakers, and Charter of Proposals, GCUA.
82 Emily Robinson, Camilla Schofield, Florence Sutcliffe-Braithwaite and Natalie Thomlinson, 'Telling stories about post-war Britain: Popular individualism and the "crisis" of the 1970s', *Twentieth Century British History*, 28 (2017), 268–304.
83 Jim Phillips, Valerie Wright and Jim Tomlinson, 'Deindustrialization, the Linwood Car Plant and Scotland's Political Divergence from England in the 1960s and 1970s', *Twentieth Century British History*, 30 (2019), 399–423.
84 R. F. Butler, 'Talbot UK', January 1981, National Records of Scotland, SEP 4/4005.

85 Valerie Walkerdine, 'Transmitting class across generations', *Theory & Psychology*, 25 (2015), 167–83.

86 Huw Beynon, Rhys Davies and Steve Davies, 'Sources of variation in trade union membership across the UK: The case of Wales', *Industrial Relations Journal*, 43 (2012), 200–21.

87 Gregor Gall, 'Still brothers and sisters in arms? A note on trends in union membership and statistics', *Scottish Labour History*, 53 (2018), 73–83.

88 Tim Strangleman, 'Deindustrialisation and the historical sociological imagination: Making sense of work and industrial change', *Sociology*, 51 (2017), 466–82.

9

Where was entrepreneurship in post-war Britain? Freedom, family and choice in modern British shopping cultures

Sarah Mass

If British historians were pressed to name the archetypal entrepreneur of the post-war age, many would settle on John Bloom. Bloom was a pioneer of home washing machines in Britain. He started by selling discount models door-to-door in 1958, before moving to newspaper direct sales of Dutch-made twin tub machines in 1958 and 1959. The heights of Bloom's notoriety came in the early 1960s, when he transformed the failing Rolls Razor safety razor company into a modern consumer durable firm. The Rolls Razor business had factories in Swansea and Aycliffe, in addition to a demonstration-manufacturing hub in Cricklewood, London. Connected to these sites were 400 self-employed salesmen and an advertising budget of £2 million, much of it going to the *Daily Mirror.*[1] For these innovations and the modes of their implementation, scholars of enterprise culture point to Bloom as a 'pure case' of entrepreneurship. He not only occupied a stereotypically 'outsider' position in a business that was controlled by manufacturing interests and their retailer allies, but he also sold his own persona right alongside his product.[2] His 1971 autobiography, *It's No Sin to Make a Profit*, pioneered the genre of British entrepreneurial memoir, a tale of singular triumph over an inefficient and archaic marketplace.[3]

Depending on their methodological orientation, scholars of neoliberalism attribute different causal weight to the John Blooms of late capitalism. For those working in the vein of governmentality, the enterprising or entrepreneurial self is the mode by which neoliberalism becomes generalised within a society, linking functionally different schools of economic thought.[4] In management, organisational and workplace studies, scholars argue that the entrepreneurial driving forces of 'competition' and 'excellence' create distinct subjectivities in neoliberal societies; Margaret Thatcher's 1980s enterprise culture and the post-2008 precarious labour market are two of the most trenchant research areas.[5] Across these subfields, 'entrepreneurs' are always ideal types embodying private, possessive, competitive and enterprising values.[6] The social atomisation of the entrepreneur is both the means and the end to neoliberalism's scalar potential: all it takes is one visionary to break free of accepted 'group think' and transform non-market areas of life into enterprise arenas.

In line with ongoing critiques of these models that tacitly accept the entrepreneur as a cult of personality, this chapter turns to the social relations that undergird individualist narratives, paying particular attention to the roles played by gender, family and place in the ascendency of 'enterprise culture' in post-war economic life.[7] If, in the words of one obituarist of John Bloom, the washing machine magnate 'launched two revolutions, one in the kitchen . . . and the second in the high street',[8] what happens when we frame this enterprise revolution of individual freedom and economic competition as contingent and fermenting in various arenas of British society?

For example, Bloom capitalised on wider political and social forces that were destabilising the balance of power in late 1950s and early 1960s economic life. The first was the rising demand for consumer durables and the proliferating ways in which ordinary families could make this dream of the 'good life' a reality. The mass diffusion of household appliances in Britain became possible by the late 1950s and early 1960s, when the country reached the real income per head attained by the US 30 years earlier.[9] Yet, for many consumers, the cost of modern durables still outpaced their real wages, so purchasing items such as washing machines was as often dependent on credit as it was on ready cash. In 1958, a survey found that nearly two-thirds of under-45-year-olds approved of buying on credit. Bloom's business model was built almost entirely on this increasing cultural openness to credit and hire purchase, as well as the (often controversial) legislative changes that allowed consumers to put smaller deposits down on items such as washing machines, refrigerators and televisions.[10]

The rationale of 'price competitiveness' was also becoming a consumerist cry in the 1950s and 1960s. The Tories partially demolished Resale Price Maintenance (RPM) in 1956, before it was completely abolished in 1964. For the first half of the twentieth century, RPM had ensured that branded goods would be sold at a minimum price that was advantageous not only to production interests, but also to small retailers.[11] The demise of RPM is remembered by retail and business historians as the final blow to small shopkeepers and the moment when commercial interests in British retail swung from manufacturing to large-scale retail-distributors such as Tesco and Woolworth's.[12] John Bloom railed against RPM, employing iconoclastic advertising schemes and trading stamps as a way to subvert price minimums.[13] All these bombastic initiatives reflected his belief that entrenched business interests could not and would not give consumers 'value for money'. Like hire purchase and RPM, trading stamps were fiercely debated in the Commons in the late 1950s and early 1960s, with the figure of Bloom hanging over disagreements about the freedom of the market.

In public, Bloom promoted himself as a 'friend of the family' whose methods suited the everyday consumer when entrenched business interests would not. In reality, he benefited from early, elite entanglements between Conservative politics and neoliberal policy influencers. Rolls Razor's board of directors included Tory MP Richard 'Reader' Harris, and the company counted among its allies Ralph Harris, director of the Institute of Economic Affairs (IEA). Both Harris the MP and Harris the think-tank director helped deflect criticism of Rolls Razor in the early to mid-1960s, turning consumer choice and enterprise initiative against political and professional interest groups.[14] For these reasons, media historian Adrian Johns found it unsurprising that the IEA tract 'Piracy as a media force' (1967) held up Bloom as an archetypal pirate of the 1960s.[15] By revealing the self-interest of retail and distribution monopolies, Bloom undercut the moral high ground of entrenched commercial interests.

Historians frame the decade after rationing (1954–64) as the key moment when British politicians shifted their rhetorical appeals to the affluent consumer's pocketbook, often to the detriment of party bases.[16] Scholarship has focused on this tension in the left, where a practice such as RPM drove wedges between wings of the Labour Party and between Labour and their Co-op allies, split as these groups were over workers' rights, wholesale interests and consumer protection.[17] Yet the right faced their own unique challenges around price maintenance. The debate forced the Tories to reckon with 'private enterprise' as either a value that wedded them to their small business voting bloc, or a political economic worldview that might portend a more multinational, corporate future.[18] Whether or not Tories' openness to consumer credit and relaxing of price regulations can be explained by a coherent and enthusiastic uptake of distinctly neoliberal ideas is a live question.[19] Yet there was no doubt that when Rolls Razor went into liquidation in July 1964 – three months before Labour won the general election – critics of Tory policy used Bloom as a cudgel against the freewheeling economic culture he had cultivated within pockets of the Conservative Party.[20] Harold Wilson used Bloom's downfall as a metaphor for Tory political insolvency, while the *New Statesman* prophesised that:

> The rise and fall of Mr John Bloom, may well be regarded, by future historians, as a suitable moral tale to append to 13 years of Tory rule. Here was an ambitious young man who grew up in the Opportunity State and absorbed its atmosphere of unrestrained commercialism almost in the schoolroom.[21]

In the process of decentring the entrepreneurial self from histories of enterprise in post-war Britain, this chapter also seeks to trouble the common historical narrative explored above, where the axis of influence around politicised consumerism ran between figures such as Bloom and party self-fashioning. Rather, I introduce the more everyday idea of post-war 'flexible retailing' – the belief that buying and selling should be freed from political, economic and even temporal and spatial constraints. The rise of 'choice' was not merely taken up by factions of the two major political parties, emerging think tanks or self-service and discount retailers; 'choice' in shopping was integral to the more gradually unfurling politics of place in post-war Britain.[22]

I will focus, therefore, on the material conditions that produced low-cost and, more importantly, flexible retailing activity on the margins of consumer culture from the 1950s to the early 1970s, examining in particular how this activity was driven by women's shifting relationships to the spaces and temporalities of consumer culture. American labour historian Emily LaBarbera-Twarog has recently explored how the late modern housewife became both 'a political constituency group and an imagined ideal'.[23] LaBarbera-Twarog excavates a rich history of consumer activism that pre-dated the conservative women's movement in the US, but whose calls ultimately served as the handmaiden of this political culture on the right. This chapter will take up a similar line of research questioning: how did a British shopping landscape forged in the social democratic ethos of family provisioning ultimately become a terrain of critique for state intervention in the consumer market?

Setting the market 'free' from state intervention is a core feature of neoliberal political economic rhetoric (even if, in reality, the creation and stimulation of competition within markets often required forceful action from the strong state). This chapter argues that flexible retailing's focus on the needs and desires of the 'forgotten consumer' and, moreover, the 'forgotten seller' is an understudied aspect of where and why entrepreneurialism has become a pillar of Britain's late modern social and cultural formation. Mike French and John Davis have explored the deep fermentation of anti-collectivism among groups such as commercial travellers and mini-cab drivers, men who made their own schedules and were defined by their spatial freedoms.[24] Exploring the antecedents of what we now recognise as the 'gig economy', these studies help explain how the rise of individual mobility and the coming of a post-industrial economy fed one another in the mid- to late twentieth century. Yet they both largely overlook how individualist disruptors often succeeded by romanticising the small-scale, even communal, commerce of the past. Scholarship on direct sales and club trading in the Americas and the rise of Walmart as a form of regional commercial populism helps us understand how retail entrepreneurs squared the freedom of the market with nostalgia for family and community in the mid- to late twentieth century.[25] While the religious and political landscape of Britain and Europe at this moment does not facilitate easy comparisons with the US case, this chapter argues that flexible retailing did engender a politics that pitched the 'hard working family' against the excesses of state planning and public spending. John Bloom did not emerge on the consumer market in a vacuum; his success was predicated on a set of demands and needs in the shopping landscape that emerged from the domestic budget and the politics of place.

My focus will be on two moments before and after the early to mid-1960s, when debates around consumerism, credit and affluence clashed in the public sphere. The first case study is the popularity of mobile trading in 1950s Harlow New Town; the second is the growth of Sunday open-air market trading around the Home Counties in the 1970s. Both of these flexible retailing trends were celebrated by their backers as simple solutions to consumer problems created by the local state. In Harlow, residents' associations critiqued the Development Corporation for failing to build enough brick-and-mortar shops to keep the cost of living in the New Town affordable. In the state's absence, mobile shops provided the retail competition and convenience that local authorities had failed to provide. Twenty years later, in the Home Counties, the issue revolved around local authorities' undue policing of open-air markets, ventures that capitalised on consumer demand and underused land. More so than the debate over mobile trading in the 1950s, the debate over open-air markets in the 1970s bled into local political life, and the chapter will end with a biographical survey of market organiser-turned-civic activist Wendy Hobday. As a small business owner, Hobday developed a two-pronged critique of state intervention in retailer–consumer relations (as an entrepreneur) and profligate spending (as a ratepayer). On the surface, Hobday appears to combine the radical retailing of John Bloom with the conservative values of Margaret Thatcher; yet this chapter will show that Hobday is much more than a curious amalgamation of impulses that animated individuals on the British right: her commercial and political causes tapped into the very way that shopping choice was built into the ordinary landscapes of post-war Britain.

Mobile shops and Harlow New Town

The early days of Britain's New Towns have been extensively covered in social and cultural, political, architectural and economic histories.[26] Scholars have predominantly focused on the intertwined debates over the politics of rehousing and the visions of architect-planners: to what extent did New Towns make a conscious break with the past styles and familiar rhythms of British urban life in order to fit the post-war ideals of social democracy? Less studied, however, have been the stopgap measures that Development Corporations developed for provisioning these new communities, in particular the question of how far the state should control business enterprise in order to direct commercial growth.[27]

On paper, the building of brick-and-mortar shops in New Towns was part of the planned socio-economic landscape: the Final Report of the New Towns Committee declared one shop for every 100–150 residents as the ideal ratio.[28] However, the high cost of labour, building materials and licensing restrictions meant that Development Corporations fell far below this number, especially in the first stages of building. The same was true in new council housing developments. When Peter Wilmott and Michael Young travelled to the new estate of Greenleigh, Essex, in the early 1950s, they found one shop for every 300 residents, a far cry from the one shop for every 44 residents to which the former Bethnal Green dwellers were accustomed.[29]

Enterprising mobile shops travelled to these New Towns and new estates – as well as to rural or bomb-damaged areas – in these initial days of constrained central funding for non-essential construction. The National Chamber of Trade estimated that by 1963 there were 11,700 mobile shops with an annual turnover of nearly £100 million, which trebled their profits at the outset of the decade.[30] *The Guardian* referred to these kitted-out vans carrying groceries and other essentials as 'the new pedlars', an economic force that at once harkened back to a world of peripatetic trading while also acknowledging the new retail geography of post-war Britain.[31] While these traders conjured up images of retailing practices gone-by, mobile shops were often offshoots of modern companies that had to adjust to the contemporary realities of working-class residential dispersal. For example, the Co-operative was the largest player in mobile shop activity; by 1958, they owned half of the mobile shops in operation, their growth far outstripping the building of Co-op permanent stores.[32] The viability of mobile shops, in fact, created a feedback loop of growth between chain stores and British automobile manufacturing: along with the Co-operative's own manufacturing arm, firms such as Smith's Delivery Vehicles, Austin Crompton Parkinson and Midland Vehicles tailored their commercial vehicle production to vans, a development that ensured Britain would 'far [outstrip] the rest of Europe in making "the shop that comes to you"'.[33]

Mobile shops were sites of retail innovation, but they also tethered their users to older forms of shopping. The Co-operative was one key operator in this subsection of the retail economy, joined by a fleet of Women's Institute (WI) retail vans.[34] In addition, there were links between mobile trading and the deprivations of rationing during and after the Second World War.[35] Many 'shops on wheels' – like John Bloom – initially launched as distributors for army surplus goods.[36] On a more affective level, the feeling of trust and loyalty that residents held towards these itinerant traders was often quite strong. In the Scottish New Town of Glenrothes, residents were particularly loyal to the mobile traders who had seen them through the difficult period in the late 1940s and early 1950s, when the last days of rationing overlapped with a lack of shops. In residents' words, it would be 'plain thankless' to disregard the service that mobile shops had provided by reregistering with the new permanent shops slowly taking shape in the New Town.[37] By the 1960s, the affective value of the mobile shop existed in relation to a stark new world of supermarkets, with the National Chamber of Trade identifying the 'great intangible in the mobiles' success' as the 'value' that 'housewives put on the personal contact with a roundsman as an alternative to helping themselves among the anonymous, jostling crowd in a confusing neon-lit store'.[38]

Due to low-cost, quick start-up features of mobile shops, many local authorities treated their licensing with indifference. If enterprising traders could fill a consumer need that the cash-strapped state could not, there was little point in regulating their activity in the cul-de-sacs and half-built sites of New Towns and new estates. In Newport and Glasgow, for example, authorities integrated mobile shops into the economic scheme of their new housing estates, encouraging mobile shops as competition drivers and factoring these outlets' usage into their calculations of how many brick-and-mortar shops to provide for residents.[39]

Small shopkeepers – squeezed between these popular informal solutions and the ascendant chain stores – greeted the indifference of local authorities with condemnation. Shopkeepers accused the state of supporting 'unfair competition' from mobile shops, referring to the 'poaching', 'pirating' and 'invasion' that these units brought to new communities.[40] While shopkeepers were subjected to the 'handicap' of shop licensing alongside high labour and material costs, mobile traders could commit minimal capital and meet low overheads by moving from site to site. In the Scottish New Town of East Kilbride, brick-and-mortar traders complained to the Development Corporation about the influx of mobile traders who took advantage of a captive market; one notorious mobile shop commuted every day from neighbouring Ayrshire because the potential profit outweighed the travel costs.[41]

Mobile retailers thus capitalised on a moment of weakness and indecision by small shopkeepers, larger firms and the local state. They met a neglected demand within the market, right when the era of rationing gave way to a period of plenty, when 'enterprise [was] finding outlets in a number of hitherto unattempted directions'.[42] Advertisements for mobile vans in national newspapers reminded prospective mobile traders to 'follow the housewife', not to let trade 'slip through your fingers' and to 'be prepared for increased business'. Van manufacturers – dependent on these outriders for their own business success – therefore focused on nimbleness and alacrity as the traits that would set 1950s retailers in good stead with their imagined consumers. These advertisements, taken alongside the inaction by many local authorities, suggest if not cooperation, then at least an early detente between the freedom of the market and the economic planning of the state. Although Lord Beveridge had imagined the New Towns as a 'housewife's paradise', where the Development Corporation would play a key role in providing amenities for young families, the widespread use of the 'shop on wheels' shows that the fixity of new economic space was shaken from these new communities' inception.[43] In the press, the 'enterprising trader' was referred to multiple times as a figure not to be hindered by vested interests; nor could the mobile shop be held back by building licences, rates and hours legislation that applied to brick-and-mortar shops.[44] The mid-1950s was, therefore, a moment when the role of the state in shaping the physical landscape of the retail economy was insufficient and flexible. Mobile shops capitalised on this insufficiency by compelling both entrenched business and the state to reconsider the relationship between consumer demand and the fixity of the built environment.

From the inception of Harlow New Town, its founders imagined this community in the north-east of London's metropolitan green belt to be a self-contained commercial unit, one whose shopping core would suit the practices and budgets of its new residents. Part of this plan was the support for more informal and low-cost retail outlets. In the internal correspondence of the Development Corporation, officials commented on the common sense of allowing stall-holding to take place in the Market Square *before* brick-and-mortar shops moved in, as this would attract a cheaper trader and a shopping crowd.[45] In the early days of town construction, the Corporation received interest from prospective mobile traders in Ilford, North Finchley and Clapton, all London traders eager to follow their customers into the New Towns around the capital.[46] For those planners tasked with developing networked amenities from scratch, these mobile entrepreneurs were viable alternatives to the larger stores, which were not only constrained by high licensing, labour and material costs, but also tended to refrain from committing to a new consumer market before a steady resident demand was guaranteed.

The openness to flexible retailing, however, was not driven solely by planner–retailer relationships, but by the everyday demands of Harlow's new housewives, overwhelmingly drawn from the working-class districts of London. For shopkeepers in the 1950s, mobile shops had become a catch-all symbol of housewives' passiveness in the consumer market: those who relied on these outlets were 'bone idle', seeing as they did not even need to 'comb their hair' to do the family shopping.[47] Angry housewives responded to these comments from the President of the National Union of Small Shopkeepers by espousing their own agency: 'running a house efficiently is a housewife's business, and, as with any other business, she buys in what she considers to be the best market'.[48] In Harlow, local journalists referred to shopping facilities as the 'single greatest factor' in the lives of Harlow's women, an issue around which they engaged the state and the press. The slow development of the central shopping precinct and the uneven growth of neighbourhood sub-units such as The Stow generated petitioning from local Labour women.[49] While affluent out-of-town shoppers came to use the facilities at The Stow, its pricing and selection did not suit the recent transplants to Harlow itself.[50] To fill this retail void, the Essex WI established the first WI branch market in a New Town, in 'recognition of the needs and difficulties of housewives moved from their own environment to form a new community'.[51] Along with the stopgap solutions that linked country to town, many of these housewives wanted to travel closer to bustling market areas they knew from their childhood. Women demanded bus services to the nearest market centre in Romford, or in some cases travelled all the way back to London street markets in efforts to convince traders to commute and sell cheap consumer goods in Harlow from vans and barrows.[52] Post-war sociology has tended to reinforce the belief that urban dispersal and the lack of a local shop or pub made the lives of women and families more insular and isolated.[53] We should attend, however, to the interventions that housewives made in their local retail markets, organising and advocating for low-cost shopping opportunities that joined together their tight-knit urban districts in London with their new life in overspill and purpose-built communities.

In the mid-1950s, the Development Corporation and the Harlow housewife who suffered 'queuing . . . far beyond moderation' were locked in a battle over the role of enterprise in the socio-economic development of the town. In a shift from their earlier policy, the Development Corporation would *not* sanction a temporary market until their 'official' informal shopping outlet – the Market Square – opened in spring 1956. Consumers and traders alike found ways to work around the local state. In the year before the Market Square opened, there was an increase in trading from private homes, as well as concern around the rising numbers of mobile barrow traders who congregated on Corporation-owned land, in effect creating unsanctioned markets.[54] Consumer demand on these retail fringes built up to such an extent that, when the municipal retail market did open in May 1956, the market department was compelled to reach out to these occasional barrow sellers, asking them to become licensed traders and thus bring their existing customer bases into the official market space.

Mobile shops began on the fringes of the post-war built landscape, but over time they became part of the metaphorical and material core of retail life. Whether individual traders or known names in the world of collective commerce (the Co-op, the WI), mobile operators sold in-demand items and the promise of shopping choice to post-war consumers. Mobile shops' success in locales such as Glenrothes, Glasgow and Harlow shows how retail flexibility disrupted the built landscape of post-war provisioning, with 'forgotten' shoppers and enterprising sellers counterbalancing the planning eye of the British state.

Sunday markets and Wendy Hobday

Harlow in the mid-1950s shows us how the citizen-consumer demand for flexible retailing became a built-in feature of post-war society, to which the state responded unevenly and to which select mobile shops responded enthusiastically. The case of Sunday markets in the 1970s demonstrates how citizen-entrepreneurs politicised this practice to critique the very efficacy of the state in shopping cultures. Two related developments from the mid-1960s to the early 1970s redoubled the focus on shopping as a flexible component of everyday life. The first was the continuing rise of the 'working family' as a dynamic actor in the British political economy. By 1971, over half of married women were employed outside the home. Dolly Smith Wilson has attributed the growth of this demographic group to 'the material and emotional attractions associated with affluence'.[55] The shifting terrain of female employment affected how political parties discussed not only how housewives brought money into the home, but how and when they spent money outside the home. For example, the Conservative manifesto of 1964 did not merely include the abolition of RPM as a policy that would gear the market towards consumers' interests; the party also vowed to review shop hours which were 'particularly inconvenient for the growing number of women at work'.[56] From the mid-1960s to the mid-1970s, Conservative and Labour governments tapped trade organisations and the ever-expanding network of consumer groups in efforts to understand the pros and cons of tailoring shopping to favour the schedules of working women, particularly extending hours past 7.00 p.m. on Fridays and Saturdays and liberalising some forms of Sunday trading.[57]

The continuing breakdown of gendered divisions of labour and temporal divisions of consumption facilitated the second development of this period: the recognition that non-work shaped the late modern British landscape.[58] John K. Walton, for example, has pinpointed the early 1970s as the moment when the industrial weekend essentially 'broke down' under the demands for family leisure and the ubiquity of car culture.[59] By the early 1970s, the freedom of the average British family to spend weekend time together outside the home put pressure on urban and suburban green belt locations: in 1973 one survey estimated that on a summer Sunday, there were nine million countryside day trips made in Britain.[60] As time and mobility became markers of freedom and choice, underdeveloped areas of land along Britain's town and city fringes became sites of concern among policymakers and planning officials.

Quasi-legal Sunday markets emerged at the metaphorical intersection of these shifting tastes and demands in the consumption and leisure arenas. Sunday markets were technically made legal with the 1969 repeal of the 1448 Sunday Fairs Act, which had forbidden these types of commercial gatherings on the Christian Sabbath.[61] Like the mobile traders discussed in the first half of this chapter, Sunday market traders in the 1970s grew their business models in spaces of the built environment that went overlooked or unregulated by the local state. Markets were predominantly held on the 'urban fringe' of towns or cities, where planning regulations were neglected and competing retailers were sparse.[62] Many traders congregated on underused football car parks and greyhound racing stadiums, sporting sites where owners needed to maximise land-use revenue to compensate for shifting leisure tastes.[63] Other Sunday markets were more rural in character, taking place on farms or disused RAF fields across England that were reachable only by private car or hired coach. As cultural and economic innovations, Sunday markets were part of the retail landscape that included supermarkets, discount warehouses, do-it-yourself stores and other forms of out-of-town shopping that appealed to the car-owning family.[64] Open-air Sunday markets resonated with consumers in the 1960s and early 1970s on two levels: they were an outlet for Britons' simultaneous unparalleled leisure spending power and the impulse to 'make ends meet' in an era of rising prices.[65]

This consumer demand for more varied and accessible shopping underwrote 'Wendy Fair', the market firm owned and operated by Ken and Wendy Hobday. Wendy Fair began making headlines in the local and national press in summer 1973. It joined the scrum of Sunday markets that had been growing in competitiveness and popularity since the late 1960s, attracting hundreds of stalls and tens of thousands of customers during their busiest seasons. The Hobdays, owners of a lighting store in Hillingdon, opened Sunday markets near Heathrow Airport and on disused RAF airfields in Buckinghamshire and Hampshire in the early to mid-1970s.[66] Almost immediately, these enterprises attracted the ire of local authorities and local shopkeepers, who argued that holding an open-air market on a Sunday not only contravened trading laws but, in the case of Buckinghamshire, also interfered with county-wide proposals to protect green belt land and slow the environmental degradation brought on by changes in land use and the growth of motor traffic.[67] Wendy Fair, like other market firms, worked through a variety of planning and legal loopholes to keep their rogue business open to eager buyers and sellers. This included rotating the location of the market, employing stallholders as 'department managers' to contravene labour law, and even attempting to register as a 'Jewish company' in order to receive Sunday trading exemption. After incurring fines of more than £1,000, the Hobdays 'took the best legal advice' and decided to transform Wendy Fair into a club trading firm, meaning that customers would pay a nominal fee (between 10 and 20 pence), thereby protecting the company from the regulations of the Shops Act.[68]

More than any other Sunday market firm, Wendy Fair and the Hobdays relied on the club trading model as a method of circumventing shopping hours and labour legislation. They also built up their retail outlet to be far more than a space of simple buying and selling; it was a space of collective non-work. Alongside the stalls selling discount or second-hand home goods, toys and food, Ken and Wendy Hobday also provided steam organs and hot-air balloons, appealing to pleasure-seeking families.[69] The Hobdays dotted their markets along the semi-rural and rural London green belt locales; these choices took advantage not only of underdeveloped land, but also of car-owning young couples who wanted to shop for pleasure together on the weekend, and of young families seeking outdoor leisure. The *Sunday Telegraph* described this new retail environment 'on the runways built for war' in positively Dunkirk-esque terms: 'traders were fighting the archaic laws that forbid the sale of . . . goods on a Sunday and defending the principle of free trading, working when you want to and not when you are told to'.[70] The Hobdays, thus, were the plucky entrepreneurs versus an overbearing state, whose land-use planning regulations and army of shops inspectors were needlessly interfering with the modern needs and desires of hard-working families. At one Hobday market, where 'a lot of the women work[ed] during the week' and left the weekend for housework and shopping, the appeal of Sunday markets was their capacity to bend to the modern working family schedule.[71]

Although the Hobdays were equal partners in the running of Wendy Fair, it was Wendy who elevated independent market trading to a political cause. In addition to her roles operating the string of Wendy Fair markets and running the family lighting shop, Hobday was an active participant in local Hillingdon civil society. She was a member of the Hillingdon Residents' Federation and the Ruislip Residents' Association. In the press coverage of Hobday's amenity activism, her role as a 'local mother' or 'mother of seven' was always at the core of her public persona.

In February 1974, Hobday made her initial entry into national politics when she ran as an independent Conservative candidate for Ruislip-Northwood. One of 143 women running for Parliament (up from 80 at the previous general election), Hobday had defected from the local

Conservative group, marking the first time that the Tories had 'broken ranks' since the Ruislip-Northwood constituency was created in 1950.[72] Running on a broadly 'power to the local people' campaign, Hobday focused on causes that had animated her civic activism in her previous political life: protesting against Compulsory Purchase Orders (CPOs) by the council in the name of public housing and opposing incursions on the green belt. Scaling up to national and international issues, Hobday subscribed to a largely popular consumerist platform that included better protections and prices for consumers, a critical investigation of Common Market membership and the exploration of North Sea oil for the 'benefit of the nation'.

Hobday lost her deposit that February when the establishment Tory MP, Petre Crowder, was returned. This initial setback did not dampen her political ambitions. When a second general election was called in October 1974, Hobday joined with the newly formed United Democratic Party. Comprising disaffected Tories – many of whom had likewise run in the February election as independent Conservatives – the United Democratic Party had its roots in the Conservative heartlands of the South of England (primarily around Somerset and East Anglia).[73] Candidates ran on opposing existing Tory policy, especially Britain's entry into the Common Market. For example, one of Hobday's promises as candidate and south-eastern region chairperson-organiser was to 'set the British people free from bureaucrats' control, whether it be from Brussels, Whitehall or County Hall', in a nod to her roots in local residents' activism.[74]

Hobday was among those small businesspersons whom Andrew Gamble called the base of the Enoch Powell-led Conservative rebels in the late 1960s and early 1970s.[75] Just as the economic facets of Powellism eschewed all state intervention for the benefit of small capital, the primacy of 'freedom' and 'choice' repeatedly returns in Hobday's everywoman political outlook. Whether it was a focus on cutting down bureaucratic institutions, the rights of the homeowner to oppose a CPO, or the importance of grammar schools and school choice, Hobday made the ordinary person railing against the structures and institutions of post-war life the key voter in her campaign. When her share of the vote moved little from its February levels, Hobday then threw her political efforts back into the local realm. As a critical player in ratepaying campaigns in the mid-1970s, Hobday drew on her background in small business and her persona as a 'common sense' housewife to protest the increase in homeowners' and business rates against the spending habits of Hillingdon Council. In methods that mirrored her tactics at Wendy Fair, Hobday helped organise subscriptions to mitigate the legal costs of withholding rates, constantly searching for stipulations in local government acts that would allow a private citizen to protest against state policy and spending.

In 1978 borough elections, Hobday combined her small business background with her ratepaying activism by launching a hyper-local organisation in Hillingdon, the 'We Mean Business' group, backed by the National Federation of the Self Employed.[76] The group members came from eclectic backgrounds: small business owners like the Hobdays, but also trade unionists, tradesmen and professionals. The cause that united the group was, again, the belief that standard party politics no longer represented the views of constituents. Profligate spending and obfuscated council deals had increased the distance between the electorate and political power; only by 'taking the politics out of government' would there be a local council that worked for the many. Although 'non-party' in name, the manifesto of the group previews many of the tenets of the Thatcherite national project that would enter Downing Street in less than a year: 'pruning out of all dead wood' and 'removal of political animals', the encouragement of home ownership in 'all its aspects', curtailing closed shop trade union policies, reducing the borough debt, law and order policing, and the stimulation of small businesses as the root of tackling unemployment.[77]

Hobday was an entrepreneur in the mould of Bloom: she claimed the British state's anachronistic interference in retail markets was a hindrance to the freedom of the British shopping family. Linking her tactics and politics to an earlier history of enterprise culture rooted in alternative uses of lived space, however, reveals new facets of the development of neoliberal logics in everyday life. By starting this story with retail provisioning in late 1940s and 1950s New Towns, we see how, from their inception, proposals to plan and rationalise shopping space often clashed with the immediate, day-to-day needs of consumers. The mobile shop, the self-proclaimed saviour of the under-provisioned family, was thus a curious case of anachronistic retail that had contemporary purchase. Fast-forward to the 1970s, when support for state intervention in economic relations and the built environment was fraying at the national and local political level. Wendy Hobday harnessed her dual identity as retail disruptor and concerned housewife to galvanise a renewed vision of 'collective' consumerism and leisure outside social democratic structures and in opposition to outdated laws. Figures such as Wendy Hobday expand the actors who count as entrepreneurs in the post-war period. She leveraged 'freedom' and 'choice' not merely as free-market signals, but as values that had their roots in the spatial and temporal autonomy of family life in late modern Britain.

Conclusion

This chapter opened with the iconoclasm of John Bloom, a retail hero in Britain's 'age of affluence'. From a twenty-first-century perspective, Bloom's entrepreneurialism both embodies and anticipates many of the accepted timelines of post-war Britain: the short life of social democracy, a national polity comprised of 'consumers' rather than 'producers' and, most germane to the contents of this volume, the implication of proto-neoliberal thought within various corners of the political and social right. Bloom was a pioneer of direct sales in Britain, a model of retail that depended on disrupting the very spaces of buying and selling in order to keep overheads low and sales buoyant. The art of the 'deal', then, was not made in the high street, the shopping precinct or the showroom; it was closed through the newspaper advertisement, the catalogue and the parlour. Bloom's focus on *choice* in his business model was one instance of a larger trend in diffuse methods of sale in the 1950s through the 1970s: the modern British housewife should have the best products and best prices available without the interference of state or vested interests.

The posthumous evaluations of Bloom's legacy tend to draw a direct line between his disruptive vision in the 1950s and 1960s and today's discount retail entrepreneurs,[78] whether those are pound shop fixtures on the high street or the 'anytime, anywhere' methods of Amazon. I have told a different story in this chapter, one that places emphasis on how a market for 'freedom' and 'choice' in retailing was collectively created, not individually invented. Even the self-promoting Bloom could see that change in the consumer market was made through infiltrating its pre-existing communal spaces. His prodigious *Daily Mirror* advertisements rely, often, on appealing to the lone housewife or the married couple. In the second half of 1962, Rolls Razor's *Daily Mirror* advertising chose to target the British housewife in those moments of community and exchange that defined her larger homosocial network.[79] Quarter- or half-page advertisements include groups of women discussing Rolls Razor's merits across hedges in their interwar suburban housing, or while sitting in a row opposite prams with babies who remind the reader that 'Mummy did not have to drag off to the shops. She just saved oodles of boodle by buying DIRECT FROM FACTORY and by-passing all middlemen's costs.'[80] Advertisers didn't always imagine that their consumers stayed within the confines of the residential neighbourhood; other versions show women discussing the merits of twin-tub washing machines in their local hairdresser or while being waited upon in a shoe shop.[81]

The most striking pages, however, are those that place Rolls Razor at the heart of women's sociable, non-shopping lives: a women's choir reading off the literal 'praises' of Rolls Razor from the hymn books, or a collective of smartly dressed women, gathered with placards, who appear to be marching for the company. Women's calls to 'Join Us! Join Us!' are, on one level, group-think marketing. Yet read on a different rhetorical level, this message evokes the ordinary networks and landscapes through which demands for 'flexible' retailing grew in voice between the 1950s and the 1970s. By integrating the lesser-known activism of the housewives of Harlow and the causes of Wendy Fair into the familiar story of the heroic entrepreneur, we are better equipped to see how demand for commercial flexibility in post-war retail and shopping life was generated through collective action, not just through an outriding disruptor.

Notes

1 Margaret Laing, 'The electric man', *The Sunday Times Colour Magazine* (22 March 1964).
2 Peter Armstrong, 'Entrepreneurial competition in the pure case: John Bloom and Jim Elkins', in Peter Armstrong, *Critique of Entrepreneurship: People and policy* (Basingstoke, Palgrave Macmillan, 2005), 45–60.
3 See memoirs of Jack Cohen, Richard Branson, James Dyson and Chris Edwards for legacies of the genre.
4 Nikolas Rose, 'Governing the enterprising self', in Paul Heelas and Paul Morris (eds), *The Values of Enterprise Culture: The moral debate* (London, Unwin Hyman, 1992), 141–164; and Ulrich Bröckling, *The Entrepreneurial Self: Fabricating a new type of subject* (Los Angeles, SAGE, 2016).
5 Paul Du Gay, *Consumption and Identity at Work* (Los Angeles, SAGE, 1996); and Christina Scharff, 'The psychic life of neoliberalism: Mapping the contours of entrepreneurial subjectivity', *Theory, Culture & Society*, 33 (2016), 107–22.
6 Du Gay, *Consumption and Identity*, 62.
7 John Patrick Leary, *Keywords: The new language of capitalism* (Chicago, Haymarket Books, 2018), 138; Friederike Welter, 'Contextualising entrepreneurship: Conceptual challenges and ways forward', *Entrepreneurship, Theory & Practice*, 35 (2011), 165–84; and Tony J. Watson, 'Entrepreneurial action and the Euro-American social science tradition: Pragmatism, realism and looking beyond "the entrepreneur"', *Entrepreneurship & Regional Development*, 25 (2013), 16–33.
8 'Obituary: John Bloom', *Daily Telegraph* (6 March 2019), 29.
9 Sue Bowden and Avner Offer, 'Household appliances and the use of time: The United States and Britain since the 1920s', *Economic History Review*, 47 (1994), 725–48, at 730.
10 Stuart Aveyard, Paul Corthorn and Sean O'Connell, *The Politics of Consumer Credit in the UK, 1938–1992* (Oxford, Oxford University Press, 2018), 72–92.
11 See Janice Winship, 'Culture of restraint: The British chain store 1920–1939', in Michelle Lowe, Daniel Miller, Frank Mort and Peter Jackson (eds), *Commercial Cultures: Economies, practices, spaces* (Oxford, Berg, 2000), 15–34 for an overview of the British case. For international examples of the importance of fixed prices for diverse varieties of economic populism, see Bethany Moreton, *To Serve God and Walmart: The making of Christian free enterprise* (Cambridge, MA, Harvard University Press, 2010), 6–23; and Jan Logemann, *Trams or Tailfins? Public and private prosperity in postwar West Germany and the United States* (Chicago, University of Chicago Press, 2012), 48–9.
12 Helen Mercer, 'The making of the modern retail market: Economic theory, business interests and economic policy in the passage of the 1964 Resale Prices Act', *Business History*, 59 (2017), 778–801, at 793; and Helen Mercer, 'Retailer–supplier relationships before and after the Resale

Prices Act, 1964: A turning point in British economic history?', *Enterprise & Society*, 15 (2014), 132–65, at 152.

13 Originating in the US, trading stamps were tokens given out by retailers to establish customer loyalty. They could be collected and exchanged for a wide range of consumer durables from the stamp-issuing company. In Britain, Green Shield controlled over 60 per cent of the trading stamp business in the early 1960s. See Carlo Morelli, 'Constructing a balance between price and non-price competition in British multiple food retailing, 1954–1964', *Business History*, 40 (1998), 45–61, at 54.

14 In the case of backbencher Reader Harris, this meant going against members of his own party. See his response to Philip Goodhart (C, Beckenham) where Harris states that Goodhart is in the pocket of the Retailing Trading Standards Association, organisations that are unprepared for the fact that 'methods of selling in this country are changing. The old method of selling through a small retail shop in each town is disappearing. The supermarket is coming, and the small shopkeeper is being pushed out . . . Direct sellers are here to stay, and I think that the new methods of selling are, by and large, to the advantage of the public.' Commons Sitting of Friday, 8 December 1961. Fifth Series, Volume 650, columns 1796–7; and Ralph Harris, 'Letter to the Editor: A Competitive Market', *The Times* (22 July 1964), 11.

15 Adrian Johns, 'Piracy as a business force', *Culture Machine*, 10 (2009), 53–4.

16 The literature here is vast; see Lawrence Black, *Redefining British Politics: Culture, consumerism and participation, 1954–1970* (Basingstoke, Palgrave Macmillan, 2010) for a definitive account.

17 Black, *Redefining British Politics*; and David Stewart, '"The people's main defence against monopoly"? The Co-op, the Labour Party and Resale Price Maintenance, 1918–1964', in Emmanuelle Avril and Yann Béliard (eds), *Labour United and Divided from the 1830s to the Present* (Manchester, Manchester University Press, 2018), 101–21.

18 Richard Findley, 'The Conservative Party and defeat: The significance of Resale Price Maintenance for the general election of 1964', *Twentieth Century British History*, 12 (2001), 327–53; Stuart Mitchell, 'Resale Price Maintenance and the character of resistance in the Conservative Party: 1949–64', *Canadian Journal of History/Annales canadiennes d'histoire*, 40 (2005), 259–88; and Mercer, 'Making of the modern retail market'.

19 Christopher Payne is one of the few scholars who draws direct lines between the language of consumerism and credit during this period and the rise of neoliberalism. See Christopher Payne, *The Consumer, Credit and Neoliberalism: Governing the modern economy* (London, Routledge, 2011).

20 The failure of Rolls Razor was due to a combination of a postal strike disrupting orders, big retail competitors adapting to price cutting and bankers losing confidence in Bloom's hire purchase scheme.

21 'The Blooms and the Bowgroupers', *New Statesman* (24 July 1964), 105.

22 For a critique of top-down approaches to the New Right, see Lawrence Black, '1968 and all That(cher): Cultures of conservatism and the New Right in Britain', in Anna von Der Goltz and Britta Waldschmidt-Nelson (eds), *Inventing the Silent Majority in Western Europe and the United States* (Cambridge, Cambridge University Press, 2017), 356–76.

23 Emily E. LaBarbera-Twarog, *Politics of the Pantry: Housewives, food, and consumer protest in twentieth-century America* (Oxford, Oxford University Press, 2017), 2.

24 Mike French, 'Slowly becoming sales promotion men? Negotiating the career of the sales representative in Britain, 1920s–1970s', *Enterprise & Society,* 17 (2016), 39–79; and John Davis, 'The London cabbie and the rise of Essex man', in Clare V. J. Griffiths, James J. Nott and William Whyte (eds), *Classes, Cultures, and Politics: Essays on British history for Ross McKibbin* (Oxford, Oxford University Press, 2011), 102–20.

25 Jessica Burch, '"Soap and hope": Direct sales and the culture of work and capitalism in postwar America', *Enterprise & Society*, 17 (2016), 741–51; Jessica Burch, *Door-to-Door Capitalism: Direct selling in America from the New Deal to the internet age* (New York, Columbia University Press, forthcoming); Peter S. Cahn, *Direct Sales and Direct Faith in Latin America* (Basingstoke, Palgrave Macmillan, 2011); and Moreton, *Serve God and Walmart*.

26 Mark Clapson, *Invincible Green Suburbs, Brave New Towns: Social change and urban dispersal in postwar England* (Manchester, Manchester University Press, 1998); Andrew Homer, 'Creating new communities: The role of the neighbourhood unit in post-war British planning', *Contemporary British History*, 14 (2000), 63–80; and John Boughton, *Municipal Dreams: The rise and fall of council housing* (London, Verso, 2018), 61–138. For more recent global and

post-colonial treatments, see Rosemary Wakeman, *Practicing Utopia: An intellectual history of the New Town movement* (Chicago, University of Chicago Press, 2016); and Jesse Meredith, 'Decolonizing the New Town: Roy Gazzard and the making of Killingworth Township', *Journal of British Studies*, 57 (2018), 333–62. For contemporary studies, see Peter Wilmott, 'Housing density and town design in a New Town', *Town Planning Review*, 33 (1962), 115–27. For a new perspective that shifts the politics of housing to a grassroots perspective, see Helena Rivera, 'Political ideology and housing supply: Rethinking New Towns and the building of new communities in England' (Ph.D. thesis, University College London, 2015).

27 Although technically about overspill estates and not New Towns, one exception has been the recent work from James Greenhalgh, particularly chapter 3 in James Greenhalgh, *Reconstructing Modernity: Space, power, and governance in mid-twentieth century British cities* (Manchester, Manchester University Press, 2018).

28 Anthony Goss, 'Neighbourhood units in British New Towns', *Town Planning Review*, 32 (1961), 73–4.

29 Michael Young and Peter Wilmott, *Family and Kinship in East London* (London, Routledge, 1957), 116.

30 'Modern forms of retailing', *The National Chamber of Trade Journal* (January–February 1964), 8. In comparison, the Census of Distribution for 1961 shows that the Co-operative as a whole had a turnover of £959 million, multiples with more than 10 branches £2,586 million. However, the rate of increase over the decade fell short of the mobile shop phenomenon. The Co-operative grew at a rate of 70 per cent, larger multiples at 136 per cent. 'First Results from 1961 Census of Distribution', *Financial Times* (8 February 1963), 18.

31 'The new pedlars', *The Guardian* (28 January 1955), 8.

32 'Shops on wheels', *Financial Times* (12 February 1958), 6.

33 'Shops on wheels – and Britain leads the way', *Lancashire Evening Post* (20 September 1956), 9. Smith's of Gateshead made a splash in the mid-1950s by exporting mobile shops to the Turkish and Puerto Rican markets in efforts to 'bring down retail prices by increasing efficiency and cutting distributive overheads' in those countries. *Shields Daily News* (9 September 1954), 6; and 'Puerto Rico buys mobile shops', *Coventry Evening Telegraph* (23 July 1956), 7.

34 See Nicole Robertson, *The Co-operative Movement and Communities in Britain, 1914–1960* (London, Routledge, 2016); and Maggie Andrews, 'The WI's rural retailing and markets 1915–1939: A First World War legacy', *History of Retailing and Consumption*, 1 (2015), 89–104, on the tensions between community and consumerism in the Co-operative movement and the WI.

35 See 'Britain's "shadow larder": Food ministry is ready to meet any emergency', *Shields Daily News* (15 August 1941), 4; and 'Mobile meat shop: Birmingham's lead to the country', *Birmingham Mail* (16 February 1942), 1.

36 'Travelling shops: An Irish point of view', *The National Chamber of Trade Journal* (January 1952), 7.

37 *Fifeshire Advertiser* (24 May 1952), 5. See a similar story for the 1960s in Kirkby New Town: N. L. Chapple, 'Community–police relations in Kirkby New Town', *The Police Journal* (1976), 294.

38 'Modern forms of retailing', 8.

39 *The National Chamber of Trade Journal* (April 1957), 66; The Survey Report – The First Quinquennial Review of the Development Plan – 1960, 9, Glasgow City Archives, D-AP 1/4a; and D. R. Diamond and E. B. Gibb, 'Development of new shopping centres: Area estimation', *Scottish Journal of Political Economy*, 9 (1962), 130–46, at 144.

40 'What our readers say – a new UNO pact', *Sunderland Daily Echo and Shipping Gazette* (8 October 1948), 2; 'Mobile shops', *Harlow Citizen* (14 May 1954); 'Leeds grocers hit out at "Buccaneers"', *Yorkshire Evening News* (23 July 1958); and 'Leeds move against pirate mobile shops', *Yorkshire Evening News* (2 September 1958).

41 'Mobile shops', *Harlow Citizen* (14 May 1954).

42 *Sixty-second Annual Report of the Board of Management, The National Chamber of Trade* (London, 1959–60), 23.

43 Boughton, *Municipal Dreams*, 78–9.

44 'The new pedlars'; 'Mobile shops', *The Guardian* (27 May 1957), 2; and 'Shops on wheels', *The Guardian* (24 September 1958), 6.

45 Copy to General Manager for information, 3 January 1950, Essex Record Office (ERO) ERO A6306 Box 330, Town Centre.

46 Letters from J. H. Burke, Theresa Hart and D. Sopler to Harlow Development Corporation, ERO A6306 Box 330.
47 '"Housewife is getting lazier every day"', *Birmingham Daily Gazette* (21 June 1956), 3.
48 'Letter from Mrs. Winifred Evans', *Birmingham Daily Post* (10 December 1957), 6; and Joyce Chesterson, 'So he thinks we housewives are lazy', *Daily Herald* (4 July 1956), 6.
49 'Labour women want market', *Harlow Citizen* (12 March 1954), 7; and Memorandum from Liaison Officer to General Manager, 13 August 1954, ERO A10417 Box 10.
50 'Two-year wait for town centre shopping', *Harlow Citizen* (13 August 1954), 1.
51 'Congratulations to Harlow New Town market', *Home and Country* (January 1953), 9.
52 'Residents want shopping trips to Romford', *Harlow Citizen* (20 August 1954), 1; and 'Feathers fly in Harlow in court', *Harlow Citizen* (29 April 1955), 11.
53 Young and Willmott, *Family and Kinship*, 126.
54 'Barrow boys come to town', *Harlow Citizen* (9 September 1955), 1, 6.
55 Dolly Smith Wilson, 'A new look at the affluent worker: The good working mother in post-war Britain', *Twentieth Century British History*, 17 (2006), 206–29, at 210.
56 'The Conservative Party's manifesto for "prosperity with a purpose"', *The Times* (18 September 1964), 16.
57 'Report of the Crathorne Committee' (London, HMSO, 1964); 'Retail trading hours: Suggested provisions for amending the Shops Act, 1950' (London, HMSO, 1965); 'Shopping habits and attitudes to shop hours in Great Britain' (London, HMSO, 1975); and Economic Development Council (EDC), *The Future Pattern of Shopping* (London, HMSO, 1971).
58 For an overview of this moment, see Chris Rojek, 'The leisure society thesis and its consequences', in Chris Rojek, *The Labour of Leisure: The culture of free time* (London, SAGE, 2010), 21–52.
59 John K. Walton, 'From institution to fragmentation: The making and unmaking of the British weekend', *Leisure Studies*, 33 (2014), 209–10.
60 Nigel Curry, *Countryside Recreation, Access and Land Use Planning* (London, E & FN Spon, 1994), 85; Michael Dower, *The Fourth Wave: The challenge of leisure* (London, The Civic Trust, 1965); and Kenneth Roberts, *Contemporary Society and the Growth of Leisure* (London, Longman, 1978), 19.
61 According to the 1950 Shops Act, however, most items sold at a general goods market would still be barred.
62 J. Davidson, 'The urban fringe', *Countryside Recreation Review*, 1 (1976), 2–7.
63 The aggregate attendance at football matches halved between the early 1950s and the 1980s. Richard Holt has attributed this decline to the rise of Saturday afternoon as 'family' leisure time. Richard Holt, *Sport and the British* (Oxford, Clarendon Press, 1989), 335.
64 For a summary of these trends, see EDC, *Future Pattern of Shopping*.
65 Mark Dunton, 'Public relations and the Price Commission, 1973–74', *Archives*, 52 (2017), 12–25.
66 Roland Adburgham, 'Market men fight Never on Sunday law', *Sunday Times* (15 July 1973), 54.
67 Linda Millington, 'Why can't I sell it if they want it', *Birmingham Daily Post* (10 August 1973), 8; and Minute Book of Finance, Planning, Staff and Salaries Committees, Buckingham Rural District Council. Application no. BR/80/73 (23 May 1973), Wendy Fair Market Operators, Ruislip, Centre for Buckinghamshire Studies, DC 5/1/33.
68 Robert Millar, 'Why some faiths make big profits on a Sunday', *Daily Express* (19 July 1976), 8.
69 Adburgham, 'Market men fight Never on Sunday law'.
70 John Smalldon, 'Where Sunday is market day', *Sunday Telegraph* (8 May 1977), 7.
71 'Coventry faces market "war"', *Coventry Evening Telegraph* (24 May 1976), 1.
72 'The would-be women MPs . . . all 143 of them', *Daily Mail* (25 February 1974), 16–17; and 'Surprise rebel candidate splits Tory workers', *Ruislip-Northwood Gazette* (21 February 1974), 1.
73 David Boothroyd, *The History of British Political Parties* (London, Politicos Publishing, 2001), 325–6.
74 'Candidate helps in new party', *Ruislip-Northwood Gazette* (30 May 1974), 13; and 'Wendy Hobday, United Democrat', *Ruislip-Northwood Gazette* (3 October 1974), 11.
75 Andrew Gamble, *The Conservative Nation* (London, Routledge and Kegan Paul, 1974), 117.
76 '"We mean business" pledge to voters', *Ruislip-Northwood Gazette* (13 October 1977), 13.

77 'We mean business' – Candidates for Local Council Elections, LSC/ELL, Local Elections.
78 See obituaries in *The Guardian*, *The Times*, *Daily Telegraph* and *Financial Times*.
79 For more on the relationship between mail order and female sociability, see Sean O'Connell, *Credit and Community: Working-class debt in the UK since 1880* (Oxford, Oxford University Press, 2009), 101.
80 *Daily Mirror* (3 July 1962); and *Daily Mirror* (10 December 1962).
81 *Daily Mirror* (24 September 1962); and *Daily Mirror* (2 October 1962).

Part III
Politics

10

'The privatisation of the struggle': anti-racism in the age of enterprise

Camilla Schofield, Florence Sutcliffe-Braithwaite and Rob Waters

Neoliberalism – to the surprise of some – has seemingly been able to accommodate multiculturalism, diversity and even forms of anti-racism: as Paul Gilroy has written, '[e]ven if racism remains intractable elsewhere, it seems that neoliberal capitalism is ready to free itself from the fetters placed upon it by the historic commitment to pigmentocracy'.[1] Quinn Slobodian's work illuminates how neoliberal theorists approached 'race' and racism. He finds that explicit racism was 'not the norm' for neoliberals; like most white political theorists after the Second World War, they rejected scientific racism.[2] The key concern of thinkers such as Friedrich Hayek and Milton Friedman, however, was to find rules and institutions to insulate the global market from economic nationalism and from national democratic processes that might disrupt markets. They thus tended to think that the *market* was the ultimate neutral force that would undermine racism; but, because their priority was creating a world of rule-bound free markets, they were often lax or equivocal about racism contained within the boundaries of the nation state. Some even argued that citizens of colour without equal civil rights should only *slowly* be given those rights, in order that they should not use them to disrupt markets.[3] Just as imperialists had consigned colonised peoples to the 'waiting room' of history,[4] supposedly not yet ready for liberal democracy, some neoliberals consigned people of colour to wait patiently to come into their full rights under neoliberalism.

Slobodian's focus is on the theory of neoliberalism. In practice, neoliberal capitalism has increasingly been seen to benefit from an active association with 'diversity' and multiculturalism. In 1997, Slavoj Žižek called multiculturalism 'the cultural logic of multinational capitalism', and from the 1990s onwards, the global actors which have promoted neoliberal reforms such as privatisation (for example, the World Bank, the Organisation for Economic Co-operation and Development and the European Union), have also promoted multiculturalism.[5] Some scholars have suggested that this is simply 'cover' for a damaging economic agenda which promotes the interests of the wealthy and the global North, or an attempt to close down 'the Pandora's box of race'.[6] Others, however, have identified a more active synergy between neoliberalism, multiculturalism and diversity. Multiculturalism – albeit in an attenuated form – enables ethnic minorities to leverage their social and cultural capital and transnational networks; a diverse business can access new markets, new consumers and new ideas; and multicultural places are often more attractive to skilled workers and entrepreneurs.[7] Whatever their stance, though, most critical commentators have seen neoliberalism as, in fact, largely or wholly negative for people of colour, because they tend to be less economically advantaged and so suffer disproportionately in a neoliberal economy, because neoliberal claims to be 'post-racial' generally function to *reinforce* structures of racial discrimination and disadvantage, because commodifying ethnic diversity works against collectivist projects to transform those structures and, finally, because 'consumer multiculturalism' does little to tackle racism.[8]

In the British context, discussions of the connections between neoliberalism, multiculturalism and anti-racism have focused on analyses of New Labour. Where, as Will Kymlicka suggests, the 'first wave of neoliberals', including Margaret Thatcher, was critical of multiculturalism, equal opportunities and anti-racism, seeing these formations as 'a pathology of the interventionist welfare state',[9] later neoliberals presented themselves as anti-racist and proudly multicultural. Nisha Kapoor has argued that New Labour's ideology was the British version of the neoliberal 'post-race' discourse found in the United States under Barack Obama.[10] Other scholars, however, have emphasised the conflicting and contradictory tendencies contained within New Labour's approach to race and racism: neoliberalism was only one influence among many. New Labour, in this reading, could neither 'mourn its imperial ghosts, nor embrace a democratic and truly multicultural future'.[11] We take up this argument: while neoliberal assumptions are clearly visible in New Labour's policies and rhetoric on race and racism, New Right neoliberalism was certainly not the only ideology that shaped New Labour. There were also significant continuities with aspects of the multiculturalist, equal opportunities and anti-racist activism of the 1970s and 1980s, and with elements of the meritocratic ideology that suffused social democracy in Britain.

The possible connections between neoliberalism, multiculturalism and anti-racism in Britain, moreover, do not begin and end with New Labour. In this chapter, we also show how neoliberal rationalities operated as active ingredients of Black political culture in late twentieth-century Britain. Neoliberalism was not simply an ideology, culture or practice foisted upon Black communities from the outside. The story of Black politics in Britain in the 1980s is usually told as one of defeat and rupture. The 1970s was a moment of dynamic and radical activism, when Blackness was imagined as a *political identity* held to have the ability to unite all colonised and oppressed peoples, whatever their skin colour.[12] Some scholars have seen the incorporation of Black activists into the local state in the 1980s as co-optation, leading to the abandonment of the powerful notion of political Blackness in favour of divisive organisation on the basis of different 'ethnicities', with groups competing rather than working collectively for systemic transformation.[13] In particular, Gilroy has criticised activists who, in turning activism into a career in diversity consultancy, 'accepted the privatisation of the struggle against racial inequality and hierarchy':

> . . . armed with all the tools and techniques of neoliberal revolution which are disposed to refine and enhance capitalist control of social and cultural life rather than to feed the possibilities of any alternative to it.[14]

Other scholars have looked more favourably on the anti-racist work of activists working in and with local authorities in the 1980s; but, on this view, Thatcher's abolition of the Greater London Council (GLC) and cuts to local authority budgets in the later 1980s appear as moments of profound defeat.[15] A third strand in the literature on Black politics in the 1980s suggests that Thatcherism drew to the fore traditions of 'hustling' and entrepreneurship with a long history in Black culture, marginalising traditions of collectivism.[16] When the 1980s is identified as a moment of defeat, then, Thatcherism and/or neoliberalism generally appear as the key antagonists. In this chapter, however, we set out a more nuanced story, alert to the successes of Black and ethnic minority activism in the 1980s and 1990s alongside the failures, and to continuities and radical inheritances.

It is important to recognise that Black and anti-racist activism in the 1970s and 1980s was far from homogeneous, with a radical, anti-capitalist and anti-imperialist end and a more moderate, ameliorative end: there were more and less radical versions of equal opportunities, self-help, multiculturalism and anti-racism, and vigorous debates between different tendencies. 'Equal opportunities' could mean removing formal barriers to opportunity, or actively working to ensure disadvantaged groups had substantive opportunities.[17] 'Self-help' initiatives – which were on the rise in urban communities in Britain in the 1970s – could emphasise the importance of radical, autonomous collectives but were also often understood in very different political terms as a model of 'self-improvement', sometimes even inhabiting the moralising (and often highly racialised) discourse of the deserving and undeserving poor.[18] Self-help thus had both individualistic and collectivist forms. In the 1970s and early 1980s, the more radical versions of these ideologies were in the ascendant; this changed in the 1980s, under the influence of Thatcherism – and several other forces. In accounting for the trajectory of Black activism in Britain in the 1980s, we must pay attention to more than simply Thatcher. In the late 1970s, many activists of the New Left decided to go 'into the state', feeling this was crucial to achieving many of their goals; in the early 1980s, the New Urban Left entered its most fertile period. After the uprisings of 1980 and 1981, the Thatcher governments were forced to significantly expand funding for inner-city areas. It was in this context that Black activism in Britain was reoriented, and less radical versions of multiculturalism, anti-racism and Black enterprise traditions were drawn to the fore; these were not, however, simply impositions from outside 'authentic' Black radicalism, and this rearticulation should not be seen as a simple capitulation to neoliberalism.

In this chapter we work backwards. First, we examine the New Labour years, showing how a complex array of anti-racist, equal opportunities and multicultural ideologies shaped New Labour policymaking, alongside a celebration of 'ethnic minority enterprise'. We then move back to the post-1981 period and trace the pre-history and development of these ideas in the New Urban Left and the activist circles of the 1980s; finally, we move back in time again, to examine the Black enterprise culture of the pre-Thatcher period.

Anti-racist ideology and practice in New Labour's Britain, *c.* 1997–2010

At the turn of the millennium, the chair of the Commission for Racial Equality (CRE), Herman Ouseley, commented on the 'mood of optimism' that accompanied New Labour's election.[19] Trevor Phillips, too, speaking in 2009 as chair of the Equality and Human Rights Commission (EHRC), depicted New Labour as transformational: '[Y]ou had a government which was full of people who saw being in the right place on race and racial discrimination as a symbol of progressive politics.'[20] In 1998, Gordon Brown celebrated 'a multicultural multi-ethnic and multinational Britain',[21] and just months after the party's election victory in 1997, Jack Straw commissioned the Macpherson Inquiry into the botched investigation of the murder of Stephen Lawrence. Macpherson concluded, in explicit contrast to the Scarman report into the disturbances in Brixton in 1981, that the Metropolitan Police Service was institutionally racist.[22] The Race Relations (Amendment) Act 2000 responded to Macpherson's recommendations; monitoring began of the recruitment and retention of ethnic minority staff in public services, and racial awareness training was promoted. New Labour's self-image was, thus, proudly multicultural and anti-racist. Yet, particularly after 2001 – the year that saw the 9/11 attacks as well as the resurgence of a language of crisis around 'community relations' and public order after the Bradford and Oldham riots – many scholars identified continuities with the Thatcherite approach to race.[23] New Labour rhetoric began to focus more on 'integration' and 'belonging and identity'.[24] Policies known to disproportionately affect Black people, such as encouragement of plea bargaining, were introduced in order to seem 'tough on crime', and Macpherson's recommendations were deprioritised.[25] New Labour's approach to asylum seekers intensified previous Conservative governments' hostile policies.[26] The rhetoric of the 'war on terror' and 'clash of civilisations' demonised Muslims,[27] and the language of race and ethnicity was 'increasingly effaced from discussion'.[28] But we should not entirely dismiss the testimonies of Ouseley and Phillips: what they suggest is that alongside the influence of neoliberal rationalities (and older Conservative/conservative discourses on race) we can also see, in the New Labour years, continuities with the New Urban Left and the Black and anti-racist activism of the preceding decades – if usually with the less radical elements within those formations. This becomes clear if we examine case studies drawn from the public sector: judicial appointments and the Public Sector Equality Duty.

Attempts to create a more diverse judiciary had roots in the 1990s but gained momentum when the Constitutional Reform Act 2005 set up a new non-departmental public body, the Judicial Appointments Commission (JAC), with the duty to select candidates 'on merit' and to 'have regard to the need to encourage diversity in the range of persons available for selection for appointment'.[29] Its first chairman, Baroness

Usha Prashar, sat on the Race Relations Board between 1971 and 1976 and was assistant director and then director of the Runnymede Trust between 1976 and 1984 (a body Trevor Phillips later chaired, from 1993 to 1998).[30] Merit and diversity were consistently emphasised in the work of the Commission. The JAC was to deliver a more diverse – but definitely meritocratic – judiciary, by working to recruit from as wide a pool as possible, encouraging any eligible candidate to consider a judicial appointment, and ensuring selection processes were fair and transparent, in order to ensure no old boys' networks or assumptions about what a judge 'should' look like could influence appointments. To this end, the Commission developed new selection processes and undertook outreach activities with a range of partners, including the Black Solicitors Network, the Society of Asian Lawyers, the Association of Women Barristers and the Group for Solicitors with Disabilities. The goal was a more diverse judiciary, but the JAC emphasised that diversity was good *not* because it improved the quality of judicial decisions or even the public legitimacy of the judiciary, but because '[i]f you draw from a wider pool of people, you have a better choice, and you are more likely to improve rather than diminish the quality of the pool of judicial appointments'.[31] The social justice arguments for such policies were, thus, marginalised, but the Committee did undertake some forms of 'positive action' in order to try to create more meaningful 'equal opportunity' for potential judicial candidates.

The JAC's duty to promote diversity was backed up by a duty introduced in the Race Relations (Amendment) Act 2000 that required *all* public bodies to work proactively to eliminate racial discrimination and promote 'equality of opportunity'.[32] This was an important step forward, but, importantly, the 2000 Act built on the requirement introduced in 1976 that *local authorities* should encourage equal opportunities and counter discrimination.[33] In 2010, the Equality Act brought together all protected categories, including ethnicity, sex and disability, in one legal framework, with a standard Public Sector Equality Duty now applying across all. In developing the Act, efficiency and business sense were emphasised: public bodies were to be allowed to focus on 'a limited number of priority areas',[34] and equality was justified not only on the basis of 'principle' – a 'basic right' of each individual – but also as necessary for 'social cohesion' and for a strong 'modern economy', which would benefit from 'a culture of equality which brings employers the widest labour pool' and from 'diversity' which would make Britain 'outward facing' and more globally competitive.[35] This rhetoric chimed with Trevor Phillips's emphasis, as chair of the CRE between 2003 and 2006, on diversity as a 'business problem'.[36] It also fit with an increasing public celebration of entrepreneurs such as Tim Campbell, a young British man of African-Caribbean heritage who in 2005 won the first UK series of the business reality show *The Apprentice*; two years later, Campbell served as one of the government's first Social Enterprise Ambassadors, as part of a programme that ran between 2007 and 2010 and which aimed to use business solutions to confront social problems.[37] Some scholars have seen all this as evidence of the triumph of enterprise and efficiency over justice. Kapoor argues that the process of legal 'simplification' in fact 'meant watering down, thinning out and erasing detail', reducing race to just one axis of equality among many.[38] But it is important to recognise that the equal opportunities ideology of social democracy infused New Labour's policies at least as much as the logic of neoliberalism. New Labour's reforms built upon the legislation of the 1970s and were fundamentally premised on a modernist belief in the possibilities of planning and bureaucracy to reform capitalism – to create a *fair* market or 'free competition' between individuals.[39]

The expansion of the Public Sector Equality Duty under New Labour also led to the expansion of a technique developed at the heart of the New Urban Left in the 1980s: the 'equality impact assessment', pioneered by Linda Bellos as leader of Lambeth Council. Bellos, a radical Black feminist and gay rights activist, sometime member of the *Spare Rib* editorial collective, GLC worker and Labour Party Black Sections activist, became a local councillor for Lambeth in 1985 and council leader in 1986.[40] In 1988, forced by central government to make budget cuts of 25 per cent, she demanded information on the differential impact of each type of council spending on different social groups and used this data to prioritise services used by those most in need.[41] After leaving local government, Bellos founded Diversity Solutions Ltd, training organisations on diversity, including how to complete equality impact assessments.[42] Interviewed in 2017, she highlighted the way her work in the GLC convinced her of the need to 'empower' third sector groups by giving them the information, tools and skills they needed to navigate employment and equal opportunities legislation,[43] an experience which doubtless informed her work as a consultant. The emphasis on data and monitoring in Bellos's work reflected the pragmatism of anti-racist praxis in the 1980s; this was a strategy that persisted – and indeed grew, under the expanded Public Sector Equality Duty – in the 2000s.

Individuals such as Prashar and Bellos might be seen by some to embody the ideal neoliberal subject, having turned work in the race relations industry and local government in the 1970s and 1980s into portfolio careers in the public and third sectors, and running their own consultancies. The work of such consultants and diversity professionals – not least, their rhetorical focus on 'diversity' rather than substantive 'equality' – has been widely critiqued. Yet some studies have been more measured in their conclusions. Interviewing Australian 'diversity' practitioners in the early 2000s, Sara Ahmed argued that the language of 'diversity' could be put to transformative use.[44] Gill Kirton and Anne-Marie Greene, in their close analysis of 'diversity professionals' in Britain in the 2000s and 2010s, argue similarly that though 'the business case has undoubtedly influenced this field of professional practice, the field's origins in the social justice activism of historically marginalised groups have left a legacy';[45] these professionals 'bring personal experiences of marginalisation, under-representation, and discrimination' to their approach and should be seen as 'tempered radicals'.[46] There were always more and less radical versions of equal opportunities, multiculturalist and anti-racist ideology and practice, and it was the less radical versions of these that infused New Labour, but the legacy of social democracy and of the New Urban Left is visible in the New Labour project; the category of neoliberalism is not a sufficient explanation.

An 'anti-racist' moment? Britain after 1981

Pragna Patel, a founding member in 1979 of the feminist group Southall Black Sisters (SBS), remembers the Thatcher era as the moment 'when the GLC was at its best, had a lot of influential people within it, feminists and others who'd gone in'.[47] Convinced that the levers of state power were needed to achieve many of their goals, from the late 1970s many radicals shaped by the New Left entered into the state and – as the central government began to defund local authorities – were on the frontline of a battle between central and local government that raged throughout the 1980s. 'Despite Thatcherism, despite the really bleak landscape that was around us', Patel recounts, this was also a moment of possibility, with local authorities setting up women's centres, race committees and equalities committees. In 1983, funding from the GLC helped to establish the Southall Black Women's Centre. Working with the GLC was, in Patel's view, essential training for work at the national level with the New Labour government – their greatest achievement came, she noted, in 2002 when SBS pushed through a major piece of reform in immigration law that recognised the plight of women suffering domestic violence who held insecure status.[48]

The 1981 urban uprisings pulled more activists into the local state; Linda Bellos, for example, recalled this as a key moment. She was 'furious' about discriminatory policing, 'pained by the criminalisation of a significant percentage of Black boys for being Black', and, looking back, she saw this as 'one of the reasons I came to the view about joining the GLC'.[49] Ambalavaner Sivanandan, Gilroy and others have critiqued the incorporation of anti-racism into the state, and the later emergence of a generation of 'diversity professionals', seeing these developments as representing a loss of radicalism or, in the language of social movement theory, co-optation.[50] As Sivanandan points out, this was not a process that began after 1981: it was already underway with the Community Relations Councils and the Community Relations Commission of the 1960s.[51] But, as Bellos makes clear, 1981 did mark a moment of rupture and transformation. While police harassment of young Black people continued to be a major galvanising issue, grassroots efforts to combat extreme levels of unemployment in areas such as Brixton also produced an unstable coalition of Black community workers and a government concerned with economic development in the 'inner city'. In this section, we show how the Thatcher years rearticulated Black and anti-racist activism, drawing enterprise to the fore and encouraging the further professionalisation of the race relations industry, but also how radicalism persisted in the decade.

From 1979, a shift could be discerned in the approach of the CRE. The Commission had long promoted training and employment, not least through its self-help fund, initiated in 1975, which funded organisations such as Brixton Melting Pot Foundation from the late 1970s onwards.[52] But 'enterprise', not mentioned in the Commission's reports for 1977 or 1978, was newly on the agenda under Thatcher.[53] Giving evidence in Parliament on 30 March 1981 – just days before the start of the uprisings in Brixton that year – the CRE noted it was refocusing its strategy on promoting 'minority business enterprise'.[54] After the 1981 uprisings, a further and highly significant shift occurred: 'black alienation' went to the top of the policy agenda,[55] and money was funnelled into a range of anti-racist, self-help and community projects through the Urban Programme. Begun by Labour in 1968 to fund social projects in inner-city areas, and expanded in 1978 to fund economic and environmental projects as well, funding for the Programme increased significantly after 1981, from £165 million in 1979–80 to £348 million in 1984–5.[56] The proportion of funding to Black projects also rose dramatically: in 1981–2, 20 per cent of Programme funding for voluntary organisations went to Black groups; by 1986, half of all funding did.[57] This was an essentially pragmatic move: the Tories needed to be seen to be achieving something in the inner cities.[58] Indeed, Thatcher's close advisers were often scathing about 'black enterprise' programmes: after the Tottenham and Handsworth disturbances of 1985, one suggested that funding to support 'new entrepreneurs' would simply expand 'the disco and drug trade'.[59] Nevertheless, funding expanded; it also shifted increasingly towards projects associated with employment, business and enterprise, as well as projects celebrating the cultural identities of particular ethnic groups (rather than projects driven by the collectivist ideology of Blackness).[60]

A critical further goal of the Thatcher governments was to create more Black 'leaders' and integrate them into the state.[61] As Sir George Young, Conservative minister responsible for race relations, put it, '[w]e've got to back the good guys, the sensible, moderate, responsible leaders of ethnic groups'; funding their projects would increase their legitimacy, ensuring people of colour did not 'turn to the militants'.[62] This was linked to a wider commitment to 'create a black middle class' who would 'exercise responsible and creative leadership in their own community'.[63] Kalbir Shukra calls this a strategy of 'repression and containment';[64] funding was designed to flow to moderates and develop a Black middle class, while hard, targeted policing of Black people, especially Black boys and young men, continued. Yet examining the ideas and careers of several 'race relations professionals' serves to demonstrate that the 'containment' was not always complete.

Herman Ouseley had been a local government officer since 1963, working in town planning; he was Race Relations Adviser to Lambeth Council between 1979 and 1981, and the first Principal Race Relations Advisor to the GLC from 1981 to 1984. Though Ouseley could be seen as an anti-revolutionary, a man *of* the administration of the state, that view diminishes his contribution to the history of Black resistance. In 1981, he argued against Lambeth Council's 'divide and rule' strategy of giving competitive grants to local Black groups and, to strengthen the collective lobbying power of these groups, helped develop an umbrella organisation – independent of the local Community Relations Council – called the Consortium. As he explained:

> The black self-help programmes and the Consortium's overviewing thrusts are providing individuals with the confidence, skills and expertise to develop an awareness of 'the system' in order to get access to it and to manipulate it accordingly.[65]

Ouseley's vision of Black emancipation in 1981 was the 'confidence, skill and expertise' to manipulate the system, but it was also predicated on collective action and on challenging, as well as working within, the state. Ouseley developed his analysis further in a book co-authored with Usha Prashar and Daniel Silverstone in 1981 and titled *The System*, which examined the work of local authorities – particularly Lambeth – on race. It argued that local authorities which declared a 'colour blind' approach were likely failing to meet the duty placed on them by the 1976 Race Relations Act to eradicate racial discrimination. 'The system', Ouseley, Prashar and Silverstone argued, perpetuated conscious and unconscious racism. Only those local authorities that took *positive action* – usually through establishing a race unit, as Lambeth had done – could 'demonstrate to black people that their different and special needs would be identified, adequately considered and provided for'.[66] The book contributed to a new field of professional anti-racist practice and what Gilroy would describe as the new neoliberal 'managerialist ideology' of anti-racism.[67] But the title is also significant: 'the system', in Ouseley et al's reading, was 'organizational arrangements within large companies and institutions', 'bureaucratic procedures' as well as the 'attitudes, actions and practices' of managers.[68] 'The system' in radical Black circles was regularly used to denote the wider political economy and hegemonic racist ideology. Here it was reduced to the size of a (manageable) organisation.[69] The radical language of Black Power was marshalled to moderate ends.[70]

Ouseley et al. did not see 'positive action', however, as 'unradical'. Prashar, for example, in *Scarman and After* (1984), criticised the Scarman report into the Brixton disturbances in 1981 for 'underestimat[ing]' the impact of 'institutional racism' and 'ignor[ing] the Government's racist immigration laws'; she called for 'positive action' to tackle racism and discrimination and emphasised that such action needed to be supported by government leadership and funding.[71] Prashar argued for the monitoring of the ethnicity of civil service staff to measure and combat discrimination in hiring (a policy which had been rejected by the Thatcher government in 1981). In the study *Sickle Cell Anaemia*, Prashar and her co-authors developed further the case for widespread problems with 'the system', and the need for positive action to remedy this.[72] They highlighted the flagrant discrimination which meant much less money was spent on sickle cell than was spent on much rarer diseases (such as phenylketonuria) that did not predominantly affect Black people. Surveying provision for sickle cell sufferers in 101 health districts in England, they found that provision was inadequate, and that the seven existing sickle cell centres had only been set up because of pressure from Black communities, all with only short-term funding. The authors concluded that Black people 'rightly feel discriminated against and allege that there is racism in the NHS'; they set out proposals for the organisations and services needed, as well as long-term funding.[73] Positive action, in Prashar's analysis, was vital, and this went beyond a liberal understanding of the need to remove formal barriers: Prashar argued for programmes to actively create equal opportunities and necessary services.[74]

Another contribution to *Scarman and After*, from Devon Thomas, demonstrates how the economic concerns of Black activism could be in tune with elements of the Thatcherite 'enterprise culture' and yet be motivated by much more radical, transformative intentions. Thomas, whose parents had been very active in the Garveyite movement in 1930s Jamaica, first began community work when he helped to establish an early Black youth club, the Allardyce, in Brixton with Linton Kwesi Johnson.[75] Thomas worked alongside Ouseley at Lambeth Council in the early 1980s as Lambeth's first 'economic development officer', creating temporary jobs for the unemployed, 'three quarters of whom are black' (the chair of Lambeth's new subcommittee on unemployment was a young councillor by the name of Peter Mandelson).[76] Thomas was also a member of the radical Brixton Defence Committee, which campaigned for amnesty for all those arrested in the riots; its leader, Rudy Narayan, argued the Black community did not need an inquiry to know that policing was racist, and called for the Black community to boycott the official Scarman inquiry, on the grounds that it was an attempt to dissipate Black protest.[77]

In 1981, soon after the uprising, Thomas held a conference, 'Why so few Black businesses?', which was filmed as an hour-long special for *The Money Programme* on BBC Two. Conference participants spoke of having been refused capital by banks despite their good financial track records and sound business proposals: racist barriers to the mainstream economy were why young people were, as Thomas put it, 'in the street burning down the place'.[78] A few years later, in *Scarman and After*, Thomas offered a vision of Black empowerment through the private sector, lamenting that while '10 per cent of whites and a similar percentage of Asians' were involved in their own 'self-employment, small business or co-operative enterprise', only 3 per cent of West Indian people were similarly engaged. The limits of Black 'self-generated economic activity', he argued, 'constrains our ability to mobilise influence and power and independent political and social activity'. Rejecting commonplace views of Brixton as a place of 'dereliction, despair and apathy', Thomas emphasised that the 'community . . . is and always has been very active and dynamic', seeing the seeds of transformation in Brixton's already existing community organisations, such as the Melting Pot Foundation or the Brixton Neighbourhood Community Association. West Indian community and self-help groups were already, Thomas argued, looking to become 'independently self-sustaining' by 'trying to apply their previous experience in other fields to that of the world of business'.[79] While, Thomas thought, 'the black community has evolved a whole range of strategies to redirect local and central government finance', the more difficult task remained: influencing 'those in this society who control the *private* sector'.[80] By 1984, Thomas had already founded the South Bank Inner City Centre, a think tank and economic development organisation focused on 'black economic empowerment', in partnership with South Bank Polytechnic and the GLC. With funding from Prudential Life Insurance, it built a science park for new technology companies – the first inner-city science park in Britain – on the 'bombsite' at Elephant & Castle roundabout; it later built 11 more business parks around London and across the country. The turn to 'enterprise' under Thatcher did not simply represent a capitulation: it can also be seen to represent a continuation of a Black self-help tradition, an argument for economic empowerment and the 'black pound'. In the early 1990s, Thomas went on to be substantially involved in the 'Brixton City Challenge', writing the regeneration strategy for the area. Since then, he has continued to work to support Black-owned businesses in Brixton, serving as Director of the independent agency Lambeth Enterprise, Director of Lambeth Business Advisory and Chair of the Brixton Business Forum.[81]

From the mid-1980s, the attack on local government – its powers and funding – intensified; the GLC was abolished in 1986. Thatcher, however, needed to appear to be achieving progress on inner-city problems, so she launched the repackaged 'Action for Cities' in her third term; spending was focused even more on business and enterprise, and local authorities were edged out.[82] For Thatcherites, urban poverty was the result of 'market failure' in the city. The City Action Teams (CATs) originated within the Department of the Environment in 1985 in response to the urban unrest in that year: the government rolled out 'Task Forces' in eight inner-city areas to stimulate Black business activity. The aim was not to spend large amounts of government funding, but to 'create' an enterprise culture among Black people, as well as an infrastructure specifically for Black business. The focus was supposed to be on unleashing entrepreneurial energy and developing urban space, not resisting racism. In Liverpool, the Task Force created a business park, hotel and conference centre; in Leeds, a design centre comprising small studios, workshops and galleries. The activists involved did not see this as necessarily lacking in radical and transformative potential, however. In its first year, the Director of North Kensington's Task Force, Colin Francis, insisted in a local paper that he did not just represent another 'ministerial public relations exercise' or 'white man in a black skin': the project was 'about helping people to help themselves', and he was 'an ambassador for black people'. Like Thomas, Prashar and Ouseley, Francis viewed his role as a form of social justice work: 'I don't have to be here. I could be working for some bank, paying off a big mortgage. But I chose to come back to the community, to give something back.' Like Thomas, he believed the private sector was the key to achieving Black liberation: 'Unless people get an economic base in society, things will never change . . . We want to establish seeds of independence.'[83]

The 'community enterprises' still receiving financial support from the state by the early 1990s tended to be those training unemployed youth, especially Black youth: as local authority funding dried up, many turned to the Department for Education/Training, and so 'changed their role'.[84] The Conservative government did not want to abolish the CRE, but rather hoped it would suffer a 'slow death' as a result of cutting its budget each year and restricting its influence.[85] Under Ouseley, the CRE worked to adapt to this unfavourable environment by shifting its emphasis from 'appeals to social justice and tougher legislation to forming a government–business consensus around the idea of being "fair" to the disadvantaged', arguing that this would benefit 'human resources optimization and organizational efficiency generally'.[86] The 1995 campaign 'Racial Equality Means Business' argued that an 'organisation's competitive edge' depends on being able to reach out 'to all sectors of the community, as employees, customers, clients and suppliers';[87] alongside the 'legal and moral reasons for racial equality', Ouseley argued, there was 'a strong business case'.[88] Looking back on the end of his chairmanship of the CRE, Ouseley noted in 2000 that, with the decline in anti-racist programmes in the public sector, 'many people had to fend for themselves and get involved in enterprise culture'.[89] Importantly, race relations legislation gave many a way into enterprise. While funding to local government was cut under Thatcher, the key provisions of the legislation of 1965, 1968 and 1976 were not abolished: they remained in place, creating a framework for race relations professionals who could help the public sector and, increasingly, the private sector navigate the law and 'maximise efficiency'. As discussed above, Linda Bellos founded Diversity Solutions Ltd, and many others followed a similar path; for example, Chris Mullard, secretary of the Campaign Against Racial Discrimination and community relations officer in Durham, founded Focus Consultancy in 1986; David Dine, a Black social worker in Brent Council in the 1980s and later Chair of Ujima Housing Association, founded DD Consultancy in 1994; and Herman Ouseley was Managing Director and then President of Different Realities Partnership Ltd, which focused on equality, diversity and human resources, between 2000 and 2010.

In March 1983, Sivanandan was a keynote speaker at the GLC Ethnic Minorities Unit Consultation on Challenging Racism, a huge conference bringing together professional activists and intellectuals, partly organised by Ouseley. Sivanandan began his talk by describing himself as 'a heretic' of the GLC Unit, 'a disbeliever' in the efficacy of ethnic policies to alter 'the monumental and endemic racism' of British society.[90] He repeated his seminal critique of government programmes for ethnic minorities: they were 'a tool to blunt the edge of black struggle' and divide Black people into different cultural groupings. Government efforts to support a 'nascent black bourgeoisie' were a strategy of political containment.[91] Yet to position radicals such as Sivanandan in perpetual opposition to an anti-racist 'black bourgeoisie' made up of people such as Ouseley – and to view Sivanandan's radical critique as the final word on the progressive potential of anti-racism in local government – is to ignore the robust ideological debate and diverse strategies of Black resistance in a time of crisis. Later in his talk, Sivanandan advocated pragmatism, a revolution from inside the house:

> Don't let's be purists and stand outside, for we can't fight the system bare-handed. We don't have the tools, brothers and sisters; we've got to get the tools from the system itself and hope that in the process five out of ten of us don't become corrupt.[92]

If the GLC was prepared to give Black activists the tools, it was time to take them. Seeing Black activism in the 1980s as divided into the incorporated 'professionals' and the authentic radicalism of those who remained outside the state is to ignore the fact that these activists often worked in the same spaces and towards the same ends. Government funding did change the ecology of Black and anti-racist activism and ideology, but there were continuities and important legacies which should be remembered alongside the defeats. 'Enterprise' was emphasised under Thatcher in ways that it had not been in the Black activism of the preceding decade, and here we can certainly identify the influence of the neoliberal context. But, as we demonstrate in the final section of this chapter, there were also precursors to the emphasis on enterprise in the Black activism of the 1970s.

Black politics and Black enterprise culture in the 1970s

Among the advocates of Black enterprise in the 2000s was Tony Wade, a businessman from Montserrat who had migrated to Britain in 1954 and made his money in the Black cosmetics and haircare industry. In a history of Black British enterprise published in 2003, Wade prefaced his narrative by explaining that his ultimate aim was to show how Black Britons could incorporate 'our human capital investment to the UK economy' and contribute 'to the nation's wealth creation'.[93] His celebration of Black Britain, and of the post-colonial migrations of which he was a part, was couched in the language of added value: 'Each wave of immigrants has enriched the cultural and social fabric of British society, and represents building blocks of prosperity.'[94] In this respect, Wade is identifiably a Black neoliberal, but he was not made one in the 2000s. Digging into his history, we find a politics of Black British neoliberalism *avant la lettre*, reaching back half a century – a politics that bears a closer relationship to post-war forms of Black collectivism than we might imagine.

Wade was a passionate supporter of Tony Blair and, before that, of Margaret Thatcher; in 1984, he was a guest at Downing Street.[95] Wade was, in many ways, a natural Thatcherite. Even in the early 1960s, when the post-war settlement still held strong, he would argue against state ownership with his Labour-supporting wife and promote the virtues of private property.[96] Like Thatcher, Wade believed that a stake in society was secured by a stake in the economy. In 1980, he argued, in an idiosyncratic rendition of Marcus Garvey's politics, that the lesson to take from what he called 'the Garveyist spirit of self-help, enterprise and risk-taking' was that the road to racial equality must come by 'owning a stake in the British economy'.[97] In the same speech, delivering what Wendy Brown might recognise as a classically neoliberal rationality, Wade articulated the challenge facing Britain's Black communities as a challenge of resource maximisation:

> . . . we must . . . prepare to gird our loins, and use every opportunity to utilise our skills and distinctive competencies to create and build our own business, our own markets and ultimately create our own wealth.[98]

He also presented this as something to which West Indians were particularly suited. Entrepreneurialism, he argued, was characteristically West Indian: this 'spirit of self-initiative, enterprise and risk-taking . . . brought most of us to Britain'.[99] Mobilising this entrepreneurialism,

Wade argued in 1982, was the solution to the problem of Black disadvantage. It would mean that 'the leaders in industry and commerce' should be the key movers in building 'a healthier and a more harmonious society'.[100]

Wade's vision of the reparative power of work and enterprise was shared by other members of the small but influential Black business community in 1960s and 1970s Britain. Wade's big break in business came through his involvement in Dyke and Dryden Ltd, which he joined as a partner in 1968. Formed three years earlier in Tottenham by Len Dyke and Dudley Dryden, Dyke and Dryden specialised in records, haircare and cosmetics. It was among the most successful Black British businesses operating at the time,[101] and Dyke, Dryden and Wade each received an extensive public platform in the Black press, particularly in the business- and professional-supporting weekly newspaper *West Indian World*, and in the magazine *Westindian Digest*. This public platform was not only a recognition of Dyke and Dryden's success (or of the publications' need for advertising revenue from the business); it was due to the work of Dyke, Dryden and Wade in race relations, Black community development, uplift politics and anti-racist campaigning. The link between business and community work is important. All three men were champions, simultaneously, of Black business and Black social work. Both Dyke and Dryden, arriving from Jamaica in the 1950s, were founding members of the West Indian Standing Conference (WISC), formed following the 1958 white riots to promote West Indian integration and welfare. In 1963, Dyke co-founded the North London West Indian Association (NLWIA), which echoed the WISC's ambitions; it became most significant for its campaigns against the streaming of Black children into schools for the 'educationally sub-normal'.[102] Dryden also founded the Hackney Council of Citizens, the forerunner to the Hackney Community Relations Council, in 1966.[103] Both Dyke and Dryden campaigned tirelessly on behalf of young Black people targeted by the police, spending their Sundays patrolling the streets of Hackney and Haringey, monitoring police activities.[104] Wade pursued similar community initiatives. In the 1950s, he was a part of the international friendship movement, founding the Finsbury Park Methodist Church International Fellowship. A decade later, he became active in both the NLWIA and the WISC, for which he served as Housing Officer.[105]

Alongside these political preoccupations, the three men also sponsored annual Dyke and Dryden Beauty Competitions, 'to give black girls an opportunity to win prizes and develop their femininity and project our Black and Beautiful image'.[106] The contest became a key event in the social calendar of West Indian business and community leaders in London, and an opportunity for the Dyke and Dryden men to deliver speeches on their ideas about community development.[107] The promotion of community work and the promotion of an individual work ethic, however, were of a piece here: 'Involvement in community social affairs', Wade explained in his memoir, 'provided a platform to spread the merits of disciplined hard work'.[108] Hard work was repeatedly underlined in the pronouncements of the West Indian business leaders. 'Hard work made us successful', Dyke and Dryden told *West Indian World*, in an interview in which they underlined their credentials as community leaders.[109] 'All it needs is hard work. Sometimes I work 24 hours a day', Stuart Weathers, the Jamaican owner of a successful Clapham plumbing business, told the journalist Mike Phillips, in a similar move.[110] There is a clear congruity with Thatcherism here; but we should not overlook the fact that the ideology of meritocracy was also deeply woven into the fabric of social democracy in Britain, in the Race Relations Acts of the 1960s and the framework they created for individuals to challenge discrimination in order to win equality of opportunity.[111] The social democratic vision of meritocracy emphasised overcoming structures of inherited privilege by reforming those structures to give those with talents the ability to use them; the Thatcherite version placed far more emphasis on overcoming adversity though hard work.[112] Dyke and Dryden emphasised the *virtue* of hard work, but they also worked to dismantle structures of discrimination. Their message was that in a racist society, Black people could only rely on themselves: they needed to work hard as well as working collectively.

For men such as Dyke and Dryden, hard work was not only the key to individual success; it was also vital to the collective 'uplift' of Black Britain, through the pride that successful Black businesses offered, the clout they commanded in social and political affairs, and the possibility they offered for further prosperity in Black communities. For Vince Howard, owner of the successful West End club Gilly's, 'the powerful new movement to improve the position of blacks in business' was evidence of an 'enlightened age'. He urged papers such as *West Indian World* to 'encourage Black people to support Black businesses, and for Black businessmen to play a positive part in alleviating the Black Community from its present situation'.[113] In 1978, Mike Phillips reported the growing 'assumption that it's possible to create an immigrant middle class which would owe its prosperity to hard work and ingenuity', and which would in turn be the base for better political leadership (this assumption, as we have seen, intensified in Thatcherite circles after 1981).[114] The often-cited model to follow was the Jewish migrants of the late nineteenth century, to whom Len Dyke, as early as 1966, pointed as justification for the need for more West Indians to work hard, 'get into business' and thus have an 'impact' in British society.[115] Thatcher, of course, would also frequently celebrate the Jewish community on these grounds.[116]

The UK Caribbean Chamber of Commerce (CCC), formed in early 1977, became a primary vehicle for this Caribbean business–political class to promote their version of enterprise-driven self-help. Like Wade, the CCC presented entrepreneurialism as characteristically West Indian:

> Let us remember that the slaves who went to the Americas came from West Africa with a long history and tradition of business in gold, silk, precious stones, salt, copper, palm oil, hides and skins, ivory, dye-woods and hardwoods.[117]

The lesson was that Black people should be proud of their history and heritage; this was a history, however, which emphasised precolonial Africa not as a proto-socialist society (the meaning usually given to it by Black radicals of the era), but rather as a deep-rooted 'enterprise culture'. The CCC's central purpose was to pressure the government 'to enable ethnic minority small businesses to overcome the main obstacles to their economic development': state monopolies, the unfair lending policies of the 'big five' banks and the inadequacies of inner-city policies.[118] The CCC thus sought to fight the institutional racism that held Black businesses back. This could be seen as a neoliberal anti-racism; it saw racism's degradations, as Wade put it in a speech to the CCC in 1982, in 'the harm it does both in demoralising and rending to waste skills and human resources that should be gainfully employed'.[119] The ambition to remove the barriers of institutional racism was coupled with the demand for capital investment and building capital management skills in order to allow 'the ethnic community to develop'.[120] This was a manifesto for anti-racism that the CCC pushed wherever they could gain a platform – which they often did: their activities were covered regularly in *West Indian World*, and Syd Burke's popular *Rice 'n' Peas* show on BBC Radio London broadcast their convention speeches.[121]

Beyond businesses and commercial networks, a wider culture of Black enterprise flourished around the newspaper *West Indian World* itself, and later around the magazine *Root*. *West Indian World* was founded in 1971 by Aubrey Baynes, a Vincentian journalist who had previously edited *Daylight International*, one of Black Britain's early lifestyle magazines. From 1973, its editor was the Guyanese Indian Arif Ali, who since 1971 had published the magazine *Westindian Digest*, another home for the West Indian middle class in Britain, which hosted regular features on business leaders and entrepreneurs. Ali was famous as the man behind Hansib, a publishing company that produced the first 'Who's Who'-style anthologies for leaders of business, arts and entertainment in West Indian Britain.[122] *West Indian World*, however, was the most significant output in this business-supporting culture. Its daily distribution reached 25,000 per week, covering England and Scotland, within six months of its inauguration, and even by 1980, when it was past its peak, it was selling 10,000 weekly copies.[123] It is in the pages of *West Indian World* that we can most easily see the thriving world of Black business in the 1970s. The newspaper regularly profiled Black hairdressers and barbers, stores and distributors, estate agents and market traders – many of them the paper's own advertisers. It celebrated each new business venture and was a firm believer in the importance of establishing a Black professional and business class for the furtherance of good 'race relations'. It also conducted regular 'buy black' campaigns, admonishing those who spent their money with businesses known for racial discrimination or for investments in South Africa or Rhodesia. *Root*, founded in 1979 by former *West Indian World* journalist Hal Austin, had less to say on the ethics of consumption but shared with *West Indian World* a prioritisation of what it called 'the black achiever', celebrating money-making and advertising luxury commodities to its readers, including 'good food, quality wine bars, pioneering fashion, nice music, stylised home décor, relaxing travel, the lot'.[124]

These celebrations of Black entrepreneurialism and consumption drew the ire of many Black radicals. *Root*, for example, was criticised by the Black feminist group the Organisation of Women of African and Asian Descent (OWAAD) for suggesting to its readers that 'by aspiring to [this] kind of lifestyle . . . their lives will somehow miraculously improve'.[125] While *Root* talked in the language of 'collective suffering' that was prominent in the Black politics of these years, OWAAD objected that *Root*'s was a cynical appropriation of such language. Black advocates of 'enterprise and self-help' in the 1970s were swimming against the tide of Black activism in the period and were frequently and hotly criticised for it.[126] Despite these skirmishes around the language of Blackness and Black community, there was a substantial overlap between the concerns with enterprise, work ethic, entrepreneurialism and profit that defined the Black business networks and cultures discussed in this section, and the priorities of sections of the Black Power movement who would, nonetheless, seek to distance themselves from this business culture. The first, most obvious overlap is the organisations from which both emerged.

The WISC included not only Dyke, Dryden and Wade, but Neville Maxwell, whose *The Power of Negro Action* (1965) signalled an early turn to the new Black liberation politics cohering around Malcolm X in the US, and Joseph Hunte, whose *N[***]r Hunting in England?* (1966) marked the start of a protracted effort at monitoring racist policing that defined the Black Power era.[127] The NLWIA was a home not only for Dyke and Wade, but also for the Trinidadian labour activist and poet John La Rose; the radical lawyer Rudy Narayan, head of the Brixton Defence Committee in 1981; and many other key figures of London Black radicalism. *West Indian World*, moreover, included among its regular contributors Narayan, the prominent Black Power activist Roy Sawh and the Black Panther movement photographer Neil Kenlock, who also went on to co-found *Root*.

To see these crossovers is to see that the history of Black anti-racist work is not one only of the social democratic or liberationist left; indeed, even Black liberation projects could appear in guises that shared many common assumptions with emergent Black neoliberalisms. Ideas about the role of work, entrepreneurialism and the logic of the market in securing racial equality found surprising accommodation within the movement for civil rights in Britain and even had affinities with parts of the movement for Black liberation. This was most obviously so in the self-help initiatives, particularly hostels and youth centres, that sprang up across Britain's multicultural cities in the wake of Black Power in the 1970s, often led by figures who had become active through Black Power organisations.[128] There was nothing intrinsically neoliberal about the philosophy of self-help practised here, but these institutions did emphasise the virtues of self-improvement, responsibility and industriousness. The hostels were places to learn skills. This apprenticeship system, as Devon Thomas remembers, was a strategic response to the racism of British schooling.[129] At Dashiki in Notting Hill, young people were taught motor mechanics, electrical engineering, welding, radio and television engineering, photography, plumbing, painting and decorating, brick laying, carpentry, dress making, typing and secretarial skills, beautician skills, driving, tailoring and African and Caribbean arts.[130] At Melting Pot in Brixton, they trained in heavy goods driving and operated their own garments factory, specialising in Caribbean styles; the ambition was 'training up Westindians for better jobs'.[131]

This was not simply about making economically useful citizens, even if this was the premise upon which these projects won government and charitable funding. Notting Hill's Unity House, for example, maintained that the young people it worked with only came there because 'they would rather break bricks for an organisation or business run by black people, than be caught up in one of the "shit jobs" they might be offered at the labour exchange'. They certainly saw more purpose in supporting 'the youngsters on the street' in opposition to 'baton-wielding police' than in skills training for jobs that either did not exist or would be denied to Black people anyway.[132] The self-help hostels, moreover, were often pitched as efforts in collectivism, where, as Dashiki put it, 'personal greed' was to be dispensed with and 'everyone is prepared to respond in any way necessary, beneficial to black people's collective interest'.[133] Black self-help, as Paul Gilroy has insisted, has historically been articulated in individual and collective registers simultaneously.[134] The relationship between individual and collective prosperity was different across different parts of the Black self-help movement. In Dashiki's iteration, the job of self-help was to offer a different route to self-fulfilment for the Black middle class, who 'may have to take a fall in positions and earnings; but an increase in their self-respect and a sense of contributing to the cause of a world-wide struggle for total and complete human respect of our people'.[135] In Dyke and Dryden's, by contrast, a Black middle class making money was a virtue in itself and a benefit for the wider community. Dyke formed the business because he and Dryden 'saw the need for a black business coming up as an economic status for the black people'.[136] The crossovers, nonetheless, are important.

Conclusion

In this chapter, we have traced the different forms that neoliberal rationalities took in different spheres, but we have also suggested that neoliberalism is not a sufficient category to explain New Labour's policies on race and racism, the transformation of anti-racist activism in the 1980s or Black enterprise culture in the 1970s. We must view neoliberalism not as a conspiratorial agent – or an all-encompassing political and economic force that destroys the progressive potential of everything it touches – but instead as one ideological formation intersecting with (and itself transformed by) many others. Neoliberal rationalities shaped the public sector under New Labour, to be sure: diversity was cast as positive because it maximises quality; race was reduced to one among many axes of diversity, and activists became diversity professionals. But we should also recognise longer continuities: the meritocratic assumptions deeply rooted in the post-war social democratic state, and given form in the Race Relations legislation of the 1960s and 1970s, persisted into the 2000s alongside ideas and practices drawn from the New Urban Left and the multiculturalism and anti-racist activism of the 1970s and 1980s. Anti-racist activism and Black enterprise traditions were rearticulated under Thatcher, but neoliberal ideology was far from the only force shaping the transition. Finally, neoliberalism did not come from nowhere: it found roots in already existing elements of Black culture. We should not see 'enterprise culture' as simply foisted on Black Britons by Thatcher; rather, we need to understand how Black vernacular cultures, social and political practices and institutions became articulated to an emergent neoliberal hegemony.

Notes

1 Paul Gilroy, '". . . We got to get over before we go under . . . ": Fragments for a history of Black vernacular neoliberalism', *New Formations*, 80/81 (2013), 23–38, at 24.
2 Quinn Slobodian, *Globalists: The end of empire and the birth of neoliberalism* (Cambridge, MA, Harvard University Press, 2018), 172.
3 In this chapter, we use the anachronistic 'people of colour' because, as we discuss later in this introduction, in the period under discussion, the terms 'Black' and 'ethnic minority' had specific, politically laden and deeply contested meanings.
4 Dipesh Chakrabarty, *Provincializing Europe: Postcolonial thought and historical difference* (Princeton, NJ, Princeton University Press, 2008).
5 Slavoj Žižek, 'Multiculturalism, or, the cultural logic of multinational capitalism', *New Left Review* (September–October 1997), 28–51. See Will Kymlicka, 'Neoliberal multiculturalism?', in Michèle Lamont and Peter A. Hall (eds), *Social Resilience in the Neoliberal Era* (Cambridge, Cambridge University Press, 2013), 99–125, at 109.
6 Michael Omi and Howard Winant, *Racial Formation in the United States: From the 1960s to the 1990s* (New York, Routledge, 1994), 47.
7 Kymlicka, 'Neoliberal multiculturalism?', 109–10. See also Gurminder K. Bhambra, 'Whither Europe? Postcolonial versus neocolonial cosmopolitanism', *Interventions: International Journal of Postcolonial Studies*, 18 (2016), 187–202.
8 Elizabeth Buettner, '"Going for an Indian": South Asian restaurants and the limits of multiculturalism in Britain', *Journal of Modern History*, 80 (2008), 865–901, at 899; and David Goldberg, *The Threat of Race: Reflections on racial neoliberalism* (Oxford, Wiley-Blackwell, 2009).
9 Kymlicka, 'Neoliberal multiculturalism?', 107, 109.
10 Nisha Kapoor, 'The advancement of racial neoliberalism in Britain', *Ethnic and Racial Studies*, 36 (2013), 1028–46, at 1035.
11 Les Back, Michael Keith, Azra Khan, Kalbir Shukra and John Solomos, 'The return of assimilationism: Race, multiculturalism and New Labour', *Sociological Research Online*, 7 (2002), 1–10, para 5.7.
12 Rob Waters, *Thinking Black: Britain, 1964–1985* (Oakland, University of California Press, 2019).
13 Markus Holdo, 'Cooptation and non-cooptation: Elite strategies in response to social protest', *Social Movement Studies*, 18 (2019), 444–62; A. Sivanandan, 'RAT and the degradation of Black struggle', *Race & Class*, 26 (1985), 1–33; and Paul Gilroy, 'The end of anti-racism', *Journal of Ethnic and Migration Studies*, 17 (1990), 71–83.
14 Gilroy, 'Fragments', 35.
15 Sally Davison and George Shire, 'Race, migration and neoliberalism: How neoliberalism benefits from discourses of exclusion', *Soundings: A Journal of Politics and Culture*, 59 (2015), 81–95, at 87.
16 Gilroy, 'Fragments'; see also Stuart Hall, 'Aspiration and attitude: Reflections on Black Britain in the nineties', *New Formations*, 33 (1998), 38–46.

17 Nick Jewson and David Mason, 'The theory and practice of equal opportunities policies: Liberal and radical approaches', *Sociological Review*, 34 (1986), 307–34.
18 For a radical perspective on Black 'self-help', see Mike Phillips, 'Separatism or Black control?', in Ashok Ohri, Basil Manning and Paul Curno (eds), *Community Work and Racism* (London, Routledge and Kegan Paul, 1982), 103–20. See also Robbie Shilliam, *Race and the Undeserving Poor: From abolition to Brexit* (New York, Columbia University Press, 2018).
19 Herman Ouseley interviewed by Kwesi Owusu, 'The Commission for Racial Equality and the politics of race relations: An interview with chairman Sir Herman Ouseley', in Kwesi Owusu (ed.), *Black British Culture & Society: A text reader* (New York, Routledge, 2000), 425–35, at 429 (no date of the actual interview).
20 Trevor Phillips interviewed by Rob Berkeley (7 April 2009) for *The Struggle for Race Equality: An oral history of the Runnymede Trust, 1968–2008*, British Library Sound Archive.
21 Gordon Brown, 'The SNP nightmare', *The Guardian* (12 November 1998).
22 Stuart Hall, 'From Scarman to Stephen Lawrence', *History Workshop Journal*, 48 (1999), 187–97.
23 Tahir Abbas, 'Recent developments to British multicultural theory, policy and practice: The case of British Muslims', *Citizenship Studies*, 9 (2005), 154–9.
24 David Blunkett, 'Preface', in *Secure Borders, Safe Haven: Integration and diversity in modern Britain* (London, Home Office, 2002).
25 James Whitfield, *Unhappy Dialogue: The Metropolitan Police and Black Londoners in post-war Britain* (London, Routledge, 2004), 175.
26 Liz Fekete, 'The emergence of xeno-racism', *Race and Class*, 43 (2001), 23–40.
27 Antonio Perra, 'Prevent, Muslim identity, and the normalisation of neoliberalism', *Renewal: A Journal of Social Democracy*, 26 (2018), 83–95.
28 Kapoor, 'Advancement', 1035.
29 Judicial Appointments Commission, *Annual Report 2006/7*, 2.
30 Prashar always used the gendered 'chairman' to describe her role, as in the JAC's annual reports.
31 Judicial Appointments Commission, *Annual Report 2006/7*, 30.
32 Race Relations (Amendment) Act (2000), para. 2.1.1.
33 Race Relations Act (1976), para. 71.
34 *Discrimination Law Review: A Framework for Fairness: Proposals for a Single Equality Bill for Great Britain: A consultation paper* (London, DCLG, 2007), 88–9.
35 *Framework for a Fairer Future: The Equality Bill* (London, DCLG, June 2008), Cmnd 7431, 5.
36 'Racial diversity is a business problem', *Personnel Today* (29 April 2003), 8.
37 See Gilroy, 'Fragments', 23–4; and David Ainsworth, 'Saying goodbye to the social enterprise ambassadors', *Thirdsector* (15 September 2010), https://www.thirdsector.co.uk/saying-goodbye-social-enterprise-ambassadors/finance/article/1027941 (accessed 21 June 2021).
38 Kapoor, 'Advancement', 1037.
39 On the social democratic approach to racial equality and public policy, see John Solomos, 'Equal opportunities policies and racial inequality: The role of public policy', *Public Administration*, 67 (May 1989), 79–93.
40 Linda Bellos interviewed by Aviah Day (7 March 2017) for The GLC Story Oral History Project, http://glcstory.co.uk/listen-to-interviews/ (accessed 21 June 2021).
41 Jess McCabe, 'Linda Bellos: The enduring impact of accountable leadership', *Make/Shift*, 14 (2013), 36–7.
42 Jess McCabe, 'Back in action', *Inside Housing* (31 May 2013).
43 Bellos interviewed by Day.
44 Sara Ahmed, 'The language of diversity', *Ethnic and Racial Studies*, 30 (2007), 235–56.
45 Gill Kirton and Anne-Marie Greene, 'Telling and selling the value of diversity and inclusion: External consultants' discursive strategies and practices', *Human Resource Management Journal*, 29 (2019), 676–91, at 678.
46 Gill Kirton, Anne-Marie Greene and Deborah Dean, 'British diversity professionals as change agents: Radicals, tempered radicals or liberal reformers?', *International Journal of Human Resource Management*, 18 (2007), 1979–94.
47 Pragna Patel, 'Sisterhood and after: The Women's Liberation Oral History Project' (2011), British Library.
48 Patel, 'Sisterhood and after'.
49 Bellos interviewed by Day.

50 Holdo, 'Cooptation'; Gilroy, 'End of anti-racism'; and Sivanandan, 'RAT'. See also Kalbir Shukra, 'Ethnic pluralism and Black perspectives', in Kalbir Shukra, *The Changing Pattern of Black Politics* (London, Pluto Press, 1998), 50–69.
51 Sivanandan, 'RAT', 4.
52 Home Affairs Committee, Race Relations and Immigration Sub-Committee, *The Operation and Effectiveness of the Commission for Racial Equality, Minutes of Evidence* (London, CRE, 30 March 1981), HC 259-i, 35, 54; for funding to these groups in 1978–9, see *Annual Report of the Commission for Racial Equality, January to December 1978* (London, CRE, 1979), 50.
53 *First Report of the Commission for Racial Equality, June 1977 to December 1977* (London, CRE, 1978) or the *Annual Report of the CRE, 1978.*
54 *Operation and Effectiveness of the Commission for Racial Equality*, 6.
55 Paul Gilroy, *'There Ain't no Black in the Union Jack': The cultural politics of race and nation* (London, Routledge, 1992), 178.
56 National Audit Office, *Report by the Comptroller and Auditor General, Department of the Environment: Urban Programme* (London, House of Commons, 1985), appendix 2.
57 Keith Tompson, *Under Siege: Racism and violence in Britain today* (London, Penguin, 1988), 95. Keith Teare, now a highly successful technology entrepreneur, wrote this book under the pseudonym Keith Tompson.
58 Otto Saumarez Smith, 'Action for cities: The Thatcher government and inner-city policy', *Urban History*, 47 (2020), 274–91.
59 Alan Travis, 'Oliver Letwin blocked help for Black youth after 1985 riots', *The Guardian* (30 December 2015).
60 *Report by the Comptroller and Auditor General,* 2; Floya Anthias and Nira Yuval-Davis, *Racialised Boundaries: Race, nation, gender, colour and class and the anti-racist struggle* (London, Routledge, 1993), 181.
61 Tompson, *Under Siege*, 93–4
62 Tompson, *Under Siege*, 91.
63 Lord Scarman, *New Society* (February 1986).
64 Shukra, 'Ethnic pluralism and Black perspective', 54.
65 Herman Ouseley, 'A local black alliance: Consortium of Ethnic Minority Groups in Lambeth', in Ashok Ohri, Basil Manning and Paul Curno (eds), *Community Work and Racism* (London, Routledge and Kegan Paul, 1982), 160–7, at 166.
66 Herman Ouseley, Daniel Silverstone and Usha Prashar, *The System* (London, Runnymede Trust and South London Equal Rights Consultancy, 1984), 15.
67 See Gilroy, 'The end of anti-racism'.
68 Ouseley et al., *The System*, 11.
69 Shukra, 'Ethnic pluralism and Black perspectives', 64.
70 Shukra sees a parallel in the use of 'black' in, for example, the Labour Party Black Sections in the 1980s: 'black' was related to the 1960s' 'black power' and 1970s' 'black autonomous organization', but now ethnic difference was recognised *within* the category Black; it was not 'a single political identity stemming from resistance to racism' but 'a mechanism through which the separate ethnic groups can be called together, coordinated and linked'. Shukra, 'Ethnic pluralism and Black perspectives', 61–2.
71 Usha Prashar, 'The need for positive action', in John Benyon (ed.), *Scarman and After: Essays reflecting on Lord Scarman's report, the riots and their aftermath* (Oxford, Pergamon, 1984), 209–10.
72 Usha Prashar, Elizabeth Anionwu and Milica Brozović, *Sickle Cell Anaemia: Who cares?* (London, Runnymede Trust, 1986).
73 See also Usha Prashar and Shān Nicholas, *Routes or Roadblocks?: A study of consultation arrangements between local authorities and local communities* (London, Runnymede Trust, 1986).
74 See Jewson and Mason, 'Theory and practice of equal opportunities'.
75 Devon Thomas interviewed by Zena Edwards (22 April 2017) for The GLC Story Oral History Project, http://glcstory.co.uk/listen-to-interviews/ (accessed 21 June 2021).
76 Robert Chessyre and George Brock, 'Living behind the front line of violence', *The Observer* (19 April 1981).
77 Chessyre and Brock, 'Living behind the front line'.
78 Thomas interviewed by Edwards.

79 Devon Thomas, 'Black initiatives in Brixton', in John Benyon (ed.), *Scarman and After: Essays reflecting on Lord Scarman's report, the riots and their aftermath* (Oxford, Pergamon, 1984), 184–90, at 188.
80 Thomas, 'Black initiatives in Brixton', 189.
81 Thomas interviewed by Edwards.
82 Saumarez Smith, 'Action for cities', 287–9.
83 'Straight talk from the new task force boss', *Kensington Post* (20 August 1987).
84 Anthias and Yuval-Davis, *Racialised Boundaries*, 183.
85 Herman Ouseley interviewed by Louise Brodie (12 March 2012), British Library Sound Archive.
86 Peter Gibbon, 'Equal opportunities policy and race equality', in Peter Braham, Ali Rattansi and Richard Skellington (eds), *Racism and Antiracism: Inequalities, opportunities and policies* (London, Sage Publications, 1992), 235–51, at 235.
87 *Racial Equality Means Business* (London, CRE, 1995).
88 *Racial Equality Means Business.*
89 Ouseley interviewed by Owusu, 432.
90 A. Sivanandan, 'Challenging racism: Strategies for the '80s', *Race & Class*, 15 (1983), 1–11, at 1.
91 Sivanandan, 'Challenging racism'.
92 Sivanandan, 'Challenging racism', 8.
93 Tony Wade, *Black Enterprise in Britain* (London, TCS, 2003), 11.
94 Wade, *Black Enterprise*, 11.
95 Tony Wade, *The Adventures of an Economic Migrant* (Kingston, Ian Randle Publishers, 2007), 89.
96 Wade, *The Adventures of an Economic Migrant*, 57.
97 Tony Wade, speech to the UK Caribbean Chamber of Commerce, 1980, reproduced in *Adventures*, 107. Gilroy discusses such readings of Garvey in 'Fragments', 27.
98 'Both persons and states are expected to comport themselves in ways that maximize their capital value in the present and enhance their future value . . . through practices of entrepreneurialism, self-investment, and/or attracting investors': Wendy Brown, *Undoing the Demos: Neoliberalism's stealth revolution* (New York, Zone Books, 2015), 22.
99 Tony Wade, speech to the Caribbean Chamber of Commerce at their 5th annual dinner, 30 January 1980, reproduced in Tony Wade, *How They Made a Million: The Dyke and Dryden story* (London, Hansib, 2001), 18.
100 Tony Wade in UK Caribbean Chamber of Commerce *Annual Report*, 6 (June/July 1982), reproduced in Wade, *How They Made a Million*, 13.
101 In a list of Britain's top twenty Black millionaires published by *The Times* in 1992, Dyke and Dryden came in position 16, their wealth largely topped by entertainers and sportspeople ('200 millionaires in Britain are Black', *The Times* (7 November 1992), 9.
102 'A decade of Dyke and Dryden', *West Indian World* (5 June 1975), 12–13. On the North London West Indian Association's education campaigns, see Bernard Coard, *How the West Indian Child Is Made Educationally Sub-Normal: The scandal of the Black child in schools in Britain* (London, Caribbean Education and Community Workers Association, 1971).
103 *Launch of the Dudley Dryden Reference Library, 16 December 1994* (London, Hackney Racial Equality Council, 1994), Hackney Archives, C. L. R. James Library, Dalston, 301 P. Y 9724, Y13181.
104 'Decade of Dyke and Dryden', 12–13.
105 Wade, *Adventures*, 31–2.
106 Tony Wade quoted in 'Decade of Dyke and Dryden', 12–13.
107 'Miss Dyke and Dryden 1971', *West Indian Digest* (October–November 1971), 57–8. See also 'The crowning of Miss Dyke and Dryden', *West Indian Digest* (November 1972), 14–15.
108 Wade, *Adventures*, 41.
109 'Hard work made us successful', *West Indian World* (1 May 1974), 22.
110 Mike Phillips, 'West Indian businessmen', *New Society*, 44 (18 May 1978), 354.
111 Emily Robinson, Camilla Schofield, Florence Sutcliffe-Braithwaite and Natalie Thomlinson, 'Telling stories about post-war Britain: Popular individualism and the "crisis" of the 1970s', *Twentieth Century British History*, 28 (2017), 297–302.
112 Jewson and Mason, 'Theory and practice of equal opportunities'.
113 'Top London club proprietor hits out at disloyal Blacks', *West Indian World* (16 July 1976), 1, 11.

114 Phillips, 'West Indian businessmen'.
115 Len Dyke in *The West Indians* (BBC, 1966).
116 Margaret Thatcher, *The Downing Street Years* (London, HarperCollins, 1993), 509; and Charles Moore, *Margaret Thatcher: The authorized biography, volume 1: Not for turning* (London, Allen Lane, 2013), 137.
117 Home Affairs Committee, Race Relations and Immigration Sub-Committee, *Session 1980–1981, Racial Disadvantage, Minutes of Evidence*, 906.
118 Home Affairs Committee, Race Relations and Immigration Sub-Committee, *Session 1980–1981, Racial Disadvantage, Minutes of Evidence*, 906.
119 Wade in *Annual Report*, 6 (June/July 1982), reproduced in Wade, *How They Made a Million*, 13.
120 Wade, *How They Made a Million*, 13.
121 In 1980, Burke broadcast Wade's full address to the CCC's annual convention. See Wade, *How They Made a Million*, 19.
122 *Westindians in Great Britain* (London, Hansib, 1973); *Westindians in Great Britain: 1973–74*, 2nd ed. (Hoddesdon, Westindian Digest, 1974); *Westindians in Great Britain: 1975–76*, 3rd ed. (London, Hansib, 1975); *West Indians in Britain: A Caribbean impact on the United Kingdom*, 4th ed. (London, Hansib, 1979).
123 Editorial, 'After six months', *West Indian World* (10 December 1971), 6. See also Lionel Morrison, *A Century of Black Journalism in Britain: A kaleidoscopic view of race and the media (1893–2003)* (London, Truebay, 2007), 34; and Caribbean Chamber of Commerce, 'West Indian Enterprise in the UK', memorandum submitted to the House of Commons Race Relations and Immigration Sub-Committee, in House of Commons Home Affairs Committee, *Race Relations and Immigration Sub-Committee: Session 1980–81. Racial Disadvantage, Minutes of Evidence, Thursday 11 December 1980* (London, HMSO, 1980), 907.
124 Quoted in '*Root* is a four-letter word', *Forwaad!* (November 1979), 11–12.
125 '*Root* is a Four-Letter Word', 11–12.
126 For similar critiques of *West Indian World*, see Barbara Beese and Leila Hassan, 'A review of *Westindian World*', *Race Today* (September 1976), 188, 189; *Black Voice*, 3, 5 (1972), 3, cited in Savannah Blake, '"Kill the bill": The 1971 Immigration Act and the opposition of the Black British press' (undergraduate dissertation, Queen Mary University of London, 2020), 26.
127 Neville Maxwell, *The Power of Negro Action* (London, Neville Maxwell, 1965); and Joseph A. Hunte, *N[***]r Hunting in England?* (London, West Indian Standing Conference, 1966).
128 In Manchester, Ron Phillips, the leader of the local Universal Coloured People's Association, opened George Jackson House. In Birmingham, a group of Pan Africanist social workers established Harambee House. London boasted the largest concentration of these institutions, beginning with Michael X's Black House in Islington in 1969, and followed by Dashiki and Unity House in Notting Hill, Melting Pot in Brixton, Westindian Concern in Hoxton and Harambee in Holloway, each established by former Black House workers. Many of these organisations were united, in 1978, by the National Federation of Self-Help Organisations, which was opened at Melting Pot under the directorship of Vince Hines, one of Michael X's former right-hand men.
129 Thomas interviewed by Edwards.
130 *Dashiki and Homeless Black Young People: The Dashiki Council Annual Report, 1973–4*, p. 9, AST 36/1417 (2/ (incl. Annual Report booklet).
131 'Amazing story of Melting Pot', *West Indian World* (11 March 1973), 14; and 'Homeless Black youths creating problems in Westindian community', *West Indian World* (29 May 1974), 4.
132 Tony Sealy, 'Job creation! Work experience! Urban aid! These schemes are not meant to work for Blacks', *West Indian World* (24 September 1976), 13.
133 *Dashiki and Homeless Black Young People: The Dashiki Council Annual Report, 1973–4*, p. 6, AST 36/1417 (2/ (incl. Annual Report booklet).
134 Gilroy, 'Fragments', 26–7.
135 Vince Hines, 'The time must be considered', *West Indian World* (1 November 1974), 5.
136 'Hard work made us successful'.

11

Neoliberalism and the Labour Party

Mark Wickham-Jones

Writing in *The Times* in June 2002, Peter Mandelson announced: 'We are all "Thatcherite" now.'[1] Mandelson was a senior Labour politician and close adviser to Prime Minister Tony Blair (although in January 2001 he had resigned from the Cabinet for the second time). Emphasising the need for deregulation and greater flexibility, by 'Thatcherite' he appeared to mean something close to neoliberal: '[G]lobalisation punishes hard any country that tries to run its economy by ignoring the realities of the market or prudent public finances.' On the same day that Mandelson offered his provocative pronouncement, Blair gave a set-piece speech on welfare reform. He insisted that his administration offered a radically new position on the subject, one that broke with the party's past. It was an approach based on responsibilities, creating 'a dynamic labour market': 'We have changed the culture of the welfare state.'[2]

The notion that Labour had turned towards neoliberalism was hardly surprising. In February 1988, Tony Benn, a long-standing Labour MP, recorded in his diary an account of a joint meeting of the party's Shadow Cabinet and National Executive Committee (NEC), called to discuss the draft of a new statement of aims and values. Describing the text as 'insubstantial', Benn recorded his concern as Roy Hattersley, Labour's deputy leader and one of the authors of the document, said that 'he thought we [Labour] were in error to criticise market forces, and we must avoid the libel that we wanted a command economy'.[3] Benn was not alone: others (including members of the party's right wing) queued up to criticise the draft as being far too supportive of the market and putting too much emphasis on individual freedom.[4] Changes were made, but the final document offered a clear endorsement of the market mechanism as the basis for the economic organisation of most goods and services.[5] A few months later, when Labour published its new policy documents, Benn was glum about the party's trajectory: 'This is the Thatcherisation of the Labour Party. We have moved into the penumbra of her policy area and our main argument is that we will administer it better than she will.'[6]

In May 1989, following two days of discussions, marking the culmination of the party's two-year-long Policy Review, Benn was equally gloomy, writing: '[T]he NEC has abandoned socialist aspirations and any idea of transforming society: it has accepted the main principles not only of capitalism but of Thatcherism.'[7] The Labour leadership had just agreed, against Benn's vehement but marginalised protests, a new programme, outlined in *Meet the Challenge, Make the Change*, and heralded by many as marking a decisive change in the party's outlook. The opening pages of the text stated: 'Of course, private business can be the most efficient way of producing and distributing many goods and services.'[8] For the veteran left-winger, the Policy Review marked a fundamental transformation of Labour: in effect, it had become a party defined by its neoliberalism, that is, put rather starkly, by the extent of its commitment to free-market capitalism. (Benn did not use the term neoliberal.)

With the advent of Tony Blair's leadership of Labour in 1994, scholars and others claimed that the party was neoliberal in its orientation. As a letter writer to the *Glasgow Herald* put it in March 1995, '[t]here is nothing modernising about the new Labour Party. It is simply joining the neoliberal bandwagon.'[9] To signal the far-reaching extent of its underlying reorientation, Blair rebranded the party as 'New Labour'. To demonstrate the break with its past, he insisted on the reform of Clause IV of the party's constitution (its historic and sweeping commitment to public ownership) and he appeared to relish emphasising his pro-market credentials at every available opportunity. Within a year of becoming leader, giving the Mais Lecture in the City of London on 22 May 1995, Blair mapped out a minimalist economic strategy that resonated firmly with neoliberalism. He prioritised the fight against inflation, criticised Labour's Keynesian-oriented past and, insisting that 'capital flows . . . can swiftly move against policies which fail to win investors' confidence', concluded governments had minimal policy autonomy.[10] In developing the party's policies in this period, fulsome support came from Labour's Shadow Chancellor, Gordon Brown. He told one audience in 1994 that 'the old-style corporatism offered no solution'.[11] He continued: 'Labour will not take risks with inflation and we reject old quick-fix solutions of tax, spend and borrow.'[12]

For many, Blair's adoption of a neoliberal paradigm became even more forthright following his landslide general election victory in May 1997. When the Japanese firm Fujitsu closed a factory in his Sedgefield constituency in the north-east, the new Prime Minister was blunt (and unapologetic): 'It's totally dishonest', he said defiantly, 'to pretend governments can prevent such decisions . . . let us not kid ourselves. In certain sectors there will be an impact . . . We can't as the government do much about the twists and turns of world markets in an increasingly globalised economy.'[13] Giving his own Mais Lecture in 1999, Brown emphasised market credibility and endorsed Milton Friedman's 1968 monetarist analysis (claiming 'conclusive evidence for this proposition').[14]

In this chapter, I examine the nature of Labour as a neoliberal political party. I start with an outline of three influential social scientists, among the many, who have examined the link between social democracy and neoliberalism: Adam Przeworski, Colin Hay and Stephanie Mudge. In one way or another, each has suggested that, in recent decades, in conceptual terms reformist politics in the UK have collapsed into a residual neoliberalism. In subsequent sections, I detail the development of Labour's outlook over the course of the twentieth century, I discuss the attitude of the party's left and I consider the reform of Clause IV, before going on to assess whether Blair and Brown can be judged as neoliberals. Given the constraints of space and the ambitious extent of my coverage, readers may criticise my account for a lack of depth. But these are important issues covering much of the party's history. Let me emphasise that I do not intend to resolve the question of Labour's neoliberal turn. I hope this chapter will be taken as it is intended: as a plausible explanation of the party's politics that might contribute to further debate. Put starkly, my central aim is to ask: how far has Labour embraced neoliberalism?

In this discussion it is important, of course, to be clear about what I mean by the term neoliberalism. As the editors of this volume note, analyses of neoliberalism often fall back on an overly reductionist conception of the term based somewhat clumsily around free markets. Mudge offers a more layered definition of the term as an intellectual project that comprises a set of distinct policies (including, among other measures, deregulation, monetarism and privatisation) and some sort of political and normative commitment to markets. Manifestly, markets are central to the neoliberal endeavour: Mudge argues that neoliberalism embodies 'an unadulterated emphasis on the (disembedded) market as the source and arbiter of human freedoms'.[15] Several scholars have documented the complicated and nuanced history of neoliberal thought, from its emergence within the Mont Pèlerin Society to its dissemination among policymakers during the 1970s and 1980s.[16] In his account of neoliberal debates during the 1940s, Ben Jackson elaborates an intricate definition that highlights the complexity of the term and its contextual development: the neoliberal project has evolved in fundamental ways during the second half of the twentieth century.[17] (For more on this, see Jackson's chapter in this volume.) Both Mudge and Jackson share an emphasis on the historical nature of the term 'neoliberalism', its intricacies and its normative character.

Perspectives on Labour and neoliberalism

Writing in *New Left Review*, in 1980, Adam Przeworski offered a bold, sweeping and ultimately influential account of the development of social democratic politics.[18] Although he did not deploy the word 'neoliberal', the thrust of his argument and the importance he placed on such an outlook were straightforward. Moreover, while he subsequently formalised the analysis with the development of a sophisticated model and offered some emendations of his argument, the core elements remained pretty much the same throughout his later writings.[19] Przeworski's suggestion was that, under capitalism, reformist governments would encounter profound structural constraints, the effect of which was to force them to abandon their social democratic aspirations. He argued that any government, radical or not, needed to ensure a prosperous economy in order both to generate resources for its policies and to maintain electoral support. But growth under capitalism relied upon investment, which in turn required a profit incentive. Ensuring a sufficient rate of profit for growth therefore meant, put starkly, that governments needed to offer neoliberal-orientated (that is market-friendly) policies: 'The very capacity of social democrats to regulate the economy depends upon the profits of capital. This is the structural barrier which cannot be broken: the limit of any policy is that investment and thus profits must be protected in the long run.'[20] Such, Przeworski concluded, were the structural constraints of capitalism.[21] His writings abound with similar, simple statements.

Following publication of the more formal account, working with Michael Wallerstein, Przeworski revised his model, now framing it explicitly in terms of neoliberalism: 'At this moment', Przeworski and Wallerstein wrote, presumably with a degree of provocation in mind, 'the reader may remark that this is the neoliberal theory as well. It is.'[22] (Przeworski and Wallerstein noted a difference between neoliberals and their own variant of rational choice Marxism concerning the power that groups might enjoy.) Przeworski and Wallerstein argued that some – limited – redistribution was possible. But they remained doubtful about the social democratic prospect, putting particular emphasis upon mobility (could capital flows be taxed effectively?) and upon anticipations of radical measures. More importantly perhaps, their analysis remained couched in a pessimistic language, noting the constrained framework that must confront social democrats. In a sense, whatever the fine detail of their model (that some reformism might be possible), most readers associated Przeworski with the stark nihilism of his original argument, an association of which he did little to disabuse them. In a retrospective, the American political scientist opined gloomily: 'Does social democracy make a difference? It is only natural to expect that most of the time it would not.'[23]

By the time of the retrospective, Przeworski offered an explicitly historical account: he suggested that, for social democrats, revolutionary aspirations (by which I assume he meant aspirations for wholesale and abrupt measures) would give way to reformist ones, and that this approach, in turn, would pave the way for remedialism. Reformism (based around the notion of gradual, cumulative measures) gave way to policies aimed at correcting and limiting but not challenging market difficulties. In effect, reformism dissolved into neoliberalism. For Przeworski, such a position was accompanied by 'resignation', an acceptance on the part of social democrats that there were fundamental issues that they could not resolve. Social democratic parties such as Labour might begin with radical intentions, usually revolving around a programme of public ownership. But, Przeworski argued, nationalisation was neither sufficiently electorally popular nor developed as a strategy to provide a viable approach. Instead, left-wing parties would drift steadily into market-oriented policies: public ownership 'has turned out to be electorally unfeasible; radical redistributive policies result in economic crises which are not in the interests of wage-earners; and general affluence can be increased if capitalists are made to cooperate and wage-earners are continually disciplined to wait'.[24] The market became an essential aspect of economic strategy: its 'informational role is crucial' (though Przeworski noted that other forms of ownership than either that of shareholders or the state might have been developed).[25] His definition of neoliberalism focused on 'the claim that markets spontaneously maximise the welfare of society, or at least "efficiency", with only minimal regulation'.[26]

To be sure, as a political scientist Przeworski did not engage with the case of British Labour in any depth (though he did quote from its history). But the application of his analysis to the UK was clear-cut. Social democracy as a reformist concept was an exhausted historical phenomenon. Labour was, effectively, neoliberal. By 2001, Przeworski's conclusion was that, whatever Tony Blair's claim about negotiating a distinct 'Third Way', Labour had become such a party, following the policies of its Conservative predecessors.[27] Moreover, he presented this drift to neoliberalism as self-evident: describing the policy transformation, he concluded, '[t]he reader knows the rest, so I stop'.[28] He qualified the analysis to the extent that governments would try to offset the impact of globalisation (through, among other measures, protection against import penetration). There might be debate about the ideas underpinning social democracy, but Przeworski insisted that policies had, in practical terms, converged. Indeed, in the extent of their resignation, social democrats had abandoned some of their remedialism.

In a sequence of publications from the mid-1990s into the 2000s, focusing much more directly on the case of Labour, Colin Hay reached a broadly similar conclusion: that the party had become neoliberal.[29] There were two central aspects to Hay's account. Firstly, Labour had abandoned reformism (in the form of Keynesian social democracy) in favour of a Thatcherite free-market-based approach to policy. Dismissing the notion that such a process represented the modernisation of reformism, Hay emphasised a range of factors shaping such an outcome, including the direct impact of Thatcherism and Labour's Downsian-like quest for the centre ground of British politics and the median voter. As with Tony Benn's position, quoted in my introduction, Hay took Labour's 1987–9 Policy Review to be a critical episode in this transformation.[30] He argued:

> By the completion of the Policy Review – and, perhaps, some time before that – Labour had ceased effectively to be a social democratic party, committed as it had by then become to a pervasive neoliberal economic orthodoxy and to a basic acceptance of the legacy of the Thatcher years.[31]

Secondly, while Hay detailed the outcome of policy development within Labour from the 1980s onwards, he challenged the inevitability of the party's trajectory. Instead, in a series of papers, some written with Matthew Watson, he argued that a central aspect of Labour's accommodation with neoliberalism was the manner in which Labour elites had deliberately *constructed* a pessimistic discourse justifying their course.[32] No resignation here: the party had willingly agreed to, embraced even, its new position. As such, Labour's neoliberalism reflected the claims of senior figures that the nature of the global economy was an all-embracing and inevitable constraint upon any government, social democratic or not. Hay emphasised the extent to which politicians (most obviously Blair and

Brown) had built a narrative for neoliberalism in the rhetoric that they had articulated, using such a discourse to justify subsequent policy moderations: Labour politicians assembled 'an overarching logic of political "necessity" where the economic "realities" themselves did not warrant one'.[33] In another account with Watson, Hay argued that Labour politicians had 'internalised' the neoliberal imperative.[34] In marked contrast to Przeworski's inevitable structuralism, for Hay, the invocation of constraints (many stemming from globalisation) was a deliberate discursive strategy on the part of Labour politicians to justify an unnecessary and deeply problematic neoliberalism.[35]

Of course, Hay was by no means alone in drawing the conclusion that Labour's apparent acquiescence to Thatcherism represented the deliberate adoption of a neoliberal outlook. In a similar vein, for example, Richard Heffernan argued that Labour had been 'colonised' by the ideas of the right and so 'neoliberalised'.[36] Like Hay, Heffernan suggested that there was some agency in Labour's trajectory: the party was 'increasingly unwilling' to challenge Conservative initiatives regarding privatisation and deregulation.[37]

More recently, in *Leftism Reinvented*, Stephanie Mudge has developed an argument about social democracy's surrender to neoliberalism that echoes aspects of Przeworski's account. Like him, she advances an historically based analysis identifying different stages that the social democratic project has moved through. Socialism, she argues, gave way to Keynesianism (Przeworski's reformist phase), only for that to result in a neoliberal turn. But her causal explanation for such phases is different. While Przeworski emphasised the constraints that social democrats must confront and cannot overcome, Mudge places much more weight on the role of economists within social democratic parties. In its 1918 programme, without much expert input, a radical Labour Party criticised private ownership, 'reckless "profiteering" and wage slavery'.[38] From the 1930s onwards, partly under the guidance of Hugh Dalton, the party looked towards a more Keynesian-inclined outlook, a position that became institutionalised with the emergence of, among others, Hugh Gaitskell, Evan Durbin, Douglas Jay and, subsequently, Tony Crosland.[39] In the 1960s, under pressure from theoretical developments such as monetarism, rational expectations and public choice, Keynesian economics started to unravel, at the same time that Labour's management of the British economy ran into profound difficulties. In such circumstances, guided by a new group of expert economists and by external think tanks, by the 1990s, Blair and Brown had turned Labour towards neoliberalism. One adviser, Ed Balls – later a

Labour MP and Cabinet minister – was especially important in shaping the party's outlook.[40] Left-inclined economists played a critical role in driving the neoliberal project: '[T]he tactic . . . was to refit Labour's economic strategy to the imperatives of markets.'[41]

Labour and the market

Has Labour moved towards the market over the course of its history? I noted above that neoliberalism should not be defined simply by a reductionist view of market mechanisms. At the same time, patently, market processes, profits and price incentives are important aspects of such an approach (along with other factors). Each of the three perspectives above indicates a shift towards the market on the part of British reformists during the last decades of the twentieth century. Has Labour adopted a neoliberal perspective in recent decades through its embrace of the price mechanism and private ownership?

As part of its constitutional reorganisation in 1918, Labour adopted commitments that were, on the face of it, radical and far-reaching. Most obviously, in its well-known Clause IV (section 4), the 1918 constitution pledged Labour to sweeping and comprehensive nationalisation through 'the common ownership of the means of production, distribution, and exchange and the best obtainable system of popular administration and control of each industry or service'.[42] For Przeworski and Mudge, the abandonment of such a commitment is part of the transformation towards neoliberalism.[43] But note that Clause IV said nothing about what might or might not be the role of the market mechanism in allocating goods and services. Moreover, quite what such a statement meant in practice was by no means obvious. While sweeping in its apparent ultimate objective, few commentators thought that it meant that Labour would literally abolish private ownership. Rather, they tended to take it as a signal of the party's radical intent and as some sort of general aspiration.

Many scholars concluded that the 1918 constitution defined the party's moderation. For Tom Nairn, it enshrined the party's labourist outlook: in effect, it institutionalised trade union control of Labour in a defensive and atheoretical manner.[44] Nairn pointed out that, having adopted such a commitment, the party immediately debated a resolution concerning social reconstruction that made no reference to ownership whatsoever. When a delegate complained, Sidney Webb (author of the new clause) told the conference that Labour should not go back over old shibboleths, effectively equating the clause with such a status. Nairn concluded: 'Socialism, in short, belonged in its proper place, the constitution, where it could be admired occasionally and referred to in moments of emotion.'[45] Ralph Miliband's equally critical judgement in *Parliamentary Socialism* was that Labour's new programme was a 'Fabian blueprint for a more advanced, more regulated form of capitalism', one that would humanise private enterprise.[46] Attributing the Clause IV wording to Webb, Ross McKibbin argued that the new clause was important 'precisely because of its vagueness and lack of rigour'. It had 'an umbrella function: it was an acceptable formula in a party where there was otherwise little doctrinal agreement'.[47] Rather than being a precise policy statement, its architects saw the phrase 'common ownership' as electorally popular in appealing to middle-class Fabians.

In March 1923, Philip Snowden, soon to become Labour's first Chancellor of the Exchequer, introduced a motion into the House of Commons about the capitalist system. He criticised private ownership and control and called for their gradual supersession with a system based on public ownership and democratic control.[48] But, while Snowden's goal was radical, interestingly, he also talked about 'social amelioration' (and the improvement of industrial conditions), exactly the kind of objective that Przeworski so disparaged as watered-down reformism. While Snowden was especially critical of economic monopolies and trusts, his critique was essentially empirical and his means moderate: 'There are three or four ways in which we have been dealing with the capitalist system, and all we suggest is that we should continue along these lines, but move much more rapidly.'[49]

Over the next 50 or so years, while the party formally retained Clause IV, Labour's approach to economics remained based around a combination of modest state intervention and market arrangements. There were, of course, different policy packages, and the proposed extent of public regulation across economic affairs varied. In office between 1945 and 1951, Labour did take parts of the economy into public ownership. But there was little suggestion that such public ownership was a specifically socialist endeavour designed to replace the market. Far from it: with few exceptions, nationalisation covered basic utilities, natural monopolies and essential services. In practice, public ownership neither challenged the market nor directly furthered socialism. Even at the time of this programme – the party's most interventionist phase – Hugh Dalton, Labour's second Chancellor of the Exchequer (following Snowden), told the House of Commons: '[W]e all desire that private enterprise should show itself capable over the great field that will be left to it, even after we have carried out the programme on which this government and the

Labour Party won the election.'[50] A couple of years later, Dalton told the Labour Party conference:

> Since we are operating a mixed economy in which the socialised sector is still not very large, relatively speaking, the profit motive cannot be completely removed within the private sector . . . The private sector, which is conducted for profit, would not be conducted at all, if there were no profits.[51]

Stafford Cripps and Hugh Gaitskell, successive chancellors between 1947 and 1951, professed a similar outlook. Cripps described the profit motive as an essential factor in the economy, albeit one that should be regulated.[52] Gaitskell emphasised the importance of understanding 'the nature of the pricing system' and not being 'hopelessly prejudiced against a market economy'.[53] He continued: 'To-day the party attitude in the main is that free choice must be continued and unfairness corrected rather through redistribution of income and wealth than through direct controls.'[54] Subsequently, Labour chancellors adopted a comparable position. James Callaghan reordered corporation tax to increase incentives: '[O]ne can, as I am proposing here, have a relatively low rate of tax on the profitability of the company, so encouraging it to plough back its retentions into new machinery and plant, whereas there will be a higher rate of tax on the shareholder.'[55] Roy Jenkins told the Labour conference in 1969 that the party should not 'tax people without limit . . . [while] we ought not to be ashamed of believing in taxation for worthwhile social purposes. But we certainly ought not to be a party of taxation for taxation's sake or a party which is instinctively hostile to private consumption.'[56] Between 1974 and 1979, Denis Healey made clear his commitment to a 'vigorous and profitable private sector'.[57]

This brief discussion suggests that there was no abrupt turn on the part of Labour towards the market (and so potentially towards neoliberalism). Regardless of what was in Clause IV, for decades Labour politicians took profit incentives and the price mechanism to be acceptable features of the prevailing economic arrangements, albeit ones that required some regulation. They certainly condemned 'profiteering', as Mudge noted, which I take to mean the uncontrolled accumulation of a surplus (usually through some sort of market distortion, such as monopoly). But they were much less hostile to what might be taken as a reasonable profit (that could be taxed and regulated). For Stafford Cripps, in 1945, profiteers were on a par with racketeers. At the same time, his acceptance of the market mechanism was plain: '[A] great many controls have already been removed where they are not necessary for the decent and orderly development of industry in the present economic circumstances.'[58] As Eric Shaw notes, 'Labour never sought to challenge the market as the organising principle of economic life'.[59]

Labour's left and the market

It might be expected that Labour's attitude towards the market and profits would have undergone a change during the period in which the party was dominated by its left wing, between the early 1970s and the early 1980s. At this time, Labour adopted a series of radical interventionist measures – known collectively as the Alternative Economic Strategy – revolving around the public ownership of individual firms and the introduction of planning agreements between private companies and the state.[60] But, for Stuart Holland, the economist who was the central architect of the party's new programme, competition, market processes and the pricing mechanism remained central (for some reason Holland does not figure in Mudge's account of Labour's trajectory).[61] What mattered was the public ownership of individual firms in order to inject competition into a particular sector and so challenge private monopolies – 'competitive public enterprise', as Holland termed it: 'The [new public] companies would be employed within a market economy framework in which the price mechanism remained the key resource allocation guideline.'[62] The result would be 'healthy competition'.[63] By 1976, Labour's commitment to a state holding company working within the market was mapped out: 'The NEB [National Enterprise Board] must be given the same operating freedom as other companies. It must be able to make competitive bids on the market for companies.'[64] In developing such a position, Holland was categoric: '[P]rofits are as important in modern capitalism as ever before.'[65]

Outlining Labour's approach to economic planning after the 1979 general election, Geoff Bish, Labour's left-wing research secretary, addressed the issue of the market, distinguishing between four different (though not mutually exclusive) positions. They included improving the market, anticipating it, fixing it and, finally, replacing it (what Bish termed Soviet planning). His conclusion was straightforward: through 'a judicious combination of anticipation and fixing together with some improvement', the party should come up with a plan that 'should, in my view, have a market orientation'.[66] That is, there should be no replacement of the market (Bish's fourth position). Planning in Eastern Europe had,

Bish argued, moved towards market criteria. (He was also interested in Japanese planning.) In a later paper, Bish pointed out that international trade meant the British economy needed to be competitive, which, 'unless we envisage moving toward a system of autarchy', implied a role for the market and for prices. Industrial activities should, by and large, be profitable. Accordingly, the market 'should have a very important role in industrial planning'.[67] Bish went so far as to offer a more normative defence of market processes: they could 'be a useful means of decentralising decision-making in the economy'. (In other words, he offered them the sort of informational role that Przeworski saw as crucial: my point is that Labour politicians, including left-wingers, have pretty much always held this view.) Central planners should not pass decisions downwards. Within such a framework, Bish indicated that there needed to be far greater public ownership and government intervention, while price signals might on occasion be misleading.

In the early 1980s, Labour passed on discussion of its planning policy to the Trades Union Congress–Labour Party Liaison Committee, a joint union–party structure. In September 1981, its subcommittee on Industrial Democracy and Planning discussed the relationship between planning and the operation of markets and was critical of the latter: the group's minutes recorded, 'it was argued that the market mechanism was incapable of allocating resources to meet social requirements'. But the minute went on to accept a role for market processes: 'At the same time, it was pointed out that economic planning was not meant to negate the allocative functioning of the market but rather to perform those functions more successfully.'[68] The committee noted even East European countries used information about rates of return, prices and preferences across both international and domestically focused sectors.

Tony Benn was dismissive of the discussion. In his diary, he noted that Norman Atkinson, another veteran left-wing MP, had complained that the document did not criticise markets. Bish responded: 'Well the party hasn't opposed the market mechanism for a decade or more. It hasn't been rejected by the party for years.'[69] But Benn made a more subtle point than had Atkinson: 'We should', he told his colleagues, 'therefore redefine our concept of the market mechanism and make it absolutely clear that we are talking about the difference between the big companies and the 98 per cent of companies that are medium and small businesses.'[70] Benn appeared to accept that market processes, albeit regulated and modified, could work for medium and small firms. He had made a similar point some years earlier, praising such firms and saying, 'I am a firm believer in free enterprise on this scale'.[71] In 1982, the final document tried to capture the party's position: '[I]f the political dogma of the free market offers no solution to our economic problems, neither does a planning system which tries to direct economic activity from the centre.'[72] The draft had included a further qualification, referring to 'the totally free market'.[73]

The repeal of Clause IV

At the end of his first speech as Labour leader to the party conference, Tony Blair told his audience that they must adopt a new statement of objectives. Clause IV needed to be completely rewritten. It was not, of course, a new issue. Following the party's 1959 general election, Hugh Gaitskell had tried and failed to amend it: '[S]tanding as it does on its own, this [Clause IV] cannot be regarded as adequate. It lays us open to continual misrepresentation.'[74] As leader, Neil Kinnock had had more success with the adoption of *Democratic Socialist Aims & Values*, the document that had so alarmed Benn back in 1988. In his original draft of the economic section, the Labour leader had opened by stating that change could not be left to random market forces. Hattersley felt this was 'a far too total rejection of the market: the sort of wild swing that got us into previous trouble'.[75] His position was that, while requiring regulation, markets promoted liberty and efficiency. He insisted that such a stance was at odds with a neoliberal one and that it was firmly within the traditions of Labour. Markets had no 'moral significance' other than as means to ends.[76]

Some of the criticism of the market in the new document was modified. In the final version, Labour offered an explicit, though qualified, commitment to market forces. While in some areas of activity (for example, health care and education) it was inappropriate, the document concluded, 'in the case of the allocation of most other goods and services, the operation of the market, where properly regulated, is a generally satisfactory means of determining provision and consumption'.[77] At the same time, Kinnock attempted to clarify the party's attitude to nationalisation by detailing the need for an extension of 'social' ownership. But Labour was manifestly committed to the mixed economy and to a private ownership structure. These commitments sat somewhat uneasily alongside the original Clause IV section 4 which was retained in party literature. At the party's conference in 1988, Kinnock defended the Policy Review and recognised 'the fact that the kind of economy we will be faced with when we win the election will be a market economy. That is what we have to deal with and we will have to make it work better than the Tories do.'[78] The detail of Kinnock's policy programme owed much to continental arrangements. In the same speech, the Labour leader sought to attack Margaret Thatcher's individualism and her 'no such thing as society' aphorism: 'No person other than me. No time other than now. No such thing as society, just "me" and "now".'[79] The new statement of aims had, however, little impact on the party as a whole.

Tony Blair, by contrast, was not prepared to maintain the old Clause IV in any form. Unsurprisingly, he was subsequently scathing about its wording, calling it, over a few pages, 'intellectually redundant', 'politically calamitous', 'hopelessly unreal', 'a refusal to confront reality', a 'graven image' and an 'unfettered indulgence'.[80] (Don't hold back, Tony.) He did admit that it was 'largely symbolic', but to Blair such rhetoric mattered; as he told one audience, '[r]e-writing Clause IV is an essential part of the transformation of the Labour Party'.[81] In April 1995, Labour committed itself to a new statement of aims, this time replacing the old version altogether. Gone was the promise of sweeping nationalisation. The new Clause IV offered common endeavour, community, solidarity, tolerance and respect. But it explicitly endorsed the 'enterprise of the market and the rigour of competition' as well as a 'thriving private sector and high-quality public services'.

New Labour and neoliberalism

It is easy to see why scholars presumed Labour to be a neoliberal party during the 1990s. As Colin Hay argued, there is much in the rhetoric deployed by Tony Blair and Gordon Brown that reverberates with aspects of such an approach. Each seemed determined to construct a very clear and distinct discourse. Moreover, as Adam Przeworski indicated, each placed considerable emphasis on the constraints that must confront any government.

From his election as Labour leader, Blair quickly made plain his determination to reorient the party, to tone down its policy commitments and to moderate its rhetoric.[82] Outlining its values and policies, Labour made a series of apparent concessions to the neoliberal cause, seeming to abandon many of its past radical commitments. In the wake of Labour's defeat in the 1992 general election, Gordon Brown, as Shadow Chancellor, had already mapped out changes to the party's economic strategy: '[W]e had to leave behind the old sterile conflicts between public and private sectors, between state and markets, between managers and employees . . .

we had to shed old dogmas.'[83] Blair's 1995 Mais Lecture became something of a defining statement on the economy, emphasising the market forces that a Labour administration must encounter. A year later, he told an audience in New York that 'errors in macroeconomic policy will be punished rapidly and without mercy'.[84] In the Mais Lecture, distancing himself from European-style economic arrangements, Blair appeared to accept the nature of the UK as a liberal market economy (though the speech obviously pre-dated the subsequent Varieties of Capitalism scholarly debate). He defended the 'Anglo-Saxon structure', something that had 'not stopped the US economy being dynamic and strong'.[85] Such a liberal structure, it could be presumed, lent itself to a neoliberal outlook (though see the discussion on growth models by Peter Sloman in this collection).

Repeatedly, Blair and Brown emphasised that Labour had ditched its past: 'The days of reflex tax and spend politics are over . . . we will reward work, effort and opportunity.'[86] In January 1997, the Shadow Chancellor pledged that there would be no increase in personal taxation, including the higher rate, under a future Labour government ('no return to the penal tax rates of the 1970s').[87] Writing in *The Observer*, the journalist Patrick Wintour said the decision represented 'not simply the end of socialism but of social democracy, and the whole Croslandite commitment to use public spending and tax to reduce inequality'.[88] (Wintour's argument anticipated Przeworski's claim that remedialism had replaced reformism.) Brown followed this undertaking with a promise to accept the Conservative government's existing spending limits for its first two years of office. In other words, social democracy did not mean higher public expenditure.

In criticising past Labour governments' management of the economy, Tony Blair came close to endorsing Thatcherism. The Labour leader admitted that 'serious change was required to improve competitiveness at the end of the 70s. The emphasis on enterprise, on initiative and incentive and on tackling lack of responsiveness in the public sector was necessary.'[89] On another occasion, he pronounced: 'Business runs business. There'll be no "corporatism" or "picking winners".'[90] At times, the rhetoric echoed the views of those who saw Labour as a manifestly anti-market party in its previous policy positions. Hence, Gordon Brown proclaimed that 'past Labour governments tried to counter the injustice and failings of free market forces by substituting government for market'.[91] He argued that 'the old economic policies which ended at the boundaries of the nation state . . . no longer made any sense'.[92]

In mapping out such a position, Blair and Brown were particularly concerned to assure business of their moderation (so 'building a genuine new partnership').[93] Developing the party's so-called prawn cocktail offensive of the early 1990s, they went to considerable effort to persuade firms about their limited intent.[94] Drawing on rational expectations and public choice, New Labour politicians offered a pro-market rules-based approach to economic strategy: there would be no policy surprises once the party took office. Accordingly, business could trust a Blair-led administration. The Labour leader approved the profit-making activities of the private sector: '[F]irms invest to make money and over the decades, poor returns have probably been the biggest single explanation for the UK's poor investment record.'[95] Profit needed to be sustained. During the 1997 general election campaign, Blair gave a straightforward endorsement of the market mechanism, saying: 'There is no overriding reason for preferring the public provision of goods and services, particularly where those services operate in a competitive market economy.' He continued: 'The presumption should be that economic activity is best left to the private sector, with market forces being fully encouraged to operate.'[96]

New Labour followed up this moderate agenda in office.[97] In her account of neoliberalism, Stephanie Mudge mapped out distinct policy areas including liberalisation, deregulation, privatisation, depoliticisation and monetarism.[98] In each, the Blair government can be argued to have followed a neoliberal trajectory. In terms of monetarism and depoliticisation, as Chancellor of the Exchequer, Gordon Brown immediately made the Bank of England independent. Meeting Eddie George, its Governor, to discuss interest rates after the May 1997 general election, Brown raised interest rates, only to announce that henceforth a new Monetary Policy Committee made up of bank officials and civil servants would be responsible for operational decisions. It was a standard claim of neoclassical economic theory that politicians should not be trusted with setting interest rates because of the temptation to manipulate the economy for political purposes. Brown's delegation of the decision represented a straightforward acknowledgement of the neoliberal case: in the future, the decision would be depoliticised, to the extent that it would be taken by Bank officials and economists and not by elected politicians. (There was some qualification of this position to the extent that the Chancellor still set the inflation target that the Bank should attain. For critics of Labour, it was little consolation.) In his Mais Lecture of 1999, Brown accepted much of the monetarist case, emphasised the importance of credibility, transparency and trust, and outlined a modest agenda for government aimed at the promotion of stability. He was clearly influenced in such thinking, as Mudge notes, by Ed Balls.[99]

New Labour's approach to fiscal policy was equally cautious ('an iron commitment to financial stability and fiscal prudence').[100] In opposition, Brown had mapped out several market-based rules.[101] The first, termed the 'golden rule', indicated that the government should borrow only to meet the demands of investment. The second was that the ratio of public debt to GDP should remain constant over the economic cycle. The rules were backed up during Brown's first years as Chancellor with an austere approach to taxation, though he introduced a windfall tax on the privatised utilities and increased the taxation of company dividends alongside several other revenue-raising measures. When the auction of licences for mobile phone services brought in a windfall, Brown simply used it to reduce the national debt. Corporation tax was cut. Blair claimed that any government needed to take care when raising personal taxation and went so far as to state that, 'even making allowance for that [some redistributive measures], inequalities have merit'.[102] He had earlier suggested that '[t]he public simply won't pay more taxes and spend more to fund an unreconstructed welfare system'.[103]

In terms of public spending, at times, the government appeared to take an aggressive position. Blair complained about social democrats in the past: 'We seemed to want to throw money at every problem, with little if any concern for the efficiency with which public resources were spent.'[104] New Labour placed considerable weight on the need for welfare reform. Early on, Brown signalled his intention by forcing through a Conservative-planned cut in benefit for lone parents. The administration's position was, moreover, accompanied by an aggressive rhetoric that was hostile to perceived dependency. Blair argued that 'the welfare system can discourage hard work and honesty . . . it locks people into dependency on benefits'.[105] When the government launched its welfare reform bill, Blair insisted that it marked 'a fundamental break with the past', stating that 'the days of an automatic right to benefit will go'.[106] In a similar vein, Alistair Darling, the relevant minister, stated that 'no-one has an unqualified right to benefit'. He promised that 'the new regime will be far-tougher than people thought . . . we will end the something-for-nothing approach that has characterised the past'.[107] People would be helped into work but there would be conditions and responsibilities that they would be expected to meet. In his chapter in this volume, Bernhard Rieger emphasises Blair's commitment to duty as underpinning the party's approach to welfare. In a statement co-authored with Gerhard Schröder, the German social democrat, the Labour leader maintained that '[p]ublic expenditure as a proportion of national income has more or less reached the limited of acceptability'.[108] By 2001, Roy Hattersley, the former deputy leader of the party who had promoted the market back in the 1980s, had had enough: 'Now my party not only pursues policies with which I disagree; its whole programme is based on a principle that I reject.'[109] During the general election campaign that year, Jeremy Paxman asked Blair on 11 occasions whether rising inequality was acceptable.[110] He refused to answer.

In terms of privatisation, New Labour did not maintain the bold programme associated with previous Conservative governments. Some, relatively limited, privatisations continued, however, including air traffic services, the Defence Evaluation and Research Agency and the British Nuclear Group. By and large, other than in extreme circumstances, Labour governments between 1997 and 2010 did not reverse any privatisations. They did take over Railtrack (the rail network – not the train companies) in 2002, and they did receive a stake in several banks in exchange for public funds during the financial crisis of 2008–9. The government made widespread use of the Private Finance Initiative (PFI), under which private capital was used to fund many hospital, education and other construction projects. The PFI traded immediate investment funds (which did not appear as public liabilities) for repayment over several decades. Blair insisted that it did not amount to privatisation and that his approach was simply pragmatic: 'Where it works and delivers a better public service, use it; where it doesn't, don't.'[111]

Regarding liberalisation and deregulation, Labour launched several initiatives. During his second term in office, Blair established foundation hospitals, which enjoyed greater financial autonomy in their decision-making, with market-based incentives. Top-up fees were introduced into higher education. It was in such a context that Mandelson made his claim about a Thatcherite Labour Party, referring to 'the urgent need to remove rigidities and incorporate flexibility in capital, product and labour markets'.[112] Repeatedly and unashamedly, Brown made the case for markets: acknowledging their extension under Labour, he claimed that 'where there was insufficient competition our aim should be to enable markets to work better'.[113] Making them work better meant more competition, increased enterprise, better information, less regulation where possible and more flexibility. In opposition, Blair had been critical of 'Eurosclerosis', perceived institutional inflexibilities on the Continent: 'We do not want to import the rigidities apparent in some European economies.'[114] In office, he developed the notion of flexible labour markets as a central aspect of economic strategy (see Peter Sloman's chapter in this volume). To critics, such arrangements simply institutionalised low pay. Blair told the Confederation of British Industry in 2001 that 'the UK has among the least regulated product and labour markets of any industrialised countries . . . It will stay that way.'[115]

At certain points, Tony Blair tried to map out a Third Way as a distinct position between the left and the right, one that would offer a theoretical underpinning to his policy trajectory. The Third Way (a concept that Gordon Brown did not subscribe to) reached its height in 1998 in a Fabian pamphlet, several speeches and the statement jointly authored with Schröder. But many commentators concluded that the terrain detailed by Blair was largely a reworked neoliberalism. While he committed himself to the public interest, Blair emphasised dynamic, competitive markets, acknowledging 'that the private sector, not government, is at the forefront of wealth creation and employment generation'.[116] With Schröder, he criticised high public spending, indicated that too much effort had gone to correcting market failures and condemned the belief in government intervention: '[T]he weaknesses of markets have been overstated.'[117] It was as part of an attempted reboot of the Third Way that Mandelson offered his 2002 judgement about Thatcherism.

Assessing New Labour's neoliberalism

Care needs to be exercised, for several reasons, however, in assuming New Labour's trajectory to be conclusively neoliberal.[118] Firstly, having mapped out a cautious approach to public spending for its first years in office, such a stance was not sustained. From July 2000 onwards, the Blair administration implemented some significant increases in public expenditure. While the administration maintained a rhetoric of having broken with 'tax and spend', spending in some areas, including health care and education, went up substantially. Doubling in cash terms, health care expenditure rose from around 6.5 per cent of GDP to just under 10 per cent by 2010 (partly as a result of the recession). Overall, between 2000/1 and 2007/8, public spending as a percentage of GDP increased from 36.9 to 41.1. Funding of public services increased year by year by 4.4 per cent in real terms, more than the 0.7 per cent rise per annum under the Conservatives between 1979 and 1997.[119] Moreover, the fiscal rules announced by Brown proved far less constraining than might have been the case. With regard to the first, the government did not define investment; concerning the second, Treasury ministers avoided offering a commitment to the exact terms of the economic cycle. In any case, when circumstances demanded, during the economic crisis of 2008–9, the government accepted that the rule could not be maintained. It is worth noting, too, how the financial crisis reshaped the image of Labour in office. Having frequently been considered as an austere proto-Thatcherite government, it came to be seen as profligate in public spending, unremittingly increasing expenditure with little regard for efficiency or sustainability.

Secondly, a similar pattern characterised the government's approach to taxation. Having offered a cautious rhetoric (and in 1999 having cut income tax), Labour proved prepared to raise tax (as noted above) in myriad ways – sometimes called stealth taxes because they did not have an immediate impact on pay packets. In 2002, Brown increased national insurance contributions specifically to fund the National Health Service, something that was well received by the public: according to one pollster it was 'the most popular tax rise ever'.[120] Spending increases were also funded by borrowing as well as by growth. Further tax increases, including of the higher rate of income tax, took place during the 2008–9 financial crisis. Of course, until that economic crisis, Labour's fiscal position also reflected buoyant tax receipts in a growing economy, especially those from the financial sector. Critics questioned the sustainability of such a model as well as the government's reliance on increased debt (especially household liabilities).[121]

Thirdly, between 1997 and 2010, Labour made a series of significant interventions in the operation of the market economy. Brown introduced a 'New Deal' to assist the long-term unemployed back into the labour market through a Gateway process to prepare them for work and several options to guide them into employment (see Bernhard Rieger's contribution to this volume). Employers were given subsidies to take on workers. Subsequently, the programme was embedded and extended to other groups. In terms of its impact, there was considerable debate as to how effective the various New Deal programmes were. Nevertheless, the theory underlying them was a straightforward rejection of the notion that labour markets were efficient and could spontaneously adjust to reduce unemployment. I noted in my introduction Tony Blair's reaction to the closure by Fujitsu of a factory in his constituency. The bleak position he articulated was certainly at odds with the argument underpinning the myriad New Deal programmes. These programmes concluded that market corrections would not tackle unemployment for all sorts of reasons (such as rigidities, information asymmetries, differential time horizons and skills deficiencies) without sustained government intervention.

Following on from the New Deal, Brown attempted to integrate the tax and benefits system more fully, thereby ensuring that people had incentives to take employment. In 1998, he introduced the Working Families Tax Credit (WFTC), which offered supplementary payments to those taking low-paid jobs. Again, the approach was based on the notion that markets, as presently structured, did not operate efficiently: they created a poverty trap where people might be better off on benefit because of the tax liabilities associated with work. Tax credits offered an automatic top-up to market wages. The WFTC was developed into a Working Tax Credit and a Child Tax Credit as well as improved maternity care and the Sure Start programme (which assisted with childcare arrangements). By 2007, six million families benefited from tax credits of one kind or another. Labour also introduced a statutory minimum wage (see Jim Phillips's analysis in this volume). While there was debate about its effectiveness, again the theory underlining the measure was at odds with neoliberalism. (It is, of course, important to note that some aspects of such measures were problematic – notably the punitive element of the New Deal in the form of withholding benefit from those who did not cooperate.) In his chapter in this volume, Jim Tomlinson offers an account of governmental interventions in the labour market (concerning benefits and wages) as well as in housing.

Fourthly, there was a pronounced redistributive aspect to some of New Labour's measures (see Sloman's chapter in this volume for a sustained discussion of this point). The New Deal, tax credits and minimum wage were all intended to help the less well-off. Regarding child poverty, Labour chose a relative target (thereby endorsing a redistributive goal): between 1998/9 and 2009/10, the level of child poverty fell from around 26 per cent to 20 per cent.[122] In 2000, one commentator stated of the budget measures: 'These are very, very substantial changes. It really is a dramatic change . . . I can't think of any economic measure giving such a large group of the population gains on this scale in 20 years of tax and benefits policy.'[123] Another termed it 'redistribution by stealth'.[124] Such a pattern continued into Labour's second and third terms in office, beginning in 2001 and 2005 respectively. Curiously, at much the same time that he embraced Thatcherism, Peter Mandelson told readers of a new version of his book, *The Blair Revolution*, that 'there is much of Croslandism that is still relevant to Labour thinking . . . promotion of equality through the increased public spending that growth permits'.[125] To be sure, the inequalities in British society did not improve markedly. Labour did not reverse the increased inequality of the 1980s, as evidenced by a rising Gini coefficient, but they did stabilise it (as illustrated by figure 4.1 in Peter Sloman's chapter in this volume).[126] At the level of decile groups, real income went up for the second, third and fourth bands by more than it did for the seventh, eighth and ninth groups, demonstrating greater equality between these groups. But this pattern was countered by the performance of the first band, the very weakest (whose real income fell) and by the growth of the top band, the richest.[127] Such an outcome reflected, in part, how market pressures in a globalised world were accelerating such disparities and the fact that Labour's approach focused on some disadvantaged groups at the expense of others. Reducing unemployment was the main route by which those in poverty would become better off (that is through the provision of work).

A last point to make is that, even in its neoliberally oriented rhetoric, New Labour's endorsement of the market was frequently qualified. Both Blair and Brown noted the extent to which the market needed regulating, argued that its operation frequently produced significant failures and asserted that it should not be judged in isolation from its relationship to the state and to society. For example, in 1994, Brown claimed that 'the British free market, without effective intervention, has proved to be a static, brittle and second rate model of economic development'.[128] Explicitly critiquing the notion that markets worked automatically and that any interference in them was problematic, he attacked the right and their commitment to unregulated laissez-faire.[129] Even in declaring the universalism of the Thatcherite position in 2002, Peter Mandelson attacked 'old laissez-faire notions of indiscriminate tax cuts and rolling back the state'.[130] He put considerable emphasis on social justice as a guiding value. When *The Guardian* asked Blair whether narrowing inequalities was one of his government's objectives, he was unambiguous, replying '[y]es, of course it is'.[131] In this volume, Jim Tomlinson suggests that Labour inherited a set of structures that hindered the implementation of neoliberal measures. Alongside such a constraint, I am less certain of the neoliberal intent of New Labour's agenda.

Conclusion

After 2015, with Jeremy Corbyn as leader and John McDonnell as Shadow Chancellor, Labour moved away from aspects of the economic model that the party had articulated during the 1990s and 2000s. Given their background on the left of Labour, as well as the economic difficulties that the Brown administration had run into, and the party's electoral defeats in 2010 and 2015, such a shift in trajectory was unsurprising. In speeches,

McDonnell made the case for greater government intervention, increased public ownership and higher taxation at the same time as promising an end to the PFI.[132] Furthermore, he was clear in linking New Labour with neoliberalism, effectively blaming the Brown administration's market-based approach for the economic crisis of 2008–9. Whether McDonnell's approach amounted to a break either with the market mechanism or with the kind of measures the party had adopted in the past is another matter. His call for increased public ownership effectively amounted to limited renationalisation and did not involve anything like the scale of intervention associated with the Alternative Economic Strategy. His proposal for 'Inclusive Ownership Funds', based on the distribution of profits across a firm's workforce, bore some similarities to a scheme developed by Labour in the early 1970s.[133] Incidentally, the suggestion in the 1970s that Labour might develop capital-sharing was vehemently opposed by many left-wingers in the party because it would encourage profit-making while undermining traditional public ownership and socialist consciousness, thereby legitimating capitalism. However, no one appeared to have accused McDonnell of neoliberalism on the basis of his proposal for collective funds in the late 2010s.

In this chapter, I have examined Labour's relationship with neoliberalism. Has Labour turned into a neoliberal party? It depends, in part, on what is meant by the term neoliberalism. If it represents a residual belief in the market mechanism, then I think that Labour has always, despite the lofty ambitions of Clause IV, been a neoliberal party. If the term means something more complex, the conclusion is less clear. Przeworski equates neoliberalism with a belief that markets spontaneously maximise welfare, while Mudge sees it as a belief in markets as the source and arbiter of human freedoms. I am unpersuaded that New Labour would meet such a threshold: for all its endorsements, the party neither advocated markets as extemporaneously and naturally meeting human needs, nor did it believe that markets would sponsor freedom, without a considerable role alongside them for the state. For all their support of markets, neither Blair nor Brown offered the kind of principled normative support of markets that might be expected of neoliberalism. While their position was manifestly supportive, it was also empirical, pragmatic and qualified. Stephanie Mudge rightly emphasises the importance of policy advisers (and party officials), a much-neglected aspect of Labour's policy development. But it is not clear to me that their contribution during the New Labour years was to determine a neoliberal trajectory. Frequently, the importance of economists was to legitimate and signal the detail of policy on the basis of decisions already taken.

In reaching such a conclusion, I do not deny that New Labour moved towards a more market-friendly position – as the party has done at other points in its past. Such a development has also reflected the context in which the party has governed, one reflecting the considerable deindustrialisation within the British economy. Some of the inequality commonly associated with neoliberalism has resulted from the polarisation of a deindustrialised workforce and its impact on incomes (see the chapters by Jim Phillips and Jim Tomlinson in this volume).[134]

The above discussion indicates that both Blair and Brown did, as Colin Hay has argued, offer a discourse that resonated with aspects of neoliberalism. But, in contrast to Hay, I conclude that in Labour's policies there remained significant commitments to tax and spend and to intervention in the economy, as well as to a redistributive impulse. Indeed, at times, despite its appearance, Labour's rhetoric was not deployed to justify a neoliberal programme. Rather, the party's discourse hid a more radical approach to practical policy measures. As such, in the study of New Labour, it is important to separate policy pronouncements from practical interventions (in much the same way as the 1918 Clause IV can be separated from the party's then attitude to the market mechanism). In particular, as Chancellor between 1997 and 2007 and as Prime Minister from then until 2010, Brown was able to offer a range of distinct policy positions, some of which were manifestly at odds with the party's rhetoric. A *Times* leader on the same day as Mandelson's claim about Labour's Thatcherism complained about the Blair government that 'it offers slogans when it cannot decide how to act. It says it will embrace the private sector to deliver healthcare yet shows little progress . . . Enough of talking. It is time now to do.'[135]

Overall, there is considerable continuity, over the course of the party's history, in Labour's attitude to the market and to capitalism. While Tony Benn complained about the apparent rightward turns taken by Labour in the late 1980s, he also noted the enduring similarity of the party's outlook. A day before the comment in May 1989 which I quoted in my introduction, he wrote despairingly: 'Looking back on it, I must recognise that the Labour Party has never been a socialist party, it has never wanted social transformation.'[136]

Notes

1 Peter Mandelson, 'There's plenty of life in the "new" Third Way yet', *The Times* (10 June 2002), 16. My thanks to Ben Jackson and Florence Sutcliffe-Braithwaite for comments on a draft of this chapter.

2 Tony Blair, 'Speech on welfare reform', *The Guardian* (10 June 2002), https://www.theguardian.com/society/2002/jun/10/socialexclusion.politics1 (accessed 21 June 2021).
3 Tony Benn, 5 February 1988, *The End of an Era* (London, Hutchinson, 1992), 537.
4 Colin Hughes and Patrick Wintour, *Labour Rebuilt* (London, Fourth Estate, 1990), 64–75.
5 Labour Party, *Democratic Socialist Aims & Values* (London, Labour Party, 1988), 10.
6 Benn, 25 May 1988, *End of an Era*, 546.
7 Benn, 9 May 1989, *End of an Era*, 568.
8 Labour Party, *Meet the Challenge, Make the Change* (London, Labour Party, 1989), 6.
9 Paul Laverty, 'Letter to the editor', *Glasgow Herald* (17 March 1995), 18. Laverty scripted *I, Daniel Blake*.
10 Tony Blair, The Mais Lecture (22 May 1995), 10. (Unpublished Labour Party speeches are in the author's private collection.)
11 Gordon Brown, 'New policies for the global economy' (26 September 1994), 7 (unpublished Labour Party speech).
12 Brown, 'New policies for the global economy', 8.
13 Quoted by Philip Webster and Paul Wilkinson, 'Flying Squads to help jobless', *The Times* (17 September 1998).
14 Gordon Brown, The Mais Lecture (October 1999) (unpublished Labour Party speech).
15 Stephanie Mudge, 'What is neo-liberalism', *Socio-Economic Review*, 6 (October 2008), 703–31, at 704.
16 See, for example, Philip Mirowski and Dieter Plehwe (eds), *The Road from Mont Pèlerin: The making of the neoliberal thought collective* (Cambridge, MA, Harvard University Press, 2009); and Quinn Slobodian, *Globalists: The end of empire and the birth of neoliberalism* (Cambridge, MA, Harvard University Press, 2009).
17 Ben Jackson, 'At the origins of neo-liberalism: the free economy and the strong state, 1930–1947', *Historical Journal*, 53 (2010), 129–51.
18 Adam Przeworski, 'Social democracy as a historical phenomenon', *New Left Review*, I/122 (1980), 122.
19 Adam Przeworski, *Capitalism and Social Democracy* (Cambridge, Cambridge University Press, 1985), 171–204; and Adam Przeworski and Michael Wallerstein, 'The structure of class conflict in democratic capitalist societies', *American Political Science Review*, 76 (1982), 215–38.
20 Przeworski, 'Social democracy as a historical phenomenon'.
21 Desmond King and Mark Wickham-Jones, 'Social democracy and rational choice Marxism', in Terrell Carver and Paul Thomas (eds), *Rational Choice Marxism* (Basingstoke, Palgrave, 1995), 200–30.
22 Adam Przeworski and Michael Wallerstein, 'Structural dependence of the state on capital', *American Political Science Review*, 82 (1988), 11–29, at 13. Interestingly, in their abstract they used the term 'neoclassical' rather than neoliberal.
23 Adam Przeworski, 'How many ways can be third?', in Andrew Glyn (ed.), *Social Democracy in Neoliberal Times* (Oxford, Oxford University Press, 2001), 312–33, at 312.
24 Przeworski, *Capitalism and Social Democracy*, 43. Przeworski took out the word 'only' from the *New Left Review* article appearing before the word if ('only if capitalists . . .).
25 Przeworski, 'How many ways can be third?', 323.
26 Adam Przeworski, 'Choices and echoes: Stability and change of policy regimes', in Hideko Magara (ed.), *Economic Crises and Policy Regimes* (Cheltenham, Edward Elgar, 2014), 33–55, at 33. He also notes the neoliberal critique of the state and of state intervention.
27 Przeworski, 'How many ways can be third?', 312
28 Przeworski, 'How many ways can be third?', 321.
29 For the fullest statement of Hay's approach, see Colin Hay, *The Political Economy of New Labour* (Manchester, Manchester University Press, 1999).
30 Colin Hay, 'Labour's Thatcherite revisionism: Playing the "politics of catch-up"', *Political Studies*, 42 (1994), 700–7.
31 Hay, *Political Economy of New Labour*, 42.
32 See, for example, Colin Hay, 'The invocation of external economic constraints', *The European Legacy*, 6 (2001), 233–49; and Matthew Watson and Colin Hay, 'The discourse of globalisation and the logic of no alternative: Rendering the contingent necessary in the political economy of New Labour', *Policy and Politics*, 31 (2003), 289–305.
33 Watson and Hay, 'The discourse of globalisation', 294.

34 Colin Hay and Matthew Watson, 'In the dedicated pursuit of dedicated capital', *New Political Economy*, 3 (1998), 407–26, at 407.
35 In later work, Przeworski edged away from inexorable structural constraints and towards a similar position to that of Hay, noting: 'There seems to be no politician who does not proclaim that globalisation narrowly circumscribes their margin of manoeuvre . . . most of the effects attributed to globalisation are due to something else.' Przeworski, 'How many ways can be third?', 330.
36 Richard Heffernan, *New Labour and Thatcherism* (Basingstoke, Palgrave, 2001), 157.
37 Heffernan, *New Labour and Thatcherism*, 168.
38 Quoted by Stephanie Mudge, *Leftism Reinvented: Western parties from socialism to neoliberalism* (Cambridge, MA, Harvard University Press, 2018), 47.
39 Mudge, *Leftism Reinvented*, 150–5. It is important to note that Mudge's book offers a detailed and comparative discussion of these themes.
40 Mudge, *Leftism Reinvented*, 345–8.
41 Mudge, *Leftism Reinvented*, 348.
42 Labour Party, *Rule Book 1988–1989* (London, Labour Party), 6–7.
43 See also Heffernan, *New Labour and Thatcherism*, 21.
44 Tom Nairn, 'The nature of the Labour Party', in Perry Anderson and Robin Blackburn (eds), *Towards Socialism* (London, Fontana, 1965), 159–220, at 179–84.
45 Nairn, 'The nature of the Labour Party', 184.
46 Ralph Miliband, *Parliamentary Socialism* (London, Merlin, 1961), 62. See also David Coates, *The Labour Party and the Struggle for Socialism* (Cambridge, Cambridge University Press, 1975), 18–21.
47 Ross McKibbin, *The Evolution of the Labour Party, 1910–1924* (Oxford, Oxford University Press, 1974).
48 Philip Snowden, *Hansard* (20 March 1923), col. 2472.
49 Snowden, *Hansard* (20 March 1923): 'We want no further step forward until the previous step which we took has been justified by its success.'
50 Hugh Dalton, *Hansard* (25 October 1946), col. 2298.
51 Labour Party, *Annual Conference Report* (1948), 149.
52 Stafford Cripps, *Hansard* (16 November 1948), col. 324.
53 Hugh Gaitskell, *Recent Developments in British Socialist Thinking* (London, Co-operative Union, 1955), 21.
54 Gaitskell, *Recent Developments in British Socialist Thinking*, 33.
55 James Callaghan, *Hansard* (10 May 1965), col. 200.
56 Labour Party, *Annual Conference Report* (1969), 255.
57 Denis Healey, *Hansard* (2 August 1976), col. 1242.
58 Stafford Cripps, *Hansard* (5 December 1945), col. 2375.
59 Eric Shaw, *The Labour Party Since 1979* (London, Routledge, 1994), 5.
60 Mark Wickham-Jones, *Economic Strategy and the Labour Party* (Basingstoke, Palgrave, 1996).
61 Stuart Holland, *The Socialist Challenge* (London, Quartet, 1975).
62 Stuart Holland, 'The new economic imperatives', internal Labour Party memorandum, RD: 473/November 1972, Labour Party Archive, People's History Museum, Manchester, 7.
63 Labour Party, *The National Enterprise Board* (London, Labour Party, 1973), 16.
64 Labour Party, *Labour's Programme 1976* (London, Labour Party, 1976), 27.
65 Holland, 'The new economic imperatives', 1.
66 Geoff Bish, 'Planning aims and priorities', memorandum, RD322/March 1980, Labour Party Archive, 4.
67 Geoff Bish, 'Industrial planning: Some basic assumptions and questions', RD725/February 1981, Labour Party Archive, 2.
68 TUC–LP Liaison Committee Planning and Industrial Democracy Sub-Committee, minutes, 21 September 1981, Labour Party Archive, 2.
69 Benn, 21 September 1981, *The End of an Era*, 150.
70 Benn, 21 September 1981, *The End of an Era*, 151.
71 Maurice Corina, 'Mr Benn favours smaller companies to develop "real enterprise and initiative"', *The Times* (15 June 1974), 19.
72 TUC–LP Liaison Committee, *Economic Planning and Industrial Democracy* (London, Labour Party, 1982), 6.

73 'Draft interim report', RD2319/April 1982, Labour Party Archive, 4.
74 Labour Party, *Annual Conference Report* (1959), 112.
75 Roy Hattersley, annotated draft copy, 'Statement of Aims & Values' (in author's possession, no date), 15.
76 Roy Hattersley, Eighth Hannah Arendt memorial lecture, University of Southampton (17 February 1987).
77 Labour Party, *Democratic Socialist Aims & Values*, 10.
78 Labour Party, *Annual Conference Report* (1988), 64
79 Labour Party, *Annual Conference Report* (1988), 63.
80 Tony Blair, *A Journey* (London, Hutchinson, 2010), 76.
81 Tony Blair, 'The rights we enjoy reflect the duties we owe' (22 March 1995), 1 (unpublished Labour Party speech).
82 Mark Wickham-Jones, 'How the Conservatives lost the economic argument', in Andrew Geddes and Jonathan Tonge (eds), *Labour's Landslide* (Manchester, Manchester University Press, 1997), 100–18.
83 Gordon Brown, 'The dynamic market economy' (1 May 1995), 1 (unpublished Labour Party speech).
84 Tony Blair, British American Chamber of Commerce (11 April 1996), 4 (unpublished Labour Party speech).
85 Blair, Mais Lecture, 16.
86 Blair, speech, British American Chamber of Commerce, 5.
87 Gordon Brown, 'Preparing Britain for the future' (4 September 1996), 4; and Gordon Brown, 'Equipping Britain for the future' (31 January 1997) (unpublished Labour Party speeches).
88 Patrick Wintour, 'Gordon Brown has delivered his real tax bombshell', *The Observer* (26 January 1997).
89 Blair, speech, British American Chamber of Commerce (11 April 1996), 4–5 (unpublished Labour Party speech).
90 Tony Blair, 'Making Britain competitive in a world economy' (21 January 1997), 3 (unpublished Labour Party speech).
91 Brown, 'New politics for the global economy', 2.
92 Gordon Brown, London International Financial Futures and Options Exchange City lecture (19 November 1996), 3 (unpublished Labour Party speech).
93 Blair, 'Making Britain competitive in a world economy', 1.
94 Mark Wickham-Jones, 'Anticipating social democracy, pre-empting anticipations', *Politics and Society*, 23 (December 1995), 465–94.
95 Tony Blair, The LIFFE/City of London Corporation lecture (16 September 1996), 17 (unpublished Labour Party speech).
96 Tony Blair, Corn Exchange, London (7 April 1997) (unpublished Labour Party speech).
97 Mark Wickham-Jones, 'Exorcising ghosts: How Labour dominated the economic argument', in Andrew Geddes and Jonathan Tonge (eds), *Labour's Second Landslide* (Manchester, Manchester University Press, 2002), 103–24.
98 Mudge, 'What is neo-liberalism?', 704; and Mudge, *Leftism Reinvented*, 369.
99 Ed Balls, 'Open macroeconomics in an open economy', *Scottish Journal of Political Economy*, 45 (1998), 113–32. See Mark Wickham-Jones, 'Communautés épistémiques et évolution de la stratégie économique du Parti travailliste britannique', in Michel Camau and Gilles Massardier (eds), *Démocraties et autoritarismes: Fragmentation et hybridation des régimes* (Paris, Kathala, 2009), 305–27.
100 Brown, London International Financial Futures and Options Exchange City lecture, 4.
101 Brown, 'Preparing Britain for the future', 4.
102 Tony Blair, interview transcript, *The Guardian* (11 September 2001).
103 Tony Blair, Party of European Socialists, Malmö, Sweden (June 1997), 3 (unpublished Labour Party speech).
104 Tony Blair, *The Third Way* (London, Fabian Society, 1998), 15.
105 Tony Blair, speech, Aylesbury estate, London (2 June 1997).
106 Tony Blair, 'It really is the end of the something for nothing days', *Daily Mail* (10 February 1999).
107 Alistair Darling, 'We make no apologies for our tough welfare regime', *The Independent* (10 February 1999).

108 Tony Blair and Gerhard Schröder, 'Europe: The Third Way/Die Neue Mitte', Friedrich Ebert Stiftung (June 1998), 4 (unpublished Labour Party speech).
109 Roy Hattersley, 'It's no longer my party', *The Guardian* (24 June 2001).
110 Jeremy Paxman, interview with Tony Blair (June 2001), http://news.bbc.co.uk/1/hi/events/newsnight/1372220.stm (accessed 21 June 2021).
111 Blair, interview transcript (11 September 2001).
112 Mandelson, 'Plenty of life'.
113 Gordon Brown, *Speeches 1997–2006* (London, Bloomsbury, 2006), 126.
114 Tony Blair, 'Growth through partnership' (3 July 1996) (unpublished Labour Party speech).
115 Tony Blair, CBI (November 2001) (unpublished Labour Party speech).
116 Blair, *The Third Way*, 10: 'Competition where possible, regulation where necessary.'
117 Blair and Schröder, 'Europe: The Third Way/Die Neue Mitte', 3.
118 Mark Wickham-Jones 'From reformism to resignation and remedialism?', *Journal of Policy History*, 15 (2003), 26–45; and Ken Mayhew and Mark Wickham-Jones, 'The United Kingdom's social model', in Jon Erik Dolvik and Andrew Martin (eds), *European Social Models from Crisis to Crisis* (Oxford, Oxford University Press, 2015), 144–76.
119 Mayhew and Wickham-Jones, 'The United Kingdom's social model', 150.
120 Deborah Mattinson, *Talking to a Brick Wall* (London, Biteback, 2010), 119.
121 See Colin Crouch, 'Privatised Keynesianism: An unacknowledged policy regime', *British Journal of Politics and International Relations*, 11 (2011), 382–99; and Colin Hay and Nicola Smith, 'The story of a North Sea bubble: The strange demise of the Anglo-liberal growth model in the United Kingdom and Ireland', *European Political Science Review*, 6 (2013), 401–30.
122 Mayhew and Wickham-Jones, 'United Kingdom's social model', 163.
123 Andrew Dilnot quoted by Mark Atkinson, 'Help for the poorest pensioners "most generous for 20 years"', *The Guardian* (10 November 2000).
124 Andrew Grice, 'Budget 1999: Red Gordon and the iron Chancellor sit happily together', *The Independent* (10 March 1999), 14.
125 Peter Mandelson, *The Blair Revolution Revisited* (London, Politico's, 2002), xxix.
126 Mayhew and Wickham-Jones, 'United Kingdom's social model', 162.
127 Tom Sefton, John Hills and Holly Sutherland, 'Poverty, inequality and redistribution', in John Hills, Tom Sefton and Kitty Stewart (eds), *Towards a More Equal Society* (Bristol, Policy Press, 2009), 21–46, at 25; and Mayhew and Wickham-Jones, 'The United Kingdom's social model', 163.
128 Brown, 'New policies for the global economy', 6: 'Crude free market dogma has failed because it does not encourage long term relations and commitments'.
129 Brown, 'The dynamic market economy', 3.
130 Mandelson, 'Plenty of life'.
131 Blair, interview transcript (11 September 2001) (unpublished Labour Party speech).
132 John McDonnell, speeches, Labour Party Conference (25 September 2017 and 24 September 2018); and John McDonnell, 'Introduction', in John McDonnell (ed.), *Economics for the Many* (London, Verso, 2018), vii–xviii.
133 Wickham-Jones, *Economic Strategy*, 63.
134 See also Avner Offer, 'British manual workers: From producers to consumers, c. 1950–2000', *Contemporary British History*, 22 (2008), 537–71.
135 'It's good to talk but the Government needs firmer action', *The Times* (10 June 2002), 17.
136 Benn, 8 May 1989, *The End of an Era*, 564.

12

Neoliberalism and Conservatism in Britain

James Freeman

What was the relationship between neoliberalism and Conservatism in twentieth-century Britain? Political and intellectual historians have often told the story of one by reference to the other. Until recently, for example, the main impetus for tracing 'neoliberalism' back to an international network of thinkers in the 1930s and 1940s was to explain the ideas and networks that supposedly held sway over Conservative elites in later decades.[1] In Britain, the high-water mark of neoliberal influence was normally located in the Conservative administrations governing between 1979 and 1997.[2] Accordingly, when critics or advocates of neoliberalism looked for agents of neoliberal change in Britain these were often found working in the party's orbit.

Writing about twentieth-century Conservatism has likewise been shaped by neoliberalism. The label has been used to describe shifts in party philosophy or factional power struggles.[3] It also plays a role in the literature's preoccupation with explaining 'Thatcherism'.[4] Neoliberal ideas both help distinguish Thatcherism from other Conservatisms and help tie together the aims, policies and arguments of Thatcher's governments as a local implementation of a transnational ideology. Thus, as one of many spillover effects of searching for Thatcherism's origins, neoliberalism has indirectly shaped our understanding of the party's history well before the 1970s.

But as much as these are two histories told in tandem, adequately describing the interaction between neoliberalism and Conservative politics has proven challenging. Contemporaries noted tensions between neoliberal solutions and the party's political needs, as well as an uncomfortable intellectual fit between the two on certain issues, particularly on questions of personal morality.[5] Representatives of each tradition have offered public support for the other and yet made it clear that they did not regard themselves as members.[6] Other representatives have been openly hostile, arguing that links between the two are unwelcome or tantamount to an invasion.[7] Political scientists and historians have further contributed to the catalogue of contradictions, mostly by exposing the inconsistent practice of Conservatives said to be governing as neoliberals.[8]

To make sense of the 1970s and 1980s in particular, commentators and academics institutionalised these tensions in terms such as 'the New Right' and 'Thatcherism', or in formulations such as 'the free economy and the strong state'.[9] As Ben Jackson and Robert Saunders point out, these terms are themselves historical artefacts; they were responses to the observation that the political energy of the right in this period seemingly stemmed from contacts between Conservatism and neoliberalism, aided at least in part by think tanks.[10] Rather than tie much down, these terms produced more debate. At its best, this provoked insightful, cross-disciplinary exchanges about what their alliance represented.[11] At its worst, it became self-limiting, trapping explanations of what happened within a web of contemporary terms that came to signify both the ideas said to be motivating political action and the resulting policies themselves.

As we learn more about the inner workings of Thatcher's governments, it has also become evident that these formulations imply too much coherency and too little contingency and evolution.[12] While think tanks did play a role in policy change, it is easily overstated and a much wider array of motivations, influences, interests and actors were involved.[13] New ideas were in play, but they stood in relation to longer historical processes.[14] And while the tension between Conservative and 'neoliberal' instincts did directly inform policy debates, these tensions are best thought of as ongoing, malleable, sometimes explosive, sometimes inert, and generally more unstable than the terms above implied.[15] 'Thatcherism', then, is not so much a term that denotes a stable configuration of Conservative and neoliberal ideas then implemented, as one set of possible paths Conservatives took through complex electoral and policy problems, only partly guided by an ongoing renegotiation of Conservative and neoliberal principles and arguments.

Taken together, this recent work suggests we need to think afresh about the interface between Conservatism and neoliberalism, freeing our description from the questions, timelines and models suited to explaining the Thatcher 'revolution'. Paradoxically, this does not mean ceasing to focus on the 1970s and 1980s as the period in which the two became most obviously entwined (although understanding other points of contact is important).[16] Rather, it means reading their relationship in these decades in ways that look beyond the question of 'influence'. The factors driving their relationship might be different from those that led Thatcher to power. The mechanisms shaping their interaction might lie outside the policy process. And the events and developments that put this relationship in historical perspective might involve people who do not feature in the usual backstory of Thatcherism.

This chapter begins to re-describe the relationship between Conservatism and neoliberalism in two ways. Firstly, it resets our historical perspective on their relationship prior to Thatcherism by drawing out the cumulative historiographical impact of applying models used to understand their interaction in the 1980s to earlier periods. Secondly, the chapter offers a deeper account of the interface between Conservatism and neoliberalism in the late 1970s and early 1980s. 'Interface' is a deliberate choice of term. My interest here is not the organisational structures of think tanks or academic/journalistic networks. Nor is it in establishing a chain of neoliberal influence from thinker through to policy implementation. And nor is it the wider socio-economic contexts that promoted a *general* affinity between the two. Instead, I want to isolate specific moments of contact and assess what their particular features – both medium and message – tell us about the wider interaction between Conservatives and neoliberal arguments. One way to take forward Ben Jackson's suggestion that we pay closer attention to how politicians translated abstract ideas into more 'demotic' terms, then, is to better characterise the kinds of interaction that took place between these groups as part of a speechwriting process.[17]

Neoliberalism and Conservatism before 1975

'Influence' has been the chief way of relating neoliberalism to Conservatism. While this is most obvious in accounts of think tanks' influence on Margaret Thatcher's party, three types of 'influence claim' have been made about earlier periods. Firstly, historians have detected influence in specific moments in the party's post-war history, especially in Churchill's 'Gestapo' broadcast of 1945.[18] Secondly, earlier Conservatives have been identified as converts to neoliberal thought.[19] Thirdly, there are broader claims to influence, such as those which read the 1945–51 Opposition's emancipatory rhetoric as evidence of Conservatives adding 'a dash of Hayek to their previously Keynesian tonic'.[20] The weight placed on intellectual influences varies, but this reading of rhetoric opens up a connection between Thatcherism and 1940s Conservatism.

Yet the influence model can distort neoliberals' relationship to Conservatism in earlier periods. As I have discussed elsewhere, the claim that F. A. Hayek's *Road to Serfdom* (1944) influenced Churchill's 1945 election broadcasts is unsound.[21] The speech's general line of argument was set prior to the publication of Hayek's book and it built on a tradition of argument that could produce similar conclusions to Hayek but from distinctly Conservative premises. Accordingly, reading 1945 as an inaugural moment for the party's relationship with neoliberalism omits the roles of Stanley Baldwin and other figures such as Viscount Cranbourne; they were not influenced by neoliberals, but they did develop their party's tradition of argument in directions that shaped the relationship between Conservatism and neoliberalism as the latter emerged.[22]

'Influence' also detracts from other developments in anti-statist arguments. Debate about the nationalisation of banks in the mid-1930s, for example, saw Conservatives argue that competition enshrined public control over the economy: industries worked to meet public demand and banks financed those successfully doing so. Without banks' freedom to make investment decisions, the public would lose its 'freedom of choice', and socialists looking to impose teetotalism 'in the public interest' might simply cut off breweries' credit.[23] 'Influence' does not take us very far here. A specific rhetorical need (refuting the accusation that banking elites controlled the economy) encouraged the mixing of newer arguments with older attacks on progressives. Instead, it suggests one factor promoting longer-term compatibilities – but not equivalence – between Conservative and neoliberal arguments was that interwar debate about the 'public interest' shaped both.

A second means of relating Conservatism and neoliberalism has been to use 'neoliberal' as a label to denote free-market positions.[24] This is an understandable – if problematic – shorthand in the 1970s. But without caveats, it risks anachronism or confusion with simple 'libertarian' positions when applied to earlier periods, because it homogenises neoliberal viewpoints and underplays the evolution of their positions between the 1930s and 1980s.[25] Even with caveats, the label can misrepresent episodes in the party's history. For example, the party's 1949 policy statement 'The right road for Britain' can accurately be read as a departure from the *Industrial Charter* (1947). It is not, however, evidence of a party turning towards 'neo-liberalism'.[26] In fact, the party's right criticised the document for 'rather too much adherence to the notion of a planned economy'.[27] The impression of a shift arises in part because its launch was designed to deflect that criticism.[28] Control-cutting individualism came through in the press coverage and Churchill's associated speech. His speechwriters were clear, though, that they wanted to free the economy to protect full employment and social services, not reject them.[29] The risk with using the term, then, is that it shrinks the distance between the mid-century party and neoliberals of both periods.

This labelling has been attractive because it integrates the relationship between neoliberalism and Conservatism within a wider model that understands Conservative history as a tussle between 'paternalist' and 'libertarian' instincts, arranging policies, factions and periods along that axis.[30] Little of the original chronology remains unchallenged. However, its basic plot – the libertarian strand's rise, fall and revival – set the template for claims that the influence of neoliberals under Thatcher represented either a Conservative restoration or a liberal invasion.[31] Moreover, neoliberalism has been drawn into explanations which retain the duality's concepts but complicate its narrative. For some historians, Conservatives pragmatically drew on both instincts. Jim Tomlinson described 1950s economic policy as neither 'neo-liberal' nor interventionist but 'lurch[ing] from expedient to expedient' in pursuit of 'liberty with order'.[32] Alternatively, Harriet Jones identified a 'reinvigorated neo-liberal Conservatism' in 1950–1, but one restrained by the electorate's support for social services.[33] To others, the 'two souls' of Conservatism were reconciled by a higher principle, such as the preservation of social order, or by seeing conflicting rhetoric as a proxy for a deeper debate about the effectiveness of civil society's institutions.[34]

In later periods, related theories have helped explain why Conservatives were attracted to neoliberalism. Neoliberal theory, it can be argued, was one part of a political project to construct a cross-class electoral alliance, and the link between new ideas and economic circumstances is captured in the idea that Conservatives were attracted to neoliberalism as a way to navigate the crisis of Keynesian social democracy or legitimise a counter-inflationary strategy.[35] Likewise, contradictions between Conservatism and neoliberalism can be lessened by seeing the latter as a tool for pursuing a higher statecraft.[36]

But in earlier periods, the duality model and the theories attached to it have obscured the relationship between Conservatism and neoliberalism. The duality oversimplifies the ideological breadth of mid-century Conservatism.[37] In particular, the temptation to focus on 'libertarian' periods or factions misses important developments that rendered *mainstream* Conservatism much more compatible with neoliberalism. For instance, it was R. A. Butler who began to make important connections between welfare, choice and moral virtue. As Home Secretary, he argued that, although he did *not* think crime was 'entirely due to the . . . Welfare State', it was important to recognise that crime had risen despite prosperity and that material satisfaction had not ensured 'moral progress'.[38] Several years later, through debates that (re)established the family as key to preventing delinquency, he made the case for the 'proper balance between State-help and self-help' on the grounds that the family's role was to transmit 'manners and morals', and that the family could not be expected to 'remain vigorous and vital if it comes to rely on the State'.[39]

The language of pragmatism also fosters unhelpful arguments about sincerity. In the early post-war period, Churchill's party is said to have not been committed to its libertarian rhetoric.[40] Later, in a highly politicised version, Edward Heath is either guilty of having betrayed the neoliberal policies his rhetoric in opposition suggested, or of having 'allow[ed] himself to be pushed into a more doctrinaire right-wing rhetoric'.[41] In both instances, the reading of Conservative rhetoric as 'neoliberal' sets up a false standard in which it is only sincere if it reflects 'neoliberal' policies. These arguments have several weaknesses. Firstly, they misconstrue the motivations of the rhetoric said to reflect neoliberalism. Because the emancipatory rhetoric of 1940s Conservatism reflected a diagnosis of Britain's economic situation, not abstract views of the state, leading Conservatives could call for both deep cuts to public spending and a corporatist Industrial Parliament.[42] Secondly, by underestimating Conservative commitment to principles, they ignore important developments. During the economic crisis of 1961, for example, the principle of a 'free society' acted as an important brake on intervention. Conservatives stressed that their pay pause needed to be voluntary to preserve the free society, in contrast to their opponents who allegedly desired a 'Fascist society where we would impose our will'.[43] Well into 1962, the Cabinet's private and public framing of the crisis centred on the challenge of how to control inflation without sacrificing freedom, and Harold Macmillan put his New Approach (an Incomes Commission) to the Cabinet as an answer to whether it was possible to meet their economic objectives 'in a free society'.[44] Even though the policy itself was the antithesis of neoliberalism, the arguments made at the time about the balance of freedom and responsibility became a major site of connection between later Conservatives and neoliberals. Thirdly, because they ignore this heritage, accusations of insincerity forget that freedom rhetoric was *not* the exclusive property of the New Right in 1960s Britain;

Conservatives with different beliefs were making different arguments about freedom and its conditions. Heath's speeches on the Great Divide owed as much to Macmillan's earlier rhetoric as they did to Enoch Powell's. A key step in breaking the hold of Thatcherism over the relationship between Conservatism and neoliberals, then, is reading the rhetoric of earlier periods on its own terms.

The image of a party with competing instincts has informed a final model for relating neoliberalism and Conservatism, one less concerned with direct 'influences' than with identifying 'resonances' between the two to help explain Thatcherism. Individual policies associated with Thatcher's governments have been shown to have a much longer lineage, suggesting the novelty of Thatcher's governments lay in their ability to implement neoliberal-inflected versions of long-standing aims given more fortuitous circumstances.[45] More broadly, E. H. H. Green saw Thatcherism as a product of 'trends in the Conservative Party's subculture since 1945', and others have built on his insight to claim that Thatcher used her party's traditions – especially that of the One Nation Group – to 'domesticate' the American New Right.[46] In Jackson's more nuanced model, neoliberalism's success is partly down to how effectively it was 'translated into diverse neo-liberalisms' suited to party traditions.[47]

This 'resonance' model is the best platform on which to build an understanding of neoliberalism's relationship with Conservatism that connects developments from different periods without falling into teleology. It does need modification, though. There is a natural bias towards exploring more obvious precursors or claimed connections. As such, the danger is that the approach mirrors other approaches to Thatcherism, emphasising headline policies, economics and the state over other connections. Too little attention has been paid, for example, to the increasing advocacy of an emotional politics of conflict in 1960s Conservatism, or the tendency to ground virtue in the characteristics of an agricultural community, not just the imagined virtues of the urban middle class. Furthermore, to escape the one-directional 'influence' model, we need to assess how far changes in neoliberal thought itself created new connections with Conservatism. Melinda Cooper's work on 'family values' and Jackson's analysis of neoliberals' reliance on the breadwinner model indicate ways forward,[48] but the literature on neoliberals' views of tradition and religion remains disconnected from political histories. Finally, the way to construct a history of the relationship between neoliberalism and Conservatism outside Thatcherism's origin story is to see these developments as a process in which two traditions of argument gradually developed more *potential* commonalities. These were not inevitable connections: understanding the historically specific pressures that shaped how arguments developed at each stage is a pressing task. Nor did these commonalities need to end in Thatcherism. That outcome relied very much upon the agency of later actors responding to these potential links, and it is to that process which we now turn.

The interface

Interrogating policymaking has changed how historians think about the role of neoliberal and Conservative ideas in shaping initiatives under Thatcher. But the case for reading the 1970s and 1980s as a fusion of Conservatism and neoliberalism has never rested on policies alone; for Stuart Hall and others, 'Thatcherism' was expressed in the narratives, values and logics Thatcher and her allies used to win support for their programme.[49] To fully understand the interface between neoliberalism and Conservatism in the late 1970s and 1980s, then, we need to complement analysis of policy with a finer-grained understanding of the processes that generated these wider arguments. In the remainder of this chapter, I demonstrate this approach by asking what the contributions of speechwriters, advisers and Thatcher's own reading can tell us about the interface between neoliberalism and Conservatism.

Speechwriting played an important role in Thatcher's leadership. Reconfiguring the electorate's understanding of the world was seen as a precondition of victory, and considerable effort was expended on crafting the leader's message. Practically, Thatcher also used the process of speechwriting to collect and integrate viewpoints.[50] For her advisers and speechwriters, access to this process was an important way to exert influence, especially when they had less access to the party or Whitehall. To accurately describe the interface between Conservatism and neoliberalism in shaping the party's discourse, then, we need to describe these writers' roles in relating the two.

Alfred Sherman is perhaps the best-known example of a speechwriter and adviser who served as a 'conduit' for neoliberal ideas.[51] He was well connected with the network of free-market think tanks, was fluent in the ideas of neoliberal economists and had direct access to the Conservative leadership. Along with Thatcher and Keith Joseph, he founded the Centre for Policy Studies (CPS), which coordinated neoliberal-informed perspectives on policy problems and which is thought of as a 'focal point of their efforts to convert the Conservative party to the ideology of neo-liberalism'.[52]

But although Sherman is sometimes presented as 'attracted to ideological absolutism', he and other speechwriters thought of themselves as Conservatives, not neoliberal 'ideologues'.[53] Sherman described himself, and the CPS, as 'Tories first, (economic) liberals only second'. In his view, economic liberalism was not a universal 'verity'; it was dependent on circumstance and assumed certain values, ethics and social obligations.[54] Indeed, Sherman sometimes made the case for market solutions in the traditional Conservative tones of pragmatism. In 1981, for example, he privately urged the Prime Minister to refute the idea that Benjamin Disraeli would have been a 'wet' and explain that her government was neither 'monetarist' nor 'laissez-faire'.[55] Conservatives *did* believe that humankind could 'gain increasing control over its social environment'. They were just wary of the 'unexpected side-effects'. That 'indiscriminate welfare can demoralise . . . [did] not mean that we should cease to seek constructive ways of helping the unfortunate, and indeed the unworthy, because we are a Christian society'. Rather, it meant that governments must assess the impacts of such policies on recipients, taxpayers and those 'struggling to shift for themselves'. Similarly, Conservatives 'had never argued that the Government must necessarily always stand aloof from industrial and commercial matters'. They merely felt that most intervention had 'done more harm than good'.

Some might doubt Sherman's sincerity – ideologues can, after all, adapt their arguments for an audience. Yet this standpoint explains how advisers such as Sherman promoted both moral conservatism and economic liberalism to their political masters. In 1976, for example, Sherman proposed that Thatcher take a stand against pornography. Responding to the publication of *Inside Linda Lovelace* (1976), Sherman feared that the 'whole system of dykes provided by the law against the flow of pornography, anti-social fantasies, and sexual corruption [was] on the point of collapse'.[56] Much of Sherman's case echoed arguments made by Conservatives throughout the 1960s. Pornography was an evil because it normalised the treatment of people (especially women) as means rather than ends; it threatened the family – 'the basis of civilisation'; and it created a 'moral climate' in which weakened restraints on 'gratification of anti-social instincts' could spiral into other areas. Importantly, Sherman emphasised a 'populist' element to these arguments by claiming that the climate of opinion had been shifted by a small number of opinion formers, some of whom saw 'the breaking down of sexual restraints as a weapon for weakening capitalist society'. In fact, 'the majority of people fear[ed] pornography . . . But they lack[ed] the means of expressing their fear.' In place of 'so-called experts', 'ordinary people's experience and wit must be taken into account' and if the 'resentment' of mothers, housewives, parents and churches were 'organised' then pressure for action would arise. This suggests that a complex mix of advisers' beliefs and the active pitching of rhetorical opportunities may connect Thatcher's rhetoric to a wider anti-permissive reaction.[57]

As noted below, the wider use of 'populist' framings may have played a role in smoothing tensions between Conservative and neoliberal arguments. Nevertheless, there was a contradiction between Sherman's call for moralism and the freedom he advocated elsewhere. Critically, he addressed this:

> Now it may be asked: how does this square with our abjuration of paternalism, our espousal of liberty, our contention that men must work out their own salvation, must grapple with temptation? Yes we must allow people to make their own choices and live with them, but we must also protect the weak, the victim, the exploitee. Where these two duties conflict, it is the weak, the women and children, the potential victims who have the first claim on us.[58]

This should give us pause for thought about one of the main vectors through which 'neoliberal' ideas reached the Conservative leadership. The story is not necessarily one in which outsiders provided ideas which were *then* brought into tension with other currents by the leaders themselves. Instead, the individuals who connected the party with neoliberal networks did so a) from the perspective of Conservatism and b) with the potential tensions between elements of the two consciously in mind. In short, it suggests that the activity of combining these forces must be sought downstream from leaders and that an alliance model in which *different* individuals contributed to the creation of a mixed message is inadequate.

This understanding of Sherman sheds light on two more specific contributions that help characterise the interface between neoliberalism and Conservatism. Firstly, Sherman's ability to straddle both the Conservative and neoliberal worlds was precisely why Thatcher found him useful as a speechwriter. One of his typical tasks was to synthesise contributions from others, combining the words of traditional Conservative speeches with his own Conservative reading of liberal economics.[59] He was, for example, responsible for editing Lord Elton's draft of Thatcher's Iain Macleod Lecture and inserted a section that defended self-interest as moral.[60] Secondly, Sherman's social conservatism meant that he served as a conduit for a wider range of international thought. In 1979, for example, he wrote to Joseph and Thatcher about the threat posed by the 'disintegration' of the arts.[61] Those art forms directly 'contributing to violence or irresponsible behaviour [were] only a small part of the evil' – rock, punk and pop art, and the celebration of anti-heroes, were unlikely to produce a society 'at peace with itself'. He attached an issue of a broadsheet produced by the Rockford College Institute, the American conservative think tank, which précised parts of Michael Novak's *The American Vision* (1978) to claim that a 'new class' of activists, officials and entertainment elites were intent on bringing about a cultural shift. As well as promoting violence, their efforts to convince audiences that liberal morality was what 'most people think' threatened capitalism. Television's support for the 'do-it-your-way liberation ethos' was subverting 'hierarchical working relationships', and its relentless advocacy of 'having a good time and gratifying the senses' undermined the work ethic. Banning pornography was not enough; corporations had to use their influence to ensure cultural outputs reaffirmed the principles of 'thrift, honour, and virtue' that supported capitalism. What Sherman's role reveals, then, is that the individuals normally seen as carrying neoliberal ideas into British Conservatism were also carrying a neoconservative tradition, one increasingly framing its arguments in populist terms and using the language of virtues to connect public morality and the survival of capitalism.

The Letwins

More occasional advisers also played a role in bridging Conservatism and neoliberalism. In 1976, for example, Thatcher and Joseph regularly dined with the academics William and Shirley Letwin. Although the label 'neoliberal' would not apply to either in a straightforward way, the Letwins' careers had connected them with the first Chicago strand of neoliberalism,[62] and they provided Thatcher with notes that became sources for several speeches they helped write. One such paper, on the role of the state, illuminates several features of the interface between neoliberal ideas and Conservative politics that are worth unpacking.

Firstly, arguments and policies clearly influenced by the neoliberal thought collective were pitched into Conservative politics in a re-systematised form. In the Letwins' system, the organising concept became a state which 'ruled' rather than 'managed' and sought only to secure 'freedom for self-determination'.[63] Instead of maximising wealth, health or education, the state limited itself to actions which enabled people to 'preserve and develop their individual identity'. Support for that concept could be found in the writings of most neoliberal authors. But in the Letwins' version this premise acted as *the* justification for other positions that had multiple rationales in the wider neoliberal corpus. Governing through stable laws rather than arbitrary decrees was important, for example, because it was a condition of people being able to exercise self-determination in a predictable context. What Conservative leaders were presented with were somewhat truncated pathways through neoliberal arguments.

Secondly, these pathways were selected in response to rhetorical problems. Much of the Letwins' paper was designed to combat the accusation that Conservatives envisioned a weak state. This in part explains the focus on 'self-determination'; it was explicitly intended to reconceptualise the differences between political parties as not about the *extent* of the state but about its aims. Consequently, the paper foregrounded the need for a strong state: 'government concerned to rule must be strong government' to secure both individual self-determination and competition against monopoly power. This was a central spine of neoliberal argument, particularly associated with the German ordo-liberals. But the conscious emphasis the Letwins gave to it as a proleptic defence against their critics suggests that we may have underplayed the role of perceived rhetorical needs in selecting which arguments – indeed which strands of neoliberalism – were emphasised.

Similarly, the Letwins set out to combat accusations that Conservatives desired a 'free-for-all'. Accordingly, they repainted the corporatist state as a licentious anarchy in which the monopoly interests battled for control at the expense of the individual. The strong state was necessary to protect self-determination against these bullies. Likewise, to anticipate the charge that such a state would be uncaring, the Letwins agreed it should provide a minimum standard in welfare and education. This standard could even be high, provided it was a political decision. This allowed them to recast the issue as whether or not the state sought out ways in which it could avoid becoming a monopolising power or increasing dependency (the inverse of self-determination). Neoliberal policies such as a negative income tax, school and university vouchers, and health and mortgage insurance schemes were recommended as complementary ways to achieve these ends, ones which the state could support alongside its own provision to preserve opportunities for self-determination.

This was a conscious principle of rhetorical selection: the paper ends by listing the ways its earlier suggestions meet these tasks. It also accounts for a third feature: the presentation of neoliberal policies in a populist framework that layered an English nationalism onto minority–majority structures. In the Letwins' view, for example, the existence of a minority which 'could not live as adults' and take on the responsibilities of self-determination was not a sufficient reason to 'reduce the people of England to the status of children'. Self-determination also meant the championing of the 'hard common sense for which [England] was always distinguished' over the arrogance of government and experts. Accordingly, one section of the paper transitioned quickly from arguments about economic intervention to make the case against compulsory vaccination schemes. Self-determination in this context was not so much an efficiency principle or route to moral behaviour as an emotive appeal 'to restore to the people of England mastery over their own lives'. Of course, opposition to overbearing elites had long been part of the party's discourse. This was not a rhetorical layer added later, though; it was part of how more complex points derived from neoliberal points of view arrived into Conservative argument. Indeed, read alongside Roberto Romani's recent case that neoliberal thought took on a populist turn from the 1970s, the Letwins' paper suggests that one reason why neoliberalism might have been useful was the ease with which it could be assimilated into national populist frameworks.[64]

Finally, the Letwins explicitly positioned interest in neoliberal policy alternatives with reference to a *Conservative* ethos. The paper contained an entire section on 'implications for Conservatives' which re-emphasised that the latter were 'practical politicians', not 'ideologues' replacing one ideology with another. This pragmatism was said to lead Conservatives to look to alternative policies dismissed by their opponents outright, such as voucher and insurance-based schemes. Indeed, Conservatives were said to be uniquely able to examine these alternatives because they represented the nation, not interest groups. Centring the principle of self-determination played an important supporting role here because it offered proof that the party had no 'fanciful, ideological preoccupations' – seemingly its only interest was to allow the people to make decisions. This suggests that neoliberal positions and Conservative themes were not simply placed together. Their relationship is better characterised as one in which some long-standing themes of Conservative rhetoric could provide a justification for the inclusion of neoliberal alternatives.

Thatcher's reading

To explain Thatcher's mix of moral conservatism and neoliberal economics, it is tempting to emphasise her personal faith.[65] In fact, her oft-cited speeches on the links between religion, morality and free enterprise were largely written by others and rehearsed well-worn Conservative arguments. This is not to say she lacked agency; Thatcher engaged with a wide range of materials to set her speechwriters' briefs. But apocryphal stories about her dramatically directing colleagues to Hayek's *Constitution of Liberty* have detracted from a more complex picture of what she read and what this tells us about the relationship between Conservative and neoliberal thought.[66] To understand the interface between the two we need to consider the arguments made in some lesser-known texts that Thatcher read and pay closer attention to how these were interpreted.

The materials that Thatcher 'saved' in her speechwriting files suggest that books written by neoliberals informed speechwriting. It is not coincidental, though, that the clearest examples involve authors who emphasised the commonalities between Conservative and neoliberal ideas. Henry Hazlitt is a good example. An American journalist and member of the Mont Pèlerin Society (MPS) who popularised the work of the early neoliberal economist Ludwig von Mises and Hayek, parts of Hazlitt's *Foundations of Morality* (1964) can be found in Thatcher's 'ideas' folder for speeches on Conservative philosophy.[67] The specific chapter retained is important because it synthesised different neoliberal writers to reconcile liberal economics with morality. Hazlitt's argument began by asserting that free enterprise 'presupposed morality' – both because its underlying principles, such as private property, rested on morality and because enterprise needed to be conducted in a climate of morality to serve the general interest. Yet Hazlitt's central claim was that free markets strengthened morality. To this end, he framed two elements of the market economy as 'social cooperation'. Using Burke's analogy of wrestlers improving each other's skill, Hazlitt saw competition as triangular cooperation – companies spurred each other to innovate and in doing so cooperated with the consumer to lower prices.[68] He then quoted Ludwig von Mises to show that the division of labour was not an endorsement of self-interest but an acceptance that individuals could best meet the needs of others by acting in their own self-interest.[69] Crucially, this system of 'mutualism' rendered debates about altruism and egotism redundant – individuals could never know how their actions impacted others, but the system itself ensured they cooperated.

Hazlitt then marshalled together several more 'neoliberal' writers to draw out the moral benefits of this cooperation. Von Mises's student and fellow MPS member Murray Rothbard was quoted to claim friendship resulted from the free economy's social cooperation – the cooperation intrinsic to the division of labour gave scope for friendliness and other forms of cooperation to arise, whereas an economic system lacking it would reduce individuals to a violent, zero-sum scramble for resources. It also provided a strong incentive to restrain immoral behaviours, as breaches would result in less willingness to cooperate.[70] Importantly, though, it was the free economy's version of social cooperation that led to moral improvement. As a system of freedom, this cooperation was *actively chosen* by participants. Quoting Hayek, Hazlitt claimed this free choice was the precondition of moral virtue and left individuals free to voluntarily use the surplus generated by the efficient system in selfless ways.[71] The combination of these points allowed Hazlitt to argue that the free economy was a system that made people more interdependent and led to a general raising of morality through its incentives.

To be clear, 'influence' is not what is at stake here. Hazlitt's arguments had much in common with traditional Conservative explanations of how socialism demoralised individuals and how free choice improved people. However, the fact that some of the specific neoliberal texts we can be more confident Thatcher actually read were those which emphasised the compatibility of the liberal market with morality tells us two things about the interface between neoliberalism and Conservatism. Firstly, the interface involved more than raw theory – the particular glosses and arrangements given to neoliberal thought in summary texts such as Hazlitt's can help explain how and why these traditions were seen as compatible. Secondly, the tensions identified between questions of morality and liberal economics were not necessarily products of neoliberal texts colliding with Conservatism; instead, the Conservative leadership could be exposed to these ideas through explorations of that tension (and attempts to resolve it).

We must also remember that politicians did not experience the interface between Conservative and neoliberal ideas in isolation; texts belonging to neither tradition could reinforce arguments from either and bridge their arguments. One such example can be seen in criticism of social science. Attacks on the left as led by an arrogant intelligentsia planning to remake society had a long pedigree in Conservative circles, along with the idea that government schemes dehumanised people in favour of statistics. By the late 1960s, some Conservatives targeted this critique at social scientists, claiming their work on the causes of crime and other social ills undermined the intellectual foundations of responsibility.[72] For their part, neoliberals made a similar case that the application of determinist approaches from the physical sciences to human society had played a part in diminishing individual responsibility.[73]

But at least one of the ways in which Thatcher was aware of these arguments was via a piece by Paul Wilding in *New Society*.[74] Wilding, a lecturer in Social Administration, was no Thatcherite and would go on to write a defence of the welfare state. Nevertheless, Thatcher read his critique of contemporary social science and kept her annotated copy among her speech ideas papers. Wilding claimed that whereas the nineteenth-century 'idiom' attributed responsibility to individuals for their success or failure, 'environmental and social' explanations had become dominant in the twentieth century. This 'dominant idiom' meant that solutions were not aimed at changing attitudes but instead focused on better systems and planning and encouraged the general application of statistical rules to groups. This 'stress on systems and forces implies and encourages a denigration of man' [Thatcher's underlining] and when applied to issues like delinquency contributed to 'weakening the sense of individual responsibility'.

These would have been familiar arguments, and no doubt some of Thatcher's interest lay in the potential to quote a member of the field. But Wilding's piece is interesting because it connects these critiques to other arguments about the limits of government action becoming popular among those associated with a neoliberal critique of social democracy. Social science, Wilding felt, had wrongly taken conflicts between groups outside of debate, implying they could be resolved 'a-politically' as social problems through further research and funding. It implied that the solutions were technocratic and most damagingly 'contribute[d] to excessive optimism about what can be achieved through government action'. Explicitly connecting his claims with Anthony King's 'overload' thesis, Wilding wrote that the result was that 'governments have taken on an ever-widening range of responsibilities; but sadly, to use King's phrase, the reach of British government has exceeded its grasp'. Key to understanding the relationship between Conservatism and neoliberalism in 1970s Britain, then, is that it was not just members of either tradition who connected the arguments together.

Some of the annotations on Wilding's article indicate a wider practice of political reading that characterises Thatcher's engagement with these texts. There are few instances where we can be certain an annotation indicates assent or dissent, but the general patterning indicates that Thatcher read new information through the lens of her own party's traditions. Her annotation of an article by a leading American neoconservative, Irving Kristol, illustrates this point, as well as showing that she read neoliberal texts in the context of neoconservative authors attempting to couple neoliberal policies with social conservatism.

Ostensibly an 'obituary' for socialism, Kristol's real purpose was to outline the challenge facing liberal capitalism in a post-socialist world.[75] Socialism had been 'a necessary idea' because it offered 'elements that were wanting in capitalist society'. Its original 'utopian' advocates offered a secular version of a valid criticism also made by the Church:

> The essential point of this indictment was that liberty was not enough. A society founded solely on 'individual rights' was a society that ultimately deprived men of those virtues which could only exist in a political community which is something other than a 'society'. Among these virtues are a sense of distributive justice, a fund of shared moral values, and a common vision of the good life. [Thatcher's underlining]

Capitalist thinkers had not denigrated these values, but they had taken for granted the '**moral and spiritual heritage of Judaism and Christianity** [bold indicates Thatcher's paragraph/line marking]' and assumed that the '**new individualism of bourgeois society**' would not disturb this. Using a line of argument familiar to British Conservatives through the writings of T. S. Eliot, Kristol argued that capitalism had been '**able to live off the accumulated moral and spiritual capital of the past**'. However, this heritage had been spread thinner and was now bankrupt, leaving 'a spirit of nihilism' that not only dismissed traditions but also replaced the very idea of the 'good life' with the commodified 'lifestyle'.

Kristol's essay then launched into a narrative of scientific socialism's embrace of materialism, detailing how its inadequacies led to a spiral in which social democratic parties' left wings demanded ever greater control, eventually culminating in a political crisis that would either produce an authoritarian regime or liberal capitalist reaction. Thatcher no doubt welcomed his prediction that Britain was about to go down the latter path, but this still left the question: '**what can liberal capitalist society do to inoculate itself against a resurgence of anti-capitalist dissent?**' Kristol saw two areas for action. Firstly, such an inoculation could be brought about by reforming welfare to stress individual choice. The welfare state was not popular in and of itself; it reflected a 'demand for a greater minimum of political community, for more "social justice" (i.e. distributive justice), than capitalism, in its pristine, individualistic form, can provide'. In Kristol's view, a mix of voluntary and compulsory insurance schemes – those developed by neoliberal thinkers – would satisfy support for the welfare state and make such provision compatible with a liberal capitalist society. In a second area, though, 'the decline of religious beliefs and traditional values', there were fewer answers because the decline stemmed from liberal capitalism's willingness to confine such questions to private affairs. Without resolving this question, though, Kristol warned that any revival of liberal capitalism would remain fragile, leaving socialism 'putrefying' rather than seeing it 'dead and buried'.

A text such as this is important for understanding the interface between neoliberals and Conservatives for several reasons. It again suggests that we need to look beyond the 'neoliberal' international thought collective towards wider neoconservative networks. Indeed, it suggests that British Conservatives were exposed to neoconservatives' efforts to connect their own arguments to neoliberal policies.[76] This particular example also shows that Conservatives had access to different ways of thinking about the relationship between morality and neoliberal policies. Kristol does not position the two as in conflict; instead, the re-moralisation of public life and neoliberal reforms are presented as solutions to capitalism's weaknesses. Finally, it exposes the difficulty of reading the relationship between Conservatism and neoliberalism as a contrast between national and international influences. Kristol's piece was international in scope and published in an Australian magazine. However, most of its arguments had a history within British Conservatism, and it is interesting that most of Thatcher's annotations pick up lines she would have been familiar with through her national party discourse.

Conclusion

Just as historians are now exploring the development of international neoliberalism in a wider range of contexts,[77] the time has come to explore the relationship between British Conservatism and neoliberalism outside the context of explaining the origins and policies of Thatcher's governments. This does not mean abandoning the 1970s and 1980s. We should recognise, though, that the concepts used to understand those decades' politics can cloud rather than clarify the relationship between neoliberals and Conservatives in earlier periods. Instead, historians might explore (and explain) not the influence of one tradition on the other, but the developments in both traditions of argument that increased *potential* points of compatibility, regardless of whether these arguments led members of each tradition to the same policies.

An important guard against the potential for teleology in that approach is to better define the agency involved in using those potential points of connection. Acquiring a better view of the interface between neoliberalism and Conservatism in the late 1970s marks a first step in that direction. This chapter suggests that interface should be characterised as one which was Conservative in outlook and keen to select arguments that helped resolve rhetorical problems confronting the party. It carried plenty of other traffic alongside 'neoliberal' ideas, partly because those involved had their own socially conservative views and partly because the networks these individuals were connected to included neoconservatives trying to build links between moral conservatism and liberal economics. But as well as bringing some of the tensions between Conservatism and neoliberalism into the former 'at source', Conservative leaders were exposed to readings of neoliberalism or wider texts that resolved such tensions. Other parts of the interface indicate the importance of 'reinforcement' texts and selective reading through the lens of established national traditions. This is not a complete picture of the interface between neoliberalism and Conservatism, but it does indicate that some of the factors shaping their relationship become clearer when we step back from the question of policy influence to ask how the routes through which politicians experienced contact between these traditions may have affected their view of how the two could be brought together.

Finally, this chapter shows the utility of Jackson's wider suggestion in this volume that we treat the analysis of political speech and intellectual history as complementary. I would argue that the best way of achieving that integration without making one the master of the other is to forgo a search for individual 'neoliberal' lines in speeches. Instead, we should re-examine the interfaces where neoliberalism and Conservatism met, stressing how the particularities of each point of contact worked with longer-term developments to shape exchanges between the casts of political and intellectual histories.

Notes

1 Richard Cockett, *Thinking the Unthinkable: Think tanks and the economic counter-revolution* (London, HarperCollins, 1994). For a subtler account, see Daniel Stedman Jones, *Masters of the Universe: Hayek, Friedman, and the birth of neoliberal politics* (Princeton, NJ, Princeton University Press, 2012).

2 Radhika Desai, 'Second-hand dealers in ideas: Think-tanks and Thatcherite hegemony', *New Left Review*, 203 (1994), 27–64; Andrew Gamble, *The Free Economy and the Strong State: The politics of Thatcherism*, 2nd ed. (Basingstoke, Palgrave, 1994); and David Harvey, *A Brief History of Neoliberalism* (Oxford, Oxford University Press, 2005), 39–63.

3 Peter Dorey, *British Conservatism: The politics and philosophy of inequality* (London, I.B. Tauris, 2011), 118–23; and Nigel Harris, *Competition and the Corporate Society: Conservatives, the state and industry, 1945–64* (Abingdon, Routledge, 2006).

4 For a summary, see Ben Jackson and Robert Saunders, 'Introduction', in Ben Jackson and Robert Saunders (eds), *Making Thatcher's Britain* (Cambridge, Cambridge University Press, 2012), 1–22.

5 David Marquand, 'The paradoxes of Thatcherism', in Robert Skidelsky (ed.), *Thatcherism* (London, Chatto and Windus, 1988), 159–72, at 164; and Peter Jenkins, *Mrs Thatcher's Revolution* (London, Cape, 1987).

6 F. A. Hayek, *The Constitution of Liberty* (Abingdon, Routledge, 2006), 344–55; Margaret Thatcher, Speech at St Lawrence Jewry (30 March 1978), Margaret Thatcher Foundation Online (MTFO).

7 Samuel Brittan, *Capitalism and the Permissive Society* (London, Macmillan 1973); and Ian Gilmour, *Inside Right: A study of Conservatism* (London, Hutchinson, 1977).

8 Martin Durham, *Sex and Politics: The family and morality in the Thatcher years* (Basingstoke, Macmillan, 1991); and Richard Vinen, *Thatcher's Britain: The politics and social upheaval of the Thatcher era* (London, Simon & Schuster, 2010).

9 Martin Jacques, 'Thatcherism: Breaking out of the impasse', in Stuart Hall and Martin Jacques (eds), *The Politics of Thatcherism* (London, Lawrence and Wishart, 1983); and Gamble, *Free Economy and the Strong State*.

10 Jackson and Saunders, 'Introduction', 13.

11 Bob Jessop, Kevin Bonnett, Tom Ling and Simon Bromley, *Thatcherism: A tale of two nations* (Cambridge, Polity Press, 1988); and Stuart Hall, *The Hard Road to Renewal: Thatcherism and the crisis of the left* (London, Verso, 1988).

12 Stephen Farrall and Colin Hay, *The Legacy of Thatcherism: Assessing and exploring Thatcherite social and economic policies* (Oxford, Oxford University Press, 2014).

13 Adrian Williamson, *Conservative Economic Policymaking and the Birth of Thatcherism, 1964–1979* (Basingstoke, Palgrave Macmillan, 2015); Monica Prasad, *The Politics of Free Markets: The rise of neoliberal economic policies in Britain, France, Germany, and the United States* (Chicago, University of Chicago Press, 2006), 98–61; and Guy Ortolano, *Thatcher's Progress: From social democracy to market liberalism through an English New Town* (Cambridge, Cambridge University Press, 2019).

14 Amy Edwards, '"Financial consumerism": Citizenship, consumerism and capital ownership in the 1980s', *Contemporary British History*, 31 (2017), 210–29; and Emily Robinson, Camilla Schofield, Florence Sutcliffe-Braithwaite and Natalie Thomlinson, 'Telling stories about post-war Britain: Popular individualism and the "crisis" of the 1970s', *Twentieth Century British History*, 28 (2017), 268–304.

15 Aled Davies, James Freeman and Hugh Pemberton, '"Everyman a capitalist" or "free to choose"? Exploring the tensions within Thatcherite individualism', *Historical Journal*, 61 (2018), 477–501; and Florence Sutcliffe-Braithwaite, 'Neo-liberalism and morality in the making of Thatcherite social policy', *Historical Journal*, 55 (2012), 497–520.

16 Ben Jackson, 'Currents of neo-liberalism: British political ideologies and the New Right, c.1955–1979', *English Historical Review*, 131 (2016), 823–50.

17 See Ben Jackson, this volume.

18 John Ramsden, *The Age of Churchill and Eden, 1940–1957* (London, Longman, 1995), 62; Cockett, *Thinking the Unthinkable*, 91–5; and Michael Kandiah, 'The Conservative Party and the 1945 general election', *Contemporary Record*, 9 (1995), 34–5.

19 Kevin Hickson, 'Lord Coleraine: The neglected prophet of the New Right', *Journal of Political Ideologies*, 14 (2009), 173–87.

20 Richard Carr, *Veteran MPs and Conservative Politics in the Aftermath of the Great War: The memory of all that* (Farnham, Ashgate, 2013), 176, 179; and Ina Zweiniger-Bargielowska, *Austerity in Britain: Rationing, controls and consumption, 1939–1955* (Oxford, Oxford University Press, 2000), 211.

21 James Freeman, 'Reconsidering "set the people free": Neoliberalism and freedom rhetoric in Churchill's Conservative Party', *Twentieth Century British History*, 29 (2018), 522–46.

22 Stuart Ball, *Portrait of a Party: The Conservative Party in Britain, 1918–1945* (Oxford, Oxford University Press, 2013), 61.

23 Hartley Withers, *Should the Banks be Nationalised?* (London, Burrup, Mathieson & Co, 1934).

24 Dorey, *British Conservatism*, 111–26; and Harris, *Competition and the Corporate Society*, 77–84.

25 Ben Jackson, 'At the origins of neo-liberalism: The free economy and the strong state, 1930–47', *Historical Journal*, 53 (2010), 129–51.

26 Tim Bale, *The Conservatives since 1945: The drivers of party change* (Oxford, Oxford University Press, 2012), 34.

27 Ralph Assheton, 'Draft statement of policy', Churchill Archive Centre (CAC), Churchill Papers, CHUR 2/88.

28 Butler to Churchill (7 July 1949), CAC, CHUR 23/88.
29 *The Times* (25 July 1949); and Maudling to Churchill (16 July 1949), CAC, CHUR 5/26B.
30 W. H. Greenleaf, *The British Political Tradition*, Volume 2 (London, Methuen, 1983), 192–3; and David Seawright, *The British Conservative Party and One Nation Politics* (London, Continuum, 2010).
31 Norman Barry, 'New Right', in Kevin Hickson (ed.), *The Political Thought of the Conservative Party since 1945* (Basingstoke, Palgrave Macmillan, 2005), 28–50; and Andrew Denham and Mark Garnett, 'Sir Keith Joseph and the undoing of British Conservatism', *Journal of Political Ideologies*, 7 (2002), 57–75.
32 Jim Tomlinson, '"Liberty with order": Conservative economic policy, 1951–1964', in Martin Francis and Ina Zweiniger-Bargielowska (eds), *Conservatives and British Society, 1880–1990* (Cardiff, University of Wales Press, 1996), 274–88.
33 Harriet Jones, 'The Cold War and the Santa Claus syndrome', in Martin Francis and Ina Zweiniger-Bargielowska (eds), *Conservatives and British Society, 1880–1990* (Cardiff, University of Wales Press, 1996), 242–3.
34 Michael Freeden, *Ideologies and Political Theory: A conceptual approach* (Oxford, Oxford University Press, 1996), 373–8; and E. H. H. Green, *Ideologies of Conservatism: Conservative political ideals in the twentieth century* (Oxford, Oxford University Press, 2002), 279.
35 Colin Hay, 'Chronicles of a death foretold: The winter of discontent and the construction of the crisis of British Keynesianism', *Parliamentary Affairs*, 63 (2010), 446–70.
36 Jim Bulpitt, 'The discipline of the new democracy: Mrs Thatcher's domestic statecraft', *Political Studies*, 34 (1986), 19–39.
37 Kit Kowol, 'The Conservative movement and dreams of Britain's post-war future', *Historical Journal*, 62 (2019), 473–93.
38 House of Commons Debates, *Hansard* (31 October 1958), cols 495–512.
39 R. A. Butler, *Our New Frontier* (London, Conservative Political Centre, 1962), 12.
40 Andrew Gamble, *The Conservative Nation* (London, Routledge and Kegan Paul, 1974), 54–86.
41 Martin Holmes, *The Failure of the Heath Government*, 2nd ed. (Basingstoke, Macmillan, 1997); and John Campbell, *Edward Heath: A biography* (London, Cape, 1993).
42 Freeman, 'Set the people free', 543.
43 Harold Macmillan, House of Commons Debates, *Hansard* (21 November 1961), cols 1145–52, at 1147.
44 Cabinet Notebook (28 May 1962), TNA, CAB 195/21/1.
45 Aled Davies, '"Right to buy": The development of a Conservative housing policy, 1945–1980', *Contemporary British History*, 27 (2013), 421–44.
46 E. H. H. Green, *Thatcher* (London, Hodder and Stoughton, 2006), 53; and Stephen Evans, 'The not so odd couple: Margaret Thatcher and One Nation Conservatism', *Contemporary British History*, 23 (2009), 101–21.
47 Jackson, 'Currents of neoliberalism', 849–50.
48 Melinda Cooper, *Family Values: Between neoliberalism and the new social conservatism* (New York, Zone Books, 2017); and Ben Jackson, 'Free markets and feminism: The neo-liberal defence of the male breadwinner model in Britain, c.1980–1997', *Women's History Review*, 28 (2019), 297–316.
49 Stuart Hall, 'The great moving right show', *Marxism Today* (January 1979), 14–20.
50 For another example in a later context, see Oliver Daddow, Christopher Gifford and Ben Wellings, 'The battle of Bruges: Margaret Thatcher, the foreign office and the unravelling of British European policy', *Political Research Exchange*, 1 (2019), 1–24.
51 Robert Ledger, *Neoliberal Thought and Thatcherism: 'A transition from here to there'?* (London, Routledge, 2017), 155.
52 Rachel S. Turner, *Neo-Liberal Ideology: History, concepts and policies* (Edinburgh, Edinburgh University Press, 2008), 96.
53 Ledger, *Neoliberal*, 41, 155.
54 'Credo' (18 November 1974), Royal Holloway Archives and Special Collections (RH), Sherman Papers (SHER) Box 7.
55 'Tory politics' (22 April 1981), SHER 8/4.
56 Alfred Sherman, 'Notes for a speech on pornography' (6 February 1976), CAC, THCR 5/1/3/4.
57 Matthew Grimley, 'Thatcherism, morality and religion', in Ben Jackson and Robert Saunders (eds), *Making Thatcher's Britain* (Cambridge, Cambridge University Press, 2012), 78–94.
58 Grimley, 'Thatcherism, morality and religion'.

59 'The Conservative ideal' (9 May 1979), SHER 6/2.
60 Alfred Sherman, 'Self interest and public interest' (23 May 1977), CAC, THCR 5/1/2/145.
61 Sherman to Thatcher and Joseph (22 March 1979), RH, SHER 8/2.
62 Roger Middleton, 'Letwin, William Louis [Bill] (1922–2013)', *Oxford Dictionary of National Biography* (Oxford, Oxford University Press, 2017).
63 William Letwin and Shirley Letwin, 'The role of the state', CAC, THCR 5/1/3/1.
64 Roberto Romani, 'Varieties of neoliberalism: On the populism of laissez-faire in America, 1960–1985', *Global Intellectual History* (Advance Access, 2019) DOI: 10.1080/23801883.2019.1588198.
65 Graeme Smith, 'Margaret Thatcher's Christian faith: A case study in political theology', *Journal of Religious Ethics*, 35 (2007), 233–57.
66 John Ranelagh, *Thatcher's People: An insider's account of the politics, the power and the personalities* (London, Fontana, 1992), ix.
67 Henry Hazlitt, *The Foundations of Morality* (1964), CAC, THCR 5/1/3/4.
68 Hazlitt, *The Foundations of Morality*, 307.
69 Hazlitt, *The Foundations of Morality*, 313.
70 Hazlitt, *The Foundations of Morality*, 320–1.
71 Hazlitt, *The Foundations of Morality*, 322–3.
72 Angus Maude, *The Common Problem* (London, Constable, 1969).
73 F. A. Hayek, *The Constitution of Liberty* (Abingdon, Routledge, 2006), 64–6.
74 Paul Wilding, 'Objections to social science', *New Society* (8 April 1976), CAC, THCR 5/1/3/1.
75 *Quadrant*, 21 (1977), CAC, THCR 5/1/3/2.
76 Jacob Hamburger and Daniel Stienmetz-Jenkins, 'Why did neoconservatives join forces with neoliberals? Irving Kristol from critic to ally of free-market economics', *Global Intellectual History*, 6 (2021), 215–30.
77 Quinn Slobodian, *Globalists: The end of empire and the birth of neoliberalism* (Cambridge, MA, Harvard University Press, 2018).

Part IV
Political Economy

13

Organised business and the rise of neoliberalism: the Confederation of British Industry 1965–1990s

Neil Rollings

> Let there be no going back.
>
> - No going back to the days of industrial relations chaos.
> - To the bogus sham that was the Corporate State; to useless so-called 'agreements' that no one can deliver where it matters, on the ground at local level.
> - To nationalisation . . .
> - To the poisonous politics of envy.
>
> Let there be no going back, in short, to the dreary dreadful days of failure.[1]

John Banham, the Director-General of the Confederation of British Industry (CBI), wound up the 1990 CBI annual conference with these words. Shortly afterwards, the CBI published *Business Agenda for the 1990s,* which repeated this message, contrasting itself with a similar CBI report, *The Will to Win*, published 10 years earlier. As an adviser in Number 10 Downing Street put it, '[t]he report admits that the CBI thought in corporatist terms when it published the "Will to Win" in 1981, admits the error of its ways and says we must never go back to that'.[2] *The Will to Win* was the brainchild of Sir Terence Beckett, whom Banham had succeeded in 1987, and is best known for calling for a 'bare knuckle fight' to save manufacturing industry at the 1980 CBI conference, which was widely perceived as a direct assault on the government.[3] A leading article in *The Times* marking the change from Beckett to Banham summed up the conventional picture of the relationship between the CBI and Margaret Thatcher's Conservative governments during the 1980s. Thatcher rejected engagement with the CBI and unions in the form of a corporate state, whereupon the CBI's influence 'plummeted'. Only gradually was a relationship re-established and only through the CBI acknowledging the changed circumstances, such that 'the voice of the whingeing tendency' was quietened.[4]

Many features of the conventional portrayal of Thatcherism are visible here: Margaret Thatcher's dislike of the CBI because of its association with 1970s corporatism; the resulting weakness of the CBI as it was 'cold-shouldered' by the government, and 'elbowed out' by the more supportive Institute of Directors (IoD); and that the CBI only had the ear of government once it had moved into line with the government's neoliberal view of the world.[5] This also fits the more general account of the rise of neoliberalism in the UK in which businesses feature as funders of neoliberal activities such as the Institute of Economic Affairs (IEA), but the CBI, as the voice of industry, was a bystander.

This chapter questions this dominant interpretation by showing that the position of organised business in these developments was more complex and nuanced. There were strands of business support for neoliberal ideas at the heart of the CBI from its creation, and there was less distance between the government and the CBI than is commonly believed during the 1980s. It is suggested that this has been missed in the existing historiography for three main reasons. Firstly, the relationship was private rather than public. Secondly, the contemporary media misrepresented the relationship. Thirdly, the relationship was interdependent, such that the government had to take notice of the CBI. This was because of the CBI's role in pay restraint in the absence of incomes policy (which has also been overlooked in the historiography of Thatcherism), its production of the CBI Industrial Trends Survey and, linked to this, the impact of its public pronouncements on market confidence. The chapter starts by a brief presentation of the key features of the conventional account, followed by discussion of the Industrial Policy Group (IPG). It then moves to relations between the CBI and the Thatcher governments before a section that explains why relations were closer than is commonly understood.

Conventional account

The dominant account of the role of organised business in the rise of neoliberalism in the UK is both straightforward and widely agreed. The spotlight has been on the role of ideas and on a small group of converts to neoliberal ideas working through think tanks, most notably the IEA.[6] Although Damian Cahill has criticised this ideational focus as overly simplistic and has highlighted the centrality of business in the process, even he presents the contribution of business as primarily limited to its provision of funds.[7] In the British case, Ben Jackson has examined business funding of the IEA.[8] While many large companies were consistent sponsors of the IEA, the CBI and its predecessors played no direct part in these developments.

More generally, despite there being natural affinities between the Conservative Party and the CBI, the relationship was not so straightforward.[9] With Margaret Thatcher's appointment as leader of the Conservative Party in 1975, it was the CBI's engagement in tripartite discussions and corporate-style incomes policy that was the problem. According to E. H. H. Green, Thatcher referred to corporatism or the corporate state 25 times in speeches over her career, and all were deeply critical: she even told Geoffrey Howe, her first Chancellor of the Exchequer, not to use the word corporate as it was too close to corporatism.[10] Two particular episodes are highlighted for both illustrating and exacerbating this tension. The first relates to a dispute between Campbell Adamson and the CBI's Economic Director, Barry Bracewell-Milnes, which in 1973 resulted in Bracewell-Milnes being forced to leave the organisation.[11] On leaving, Bracewell-Milnes became Economic Director of the IoD, a founder of the Selsdon Group within the Conservative Party, and active in the Adam Smith Institute and other neoliberal bodies. Apparently, '[o]ne of his proudest boasts was that he was "sacked in 1973 by Mr Campbell Adamson . . . for supporting capitalism, free enterprise and the market economy"'.[12]

However, it was the second key episode which is more commonly cited as illustrating the chasm between the CBI and Thatcherites. This was Terence Beckett's speech as the new CBI Director-General to the November 1980 CBI conference. With the government's focus on controlling inflation via monetary policy, interest rates rose, the Bank of England base rate reaching a peak that year of 17 per cent. This exacerbated the rise in the value of the pound – from $2.06 when the Conservatives came to power to a peak of $2.42 just at the time of the CBI conference – raising the price of UK exports by 17 per cent in just 18 months. British industry suffered the consequences: in August 1980, unemployment rose to over two million for the first time since 1935, with redundancies running at 20,000 jobs per week, virtually all in manufacturing industry. Industrial production and economic growth collapsed. Beckett revised his speech at the last minute to reflect the anger felt by business: 'We have got to take the gloves off and have a bare knuckle fight because we have got to have an effective and prosperous industry.'[13] The media presented his speech as 'a fierce attack on the Conservative Party and the Government's economic policies'.[14] With Beckett supposedly summoned by the Prime Minister, the speech became viewed as a 'political and PR disaster': Thatcher was 'infuriated', and Beckett and the CBI President, Ray Pennock, 'were castigated for [their] temerity' by Thatcher and afterwards stood outside Number 10 'looking positively craven'.[15] Resignations from the CBI followed.[16] Beckett and the CBI were seen to be clearly damaged by the episode. John King, one of those to resign from the CBI, mocked them: 'They went in like Brighton rock and came out like Turkish delight.'[17] Likewise, *The Times* suggested that the speech was 'ill-judged and that the degree of subsequent retraction undignified', going on to explore the awkward and uncertain role of the CBI in the government's move away from corporatism.[18]

It is unsurprising, therefore, that the CBI's status and influence are perceived as having 'withered dramatically' after 1979.[19] Not only was the CBI leadership regarded by Thatcher as 'unreconstructed bastions of corporatism', but they were also seen as being in cahoots with the wets in Cabinet, notably Jim Prior, the Secretary of State for Employment.[20] Her advisers were equally scathing. One noted that '[t]he CBI were loathed more than the Bank of England', while Alfred Sherman, one of Thatcher's closest advisers, claimed that '[a]s a *patronat*-style appendage of the corporate state, [the CBI] served no purpose and should be closed down as soon as possible'.[21] Instead, it is argued, she consulted ideologically sympathetic businessmen directly or used the overtly free-market IoD as her route to business opinion.[22] Walter Goldsmith, the Director-General of the Institute, used every opportunity to play up his support for the government to contrast with the complaints emanating from the CBI.[23] Indeed, his replacement in 1984, John Hoskyns, had come directly from heading the Policy Unit at Number 10.

The period to 1983 was one where conflict between the CBI and the government was 'a marked and continuous feature' and where 'the level of conflict had been deep and mistrust had been more evident than cooperation', according to one account from a Thatcherite sympathiser.[24] It was only when the CBI's position shifted to one more clearly in line with that of the Conservative government that it was able to regain some of its status. Even then, although Stephen Wilks refers to the emergence of a new 'corporate state', collective business representation tends to be seen as relatively weak, with the emergence of direct lobbying by individual firms.[25] A further complication was that the CBI was firmly in favour of deeper European integration, in contrast to the IoD and many on the right of the Conservative Party. Thus, the 1980s marks a clear turning point in the existing historiography, as a moment when the status of the CBI was permanently damaged, and what improvement there was flowed from the CBI rejecting its past, illustrated by Banham's speech quoted at the start and the CBI's *Business Agenda for the 1990s*.

An alternative interpretation

It is argued here that there are fundamental flaws with this existing account. While there were repeated tensions between Conservative ministers, including Thatcher, and the CBI, the differences were not as great as presented in the historiography. We begin with the creation of the CBI in 1965. This involved the merger of the Federation of Business Industries with the British Employers' Confederation and the National Association of British Manufacturers, which represented small business. There was a concern that the cost of becoming the voice of industry was that the voice of big business would be watered down, as would the ability of the CBI to speak frankly. Tensions were building between the CBI and the 1964–70 Labour governments, with business increasingly frustrated at the growing intervention in the economy and becoming more vocal in its criticism of government policy.[26] As a result, leading businessmen and the Economic Director of the CBI, Arthur Shenfield, came together to create the Industrial Policy Group in 1967. The group was the brainchild of Shenfield, who became its Director, and Sir Paul Chambers, the Chairman of Imperial Chemical Industries (ICI) (1960–8), who became IPG Chairman. Shenfield was active in the Mont Pelèrin Society (MPS), having been its Secretary and later becoming its President. Chambers had good links with the IEA.[27] All of the members headed large, well-known British companies and most were active in the CBI and other business organisations. The IPG's membership changed over time but remained at around 20 in number. Table 13.1 sets out the early membership. In 1969, Shenfield was succeeded as Director by John Jewkes, ex-Professor of Economics at Oxford University and another MPS President. Jewkes 'sympathised with the aims of the Group' and believed his views on the importance of 'a vigorous system of private enterprise' were 'similar to those held by the members of the Group'.[28] Indeed, Boswell and Peters considered the IPG to be 'the most formidable liberationist [neoliberal] challenge to the revisionist ascendency in this period'.[29]

In all, the group published 10 reports before being wound up in 1974. Its objective, as set out by Shenfield, was 'to study the cause of the

Table 13.1 Members of the Industrial Policy Group in January 1968

Sir Paul Chambers	Chairman ICI
Henry Lazell	Chairman Beecham
Lord Cole	Chairman Unilever
David Barran	Chief Executive Shell
Lord Boyd	Chairman Guinness
Sir Joseph Lockwood	Chairman EMI
A. F. McDonald	Chairman Distillers
John Partidge	Chairman Imperial Tobacco
Lord Netherhope	Chairman Fisons
Sir William McEwan Younger	Chairman Scottish and Newcastle Breweries
Sir Charles Wheeler	Chairman AEI
Sir Peter Runge	Senior Director Tate and Lyle
Sir George Bolton	Chairman Bank of London and South America
Sir Cyril Harrison	Chairman English Sewing Cotton
Sir Nicholas Cayzer	Chairman British and Commonwealth Shipping
Sir Reay Geddes	Chairman Dunlop
Sir Maurice Laing	Deputy Chairman John Laings
Lord Pilkington	Chairman Pilkingtons
Sir John Nicholson	Chairman Ocean Steam Ship Co.
Lord Sieff	Chairman Marks and Spencer
Gordon Richardson	Chairman J. Henry Schroder
R. G. Soothill	Chairman Turner and Newall
John Davies	CBI Director-General (*ex officio*)
Sir Stephen Brown	CBI President (*ex officio*)

Source: MRC MSS200/C/3/DG1/44, IPG meeting, 4 January 1968.

country's malaise and to make their views public'. 'The "malaise" or weakness in the British economy', he continued, 'is deep-seated and its origins go a long way back – perhaps half a century or more', going on to explain the relatively poor productivity performance of British industry in terms of restrictive practices, particularly those of trade unions, the policy of full employment, a lack of private investment due to excessive government expenditure and the tax system.[30]

However, the IPG's relationship with the CBI proved ambiguous, as the leadership of the CBI were reluctant to break with political neutrality in public. Having the CBI President and the Director-General in the group *ex officio* meant that any IPG publications might be regarded as having official CBI approval. Indeed, the final IPG report was published with a note of dissent from the CBI President and Director-General. Nevertheless, at the outset *The Times* believed that the IPG 'may well develop into an unofficial inner cabinet of the CBI'.[31] Moreover, its office was in the CBI's building and its papers were commented upon by CBI staff prior to publication. Shenfield even continued to use CBI headed paper until his retirement in 1969. Originally it was talked about as 'Shenfield's Research Unit' within the CBI and received CBI funding.[32]

Clearly, then, the IPG was not a mouthpiece of the CBI, but it was present at the heart of the CBI from its creation, while having members who were clearly sympathetic to neoliberal thinking. Its members' influence continued even as it was being wound up. IPG members took a leading role in manoeuvres which restricted Adamson's freedom, one of which was the creation of the President's Committee, a body of senior industrialists to advise the CBI President.[33] Significantly, the initial committee contained six ex-IPG members as well as other critics of the way the CBI had been operating.[34]

The Thatcher governments

During the 1970s the CBI remained committed to tripartite discussions. However, in private the CBI moved much closer to the Conservative Party, meeting the shadow ministers increasingly often and sharing draft policy statements for comment prior to publication.[35] A senior CBI committee was set up to explore the changes needed in 'the balance of power' with trade unions.[36] And, even in public, the CBI was uncompromising in its critique of the Bullock Report on industrial democracy.[37] At the CBI Council meeting following the 1979 election, it was clear where political sentiment lay: a spontaneous round of applause followed Lord Watkinson's remark that:

> . . . the new Prime Minister had put her trust in the principles which the CBI stood for, and could be expected to act to back this up. The CBI and its members must justify this trust by making their ideas work. Every company board should therefore consider what it would do to this end.[38]

Yet, at the first meeting with the Prime Minister, the CBI leadership made clear their concerns about the impact of the high rate of interest.[39] As the economic situation deteriorated, so criticism became more vehement and the calls for a reduction in the rate of interest more desperate. Nevertheless, many Thatcherites also believed interest rates were too high. John Hoskyns, now working in Number 10, believed that '[o]nly ministers and civil servants devoid of business experience could think that the private sector could adjust to such ham-handed policy without suffering great damage'.[40] It is in this context, with manufacturing output and employment falling sharply, that Beckett's 'bare knuckle fight' speech needs to be placed. The government was not surprised, therefore, to be facing attacks at the conference: ministers had been warned that the CBI leadership, caught between the membership and the government, might feel obliged to say some unpleasant things.[41] Six months before Beckett's speech, the Prime Minister's office was informed that Sir John Greenborough, the then CBI President, had given 'a distinctly tougher' speech at the CBI dinner owing to 'increasing pressure from CBI firms'.[42] Even before then, Greenborough had made clear that the CBI's concerns were rising and there was growing pressure from members for action to alleviate industry's problems, including a reduction in interest rates.[43]

As the summer progressed, that pressure mounted. In September, Ray Pennock, Greenborough's successor, met with Thatcher. He explained industry's problems and the need for help from the government.[44] A month later, Geoffrey Howe was warned by his special adviser that 'government policies are quite likely to get a very rough ride at the [CBI] Conference'.[45] Only days afterwards, Howe heard directly from the CBI about the very real fears of industry and the pleas for action. At the end of the meeting he 'thanked the CBI for their forceful and persuasive presentation. The diagnosis was clear enough; the right answers, as he had attempted to show, were less easy to find.'[46] Not long after (and just days before the CBI conference) Beckett and Pennock took the opportunity to warn the government again that they might be forced to say some harsh things at the conference and to suggest that a further meeting with the Chancellor might be in order.[47] In reply, they were told that Howe would be happy to see them, that he was 'certainly well aware of the likelihood of disquiet' at the conference and that he 'would not feel affronted by suggestions that the government ought to do more to control monetary growth by limiting its own borrowing and curbing expenditure and public service pay increases'.[48]

The next day, Howe's special adviser, Adam Ridley, reported that, in Pennock's conference speech:

> He will express unstinting admiration for the PM personally (he stressed the word personally), and his own and the CBI's complete support for the fundamental objectives of the government's policy . . . He will then go on to say, however, that there are certain things he must point out to the government.[49]

Ridley stressed to Pennock that he would be 'at his [Pennock's] disposal throughout the conference should he wish me to see anybody, attend any meetings or be helpful in any other way that might occur to him'. That the Chancellor's special adviser was willing to go to such lengths illustrates the extent to which the government was working together with the CBI leadership at this time.

Similarly, while Beckett's speech did cause ructions in the government, including with the Prime Minister, what followed was not evidence of any breakdown in relations, nor of Pennock and Beckett being called into Number 10 and 'given the full handbag treatment'.[50] Firstly, the meeting was called for by the CBI, not by Thatcher.[51] Secondly, the minute of the meeting paints a very different picture: the overall tone was one of a constructive discussion. Thatcher listened to the industrialists' position for the first 25 minutes of the hour-and-a-half meeting 'in a rare mood of restraint'.[52] Pennock opened by pointing out that while the CBI conference supported the government's basic aims, 'they questioned whether the government fully understood the gravity of the industrial situation'.[53] Beckett then outlined what he had learned on his tour of the regions prior to the conference and his plans for a medium-term strategy for industry to complement the government's monetary strategy. It was only then that the Prime Minister spoke, explaining that, while industry's problems were largely outside the remit of government influence, 'the government were determined to get interest rates down as soon as possible – to give hope to industry if nothing else'. Thatcher did not offer much prospect of respite and there were clear differences of opinion, but there was no 'handbagging' of the CBI representatives. Moreover, Thatcher's reaction to the meeting was positive: 'You have probably heard by now that I had a useful meeting with him [Beckett] and with Ray Pennock.'[54] And in another letter she wrote: 'I agree with you that the Government and CBI must work together for the longer term success of industry. I had a fairly lengthy and rather good talk a few days ago with Terry Beckett and Ray Pennock; we are not really far apart in my view.'[55] Indeed, she added, 'Ray Pennock's [conference] speech was very practical and very good. He is a marvellous President.'[56]

This working relationship continued. Geoffrey Howe's 1981 budget is infamous for its controversial nature, and for prompting the critical letter to *The Times* signed by 364 economists. The CBI were critical but, given the state of the economy, nothing like as much as many others and always with qualification. At a private meeting with the Prime Minister and the Chancellor, Pennock opened by making clear that the CBI were not 'moving into confrontation with the government', but, thereafter, he made clear the CBI's dismay in robust terms.[57] Likewise, Beckett, having also stressed that there was no desire for confrontation, told the Prime Minister that 'the Budget was of no net help to industry, and it was not in any way an *industrial* budget'. The meeting closed with Sir Terence noting:

> Although the government's and the CBI's analysis of the underlying situation seemed to be identical, their view remained that the budget had been misjudged. He hoped that the government fully understood their concern; but at least the assurance that the government wanted to reduce interest rates was helpful.[58]

What is more significant in many respects was that the CBI leadership could get to see both the Prime Minister and the Chancellor just one day after making the request. Again, there is no evidence that there had been a breakdown in relations, nor that the CBI had been sidelined. On other occasions the CBI leadership was able to get access to senior ministers, including the Prime Minister, even when there was no time immediately available in the diary.[59] In all, between Thatcher's election in May 1979 and the end of 1982, the CBI leadership met with her 21 times, of which 14 were small private meetings.[60] Added to regular meetings with the Chancellor of the Exchequer, which Donald MacDougall estimated as occurring on average every six weeks, and with other ministers, there seems to have been a close working relationship just at the time when the historiography talks about the extent of division.[61] Indeed, one effect of Beckett's speech was to strengthen this dialogue. 'A frank and realistic discussion' over 'a relatively intimate' private lunch for the CBI leadership and Geoffrey Howe at the start of December 1980 was followed by a meeting later that month.[62] There it was agreed that fairly regular private informal meetings between senior economic ministers and the CBI were needed 'to permit a real exchange of views' to ensure mutual understanding.[63]

Just as Beckett's 'bare knuckle fight' speech did not lead to a breakdown in the working relationship between ministers and the CBI, so the 1991 depiction of the 1981 CBI publication *The Will to Win*, with which this chapter opened, does not stand up to scrutiny either. The initiative for the document came from Beckett himself, and the aim was to develop a medium-term strategy to provide a clearer sense of direction for the next five years for CBI members.[64] A summary of its likely shape was sent to the Prime Minister, and she met with Pennock and Beckett to discuss it at the start of February. An advance copy was sent to her a month later.[65] Once the budget was out of the way, Pennock and Beckett again met with the Prime Minister to discuss the document.[66] The CBI paper set out 50 action points for the government, trade unions and industry. Government officials believed that the document should be welcomed for the emphasis it placed on industry's role in restoring the UK's economic prosperity: 'While the government is not prepared to contemplate any dramatic changes in its policy towards industry, it is anxious to maintain a "constructive dialogue" with the CBI.'[67] More specifically, the CBI's analysis on pay and on competitiveness were flagged for praise: 'We think the CBI leaders deserve congratulations for being willing to tell their members in fairly forthright terms what they should be doing.'[68] While there were elements of *The Will to Win* which were not in line with the government's outlook, notably on reflation, it would be hard to describe it as corporatist and significantly out of line with government thinking, especially on pay bargaining.

And that picture of broad agreement but with differences on particular aspects of policy remained evident for the rest of the decade. One government official, reporting on the 1984 CBI conference, summed up the situation:

> There was throughout the discussions an obvious sympathy for the government. While government policies were criticised, sometimes in a hard and uncompromising manner, these criticisms were almost invariably prefaced by general remarks to the effect that the speaker still supported the broad thrust of government policies.[69]

Many examples of just this situation can be found.[70] As a 1987 Treasury brief put it:

> CBI have various complaints – about rating reform, electricity prices, interest rates, exchange rates, corporation tax, public sector investment and the employment bill – but they freely admit that these are all heavily outweighed by the healthy state of the economy.[71]

There is considerable continuity in the working relationship that existed between the Conservative governments and the CBI throughout the 1980s.

Explaining the working relationship

So far, evidence has been presented showing that the CBI was able to get access to the heart of the Conservative government and that, despite differences, there were common understandings which underpinned that working relationship. This begs two questions: if the relationship was not so bad as commonly believed, why was this the case? And why has the historiography emphasised division? Various factors are relevant here. One factor has been the dominance of ideologically focused accounts in establishing the narrative of the rise of neoliberalism in the UK.[72] Secondly, there was the media coverage, which tended to play up the differences between the CBI and ministers. As already mentioned, Beckett pointed to this over his 'bare knuckle fight' speech, and Pennock believed '[i]t was clear that the media were looking for opportunities to show the government and the CBI in disagreement with each other, and that they would not shrink from selective reporting.'[73] It became a fairly common refrain to point to press misrepresentation of CBI views.[74]

Thirdly, and more importantly, there was an interdependent relationship between the government and the CBI. The government relied on the CBI in certain respects and these coloured its dealings with the organisation. This was most important during the first Thatcher government. The Prime Minister was determined not to have an incomes policy – wage inflation was a symptom rather than a cause of inflation – and this was a key test of Thatcherism. 'Under Thatcher', Green has argued, 'wage negotiations were left to management and the private sector was not even addressed indirectly'.[75] The validity of the second half of the sentence is questionable. By the late 1970s, 74 per cent of all manufacturing firms were members of the CBI, rising to 88 per cent of firms employing more than 1,000 employees.[76] The CBI had a key role in encouraging its members to show pay restraint, and the government was aware of this: it needed the CBI to be effective in helping to achieve this. Hence, sustaining a constructive dialogue with the CBI was crucial.[77] This was particularly the case in 1981, with the prospect of emerging from the recession. As Howe was briefed:

> This will be an important meeting in terms of concerting views and action with the CBI on the next pay round. Given that the

government will not want to be promulgating pay norms, the CBI have an important role to play in communicating the right message to the private sector. It is important that the government and the CBI are as far as possible at one both on what this message should be and on what is necessary to ensure that the case does not go by default. One objective of the meeting will be to ensure that there is a clear understanding with the CBI about this. Another, which is hardly less important, will be to get the CBI's views on what economic ministers and the government generally need to do and say to facilitate a satisfactory outcome on pay over the coming year.[78]

Two years later, Margaret Thatcher and her advisers were again emphasising the importance of the CBI's role in getting across to its members the importance of pay restraint and, in return, '[s]he would welcome further such exchanges between the government and the CBI'.[79] Indeed, the discussion of the CBI's approach to each annual pay round remained one of the main reasons for senior ministers, including Margaret Thatcher, to meet with the CBI leadership.[80]

Nor was pay the only issue which illustrated the dependence of the government on the CBI. The CBI also published its Industrial Trends Survey. This survey was begun in 1958 and was originally published three times per year.[81] By 1984, the survey appeared quarterly, used a panel of 1,700–1,800 firms covering 56 per cent of manufacturing employment, and could rely on most of the larger firms replying regularly.[82] The scale, nature (including data rather than just business opinion) and longevity of the survey gave it, and the CBI, authority not accorded to other business surveys, such as that by the IoD begun in 1983.[83] Its significance was such that in the 1980s the Chancellor would usually receive a briefing on it prior to publication.[84] The survey would also sometimes be the prompt for the CBI to meet with senior ministers.[85]

It was not just the content of the survey that mattered. The tone of the language which the CBI were likely to use in their press conferences and press releases was also crucial. Ministers and government officials were concerned that the CBI downplayed any positive news to 'eke out as much gloom as possible'.[86] The role of ministers was to counter this. As Thatcher noted to Sir James Clemminson in 1985:

> I am sure we are agreed on the importance of presenting your surveys with great care and in a balanced way . . . The prospects . . . of continued prosperity for business are not assisted by propagating the idea that the expansion is about to end, which can only damage

> business confidence. It would also be helpful if, as you say, you can keep your pressure on interest rates 'very low key'. High key pressure makes it harder not easier to lower interest rates, for markets may think that the government has been pushed into taking risks with inflation, which could be very damaging.[87]

Seven years later, her successor, John Major, was making the same point about the importance of presentation for maintaining market confidence to one of Clemminson's successors, encouraging the CBI to highlight any signs of recovery.[88] Back in 1982, an official highlighted the CBI's responsibilities here:

> Perhaps the most important point to make is that they can by their statements help or hinder the recovery. They, of course, have a duty to represent their members' interests as they best see fit. But it does not do them or anyone else a service to encourage gloom simply in order to try to bring pressure to bear on the government. That only weakens confidence still further. The cycle can then become self-reinforcing and the recovery itself is damaged . . .
>
> The CBI, like the government itself, has a duty to weigh its words with care. It has public responsibilities.[89]

Throughout the period of the Thatcher governments, and later, the government remained dependent on the CBI. If the government wanted the CBI to take its public responsibilities seriously, ministers could not ignore the organisation. It had to rely on the CBI presenting a suitable message of pay restraint to its members, particularly during the first Thatcher government, but it also depended on the CBI's public discourse because of its potential impact on market confidence, especially when the economy was fragile. This provided to the CBI leadership a means of access to ministers at the heart of the government and allowed it to maintain its traditional insider lobbying, which was meant to have disappeared during the Thatcher governments. Instead, the CBI still had opportunities to make its case in small private meetings with the Prime Minister and senior economic ministers.

Conclusion

This chapter has shown that the depiction of the CBI as having been ignored by Margaret Thatcher and her like-minded ministers after 1979 because of its corporatist mindset is overly simplistic and sweeping. This interpretation has been accepted unquestioningly to date – even by the CBI itself – yet appears on the basis of the research presented here to be fundamentally flawed. It is flawed in the way it presents organised business in the form of the CBI; it is flawed in its depiction of the way Thatcher and other senior ministers viewed the CBI; and it is flawed in its presentation of the nature of the relationship between the two groups of actors. From its outset, the CBI faced internal tensions over the desired direction of economic policy. As the case of the IPG illustrates, some senior industrialists were happy to support neoliberal arguments, especially ones about the value of free enterprise, and to employ, and engage with, leading neoliberal activists. The way in which they were able to constrain the freedom of Campbell Adamson in 1974 through the creation of the President's Committee shows that their influence remained real.

With this in mind, it is less surprising that the working relationship between the CBI and the Thatcher governments endured despite the economic pressures pulling them apart in the early 1980s. The relationship was not without its tensions and misunderstandings, but there was a genuine desire from both parties to maintain a constructive dialogue and to get past any difficulties. It is easy to understand why the CBI would want access to Thatcher and her economic ministers, but given the existence of the IoD as an alternative source of business advice, what could the CBI offer to the government? The existing dominant account suggests very little, dismissing the CBI as largely irrelevant in the 1980s. This was not the case: the Prime Minister, the Chancellor and their officials recognised that the CBI had a key position in British society and the government had to work with it if the government was to achieve its goals. This dependency was sufficiently recognised to ensure that dialogue continued and remained constructive and suitably regular.

This should not be surprising. There were natural affinities between the Conservative government and the CBI which did not disappear. Cahill is right to remind us that all forms of neoliberalism are embedded. This also means that influences other than ideology are important in understanding the spread and implementation of neoliberal ideas. Just as business's involvement in this process was more than simply funding think tanks, so one must also not forget that Thatcher was a politician and that she could not ride roughshod over everyone if she was to achieve the changes she desired for the UK. Pragmatic politics and material interests remained important throughout the 1980s. On that basis, the CBI remained a key actor with which to maintain an understanding, even if Thatcher personally preferred the company of the IoD. It also means she was able to see the significance of encouraging the CBI to disseminate a message of pay restraint to its members, although this does not seem congruent with neoliberal thinking on the causes of, and cures for, inflation: a politician of conviction perhaps, but one who appreciated the value of consensus-building with sympathetic vested interests.

This last point suggests that the conventional account overstates the extent to which 1979 was a turning point in the relationship between the government and the rest of society: there were continuities. Broader implications for our understanding of the development of neoliberalism in the UK, and beyond, flow from this. Firstly, it highlights the interaction between ideas and material interests in which business did more than simply supply funds to neoliberal think tanks. There is a need to recognise the complex and diverse ways in which ideas and material interests interacted, rather than to see them as alternative interpretations of neoliberalism. Secondly, building on this first point, the account given here questions a rigid focus on intellectuals and ideas when defining who should be included in the ambit of neoliberalism. Some businessmen directly promoted neoliberal ideas themselves, as illustrated here through the example of the IPG. At the same time, and thirdly, this account reasserts the diversity inherent in the thinking found in neoliberal circles, where there could be agreement on the broad goals but sharp disagreement on particular policies. Here the CBI, and business more generally, found it difficult to accept monetarism, but so did others in neoliberal circles. On the other side of the coin (and not elaborated here for reasons of space), the CBI was highly critical of the Conservative governments' efforts to control public expenditure and to roll back the state. Lastly, the interdependent relationship between the government and the CBI cautions against overly simplistic depictions of the Thatcher governments as a limited but strong and independent government operating separately from a free economy. In contrast, in this case, the Thatcher governments' necessary reliance on the CBI to achieve their policy goals evokes an awareness of the constraints on their power and independence.

Notes

1 'Investing for the New Europe', 6 November 1990, 7–8, TNA: PREM 19/3395, P.242.90.

2 'Competing in the New Europe: John Banham's presentation to the Prime Minister, Friday, 26 April', Howell Harris Hughes to Sarah Hogg, 24 April 1991, TNA: PREM 19/3395. See also Confederation of British Industry, *A Business Agenda for the 1990s* (London, CBI, 1991); and CBI, *The Will to Win* (London, CBI, 1981).

3 'Director-General's national conference speech 1980', Beckett, 11 November 1980, TNA: PREM 19/490.

4 'A changed culture', *The Times* (10 November 1986), 17.

5 Andrew Bowman, Julie Froud, Sukhdev Johal, Michael Moran and Karel Williams, 'Business elites and undemocracy in Britain: A work in progress', in Glenn Morgan, Paul Hirsch and Sigrid Quack (eds), *Elites on Trial* (Bingley, Emerald Group Publishing, 2005), 321; Martin Adeney, 'Beckett, Sir Terence Norman', *Oxford Dictionary of National Biography*, https://doi.org/10.1093/ref:odnb/106777 (accessed 1 August 2017); Keith Middlemas, *Power, Competition and the State, Volume 3: The end of the postwar era: Britain since 1974* (Basingstoke, Macmillan, 1991), 306; and Peter Kerr, *Postwar British Politics: From conflict to consensus* (Abingdon, Routledge, 2001), 205.

6 Richard Cockett, *Thinking the Unthinkable: Think-tanks and the economic counter-revolution, 1931–83* (London, HarperCollins, 1994).

7 Damian Cahill, *The End of Laissez-Faire? On the durability of embedded neoliberalism* (Cheltenham, Edward Elgar, 2014); and Damian Cahill and Martijn Konings, *Neoliberalism* (Cambridge, Polity Press, 2017), 102.

8 Ben Jackson, 'The think-tank archipelago: Thatcherism and neo-liberalism', in Ben Jackson and Robert Saunders (eds), *Making Thatcher's Britain* (Cambridge, Cambridge University Press, 2012), 43–61.

9 See E. H. H. Green, *Thatcher* (London, Hodder and Stoughton, 2006), 64.

10 Green, *Thatcher*, 113.

11 For more on this episode, see Neil Rollings, 'Cracks in the post-war Keynesian settlement? The role of organised business in Britain in the rise of neoliberalism before Margaret Thatcher', *Twentieth Century British History*, 24 (2013), 637–59; and Neil Rollings, 'Between business and academia in post-war Britain: Three advocates of neoliberalism at the heart of the British business community', in Roger E. Backhouse, Bradley W. Bateman, Tamotsu Nishizawa and Dieter Plehwe (eds), *Liberalism and the Welfare State: Economists and arguments for the welfare state* (Oxford, Oxford University Press, 2017), 101–17.

12 'Obituary: Barry Bracewell-Milnes', *Daily Telegraph* (24 July 2012), https://www.telegraph.co.uk/news/obituaries/finance-obituaries/9424562/Barry-Bracewell-Milnes.html (accessed 19 February 2020).

13 'Director-General's National Conference speech 1980', Terence Beckett, 11 November 1980, TNA: PREM 19/490. See also Donald MacDougall, *Don and Mandarin* (London, John Murray, 1987), 254–5.

14 Patricia Tisdall, 'CBI leader attacks "narrow" Tory policies', *The Times* (12 November 1980), 1.

15 Adeney, 'Beckett'; and Middlemas, *Power, Vol. 3*, 306. Similar imagery can be found in press references to the episode.

16 *Financial Times* (14 November 1980), 1.

17 Quoted in Wyn Grant, 'Representing capital: The role of the CBI', in Roger King (ed.), *Capital and Politics* (London, Routledge and Kegan Paul, 1983), 72.

18 *The Times* (20 November 1980), 15.

19 Kerr, *Postwar British Politics*, 205; and Henk Overbeek, *Global Capitalism and National Decline: The Thatcher decade in perspective* (London, Unwin Hyman, 1990), 202.

20 'The love affair with Labour is heart on the sleeve stuff', *The Guardian* (2 November 1999), https://www.theguardian.com/business/1999/nov/02/labourparty.politics1 (accessed 23 June 2021); and Charles Moore, *Margaret Thatcher: The authorized biography, Volume 1: Not for turning* (London, Allen Lane, 2013), 534.

21 Quoted by Martin Holmes, *The First Thatcher Government 1979–1983: Contemporary Conservatism and economic change* (Brighton, Wheatsheaf, 1985), 157; and John Hoskyns, *Just in Time: Inside the Thatcher revolution* (London, Aurum Press, 2000), 345.

22 Wyn Grant, 'Business interests and the British Conservative Party', *Government and Opposition*, 18 (1980), 143–61; Neil J. Mitchell, 'The decentralization of business in Britain', *Journal of Politics*, 52 (1990), 622–37; and Rob Baggott, 'From confrontation to consultation? Pressure group relations from Thatcher to Major', *Parliamentary Affairs*, 48 (1995), 484–502. One other important difference between the CBI and the IoD was that the former had only company or trade association membership, while the IoD had individual membership.

23 Dennis Kavanagh, *Thatcherism and British Politics: The end of consensus?* 2nd ed. (Oxford, Oxford University Press, 1990), 91–2; and Jonathan Boswell and James Peter, *Capitalism in*

Contention: Business leaders and political economy in modern Britain (Cambridge, Cambridge University Press, 1997), 154–7.

24 Holmes, *First Thatcher Government*, 154, 161.

25 Stephen Wilks, *The Political Power of the Business Corporation* (Cheltenham, Edward Elgar, 2013), 105–13; and Michael Moran, *Business, Politics and Society: An Anglo-American comparison* (Oxford, Oxford University Press, 2009).

26 Anthony Sampson, *The New Anatomy of Britain* (London, Hodder and Stoughton, 1971), 571, 612.

27 John Jewkes, Paul Chambers and Lionel Robbins, *Economics, Business and Government: Addresses given at a dinner on 13 January 1966 to mark the IEA's 10th year* (London, IEA, 1966).

28 John Jewkes, 'Entrepreneurs on the defensive: The Industrial Policy Group: The failure of an experiment', in John Jewkes, *A Return to Free Market Economics?* (London, Macmillan, 1978), 174.

29 Boswell and Peters, *Capitalism*, 76.

30 'Industrial Policy Group memorandum no. 1', 26 March 1968, Modern Records Centre, University of Warwick (MRC) MSS200/C/3/DG1/42.

31 'Industrialists form policy group to study economy', *The Times* (12 October 1967), 17.

32 John Whitehorn, 'Company law and worker participation', 15 August 1967, MRC MSS200/C/3/DG1/44.

33 Middlemas, *Power, Vol. 3*, 27.

34 Wyn Grant and David Marsh, *The Confederation of British Industry* (London, Hodder and Stoughton, 1977), 104–5.

35 Middlemas, *Power, Vol. 3*, 186–7, 211–15; and Green, *Thatcher*, 72. See also A. K. Rawlinson, 'Conversation with Sir Donald McDougall', 9 April 1979, TNA: T 371/1043.

36 Middlemas, *Power, Vol. 3*, 187.

37 Jim Phillips, 'Business and the limited reconstruction of industrial relations in the UK in the 1970s', *Business History*, 51 (2009), 801–16.

38 CBI Council minutes, 17 May 1979, MRC: MSS200/C/3/53/1/2, C.32.79.

39 Sir Adrian Cadbury, 'Record of a meeting between the Prime Minister and the CBI', 9 July 1979, TNA: T 390/410.

40 Gerald Frost, *Making Things Happen: The life and original thinking of Nigel Vinson* (London, Biteback, 2015); and Hoskyns, *Just in Time*, 161.

41 P. V. Dixon to Howe, 'CBI', 17 December 1980, TNA T 390/724. See also Jock Bruce-Gardyne, *Mrs Thatcher's First Administration: The prophets confounded* (London, Macmillan, 1984), 65; and Nigel Lawson, *Memoirs of a Tory Radical* (London, Biteback, 2010), 48.

42 'Prime Minister's meeting with the CBI', M. A. Hall to Tim Lankester (Private Secretary to the Prime Minister), 30 May 1980, TNA: T 390/595.

43 'Note of a meeting at No. 11 Downing Street: 5 pm, Friday 16th May 1980', TNA: T 390/595.

44 'Note of a meeting between the Prime Minister and Sir Ray Pennock at 1600 hours on Friday 12 September at 10 Downing Street', Lankester, 15 September 1980, TNA: T 390/596.

45 'CBI conference and pay announcement', Adam Ridley to Howe, 16 October 1980, TNA: T 390/596.

46 'Note of a meeting held at 11 Downing Street with the CBI on Thursday, 23 October 1980', P. S. Jenkins, 23 October 1980, TNA: T 390/596.

47 'CBI conference', P. V. Dixon to Howe, 6 November 1980, TNA: T 390/724.

48 'CBI conference', P. V. Dixon to Howe, 6 November 1980, TNA: T 390/724.

49 'CBI conference', Ridley to Howe, 7 November 1980, TNA: PREM 19/490.

50 Margareta Pagano, 'We've got to show that business is a force for good', *The Independent* (5 June 2011), http://www.independent.co.uk/news/business/analysis-and-features/weve-got-to-show-that-business-is-a-force-for-good-2293044.html (accessed 23 June 2021).

51 'CBI conference', attached to A. J. Wiggins (Treasury) to Lankester, 11 November 1980, TNA PREM 19/490.

52 *The Times* (13 November 1980), 1.

53 Record of a meeting, 12 November 1980, TNA: PREM 19/490.

54 Thatcher to M. J. Verey, 17 November 1980, Margaret Thatcher Foundation online archive (MTF), http://www.margaretthatcher.org/document/119887 (accessed 23 June 2021).

55 Thatcher to Sir John Clark, 25 November 1980, MTF, http://www.margaretthatcher.org/document/119897 (accessed 23 June 2021). Pennock had also briefed the Chancellor of the Exchequer's adviser on his speech prior to the conference ('CBI conference', Adam Ridley to Geoffrey Howe, 7 November 1980, TNA: PREM 19/490).

56 'Record of a meeting', 12 November 1980, TNA: PREM 19/490.
57 'Record of a meeting between the Prime Minister and the President of the Confederation of British Industry at 1615 hours on Friday, 13 March at 10 Downing Street', 16 March 1981, TNA: T 366/760.
58 'Record of a meeting between the Prime Minister and the President of the Confederation of British Industry at 1615 hours on Friday, 13 March at 10 Downing Street', 16 March 1981, TNA: T 366/760.
59 Ian Gow to the Prime Minister, 8 September 1982, TNA: PREM 19/1062.
60 Note at end of the file, TNA: PREM 19/1062.
61 MacDougall, *Don and Mandarin*, 246
62 Greenborough to Howe, 3 December 1980, TNA: T 390/724.
63 'Note of a meeting at No. 11 Downing Street on Thursday, 18 December 1980 at 5.45 pm', TNA: T 390/724.
64 Pennock to Clive Whitmore, 26 January 1981, TNA: PREM 19/490.
65 Beckett to Thatcher, 2 March 1981, TNA: PREM 19/490.
66 Lankester to John Wiggins (Treasury), 14 May 1981, reporting on the meeting, TNA: PREM 19/490.
67 'Brief on CBI discussion paper on the Will to Win (TWTW)', undated but May 1981, TNA: T 440/76.
68 'Brief on CBI discussion paper on the Will to Win (TWTW)', undated but May 1981, TNA: T 440/76.
69 'CBI conference: Sunday 4 November to Tuesday 6 November', A. Lovell, undated but November 1984, TNA: T 471/105.
70 For example, Thatcher to Clemminson, 5 August 1985, TNA: PREM 19/3395; and Clemminson to Thatcher, 20 November 1985, TNA: PREM 19/3395.
71 'Dinner for the CBI, Monday 30 November 1987', unsigned and undated, TNA: T 640/856.
72 For questioning of this perspective, see Cahill, *End of Laissez-Faire?*; and Middlemas, *Power, Vol. 3*, 279.
73 'Note of a meeting at No. 11 Downing Street on Thursday, 18 December 1980 at 5.45 pm', TNA: T 390/724.
74 For example, 'CBI Annual Conference 1983', by J. Anson (Treasury), 9 November 1983, TNA: T 471/99; 'Note of a meeting in No. 11 Downing Street at 6.00pm on Tuesday, 17 November', by A. C. S. Allan, comment by John Banham, 19 November 1987, TNA: T 640/856; and 'The CBI', Sarah Hogg to John Major, the Prime Minister, 25 April 1991, TNA: PREM 19/2295.
75 Green, *Thatcher*, 126.
76 Grant, 'Business interests', 146–7.
77 Treasury untitled brief for meeting with CBI, 13 March 1981, TNA: PREM 19/490; 'CBI reaction to the budget', George Younger, Secretary of State for Scotland, to Howe, 25 March 1981, TNA: T 390/724; and 'Brief on CBI discussion paper on the Will to Win (TWTW)', John Wiggins to Caroline Stephens, 8 May 1981, TNA: PREM 19/490.
78 'Prospects for the next pay round', brief included in T. J. Burr, 'Economic ministers meeting with the CBI', 5 June 1981, TNA: T 440/76. The meeting had been given this purpose since April 1981 ('Post-Easter meetings with the CBI', D. B. Andren, 24 April 1981, TNA: T 440/76).
79 'Meeting with the CBI', Robin Butler to John Kerr, 27 June 1983, TNA: PREM 19/1062. See also Bernard Ingham (the Prime Minister's press secretary) to the Prime Minister, 21 June 1983, TNA: PREM 19/1062.
80 For example, 'CBI pay presentations: Letter from Sir T Beckett', Carolyn Sinclair, 7 August 1984, TNA: T 471/102.
81 D. R. Glynn, 'The CBI Industrial Trends Survey', *Applied Economics*, 1 (1969), 183–96.
82 B. C. Rosewell, 'The CBI Industrial Trends Survey and capacity working', in Derek Bosworth and David Heathfield (eds), *Working below Capacity* (London, Palgrave Macmillan, 1987), 3–22.
83 Grant and Marsh, *CBI*, 210; and 'Institute of Directors: "Business Opinion Survey"', A. Smith, 7 November 1983, TNA: T 471/114. The CBI survey still continues today and regularly receives press coverage.
84 See 'CBI Quarterly Trends Survey – July', R. I. G. Allen, 2 August 1982, TNA: T 440/76; 'Early briefing on the October CBI Industrial Trends Survey', I. Williams, 18 October 1982, TNA: T 440/128; and 'CBI Quarterly Trends Survey – January', R. I. G. Allen, 31 January 1983, TNA: T 440/128.

85 For example, 'Meeting with the CBI', Alex Allan, 23 July 1992, TNA: PREM 19/3807.
86 'CBI Quarterly Trends Survey – January', R. I. G. Allen, 31 January 1983, TNA: T 440/128; and 'CBI Quarterly Trends Survey – July', R. I. G. Allen, 2 August 1982, TNA: T 440/76.
87 Thatcher to Clemminson, 5 August 1985, TNA: PREM 19/3395.
88 'Meeting with the CBI', Alex Allan, 23 July 1992, TNA: PREM 19/3807.
89 'Prime Minister's meeting with the Scottish CBI', D. R. Norgove, 25 August 1982, TNA: T 440/76.

14

The roots of Britain's financialised political economy

Aled Davies*

The collapse of the global financial system in 2008 may be regarded as the beginning of the end of the neoliberal age. This catastrophic event, caused by the transmission of US mortgage defaults throughout the complex network of transnational financial markets, profoundly undermined a core neoliberal assumption that markets were always rational and efficient and revived 'the state' as the only economic actor capable of saving capitalism from destruction.[1] While the crisis did not lead to a coherent, radical break with the neoliberal norms that governed national economies and the global economic order, these norms have been continually destabilised in the subsequent decade by the political forces unleashed by the legacy of the crash.[2]

In its 'death', as in life, neoliberalism was closely bound up with the fortunes of finance. The political revolutions of Margaret Thatcher and Ronald Reagan, which heralded the birth of the neoliberal age at the start of the 1980s, coincided with the liberalisation and globalisation of financial markets. Given this synchronicity, we cannot analyse one without the other. Indeed, many scholars have already interrogated the relationship between triumphant global finance and the political economy of neoliberalism in the late twentieth century. For some, such as the Marxist economists Gérard Duménil and Dominique Lévy, neoliberalism was simply 'the ideological expression of the return to hegemony of the financial fraction of the ruling class'.[3] In this account, the crisis of Fordist accumulation in the late 1960s served to *financialise* capitalism, which in turn forced changes to the way in which it was managed and regulated by introducing neoliberal economic policies.[4] This materialist account has, however, been challenged by those who see the liberation of finance as a product of a neoliberal ideology that claimed that impediments to financial markets were inefficient and contrary to individual liberty.[5] The key question, therefore, is whether neoliberalism was a cause or an effect of 'financialisation'.

A financialised growth model

Britain's economy in the late twentieth and early twenty-first centuries can be described as having been 'financialised', by which is meant that the financial sector, and financial-type activities, had become increasingly dominant within British capitalism. This took two particularly salient forms: a globally oriented financial sector with a hegemonic position within the structure and government of the nation's economy, and a reliance on private mortgage borrowing to sustain economic growth.[6] At the turn of the millennium, the UK was distinctive among the world's leading economies for having an especially large financial sector with a predominantly global character, based in (but not confined to) the City of London.[7] On the eve of the 2008 financial crisis, banks in London were responsible for 20 per cent of global cross-border lending and held one-fifth of all international bank assets. In 2007, London could claim a 46 per cent share of global foreign equity trading, a 70 per cent share of international bond trading and a 47 per cent share of the entire world's cross-border derivatives turnover. The nation's capital was at the heart of the global financial system. In 2007, financial and professional services accounted for 11 per cent of UK GDP, and the trade surplus in financial services equalled £35.6 billion.[8] Employment in financial services peaked and remained at roughly 1.2 million after 1990, and the financial sector's share of total profits in Britain reached 20 per cent in the 2000s (compared with roughly 5 per cent in the 1950s and 1960s).[9]

Since the financial crisis, critics such as John Cristensen, Nicholas Shaxson and Duncan Wigan have argued that this large financial sector is a national curse that has:

> . . . crowded out manufacturing and non-financial services, leeched government of skilled staff, entrenched regional disparities, fostered large-scale financial rent-seeking, heightened economic dependence, increased inequality, helped disenfranchise the majority and exposed the economy to violent crises.[10]

Furthermore, the liberalised, market-based financial system is alleged to have imposed its short-term priorities on the real economy, which has weakened the long-term prospects of British industry.[11] However, such criticism had little purchase in the decades preceding the financial crash, as the City was embedded in a political consensus committed to championing its global role. To maintain and promote the City, financial services were insulated from 'excessive' taxation and regulation. The creation of the Financial Services Authority in 2001 was an attempt to replace the supposedly 'burdensome' system that had preceded it.[12] Furthermore, threats from abroad were vigorously resisted. Take, for example, the response of the Labour government to the idea of a European Union withholding tax on savings in 1998, which was designed to reduce tax avoidance. The City's political representatives argued that such a move would be damaging to its international bond business, and so the Chancellor of the Exchequer, Gordon Brown, unilaterally abolished the UK's tax on international bond interest, which in turn forced the EU to agree to a watered-down agreement based on the greater international exchange of information.[13] Not only was the City seen as a key asset, but it was celebrated by Brown for embodying Britain's 'enduring qualities' of 'creativity', 'enterprise', 'openness to the world' and a 'belief in duty and fair play'.[14] In the age of apparently inevitable, unstoppable globalisation, the City demonstrated to the rest of the country the need to 'think globally' and to embrace 'the vigour, ingenuity and aspiration . . . that [was] the hallmark of [the City's] success'.[15]

Beyond London's position as a key node in the network of globalised finance, by the end of the twentieth century the provision of credit to the domestic economy through a liberalised financial system had become essential to the national model of economic growth. Easy access to credit, primarily used to buy property, was central to what Colin Hay has characterised as the 'Anglo-liberal growth model'.[16] Households borrowed to acquire property that could be expected to appreciate in value, and which would in turn enable them to 'move up the housing ladder', withdraw equity to fund present consumption, or save for retirement.[17] The latter factor became especially important as generous employer-based pension schemes were dismantled and state retirement benefits dwindled.[18] High costs and constraints on borrowing had been reduced by the integration of the UK mortgage market within a transatlantic financial system, which introduced the American practice of mortgage securitisation.[19] This economic model has been described, by Avner Offer and James Wood respectively, as a 'property windfall economy'[20] and a 'mortgage-led accumulation regime'.[21] Colin Crouch has characterised it as a system of 'privatized Keynesianism', in which demand in the economy was no longer maintained by governments taking on the burden of debt to fund growth-provoking expenditure, but instead indebtedness was devolved to individuals (whose wages, on average, had stagnated since the 1980s, but who benefited from rising house prices).[22] House price inflation was tolerated because it provided the necessary spur to encourage borrowing, as well as delivering nominal capital gains to a home-owning electorate. As Offer points out, this growth model seemed to produce more winners than losers, and so generated broad popular support.[23]

How, and why, did this financialised economic model emerge? One popularly held view is that it was the deliberate creation of the Thatcher governments and their implementation of an ideological commitment to unfettered market competition, combined with a radical attempt to create a home-owning society. Indeed, two achievements that are often identified as embodying Thatcherism are the enforced sale of council houses at a discount (the 'Right to Buy') and the de-cartelisation of the London Stock Exchange in the so-called Big Bang of 1986. It is certainly the case that the actions of the Thatcher governments served to create the financialised economic model, and it is also undeniably true that the Thatcher governments contained many neoliberal partisans who championed this. However, these governments did not operate in a vacuum, and to develop a more accurate understanding of their achievements it is essential to situate them in a longer-term historical context. This chapter will argue that the financialised growth model is best understood as an emergent political-economic strategy in which the Thatcher governments acquiesced to processes of 'financialisation' that had been underway throughout the post-war decades. In particular, the chapter will focus on the re-globalisation of finance through the City of London in the 1960s and 1970s, as well as the substantial demand for mortgage finance generated by the post-war political consensus in favour of expanding home ownership. The confluence and fusion of these two processes during the crisis of the industrial economy in the early 1980s established the financialised growth model that underpinned the political-economic settlement of Britain's neoliberal age.

Re-globalising finance

Despite the supposed novelty and hyper-modernity of late twentieth-century globalisation, it was in fact a part-revival of an economic order that had prevailed at the turn of the nineteenth and twentieth centuries.[24] The City of London had been at the heart of the late nineteenth-century global economy: it provided the capital for economic development, markets for trade, a mechanism for international payments, means of global shipping and insurance and a trusted currency backed by the gold standard.[25] The First World War, and the ensuing political chaos of the interwar decades, destroyed this liberal order and destabilised London's position as a financial centre. Most significantly, after the financial crisis of 1931, government-mandated controls on capital prevented the free movement of money across political borders.[26] The City's merchant banks were subsequently trapped within the limitations of the sterling area (a group of mostly British colonies and post-colonial states that pegged their currencies to the pound).[27] The City's partially de-globalised status was subsequently cemented by the Bretton Woods agreement in 1944, which arranged to fix international exchange rates and, importantly, permitted the continued control of capital flows to support the legitimate pursuit of domestic-focused, employment-maximising macroeconomic policies by national governments.[28]

By the 1950s, the prospects for the City's role as an international financial centre looked bleak. The costs to Britain of maintaining sterling as an international currency became increasingly intolerable as efforts to maintain confidence in the pound forced governments to adopt restrictive economic policies at the expense of their intended aims of national economic modernisation and social reform.[29] Meanwhile, as Britain's imperial financial inheritance crumbled in the face of domestic political pressure, the US dollar had become the dominant currency for trade and investment – reflecting the USA's hegemonic position in the post-war global order.[30] At this juncture, the City's banking elite was forced to find a way to reconcile the decline of sterling with the new dollar dominance. Financial historians have long understood that it was the City's response to this structural change to the international economy that laid the foundations for its revitalisation as a global financial centre. The revival of the City did not begin with the Thatcher government's deregulatory agenda in the 1980s, but with the creation of the so-called Eurodollar market during the years of post-war political consensus.[31]

The Eurodollar market was one in which dollars could be deposited and lent outside the exchange controls imposed on both sterling and the dollar. This was achieved by treating the dollars as technically 'offshore' on the balance sheets of banks based in London, and so not subject to national regulation. These dollars that had accumulated overseas arose from the combined effects of a cap on domestic interest rates, a balance of payments deficit and the multi-nationalisation of American firms. Gary Burn has demonstrated that the creation of the Eurodollar market – a global financial market outside the control of national states – was the product of a deliberate attempt by the Bank of England and London's banking fraternity to re-establish the freedoms that the global City had lost since 1931. The market was only able to develop because the Bank of England permitted it to do so and encouraged its growth.[32] The success of the Eurodollar market divorced the City from its reliance on sterling, which enabled London to operate freely as a post-imperial financial centre. As P. J. Cain and A. G. Hopkins put it:

> As the good ship sterling sank, the City was able to scramble aboard a much more seaworthy young vessel, the Eurodollar.[33]

The triumph of the Eurodollar was, at once, a victory and a defeat for the gentlemanly financial order that had originated in the nineteenth century. Its commitment to a globally oriented City, liberated from the demands of national economic management, had been sustained and championed by the nominally nationalised Bank of England throughout the mid-century of financial de-globalisation. Once the Eurodollar market had been established, however, British banks were quickly displaced by American and other foreign banks that flooded into London to participate in the financial free-for-all.[34] Ironically, the rebirth of the global City through the Eurodollar market went hand in hand with the 'death of gentlemanly capitalism'.[35]

Beyond revitalising the City, the liberation of finance from national boundaries via the Eurodollar market had a profoundly destabilising effect on the global economic order that had been constructed following the Second World War. The accumulation of vast pools of short-term funds outside national control exposed fixed exchange rates to increasingly intense and rapid speculative attacks. The effect was to erode the capacity of nation states to pursue domestic-focused economic policies. This has been demonstrated by Scott Newton, who has shown how the sterling crises of the 1960s were made more severe and more unmanageable by the unforgiving flows of 'hot money' enabled by the Eurodollar market.[36] Speculation against the US dollar and sterling undermined the Bretton Woods order of fixed exchange rates and led ultimately to the system's collapse in 1971. The subsequent worldwide explosion in prices dictated that governments were compelled to demonstrate their commitment to controlling inflation to the judge and jury of global financial flows. The result was an enforced abandonment of Keynesian policies intended to minimise unemployment, and the adoption of a harsh discipline of monetarist policies designed to reduce inflation. In Britain, where the

Thatcher government inherited a system of monetary targets that had been unwillingly adopted by its Labour predecessor in 1976, this proved disastrous for large sections of British industry.[37] Rocketing interest rates and the resulting exchange rate appreciation of the pound, exacerbated by the UK's new role as a major oil exporter during the second oil shock, resulted in an unemployment rate of over three million and pushed many export-manufacturing industries to the wall.[38]

While Eurodollars wreaked havoc and eventually destroyed the post-war Bretton Woods order, the re-globalisation of London was presented as an opportunity for the British state. While nurturing the Eurodollar market, the Bank of England also sought to promote the importance of the global City to the national economy. In 1967, a committee was formed called the Committee on Invisible Exports. Funded and managed at arm's length by the Bank of England, the committee was made up of senior City figures and was led by the financial journalist William Clarke. The committee sought to counter the notion that the City was a hindrance to the national economy, and to do this it argued that London's globally oriented financial services sector was invaluable to Britain because it generated foreign income that contributed to the nation's balance of payments. The committee ran a highly successful and influential campaign that persuaded Britain's governing elite in the 1960s and 1970s that allowing London the freedom to operate globally (not just in banking, but in a whole range of financial and commercial services) would be beneficial to the nation (rather than harmful – as had allegedly been the case when London's international role was bound up with sterling).[39] The power of this argument was that it even came to be deployed by the British state to accelerate the destruction of the remnants of the City's gentlemanly order: the Big Bang deregulation of the London Stock Exchange was a deliberate attempt to internationalise the market so that it would begin to compete for business with other financial centres, especially New York, and therefore generate foreign income.[40] One reason for the effectiveness of this argument was that it successfully conflated the interests of the globally oriented elements of the financial sector with the service sector of the entire economy (which had been growing throughout the twentieth century).[41] The Committee on Invisible Exports, and in particular its spin-off the Liberalisation of Trade in Services committee, positioned itself (somewhat disingenuously, but politically effectively) as the champion of the entire service sector.[42]

This is not to say that by 1979 a financial service exporting strategy, with the City at its centre, had been adopted by the British state at the expense of manufacturing industry. The Conservatives under Thatcher had in fact entered government committed to industrial revival.[43] It was not until the disastrous effects of the monetarist macroeconomic experiment that the government was forced to rely on the overseas provision of global financial services for national economic prosperity. The evidence of this can be found in the Chancellor of the Exchequer Nigel Lawson's combative contribution to the House of Lords Select Committee on Overseas Trade in 1985. Presented with the evidence of Britain's crumbling industrial base, he argued that it mattered less than critics claimed because Britain in fact had a comparative advantage in providing services to the rest of the world. Lawson told the committee:

> There is no adamantine law that says we have to produce as much in the way of manufactures as we consume. If it does turn out that we are relatively more efficient in world terms at providing services than at producing goods, then our national interest lies in a surplus on services and a deficit on goods.[44]

This argument had been developed by the invisibles committee over the preceding two decades and was readily available as a tool for giving a positive, progressive spin to the government's economic policies. Lawson's pursuit of this argument must be situated in the context of the continuing failure of the government's economic policies (unemployment remained above 10 per cent and the UK's trade balance in manufactures had been in deficit since 1983).[45] It was a politically necessary attempt to justify the speed of the deindustrialisation that had taken place over the previous six years. It is notable, however, that in their evidence to the House of Lords committee the British Invisible Exports Council expressed scepticism that service exports would ever be an ample substitute for the loss of manufactured exports.[46] Meanwhile, Baron (Arnold) Weinstock, the managing director of General Electric Company (GEC), was indignant in response to Lawson's apparent indifference to the fate of British industry and condemned the vision of future economic prosperity outlined by the Chancellor. He told the committee, with evident distaste, that:

> We will be servicing, presumably, the production of wealth by others. We will supply the changing of the guard, we will supply the Beefeaters around the Tower of London. We will become a curiosity. I do not think that is what Britain is about; I think that is rubbish. What service industries are there going to be in Wigan, or in Bolton, or at Smethwick?[47]

As Barry Supple has noted, Weinstock's condemnation drew on a long-standing critique of the service sector that can be traced back to Joseph Chamberlain and the Tariff Reform campaign at the beginning of the century.[48] Yet it also presaged the geographical and cultural tensions that were subsequently to develop over the following decades, factors that would lead ultimately to the political storms that would engulf the neoliberal order in the 2010s.[49]

The international economic order that had been planned at the Bretton Woods conference in 1944, and that had been imperfectly implemented in the post-war decades, suppressed global finance to assist national governments in the pursuit of the social democratic aims of sustained economic growth, full employment and redistribution. The banking institutions of the City of London, wedded to an ideal of financial liberalism inherited from the age of British imperialism, successfully reconstructed global finance under the auspices of US dollar hegemony. The result was to destroy the international framework that had underpinned the social democratic age. The harsh conditions unleashed by re-globalised finance inadvertently washed away the remnants (if not the ideals) of the City's gentlemanly order and, even more significantly, accelerated the deindustrialisation of Britain. For the British state, commandeered by Conservative governments under the influence of neoliberal ideas, the only feasible course of action appeared to be to embrace global finance as the centrepiece of a new, post-industrial national economic strategy.

Liberating the mortgage market

The domestic component of Britain's financialised growth model in the late twentieth century – liberalised access to mortgage borrowing to purchase appreciating property assets – is commonly attributed to the deregulatory agenda of the Thatcher governments. However, despite the undoubted liberal market orientation of the Thatcherite agenda, the deregulation of the mortgage market was in fact unplanned. Instead, we should see it as a product of two factors that were fused together by the adoption of monetarist economic policies in the late 1970s: a public demand for mortgages generated by the post-war expansion of home ownership and the re-globalisation of finance.

Owner-occupation became the dominant form of tenure in Britain during the post-war decades. This profound economic and social change was largely attributable to the combined effects of economic affluence and a political consensus in favour of home ownership, which provided tax exemptions and subsidies for owner-occupiers (see also Guy Ortolano's chapter in this volume).[50] Home ownership also came to be associated with independence, autonomy and social status.[51] Given the substantial cost of house purchase, potential buyers required credit that could be paid back over a long term: a mortgage. This meant that as the desire for home ownership grew, the demand for mortgages increased. In the post-war period mortgages were provided by specialised financial institutions: building societies. These were mutually owned institutions that pooled the savings of their members and then provided mortgages to those members once they had saved for a deposit.[52] These societies sat within a wider domestic financial system which, although not under direct state control, was subject to a semi-formal regulatory regime designed to aid the implementation of demand management and industrial development policies. In particular, governments sought to direct credit to export-oriented industries in order to help overcome the nation's recurrent balance of payments deficit and to maintain the sterling exchange rate. In essence, the financial system was strictly compartmentalised and organised by a range of semi-private cartels.[53] Most significantly, the banking system was subjected to instructions from government on how much it could lend, and to what sectors of the economy. This influence over lending was operated through an oligopoly of clearing banks that agreed not to compete with each other on price.[54] Banks were prevented from engaging in mortgage lending, and instead the system of housing finance was confined to the building societies.[55] Like the clearing banks, the building societies did not compete with each other on price – they agreed instead to a system of recommended interest rates through the Building Societies Association (BSA).[56] This uncompetitive practice, and the exclusion of banks from the mortgage market, was tolerated because it made it easier for governments to manage the allocation of credit in accordance with the perceived needs of the overall economy.[57] It also prevented credit-fuelled house price inflation.

Despite the submission of the mortgage market to the imperatives of economic management, the building societies cartel was successful in enabling the growth of home ownership. By the late 1960s, however, growing demand for mortgage finance, combined with fluctuating interest rates, generated recurrent political crises. Given the need to meet the demand for home ownership in the age of affluence, Labour and Conservative governments were burdened with the responsibility of maintaining the supply of mortgages *and* limiting their cost.[58] While the cartelised building society sector allowed governments to exercise influence over mortgage lending, it also exposed the government to public criticism. Because the building societies were dependent on a narrow funding model (they could only access savings deposits from the British public), if they wanted to increase their lending they had to attract more savings into their specialised compartment of the financial system. Members of the public wanting to obtain a mortgage could only do so if building societies had accumulated sufficient deposits. If not, potential borrowers were forced to wait until funds were available, which resulted in the formation of so-called mortgage queues.[59] The existence of such queues was determined by the wider environment of monetary policy: if the interest rate offered on building society deposits was lower than other locations for savings (for example banks), savers would move their money to get a higher rate of return. The result was that the societies would then not have sufficient funds to offer mortgages, and so queues would form every time the government increased interest rates according to wider macroeconomic requirements. This would, in turn, lead the BSA to announce their intention to increase the building societies' recommended rate of interest in order to clear their mortgage queues. But if building societies increased their interest rates, the cost of mortgage borrowing would also have to increase. In a note to the Prime Minister in April 1974 the Cabinet Secretary, John Hunt, summarised the problem facing the government:

> The mortgage question must surely command very high priority. The basic problem is to find acceptable means of insulating house purchasers from the money market while at the same time ensuring an adequate supply of mortgage finance. If market rates of interest are high the most obvious method of protecting house purchasers is by some form of Exchequer subsidy . . . If the mortgage rate is kept at a lower level than the market justifies, without any subsidy, then adequate finance for house purchases will not be forthcoming, with the result that there will be a mortgage famine and a decline in the house building programme.[60]

To overcome the trade-off between increasing lending rates and limiting the supply of mortgages, governments provided loans to the building societies until interest rates fell back to a level that enabled the societies to attract deposits once again. In April 1973, when the BSA proposed increasing their rates, the *Daily Mirror* described the move as 'political dynamite'.[61] The only way to prevent the societies from increasing the costs of mortgages was to provide a £15 million government subsidy.[62]

A year later, in 1974, the societies accepted (after some cajoling) a £500 million loan from the new Labour government to prevent a proposed increase in the mortgage rate to 11 per cent.[63] This solution to the problem was only feasible, however, if governments had the budgetary freedom to provide loans to the societies. The post-1976 monetarist constraints on government expenditure removed this option, and governments were forced to relinquish control over mortgage rates. In June 1979 the Thatcher government, as enthusiastic as its predecessors had been to continue to expand home ownership (combined with an ideological commitment to eliminating the public rental sector), was faced with the threat of an increase in the recommended mortgage rate (the bank rate had risen to 15 per cent in an effort to control the 'money supply').[64] The Chancellor, Geoffrey Howe, informed the Prime Minister that the only two options available to prevent such an increase, which she feared would deter potential home buyers, were to pay an interest rate subsidy to borrowers (at the cost to the exchequer of an estimated £25 million per percentage point per month) or to loan between £100 million and £150 million a month to the societies. Yet the constraints on public expenditure, which were central to the government's monetarist economic policy, meant that neither option was feasible.[65] Kenneth Berrill, head of the Central Policy Review Staff (CPRS), argued that for the government to intervene would tarnish its 'genuinely new approach to our post-war malaise'. 'Everybody', he said, was 'waiting to see if the Government has the strength of its convictions: not least the Unions'.[66] The influential City analyst Gordon Pepper informed Thatcher's private secretary that any government subsidy to the building societies would signal to the financial markets that the government was 'moving away from its firm intentions on monetary discipline'.[67] John Hoskyns, a key adviser to Thatcher, warned the Prime Minister that 'to preach economic realism and urge people to abandon the dream world etc., and then try to subsidise mortgage rates would invite ridicule'.[68] The constraints imposed on the government by its commitment to controlling inflation through reducing government expenditure and tight monetary policy disabled the government's ability to manage mortgage costs.

Abolition of the building society interest rate cartel would not solve the problem of the rising cost of borrowing in 1979. Nevertheless, there was some pressure on the government to take such action. The BSA's uncompetitive practices, and particularly its recommended rate, had drawn cross-party criticism since the late 1960s. In 1980 the Tory Bow Group proposed a rationalisation of the financial system so that the advantages afforded to building societies (favourable tax treatment, in addition to the cartel) would be removed and the societies incorporated within the banking system.[69] The report of the Committee to Review the Functioning of Financial Institutions, set up under the chairmanship of Harold Wilson to consider possible reform of the national financial system, also endorsed abolishing the cartel to create a more competitive financial system.[70] Yet despite the ideological commitments of the first Thatcher government, such a move was resisted. Shortly after Margaret Thatcher arrived in Downing Street, the CPRS proposed breaking up the building society cartel in order 'to help avoid the periodic mortgage famines which have been a common feature since the war'.[71] Thatcher's response was that while she did not like the cartel, she was 'fearful of encouraging competition with the present structure in management of the societies [Thatcher's underlining]', which she believed to be poor.[72] Harold Wilson had been equally scathing of the building societies during his tenure at Number 10, describing them as 'hidebound', 'fuddy-duddy' and 'ossified'.[73] The quality of building society management was not, however, the primary concern. A key worry, expressed by Nigel Lawson, then Financial Secretary to the Treasury, in a speech to the BSA conference in May 1980, was that by creating a unified mortgage market the building societies would increase their interest rates and this would remove the mechanism by which mortgage costs had been made affordable since the war.[74] It was also recognised that to create a unified mortgage market would likely result in increased house prices, as had occurred during the brief experiment in the liberalisation of bank lending under the Heath government.[75] It was a major concern, too, that to lose control over mortgage lending would weaken the government's ability to control the money supply, which at that time was the central aim of macroeconomic policy.[76]

Once again, however, the imperatives of monetarism had unintended consequences. Anti-inflationary policies had attracted foreign capital into Britain in 1979, which, combined with North Sea oil, had the damaging effect (for British exporters) of appreciating the sterling exchange rate. The government was unable to abandon its monetarist policies and so instead decided that the most effective way to reduce the exchange rate would be to allow foreign outflows of capital. Exchange controls, which had been in place in various forms since the 1930s, were abolished in October 1979.[77] The corollary of this final capitulation to re-globalised finance was that any government limits on the domestic banking system were deemed to be no longer operable. Banks could simply evade government controls by freely moving their money abroad, and so they were abandoned as useless. Geoffrey Howe's Treasury advisers were divided over whether removing controls on bank lending would see the clearing banks enter into the mortgage market in any significant way.[78] Lawson expressed concern that the banks would begin to offer mortgages, which would have the adverse side effect of increasing the money supply.[79] Without any formal controls, the Chancellor was forced to rely on making requests to the banks that they restrain their lending in the mortgage market.[80] However, these requests went unheeded and the banks, with their ability to source wholesale funds in the now-global money markets, began to undermine the building societies' dominance. In 1982 over a third of all new mortgage lending was provided by banks.[81] The competitive pressure brought to bear on the building societies served to break down the cartel arrangements.[82] It also prompted the building societies, which were traditionally wedded to their mutual ownership structure and their reliance on retail deposits, to lobby the government for the freedom to operate as banks. This was so that they could defend their market share in the newly competitive environment of Britain's globalised domestic financial system.[83] Significantly, by 1988 new legislation enabled the building societies to obtain up to 40 per cent of their funding from wholesale sources.[84] They were also given the freedom to demutualise and become banks, an opportunity that many embraced.[85]

The liberalisation of mortgage lending in Britain may have accorded with the free-market principles of Thatcherism, but it was, in fact, imposed on the post-1979 Conservative government by the exigencies of its monetarist macroeconomic policy, which itself was a response to globalised finance. The aims of the first Thatcher government were no different from those of its Labour predecessors: to satisfy the public demand for affordable homes to buy, and credit to buy them with. It was only as time went on that the government realised that a combination of higher mortgage rates and rising house prices could be politically acceptable and, indeed, provide the basis for continued electoral dominance. The government's failure to achieve broad-based economic growth in the wake of the monetarist experiment had left it without a coherent economic strategy for future prosperity. Tim Congdon wrote in *The Times* in 1986:

> The Conservatives are asking themselves how they can secure re-election. Unless the economy recovers more vigorously, unemployment will remain at over three million . . . How does it escape? Is there any mechanism still available for strengthening demand and improving business conditions in time to swing enough votes in its direction?[86]

As interest rates came down in the mid-1980s, a mortgage lending bonanza ensued that allowed more and more people to borrow to purchase houses that were increasing in value.[87] The Thatcher government's escape route was found in appreciating house prices, which not only made substantial numbers of voters feel more prosperous, but also encouraged greater consumption that in turn generated economic growth.

The demand for home ownership, and the desire for easy access to mortgage credit, was entrenched during the years of the post-war consensus. Government attempts to maintain both the supply and the cost of mortgages were rendered impossible by severe limits on government spending and tight monetary policies dictated by monetarism after 1976. The 'mortgage-accumulation regime' that emerged in the mid-1980s was an unintended product of the globalisation of finance, which intersected with this deep demand for home ownership.[88] In the post-monetarist, post-industrial economy of the mid-1980s, easy access to credit to purchase properties appreciating in value emerged as an effective way to achieve a politically stable form of 'inclusive' economic growth.

Conclusion

Britain's late twentieth-century financialised economic model was forged in the 1980s. It was not, however, simply the product of an ideological commitment to free markets by the Thatcher governments. Instead, we must situate these governments in a historical context that recognises the importance of processes of 'financialisation' that had been underway throughout the post-war decades. This chapter has highlighted two of these: the incorporation of large sections of the British public within the financial system as mortgagors (or potential mortgagors), and the re-globalisation of finance through the Eurodollar market. The latter was the most fundamentally important development: uncontrolled cross-border financial flows managed by banks in London destabilised the international economic framework that provided the basis for post-war social democracy and thus created the most important material condition for the transition towards neoliberalism.

The argument presented in this chapter challenges the temporal framing of a transition from post-war social democracy to neoliberalism having taken place around the time of the election of the first Thatcher government. Although profound changes to Britain's political economy did take place in the 1980s, it is evident that these had deep roots that pre-dated 'Thatcherism': the globalisation of the City of London was a 1960s revival of Britain's pre-1931 liberal-imperial position in the world economic order (albeit within the wider frame of US financial hegemony); and the demand for mortgages took off in the 1930s and became deeply embedded in the post-war political consensus. This does not mean that there was nothing novel about the Thatcher years, but what was new was not created *ex nihilo*.

Furthermore, this chapter should remind us not to lose sight of the material conditions in which neoliberal ideology, as well as neoliberal social and cultural practices, developed. This does not mean that we must revert to a simplistic materialist analysis in which the economic fundamentals are deemed to be direct determinants of politics, society and culture. Clearly, the material conditions prevailing in the 1970s and 1980s were themselves produced by 'non-economic' factors, such as the institutional and cultural hangover of British imperialism in the City, or the multiple meanings and values attached to home ownership in British culture. It is also true that new ideas, especially neoliberal economic theories (for example monetarism), could be drawn upon to make the new conditions comprehensible and manageable. Yet histories of neoliberalism that focus solely on neoliberal ideas about capitalism, but fail to pay attention to the contemporaneous dynamics of capitalism, will only provide a limited analysis of the late twentieth century.

Notes

* I am grateful to Ben Jackson, Florence Sutcliffe-Braithwaite and the attendees of the Modern British History Seminar at the University of Oxford for their comments on this paper.

1 Adam Tooze, *Crashed: How a decade of financial crises changed the world* (London, Allen Lane, 2018).

2 On the persistence or otherwise of neoliberalism, see Colin Crouch, *The Strange Non-Death of Neoliberalism* (Cambridge, Polity Press, 2011); and Tom Hunt and Liam Stanley, 'From "there is no alternative" to "maybe there are alternatives": Five challenges to economic orthodoxy after the crash', *Political Quarterly* 90/3 (2019), 479–87. On the political impact of the crisis, see John B. Judis, *The Populist Explosion: How the great recession transformed American and European politics* (New York, Columbia Global Reports, 2016).

3 Gérard Duménil and Dominique Lévy, 'Costs and benefits of neoliberalism: A class analysis', *Review of International Political Economy*, 8 (2001), 578–607.

4 See, for example, Giovanni Arrighi, *The Long Twentieth Century: Money, power, and origins of our times* (London, Verso, 1994); and John Bellamy Foster, 'The financialization of capitalism', *Monthly Review*, 11 (2007), 8–10.

5 David M. Kotz, 'Financialization and neoliberalism', in Gary Teeple and Stephen McBride (eds), *Relations of Global Power: Neoliberal order and disorder* (Toronto, University of Toronto Press, 2010), 1–18. On the globalising project of neoliberalism, see Quinn Slobodian, *Globalists: The end of empire and the birth of neoliberalism* (Cambridge, MA, Harvard University Press, 2018).

6 As a concept, financialisaton also encompasses a range of other phenomena, such as the restructuring of 'non-financial' firms according to financialised logics. For a review of the

broader literature on financialisation, see Natascha van der Zwan, 'Making sense of financialization', *Socio-Economic Review*, 12 (2014), 99–129; and Gerald F. Davis and Suntae Kim, 'Financialization of the economy', *Annual Review of Sociology*, 41 (2015), 203–21.

7 David Edgerton, *The Rise and Fall of the British Nation: A twentieth-century history* (London, Allen Lane, 2018), 470–5.

8 Leila Simona Talani, *Globalization, Hegemony and the Future of the City of London* (London, Palgrave Macmillan, 2012), 172–7; and Tony Norfield, *The City: London and the global power of finance* (London, Verso, 2016), 71.

9 Tony Dolphin, 'Don't bank on it: The financialisation of the UK economy', *IPPR* (2012), 18–21.

10 John Cristensen, Nicholas Shaxson and Duncan Wigan, 'The finance curse: Britain and the world economy', *British Journal of Politics and International Relations*, 18 (2016), 256.

11 Will Hutton, *The State We're In*, 2nd ed. (London, Vintage, 1996), 132–68; and Mariana Mazzucato, *The Value of Everything: Making and taking in the global economy* (London, Allen Lane, 2018), 161–88.

12 Ed Balls, 'The City as the global finance centre: Risks and opportunities' (14 June 2006), https://webarchive.nationalarchives.gov.uk/20100407165232/http://www.hm-treasury.gov.uk/speech_est_140606.htm (accessed 19 February 2019).

13 Antony Seely, 'EU Savings Directive: Background history', *House of Commons Library*, 17 October 2012.

14 Gordon Brown, 'Speech at the Mansion House' (15 June 2000), https://webarchive.nationalarchives.gov.uk/200012072253/http://www.hm-treasury.gov.uk:80/press/2000/p75_00.html (accessed 19 February 2019).

15 Glenn Morgan, 'Supporting the City: Economic patriotism in financial markets', *Journal of European Public Policy*, 19 (2012), 379–80; on New Labour's attitude to globalisation, see Matthew Watson and Colin Hay, 'The discourse of globalisation and the logic of no alternative: Rendering the contingent necessary in the political economy of New Labour', *Policy & Politics*, 31 (2003), 289–305; and Mark Wickham-Jones, this volume.

16 Colin Hay, *The Failure of Anglo-Liberal Capitalism* (London, Palgrave Macmillan, 2013).

17 Avner Offer, 'Narrow banking, real estate, and financial stability in the UK, c.1870–2010', in Nicholas Dimsdale and Anthony Hotson (eds), *British Financial Crises since 1825* (Oxford, Oxford University Press, 2014), 170.

18 Hay, *Failure of Anglo-Liberal Capitalism*, 26; John Doling and Richard Ronald, 'Home ownership and asset-based welfare', *Journal of Housing and the Built Environment*, 25 (2010), 165–73; and Stuart G. Lowe, Beverley A. Searle and Susan J. Smith, 'From housing wealth to mortgage debt: The emergence of Britain's asset-shaped welfare state', *Social Policy & Society*, 11 (2011), 105–16.

19 Michael Pryke and Christine Whitehead, 'An overview of mortgage-backed securitisation in the UK', *Housing Studies*, 9 (1994), 75–101; on 'transatlantic finance', see Tooze, *Crashed*, 72–90.

20 Offer, 'Narrow banking', 170.

21 J. D. G. Wood, 'The integrating role of private homeownership and mortgage credit in British neoliberalism', *Housing Studies*, 33 (2018), 1002–3.

22 Colin Crouch, 'Privatised Keynesianism: An unacknowledged policy regime', *British Journal of Politics and International Relations*, 11 (2009), 382–99.

23 Offer, 'Narrow banking', 170.

24 Kevin O'Rourke and Jeffrey Williamson, *Globalization and History: The evolution of a nineteenth-century Atlantic economy* (Cambridge, MA, MIT Press, 1999).

25 Youssef Cassis, *Capitals of Capital: The rise and fall of international financial centres* (Cambridge, Cambridge University Press, 2010), 83–101.

26 On the instability of the international monetary system in the interwar period, see Barry Eichengreen, *Globalizing Capital: A history of the international monetary system*, 2nd ed. (Princeton, NJ, Princeton University Press, 2008), 43–90.

27 Ian M. Drummond, *The Floating Pound and the Sterling Area, 1931–39* (Cambridge, Cambridge University Press, 1981), 1–27.

28 The literature on the Bretton Woods era is extensive. See Eichengreen, *Globalizing Capital*, 91–133; Jeffry A. Frieden, *Global Capitalism: Its rise and fall in the twentieth century* (New York, Norton, 2006); 278–320; and John Gerard Ruggie, 'International regimes, transactions, and change: Embedded liberalism in the postwar economic order', *International Organization*, 36 (1982), 379–415.

29 On the post-war history of sterling, see Catherine Schenk, *The Decline of Sterling: Managing the retreat of an international currency, 1945–1992* (Cambridge, Cambridge University Press, 2010).

30 Barry Eichengreen, *Exorbitant Privilege: The rise and fall of the dollar and the future of the international monetary system* (Oxford, Oxford University Press, 2011), 39–68.

31 Catherine Schenk, 'The origins of the Eurodollar market in London, 1955–63', *Explorations in Economic History*, 2 (1996), 1–19; Richard Roberts and David Kynaston, *City State: How the markets came to rule the world* (London, Profile, 2001), 88–92; Eric Helleiner, *States and the Reemergence of Global Finance* (Ithaca, NY, Cornell University Press, 1994); Gary Burn, *The Re-emergence of Global Finance* (London, Palgrave Macmillan, 2006); and Jeremy Green, 'Anglo-American development, the Euromarkets, and the deeper origins of neoliberal deregulation', *Review of International Studies*, 42 (2016), 425–49.

32 Burn, *Re-emergence of Global Finance*. The Bank also defended the Eurodollar market from regulatory threats at the international level; see Carlo Edoardo Altamura, *European Banks and the Rise of International Finance: The post-Bretton Woods era* (Abingdon, Routledge, 2017).

33 P. J. Cain and A. G. Hopkins, *British Imperialism, 1688–2015*, 5th ed. (Abingdon, Routledge, 2016), 679.

34 For the best account of the changing make-up of the City of London in the final quarter of the twentieth century, see David Kynaston, *The City of London, Volume 4: A club no more, 1945–2000* (London, Pimlico, 2002), 415–790.

35 Philip Augar, *The Death of Gentlemanly Capitalism* (London, Penguin, 2000).

36 Scott Newton, 'The sterling devaluation of 1967, the international economy and post-war social democracy', *English Historical Review*, 125 (2010), 912–45; and Scott Newton, 'Sterling, Bretton Woods, and social democracy, 1968–70', *Diplomacy & Statecraft*, 24 (2013), 427–55.

37 Aled Davies, *The City of London and Social Democracy: The political economy of finance, 1959–1979* (Oxford, Oxford University Press, 2017), 181–214.

38 Jim Tomlinson, 'Mrs Thatcher's macroeconomic adventurism, 1979–1981, and its political consequences', *British Politics*, 3 (2007), 5–6.

39 Davies, *City of London*, 140–80.

40 On the causes of the 'Big Bang', see Christopher Bellringer and Ranald Michie, 'Big Bang in the City of London: An intentional revolution or an accident?', *Financial History Review*, 21 (2014), 111–37.

41 Robert Millward, 'The rise of the service economy', in Roderick Floud and Paul Johnson (eds), *The Cambridge Economic History of Modern Britain, Volume 3: Structural change and growth, 1939–2000* (Cambridge, Cambridge University Press, 2004), 238–66.

42 William Clarke to C. W. McMahon (Deputy Governor), 'Liberalisation of trade in services', 5 November 1981, Bank of England Archive: 16A21/1.

43 The Thatcherite view was that industrial revival could be achieved through market reforms. See, for example, Alfred Sherman MSS, 'Minute on the committee on Industrial Policy', 9 June 1977, Royal Holloway Library, Box 13. Williamson has argued, however, that the Conservatives 'embraced' deindustrialisation: Adrian Williamson, *Conservative Economic Policymaking and the Birth of Thatcherism, 1964–1979* (Basingstoke, Palgrave Macmillan, 2015), 143–7.

44 Minutes of Evidence, HM Treasury, Chancellor of the Exchequer, 15 May 1985, *Report of the Select Committee on Overseas Trade, House of Lords, Session 1984–5, Volume 2, Oral Evidence* (London, HMSO, 1985).

45 Michael Kitson and Jonathan Michie, 'Britain's industrial performance since 1960: Underinvestment and relative decline', *The Economic Journal*, 106 (1996), 198.

46 Minutes of Evidence, 'British Invisible Exports Council', 20 March 1985, *Report of the Select Committee on Overseas Trade*; The Committee on Invisible Exports was renamed as the 'British Invisible Exports Council' in 1983, 'British Invisibles' in 1990, 'International Financial Services London' in 2001 and 'TheCityUK' in 2010.

47 Minutes of Evidence, Lord Weinstock, 24 April 1985, *Report of the Select Committee on Overseas Trade*.

48 Barry Supple, 'Fear of failing: Economic history and the decline of Britain', *Economic History Review*, 47 (1994), 451.

49 Jim Tomlinson, 'Brexit, globalisation and de-industrialisation', *The Long Run* (29 March 2017), https://ehsthelongrun.net/2017/03/29/brexit-globalisation-and-de-industrialisation/ (accessed 19 February 2019).

50 Peter Malpass and Alan Murie, *Housing Policy and Practice*, 5th ed. (Basingstoke, Palgrave Macmillan, 1999), table. 4.3; Ben Jackson, 'Revisionism reconsidered: "Property-owning

democracy" and egalitarian strategy in post-war Britain', *Twentieth Century British History*, 16 (2005), 431; Guy Ortolano, this volume; and Aled Davies, '"Right to Buy": The development of a Conservative housing policy, 1945–1980', *Contemporary British History*, 27 (2013), at 423–5.

51 See Jon Lawrence, *Me, Me, Me: The search for community in post-war England* (Oxford, Oxford University Press, 2019), 111, 190–3; and Emily Robinson, Camilla Schofield, Florence Sutcliffe-Braithwaite and Natalie Thomlinson, 'Telling stories about post-war Britain: Popular individualism and the "crisis" of the 1970s', *Twentieth Century British History*, 28 (2017), 268–304. If we accept the argument of Robinson et. al. that a popular, aspirational form of individualism developed in Britain in the 1960s and 1970s, it is not clear whether home ownership was a cause or an effect of the phenomenon. Despite its significance in the twentieth century, the history of home ownership in Britain has received only limited attention; see Peter Scott, *The Making of the Modern British Home: The suburban semi and family life between the wars* (Oxford, Oxford University Press, 2013).

52 Offer, 'Narrow banking', 162–4.

53 For a useful summary of the post-war financial system, see Gregory W. Fuller, *The Great Debt Transformation: Households, financialization, and policy responses* (Basingstoke, Palgrave Macmillan, 2016), 55–9.

54 Duncan M. Ross, 'Domestic monetary policy and the banking system in Britain, 1945–71', in Ranald Michie and Philip Williamson (eds), *The British Government and the City of London in the Twentieth Century* (Cambridge, Cambridge University Press, 2004), 298–321.

55 Offer, 'Narrow banking', 162–4.

56 *Report of the Committee to Review the Functioning of Financial Institutions,* Cmd. 7937 (London, HMSO, 1980), 107.

57 Peter M. Scott and James T. Walker, '"Stop–go" policy and the restriction of postwar British house-building', *Economic History Review*, 72 (2019), 716–37.

58 For a history of mortgage politics in the 1960s, see Stuart Aveyard, Paul Corthorn and Sean O'Connell, *The Politics of Consumer Credit in the UK, 1938–1992* (Oxford, Oxford University Press, 2018), 55–67.

59 Peter Malpass, *Housing the Welfare State: The development of housing policy in Britain* (Basingstoke, Palgrave Macmillan, 2005), 121–2.

60 John Hunt to Prime Minister, 'Building societies (C(74) 20 and 22)', 3 April 1974, TNA: PREM 16/129.

61 Victor Knight and Roy Assersohn, 'The big home loans gamble', *Daily Mirror* (5 April 1973).

62 Margaret Stone, 'Building society chief outlines dilemma in shortfall of funds', *The Times* (23 January 1974).

63 Anthony Crosland, Statement to the House of Commons, 10 April 1974, TNA: PREM 16/129; for a more detailed account of the building societies crisis in the 1970s, see Aveyard et al., *Politics of Consumer Credit*, 156–61.

64 Margaret Thatcher to the Chancellor, 24 June 1979, TNA: PREM 19/33.

65 Geoffrey Howe to Prime Minister, 'Mortgage rate', 25 June 1979, TNA: PREM 19/1269.

66 Sir Kenneth Berrill to Mr Lankester, 'Mortgage rates', 29 June 1979, TNA: PREM 19/1269.

67 Tim Lankester to Prime Minister, 'My lunch with Gordon Pepper', 4 July 1979, TNA: PREM 19/1269.

68 John Hoskyns to Prime Minister, 'Mortgage rates', 4 October 1979, TNA: PREM 19/1269.

69 Financial Editor, 'The argument about building society funds', *The Times* (8 January 1980).

70 *Report of the Committee to Review the Functioning of Financial Institutions*, Cmd. 7937, 107–14.

71 Sir Kenneth Berrill to Mr Stowe, 'Building societies', 22 May 1979, TNA: PREM 19/1269.

72 Thatcher annotations, Sir Kenneth Berrill to Mr Stowe, 'Building societies', 22 May 1979, TNA: PREM 19/1269.

73 'Why look a gift horse?', *Daily Mirror* (10 April 1974); and Harold Wilson to Chancellor of the Exchequer, 27 March 1974, TNA: PREM 16/129.

74 Margaret Stone, 'Lawson warning to building societies', *The Times* (9 May 1980).

75 Malpass, *Housing the Welfare State*, 97; and Duncan Needham, *UK Monetary Policy from Devaluation to Thatcher* (Basingstoke, Palgrave Macmillan, 2014), 46–77.

76 Nigel Lawson, *The View from No. 11: Memoirs of a Tory radical* (London, Bantam Press, 1992), 86–7.

77 Jack Copley, 'Why were capital controls abandoned? The case of Britain's abolition of exchange controls, 1977–1979', *British Journal of Politics and International Relations*, 21 (2019), 403–20.

78 J. M. Bridgeman to Mr Ryrie, 'Bank lending: Reintermediation and intermediation. A case for control?', 10 June 1980; and W. S. Ryrie to Chancellor of the Exchequer, 'Bank lending: Reintermediation and intermediation', 13 June 1980, TNA: T 386/637.
79 'Bank lending: Reintermediation and intermediation', 16 June 1980, TNA: T 386/637.
80 'Note of a meeting held at No. 11, Downing Street . . .', 3 July 1980, TNA: T 386/637.
81 Mark Boleat and Bev Taylor, *Housing in Britain*, 3rd ed. (London, Building Societies Association, 1993), 28.
82 Lawson, *View from No. 11*, 627–8.
83 Brian Lund, *Housing Politics in the United Kingdom: Power, planning and protest* (Bristol, Policy Press, 2016), 132–3.
84 Malpass, *Housing the Welfare State*, 121–2.
85 Mark Stephens, 'Building society demutualisation in the UK', *Housing Studies*, 16 (2001), 335–52.
86 Tim Congdon, 'Will the house-buying boom save Thatcher?', *The Times* (17 June 1986).
87 M. Ball, 'The 1980s property boom', *Environment and Planning A*, 26 (1994), 671–95.
88 Wood, 'The integrating role of private homeownership'.

15

Begrudging neoliberalism: housing and the fate of the property-owning social democracy

Guy Ortolano*

By 'begrudging' neoliberalism, I mean two things. Firstly, the term refers to the historian's unease in adopting such a notoriously woolly concept. The intellectual historian Daniel Rodgers, for example, faults 'neoliberalism' on both conceptual and pragmatic grounds, as a word 'accelerating through too many meanings, employed in too many debates, gluing too many phenomena together, and cannibalising too many other words around it', its very invocation rendering 'it harder to see both the forces at loose in our times and where viable resistance can be found'.[1] David Edgerton, echoing Voltaire on the Holy Roman Empire ('in no way holy, nor Roman, nor an empire'), charges that to 'call the new order neoliberalism is to flatter it, for there was little original or new, or liberal, about it'.[2] Partly for these reasons, and following the example of Avner Offer, when presented with the option I prefer to cite, as more precise and less polemical, 'market liberalism' instead.[3] And yet, if the task at hand is not primarily terminological, but rather to engage broader conversations about political life in the late twentieth century, 'neoliberalism' has come to serve as the banner under which, begrudgingly, we now gather.[4]

The second meaning of 'begrudging' neoliberalism refers to the position of public sector actors who, as the 1970s became the 1980s, found themselves accommodating priorities contrary to their own. Broadly speaking – though mindful of G. M. Young's admonition against forcing 'historic movements into exaggerated symmetry' – the second half of the twentieth century saw a shift in the relative authority of social democracy and neoliberalism.[5] If social democracy aimed to reduce collective inequality by removing aspects of social and economic life from the market, neoliberalism aimed to increase individual freedom by removing aspects of social and economic life from the state. In explaining the transition from the former to the latter, neoliberalism's historians tend to focus upon the right. The heroes (or anti-heroes) of these accounts are the liberal economists, financial journalists, conservative politicians and think-tank intellectuals who nurtured ideas and policies that achieved ascendance during the century's closing act.[6] Yet in the effort to secure not merely an altered set of policies, but an altered way of thinking, an equally significant development came when even that movement's critics found themselves enacting neoliberal policies.

Consider the case of housing. Housing figured centrally both to the welfare state from 1945, and to Margaret Thatcher's Britain from 1979. As the post-war Labour government's minister of housing as well as health, Aneurin Bevan sought to turn housing into a universal service; as Thatcher's first Secretary of State for the Environment, Michael Heseltine believed that owner-occupation would 'strike at the heart of Labour's concept of how society should be ordered'.[7] In the aftermath of Thatcher's polarising decade, the sociologist Peter Saunders adopted this dichotomous reading of housing policy, depicting owner-occupation as a 'counter-revolution' against 'the left's commitment to social engineering'.[8] This perspective associates the left with council housing and the right with private ownership, making the trajectory from the former to the latter appear to be the triumph of Conservative initiatives. Yet, as Aled Davies discusses in this volume from a different perspective, social democrats had long supported owner-occupation as part of a mixed housing system that included private owners alongside public renters – a programme referred to here as a *property-owning social democracy*. From the mid-1970s, in the wake of recession and retrenchment, some public sector actors discerned an opportunity to advance their existing goal of extending owner-occupation. In time, however, this shift in emphasis developed into an end unto itself, so that these social democratic actors soon found themselves enacting neoliberal policy goals. In this light, the ascendance of neoliberalism resulted not only from the exertions of its champions, but also from the begrudging acquiescence of its critics.

The argument that follows develops in four parts. The first part elaborates upon the 'property-owning social democracy', identifying this long-standing position as still viable through the 1970s. The second part examines efforts to realise the property-owning social democracy in a significant sector of municipal housing, the 32 New Towns designated by the British state between 1946 and 1970. Focusing on the most ambitious of these projects, Milton Keynes, this section reveals the ways in which, during the late 1970s, public sector actors adapted social democratic priorities in response to economic and political pressures. The third part follows these adaptations as they developed into ends unto themselves, as housing sales took priority over measures that could forestall socio-spatial polarisation. The fourth part recaps the argument, before indicating the general account of neoliberalism that this analysis makes available: one that features a more dynamic social democracy and a more contingent neoliberalism, and that accordingly accounts for the tactical accommodations that helped secure the ascendance of the latter.

The property-owning social democracy

With the decline of private landlords after the First World War, Britain's housing system became increasingly organised around a combination of municipal renters and owner-occupiers. From 1919 to 1980, the country's housing patterns converged towards this 'dual tenurial system'.[9] Despite their differences in emphasis, both Labour and the Conservatives accepted a role for each sector. Thus, while Bevan prioritised public provision, he called owner-occupation 'an excellent thing' and assumed it would persist.[10] His Tory successor, Harold Macmillan, favoured owner-occupation but also depended upon local authorities' construction to meet his annual building targets.[11] Labour's 1959 manifesto pledged to assist prospective buyers, a commitment that subsequent Labour manifestos only strengthened.[12] As Aled Davies shows, it often fell to local Labour councils to finance housing purchases: in Sheffield, for example, the Labour council provided more than ten thousand housing loans during the early 1960s.[13] Labour's 1965 white paper, *The Housing Programme, 1965–1970*, acknowledged owner-occupation as Britain's 'normal' housing tenure, and Harold Wilson's governments committed to extending it. Upon regaining office in 1974, Labour spent nearly as much on homeowners' tax relief as on local authorities' housing.[14] These investments from the left did not amount to tactical concessions, much less ideological surrenders. They represented, rather, a British iteration of transnational efforts to extend property throughout the popular classes, from African Americans in the US to late colonial Africans to the favelas of Brazil.[15]

In other words, advocating a role for the state in housing did not negate a simultaneous commitment to owner-occupation. Rather, the commitment to both enjoined the state to foster home ownership along social democratic lines, forging a property-owning social democracy.[16]

In the light of this position, the mere fact of council house sales on either side of 1979 did not represent a continuity in policy, since these superficially similar policies served contrary ideological agendas. The Conservative vision of a property-owning democracy sought to attach citizens to capitalism through home ownership – despite turning public housing into a second-class tenure, and despite the polarisation of property and wealth that resulted. The property-owning social democracy, by contrast, aimed to achieve a more equitable distribution of property and wealth, by placing renters alongside owners in a balanced social whole.

This ideal of 'balance' was integral to the property-owning social democracy. Balance had figured in political thought since Aristotle's *Politics*, which depicted extremes of wealth as damaging to the polity; it functioned similarly in Thomas More's *Utopia*, which imagined the elimination of the extremes plaguing More's own Europe.[17] Entering the twentieth century, balance defined town and country planning, beginning with the field's foundational text. Ebenezer Howard's *A Peaceful Path towards Real Reform* (1898) celebrated balance in its famous illustration of 'The Three Magnets', which resolved the evils of town ('foul air') and country ('lack of drainage') in the perfect symmetry of town–country ('pure air' and 'good drainage').[18] In the context of a social democratic vision for housing, 'balance' referred both to a more equitable distribution of wealth-in-property between the top and bottom of society, and to the integration of renters alongside owners in a healthy polity. The former commitment was distributive, the latter communitarian, and together they testified to housing's indispensable role in achieving social democratic goals.[19]

In practice, however, balance proved elusive. Bevan worried that the sale of council housing would divide renters and owners along class lines. He deplored this connection between public provision and financial need, in housing no less than health.[20] Housing scholars know the dynamic that worried Bevan as 'residualisation'.[21] Residualisation threatened whenever public provision became divorced from general needs and consequently acquired stigma. From the late 1960s, when Labour's housing minister, Anthony Greenwood, resumed Bevan's former practice of denying Tory councils' applications to sell municipal properties, he did so in part to retain the state's capacity to provide housing, but also to forestall the public sector's residualisation.[22] These denials made it possible for the Conservatives to depict Labour as hostile to owner-occupation. 'The Labour Party', they charged in 1983, 'is still fighting a rear-guard action against wider home ownership'.[23] But that interpretation wrongly conflates positions on the sale of council housing under the terms of 1980 Housing Act with positions on home ownership generally.

The alternative to the property-owning democracy was not, as the Conservatives would have it, universal public accommodation, but the property-owning social democracy: a managed housing system including both the public and private sectors. That system required oversight, in the form of an authority that could forestall residualisation while still facilitating ownership. With this programme in mind, the 1970s appear to be a fertile moment featuring a range of possibilities – including, but not limited to, the right to buy. This field of possibilities reflected the cross-party consensus in support of home ownership: 'a deep and natural desire', according to a Tory white paper; 'a basic and natural desire', echoed Labour.[24] At the same time, the state's housing commitments were expanding. A few enterprising local authorities bolstered their housing stocks by purchasing entire streets of flats, while – as Peter Shapely has shown – municipal tenants increasingly demanded the quality housing and routine maintenance that a social democracy promised.[25] Some policy reforms brought unintended consequences, as when the 1977 Housing (Homeless Persons) Act enshrined a right to housing in the council sector for the homeless, only to exacerbate the residualisation of the housing sector to which they had won access.[26] Meanwhile, new initiatives were emerging without obvious ties to right or left, private or public, owning or renting. New legislation enhanced the ability of ancient institutions, 'housing associations', to invest in what would later become known as the 'social housing' sector – an obscure innovation dealing with a fraction of the market, but one that would figure centrally in housing policy from the 1980s.[27]

During the 1970s, though, the effective achievement of universal housing, combined with economic pressures impacting both the public and private sectors, stimulated a context in which inherited commitments and disruptive innovations coexisted. This too-brief overview of that history has aimed to unsettle the presumption of a left/right divide over home ownership, while recovering possibilities other than those that followed from the 1980s Housing Act. In this fluid policy context, departures from Bevan's 1940s did not necessarily point to Thatcher's 1980s. How, then, did that particular end come about? Answering that question requires a shift in focus, from housing policy in general to housing policy on the ground – for instance, in Treasury-financed developments spread across all four nations of the UK, the New Towns.

A dynamic social democracy

By 1966, Britain's New Towns housed three-quarters of a million people.[28] But this achievement overwhelmingly came through rental accommodations, posing a problem for those who sought a balance among classes and between tenures. Among the most significant of the authorities responding to this challenge was the Milton Keynes Development Corporation (MKDC), established in 1967 and in existence until 1992. Charged with developing a 'new city' of 250,000 residents between Birmingham and London, MKDC had the misfortune of embarking upon that task amid a series of escalating funding crises. The development corporation's leadership struggled to navigate those crises while still achieving housing balance.

The challenge was previewed in the New Town of Stevenage. Designated in 1946, 90 per cent of Stevenage's housing had been built for rent.[29] In 1966, however, a survey found that nine residents in ten favoured sales to sitting tenants. Two years later, consistent with the vision of a property-owning social democracy, the Labour government authorised those sales, only for Stevenage's development corporation to meet difficulty finding buyers. It turned out that there was a difference between expressing an interest in buying, as an abstract proposition, and producing a deposit. Having failed to realise the promised market, the development corporation took steps to create one. They launched a campaign advertising the ease and benefits of home ownership, while offering their residents discounts of up to 20 per cent off their home's market value. Sales promptly took off, eventually extending to nearly one home in every three. By 1974, rates of home ownership in Stevenage had trebled.[30]

Then, in 1974, the Labour government suspended sales, creating an opportunity to assess the impact of liberalising sales in a discrete time and place. During this six-year period, the town's most affluent renters bought their homes. These proud new owners reaped economic and psychological rewards, gaining an investment along with the satisfactions of home ownership. These benefits, however, came at a cost, in those publicly subsidised discounts: 20 per cent below what the corporation would have yielded had they sold at market rates. Then, after five years, these new owners could sell their homes and keep that subsidy – effectively a hidden cash transfer, shifting public investments into individuals' pockets. Meanwhile, as Stevenage shed its public housing stock, housing wait lists doubled, stimulating the rental market. That market fostered the development of a phenomenon that had barely existed previously, private landlords: profit-making purveyors of rental housing that, just a few years earlier, the local authority had managed. But if this experiment revealed some of the problems attendant upon the sale of municipal housing, it also attested to the policies that could forestall those problems: a public authority managing the distribution of sales, while simultaneously maintaining a viable rental sector.

Thirty miles away, at precisely the same time, the builders of Milton Keynes were determined to get housing right. Far from an innovation of later housing acts, home ownership was inscribed in the New Town's DNA. 'The Minister of Housing and Local Government . . . has asked that at least 50% of households in the new city should own their own homes', read the master plan of 1970. 'The Corporation endorses this aim and has accepted it as a fundamental guide to policy.'[31] The pursuit of 'balance' figured centrally. Social integration, the planners believed, fostered social cohesion. 'We must, at literally all costs, build a balanced city', the chairman insisted, long before the first trench was ever dug.[32] The master plan pledged to forestall economic polarisation, by distributing the city's services evenly across the city.[33] The planners wanted residents to mix with one another. Following the war, Bevan and the Labour Party had primarily imagined this mixing in terms of class, but the social axes requiring mixing had since proliferated.[34] Milton Keynes's planners now sought balance within, as well as between, classes, aiming to cultivate a diversity of races and generations no less than income groups.[35]

But after 10 years, Milton Keynes had achieved an ownership rate of just 30 per cent – a disappointment, but not a crisis. However, policies from London soon sent MKDC into a panic. In 1976, Labour's secretary of state for the environment, Peter Shore, announced a policy shift that posed an existential threat for Britain's New Towns programme. After 30 years of dispersal, in which New Towns had enjoyed a privileged role, Shore announced a focus on inner cities instead. He wanted smaller New Towns, serving older cities, partly by absorbing their most disadvantaged populations.[36] Eleven days later, the Prime Minister issued a sobering lecture of his own. 'The cosy world we were told would go on for ever', Jim Callaghan informed his party's conference on 28 September 1976, 'where full employment would be guaranteed by a stroke of the Chancellor's pen, cutting taxes, deficit spending – that cosy world is gone'.[37] The autumn became consumed by negotiations with the International Monetary Fund, leading to Denis Healey's painful mini-budget of 15 December 1976. That budget halved the next year's New Town housing starts. Shore twisted the knife, slashing Milton Keynes's planned growth by 100,000 residents over the next 10 years, part of an overall reduction among all third-generation New Towns by nearly 400,000.[38]

Squeezed between Shore's priorities and Healey's economies, 1976/7 marked the end of an era for Milton Keynes. The New Town's very survival required a new commitment, to 'profitability and growth': *profitability* to offset the cuts from Healey's budgets, and *growth* to alleviate the crisis of confidence following Shore's priorities.[39] Both profitability and growth could be served, the development corporation concluded, by building and selling houses. In a development that had grown by 35,000 people in 10 years, nearly doubling the area's initial population, the corporation now sought to add another 75,000 over the next decade.[40] In the light of these trends, the most promising opportunity for growing owner-occupation lay less in transferring rentals – which would change tenures, but not increase numbers – than in building new sale housing. The corporation pledged to turn Milton Keynes into 'a rallying point for investment in industry, commerce, housing, and the environment', indeed a new 'centre for the building industry' nationwide.[41] In order to achieve these goals, they established a new department, the Private Housing Unit.[42] The Private Housing Unit accelerated dealings with developers, aiming to treble 1976's construction of homes for sale.[43]

In addition to building houses, they needed to sell them. The Private Housing Unit doubled as a marketing unit, turning renters into owners. The general manager, Fred Roche, wrote to every renter in the city, alerting them to new opportunities for buying their homes.[44] MKDC became a fixture at area home shows, and the Private Housing Unit erected an installation in central Milton Keynes advertising the benefits of home ownership.[45] These measures worked. In 1976, the city had sold just 200 homes, but by 1978 that figure had more than trebled – and they were on pace to reach 1,200 completions by 1981.[46] By that time, the city was finally approaching the rates of ownership to which its master plan aspired, helping the development corporation to achieve the profitability and growth that might secure its standing.

Early in 1979, the development corporation contemplated the possibility of a new Conservative government. Mindful of the Tories' historic suspicion towards the New Towns, a local newspaper expressed the obvious concern: 'City in danger if Tories win'.[47] But New Towns had survived many changes of government previously, and the most damaging policies had recently come not from the Conservatives, but from Labour. Navigating these crises had led the corporation to develop revenue streams independent of the Treasury, promising some measure of autonomy and, they hoped, the chance to continue building. Thus, while they harboured no illusions about the Conservatives, the city's leadership envisioned harnessing Tory zeal to further their own goals. As the election neared, they plotted a dual course. Their project would contribute to the 'restructuring, expansion, and growth of the British economy', while maintaining their commitments to 'a *balanced* social and economic structure', 'a *diversity* of social, educational, and cultural opportunities', and an ethic informed by '*social consciousness*'.[48] Having navigated economic and policy crises, and anticipating further challenges, MKDC hoped to manage – even harness – an ascendant market liberalism.

A shock city of private housing

The MKDC engineered its own survival, but on terms that knocked things badly out of balance. In May 1979, with the right-to-buy provisions of the 1980 Housing Act still more than a year away, the Conservative government liberalised New Town housing sales. Already by the summer, more than 20 per cent of tenants in Milton Keynes's 10,000 rentals had inquired about purchase; by September, 10 per cent of these inquiries were proceeding with sales – a figure exceeding all prior such sales in the New Town to date.[49] By 1983, owner-occupation locally had risen from 41 to 51 per cent and was fast bearing down on the national rate of 57 per cent.[50] By 1987, 83 per cent of new dwellings in Milton Keynes were sold, not rented – shattering the national rate of 64 per cent. At a time when public rentals still amounted to 25 per cent of new construction in England and Wales, in Milton Keynes they comprised a mere 7 per cent.[51] These trends climaxed in 1991, on the eve of MKDC's dissolution. In 1977, public rentals had comprised 70 per cent of the city's housing; by 1991, that figure had plunged to just 26 per cent. Even more striking, in 1990/1 the city oversaw the completion of 1,241 homes – including no public rentals.[52] These developments did not follow automatically from government policies, but rather represented the achievement of the development corporation's commitment to seeing those policies through.

As a shock city of private housing, Milton Keynes began to preview coming national problems. Soon after embarking upon these reforms, the development corporation discerned a previously rare problem, repossessions – which, by the 1990s, reached crisis levels nationally.[53] Not one year into the Conservatives' new policies, MKDC grew concerned about the loss of entry-level housing in the city, particularly among younger residents. As property values rose, public rentals newly converted into private homes became too expensive for first-time buyers when they next reached the market.[54] More troublingly, estates that had recently mixed renters alongside owners were increasingly becoming associated with one or the other. This segregation of tenures became exacerbated by a polarisation of incomes. On the lower end, Heseltine's elimination of 'Parker Morris' standards ensured that rental estates included lower-standard homes, while on the upper end, private developers prioritised upper-income construction at the expense of building more affordable developments.[55]

Ben Jones discusses this sorting of housing by tenure, income and class as 'socio-spatial polarization', and it had several causes.[56] Firstly, their eyes fixed on the bottom line, private developers preferred to boost property values (and thus their profits) by concentrating on middle-class developments.[57] Secondly, renters on the most prosperous estates seized upon the government's generous subsidies to convert their homes' tenures, causing those estates to shed their rental sectors. Thirdly, the development corporation's campaigns were not so much creating new pools of buyers, as subsidising tenants most interested in buying anyway. Renters on lesser-valued estates, by contrast, were denied the lavish subsidies that facilitated purchase, not because they would not or could not buy, but because the discounts that made buying possible only became available when a home's value exceeded the cost of its construction.

The depressed valuations of these homes were being set not by a neutral and unerring 'market', but by real estate appraisers. These appraisers remained unconvinced of the market viability of non-traditional, rental housing – even when the development corporation noted that these very renters comprised the most promising pool of untapped buyers. The obstacle to their purchasing consisted not of their homes' designs, but their costs – costs that stemmed, in a cruel catch-22, from the lack of discounts and mortgages enjoyed by residents on higher-valued estates. Rented homes on lesser-valued estates – precisely the population the development corporation wanted to reach – thus became frozen out of a market that, paradoxically, deemed the very homes they wanted to buy as unmarketable. At the same time, prosperous renters on other estates were converting public investments into private assets – pocketing public subsidies and privatising public buildings, while rendering their communities more exclusive.[58] These developments did not follow naturally from the workings of a market, unleashed at last, but rather from this particular system of discounts and appraisals. Socio-spatial polarisation followed.

Though the obstacles to balance were substantial, MKDC initially proved up to the challenge. If raw sales were their sole priority, they could easily have goosed them, by moving prospective buyers on lesser-valued estates (which did not qualify for discounts) into more highly valued areas. Such manoeuvres, however, would polarise wealth, segregate tenures and undermine the communities left behind, and the development corporation rejected them accordingly. In the planning director's judgement, such a gambit would represent 'a radical change of Corporation policy', 'directly contraven[ing] the Master Plan'.[59] At the same time, the development corporation pushed back against developers' demands that they relax bidding procedures and building requirements. Developers were simply seeking to minimise costs, but the corporation's general manager could respond by invoking values other than their bottom lines.[60] At other times, when building societies denied residents the mortgages necessary to make purchasing possible, the development corporation stepped in to offer mortgages of its own.[61] And when developers sought to cultivate higher-value sales by separating their customers from public renters, the development corporation mounted a campaign depicting the city as a whole – rather than its most exclusive estates – as a symbol of socio-economic arrival.[62] Building societies and private developers were not villains, but they were risk averse, and they were operating according to the logic of financial, rather than social, incentives. The development corporation, however, could function as an alternative centre of power, one with the ability to keep alternative priorities in mind.

In time, however, the capacity to defend those priorities eroded. In summer 1979, even while welcoming the government's sales procedures, New Towns nationally faced budget cuts of 5 per cent. In Milton Keynes, these cuts impacted on roads and rental housing, but no sooner had the board adjusted than the minister announced a new round of staff cuts as well.[63] The development corporation began losing its most valued staff, including its general manager and planning director, who could readily see opportunities moving to the private sector.[64] Whitehall next instructed all New Town development corporations to sell £120 million-worth of holdings within a year; when they managed only half that figure, the shortfall was added to the next year's even more ambitious £270 million target. As MKDC sold off its assets, even more profound changes arrived.[65] The era of public housing was finished, the housing minister announced in 1980, a sentiment echoed by the Prime Minister. '[A]s regards the traditional post-war role of government in housing', Thatcher declared, 'the state should be withdrawn . . . just as far and as fast as possible.'[66]

The accommodations that this policy demanded evacuated the city's founding goals of all their content. By the mid-1980s, to the extent that they still paid lip service to the goal of 'balance', that concept's meaning had altered beyond all recognition. 'Balance' no longer referred to the integration of tenures, classes, generations and races, as in 1970, but rather to bringing a diversity of incomes into the private market. *The housing market*, not the city or its residents, now figured as the entity in need of balance. In adjusting to this altered calculus, the policy became an end unto itself. In 1987, 2,600 residents applied for rental accommodation. During the city's founding decade, the development corporation would have met these needs through its rental sector. Now, they handled these applications differently. Just 400 of 2,600, they determined, consisted of proper (mostly elderly) renters, whereas 2,200 remained 'economically active' – all but 500 of whom, upon further examination, should be directed onto the private market. Partly through such techniques, Milton Keynes was by this time smashing national sales trends, en route to reversing 1977's ratio of renters to owners. Such achievements were made possible by turning a pool of 2,600 renters into a new market of 1,700 buyers.[67]

'The new town development corporations have always been ready to be pioneers', the Conservative housing minister declared in 1979.[68] Indeed, New Towns pioneered the new regime of housing. In that new regime, liberalised mortgages increased repossessions, the housing market sent prices soaring, private landlords made a comeback and the right to buy exacerbated socio-spatial polarisation. MKDC had valorised owner-occupation since its founding, but it had also remained committed to – and capable of – managing the social consequences that followed from that goal. During the 1980s, however, the government's campaign against the welfare state included an assault upon its spatial balancing. Cuts in funding, staff and public rentals transformed the development corporation's role, from providing oversight and management to leveraging sales and investment, evacuating its capacity to advance goals other than the private sector's profits. In Milton Keynes, as in Britain, home ownership and private investment figured prominently in the housing system before 1980. But so, too, did a commitment to balance – and the mechanisms for achieving it – that differentiated housing's ultimate trajectory from the alternative represented by the property-owning social democracy.

Begrudging neoliberalism

During most of the twentieth century, though private landlords never vanished, Britain's housing pattern became increasingly characterised by a duopoly between public sector renters and private sector owners. Rather than reading these tenures through political lenses, associating public rentals with the left and private ownership with the right, I have called attention to a programme that I call the 'property-owning social democracy'. This concept conveys the way in which private ownership always figured in the left's vision for housing, if not on the same terms as in the right's more famous 'property-owning democracy'. The property-owning social democracy embraced a mixed tenurial system, in which the government retained a role in managing both public rentals and private sales. The goal was neither universal ownership nor universal municipalisation, but rather balance – of tenures, incomes and races; within communities, and across the country – in the face of the polarising forces that the private market encouraged.

Possessed of these goals, mindful of these dynamics and embarking upon a substantial housing programme, MKDC aimed to get housing right. But the goal of balance proved difficult to realise, even before mounting economic and political pressures from 1976 threatened the development corporation's existence. In response to those challenges, MKDC became committed to achieving profitability and growth, to which end they prioritised the development and sale of housing. This initiative succeeded so thoroughly that, by 1979, they could cautiously welcome new Conservative policies favouring home ownership. That powerful current, however, soon pulled them off course, as the priorities of developers and the government undermined this public sector body's ability to pursue the social goals at the heart of the property-owning social democracy. Social democratic actors thus anticipated, accommodated and – eventually – enacted neoliberal ends.

But rather than inevitably producing neoliberalism's triumph, these crises of the 1970s stimulated innovations on the left as well as the right. As Daisy Payling, Stephen Brooke, Andrew Seaton and many others are now showing, social democratic housing innovations found echoes in other sectors, too.[69] Together they attest to a social democracy neither exhausted nor moribund, but instead capable of responding to novel challenges. In the case of housing, though, as public sector actors sought to manage this swirling economic and political environment, they made calculations and entered alliances that compromised their first intentions. Strategies aimed at securing the survival of a public sector housing programme unwittingly exacerbated socio-spatial polarisation. This process resulted not from the emergence of 'neoliberal subjectivities', but from the accommodation of neoliberal polices – after all, as we have seen, home ownership had fit within a social democratic politics no less than its alternative.[70] Ultimately, then, the history of housing offers a less deterministic account of a seminal ideological change: one that includes contingency as well as structure, irony as well as agency, and the public sector as well as the private, as social democratic actors begrudgingly accommodated neoliberalism.

Notes

* An early version of this chapter was delivered as the keynote lecture at the King's Contemporary British History conference, King's College London, 2 July 2018; I am grateful to the conference organisers, particularly David Edgerton, for that invitation. For written feedback, I must thank Aled Davies, Ben Jackson, Peter Mandler, Andrew Seaton and Florence Sutcliffe-Braithwaite. Quotations from the Centre for Buckinghamshire Studies collections are reproduced with permission of the Homes and Communities Agency, the Buckinghamshire County Council and the Centre for Buckinghamshire Studies. This chapter draws from my book: Guy Ortolano, *Thatcher's Progress: From social democracy to market liberalism through an English New Town* (Cambridge, Cambridge University Press, 2019).

1 Daniel Rodgers, 'The uses and abuses of "neoliberalism"', *Dissent* (Winter 2018), https://www.dissentmagazine.org/article/uses-and-abuses-neoliberalism-debate (accessed 17 February 2019).

2 David Edgerton, *The Rise and Fall of the British Nation: A twentieth-century history* (London, Allen Lane, 2018), 491. Edgerton's chapter in this volume, of course, applies equal pressure upon neoliberalism's vexed relation, 'social democracy'. In the former's defence, see Philip Mirowski, 'Defining neoliberalism', in Philip Mirowski and Dieter Plehwe (eds), *The Road from Mont Pèlerin: The making of the neoliberal thought collective* (Cambridge, MA, Harvard University Press, 2009), 417–55.

3 Avner Offer, 'The market turn: From social democracy to market liberalism', *Economic History Review*, 70/4 (2017), 1051–71; and Ortolano, *Thatcher's Progress*.

4 Thanks to Andrew Seaton for clarifying discussions of this point.

5 G. M. Young, *Victorian England: Portrait of an age* (New York, Oxford University Press, 1971), 10–11; and Tony Judt, *Ill Fares the Land* (New York, Penguin, 2010).

6 See, in addition to Mirowski and Plehwe (eds), *Road from Mont Pèlerin*, Richard Cockett, *Thinking the Unthinkable: Think-tanks and the economic counter-revolution, 1931–1983* (London, HarperCollins, 1994); Ben Jackson, 'The think-tank archipelago: Thatcherism and neo-liberalism', in Ben Jackson and Robert Saunders (eds), *Making Thatcher's Britain* (Cambridge, Cambridge University Press, 2012), 43–61; Daniel Stedman Jones, *Masters of the Universe: Hayek, Friedman, and the birth of neoliberal politics* (Princeton, NJ, Princeton University Press, 2012); and Quinn Slobodian, *Globalists: The end of empire and the birth of neoliberalism* (Cambridge, MA, Harvard University Press, 2018).

7 Michael Heseltine, *Life in the Jungle: My autobiography* (London, Hodder and Stoughton, 2000), 187.

8 Peter Saunders, *A Nation of Home Owners* (London, Unwin Hyman, 1990), 14, 6.

9 Martin Daunton, *A Property-Owning Democracy? Housing in Britain* (London, Faber and Faber, 1987). For the place of private landlords, see Phil Child, 'Landlordism, rent regulation, and the Labour Party in mid-twentieth century Britain, 1950–64', *Twentieth Century British History*, 29 (2018), 79–103.

10 Keith Bassett, 'The sale of council houses as a political issue', *Policy and Politics*, 8 (August 1980), 290–307, at 300; and Alison Ravetz, *Council Housing and Culture: The history of a social experiment* (New York, Routledge, 2001), 96.

11 Peter Weiler, 'The Conservatives' search for a middle way in housing, 1951–1964', *Twentieth Century British History*, 14/4 (2003), 360–90, especially 387–8.

12 Bassett, 'Sale of council houses', 301.

13 Aled Davies, '"Right to buy": The development of a Conservative housing policy, 1945–1980', *Contemporary British History*, 27 (2013), 421–44, especially 429–30.

14 John Burnett, *A Social History of Housing, 1815–1985*, 2nd ed. (London, Methuen, 1986), 287–9.

15 With thanks to Nathan Connolly. See Jessica Gordon Nembhard, *Collective Courage: A history of African American cooperative economic thought and practice* (University Park, Pennsylvania State University, 2014); Elizabeth Colson, 'The impact of the colonial period on the definition of land rights', in Victor Turner (ed.), *Colonialism in Africa, 1870–1960*, Volume 3 (Cambridge, Cambridge University Press 1971), 193–255; and Bryan McCann, *Hard Times in the Marvelous City: From dictatorship to democracy in the favelas of Rio de Janeiro* (Durham, NC, Duke University Press, 2014). See also Elizabeth A. Roistacher, 'Housing and the welfare state in the United States and Western Europe', *The Netherlands Journal of Housing and Environmental Research*, 2 (1987), 143–75.

16 For related points, see Jim Tomlinson, 'A new political arithmetic?', *Social History*, 40 (2015), 5–14, especially 13; Jeremy Nuttall, 'Tony Crosland and the many falls and rises of British social democracy', *Contemporary British History*, 18 (2004), 52–79, especially 54–5; Ben Jackson, 'Revisionism reconsidered: "Property-owning democracy" and egalitarian strategy in post-war Britain', *Twentieth Century British History*, 16 (2005), 416–40, especially 416; and David Matless, 'Appropriate geography: Patrick Abercrombie and the energy of the world', *Journal of Design History*, 6 (1993), 167–78.

17 Aristotle, *Aristotle's Politics: Writings from the complete works: Politics, economics, Constitution of Athens*, ed. Jonathan Barnes (Princeton, NJ, Princeton University Press, 2016); and Thomas More, *Utopia*, ed. Robert M. Adams (New York, Norton, 1991).

18 Ebenezer Howard, *To-morrow: A peaceful path to real reform* (London, Swan Sonnenschein, 1898); and Ebenezer Howard, *Garden Cities of To-morrow* (London, Swan Sonnenschein, 1902); for the illustration, see http://urbanplanning.library.cornell.edu/DOCS/howard1.gif (accessed 23 February 2019).

19 Thanks to Ben Jackson.

20 James Meek, 'Where will we live?', *London Review of Books* (9 January 2014), 8.

21 Peter Malpass, *Housing and the Welfare State: The development of housing policy in Britain* (New York, Palgrave Macmillan, 2005), 111, attributes the term to Alan Murie, 'Council house sales mean poor law housing', *Roof*, 2 (March 1977), 46–9. See also Ben Jones, 'Slum clearance, privatization, and residualization: The practices and politics of council housing in mid-twentieth-century England', *Twentieth Century British History*, 21 (2010), 510–39; and Ray Forrest and Alan Murie, *Selling the Welfare State: The privatisation of public housing* (London, Routledge, 1988), 65–85. For a counter-argument, differentiating between residualisation and polarisation, see Saunders, *Nation of Home Owners*, 315–21.

22 Davies, '"Right to buy"', 430. He was also responding, more immediately, to his own party's backbenchers who opposed Conservative councils' new-found zeal for sales: Bassett, 'Sale of council houses', 302.

23 Conservative Party, *The Conservative Manifesto 1983* (1983), http://www.politicsresources.net/area/uk/man/con83.htm (accessed 23 April 2017).

24 Saunders, *Nation of Home Owners*, 59.

25 Andy Beckett, *Promised You a Miracle: Why 1980–1982 made modern Britain* (London, Allen Lane, 2015), 220; Ravetz, *Council Housing and Culture*, 199–200; and Peter Shapely, *The Politics of Housing: Power, consumers, and urban culture* (Manchester, Manchester University Press, 2007).

26 Nicholas J. Crowson, 'Revisiting the 1977 Housing (Homeless Persons) Act: Westminster, Whitehall, and the homelessness lobby', *Twentieth Century British History*, 24 (2013), 424–47.

27 Meek, 'Where will we live?', 12–16.

28 The precise figure, not including Craigavon in Northern Ireland, was 741,260 residents by April 1966: J. B. Cullingworth and V. A. Karn, *The Ownership and Management of Housing in the New Towns* (London, HMSO, 1968), x.

29 David Truesdale, 'House sales and owner-occupation in Stevenage New Town', *Policy and Politics*, 8 (1980), 318–23; unless otherwise noted, details in this paragraph and the next derive from Truesdale.

30 Cullingworth and Karn, *New Towns*, x.

31 Milton Keynes Development Corporation (MKDC), *The Plan for Milton Keynes* (London, Routledge, 1970, 2013), 53.

32 Jock Campbell to Anthony Greenwood, 20 December 1967, Centre for Buckinghamshire Studies (CBS), AR 103/87 1/2 [MK 2].

33 MKDC, *The Plan for Milton Keynes*, 16, 38.
34 David Donnison, 'Social development of Milton Keynes', 6 March 1968, CBS, AR 103/87 1/8 [MK8]; and Melvyn Webber and P. Cowan, 'Milton Keynes in Britain's urban future', 7 March 1968, CBS, AR 103/87 1/8 [MK8].
35 'Notes on the seminar on Milton Keynes', July 1970, CBS, MKDC, Lib 47–49, Ref 48/15, 12–13.
36 'Third generation New Towns', 29 July 1977, CBS, MKDC, Box GM A4, File 122/2/1.
37 James Callaghan, *Time and Chance* (London, Politico's, 2006), 426.
38 Terence Bendixson and John Platt, *Milton Keynes: Image and reality* (Cambridge, Granta, 1992), 184, 188; Shore, quoted in a DoE press release, 'Third generation New Towns', 29 July 1977, CBS, MKDC, Box GM A4, File 122/2/1.
39 David Prior, 'Employment – a marketing and promotional strategy', 23 May 1978, CBS, MKDC, Box GM A5 A6, File 122/3/8.
40 'Milton Keynes – encouragement for private developers', *Building Trades Journal*, 11 February 1977, table 1, consulted in CBS, MKDC, Lib 28–30, Ref 30/10.
41 'Milton Keynes – encouragement for private developers', *Building Trades Journal*, 11 February 1977. For precedents, see Peter Shapely, 'Governance in the post-war city: Historical reflections on public–private partnerships in the UK', *International Journal of Urban and Regional Research*, 37 (2013), 1288–1304.
42 Report of the Private Housing Steering Committee, 30 May 1977, CBS, MKDC, Legal A62, Ref 00551/69/1 A62/1.
43 Bill Beesley, 'MKDC speeds up sale housing programme', 17 April 1978, CBS, MKDC, Box PHU A2, A4, A6, A16, File 00136/27 A16/3; [Report of the Private Housing Steering Committee].
44 Jane Chapman, 'Buying your home as a sitting tenant – attractive new scheme', 5 June 1979, CBS, MKDC, Box PHU A2, A4, A6, A16, File 00136/27 A16/3.
45 Chapman, 'Buying your home as a sitting tenant'; and Beesley, 'MKDC speeds up sale housing programme'.
46 [Report of the Private Housing Steering Committee]; and Bill Beesley, 'More new developers expand private housing programme', 8 November 1979, CBS, MKDC, Box PHU A2, A4, A6, A16, File 00136/27 A16/3.
47 'City in danger if Tories win', *Milton Keynes Express* (6 April 1979), quoted in Janina Gosseye, 'Milton Keynes' centre: The apotheosis of the British post-war consensus or the apostle of neo-liberalism?', *History of Retailing and Consumption*, 1 (2015), 209–29, at 225.
48 Lee Shostak, 'Here comes Maggie . . . so what are we going to do', [n.d.], 1–2; Fred Roche, 'Broadway seminar 26th/27th March 1979', 2 April 1979. Personal copies, with thanks to Lee Shostak; emphases mine.
49 'Opening of central Milton Keynes by the Prime Minister', 25 September 1979, 45–6, CBS, MKDC, Box AR 117/2006 8298/3/4–5, 8298/4/1–4, File 8298/4/3.
50 MKDC, 'Household survey', 1983, CBS, MKDC, Section MK/Lib/157 Bucks CRO Box 1, Item MK/Lib/155/26.
51 'Background information, housing in Milton Keynes', 12 May 1987, CBS, MKDC, Box PHU A2, A4, A6, A16, File 664/7/3 A4/5.
52 'Milton Keynes – encouragement for private developers'; and Bendixson and Platt, *Milton Keynes*, 274.
53 Circular 577 Ad Hoc Committee, 'Policy on mortgage arrears', [n.d.], CBS, MKDC, MK 39, Ref 00930/23/4; Lee Shostak, 'Sales to sitting tenants: Progress and issues', 26 March 1980, CBS, MKDC, Box MK 39, File 00930/23/4; and Michael Crick, *Michael Heseltine: A biography* (London, Hamish Hamilton, 1997), 200.
54 Lee Shostak, 'Sales to sitting tenants: A discussion paper', 12 February 1980, CBS, MKDC, MK 39, Ref 00930/23/4; and New Towns Circular 577 Ad Hoc Committee, 'Valuation of rental properties for sale to sitting tenants', 1 November 1979, CBS, MKDC, MK 39, Ref 00930/23/4.
55 Shostak, 'Sales to sitting tenants: A discussion paper'; and Bendixson and Platt, *Milton Keynes*, 215–17.
56 Jones, 'Slum clearance, privatization, and residualization', which in turn credits Chris Hamnett, 'Housing the two nations: Socio-tenurial polarization In England and Wales, 1961–81', *Urban Studies*, 21 (1984), 389–405.
57 Jeff Bishop, 'Private sector housing – relevant results', 3 June 1981, CBS, MKDC, Box PD A75, A77, Ref 00157/8/2 A75/3.
58 Shostak, 'Sales to sitting tenants: Progress and issues'.
59 Shostak, 'Sales to sitting tenants: Progress and issues'.

60 Correspondence between Roche and J. M. Sparrow, 12 April 1979 to 18 May 1979, CBS, MKDC, Box PHU A2, A4, A6, A16, File 00136/27/3 A16/2.

61 Taylor, 'Sales to sitting tenants policy', 6 March 1980, CBS, MKDC, MK 39, Ref 00930/23/4.

62 Bishop, 'Private sector housing – relevant results'.

63 'Public expenditure cuts', 29 June 1979, CBS, MKDC, Box 8125/17, 1 of 2, File 8125/17/2; and Tasker, 'Secret minutes of 1 August 1980', 13 August 1980, CBS, MKDC, Box GM A5 A6, File 122/3/8.

64 Bendixson and Platt, *Milton Keynes*, 205–7.

65 G. G. Anderson, 'Disposal of assets – disposals programme 1979/80, 1980/81', 1 July 1980, CBS, MKDC, Box GM A5 A6, File 122/3/8.

66 Bendixson and Platt, *Milton Keynes*, 199; and Margaret Thatcher, *The Downing Street Years* (London, HarperCollins, 1995), 600.

67 'Background information, housing in Milton Keynes'.

68 John Stanley, 'Homeownership in the New Towns', 6 July 1979, CBS, MKDC, Box GM A5 A6, File 00031/10/3.

69 Examples include, chronologically, Daisy Payling, '"Socialist Republic of South Yorkshire": Grassroots activism and left-wing solidarity in 1980s Sheffield', *Twentieth Century British History*, 25 (2014), 602–27; Stephen Brooke, 'Space, emotions, and the everyday: The affective ecology of 1980s London', *Twentieth Century British History*, 28 (2017), 110–42; Daisy Payling, 'City limits: Sexual politics and the New Urban Left in 1980s Sheffield', *Contemporary British History*, 31 (2017), 256–73; and Andrew Seaton, 'The National Health Service and the endurances of British social democracy, 1948 to the Present' (Ph.D. thesis, New York University, 2021).

70 For a parallel logic, on individualism rather than home ownership, see Emily Robinson, Camilla Schofield, Florence Sutcliffe-Braithwaite and Natalie Thomlinson, 'Telling stories about post-war Britain: Popular individualism and the "crisis" of the 1970s', *Twentieth Century British History*, 28 (2017), 268–304.

16

Afterword: British neoliberalism and its subjects

Tehila Sasson

Is neoliberalism a useful historical and analytical term? Despite the title of this volume, the majority of its chapters reject the term – or at the least are sceptical of it. David Edgerton, in the first chapter, is perhaps the most hostile, suggesting the label 'neoliberal' is 'best dispensed with'. I too was sceptical of its usefulness beyond the history of political and economic thought. After reading this volume, however, I am convinced that neoliberalism – or rather what we may call 'neoliberal rationality', the economic reason that extended economic values, ideas and practices to various spheres of life – offers a powerful and fruitful framework for all kinds of historians.[1] In their efforts to do away with or propose caveats to the term, the chapters in this volume inadvertently demonstrate that neoliberalism does, in fact, afford historians a useful – even if provocative – framework to investigate the changing relationship between the state, economy and society in the second half of the twentieth century. As Stuart Hall has put it, 'there are enough common features to warrant giving [neoliberalism] a *provisional* conceptual identity'.[2] Just like liberalism, neoliberalism was never one single, coherent system of thought or policies. Its richness lies in the multiple iterations it developed and how it intersected with other economic and political transformations in the late twentieth century.

Broadly speaking, the chapters in this volume represent two types of scholarship: the first examines political and economic policies and ideas, and the second uses the lens of social and cultural history. In this afterword, I will consider some of the common threads that emerge from both types of work, and I will read with them and beyond them in order to assess what was distinctive about British neoliberalism; what we can learn from them about the active role of the British state and British governments in facilitating neoliberalisation; what this shows us about what happened to the welfare system and the development of the welfare state under neoliberalism; and what it illuminates about the exact place of entrepreneurship, the flexible labour market and self-employment in Britain.

I argue that we cannot understand the neoliberal rationality in Britain without considering how it developed alongside and was shaped by global and post-imperial transformations in the economy, in particular deindustrialisation and financialisation. These two transformations were never only nationally bounded but were a product of the economics of decolonisation and its enduring effect on British financial and credit institutions, trade agreements, and migratory and labour regimes.[3] The conjuncture of neoliberal rationality with the political economy of both deindustrialisation and financialisation had a profound effect on economic and party policies, as much of the excellent work of British historians, represented in this volume, has demonstrated.[4] Equally important, however, was how this conjuncture transformed British society and especially its gendered and racial formations. I will show that considering the post-imperial legacies of deindustrialisation and financialisation reveals the connections between the long and lasting effects of the end of empire on labour and financialised regimes and the racialised and gendered forms of neoliberal capitalism in Britain. These connections are some of the most distinctive features of British neoliberalism.

Examining neoliberalism from the perspective of ideas, politics, economics, society and culture highlights the multiple lives of neoliberal rationality in Britain; it demonstrates that there is no single 'origin story' for neoliberal rationality but many points of convergence – and it is this convergence which makes neoliberalism a useful analytical category. It also, crucially, helps us understand why proclamations of neoliberalism's deaths, notably in 2008, 2016 and 2019, are somewhat premature and how neoliberal rationality has continued to shape contemporary Britain.[5]

*

The first body of scholarship about the history of neoliberalism in Britain comes from economic, political and intellectual historians. This scholarship forms part of a burgeoning literature that moves away from narrow (and popular) understandings of the neoliberal project as anti-statist and instead shows that neoliberalism was a project that aimed to transform the state. A new generation of historians such as Ben Jackson and Quinn Slobodian have demonstrated that neoliberalism – both in Britain as well as in Europe and the US – was never a libertarian project.[6] Quite the opposite: in Britain, as elsewhere, neoliberalism depended upon a strong state to transform market and social relationships through laws and policies. Many neoliberal economists and policymakers saw the state as a crucial agent to facilitate their reforms. Just as the state was central to the great transformation of laissez-faire capitalism in the late eighteenth century,[7] so was it crucial to the shift to neoliberal economics in the late twentieth century.[8] Neoliberal thinkers such as Walter Eucken and Wilhelm Röpke, for example, often assigned 'an important role for the state in maintaining market freedom' through anti-monopoly policies.[9] Neoliberalism was different from liberalism precisely because it acknowledged that some form of economic management was necessary to create competitive markets and to secure political support for them.

Take, for example, the story of unemployment benefits under Margaret Thatcher. As Jim Tomlinson's chapter argues, the rapid deindustrialisation of Britain from the late 1970s to the 1980s was a critical motor in shaping state interventions in labour and housing markets regardless of Thatcherite privatisation rhetoric. The Thatcher governments in fact increased spending on wage and housing subsidies, 'a major problem for the ambition to reduce public spending in the post-crash "austerity" era, given their scale'. For Tomlinson this proves that 'neoliberal plans for state retreat' clashed with 'the effects of the shifts in the labour market as a consequence of deindustrialisation'. He separates deindustrialisation from neoliberal rationality, arguing that neoliberals had to concede their ambitions to supposedly 'roll back' the state. But there is perhaps another way to tell this story, where neoliberals – in response to deindustrialisation – created a new infrastructure for the deregulation of the labour market. As we learn from Bernhard Rieger's chapter, the British state had a crucial role in shaping neoliberal labour. Thatcher's unemployment policies 'mobilised state institutions to promote market mechanisms in new social contexts'. In a period of rapid deindustrialisation, the Thatcher government used state action to inject the labour market with a new neoliberal mentality and redefined the causes of unemployment. Instead of treating unemployment as the product of deindustrialisation, which lowered the demand for waged workers, the Thatcher government argued that the price of labour was too high. In this logic unions' bargaining power was too strong and they demanded wages that were higher than market value. The Thatcher government therefore created a new benefit system that imposed income tax on unemployment benefits and kept them at a minimum, regardless of inflation. The idea was 'to remove distortions in the play of supply and demand on the labour market'. This set of policies on unemployment benefits should not be seen as a moment where the state was rolled back, nor as a moment where Thatcherites failed to roll back the state as much as they wanted; rather, this was a moment when the state actively pushed more people to seek employment at a lower wage.

Instead of limiting the state's reach, as we learn from Jim Phillips's chapter, the neoliberal project in Britain was focused on 'the narrowing of industrial democracy'. The Thatcher government used the power of the state to weaken the bargaining power of unions and strengthen the power of the employer. Following Friedrich Hayek, the Thatcher government believed the monopoly of unions was detrimental to the functioning of markets and that the state should actively design policies to dismantle them.[10] Phillips looks at laws and policies such as the Employment Act of 1980, which restricted picketing and eroded workplace rights. Furthermore, in subsequent laws of 1982 and 1988 the Thatcher governments targeted the closed shop, which – following Hayek – Thatcherites saw as 'a coercive attempt by unions to impose costs on workers, employers and the public more broadly'. The state bolstered the sovereignty of the employer. It used its power during the miners' strike of 1984–5 to police strikers, to prevent them from blockading power stations and collieries, and to provide financial incentives to strike-breakers. These were actions that were not against neoliberal rationality but rather closely adhered to it. As Jackson suggests, actually existing neoliberalism never mapped perfectly onto ideology, but from the late 1970s neoliberal ideas profoundly shaped the 'conceptual space in which [political] decision-making takes place'. Reconstructing how some ideas were transformed into policies at the particular moment of deindustrialisation provides a fruitful ground for understanding the political histories of neoliberalism in Britain.

And it was not only the narrowing of industrial democracy. Neoliberal rationality also remade the British welfare state. As Peter Sloman's chapter shows, British policymakers used neoliberal ideas to financialise and limit the reach of welfare services through transfer payments. Sloman traces how Milton Friedman's idea of Negative Income Tax (NIT) came to shape British welfare policies in the last third of the twentieth century. For Friedman, NIT was a monetary alternative to the service-based welfare system. NIT provided a cash transfer that allowed citizens to choose how to spend their benefits and, at the same time, incentivised people to not be dependent on them. Based on Friedman's idea of NIT among others, from 1979 the British government developed a system of means-tested benefits and tax credits for low- and middle-income households that would alleviate 'the inequality generated by a financialised and service-based liberal market economy'. As British industrial output declined and unemployment numbers rose,[11] cash transfers helped legitimise free-market reforms. For example, cash transfers for housing provided a form of welfare while at the same time they legitimised the introduction of new policies such as the Poll Tax, which exacerbated inequalities. These tax-based transfer payments also became the basis for New Labour's welfare policies and, as Sloman suggests, serve as the origins of the contemporary Universal Credit system. Tackling the problem of poverty through cash transfers 'played an important role in reconciling Labour politicians (and voters) to market liberalism'. Rather than a complete assault on welfare, as Sloman's chapter for example shows, neoliberalism in Britain devised its own alternative to welfare through what the economist John Kay called 'redistributive market liberalism'.[12]

In fact, while neoliberalism is often thought to be antithetical to welfare, one of the major contributions of historians in this volume has been to show that neoliberal thinkers and reformers often sought to revise rather than abolish welfare altogether. Many of the chapters in this volume move away from using 'Thatcherism' as an exclusive frame to study the origins of British neoliberalism; instead, they trace the neoliberal project back to as early as the 1940s and still see it developing in the 1990s and 2000s. In this view, neoliberalism was a project that had its roots in earlier decades of social democracy and stretched well beyond Thatcher's government to include Third Way politics. As Guy Ortolano suggests, 'the ascendance of neoliberalism resulted not only from the exertions of its champions, but also from the begrudging acquiescence of its critics'. Neoliberalism was a much more contingent phenomenon than we might think. Policies often associated with neoliberalism, such as the privatisation of housing, were not exclusively a Thatcherite story. They had roots both in liberal programmes in the early twentieth century as well as in the social democratic project of the post-war period. It is how these policies were interpreted and elaborated during the 1980s and 1990s that offers us a better understanding of British neoliberalism, or, to borrow from the American historian Amy Offner, how the mixed economy of welfare was sorted between the private and public.[13] In Ortolano's chapter, neoliberal policies had a very localised position in the New Towns such as Milton Keynes, where the notion of a property-owning democracy moved from a social democratic programme of the mixed economy to a neoliberal project that would create rafts of self-reliant citizens as homeowners with different stakes in the economy, shifting towards more Thatcherite views on welfare, work and the state.[14]

Aled Davies's chapter also focuses on Britain's social democracy, tracing how neoliberalism's origins intersected with an earlier turn towards financialisation.[15] Focusing on the story of the mortgage market, Davies shows that the political economy of home ownership began not with the Thatcherite 'Right to Buy' but with the financialisation of the British economy, a process which he dates back to the 1960s and 1970s. It was the re-globalisation of finance through the City of London in these decades, and the substantial demand for mortgage finance that followed, he argues, which created the infrastructure for the neoliberalisation of Britain. The push for home ownership was not only a major example of privatisation, but a development that reorganised the British economy around credit and finance. The case provides an interesting comparison with the history of the mortgage market in the US and pre-dates it. The so-called mortgage-led accumulation regime that was partially responsible for the 2008 crash had its origins not only in the ideological Thatcherite programme to liberalise the British economy but also in the crisis of the industrial economy.[16] Ortolano and Davies focus on the earlier, social democratic origins of home ownership, but the history they tell us provides us with some crucial insights into the deeper roots of what some scholars have recently termed 'the asset economy' of the 1990s; that is, the story of how property accumulation came to replace waged employment as a generator of capital, wealth and generational inequality in Britain.[17]

If Ortolano's and Davies's chapters show how some of the origins of neoliberalism can be located in Britain's social democracy, then other chapters follow it all the way to the 'post-Thatcherite landscape', as the editors call the period post-1990 in the introduction to the volume. Many of the chapters analyse the transformations of British neoliberalism beyond the Thatcher and the Major governments. They interrogate how neoliberal rationality morphed with the Blair government and came to inform New Labour politics. In her chapter on childcare policies, for example, Helen McCarthy shows that despite Blair's commitment to break from Major's government, in the case of childcare policy the Blair governments nevertheless relied on 'traditional forms of family-based care'. The state only supplemented what Blair saw as primarily family (and therefore women's) responsibility. Similarly, according to Sloman, New Labour did not substantially transform Conservative legislation on benefits and still used the tax system to tackle the problem of poverty through the Working Families Tax Credit. Rieger also demonstrates that Blair's government kept much of the Conservatives' employment policy and its disciplinary strategy, the Jobseeker's Allowance, albeit emphasising 'the programme's supportive rather than punitive intentions'. As Mark Wickham-Jones emphasises in his chapter, there is a long continuity in Labour's acceptance of markets and capitalism, going right back to the early years of the twentieth century; nevertheless, there are substantive ways in which Third Way politics was shaped by Thatcherite reforms and influenced by neoliberal rationalities. This points to the importance, then, of recognising the multiple lives that neoliberalism had in Britain after the 1970s.

*

While the majority of the contributions in this volume focus on how neoliberal rationality has shaped economic and welfare policies, the remaining chapters consider how it has come to transform the social. These chapters tend to reject the term neoliberalism or qualify its utility as a category with which to understand late twentieth- and early twenty-first-century Britain, but they nonetheless offer rich insights into what a social history of neoliberalism in Britain might look like, focusing on two crucial yet understudied categories of the British economy and especially of neoliberalism: gender and race.

Gender has only recently been taken on by historians of neoliberalism as a category of analysis. Historians have argued that Anglo-American neoliberalism often fused social conservatism and traditional morality with market liberalism.[18] Florence Sutcliffe-Braithwaite, for example, has revealed that neoliberal welfare policies placed family responsibility at the heart of their reforms of the national insurance system. In her chapter on feminism, family and work, however, McCarthy disagrees with this analysis and argues that family responsibility was not particularly unique to the last decades of the twentieth century. She suggests that an emphasis on family responsibility has characterised British social policy throughout the twentieth century. Both liberal feminism in the interwar period as well as the post-war welfare state, she shows, saw childcare as a maternal responsibility, framing women's real work as childrearing. When in the 1940s and 1950s welfare experts and policymakers began to perceive (white, middle-class) women as wage-earners, they nonetheless kept this maternalist framework in social provisions. The 1970s and 1980s, McCarthy argues, did not depart from the previous period. '[S]tate-endowed mothers and the eternal dependants of men left a complex and contested legacy for policymaking and for women's own subjectivities in the 1980s and beyond.' The term neoliberalism, McCarthy concludes, does not capture the continuities of this history.

McCarthy's analysis illuminates the important continuity between liberal and neoliberal rhetoric in Britain, which she terms the discourse of 'responsibilisation'. She leaves out, however, some central global transformations in the political economy of the 1970s which shaped this history. These transformations played an important role in the critique of neoliberal feminism and the place of the family in neoliberal policymaking in Britain in the 1980s. While the working mother was in no way new to the 1970s,[19] by the end of the decade rates of maternal employment rose sharply, increasing demand for day care. This so-called feminisation of the workforce was a product of both changes in the divorce rate and an increase in single-parent households, and the growth of the service economy in Britain, due to structural transformations such as deindustrialisation. The transition was supported by British governments up through the 1990s, which helped to produce a supply of part-time female workers who had to take lower-skilled, lower-paid and less secure jobs, as they had few easy childcare options available to them. It was this shift that generated a new debate within feminist circles about the place of work – productive, reproductive and later even emotional labour – in women's lives.[20] The feminist so-called discovery of work, in other words, was at least partially the result of the global crisis of labour and the move to the service economy in Britain and beyond.

The feminist discovery of work created new gender norms and new demand for childcare provisions from both the Conservative and later New Labour governments. How these governments responded to and interpreted these demands was what made their policies neoliberal. In the case of childcare, as Jackson has shown elsewhere, neoliberals argued against a universal system that would support working mothers because they perceived state-sponsored childcare as an 'intrusion into family life'.[21] They saw public expenditure on childcare as encouraging mothers to work. The state should take a neutral stance, they argued, between mothers who choose to go out to work and those who wish to spend more time with their children. By the 1990s, Major's government adopted a voucher system that offered financial support to parents who wished to use the private childcare sector. The voucher system represented the neoliberal ideal of 'preserving a market for childcare services through subsidising demand rather than instituting a new universal public service'.[22] These policies designated the family as responsible for childcare, with the option of using the private market to support the white, middle-class working mother. In doing so, British governments not only helped generate a private childcare market but also inadvertently encouraged the growth of a precarious, part-time, female labour force

– often comprising women from ethnic minorities and Commonwealth immigrants – who could not afford private and expensive childcare.

The attention to women's history in the story of British neoliberalism is also at the heart of Sarah Mass's chapter on the culture of entrepreneurship. According to Mass, women, and particularly housewives, were central to the ascendency of 'enterprise culture' in economic life in Britain. Looking at entrepreneurs such as market organiser-turned-civic activist Wendy Hobday, Mass shows that the critique of state intervention in economic life had its origins in the post-war debates about the proliferation of mobile trading in New Towns such as Harlow and Sunday open-air market trading rather than the rise of individualism, which she associates with neoliberal culture.[23] Mass's chapter offers an interesting read alongside recent works by historians of neoliberalism such as Angus Burgin that date the reinvention of entrepreneurship in American social thought to the post-war decades. While the figure of the entrepreneur in economic thought was not new to this period, Burgin shows, from the 1950s Americans began to conceive entrepreneurship as broadly accessible, meaning that 'anyone, whether working within a large organization or as a sole proprietor, could display and should try to cultivate entrepreneurial role behavior'.[24] Both Mass and Burgin explore the popularity of enterprise culture beyond big industry in the post-war period, but they attribute it to different factors. For Burgin, entrepreneurship in the US was a product of a larger political economy rooted within automation and deindustrialisation; Mass looks at the urban history of consumerism in Britain, arguing that in Britain, enterprise culture developed in response to a rise in demand for consumer goods and flexible retailing.

Mass's chapter provides historians of neoliberalism with a fruitful case study to consider the emergence of what economists in the 1970s began to call 'the informal economy', although she herself does not use the term. The term emerged within an international and post-imperial context, when development economists sought new ways to explain the crisis of unemployment and the global supply of labour, especially in post-colonial economies such as that of Kenya.[25] Its emergence marked the expansion of not only what counted but also who counted as a legitimate economic actor. The shift towards the informal economy suddenly accounted for economic activities beyond the space of the factory and the male industrial worker. It allowed economists to factor in what had previously been cast as 'disguised unemployment' and include in their analyses the perennial forms of work done by women in agriculture and handicraft work within the home.[26] In the global South that transition marked the emergence of a new approach to Women in Development (and later also the Gender and Development agenda), but it also came to influence economic and policy debates about entrepreneurship in Britain. Much of the neoliberal discourse about entrepreneurship in Britain was rooted within the story of the rise of a flexible job market, and it was dependent on economic formulations which originated in post-imperial economies rather than exclusively within a domestic story about demand. Here, as in the story about the feminisation of the workforce, the post-imperial formation of the supply side was integral to the culture of entrepreneurship, structures of self-employment and the pseudo-informal economy in Britain and cannot be understood separately from it.

Thatcher's Enterprise Allowance Scheme, mentioned in both Rieger's and Sloman's chapters, is one good example of the flexible job market and how it reshaped the history of work in Britain. The Scheme was first tested in post-industrial northern communities in order to solve the problem of unemployment in the region without offering protected jobs or government resources. Entrepreneurship was seen not as some abstract ethos or new subjectivity but rather as a concrete way to generate self-employment. The neoliberal deployment of the entrepreneurial discourse and its emphasis on economic 'independence' was used to shift the burden of employment to citizens instead of investing in the industrial sector. Thus, the first generation of neoliberal policymakers in the 1980s encouraged the development and proliferation of more informal and flexible economies in Britain through entrepreneurship. Analysis of deindustrialisation has focused on changes in the demand for industrial labour. Yet we cannot think of demand in isolation from the story of supply and how the Thatcherite governments responded to changes in demand for labour and attempted to shape its supply.[27] The emergence of the informal economy as a focus of economic management was central to enterprise culture of the 1980s and the Thatcher governments' embrace of enterprise.

Enterprise culture is also the subject of Camilla Schofield, Florence Sutcliffe-Braithwaite and Rob Waters's analysis. Their chapter grapples with the relationship between race relations and neoliberalism. It seeks to show how enterprise culture was embraced by the Black community in Britain rather than imposed on it by the Thatcher and New Labour governments. Schofield, Sutcliffe-Braithwaite and Waters explore how in the 1970s an enterprise culture grew alongside a more radical, anti-capitalist tradition, out of 'the meritocratic assumptions deeply rooted in the post-war social democratic state, and given form in the Race Relations legislation of the 1960s and 1970s'. According to them, Black enterprise culture owed much to social democracy in Britain rather than simply to neoliberal policies. Schofield, Sutcliffe-Braithwaite and Waters follow the stories of entrepreneurs such as Len Dyke and Dudley Dryden and suggest that they built their multi-million-pound business enterprise alongside, and as part of, an investment in an anti-racist politics of integration rooted in the aftermath of the Notting Hill white riots in 1958. In this narrative, entrepreneurship was an investment in the community and for the community. For some members of the Black British community, entrepreneurship was a path to racial equality, a way to own 'a stake in the British economy'.[28] It is for this reason that Schofield, Sutcliffe-Braithwaite and Waters conclude that 'neoliberalism is not a sufficient category to explain New Labour's policies on race and racism, the transformation of anti-racist activism in the 1980s or Black enterprise culture in the 1970s'. The turn to entrepreneurship by individuals in the Black British community was in part the product of the politics of assimilation and integration developed from within the Black British community.

This is a rich account and the sole chapter in this volume to consider the important place of race in the history of British neoliberalism. It urges historians of neoliberalism to take the voices of the Black British community seriously and consider what enterprise culture offered its members, rather than to see enterprise culture as something that was imposed on it. Yet we still do not know why and how race relations became connected to New Labour's economic agenda or what the relationship was between race, multiculturalism and neoliberal rationality in the 1990s. Was there an inherent connection between neoliberal rationality and race relations in New Labour's Britain? And more broadly, was there a distinctive form of racial capitalism that developed in Britain which was characteristic of neoliberal rationality?

One way to answer these questions is by looking at the history of labour rather than entrepreneurship. In a recent article, for example, James Vernon has examined the relationship between race and neoliberalism by looking at their entangled history at Heathrow Airport after 1965 with the setting up of the state-financed British Airports Authority (BAA) to operate it. As Vernon argues, Heathrow was a microcosm for the post-imperial and racialised social formation of neoliberal rationality in Britain through immigration and deregulated labour regimes. Heathrow became 'Britain's de facto border', where an increasingly restrictive and racialised immigration regime developed alongside the privatisation of border control, privatisation which was often supported by government concessions and funds to expand the airport. Government contracted the management and regulation of Britain's border to the privately owned Securicor. 'Aside from detainees',

Vernon reveals, 'it was Securicor's non-unionized employees who paid the price for detention on the cheap: they received little training and were paid so poorly that they often had to work up to sixty hours a week to make a living'. In fact, many Heathrow workers – from outsourced cleaning and catering companies – were themselves often Commonwealth citizens and primarily women of colour 'who were on the front lines of economic liberalization and outsourced jobs that were poorly paid and precarious'. The racialised forms of neoliberal capitalism at Heathrow, Vernon shows, were created at a particular, post-imperial conjuncture and were shaped by the political economy of decolonisation and its aftermath; they cannot be understood outside this context.[29] As I have argued in the cases of the informal economy and the feminisation of the economy, the production of labour supply in the case of Heathrow similarly cannot be seen as an exclusively domestic story as it was shaped by post-imperial transformations in the global economy. What I am trying to suggest here is that we should consider decolonisation as an economic and not only political *process* (rather than a singular event) that pushed for deindustrialisation and shaped labour and migratory regimes in Britain as a post-colonial metropole, a story that is absent in this volume.

But there are other ways in which we might consider the entangled relationship between post-imperial legacies of race relations, the supply-side history of the British economy and neoliberal rationality, such as through the history of financialisation. My own research traces the intersection between financialisation and race relations as part of a broader story of microfinance in Britain. Microfinance was imported to Britain in the 1990s from the global South by New Labour, via the US, through non-governmental organisations such as Oxfam. It was a technique used and supported by British humanitarians in South Asia and later Latin America and Africa in the 1980s, as a response to the problem of unemployment and deindustrialisation, in order to generate self-employment in the global South. Its origins lay in post-colonial community development and the cooperative schemes most associated with (though not exclusive to) the Bangladeshi activist Muhammad Yunus and his Grameen Bank. Yunus suggested organising borrowers in small solidarity groups that would receive financial education from an aid worker and would work as a form of emotional guarantor. The idea was to teach the habitus of being a financial and indebted subject who is able to become creditworthy while still taking financial risks.

Grameen laid the groundwork for a financialised model of aid that fit closely with neoliberal theories about entrepreneurship, finance and human capital that dominated in the 1990s. Its financialised model of aid was embraced by Third Way neoliberals, who saw in it an emancipatory project to shift the burden of poverty to the poor themselves, and especially to ethnic minorities. Just as microfinance became a panacea for solving unemployment among the global poor, so, its enthusiasts argued, it could be used as a remedy for those ethnic minorities excluded from the labour market in the global North. Instead of increasing welfare dependency, its advocates argued that microfinance held the potential for generating self-employment. With microfinance the poor took responsibility for their own material conditions by becoming entrepreneurs. Microfinance was designed to connect ethnic minorities with commercial banking providers, which had traditionally excluded them, and to help build credit history. It also legitimised economic activities in the informal economy, which has often been occupied by ethnic minorities. 'In the United Kingdom', according to the activist and microfinance enthusiast Ruth Pearson,

> [t]he small 'corner shop' culture tends to be confined to the margins of the economy, particularly in localities where such activities have been the preserve of ethnic minorities. Self-employment and microenterprise has [*sic*] often been seen as 'cheating' . . . This is compounded by the hostility towards new immigration from the Commonwealth.[30]

Incorporating microfinance into welfare programmes was seen as a path out of financial exclusion as well as an opportunity to combat racial prejudice.

Microfinance, in fact, became part of a broader focus on financial and social inclusion, and it was seen as a path to solving the problem of race relations in Britain. Social scientists had already begun to explore the place of ethnic minorities in the British economy in the early 1980s; in the 1990s they began to focus on the difficulties encountered by ethnic minorities in operating their own businesses. '[T]he use of credit by people from minority ethnic groups was more limited than was justified by their financial circumstances', claimed one report by the think tank the Policy Studies Institute. 'Cultural differences and the credit industry's lack of understanding of the needs of ethnic minority communities were also felt to limit access. There were also allegations of racism in the high street credit industry.'[31] The problem of limited credit and the financial exclusion of ethnic minorities became the heart of the new political discourse of the New Labour government in 1997 through the new Social Exclusion Unit.

In New Labour's view, the problem of race and poverty in Britain was one of access to financial resources and services. Once inclusion was achieved, ethnic minorities would not only be lifted out of poverty but would also be able to integrate into the social body.

And yet New Labour's emphasis on ending financial exclusion through schemes such as microfinance overrode local forms of lending and borrowing organised by the Caribbean and Asian communities. The British Caribbean community, for example, had its own lending structures aimed at offering support to new immigrants and young families who had struggled to get credit from high street banks since the 1950s and 1960s. These 'pardner schemes', as they were called, resembled cooperatives. They were essentially rotating saving and credit associations that collected regular deposits of a fixed amount from members with a main organiser, called a 'banker', depositing these into a central fund. The banker distributed the total sum to members in a prearranged order. Other forms of community-based banking included credit unions, such as the Camberwell Credit Union, founded by a small Afro-Caribbean church group in the late 1960s and registered in 1972 under the Friendly Society Act.[32] The credit union offered a variety of financial services to the Afro-Caribbean community in the area – who had been essentially redlined from commercial banking – from life insurance to credit. These organisations helped many community members purchase consumer goods or pay for housing but were not necessarily designed to support or encourage entrepreneurial activities.

When New Labour began to invest in financial inclusion, it often did not build on these schemes but rather aimed to replace them with a mixed economy of public and voluntary aid focused on access to commercial banking. Aid schemes such as microfinance were intended to educate members of the Afro-Caribbean community to take financial risks and, in particular, to invest in starting their own businesses. Its language of financial empowerment was often paternalistic in nature, perhaps because it was imported from an aid discourse that belonged to international developments. It was part of a post-imperial legacy of development aid that was then imported back as a somewhat racialised type of welfare service offered in particular to ethnic minorities. Instead of the locally organised schemes that developed more organically to meet specific financial needs, microfinance was designed with a more market-driven purpose. Its model aimed to encourage individuals to take financial risks and open their own businesses. For its advocates, microfinance schemes offered the broad financial education and literacy that were 'essential for full social participation and survival' and increased the 'employability and employment readiness' of participants.[33] Microfinance was a path to the labour market because it offered skills that 'have transferability into the mainstream labour market and other aspects of modern life'.[34]

Microfinance fitted into a broader transformation in neoliberal rationality in the 1990s. Third Way politicians broke with Keynesianism and instead made it their mission to encourage and to train citizens to increase their 'creditworthiness' and 'employability' without offering them protected jobs or government resources. Microfinance, in fact, was a way to invest in human capital through financial mechanisms. It encouraged citizens to embrace the condition not of entrepreneurs necessarily but of *investees*, responsible for increasing their own employability and solvency.[35] The 'creditworthiness' of citizens became a way to estimate the value of human capital, based on crude speculations on their potential ability to generate income or take financial risks through credit. Microfinance offers historians of British neoliberalism one way to consider the social formations and entangled relationship between race relations, post-imperial finance and neoliberal rationality – or what I call the 'financialization of race relations' – one that is attuned to the intersection between labour, entrepreneurship and finance and the forms of community organising they came to substitute. It demonstrates both the continuities as well as the ruptures caused by decolonisation as an economic process that shaped racialised notions of economic subjects for British policymakers not only in the 1980s but also in the 1990s and 2000s.

*

Who are the subjects of the British economy and, in particular, of its neoliberal rationality? The burgeoning literature on British neoliberalism and especially its economic, political and intellectual histories – much of it represented in this volume – has demonstrated that neoliberal rationality has come to shape the British state, industrial relations, its urban landscape and welfare services. In this afterword I have also suggested that neoliberal rationality has had a profound effect on British society and particularly its gendered and racial formations between the 1960s and the 1990s. The burgeoning literature on neoliberalism has emphasised the role of politicians, intellectuals and economists in shaping its history, but there were also other grassroots, social forms of neoliberal expression that were similarly important. The categories of gender and race were central to the distinctive formations and features of neoliberal rationality in Britain and, to my mind, offer some of the most fruitful and rewarding grounds for future work on the particular configurations of neoliberalism in Britain. They reveal the relationships between flexible labour, entrepreneurship and financialisation, as well as post-imperial legacies, in shaping the British economy in the late twentieth century. Neoliberal rationality was never one consistent or totalising body of ideas. Rather, it developed and morphed in response to myriad changes in Britain's post-imperial make-up as well as shifts in global political economy – particularly deindustrialisation and financialisation – and generated new social relationships and a new understanding of British feminism, the informal economy, immigration control and race relations. We would do well to expand our understanding of who are the subjects of British neoliberalism.

Notes

1 For more on 'neoliberal rationality' as a term, see Wendy Brown, *Undoing the Demos: Neoliberalism's stealth revolution* (Brooklyn, NY, Zone Books, 2015).
2 Stuart Hall, *Selected Political Writings: The great moving right show and other essays* (Durham, NC, Duke University Press, 2017), 318.
3 I am following here in the footsteps of scholars of empire and international history, who have argued that the end of empires was not only a political but also an economic event. See, for example, S. E. Stockwell, *The Business of Decolonization: British business strategies in the Gold Coast* (Oxford, Oxford University Press, 2000); Vanessa Ogle, '"Funk money": The end of empires, the expansion of tax havens, and decolonization as an economic and financial event', *Past & Present*, 249 (2020), 213–49; and James Vernon, 'Heathrow and the making of neoliberal Britain', *Past & Present*, 252 (2021), 213–47.
4 For 'conjuncture' as a productive concept, see Stuart Hall, 'The great moving right show', in Hall, *Selected Political Writings: The great moving right show and other essays* (Durham, NC, Duke University Press, 2017), 172–99.
5 Quinn Slobodian, 'Is neoliberalism really dead?', *New Statesman* (27 October 2020).
6 For an earlier treatment of neoliberalism and the state, see Andrew Gamble, *The Free Economy and the Strong State: The politics of Thatcherism* (Basingstoke, Palgrave, 1988). For more recent notable accounts, see Ben Jackson, 'Currents of neo-liberalism: British political ideologies and the New Right, c.1955–1979', *English Historical Review*, 131 (2016), 823–50; Philip Mirowski, 'Neoliberalism: The movement that dare not speak its name', *American Affairs*, 2 (2018), 118–41; and Quinn Slobodian, *Globalists: The end of empire and the birth of neoliberalism* (Cambridge, MA, Harvard University Press, 2018).
7 Karl Polanyi, *The Great Transformation* (New York, Octagon Books, 1975); and Tim Rogan, *The Moral Economists: R. H. Tawney, Karl Polanyi, E. P. Thompson, and the critique of capitalism* (Princeton, NJ, Princeton University Press, 2017).
8 Timothy Mitchell, *Rule of Experts: Egypt, techno-politics, modernity* (Berkeley, University of California Press, 2002).
9 Jackson, 'Currents of neo-liberalism'.
10 On how neoliberals launched a similar attack against the monopoly of the European Common Market and the Eurafrica model of preferential trade agreements in the international arena through the GATT, see Slobodian, *Globalists*, chapter 6.
11 As Sloman shows in his book, the financialisation of benefits had already begun in part in the middle of the 1960s, when it was clear that poverty was still pervasive in Britain despite welfare measures. Influenced by the 'War on Poverty' in the US, welfare policies began to be fused with tax policies as computerisation offered the possibility of easier integration: Peter Sloman,

Transfer State: The idea of a guaranteed income and the politics of redistribution in modern Britain (Oxford, Oxford University Press, 2019), chapter 4.

12 John Kay, *The Truth about Markets: Why some countries are rich and others remain poor* (London, Penguin, 2004).

13 Offner shows how in the case of the US self-help housing enterprises were first created as part of a mixed economy of welfare (with origins in development projects in Colombia). Offner argues that it was only later in the 1980s that these mixed economies were 'sorted' and became co-opted to neoliberal policies. Amy C. Offner, *Sorting Out the Mixed Economy: The rise and fall of welfare and developmental states in the Americas* (Princeton, NJ, Princeton University Press, 2019), especially chapters 7–8.

14 Guy Ortolano, *Thatcher's Progress: From social democracy to market liberalism through an English New Town* (Cambridge, Cambridge University Press, 2019). For a broader history of how New Towns and neoliberal rationality fitted within a longer urban history and shaped British politics, see Sam Wetherell, *Foundations: How the built environment made twentieth-century Britain* (Princeton, NJ, Princeton University Press, 2020).

15 For more extensive treatment of the City of London and the financialisation of the British economy from the 1960s, see Aled Davies, *The City of London and Social Democracy: The political economy of finance in Britain, 1959–1979* (Oxford, Oxford University Press, 2017).

16 J. D. G. Wood, quoted in Davies's chapter.

17 Lisa Adkins, Melinda Cooper and Martijn Konings, *The Asset Economy* (Bristol, Polity, 2020); and Thomas Piketty, *Capital in the Twenty First Century,* trans. Arthur Goldhammer (Cambridge, MA, Harvard University Press, 2014).

18 Florence Sutcliffe-Braithwaite, 'Neo-liberalism and morality in the making of Thatcherite social policy', *Historical Journal*, 55 (2012), 497–520; and Melinda Cooper, *Family Values: Between neoliberalism and the new social conservatism* (Cambridge, MA, MIT Press, 2017).

19 Helen McCarthy, *Double Lives: A history of working motherhood* (London, Bloomsbury, 2020).

20 For the debates about housework, see Sarah Stoller, 'Forging a politics of care: Theorizing household work in the British women's liberation movement', *History Workshop Journal*, 85 (2018), 95–119.

21 Quoted in Ben Jackson, 'Free markets and feminism: The neo-liberal defence of the male breadwinner model in Britain, c. 1980–1997', *Women's History Review*, 28 (2019), 297–316, at 307.

22 Jackson, 'Free markets and feminism', 310.

23 For different accounts of the origins of individualism in Britain, see Florence Sutcliffe-Braithwaite and Jon Lawrence, who attribute the rise of individualism in Britain to a rejection of established class hierarchies in the 1960s and 1970s: Jon Lawrence and Florence Sutcliffe-Braithwaite, 'Margaret Thatcher and the decline of class politics', in Ben Jackson and Robert Saunders (eds), *Making Thatcher's Britain* (Cambridge, Cambridge University Press, 2012), 132–47.

24 Angus Burgin, 'The reinvention of entrepreneurship', in Raymond Haberski Jr and Andrew Hartman (eds), *American Labyrinth: Intellectual history for complicated times* (Ithaca, NY, Cornell University Press, 2019), 166.

25 The term in fact was first coined by the British anthropologist Keith Hart in 1971 and was then adopted by the economists Hans Singer and Richard Jolly at the Institute of Development Studies at the University of Sussex for a report they wrote for the International Labour Organization (ILO) about Kenya in 1972: Keith Hart, 'Informal income opportunities and urban employment in Ghana', *Journal of Modern African Studies*, 11 (1973), 61–89; and Report on an Interagency Team Financed by the United Nations Development Programme and Organised by the International Labour Office, 'Employment, income and equality' (Geneva, ILO, 1972), 504–5.

26 The economist Phyllis Deane had already pointed out this lacuna in her research in northern Rhodesia in the 1940s, but it was only in the 1970s, when Ester Boserup published her *Women's Role in Economic Development* in the midst of the revolution of second-wave feminism, that this argument was taken seriously by economic planners, policymakers and activists. See Phyllis Deane, *The Measurement of Colonial National Incomes: An experiment* (Cambridge, Cambridge University Press, 1948); and Ester Boserup, *Woman's Role in Economic Development* (London, Allen & Unwin, 1970).

27 Ken Lipartito, 'Reassembling the economic: New departures in historical materialism', *American Historical Review*, 121 (2016), 101–39.

28 Tony Wade, quoted in Schofield, Sutcliffe-Braithwaite and Waters.
29 Vernon, 'Heathrow and the making of neoliberal Britain', 217, 218, 229.
30 Ruth Pearson, 'Think globally, act locally: Translating international microcredit experience in the United Kingdom', in D. Lewis and T. Wallace (eds), *New Roles and Relevance: Development NGOs and the challenge of change* (Boulder, CO, Kumarian Press, 2000), 157.
31 Malcolm Hayday and Mary Locke, 'South–north lessons in microfinance and the role of social investment', in Ben Rogaly and Chris Roche (eds), *Learning from South–North Links in Microfinance*, Oxfam Working Paper, 35, 2000.
32 My account here, to some measure, simplifies the rich history of credit unions in Britain which were created in the 1960s by both Afro-Caribbean communities and Irish communities. In 1979 the British government passed the Credit Union Bill which was to regulate the legal structure of credit unions in Britain.
33 Pearson, 'Think globally, act locally', 158.
34 Ruth Pearson, 'Micro-credit as a path from welfare to work: The experience of the Full Circle Project, UK', in Beverly Lemire, Ruth Pearson and Gail Campbell (eds), *Women and Credit: Researching the past, refiguring the future* (Oxford, Berg, 2001), 176.
35 Michel Feher, *Rated Agency: Investee politics in a speculative age* (Cambridge, MA, MIT Press, 2018).

Select bibliography

Abbas, Tahir. 'Recent developments to British multicultural theory, policy and practice: The case of British Muslims', *Citizenship Studies*, 9 (2005), 153–66.

Addison, Paul. 'The intellectual origins of the Keynesian Revolution', *Twentieth Century British History*, 2 (1991), 89–94.

Adeney, Martin, and John Lloyd. *The Miners' Strike, 1984–5: Loss without limit* (London, Routledge and Kegan Paul, 1986).

Adkins, Lisa, Melinda Cooper and Martijn Konings. *The Asset Economy* (Cambridge, Polity, 2020).

Ahmed, Sara. 'The language of diversity', *Ethnic and Racial Studies*, 30 (2007), 235–56.

Altamura, Carlo Edoardo. *European Banks and the Rise of International Finance: The post-Bretton Woods era* (Abingdon, Routledge, 2017).

Anderson, Perry. 'The figures of descent', *New Left Review* (January–February 1987), 20–77.

Andrews, Aaron. 'Multiple deprivation, the inner city and the fracturing of the welfare state: Glasgow, c.1968–78', *Twentieth Century British History*, 29 (2018), 605–24.

Anthias, Floya, and Nira Yuval-Davis. *Racialised Boundaries: Race, nation, gender, colour and class and the anti-racist struggle* (London, Routledge, 1993).

Arestis, Philip, and Malcolm Sawyer. 'The economic analysis underlying the "Third Way"', *New Political Economy*, 6 (2001), 258–78.

Armstrong, Peter. 'Entrepreneurial competition in the pure case: John Bloom and Jim Elkins', in Peter Armstrong, *Critique of Entrepreneurship: People and policy* (Basingstoke, Palgrave Macmillan, 2005), 45–61.

Arrighi, Giovanni. *The Long Twentieth Century: Money, power, and origins of our times* (London, Verso, 1994).

Ascher, Kate. *The Politics of Privatisation* (Basingstoke, Macmillan, 1987).

Ashworth, W. *The History of the British Coal Industry, Volume 5, 1946–1982: The nationalised industry* (Oxford, Oxford University Press, 1986).

Atkinson, Anthony B. 'What is happening to the distribution of income in the UK?', *Proceedings of the British Academy*, 82 (1992), 317–51.

Atkinson, Anthony B. 'Targeting poverty', *New Economy* 5/1 (1998), 3–7.

Atkinson, Anthony B. 'The distribution of income in the UK and OECD countries in the twentieth century', *Oxford Review of Economic Policy*, 15 (Winter 1999), 56–75.

Atkinson, Anthony B. *Inequality: What can be done?* (Cambridge, MA, Harvard University Press, 2015).

Atkinson, Anthony B., and John Micklewright. 'Turning the screw: Benefits for the unemployed, 1979–1988', in Anthony B. Atkinson (ed.), *Poverty and Social Security* (Brighton, Harvester Wheatsheaf, 1989), 125–57.

Augar, Philip. *The Death of Gentlemanly Capitalism* (London, Penguin, 2000).

Aveyard, Stuart, Paul Corthorn and Sean O'Connell. *The Politics of Consumer Credit in the UK, 1938–1992* (Oxford, Oxford University Press, 2018).

Back, Les, Michael Keith, Azra Khan, Kalbir Shukra and John Solomos. 'The return of assimilationism: Race, multiculturalism and New Labour', *Sociological Research Online*, 7 (2002), 1–10.

Baggott, Rob. 'From confrontation to consultation? Pressure group relations from Thatcher to Major', *Parliamentary Affairs*, 48 (1995), 484–502.

Bale, Tim. *The Conservatives since 1945: The drivers of party change* (Oxford, Oxford University Press, 2012).

Ball, M. 'The 1980s property boom', *Environment and Planning A*, 26 (1994), 671–95.

Ball, Stuart. *Portrait of a Party: The Conservative Party in Britain, 1918–1945* (Oxford, Oxford University Press, 2013).
Barker, Kate. *Housing: Where's the plan?* (London, London Publishing Partnership, 2014).
Barr, Nicholas. *The Economics of the Welfare State* (London, Weidenfeld & Nicolson, 1987).
Barrett, Emma. 'King Caz: Cazenove, Thatcherism, and the 1980s financial revolution', *Twentieth Century British History*, 30 (2018), 108–31.
Barry, Norman. 'New Right', in Kevin Hickson (ed.), *The Political Thought of the Conservative Party since 1945* (Basingstoke, Palgrave Macmillan, 2005), 28–50.
Bassett, Keith. 'The sale of council houses as a political issue', *Policy and Politics*, 8 (August 1980), 290–307.
Beatty, Christine, and Stephen Fothergill. 'Labour market adjustment in areas of chronic industrial decline: The case of the UK coalfields', *Regional Studies*, 30 (1996), 627–40.
Beatty, Christine, and Stephen Fothergill. 'The impact on welfare and public finances of job loss in industrial Britain', *Regional Studies, Regional Science*, 4 (2017), 161–80.
Beaumont, Caitriona. *Housewives and Citizens: Domesticity and the women's movement in England, 1928–1964* (Manchester, Manchester University Press, 2013).
Beckett, Andy. *When the Lights Went Out: Britain in the seventies* (London, Faber and Faber, 2009).
Beckett, Andy. *Promised You a Miracle: Why 1980–82 made modern Britain* (London, Allen Lane, 2015).
Belfield, Chris, Daniel Chandler and Robert Joyce. *Housing: Trends in prices, costs and tenure* (London, Institute for Fiscal Studies, 2015).
Belfield, Chris, Jonathan Cribb, Andrew Hood and Robert Joyce. *Living Standards, Poverty and Inequality in the UK: 2016* (London, Institute for Fiscal Studies, 2016).
Bellringer, Christopher and Ranald Michie. 'Big Bang in the City of London: An international revolution or an accident?', *Financial History Review*, 21 (2014), 111–37.
Bevir, Mark. *New Labour: A critique* (Abingdon, Routledge, 2005).
Beynon, Huw, Rhys Davies and Steve Davies. 'Sources of variation in trade union membership across the UK: The case of Wales', *Industrial Relations Journal*, 43 (2012), 200–21.
Bhambra, Gurminder K. 'Whither Europe? Postcolonial versus neocolonial cosmopolitanism', *Interventions: International Journal of Postcolonial Studies*, 18 (2016), 187–202.
Biebricher, Thomas. *The Political Theory of Neoliberalism* (Stanford, CA, Stanford University Press, 2019).
Birch, Kean. *A Research Agenda for Neoliberalism* (Cheltenham, Edward Elgar, 2017).
Black, Lawrence. *Redefining British Politics: Culture, consumerism and participation, 1954–1970* (Basingstoke, Palgrave Macmillan, 2010).
Black, Lawrence. '1968 and all That(cher): Cultures of Conservatism and the New Right in Britain', in Anna von Der Glotz and Britta Waldschmidt-Nelson (eds), *Inventing the Silent Majority in Western Europe and the United States* (Cambridge, Cambridge University Press, 2017), 356–76.
Blackburn, Sheila. *A Fair Day's Wage for a Fair Day's Work? Sweated labour and the origins of minimum wage legislation in Britain* (Aldershot, Ashgate, 2007).
Blackhouse, Roger, Bradley Bateman, Tamotsu Nishizawa and Dieter Plehwe (eds). *Liberalism and the Welfare State: Economists and arguments for the welfare state* (Oxford, Oxford University Press, 2017).
Blakeley, Grace. *Stolen: How to save the world from financialisation* (London, Repeater, 2019).
Blundell, Richard, and Hilary Hoynes. 'Has "in-work" benefit reform helped the labour market?', in David Card, Richard Blundell and Richard Freeman (eds), *Seeking a Premier Economy: The economic effects of British reforms 1980–2000* (Chicago, University of Chicago Press, 2004), 411–45.
Blyth, Mark. *Great Transformations: Economic ideas and institutional change in the twentieth century* (Cambridge, Cambridge University Press, 2002).
Bogdanor, Vernon. 'Social democracy', in Anthony Seldon (ed.), *Blair's Britain, 1997–2007* (Cambridge, Cambridge University Press, 2008), 164–82.
Boleat, Mark, and Bev Taylor. *Housing in Britain*, 3rd ed. (London, Building Societies Association, 1993).
Booth, Alan. 'New revisionists and the Keynesian era in British economic policy', *Economic History Review*, 454 (2001), 346–66.
Boswell, Jonathan, and James Peter. *Capitalism in Contention: Business leaders and political economy in modern Britain* (Cambridge, Cambridge University Press, 1997), 154–7.

Boucher, Ellen. 'Anticipating Armageddon: Nuclear risk and the neoliberal sensibility in Thatcher's Britain', *American Historical Review*, 124 (2019), 1221–45.
Boughton, John. *Municipal Dreams: The rise and fall of council housing* (London, Verso, 2018).
Bourke, Richard. *Peace in Ireland: The war of ideas* (London, Pimlico, 2003).
Bowden, Sue, and Avner Offer. 'Household appliances and the use of time: The United States and Britain since the 1920s', *Economic History Review*, 47 (1994), 725–48.
Bowlby, Roger. 'Union policy towards minimum wage legislation in post-war Britain', *Industrial and Labour Relations Review*, 11 (1957), 72–84.
Brennan, George, and Alan Milward. *Britain's Place in the World: Import controls, 1945–60* (London, Routledge, 2003).
Brittan, Samuel. 'Redistributive market liberalism', in Samuel Brittan, *Essays: Moral, political, and economic* (Edinburgh, Edinburgh University Press, 1998), 22–32.
Bröckling, Ulrich. *The Entrepreneurial Self: Fabricating a new type of subject* (London, SAGE, 2016).
Brooke, Stephen. 'Living in "new times": Historicizing 1980s Britain', *History Compass*, 12 (2014), 20–32.
Brooke, Stephen. 'Space, emotions and the everyday: The affective ecology of 1980s London', *Twentieth Century British History*, 28 (2017), 110–42.
Brown, Joan. *Victims or Villains?: Social security benefits in unemployment* (York, Joseph Rowntree Memorial Trust, 1990).
Brown, Wendy. *Undoing the Demos: Neoliberalism's stealth revolution* (Brooklyn, NY, Zone Books, 2015).
Brown, William. 'Industrial relations in Britain under New Labour, 1997–2010: A post mortem', *Journal of Industrial Relations*, 53 (2011), 402–13.
Browne, James, and Andrew Hood. *Living Standards, Poverty and Inequality in the UK: 2015–16 to 2020–21* (London, Institute for Fiscal Studies, 2016).
Buchanan, John, Julie Froud, Sukhdev Johal, Adam Leaver and Karel Williams. 'Undisclosed and unsustainable: Problems of the UK National Business Model' (Manchester, Centre for Research in Economic and Social Change, 2009).
Buettner, Elizabeth. '"Going for an Indian": South Asian restaurants and the limits of multiculturalism in Britain', *Journal of Modern History*, 80 (2008), 865–901.
Bulpitt, Jim. 'The discipline of the new democracy: Mrs Thatcher's domestic statecraft', *Political Studies*, 34 (1986), 19–39.
Burch, Jessica. '"Soap and hope": Direct sales and the culture of work and capitalism in postwar America', *Enterprise & Society*, 17 (2016), 741–51.
Burgin, Angus. *The Great Persuasion* (Cambridge, MA, Harvard University Press, 2012).
Burn, Gary. *The Re-Emergence of Global Finance* (London, Palgrave Macmillan, 2006).
Burnett, John. *A Social History of Housing, 1815–1985*, 2nd ed. (London, Methuen, 1986).
Cahill, Damian. *The End of Laissez-Faire? On the durability of embedded neoliberalism* (Cheltenham, Edward Elgar, 2014).
Cahill, Damien, Melinda Cooper, Martijn Konings and David Primrose (eds), *The SAGE Handbook of Neoliberalism* (Los Angeles, SAGE, 2018).
Cahill, Damien, and Martijn Konings. *Neoliberalism* (Cambridge, Polity Press, 2017).
Cain, P. J., and A. G. Hopkins. *British Imperialism, 1688–2015*, 5th ed. (Abingdon, Routledge, 2016).
Calder, Angus. *The People's War: Britain 1939–1945* (London, Deutsch, 1969).
Campbell, Jim, and Emily Thomson. 'Changing role of women in the Scottish economy', in Kenneth Gibb, Duncan Maclennan, Des McNulty and Michael Comerford (eds), *The Scottish Economy* (London, Routledge, 2018), 135–51.
Campbell, John. *Edward Heath: A biography* (London, Cape, 1993).
Cassis, Youssef. *Capitals of Capital: The rise and fall of international financial centres* (Cambridge, Cambridge University Press, 2010).
Cerny, Philip G. 'The dynamics of financial globalization: Technology, market structure, and policy response', *Policy Sciences*, 27 (1994), 319–42.
Chiapello, Eve, and Luc Boltanski. *The New Spirit of Capitalism*, trans. Gregory Elliot (London, Verso, 2007).
Child, Phil. 'Landlordism, rent regulation, and the Labour Party in mid-twentieth century Britain, 1950–64', *Twentieth Century British History*, 29 (2018), 79–103.
Christensen, John, Nicholas Shaxson and Duncan Wigan. 'The finance curse: Britain and the world economy', *British Journal of Politics and International Relations*, 18 (2016), 255–69.

Christiaens, Tim. 'The entrepreneur of the self beyond Foucault's neoliberal homo oeconomicus', *European Journal of Social Theory*, 23 (2020), 493–511.

Christophers, Brett. *The New Enclosure: The appropriation of public land in neoliberal Britain* (New York, Verso, 2018).

Christophers, Brett. *Rentier Capitalism: Who owns the economy, and who pays for it?* (London, Verso, 2020).

Chwalisz, Claudia, and Patrick Diamond (eds). *The Predistribution Agenda: Tackling inequality and supporting sustainable growth* (London, I.B. Tauris, 2015).

Chwieroth, Jeffrey M. 'Testing and measuring the role of ideas: The case of neoliberalism in the International Monetary Fund', *International Studies Quarterly*, 51 (2007), 5–30.

Clapson, Mark. *Invisible Green Suburbs, Brave New Towns: Social change and urban dispersal in postwar England* (Manchester, Manchester University Press, 1998).

Clarke, Peter. *Hope and Glory: Britain 1900–1990* (London, Penguin, 1996; rev. edn 2004).

Clegg, Daniel. 'The demise of tax credits', *Political Quarterly*, 86 (2015), 493–9.

Clift, Ben, and Jim Tomlinson. 'Credible Keynesianism? New Labour macroeconomic policy and the political economy of coarse tuning', *British Journal of Political Science*, 37 (2007), 47–69.

Coates, David. *The Labour Party and the struggle for socialism* (Cambridge, Cambridge University Press, 1975).

Coates, David. 'The UK: Less a liberal market economy, more a post-imperial one', *Capital & Class*, 30 (2014), 171–82.

Cockett, Richard. *Thinking the Unthinkable: Think-tanks and the economic counter-revolution, 1931–83* (London, HarperCollins, 1994).

Cockett, Richard. 'The New Right and the 1960s: "The Dialectics of Liberation"', in Geoff Andrews (ed.), *New Left, New Right and Beyond: Taking the sixties seriously* (Basingstoke, Palgrave, 1999), 85–105.

Cohen, Joseph, and Miguel Centeno. 'Neoliberalism and patterns of economic performance, 1980–2000', *The Annals of the American Academy of Political and Social Science*, 606 (2006), 37–41.

Cooper, Melinda. *Family Values: Between neoliberalism and the new social conservatism* (New York, Zone Books, 2017).

Copley, Jack. 'Why were capital controls abandoned? The case of Britain's abolition of exchange controls, 1977–1979', *British Journal of Politics and International Relations*, 21 (2019), 403–20.

Corry, Dan. 'Where is the British centre-left now on macro policy?', *Renewal*, 21 (2013), 34–45.

Corthorn, Paul. *Enoch Powell: Politics and ideas in modern Britain* (Oxford, Oxford University Press, 2019).

Crafts, Nicholas, Ian Gazeley and Andrew Newell. *Work and Pay in 20th Century Britain* (Oxford, Oxford University Press, 2007).

Craig, David. '"High politics" and the "new political history"', *Historical Journal*, 53 (2010), 453–75.

Creighton, Colin. 'The rise and decline of the "male breadwinner family" in Britain', *Cambridge Journal of Economics*, 23 (1999), 519–41.

Crewe, Ivor. 'Values: The crusade that failed', in Dennis Kavanagh and Anthony Seldon (eds), *The Thatcher Effect* (Oxford, Oxford University Press, 1989), 239–50.

Crouch, Colin. 'Privatised Keynesianism: An unacknowledged policy regime', *British Journal of Politics and International Relations*, 11 (2009), 382–99.

Crouch, Colin. *The Strange Non-Death of Neoliberalism* (Cambridge, Polity Press, 2011).

Crowson, Nicholas J. 'Revisiting the 1977 Housing (Homeless Persons) Act: Westminster, Whitehall, and the homelessness lobby', *Twentieth Century British History*, 24 (2013), 424–47.

Curtice, John. 'Thermostat or weathervane? Public reactions to spending and redistribution under New Labour', in Alison Park, John Curtice, Katarina Thomson, Miranda Philips, Elizabeth Clery and Sarah Butt (eds), *British Social Attitudes: The 26th report* (London, SAGE, 2010), 19–38.

Cutler, Anthony, Karel Williams and John Williams. *Keynes, Beveridge and Beyond* (London, Routledge and Kegan Paul, 1986).

Daddow, Oliver, Christopher Gifford and Ben Wellings. 'The battle of Bruges: Margaret Thatcher, the Foreign Office and the unravelling of British European policy', *Political Research Exchange*, 1 (2019), 1–24.

Dardot, Pierre, and Christian Laval. *The New Way of the World: On neoliberal society*, trans. Gregory Elliot (London, Verso, 2013).

Daunton, Martin. *A Property-Owning Democracy? Housing in Britain* (London, Faber and Faber, 1987).

Daunton, Martin. *Just Taxes: The politics of taxation in Britain, 1914–1979* (Cambridge, Cambridge University Press, 2002).
Davies, Aled. '"Right to Buy": The development of a Conservative housing policy, 1945–1980', *Contemporary British History*, 27 (2013), 421–44.
Davies, Aled. *The City of London and Social Democracy: The political economy of finance in Britain, 1959–1979* (Oxford, Oxford University Press, 2017).
Davies, Aled. 'Pension funds and the politics of ownership in Britain, c.1970–86', *Twentieth Century British History*, 30 (2019), 93–105.
Davies, Aled, James Freeman and Hugh Pemberton. '"Everyman a capitalist" or "free to choose"? Exploring the tensions within Thatcherite individualism', *Historical Journal*, 61 (2018), 93–105.
Davies, Paul, and Mark Freedland. *Labour Legislation and Public Policy: A contemporary history* (Oxford, Clarendon Press, 1993).
Davies, Stephen M. 'Promoting productivity in the National Health Service, 1950 to 1966', *Contemporary British History*, 31 (2017), 47–68.
Davies, William. *The Limits of Neoliberalism* (London, SAGE, 2014).
Davin, Anna. 'Imperialism and motherhood', *History Workshop Journal*, 5 (1978), 9–65.
Davin, Anna. 'Models of equality for women: The case of state support for children in twentieth-century Britain', in Gisela Bock and Pat Thane (eds), *Maternity and Gender Policies: Women and the rise of the European welfare states 1880s–1950s* (London, Routledge, 1991), 73–92.
Davis, Angela. *Pre-School Childcare in England, 1939–2010: Theory, practice and experience* (Manchester, Manchester University Press, 2015).
Davis, Gerald F., and Suntae Kim. 'Financialization of the economy', *Annual Review of Sociology*, 41 (2015), 203–21.
Davis, John. 'The London cabbie and the rise of the Essex man', in Clare V. J. Griffiths, James J. Nott and William Whyte (eds), *Classes, Cultures, and Politics: Essays on British history for Ross McKibbin* (Oxford, Oxford University Press, 2011), 102–18.
Davison, Sally, and George Shire. 'Race, migration and neoliberalism: How neoliberalism benefits from discourses of exclusion', *Soundings: A Journal of Politics and Culture*, 59 (Spring 2015), 81–95.
Deacon, Alan. *Perspectives on Welfare: Ideas, ideologies and policy debates* (Buckingham, Open University Press, 2002).
Delap, Lucy. 'Feminist bookshops, reading cultures and the women's liberation movement in Great Britain, c.1974–2000', *History Workshop Journal*, 81 (2016), 171–96.
Denham, Andrew, and Mark Garnett. *Keith Joseph* (Chesham, Acumen, 2001).
Denham, Andrew, and Mark Garnett. 'Sir Keith Joseph and the undoing of British Conservatism', *Journal of Political Ideologies*, 7 (2002), 57–75.
Denman, James, and Paul MacDonald. 'Unemployment statistics from 1881 to the present day', *Labour Market Trends*, 104 (January 1996), 5–18.
Desai, Radhika, 'Second-hand dealers in ideas: Think-tanks and Thatcherite hegemony', *New Left Review*, 203 (1994), 27–64.
Dickens, Richard. 'Child poverty in Britain: Past lessons and future prospects', *National Institute Economic Review*, 218 (2011), R7–R19.
Doling, John, and Richard Ronald. 'Home ownership and asset-based welfare', *Journal of Housing and the Built Environment*, 25 (2010), 165–73.
Dolphin, Tony. 'Don't bank on it: The financialisation of the UK economy', *IPPR* (2012).
Dorey, Peter. *British Conservatism: The politics and philosophy of inequality* (London, I.B. Tauris, 2011).
Dorey, Peter. '"It was just like arming to face the threat of Hitler in the late 1930s": The Ridley Report and the Conservative Party's preparations for the 1984–85 miners' strike', *Historical Studies in Industrial Relations*, 34 (2013), 173–214.
Drummond, Ian M. *The Floating Pound and the Sterling Area, 1931–39* (Cambridge, Cambridge University Press, 1981).
Du Gay, Paul. *Consumption and Identity at Work* (Los Angeles, SAGE, 1996).
Duménil, Gérard, and Dominique Lévy. 'Costs and benefits of neoliberalism: A class analysis', *Review of International Political Economy*, 8 (2001), 578–607.
Duménil, Gérard, and Dominique Lévy. *Capital Resurgent* (Cambridge, MA, Harvard University Press, 2004).
Duménil, Gérard, and Dominique Lévy. *The Crisis of Neoliberalism* (Cambridge, MA, Harvard University Press, 2011).

Dunton, Mark. 'Public relations and the Price Commission, 1973–74', *Archives*, 52 (2017), 12–25.
Durham, Martin. *Sex and Politics: The family and morality in the Thatcher years* (Basingstoke, Macmillan, 1991).
Dyhouse, Carol. *Feminism and the Family in England, 1880–1939* (Oxford, Basil Blackwell, 1989).
Eatwell, John. *Whatever Happened to Britain? The economics of decline* (London, Duckworth, 1982).
Edgerton, David. *England and the Aeroplane: Militarism, modernity and machines* (London, Penguin, 1991, 2013).
Edgerton, David. *Warfare State: Britain, 1920–1970* (Cambridge, Cambridge University Press, 2005).
Edgerton, David. *Britain's War Machine: Weapons, resources and experts in the Second World War* (London, Allen Lane, 2011).
Edgerton, David. *The Rise and Fall of the British Nation: A twentieth-century history* (London, Allen Lane, 2018).
Edgerton, David, and Kirsty Hughes. 'The poverty of science: A critical analysis of scientific and industrial policy under Mrs Thatcher', *Public Administration*, 67 (1989), 419–33.
Edwards, Amy. '"Manufacturing capitalists": The wider share ownership council and the problem of "popular capitalism", 1958–92', *Twentieth Century British History*, 27 (2016), 100–23.
Edwards, Amy. '"Financial consumerism": Citizenship, consumerism and capital ownership in the 1980s', *Contemporary British History*, 31 (2017), 210–29.
Eichengreen, Barry. *Globalizing Capital: A history of the international monetary system*, 2nd ed. (Princeton, NJ, Princeton University Press, 2008).
Eichengreen, Barry. *Exorbitant Privilege: The rise and fall of the dollar and the future of the international monetary system* (Oxford, Oxford University Press, 2011).
Ellis, David. 'On taking (back) control: Lessons from community action in 1970s Britain', *Renewal*, 25 (2017), 53–61.
Emmenegger, Patrick, *The Age of Dualization* (Oxford, Oxford University Press, 2012).
Evans, Stephen, 'The not so odd couple: Margaret Thatcher and One Nation Conservatism', *Contemporary British History*, 23 (2009), 101–21.
Farrall, Stephen, and Colin Hay. *The Legacy of Thatcherism: Assessing and exploring Thatcherite social and economic policies* (Oxford, Oxford University Press, 2014).
Feher, Michel. *Rated Agency: Investee politics in a speculative age* (Cambridge, MA, MIT Press, 2018).
Fekete, Liz. 'The emergence of xeno-racism', *Race and Class*, 43 (2001), 23–40.
Feurer, Rosemary. 'The meaning of "sisterhood": The British women's movement and protective labour legislation', *Victorian Studies*, 31 (1988), 233–60.
Figes, Kate. *Because of Her Sex: The myth of equality for women in Britain* (London, Macmillan, 1994).
Findley, Richard. 'The Conservative Party and defeat: The significance of resale price maintenance for the general election of 1964', *Twentieth Century British History*, 12 (2001), 327–53.
Fleming, Peter. *The Death of Homo Economicus* (London, Pluto Press, 2017), 8–10.
Fleury, Jean-Baptiste, and Alain Marciano. 'The sound of silence: A review essay of Nancy MacLean's *Democracy in Chains*', *Journal of Economic Literature*, 56 (2018), 1492–537.
Foden, Mike, Steve Fothergill and Tony Gore. *The State of the Coalfields: Economic conditions in the former mining communities of England, Scotland and Wales* (Sheffield, Coalfields Regeneration Trust and Sheffield Hallam University, 2014).
Forder, James. *Macroeconomics and the Phillips Curve* (Oxford, Oxford University Press, 2014).
Forder, James, and Kardin Sømme. 'Explaining the fame of Friedman's Presidential Address', *Cambridge Journal of Economics*, 43 (2019), 1683–700.
Forrest, Ray, and Alan Murie. *Selling the Welfare State: The privatisation of public housing* (London, Routledge, 1988).
'Forum I: Neoliberalism as a concept of contemporary history', *Journal of Modern European History*, 17 (2019), 381–411.
Foster, John Bellamy. 'The financialization of capitalism', *Monthly Review*, 11 (2007), 8–10.
Foucault, Michel. *The Birth of Biopolitics: Lectures at the Collège de France, 1978–1979*, trans. Graham Burchell (London, Routledge, 2008).
Foundational Economic Collective. *Foundational Economy: The infrastructure of everyday life* (Manchester, Manchester University Press, 2018).
Fourcade, Marion. *Economists and Societies: Discipline and profession in the United States, Britain and France, 1890s to 1990s* (Princeton, NJ, Princeton University Press, 2009).

Francis, Matthew. '"A crusade to enfranchise the many?" Thatcherism and the "property-owning democracy"', *Twentieth Century British History*, 23 (2012), 275–97.

Frank, Thomas. *One Market under God: Extreme capitalism, market populism and the end of economic democracy* (London, Vintage, 2002).

Franklin, Jane. 'After modernisation: Gender, the Third Way and the new politics', in Anna Coote (ed.), *The New Gender Agenda* (London, IPPR, 2000), 15–22.

Fraser, Nancy. 'From redistribution to recognition? Dilemmas of justice in a "post-socialist" age', *New Left Review*, 212 (1995), 68–93.

Fraser, Nancy. 'From progressive neoliberalism to Trump – and beyond', *American Affairs*, 1/4 (2017), 46–64.

Freeden, Michael. 'The stranger at the feast: Ideology and public policy in twentieth century Britain', *Twentieth Century British History*, 1 (1990), 9–34.

Freeden, Michael. *Ideologies and Political Theory: A conceptual approach* (Oxford, Oxford University Press, 1996).

Freeman, Carla. 'Embodying and affecting neoliberalism', in Francis E. Mascia-Lees (ed.), *A Companion to the Anthropology of the Body and Embodiment* (Oxford, Wiley-Blackwell, 2011), 353–69.

Freeman, James. 'Reconsidering "set the people free": Neoliberalism and freedom rhetoric in Churchill's Conservative Party', *Twentieth Century British History*, 29 (2018), 522–46.

French, Mike. 'Slowly becoming sales promotion men? Negotiating the career of the sales representative in Britain, 1920–1970s', *Enterprise & Society*, 17 (2016), 39–79.

Frieden, Jeffry A. *Global Capitalism: Its rise and fall in the twentieth century* (New York, Norton, 2007).

Froud, Julie, Sukhdev Johal, Johnna Montgomerie and Karel Williams. 'Escaping the tyranny of earned income? The failure of finance as social innovation', *New Political Economy*, 15 (2010), 147–64.

Fuller, Gregory W. *The Great Debt Transformation: Households, financialization, and policy responses* (Basingstoke, Palgrave Macmillan, 2016).

Gall, Gregor. 'Still brothers and sisters in arms? A note on trends in union membership and statistics', *Scottish Labour History*, 53 (2018), 73–83.

Gamble, Andrew. *The Conservative Nation* (London, Routledge and Kegan Paul, 1974).

Gamble, Andrew. *Britain in Decline: Economic policy, political strategy and the British state* (London, Macmillan, 1981).

Gamble, Andrew. *The Free Economy and the Strong State*, 2nd ed. (Basingstoke, Palgrave, 1994).

Gamble, Andrew. 'Neoliberalism', *Capital and Class*, 25 (2001), 127–34.

Gamble, Andrew. 'Europe and America', in Ben Jackson and Robert Saunders (eds), *Making Thatcher's Britain* (Cambridge, Cambridge University Press, 2012), 218–33.

Gazeley, Ian. *Poverty in Britain, 1900–1965* (Basingstoke, Palgrave Macmillan, 2003).

Gazeley, Ian, Andrew Newell, Kevin Reynolds and Rebecca Searle. 'The poor and the poorest, 50 years on: Evidence from British Household Expenditure surveys of the 1950s and 1960s', *Journal of the Royal Statistical Society*, Series A, 180 (2016), 455–74.

Germann, Julian. *Unwitting Architect: German primacy and the origins of neoliberalism* (Stanford, CA, Stanford University Press, 2021).

Gerstle, Gary. 'The rise and fall(?) of America's neoliberal order', *Transactions of the Royal Historical Society*, 28 (2018), 241–64.

Gibbs, Ewan. 'The moral economy of the Scottish coalfields: Managing deindustrialization under nationalization, c. 1947–1983', *Enterprise and Society*, 19 (2018), 124–52.

Gibbs, Ewan, and Jim Phillips. 'Who owns a factory? Caterpillar tractors in Uddingston, 1956–1987', *Historical Studies in Industrial Relations*, 39 (2018), 111–37.

Giddens, Anthony. *The Third Way: The renewal of social democracy* (Cambridge, Polity, 1998).

Giddens, Anthony. *The Third Way and Its Critics* (Cambridge, Polity Press, 2000).

Gill, Rosalind. 'Culture and subjectivity in neoliberal and postfeminist times', *Subjectivity*, 25 (2008), 432–45.

Gilroy, Paul. 'The end of anti-racism', *Journal of Ethnic and Migration Studies*, 17 (1990), 71–83.

Gilroy, Paul. *"There Ain't No Black in the Union Jack": The cultural politics of race and nation* (London, Routledge, 1992).

Gilroy, Paul. '". . . We got to get over before we go under . . .": Fragments for a history of Black vernacular neoliberalism', *New Formations*, 80/81 (2013), 23–38.

Glew, Helen. *Gender, Rhetoric and Regulation: Women's work in the civil service and the London County Council, 1900–55* (Manchester, Manchester University Press, 2016).

Glyn, Andrew. 'The economic case against pit closures', in D. Cooper and T. Hopper (eds), *Debating Coal Closures: Economic calculation in the coal dispute, 1984–5* (Cambridge, Cambridge University Press, 1988), 57–94.
Glyn, Andrew. *Capitalism Unleashed: Finance, globalisation and welfare* (Oxford, Oxford University Press, 2008).
Glyn, Andrew (ed.). *Social Democracy in Neoliberal Times: The left and economic policy since 1980* (Oxford, Oxford University Press, 2001).
Glyn, Andrew, and Stewart Wood. 'New Labour's economic policy', in Andrew Glyn (ed.), *Social Democracy in Neoliberal Times: The left and economic policy since 1980* (Oxford, Oxford University Press, 2001), 200–22.
Goldberg, David. *The Threat of Race: Reflections on racial neoliberalism* (Oxford, Wiley-Blackwell, 2009).
Goos, Maarten, and Alan Manning. 'Lousy and lovely jobs: The rising polarization of jobs in Britain', *The Review of Economics and Statistics*, 89 (2007), 118–33.
Gosseye, Janina. 'Milton Keynes' centre: The apotheosis of the British post-war consensus or the apostle of neo-liberalism?', *History of Retailing and Consumption*, 1 (2015), 209–29.
Grant, Wyn. 'Business interests and the British Conservative Party', *Government and Opposition*, 18 (1980), 143–61.
Grant, Wyn. 'Representing capital: The role of the CBI', in Roger King (ed.), *Capital and Politics* (London, Routledge and Kegan Paul, 1983), 69–84.
Grant, Wyn, and David Marsh. *The Confederation of British Industry* (London, Hodder and Stoughton, 1977).
Green, E. H. H. 'The Treasury resignations of 1958: A reconsideration', *Twentieth Century British History*, 11 (2000), 409–30.
Green, E. H. H. *Ideologies of Conservatism: Conservative political ideas in the twentieth century* (Oxford, Oxford University Press, 2002).
Green, E. H. H. *Thatcher* (London, Hodder and Stoughton, 2006).
Green, E. H. H. 'The Conservative Party and Keynes', in E. H. H. Green and Duncan Tanner (eds), *The Strange Survival of Liberal England: Political leaders, moral values and the reception of economic debate* (Cambridge, Cambridge University Press, 2007), 186–211.
Green, Jeremy. 'Anglo-American development, the Euromarkets, and the deeper origins of neoliberal deregulation', *Review of International Studies*, 42 (2016), 425–49.
Greenhalgh, James. *Reconstructing Modernity: Space, power and governance in mid-twentieth century British cities* (Manchester, Manchester University Press, 2018).
Gregg, Paul, Maria Gutiérrez-Domènech and Jane Waldfogel. 'The employment of married mothers in Great Britain, 1974–2000', *Economica*, 74 (2007), 842–64.
Grimley, Matthew. 'Thatcherism, morality and religion', in Ben Jackson and Robert Saunders (eds), *Making Thatcher's Britain* (Cambridge, Cambridge University Press, 2012), 74–94.
Grover, Chris. *Social Security and Wage Poverty: Historical and policy aspects of supplementing wages in Britain and beyond* (Basingstoke, Palgrave Macmillan, 2016).
Hakim, Catherine. 'Five feminist myths about women's employment', *British Journal of Sociology*, 46 (1995), 429–55.
Hall, Peter A. 'The movement from Keynesianism to monetarism: Institutional analysis and British economic policy in the 1970s', in Sven Steinmo, Kathleen Thelen and Frank Longstreth (eds), *Structuring Politics: Historical institutionalism in comparative analysis* (Cambridge, Cambridge University Press, 1992), 90–113.
Hall, Peter A. 'Policy paradigms, social learning and the state: The case of economic policy making in Britain', *Comparative Politics*, 25 (1993), 284–92.
Hall, Peter A., and David Soskice (eds). *Varieties of Capitalism: The institutional foundations of comparative advantage* (Oxford, Oxford University Press, 2001).
Hall, Stuart. *The Hard Road to Renewal: Thatcherism and the crisis of the left* (London, Verso, 1988).
Hall, Stuart. 'Aspiration and attitude: Reflections on Black Britain in the nineties', *New Formations*, 33 (1998), 38–46.
Hall, Stuart. 'From Scarman to Stephen Lawrence', *History Workshop Journal*, 48 (1999), 187–97.
Hall, Stuart. 'The neoliberal revolution', *Soundings*, 48 (2011), 9–27.
Hall, Stuart. *Selected Political Writings: The great moving right show and other essays* (Durham, NC, Duke University Press, 2017).
Hall, Stuart, and Martin Jacques (eds). *The Politics of Thatcherism* (London, Lawrence and Wishart, 1983).

Halperin, Anna Danzier. '"Cinderella of the education system": Margaret Thatcher's plan for nursery expansion in 1970s Britain', *Twentieth Century British History*, 29 (2018), 284–308.

Hamburger, Jacob, and Daniel Stienmetz-Jenkins. 'Why did neoconservatives join forces with neoliberals? Irving Kristol from critic to ally of free-market economics', *Global Intellectual History*, 6 (2021), 215–30.

Hamnett, Chris. 'Housing the two nations: Socio-tenurial polarization in England and Wales, 1961–81', *Urban Studies*, 21 (1984), 389–405.

Harmon, Mark D. *The British Labour Government and the 1976 IMF Crisis* (Basingstoke, Palgrave Macmillan, 1998).

Harris, José. 'Enterprise and welfare states: A comparative perspective', *Transactions of the Royal Historical Society*, 40 (1990), 175–95.

Harris, José. 'From poor law to welfare state: A European perspective', in Donald Winch and Patrick K. O'Brien (eds), *The Political Economy of British Historical Experience, 1688–1914* (Oxford, Oxford University Press, 2002), 409–37.

Harris, Nigel. *Competition and the Corporate Society: Conservatives, the state and industry, 1945–64* (Abingdon, Routledge, 2006).

Harvey, David. *A Brief History of Neoliberalism* (Oxford, Oxford University Press, 2005).

Hastings, Anette, Nick Bailey, Glen Bramley and Maria Gannon. 'Austerity urbanism in England: The "regressive redistribution" of local government services and the impact on the poor and marginalised', *Environment and Planning*, 49 (2017), 2007–24.

Hay, Colin. 'Labour's Thatcherite revisionism: Playing the "politics of catch-up"', *Political Studies*, 42 (1994), 700–7.

Hay, Colin. 'Narrating crisis: The discursive construction of the winter of discontent', *Sociology*, 30 (1996), 253–77.

Hay, Colin. *The Political Economy of New Labour* (Manchester, Manchester University Press, 1999).

Hay, Colin. 'Chronicles of a death foretold: The winter of discontent and the construction of the crisis of British Keynesianism', *Parliamentary Affairs*, 63 (2010), 446–70.

Hay, Colin. *The Failure of Anglo-Liberal Capitalism* (London, Palgrave Macmillan, 2013).

Hay, Colin, and Nicola Smith. 'The story of a North Sea bubble: The strange demise of the Anglo-liberal growth model in the United Kingdom and Ireland', *European Political Science Review*, 6 (2013), 401–30.

Heath, Joseph, and Andrew Potter. *The Rebel Sell: How the counterculture became consumer culture* (Chichester, Capstone, 2006).

Heffernan, Richard. *New Labour and Thatcherism* (Basingstoke, Palgrave, 2001).

Heinemann, Kieran. 'Investment, speculation and popular stock market engagement in 20th-century Britain', *Archiv für Sozialgeschichte*, 56 (2016), 249–72.

Heinemann, Kieran. *Playing the Market: Retail investment and speculation in twentieth-century Britain* (Oxford, Oxford University Press, 2021).

Helén, Ilpo. 'Review essay: Welfare and its vicissitudes: Nikolas Rose, *Powers of Freedom*, Mitchell Dean, *Governmentality*', *Acta Sociologica*, 43 (2000), 157–64.

Helleiner, Eric. *States and the Reemergence of Global Finance* (Ithaca, NY, Cornell University Press, 1994).

Hickson, Kevin. *The IMF Crisis of 1976 and British Politics* (London, I.B. Tauris, 2005).

Hickson, Kevin. 'Lord Coleraine: The neglected prophet of the New Right', *Journal of Political Ideologies*, 14 (2009), 173–87.

Hien, Joseph, and Christian Joerges (eds). *Ordo Liberalism, Law and the Rule of Economics* (London, Bloomsbury, 2017).

Hills, John, Tom Sefton and Kitty Stewart (eds). *Towards a More Equal Society: Poverty, inequality and policy since 1997* (Bristol, Policy Press, 2009).

Hilton, Matthew, Chris Moores and Florence Sutcliffe-Braithwaite. '*New Times* revisited: Britain in the 1980s', *Contemporary British History*, 31 (2017), 145–65.

Hinton, James. *Nine Wartime Lives: Mass Observation and the making of the modern self* (Oxford, Oxford University Press, 2010).

Hinton, James. *Seven Lives from Mass Observation: Britain in the late twentieth century* (Oxford, Oxford University Press, 2016).

Hirschmann, Daniel, and Elizabeth Popp Berman. 'Do economists make policies? On the political effects of economics', *Socio-Economic Review*, 12/4 (2014), 779–811.

Holdo, Markus. 'Cooptation and non-cooptation: Elite strategies in response to social protest', *Social Movement Studies*, 18 (2019), 444–62.

Holmes, Martin. *The First Thatcher Government 1979–1983: Contemporary Conservatism and economic change* (Brighton, Wheatsheaf, 1985).
Holmes, Martin. *The Failure of the Heath Government*, 2nd ed. (Basingstoke, Macmillan, 1997).
Homer, Andrew. 'Creating new communities: The role of the neighbourhood unit in post-war British planning', *Contemporary British History*, 14 (2000), 63–80.
Hoskyns, John. *Just in Time: Inside the Thatcher revolution* (London, Aurum Press, 2000).
Howell, Chris. *Trade Unions and the State: The construction of industrial relations institutions in Britain, 1890–2000* (Princeton, NJ, Princeton University Press, 2005).
Howell, David. *British Social Democracy: A study in development and decay* (London, Croom Helm, 1976).
Howell, David. 'Defiant dominoes: Working miners and the 1984–5 strike', in Ben Jackson and Robert Saunders (eds), *Making Thatcher's Britain* (Cambridge, Cambridge University Press, 2012), 148–64.
Hunt, Tony, and Liam Stanley. 'From "there is no alternative" to "maybe there are alternatives": Five challenges to economic orthodoxy after the crash', *Political Quarterly*, 90/3 (2009), 479–87.
Hutton, Will. 'New Keynesianism and New Labour', in Andrew Gamble and Tony Wright (eds), *The New Social Democracy* (Oxford, Wiley/Political Quarterly, 1999).
Jackson, Ben. 'Revisionism reconsidered: "Property-owning democracy" and egalitarian strategy in post-war Britain', *Twentieth Century British History*, 16 (2005), 416–40.
Jackson, Ben. *Equality and the British Left: A study in progressive political thought, 1900–64* (Manchester, Manchester University Press, 2007).
Jackson, Ben. 'At the origins of neo-liberalism: The free economy and the strong state, 1930–47', *Historical Journal*, 53 (2010), 129–51.
Jackson, Ben. 'Freedom, the common good, and the rule of law: Lippmann and Hayek on economic planning', *Journal of the History of Ideas*, 73 (2012), 47–68.
Jackson, Ben. 'The think-tank archipelago: Thatcherism and neo-liberalism', in Ben Jackson and Robert Saunders (eds), *Making Thatcher's Britain* (Cambridge, Cambridge University Press, 2012), 43–61.
Jackson, Ben. 'Social democracy', in Michael Freeden and Marc Stears (eds), *The Oxford Handbook of Political Ideologies* (Oxford, Oxford University Press, 2013), 348–63.
Jackson, Ben. 'Currents of neo-liberalism: British political ideologies and the New Right, c.1955–1979', *English Historical Review*, 131 (2016), 823–50.
Jackson, Ben. 'Free markets and feminism: The neo-liberal defence of the male bread-winner model in British politics, 1980–97', *Women's History Review*, 28 (2019), 297–316.
Jackson, Ben. *The Case for Scottish Independence: A history of nationalist political thought in modern Scotland* (Cambridge, Cambridge University Press, 2020).
Jackson, Ben. 'Putting neoliberalism in its place', *Modern Intellectual History*, 17 February 2021, doi: 10.1017/S1479244321000032.
Jackson, Ben, and Robert Saunders. 'Introduction', in Ben Jackson and Robert Saunders (eds), *Making Thatcher's Britain* (Cambridge, Cambridge University Press, 2012), 1–22.
Jenkins, Jean. 'Hands not wanted: Closure, and the moral economy of protest, Treorchy, South Wales', *Historical Studies in Industrial Relations*, 38 (2017), 1–36.
Jenkins, Peter. *Mrs Thatcher's Revolution* (London, Cape, 1987).
Jessop, Bob. 'From Thatcherism to New Labour: Neo-liberalism, workfarism, and labour market regulation', in Henk Overbeek (ed.), *The Political Economy of European Employment: European integration and the transnationalization of the (un)employment question* (London, Routledge, 2003), 137–53.
Jessop, Bob, Kevin Bonnett, Tom Ling and Simon Bromley. *Thatcherism: A tale of two nations* (Cambridge, Polity Press, 1988).
Jewson, Nick, and David Mason. 'The theory and practice of equal opportunities policies: Liberal and radical approaches', *Sociological Review*, 34 (1986), 307–34.
Jones, Ben. 'Slum clearance, privatization, and residualization: The practices and politics of council housing in mid-twentieth-century England', *Twentieth Century British History*, 21 (2010), 510–39.
Jones, Ben. *The Working Class in Mid Twentieth-Century England: Community, identity and social memory* (Manchester, Manchester University Press, 2012).
Jones, Harriet. 'The Cold War and the Santa Claus syndrome', in Martin Francis and Ina Zweiniger-Bargielowska (eds), *Conservatives and British Society, 1880–1990* (Cardiff, University of Wales Press, 1996), 240–54.

Jones, Harriet, and Michael Kandiah (eds). *The Myth of Consensus: New views on British history, 1945–64* (Basingstoke, Macmillan, 1996).
Joyce, Patrick. *The State of Freedom: A social history of the British state since 1800* (Cambridge, Cambridge University Press, 2013).
Judt, Tony. *Postwar* (London, Penguin, 2005).
Judt, Tony. *Ill Fares the Land* (London, Penguin, 2010).
Kandiah, Michael. 'The Conservative Party and the 1945 general election', *Contemporary Record*, 9 (1995), 22–47.
Kapoor, Nisha. 'The advancement of racial neoliberalism in Britain', *Ethnic and Racial Studies*, 36 (2013), 1028–46.
Kavanagh, Dennis. *Thatcherism and British Politics: The end of consensus?* 2nd ed. (Oxford, Oxford University Press, 1990).
Kenny, Michael. *The Politics of English Nationhood* (Oxford, Oxford University Press, 2014).
Kerr, Peter. *Postwar British Politics: From conflict to consensus* (Abingdon, Routledge, 2001).
Kirton, Gill, and Anne-Marie Greene. 'Telling and selling the value of diversity and inclusion: External consultants' discursive strategies and practices', *Human Resource Management Journal*, 29 (2019), 676–91.
Kirton, Gill, Anne-Marie Greene and Deborah Dean. 'British diversity professionals as change agents: Radicals, tempered radicals or liberal reformers?', *International Journal of Human Resource Management*, 18 (2007), 1979–94.
Kitson, Michael, and Jonathan Michie. 'The de-industrial revolution: The rise and fall of UK manufacturing, 1870–2010', in Roderick Floud, Jane Humphries and Paul Johnson (eds), *The Cambridge Economic History of Modern Britain: Volume 2, 1870 to the present* (Cambridge, Cambridge University Press, 2014), 302–29.
Kotz, David M. 'Fincialization and neoliberalism', in Gary Teeple and Stephen McBridge (eds), *Relations of Global Power: Neoliberal order and disorder* (Toronto, University of Toronto Press, 2010), 1–18.
Kowol, Kit. 'The Conservative movement and dreams of Britain's post-war future', *Historical Journal*, 62 (2019), 473–93.
Kymlicka, Will. 'Neoliberal multiculturalism?', in Michèle Lamont and Peter A. Hall (eds), *Social Resilience in the Neoliberal Era* (Cambridge, Cambridge University Press, 2013), 99–126.
Kynaston, David. *The City of London, Volume 4: A club no more 1945–2000* (London, Pimlico, 2002).
Langley, Paul. *The Everyday Life of Global Finance: Saving and borrowing in Anglo-America* (Oxford, Oxford University Press, 2009).
Lavery, Scott. *British Capitalism after the Crisis* (Basingstoke, Palgrave Macmillan, 2019).
Lawrence, Jon. *Me, Me, Me? The search for community in post-war England* (Oxford, Oxford University Press, 2019).
Leary, John Patrick. *Keywords: The new language of capitalism* (Chicago, Haymarket Books, 2018).
Ledger, Robert. *Neo-Liberal Thought and Thatcherism: 'A transition from here to there'?* (London, Routledge, 2017).
Lemke, Thomas. '"The birth of bio-politics": Michel Foucault's lecture at the Collège de France on neo-liberal governmentality', *Economy and Society*, 30 (2001), 190–207.
Lent, Adam. *British Social Movements since 1945: Sex, colour, peace and power* (Basingstoke, Palgrave, 2001).
Lipartito, Kenneth. 'Reassembling the economic: New departures in historical materialism', *American Historical Review*, 121 (2016), 101–39.
Lockwood, Charles. 'The British New Right and the problem of public opinion, c. 1965–87' (PhD thesis, Cambridge University, 2020).
Lovenduski, Joni, and Vicky Randall. *Contemporary Feminist Politics: Women and power in Britain* (Oxford, Oxford University Press, 1993).
Lowe, Rodney. 'The replanning of the welfare state, 1957–1964', in Martin Francis and Ina Zweiniger-Bargielowska (eds), *The Conservatives and British Society, 1880–1980* (Cardiff, University of Wales Press, 1996), 255–73.
Lowe, Stuart G., Beverly A. Searle and Susan J. Smith. 'From housing wealth to mortgage debt: The emergence of Britain's asset-shaped welfare state', *Social Policy & Society*, 11 (2011), 105–16.
Lund, Brian. *Housing Politics in the United Kingdom: Power, planning and protest* (Bristol, Policy Press, 2016).

McCarthy, Helen. 'Social science and married women's employment in post-war Britain', *Past & Present*, 233 (2016), 269–305.
McCarthy, Helen. *Double Lives: A history of working motherhood* (London, Bloomsbury, 2020).
McDowell, Linda, Sundari Anitha and Ruth Pearson. 'Striking narratives: Class, gender and ethnicity in the "Great Grunwick Strike", London, UK, 1976–1978', *Women's History Review*, 23 (2014), 595–614.
MacLean, Nancy. *Democracy in Chains* (London, Penguin, 2017).
McRobbie, Angela. *The Aftermath of Feminism: Gender, culture and social change* (London, SAGE, 2009).
McRobbie, Angela. 'Feminism, the family, and the new "mediated" maternalism', *New Formations* 80/81 (2013), 119–37.
McSmith, Andy. *No Such Thing as Society: Britain in the turmoil of the 1980s* (London, Constable, 2011).
Madra, Yahya M., and Fikret Adaman. 'Neoliberal turn in the discipline of economics: Depoliticization through economization', in Damien Cahill, Melinda Cooper, Martijn Konings and David Primrose (eds), *The SAGE Handbook of Neoliberalism* (Los Angeles, SAGE, 2018), 113–28.
Malpass, Peter. *Housing the Welfare State: The development of housing policy in Britain* (Basingstoke, Palgrave Macmillan, 2005).
Marren, Brian. 'The Liverpool dock strike, 1995–98: A resurgence of solidarity in the age of globalisation', *Labor History*, 57 (2016), 463–81.
Martin, Randy. *Financialization of Daily Life* (Philadelphia, Temple University Press, 2002).
Matless, David. 'Appropriate geography: Patrick Abercrombie and the energy of the world', *Journal of Design History*, 6 (1993), 167–78.
Mattinson, Deborah. *Talking to a Brick Wall* (London, Biteback, 2010).
Mayhew, Ken, and Mark Wickham-Jones. 'The United Kingdom's social model', in Jon Erik Dolvik and Andrew Martin (eds), *European Social Models from Crisis to Crisis* (Oxford, Oxford University Press, 2015), 144–76.
Meek, James. *Private Island: Why Britain now belongs to someone else* (London, Verso, 2014).
Mercer, Helen. 'Retailer–supplier relationships before and after the Resale Prices Act, 1964: A turning point in British economic history?', *Enterprise & Society*, 15 (2014), 132–65.
Mercer, Helen. 'The making of the modern retail market: Economic theory, business interests and economic policy in the passage of the 1964 Resale Prices Act', *Business History*, 59 (2017), 778–801.
Meredith, Jesse. 'Decolonizing the New Town: Roy Gazzard and the making of Killingworth Township', *Journal of British Studies*, 57 (2018), 333–62.
Middlemas, Keith. *Power, Competition and the State, Volume 3: The end of the postwar era: Britain since 1974* (Basingstoke, Macmillan, 1991).
Middleton, Roger. *Towards the Managed Economy* (London, Methuen, 1985).
Middleton, Roger. *Government versus the Market: The growth of the public sector, economic management and British economic performance, c.1890–1979* (Cheltenham, Edward Elgar, 1996).
Middleton, Roger. *Charlatans or Saviours? Economics and the British economy from Marshall to Meade* (Cheltenham, Edward Elgar, 1998).
Middleton, Roger. 'Brittan on Britain: "The economic contradictions of democracy" redux', *Historical Journal*, 54 (2011), 1141–68.
Middleton, Stuart. '"Affluence" and the left in Britain, c.1958–1974', *English Historical Review*, 129 (2014), 107–38.
Millar, Jane, and Fran Bennett. 'Universal Credit: Assumptions, contradictions and virtual reality', *Social Policy and Society*, 16 (2017), 169–82.
Millward, Robert. 'The rise of the service economy', in Roderick Floud and Paul Johnson (eds), *The Cambridge Economic History of Modern Britain, Volume 3: Structural change and growth, 1939–2000* (Cambridge, Cambridge University Press, 2004), 238–66.
Milward, Alan S. *The Rise and Fall of a National Strategy, 1945–1963: The UK and the European Community, volume 1* (London, Routledge, 2002).
Mirowski, Philip. *Never Let a Serious Crisis Go to Waste* (London, Verso, 2013).
Mirowski, Philip. 'The political movement that dared not speak its own name: The neoliberal thought collective under erasure', Institute for New Economic Thinking Working Paper (23 September 2014), https://www.ineteconomics.org/uploads/papers/WP23-Mirowski.pdf (accessed 24 June 2021).

Mirowski, Philip. 'Postface: Defining neoliberalism', in Philip Mirowski and Dieter Plehwe (eds), *The Road from Mont Pèlerin: The making of the neoliberal thought collective* (Cambridge, MA, Harvard University Press, 2009), 417–56.
Mirowski, Philip. 'Neoliberalism: The movement that dare not speak its name', *American Affairs*, 2/1 (2018), 118–41.
Mirowski, Philip. 'The Eighteenth Brumaire of James Buchanan', *boundary 2*, 46 (2019), 197–219.
Mirowski, Philip, and Dieter Plehwe (eds). *The Road from Mont Pèlerin: The making of the neoliberal thought collective* (Cambridge, MA, Harvard University Press, 2009).
Mitchell, Neil J. 'The decentralization of business in Britain', *Journal of Politics*, 52 (1990), 622–37.
Mitchell, Stuart. 'Resale Price Maintenance and the character of resistance in the Conservative Party: 1949–64', *Canadian Journal of History/Annales canadiennes d'histoire*, 40 (2005), 259–88.
Moore, Charles. *Margaret Thatcher: The authorized biography, volume 1: Not for turning* (London, Allen Lane, 2013).
Moores, Chris. *Civil Liberties and Human Rights in Twentieth-Century Britain* (Cambridge, Cambridge University Press, 2017).
Moores, Chris. 'Thatcher's troops? Neighbourhood watch schemes and the search for "ordinary" Thatcherism in 1980s Britain', *Contemporary British History*, 31 (2017), 230–55.
Moran, Michael. *Business, Politics and Society: An Anglo-American comparison*, (Oxford, Oxford University Press, 2009).
Morelli, Carlo. 'Constructing a balance between price and non-price competition in British multiple food retailing, 1954–1964', *Business History*, 40 (1998), 45–61.
Morgan, Glenn. 'Supporting the city: Economic patriotism in financial markets', *Journal of European Public Policy*, 19 (2012), 373–87.
Morrison, Lionel. *A Century of Black Journalism in Britain: A kaleidoscopic view of race and the media (1893–2003)* (London, Truebay, 2007).
Mount, Ferdinand. 'Wedded to the absolute', *London Review of Books* (26 September 2019), 7.
Moyn, Samuel. 'Imaginary intellectual history', in Darrin McMahon and Samuel Moyn (eds), *Rethinking Modern Europe Intellectual History* (Oxford, Oxford University Press, 2014), 112–30.
Moyn, Samuel. *Not Enough: Human rights in an unequal world* (Cambridge, MA, Harvard University Press, 2018).
Mudge, Stephanie. 'What is neo-liberalism?', *Socio-Economic Review*, 6 (2008), 703–31.
Mudge, Stephanie. *Leftism Reinvented: Western parties from socialism to neoliberalism* (Cambridge, MA, Harvard University Press, 2018).
Mullins, David, and Alan Murie. *Housing Policy in the UK* (Basingstoke, Palgrave Macmillan, 2006).
Myles, John, and Paul Pierson. 'Friedman's revenge: The reform of "liberal" welfare states in Canada and the United States', *Politics & Society*, 25 (1997), 443–72.
Needham, Duncan. *UK Monetary Policy from Devaluation to Thatcher* (Basingstoke, Palgrave Macmillan, 2014).
Needham, Duncan, and Anthony Hotson (eds). *Expansionary Fiscal Contraction: The Thatcher government's 1981 budget in perspective* (Cambridge, Cambridge University Press, 2014).
Newton, Scott. 'The sterling devaluation of 1967, the international economy and post-war social democracy', *English Historical Review*, 125 (2010), 912–45.
Newton, Scott. 'Sterling, Bretton Woods, and social democracy, 1968–70', *Diplomacy & Statecraft*, 24 (2013), 427–55.
Newton, Scott. *The Reinvention of Britain, 1960–2016: A political and economic history* (London, Routledge, 2017).
Norfield, Tony. *The City: London and the global power of finance* (London, Verso, 2016).
Nuttall, Jeremy. 'Tony Crosland and the many falls and rises of British social democracy', *Contemporary British History*, 18 (2004), 52–79.
O'Conell, Sean. *Credit and Community: Working-class debt in the UK since 1880* (Oxford, Oxford University Press, 2009).
Offer, Avner. 'British manual workers: From producers to consumers, c.1950–2000', *Contemporary British History*, 22 (2008), 537–71.
Offer, Avner. 'Narrow banking, real estate, and financial stability in the UK, c.1870–2010', in Nicholas Dimsdale and Anthony Hotson (eds), *British Financial Crises since 1825* (Oxford, Oxford University Press, 2014), 158–73.

Offer, Avner. 'The market turn: From social democracy to market liberalism', *Economy History Review*, 70 (2017), 1051–71.
Offer, Avner, and Gabriel Söderberg. *The Nobel Factor: The prize in economics, social democracy, and the market turn* (Princeton, Princeton University Press, 2016).
Offner, Amy C. *Sorting Out the Mixed Economy: The rise and fall of welfare and developmental states in the Americas* (Princeton, NJ, Princeton University Press, 2019).
Ogle, Vanessa. '"Funk money": The end of empires, the expansion of tax havens, and decolonization as an economic and financial event', *Past & Present*, 249 (2020), 213–49.
Oliver, Michael J., and Hugh Pemberton. 'Learning and change in 20th-century British economic policy', *Governance*, 17 (2004), 415–41.
Ong, Aihwa. *Neoliberalism as Exception: Mutations in citizenship and sovereignty* (Durham, NC, Duke University Press, 2006).
Ortolano, Guy. *Thatcher's Progress: From social democracy to market liberalism through an English New Town* (Cambridge, Cambridge University Press, 2019).
Overbeek, Henk. *Global Capitalism and National Decline: The Thatcher decade in perspective* (London, Unwin Hyman, 1990).
Pascall, Gillian. 'Women and the family in the British welfare state: The Thatcher/Major legacy', *Social Policy & Administration*, 31 (1997), 290–305.
Payling, Daisy. '"Socialist Republic of South Yorkshire": Grassroots activism and left-wing solidarity in 1980s Sheffield', *Twentieth Century British History*, 25 (2014), 602–27.
Payling, Daisy. 'City limits: Sexual politics and the New Urban Left in 1980s Sheffield', *Contemporary British History*, 31 (2017), 256–73.
Payne, Christopher. *The Consumer, Credit and Neoliberalism: Governing the modern economy* (London, Routledge, 2011).
Peck, Jamie. *Constructions of Neoliberal Reason* (Oxford, Oxford University Press, 2010).
Peden, George. 'Neoliberal economists and the British welfare state, 1942–1975', *Journal of the History of Economic Thought*, 39 (2017), 413–27.
Pedersen, Susan. *Family, Dependence, and the Origins of the Welfare State: Britain and France 1914–1945* (Cambridge, Cambridge University Press, 1993).
Perra, Antonio. 'Prevent, Muslim identity and the normalisation of neoliberalism', *Renewal: A Journal of Social Democracy*, 26 (2018), 83–95.
Petersen, Klaus Jørn, and Henrik Petersen. 'Confusion and divergence: Origins and meanings of the term 'welfare state' in Germany and Britain, 1840–1940', *Journal of European Social Policy*, 23 (2013), 37–51.
Phillips, Jim. 'Business and the limited reconstruction of industrial relations in the UK in the 1970s', *Business History*, 51 (2009), 801–16.
Phillips, Jim. 'UK business power and opposition to the Bullock Committee's 1977 proposals for worker directors', *Historical Studies in Industrial Relations*, 31/32 (2011), 1–30.
Phillips, Jim. 'Deindustrialisation and the moral economy of the Scottish Coalfields, 1947 to 1991', *International Labor and Working-Class History*, 84 (2013), 99–115.
Phillips, Jim. *Scottish Coal Miners in the Twentieth Century* (Edinburgh, Edinburgh University Press, 2019).
Phillips-Fein, Kim. *Invisible Hands* (New York, W. W. Norton and Company, 2010).
Piketty, Thomas. *Capital in the Twenty First Century* (Cambridge, MA, Harvard University Press, 2014).
Plehwe, Dieter. 'Introduction', in Philip Mirowski and Dieter Plehwe (eds), *The Road from Mont Pèlerin: The making of the neoliberal thought collective* (Cambridge, MA, Harvard University Press, 2009), 1–42.
Plehwe, Dieter, Bernhard Walpen and Gisela Neunhöffer (eds). *Neo-Liberal Hegemony: A global critique* (London, Routledge, 2005).
Portes, Jonathan. 'Welfare and work: Continuity and change', *National Institute Economic Review*, 221 (2012), F4–F9.
Powell, Martin. 'Introduction', in Martin Powell (ed.), *New Labour, New Welfare State? The 'Third Way' in British social policy* (Bristol, Policy Press, 1999), 1–28.
Prasad, Monica. *The Politics of Free Markets: The rise of neoliberal economic policies in Britain, France, Germany and the United States* (Chicago, University of Chicago Press, 2006).
Przeworski, Adam. *Capitalism and Social Democracy* (Cambridge, Cambridge University Press, 1985).
Przeworski, Adam. 'How many ways can be third?', in Andrew Glyn (ed.), *Social Democracy in Neoliberal Times* (Oxford, Oxford University Press, 2001), 312–33.

Przeworski, Adam. 'Choices and echoes: Stability and change of policy regimes', in Hideko Magara (ed.), *Economic Crises and Policy Regimes* (Cheltenham, Edward Elgar, 2014), 33–55.
Przeworski, Adam, and Michael Wallerstein. 'Structural dependence of the state on capital', *American Political Science Review*, 82 (1988), 11–29.
Ramsden, John. 'A party for owners or a party for earners? How far did the Conservative Party really change after 1945?', *Transactions of the Royal Historical Society*, 37 (1987), 49–63.
Randall, Vicky. *The Politics of Child Daycare in Britain* (Oxford, Oxford University Press, 2000).
Ravetz, Alison. *Council Housing and Culture: The history of a social experiment* (New York, Routledge, 2001).
Reid, Alastair J. 'The dialectics of liberation: The Old Left, the New Left and the counter-culture', in David Feldman and Jon Lawrence (eds), *Structures and Transformations in Modern British History* (Cambridge, Cambridge University Press, 2011), 261–80.
Rhodes, Martin. 'Desperately seeking a solution: Social democracy, Thatcherism and the "Third Way" in British Welfare', in Maurizio Ferrera and Martin Rhodes (eds), *Recasting European Welfare States* (London, Frank Cass, 2000), 161–86.
Richards, Steve. *Whatever It Takes: The real story of Gordon Brown and New Labour* (London, Fourth Estate, 2010).
Rieger, Bernhard. 'Making Britain work again: Unemployment and the remaking of British social policy in the eighties', *English Historical Review*, 133 (2018), 634–66.
Ringrose, Jessica, and Valerie Walkerdine. 'Regulating the abject', *Feminist Media Studies*, 8 (2008), 227–46.
Riviera, Helena. 'Political ideology and housing supply: Rethinking New Towns and the building of new communities in England' (PhD thesis, University College London, 2015).
Roberts, Richard, and David Kynaston. *City State: How the markets came to rule the world* (London, Profile, 2001).
Robinson, Emily. *The Language of Progressive Politics in Modern Britain* (London, Palgrave Macmillan, 2017).
Robinson, Emily, Camilla Schofield, Florence Sutcliffe-Braithwaite and Natalie Thomlinson. 'Telling stories about post-war Britain: Popular individualism and the "crisis" of the 1970s', *Twentieth Century British History*, 28 (2017), 268–304.
Rodgers, Daniel. *Age of Fracture* (Cambridge, MA, Harvard University Press, 2011).
Rodgers, Daniel. 'The uses and abuses of "neoliberalism"', *Dissent* (Winter 2018), https://www.dissentmagazine.org/article/uses-and-abuses-neoliberalism-debate (accessed 17 February 2019).
Roistacher, Elizabeth A. 'Housing and the welfare state in the United States and Western Europe', *The Netherlands Journal of Housing and Environmental Research*, 2 (1987), 143–75.
Rojek, Chris. *The Labour of Leisure: The culture of free trade* (London, SAGE, 2010).
Rollings, Neil. 'The "Keynesian revolution" and economic policy-making: A comment', *Economic History Review*, 38 (1985), 95–100.
Rollings, Neil. '"The Reichstag method of governing"? The Attlee governments and permanent economic controls', in Helen Mercer and Neil Rollings (eds), *Labour Governments and Private Industry* (Edinburgh, Edinburgh University Press, 1992), 15–36.
Rollings, Neil. 'Cracks in the post-war Keynesian settlement? The role of organised business in Britain in the rise of neoliberalism before Margaret Thatcher', *Twentieth Century British History*, 24 (2013), 637–59.
Rollings, Neil. 'Between business and academia in post-war Britain: Three advocates of neoliberalism at the heart of the British business community', in Roger E. Backhouse, Bradley W. Bateman, Tamotsu Nishizawa and Dieter Plehwe (eds), *Liberalism and the Welfare State: Economists and arguments for the welfare state* (Oxford, Oxford University Press, 2017), 110–17.
Romani, Roberto. 'Varieties of neoliberalism: On the populism of laissez-faire in America, 1960–1985', *Global Intellectual History*, 1 March 2019, https://doi.org/10.1080/23801883.2019.1588198.
Römer, Felix. 'Poverty, inequality statistics, and knowledge politics under Thatcher', *English Historical Review* (forthcoming).
Rooney, David. 'The political economy of congestion: Road pricing and the neoliberal project, 1952–2003', *Twentieth Century British History,* 25 (2014), 628–50.
Rose, Nikolas. 'Governing the enterprising self', in Paul Heelas and Paul Morris (eds), *The Values of Enterprise Culture: The moral debate* (London, Unwin Hyman, 1992), 141–64.
Rose, Nikolas. *Governing the Soul: The shaping of the private self*, 2nd ed. (London, Free Association Books, 1999).

Rose, Nikolas, Pat O'Malley and Mariana Valverde. 'Governmentality', *Annual Review of Law and Social Science*, 2 (2006), 83–104.
Ross, Duncan M. 'Domestic policy and the banking system in Britain, 1945–71', in Ranald Michie and Philip Williamson (eds), *The British Government and the City of London in the Twentieth Century* (Cambridge, Cambridge University Press, 2004), 298–321.
Ross, Kristin. *May '68 and Its Afterlives* (Chicago, University of Chicago Press, 2002).
Rottenberg, Catherine. 'Happiness and the liberal imagination: How Superwoman became balanced', *Feminist Studies*, 40 (2014), 144–68.
Rottenberg, Catherine. 'The rise of neoliberal feminism', *Cultural Studies*, 28 (2014), 418–37.
Rottenberg, Catherine. '*Women Who Work:* The limits of the neoliberal feminist paradigm', *Gender, Work and Organisation* 26 (2019), 1073–82.
Rowthorn, Bob, and John Wells. *De-Industrialisation and Foreign Trade* (Cambridge, Cambridge University Press, 1987).
Ruggie, John Gerard. 'International regimes, transactions and change: Embedded liberalism in the postwar economic order', *International Organization*, 36 (1982), 379–415.
Runciman, Walter G. 'Has British capitalism changed since the First World War?', *British Journal of Sociology*, 44 (1993), 53–67.
Sampson, Anthony. *The New Anatomy of Britain* (London, Hodder and Stoughton, 1971).
Sandbrook, Dominic. *Seasons in the Sun: The battle for Britain, 1974–1979* (London, Allen Lane, 2012).
Sandbrook, Dominic. *Who Dares Wins: Britain, 1979–1982* (London, Allen Lane, 2019).
Saunders, Peter. *A Nation of Home Owners* (London, Unwin Hyman, 1990).
Saunders, Robert. '"Crisis, what crisis?" Thatcherism and the seventies', in Ben Jackson and Robert Saunders (eds), *Making Thatcher's Britain* (Cambridge, Cambridge University Press, 2012), 25–52.
Saumarez Smith, Otto. 'The inner city crisis and the end of urban modernism in 1970s Britain', *Twentieth Century British History*, 27 (2016), 578–98.
Saumarez Smith, Otto. 'Action for cities: The Thatcher government and inner-city policy', *Urban History*, 47 (2020), 274–91.
Scharff, Christina. 'The pyschic life of neoliberalism: Mapping the contours of entrepreneurial subjectivity', *Theory, Culture & Society*, 33 (2016), 107–22.
Schenk, Catherine. 'The origins of the Eurodollar market in London, 1955–63', *Explorations in Economic History*, 2 (1996), 1–19.
Schenk, Catherine. *The Decline of Sterling: Managing the retreat of international currency, 1945–1992* (Cambridge, Cambridge University Press, 2010).
Schofield, Camilla. *Enoch Powell and the Making of Postcolonial Britain* (Cambridge, Cambridge University Press, 2009).
Scott, Peter. 'Regional development and policy', in Roderick Floud and Paul Johnson (eds), *The Cambridge Economic History of Modern Britain, Volume 3: Structural change and growth, 1939–2000* (Cambridge, Cambridge University Press, 2004), 332–67.
Scott, Peter M., and James T. Walker. '"Stop–go" policy and the restriction of postwar British house-building', *Economic History Review*, 72 (2019), 716–37.
Seaton, Andrew. 'Against the "sacred cow": NHS opposition and the Fellowship for Freedom in Medicine, 1948–72', *Twentieth Century British History*, 26 (2015), 424–49.
Seaton, Andrew. 'The National Health Service and the endurances of British social democracy, 1948 to the present' (PhD thesis, New York University, 2020).
Seawright, David. *The British Conservative Party and One Nation Politics* (London, Continuum, 2010).
Sefton, Tom, John Hills and Holly Sutherland. 'Poverty, inequality and redistribution', in John Hills, Tom Sefton and Kitty Stewart (eds), *Towards a More Equal Society? Poverty, inequality and policy since 1997* (York, Joseph Rowntree Foundation, 2009), 21–45.
Setch, Eve. 'The face of metropolitan feminism: The London Women's Liberation Workshop, 1969–79', *Twentieth Century British History*, 13 (2002), 171–90.
Shapely, Peter. *The Politics of Housing: Power, consumers, and urban culture* (Manchester, Manchester University Press, 2007).
Shapely, Peter. 'Governance in the post-war city: Historical reflections on public–private partnerships in the UK', *International Journal of Urban and Regional Research*, 37 (2013), 1288–304.
Shapira, Michal. *The War Inside: Psychoanalysis, total war, and the making of the democratic self in postwar Britain* (Cambridge, Cambridge University Press, 2013).

Shaw, Eric. *The Labour Party since 1979* (London, Routledge, 1994).

Sheard, Sally. *The Passionate Economist: How Brian Abel-Smith shaped global health and social welfare* (Bristol, Policy Press, 2013).

Shepherd, John. *Crisis? What Crisis? The Callaghan government and the British 'Winter of Discontent'* (Manchester, Manchester University Press, 2016).

Shilliam, Robbie. *Race and the Undeserving Poor: From abolition to Brexit* (New York, Columbia University Press, 2018).

Shock, Max. 'Renewing left-wing ideas in late twentieth-century Britain: *Marxism Today*, c.1977–1994' (DPhil thesis, University of Oxford, 2020).

Shukra Kalbir. 'Ethnic pluralism and Black perspectives', in Kalbir Shukra, *The Changing Pattern of Black Politics* (London, Pluto Press, 1998), 50–69.

Sivanandan, A. 'Challenging racism: Strategies for the '80s', *Race & Class*, 15 (1983), 1–11.

Sivanandan, A. 'RAT and the degradation of Black struggle', *Race & Class*, 26 (1985), 1–33.

Slobodian, Quinn. *Globalists: The end of empire and the birth of neoliberalism* (Cambridge, MA, Harvard University Press, 2018).

Sloman, Peter. *The Liberal Party and the Economy, 1929–1964* (Oxford, Oxford University Press, 2015).

Sloman, Peter. 'Beveridge's rival: Juliet Rhys-Williams and the campaign for basic income, 1942–55', *Contemporary British History*, 30 (2016), 203–23.

Sloman, Peter. '"The pragmatist's solution to poverty": The Heath government's tax credit scheme and the politics of social policy in the 1970s', *Twentieth Century British History*, 27 (2016), 220–41.

Sloman, Peter. 'Redistribution in an age of neoliberalism: Market economics, "poverty knowledge", and the growth of working-age benefits in Britain, c. 1979–2010', *Political Studies*, 67 (2018), 732–51.

Sloman, Peter. 'Universal basic income in British politics: From a "vagabond's wage" to a global debate', *Journal of Social Policy*, 47 (2018), 625–42.

Sloman, Peter. *Transfer State: The idea of a guaranteed income and the politics of redistribution in modern Britain* (Oxford, Oxford University Press, 2019).

Smith, Graeme. 'Margaret Thatcher's Christian faith: A case study in political theology', *Journal of Religious Ethics*, 35 (2007), 233–57.

Smith, Paul. 'Order in British industrial relations: From Donovan to neoliberalism', *Historical Studies in Industrial Relations*, 31/32 (2011), 115–54.

Solomos, John. 'Equal opportunities policies and racial inequality: The role of public policy', *Public Administration*, 67 (1989), 79–93.

'Special section: Social histories of neoliberalism', *Journal of Social History*, 53 (2019), 1–132.

Spence, Jean, and Carol Stephenson. '"Side by side with our men?" Women's activism, community and gender in the 1984–85 British miners' strike', *International Labor and Working Class History*, 75 (2009), 68–84.

Springer, Simon, Kean Birch and Julie MacLeavy (eds). *The Handbook of Neoliberalism* (London, Routledge, 2016).

Standing, Guy. *The Precariat: The new dangerous class* (London, Bloomsbury Academic, 2011).

Stedman Jones, Daniel. *Masters of the Universe: Hayek, Friedman and the birth of neo-liberal politics* (Princeton, NJ, Princeton University Press, 2012).

Steensland, Brian. *The Failed Welfare Revolution: America's struggle over guaranteed income policy* (Princeton, NJ, Princeton University Press, 2008).

Stephens, Mark. 'Building society demutualisation in the UK', *Housing Studies*, 16 (2001), 335–52.

Sterber, Martina. 'Fundamentals at stake: The Conservatives, industrial relations and the rhetorical framing of the miners' strike in 1984–85', *Contemporary British History*, 32 (2018), 60–77.

Stevenson, George. 'The forgotten strike: Equality, gender, and class in the Trico equal pay strike', *Labour History Review*, 81 (2016), 141–68.

Stewart, Iain. 'On recent developments in the new historiography of (neo)liberalism', *Contemporary European History*, 29 (2020), 116–24.

Stewart, Kitty. 'Equality and social justice', in Anthony Seldon (ed.), *Blair's Britain, 1997–2007* (Cambridge, Cambridge University Press, 2008), 408–35.

Stoller, Sarah. 'Forging a politics of care: Theorising household work in the British women's liberation movement', *History Workshop Journal*, 85 (2018), 95–119.

Strange, Susan. *The Retreat of the State: The diffusion of power in the world economy* (Cambridge, Cambridge University Press, 1996).

Strangleman, Tim. 'Deindustrialisation and the historical sociological imagination: Making sense of work and industrial change', *Sociology*, 51 (2017), 466–82.

Supple, Barry. 'Fear of failing: Economic history and the decline of Britain', *Economic History Review*, 47 (1994), 441–58.

Sutcliffe-Braithwaite, Florence. 'Neo-liberalism and morality in the making of Thatcherite social policy', *Historical Journal*, 55 (2012), 497–520.

Sutcliffe-Braithwaite, Florence. *Class, Politics and the Decline of Defence in England, 1968–2000* (Oxford, Oxford University Press, 2018).

Sutcliffe-Braithwaite, Florence, Chris Hilliard, Christienna Fryar, Mo Moulton and Mark Hampton. '*Modern Britain, 1750 to the Present* by James Vernon', *Twentieth Century British History*, 30 (2019), 264–84.

Sutcliffe-Braithwaite, Florence, and Jon Lawrence. 'Margaret Thatcher and the decline of class politics', in Ben Jackson and Robert Saunders (eds), *Making Thatcher's Britain* (Cambridge, Cambridge University Press, 2012), 132–47.

Sutcliffe-Braithwaite, Florence, and Natalie Thomlinson. 'Women's activism during the miners' strike: Memories and legacies', *Contemporary British History*, 32 (2018), 78–100.

Talani, Leila Simona. *Globalization, Hegemony and the Future of the City of London* (London, Palgrave Macmillan, 2012).

Taylor, Charles. *Sources of the Self: The making of the modern identity* (Cambridge, Cambridge University Press, 1989).

Taylor, Robert. 'New labour, new capitalism', in Anthony Seldon (ed.), *Blair's Britain, 1997–2007* (Cambridge, Cambridge University Press, 2008), 214–40.

Taylor-Gooby, Peter. 'Commentary', in Stephen Farrall and Colin Hay (eds), *The Legacy of Thatcherism: Assessing and exploring Thatcherite social and economic policies* (Oxford, Oxford University Press, 2014), 100–7.

Thane, Pat. *Divided Kingdom: A history of Britain, 1900 to the Present* (Cambridge, Cambridge University Press, 2018).

Thomas, Devon. 'Black initiatives in Brixton', in John Benyon (ed.), *Scarman and After: Essays reflecting on Lord Scarman's report, the riots and their aftermath* (Oxford, Pergamon, 1984), 184–90.

Thomlinson, Natalie. *Race, Ethnicity and the Women's Movement in England, 1968–1993* (Basingstoke, Palgrave, 2016).

Thompson, E. P. 'The moral economy of the English crowd in the eighteenth century', *Past & Present*, 50 (1971), 76–136.

Thompson, Noel. 'Economic ideas and the development of economic opinion', in Richard Coopey and Nicholas Woodward (eds), *Britain in the 1970s: The troubled decade* (New York, St Martin's Press, 1996), 57–70.

Thomson, Mathew. *Lost Freedom: The landscape of the child and the British post-war settlement* (Oxford, Oxford University Press, 2013).

Todd, Selina. *The People: The rise and fall of the working class, 1910–2010* (London, John Murray, 2015).

Tomlinson, Jim. *Problems of British Economic Policy* (London, Methuen, 1981).

Tomlinson, Jim. *Hayek and the Market* (London, Pluto Press, 1990).

Tomlinson, Jim. '"Liberty with order": Conservative economic policy, 1951–1964', in Martin Francis and Ina Zweiniger-Bargielowska (eds), *Conservatives and British Society, 1880–1990* (Cardiff, University of Wales Press, 1996), 274–88.

Tomlinson, Jim. 'Mrs Thatcher's macroeconomic adventurism, 1979–1981, and its political consequences', *British Politics*, 3 (2007), 3–19.

Tomlinson, Jim. 'Tale of a death exaggerated: How Keynesian policies survived the 1970s', *Contemporary British History*, 21 (2007), 429–48.

Tomlinson, Jim. 'Thatcher, monetarism and the politics of inflation', in Ben Jackson and Robert Saunders (eds), *Making Thatcher's Britain* (Cambridge, Cambridge University Press, 2012), 62–77.

Tomlinson, Jim. *The Politics of Decline: Understanding postwar Britain* (London, Routledge, 2014).

Tomlinson, Jim. 'A new political arithmetic?', *Social History*, 40 (2015), 5–14.

Tomlinson, Jim. 'Deindustrialisation not decline: A new meta-narrative for post-war British history', *Twentieth Century British History*, 27 (2016), 76–99.

Tomlinson, Jim. 'Distributional politics: The search for equality in Britain since the First World War', in Pat Hudson and Keith Tribe (eds), *The Contradictions of Capital in the Twenty-First Century: The Piketty opportunity* (Newcastle upon Tyne, Agenda Publishing, 2016), 167–91.

Tomlinson, Jim. *Managing the Economy, Managing the People: Narratives of economic life in Britain from Beveridge to Brexit* (Oxford, Oxford University Press, 2017).
Tomlinson, Jim. 'Britain since the 1970s: A transition to neo-liberalism?', in Julian Hoppitt, Adrian Leonard and Duncan Needham (eds), *Money and Markets: Essays in honour of Martin Daunton* (Woodbridge, Boydell and Brewer, 2019), 181–98.
Tomlinson, Jim. 'De-industrialization: Strengths and weaknesses as a key concept for understanding post-war British history', *Urban History*, 47 (2020), 199–219.
Tooze, Adam. *Crashed: How a decade of financial crisis changed the world* (London, Allen Lane, 2018).
Toye, Richard. 'From "consensus" to "common ground": The rhetoric of the postwar settlement and its collapse', *Journal of Contemporary History*, 48 (2013), 3–23.
Tribe, Keith. 'Liberalism and neoliberalism in Britain, 1930–1980', in Philip Mirowski and Dieter Plehwe (eds), *The Road from Mont Pèlerin: The making of the neoliberal thought collective* (Cambridge, MA, Harvard University Press, 2009), 68–97.
Truesdale, David. 'House sales and owner-occupation in Stevenage New Town', *Policy and Politics*, 8 (1980), 318–23.
Turnbull, Peter, and Victoria Wass. 'The greatest game no more: Redundant dockers and the demise of "dock work"', *Work, Employment and Society*, 8 (1994), 487–506.
Turnbull, Peter, Charles Woolfson and John Kelly. *Dock Strike: Conflict and restructuring in Britain's ports* (Aldershot, Avebury, 1992).
Turner, Rachel S. *Neo-Liberal Ideology: History, concepts and politics* (Edinburgh, Edinburgh University Press, 2008).
van der Zwan, Natascha. 'Making sense of financialization', *Socio-Economic Review*, 12 (2014), 99–129.
Van Horn, Robert, Philip Mirowski and Thomas Stapleford (eds). *Building Chicago Economics* (Cambridge, Cambridge University Press, 2011).
Venugopal, Rajesh. 'Neoliberalism as concept', *Economy and Society*, 44 (2015), 165–87.
Vernon, James. 'The local, the imperial and the global: Repositioning twentieth-century Britain and the brief life of its social democracy', *Twentieth Century British History*, 21 (2010), 404–18.
Vernon, James. *Modern Britain: 1750 to the present* (Cambridge, Cambridge University Press, 2017).
Vernon, James. 'Heathrow and the making of neoliberal Britain', *Past & Present*, 252 (2021), 213–47.
Vinen, Richard. *Thatcher's Britain: The politics and social upheaval of the Thatcher era* (London, Simon & Schuster, 2010).
Vinen, Richard. 'A war of position? The Thatcher government's preparation for the 1984 miners' strike', *English Historical Review*, 134 (2019), 121–50.
Wade, Tony. *Black Enterprise in Britain* (London, TCS, 2003).
Wakeman, Rosemary. *Practicing Utopia: An intellectual history of the New Town movement* (Chicago, University of Chicago Press, 2016).
Walkerdine, Valerie. 'Reclassifying upward mobility: Femininity and the neo-liberal subject', *Gender and Education*, 15 (2003), 237–48.
Wall, Stephen. 'Making a single market', *Journal of European Integration History*, 16 (2010), 57–64.
Walter, Natasha. *The New Feminism* (London, Little Brown, 1998).
Waltman, Jerold. *Minimum Wage Policy in Great Britain and the USA* (New York, Algora, 2008).
Ward, Jacob. 'Financing the information age: London TeleCity, the legacy of It-82, and the selling of British Telecom', *Twentieth Century British History*, 30 (2019), 424–46.
Wass, Douglas. *Decline to Fall: The making of British macro-economic policy and the 1976 IMF crisis* (Oxford, Oxford University Press, 2008).
Wasserman, Janek. *The Austrian School* (New Haven, CT, Yale University Press, 2019).
Waters, Rob. *Thinking Black: Britain 1964–85* (Oakland, University of California Press, 2018).
Watson, Matthew, and Colin Hay. 'The discourse of globalisation and the logic of no alternative: Rendering the contingent necessary in the political economy of New Labour', *Policy & Politics*, 31 (2003), 289–305.
Weaver, Timothy P. R. *Blazing the Neoliberal Trail: Urban political development in the United States and the United Kingdom* (Philadelphia, University of Pennsylvania Press, 2016).
Weiler, Peter. 'The rise and fall of the Conservatives' "Grand Design for Housing", 1951–64', *Contemporary British History*, 14 (2000), 122–50.

Weiler, Peter. 'The Conservatives' search for a middle way in housing, 1951–1964', *Twentieth Century British History*, 14 (2003), 360–90.

Wetherell, Sam. 'Freedom planned: Enterprise Zones and non-planning in post-war Britain', *Twentieth Century British History*, 27 (2016), 266–89.

Wetherell, Sam. *Foundations: How the built environment made twentieth-century Britain* (Princeton, NJ, Princeton University Press, 2020).

Whiteside, Noel. *Bad Times: Unemployment in British social and political history* (London, Faber Press, 1991).

Whitfield, James. *Unhappy Dialogue: The Metropolitan Police and Black Londoners in post-war Britain* (London, Routledge, 2004).

Whiting, R. C. 'Income tax, the working class and party politics, 1948–1952', *Twentieth Century British History*, 8 (1997), 194–221.

Whyte, Jessica. *The Morals of the Market: Human rights and the rise of neoliberalism* (London, Verso, 2019).

Wickham-Jones, Mark. 'Anticipating social democracy, pre-empting anticipations', *Politics and Society*, 23 (1995), 465–94.

Wickham-Jones, Mark. *Economic Strategy and the Labour Party* (Basingstoke, Palgrave, 1996).

Wickham-Jones, Mark. 'How the Conservatives lost the economic argument', in Andrew Geddes and Jonathan Tonge (eds), *Labour's Landslide* (Manchester, Manchester University Press, 1997), 100–18.

Wickham-Jones, Mark. 'Exorcising ghosts: How Labour dominated the economic argument', in Andrew Geddes and Jonathan Tonge (eds), *Labour's Second Landslide* (Manchester, Manchester University Press, 2002), 103–24.

Wickham-Jones, Mark. 'From reformism to resignation and remedialism?', *Journal of Policy History*, 15 (2003), 26–45.

Williams, Karel, Colin Haslam and John Williams. 'Ford versus "Fordism": The beginning of mass production?' *Work, Employment & Society*, 6 (1992), 517–55.

Williamson, Adrian. *Conservative Economic Policymaking and the Birth of Thatcherism, 1964–1979* (Basingstoke, Palgrave Macmillan, 2015).

Willmot, Peter. 'Housing density and town design in a New Town', *The New Town Planning Review*, 33 (1962), 115–27.

Wilson, Dolly Smith. 'A new look at the affluent worker: The good working mother in post-war Britain', *Twentieth Century British History*, 17 (2006), 206–29.

Wilson, Julie A. *Neoliberalism* (New York, Routledge, 2018).

Wincott, Daniel. 'Images of welfare in law and society: The British welfare state in comparative perspective', *Journal of Law and Society*, 38 (2011), 343–75.

Wincott, Daniel. 'The (golden) age of the welfare state: Interrogating a conventional wisdom', *Public Administration*, 91 (2013), 806–22.

Wincott, Daniel. 'Original and imitated or elusive and limited? Towards a genealogy of the welfare state idea in Britain', in Daniel Béland and Klaus Petersen (eds), *Analysing Social Policy Concepts and Language: Comparative and transnational perspectives* (Bristol, Policy Press, 2014), 127–42.

Wood, J. D. G. 'The integrating role of private homeownership and mortgage credit in British neoliberalism', *Housing Studies*, 33 (2018), 993–1013.

Woodcock, Jamie. *Working the Phones: Control and resistance in call centres* (London, Pluto, 2016).

Wrigley, Chris. *British Trade Unions since 1933* (Cambridge, Cambridge University Press, 2002).

Young, Zoe. *Women's Work: How mothers manage flexible working in careers and family life* (Bristol, Bristol University Press, 2018).

Zweiniger-Bargielowska, Ina. *Austerity in Britain; Rationing, controls and consumption, 1939–1955* (Oxford, Oxford University Press, 2000).

Index

CPSIA information can be obtained
at www.ICGtesting.com
Printed in the USA
BVHW092305110222
628742BV00002B/13

9 781787 356863